Wissenschaftliche Untersuchungen
zum Neuen Testament

Herausgeber / Editor
Jörg Frey (Zürich)

Mitherausgeber / Associate Editors
Markus Bockmuehl (Oxford)
James A. Kelhoffer (Uppsala)
Hans-Josef Klauck (Chicago, IL)
Tobias Nicklas (Regensburg)

311

Lars Hartman

# Approaching New Testament Texts and Contexts

Collected Essays II

edited by

David Hellholm and
Tord Fornberg

Mohr Siebeck

Lars Hartman, born 1930; 1957 ordained priest in the Lutheran Church of Sweden; 1966 ThD and Habilitation; 1971–1990 Professor for New Testament Exegesis at Uppsala University; 1990–1995 Director of the Church of Sweden Research Department; 1995 retirement; 2011 doctor honoris causa at Helsinki University.

ISBN 978-3-16-152319-9
ISSN 0512-1604 (Wissenschaftliche Untersuchungen zum Neuen Testament)

Die Deutsche Nationalbibliothek lists this publication in the Deutsche Nationalbibliographie; detailed bibliographic data are available on the Internet at *http://dnb.dnb.de*.

© 2013  Mohr Siebeck Tübingen, Germany. www.mohr.de

This book may not be reproduced, in whole or in part, in any form (beyond that permitted by copyright law) without the publisher's written permission. This applies particularly to reproductions, translations, microfilms and storage and processing in electronic systems.

The book was typeset by Progressus Consultant AB in Karlstad, Sweden, printed by Gulde-Druck in Tübingen on non-aging paper and bound by Buchbinderei Spinner in Ottersweier.

Printed in Germany.

# Contents

Preface .................................................................................................. XI

## Exegesis and Hermeneutics

1. Commentary: A Communication about a Communication ....... 3
   1. Theoretical Presuppositions ........................................................ 3
   2. Mark 1:9–11 ................................................................................. 7
   3. Final Comments .......................................................................... 10

2. Exegetes – Interpreters? ................................................................... 13
   1. Exegeses and Interpretation ....................................................... 13
   2. Two Models .................................................................................. 14
   3. The Situation of the Text as the Focus ...................................... 18
   4. The Sender and the Text as the Focus ....................................... 20
   5. The Text as the Focus .................................................................. 21
   6. The Reader as the Focus ............................................................. 25

3. Interpreting Eschatological Texts .................................................. 29
   1. Preliminaries ................................................................................ 29
   2. Hermeneutics of Eschatology ..................................................... 31
   3. The Author and His Text ............................................................ 34
   4. A Topical Interpretation ............................................................. 35

4. Bundesideologie in und hinter einigen paulinischen Texten .... 41
   1. Begriffsbestimmung .................................................................... 41
   2. Problemstellung ........................................................................... 42
   3. Bundesideologisch gefärbte Texte .............................................. 46
   4. Resumé ......................................................................................... 54

## 5. Is the Crucified Christ the Center of a New Testament Theology?........57
1. The Problem of the Center of the New Testament .................57
2. The Crucified Christ in Paul.................61
3. The Crucified Christ in John ................64
4. Toward a NT Theology.................66

## 6. Two Early Readings of First Corinthians.................69
1. Introductory Remarks.................69
2. First Letter of Clement .................70
3. "Third Corinthians".................72
4. The Principle of Eccleastical Usage.................74
5. Résumé.................75

## 7. An Early Example of Jewish Exegesis.................77
1. The Book of the Watchers .................77
2. The Concept of Interpretation of Scripture .................78
3. 1 Enoch 10:16–11:2 .................79
4. Interpretative Techniques .................83
5. Theological Message .................85
6. Excursus .................86

# The Gospel of Mark

## 8. Grammar and Exegesis .................91
1. Modern Translations .................91
2. Ancient Grammarians.................93
3. Discussion.................94

## 9. Markus 6,3a im Lichte einiger griechischer Texte.................99
1. Die bisherige Diskussion.................99
2. Belege aus der hellenistischen Welt .................100
3. Ergebnis.................102

10. Loving "with Your Whole Heart" — Giving "Her Whole Living" .................................................................................... 103
    1. General Considerations .............................................................. 103
    2. The Structure of Mark 11:1–12:44. Some Proposals .................. 105
    3. A New Proposal ......................................................................... 110
    4. The Great Commandment and True Worship .......................... 112

11. Mark 16:1–8: the Ending of a Biography-like Narrative and of a Gospel ....................................................................... 115
    1. The Problematic Endings of Mark ............................................ 115
    2. The Function of Mark 16:1–8 as a Gospel Ending .................... 119
    3. Earlier Passages in Mark ........................................................... 121

12. „Was soll ich tun, damit ich das ewige Leben erbe?" ................. 127
    1. Das Markusevangelium für Heidenchristen ............................. 127
    2. Die Anwendung des Basileia-Begriffs ....................................... 129
    3. Die Leser/Hörer und die Gottesherrschaftsethik ..................... 130
    4. Das Ehescheidungsverbot ......................................................... 135
    5. Das Doppelgebot der Liebe ...................................................... 137
    6. Der Zukunftsaspekt .................................................................. 139
    7. Zusammenfassung .................................................................... 141

## Baptism

13. "Into the Name of Jesus" ............................................................ 145
    1. Earlier Research ........................................................................ 145
    2. Jewish Use of the l<sup>e</sup>shem- (l<sup>e</sup>shum-) formula ............................. 148
    3. Jesus as the Reference for Baptism .......................................... 152

14. La formule baptismale dans les Actes des Apôtres ..................... 155
    1. Les prépositions ........................................................................ 155
    2. Les génitifs ................................................................................ 161

15. Early Baptism – Early Christology .............................................. 165
    1. The Baptismal Formula "in(to) the name of Jesus" ................. 165

    2. The Use of Christological Titles ........................................................170

**16. Usages – Some Notes on the Baptismal Name-Formulae**........175
    1. The Formulae............................................................................................175
    2. Different Communication Situations................................................177
    3. Conclusion................................................................................................188

# Hellenistic Contexts

**17. *Psychē* – "Soul"?**...............................................................................193
    1. How do the Words נפשׁ and ψυχή Relate to Each Other?...............193
    2. The Word ψυχή in koine Greek...........................................................195
    3. The Word ψυχή in the Septuagint......................................................196
    4. Conclusions .............................................................................................201

**18. "…with the Overseers and Servants"**...........................................203
    1. The Problem............................................................................................203
    2. An Overlooked Parallel.........................................................................206
    3. Is the Comparison Valid?.....................................................................208
    4. Institutionalization?..............................................................................208
    5. The Neglecting of the *Diákonoi*........................................................210
    6. Possible Tasks of the Philippian Officials as Surmised from the Letter ......................................................................................................211

**19. "He Spoke of the Temple of His Body" (John 2:13–22)**...........215
    1. Temples and their Functions ..............................................................216
    2. Temple Imagery in John.......................................................................219

**20. Humble and Confident** ......................................................................223
    1. Introductory Remarks..........................................................................223
    2. The Representatives of the Philosophy as a Minority ..................224
    3. The Philosophy.......................................................................................224
    4. The Philosophers' Attitude to the Majority .....................................233
    5. The Majority as Confronted by the Minority..................................234

## 21. The Human Desire to Converse with the Divine ............ 237
1. What Does the Title Imply? ............ 237
2. Texts to Be Considered ............ 238
3. Main Features of the Divine ............ 238
4. Cult Sites and Images of the Divine ............ 240
5. Conclusion ............ 245

## 22. Hellenistic Elements in Apocalyptic Texts ............ 247
1. Introductory Remarks ............ 247
2. Syncretism ............ 249
3. Judaism as a Hellenistic Religion ............ 250
4. The Non-Rational Acquisition of Knowledge ............ 251
5. Astral Religion ............ 252
6. An Individual Perspective ............ 254
7. The Large Hellenistic World ............ 257
8. The View of History ............ 260
9. A Final Glance at the Small World ............ 262

## 23. The Book of Revelation ............ 265
1. Similarities in Apocalyptic Texts ............ 265
2. The Situation Behind Rev 2–3 ............ 267

## 24. Universal Reconciliation (Col 1:20) ............ 273
1. Preliminary Remark ............ 273
2. Different Problems ............ 274
3. Background to the Idea of Universal Reconciliation ............ 274
4. The Content of Col 1:15–20 ............ 281

## 25. Code and Context ............ 285
1. History of Research ............ 285
2. The Text in Its Context ............ 288
3. The Decalogue as a Structuring Factor ............ 289
4. Conclusions ............ 294

Bibliography .................................................................................................. 297
Selected Bibliography — Lars Hartman .................................................. 341
Acknowledgements ....................................................................................... 353
Index of Modern Authors............................................................................ 357
Index of Passages (selected) ........................................................................ 363

# Preface

As all Biblical scholars know all too well, much valuable research is hidden in journals that may be difficult to find. In addition, many journals are in "small" languages that most scholars cannot read. But, to be fair, journals have the great advantage that valuable research often can be published relatively quickly. The risk, however, is great that the new ideas just disappear into the void.

Much of what is written is of lasting value. As a consequence, it stands out as an important task to collect what is written by leading scholars and make it available for the scholarly community. It is thus a great honor for us to be able to publish a number of articles by our Doktorvater Lars Hartman, a widely renowned Biblical scholar. After having acquired his doctoral degree with a dissertation about the Synoptic apocalypse in 1966 and having spent a couple of semesters at Harvard Divinity School, Hartman returned to Uppsala University, where he served as professor of New Testament exegesis. His books include a study of 1 Enoch 1–5, a book of early Christian baptism, and two commentaries, on Mark and Colossians.

An earlier volume with papers by Lars Hartman was published in 1997 by Mohr Siebeck, *Text-Centered New Testament Studies. Text-Theoretical Essays on Early Jewish and Early Christian Literature* (edited by David Hellholm) as WUNT 102. We are most grateful to the publishing house that they once again have been willing to publish a number of scholarly essays by Lars Hartman. Thanks to this willingness, these essays will be easily accessible for decades to come.

No parts of Hartman's above-mentioned books are included. Together with the already published volume of essays the present volume will cover the main areas of Hartman's scholarship: basic hermeneutical topics, the gospel of Mark, early Christian baptism, and the Greco-Roman environment of the early church.

Layout, typesetting and compilation of indices has been done by Christer Hellholm of Progressus Consultant AB, Karlstad.

It is our hope that this volume, together with the earlier published collection of essays, will contribute fruitfully to the work of coming generations of Biblical scholars, and like Hartman's work be of service to the university as well as to the church.

Hammarö and Uppsala March 27, 2013 *David Hellholm   Tord Fornberg*

# Part I

Exegesis and Hermeneutics

# 1. Commentary
## A Communication about a Communication[1]

### 1. Theoretical Presuppositions

Throughout the centuries Jews and Christians have produced commentaries on their holy scriptures. The history of commentary writing is long, and a look into it confronts the student with several genres, usages and spiritual contexts that have determined the production of commentaries and their use. That history will not be taken into consideration here,[2] although it is a presupposition for the fact that some of us still put ourselves to writing such books, and, of course, for publishers to invest money in publishing them.

But what is a commentary?[3] The title of this paper seems to presuppose that we know the answer. If, however, we look up the word in Webster's dictionary, we find that it defines a commentary as, among other things, "a series of explanatory notes or annotations." Nothing is said about any exposition of a text or interpretation of it, as we would expect and as sometimes an editor of a commentary series may delineate the purpose of the series in question.[4]

Actually, however, the definition in Webster's dictionary corresponds to what a commentary was like in antiquity: notes or memoranda, for example such as for a lecture, or from a lecture (as taken down by students), or to a text, often without any systematic order. Thus, when Origen wrote commentaries, they were precisely such notes to biblical books. Commentaries belonged to the lecture hall or lay on the lecturer's desk. But if we look for a running interpretation by Origen of a biblical text, it is to his homilies that we are referred.

The preceding paragraph mentioned the "interpretation ... of a biblical *text*." When, however, Origen's commentaries and homilies deal with narratives, they

---

[1] Paper delivered at a symposium arranged by Brill Publishers on July 28, 2008 in Oslo to honor Peder Borgen for his long engagement in the board of *Novum Testamentum*.

[2] For this history see BERYL SMALLEY, "The Bible in the Medieval Schools," in *Cambridge History of the Bible* 2, Cambridge 1969, 197–220; BASIL HALL, "Biblical Scholarship: Editions and Commentaries," in *Cambridge History of the Bible* 3 (1963) 38–93; DOUGLAS R. JONES, "Commentaries: a Historical Note," in *Cambridge History of the Bible* 3 (1963) 531–535.

[3] A few contributions to the discussion of what a commentary may be are GERHARD LOHFINK, "Kommentar als Gattung," *BibLeb* 5 (1974) 1–16; RENÉ KIEFFER, "Was heißt das, einen Text zu kommentieren?," *BZ* 20 (1976) 212–216; WOLFGANG SCHENK, "Was ist ein Kommentar?" *BZ* 24 (1980) 1–20; FRANK H. GORMAN JR, "Commenting on Commentary: Reflections on a Genre," in: *Relating to the Text*, (eds.), THIMOTHY J. SANDOVAL/CARLEEN MANDOLFO, London – New York 2003, 100–119.

[4] See, e.g., the prefaces of volumes in the Sacra Pagina or Word Biblical Commentary series.

raise a question that can be put to several commentators, namely: do you comment on a text or on an event? Origen represents a common way of reading in that he identifies the contents of a narrative with an historical event, and it is this event that he discusses in his commentaries and homilies. But along with text linguists and narratologists it is useful to make a distinction between three worlds: the narrative world, the world of narration and the historical world.[5] Thus, for example, in their narratives about Jesus' entry into Jerusalem, Matthew and Luke each presents a narrative world. (Narratologists may label it the diegetic level.) The world of narration, on the other hand, is the one in which this narrative is delivered by the narrator and received by the audience. (Narratologists sometimes call it the extra-diegetic level.) In that world Matthew turns to his audience and Luke to his. The historical world, finally, is the one in which the historical Jesus appeared around 30 CE in Palestine. In consideration of these distinctions the following discussion will pertain to commenting on texts, and this is true also when we turn to commentaries on narratives.

In what follows a simple model of human communication will provide us with a number of concepts by which to analyze how a commentary functions as a piece of communication:[6]

In a given Situation and with a certain Purpose a Sender communicates a Message through a Text to a Recipient.

Let us apply this model to the passage in 1 Corinthians 1 where Paul begins to argue against the Corinthian dissension. The Sender is of course Paul, and the Recipients are the Corinthian Christian community. The Situation that determines the Text is the dissensions of the addressee. Paul's Message has primarily to do with his Purpose with regard to the Situation, namely to suppress the dissensions and to provide an argument for why they must do so. In his argument Paul also asks a couple of rhetorical questions, "Was Paul crucified for you?"; "Were you baptized into the name of Paul?" (1 Cor 1:13). These queries reflect aspects of Paul's views on Christ, on the importance of his, and on baptism, but they primarily function as elements of his argument for a message with a precise purpose in a very precise situation.

When exegetes interpret Paul's text they produce a text on Paul's text, and the result is a second communication that can be described in this way:

---

[5] See, e.g., SHLOMITH RIMMON-KENAN, *Narrative Fiction: Contemporary Poetics*, London – New York, 1983; repr. Routledge 1991, 91–95; also ELISABETH GÜLICH/WOLFGANG RAIBLE, *Linguistische Textmodelle, Grundlagen und Möglichkeiten* (UTB 139), Munich 1977, 212–238.

[6] For a more detailed version of this model and for comments on it see Gülich/Raible in the section quoted in the preceding note, and also WALLACE MARTIN, *Recent Theories of Narrative*, Ithaca – London 1986, 152–172. One aspect that is left aside here is the performance, that is, the non-linguistic side of the communication, such as gestures, voice modulation and other outward factors that can determine the reception of the audience; see GÜLICH/RAIBLE, *Linguistische Textmodelle*, 33–34. [HARTWIG KALVERKÄMPER, "Körpersprache", in: *HWR* 4 (1998), 1339–1371 (Lit.).]

Through a Text² a Sender²/the Interpreter, in a Situation² and with a Purpose² interprets a Text to a Recipient² as containing the Message of the Sender¹ with a certain Purpose¹ to Recipient¹, who is in a given Situation¹.

Applied to a New Testament professor who gives a class on 1 Corinthians, we get the following: through a Text², that is, his/her comments, a Sender², that is, the teacher in question, in a Situation², that is, in the class, interprets Paul's Text to Recipients², that is, the students, as being Paul's Message to the Corinthians, with the Purpose to eliminate the dissensions. The teacher does this with the Purpose to teach the students a bit of Pauline exegesis.

Above reference was made to Webster's definition of "commentary," which actually corresponds to what commentaries were like in antiquity. As a matter of fact modern NT exegetes are well acquainted with a commentary that meets this definition, and that, accordingly, is something else than a text-interpreting commentary of the kind presupposed in the model of interpretation above. The work in question is of course P. Billerbeck's *Kommentar zum Neuen Testament aus Talmud und Midrasch*.

Billerbeck's quotations of and references to rabbinic passages are supposed to shed light on the NT texts.⁷ But what does this material tell a present day reader about the diegetic world that, say, Mark presented to his readers? Very little, unless one presupposes that the narrative world of Mark is identical with the historical world from which Billerbeck's material is taken and which is also supposed to be similar to that of the historical Jesus.

We now turn to commentaries in the sense of the word we are used to, and, as already indicated, the model of interpretation will thereby serve as an analytic instrument. However, to mention "interpretation" means approaching a field full of philosophical and hermeneutical mines. Already words like "understand" and "interpret" are slippery and capable of several meanings. The following discussion will largely keep away from hermeneutics, but nevertheless a few words must be spent on "interpretation." Following on the previous discussion, interpretation, broadly defined, is the use of other, clarifying words to express the same contents as the text interpreted. But, in addition, the word interpretation will also be used in another, stronger sense and will stand for not just a clarifying, but a deepening of the contents of the text interpreted. This comes close to what is normally called interpretation, not least when biblical texts are concerned.⁸

Representing the matter in this way presupposes that the biblical texts do not just mean anything whatever you like. To return to the communication

---

⁷ SCHENK ("Was ist ein Kommentar?," 3–4) discusses the functions of such *annotationes-*commentaries as compared to an interpretive task; he then also refers to HERBERT BRAUN, *Qumran und das Neue Testament,* Tübingen 1966. In principle *Der neue Wettstein* can be said to belong to the same category of useful tools for doing exegesis; they do not interpret the biblical texts but can help the interpreter to do so by providing material that sheds light on vocabulary, concepts, etc.

⁸ Cf., e.g., chapter two in GERHARD SAUTER, *The Question of Meaning: A Theological and Philosophical Orientation*, Grand Rapids, Mich. – Cambridge (UK) 1995a.

model: through a text somebody, say, Paul, tells somebody, say, the Corinthians, something in a certain situation with a certain purpose. The present writer is of the opinion that it is possible for a commentator of this text to catch fairly well what Paul seems to have told his readers. This is true also of Mark as well as of Ben Sira and Epictetus. They are ambiguous only to a certain degree.

Two remarks should be added: first, the approach here adopted means focusing on what the addressees got out of the text. Secondly, the present writer is not so conceited as to believe that his interpretations are decisive answers to the question of what a text, say, by Mark, told its audience. It must also be underlined that the interpretations can become more varied when it comes to an interpretation in the stronger sense: when the interpreter tries to expand on an underlying basic ideology or on ideological implications, for instance, of the text; still, only the first communication is in view. So a present day interpreter may interpret Mark in a class, and not only try to clarify what Mark told his readers, but also attempt to translate this message, performing, say, some kind of demythologizing. The teacher is still clarifying Mark's message to his first century recipients, but wants the students to see what was at stake on a deeper level. The ideas of the text are not simply objects on a shelf in a museum of ideas but are humanly interesting, we may even dare to say, existentially interesting.

So far for interpretation. When we now go on to discuss what a commentator does when commenting a text, the model of interpretation will, as stated, determine the course of the discussion. For the sake of clarity the deliberations will be illustrated by examples from the New Testament, mostly from the Gospel of Mark.[9]

Thus, in a certain Situation Mark tells somebody something with a certain Purpose and does so through his Text. A certain commentator can be interested in different elements of that model, e.g., in the Situation, that is, in a given situation in the history of the early church. Another commentator may concentrate on the author, asking, e.g., how Mark thought, what were his biases, etc.

So a commentary is a Text$^2$ on Text$^1$, and this Text$^2$ is written with a certain Purpose with regard to a Recipient$^2$, that is, to the readers of the commentary. Thus one question to be asked when writing a commentary or studying one is: which Recipients does the writer of a commentary have in view? Pious Bible readers? Students of divinity? The guild of scholarly exegetes? A writer may not necessarily choose only one group of addressees, but the choice has consequences for where the accents of the commentary are put. Thus, if a commentary's principal recipients are supposed to be students of divinity, some energy might be spent on demonstrating how a literary analysis of the texts leads to exegetical consequences, and it also becomes important to show how the cultural back-

---

[9] The reason for the choice is very practical: a couple of years ago the present writer published a commentary on that Gospel: LARS HARTMAN, *Markusevangeliet 1–2*, Stockholm 2004–2005. An English revised version *Mark for the Nations. A Text- and Reader-oriented Commentary* is published by Wipf and Stock Publishers 2010.

ground of Recipients[1] colors the communication between the biblical author and his first addressees.

Most commentators discuss how scholarly colleagues have dealt with the different exegetical problems raised by the individual pericopes. This has also to do with the issue of the audience. When a commentary richly refers to how exegetes have dealt with a given text, this may certainly be of use to students of exegesis and can teach them how others have interpreted a given text. Referring to the scholarly discussion of course also means giving credit to the colleagues for their work.[10] But for the task of interpretation these references mean little, and the Bible-interested lay people do not bother about what Pesch or Gnilka has said concerning this or that pericope.[11]

Thus the commentator tells somebody something about a given Text. However, this Text is not, so to speak, just a naked text, but the commentator's reading of it is determined by the fact that precisely he or she is the one who reads it. This means focusing on the Sender of Text[2]. The writer in question does not only apply certain methods, such as some kind of reader-response criticism, but she or he is also a person of a certain character, being rooted in a specific scholarly and/or religious tradition, having particular experiences and prejudices, of which he or she is conscious only of some. Is the exegete who produces the commentary a rationalist, a somewhat refractory churchman, or something else entirely? The answers to such questions are not without their interest to the readers of the commentaries and can determine and indeed be most helpful in their reading.

## 2. Mark 1:9–11

When we now continue our discussion of how the factors of the interpretation model are taken into account by a commentator, we will use as an exemplary text the story of Jesus' baptism according to Mark 1:9–11.

What Mark says is communicated in an interplay between the factors involved according to the communication model. A basic factor is of course Mark's medium, the Text. In our case there are no serious problems in the manuscript tradition or any linguistic difficulties that require a discussion, and they can thus be left aside. Most commentators are not philologists and avoid tackling complicated linguistic issues. All too often they do, however, not think of using the help one can get from the older Church fathers; after all, the New Testament texts are written in their cultural environment in their language. Origen, for

---

[10] In the Mark commentary by the present writer (see the preceding note) very few such references were made, since it was presupposed that the students can easily get this information in other commentaries.

[11] See nn. 14 and 15 below.

example, was much better in Greek than we are, however much we look things up in grammars and dictionaries.[12]

As a text the passage under study has a particular compositional structure. In Mark 1:9–11 the baptism is very briefly mentioned and is immediately followed by a vision: Jesus "sees" the heaven opened and the Spirit descending on him like a dove and a voice is saying, "You are my beloved son, with you I am well pleased." This structure implies that the kernel of the story is the vision with the heavenly words. Most readers need this information – the scholarly exegete, when reading it, realizes that the colleague knows how to handle narrative structure.

One further aspect of this textual surface is that the statement on the Son has a meaningful place in the larger composition of the evangelist. The Son is first mentioned in the headline of the book that in a few traditional terms informs the reader about the main character of the following pages, Jesus, the anointed, the Son of God.[13] Then there are a few signposts along the way: via our passage, and the narrative on the transfiguration (9:2–8) on to the comment of the centurion after Jesus' death (15:39).

A particular way of focusing on the Text is to investigate its history of tradition or its redaction history. In a study of Mark this means asking how Mark has treated motifs or textual traditions that he has taken over. To some commentators this is so important that the question of what Mark's readers might have learned from the text plays next to no role. In this kind of approach the Text is analyzed in such a way that its function within communicative acts between a Sender and his Recipients is largely neglected. On the other hand, to a commentator who is mainly interested in the Text as involved in an act of communication the history of tradition and the redaction history are not as important issues. This is so, even if, in our case, there are reasons to assume that the wording of the heavenly voice is influenced by early Christian usage of the Bible (i.e., the *graphai*, or scriptures of Israel) in Christological reflection.[14] However, redaction history can shed some light on certain features of the Situation of the Markan communication, and so we will return to that topic when we consider the element of the communication model that was labeled the Situation, in which and with regard to which Mark's communication took place.

A concentration on the communication between Author/Sender and Recipients also may mean refraining from trying to look into the head of the author, in our case of Mark. It is common for the writers of commentaries to regard it their principal task to find out the personal theological tendencies of the biblical

---

[12] I had the occasion to realize this fact in "Grammar and Exegesis," in: *For Particular Reasons* (FS J. Blomqvist); eds. ANDERS PILTZ ET ALII, Lund 2003, 133–141. [No. 8 in this volume.]

[13] Thus, I prefer the longer text of Mark 1:1, assuming that "the Son of God" belongs to the original text.

[14] RUDOLF PESCH, *Das Markusevangelium 1* (HThK 2/1), Freiburg i. Br. – Basel – Vienna 1976, 92–127, assumes that behind the vision lies a so-called *Deutevision*, originating in the Jerusalem church.

author, and to do so through analyzing how, in our case, Mark has supposedly revised and edited the traditions he takes over. It can happen that commentators are so interested in the author's personal bias that they leave aside the present shape of the text, the actual means of the author's communication with his readers. He is studied as a theologian of the early church, and what he is actually doing to his addressees in a given piece of text becomes less interesting.[15]

There are other ways to reconstruct a Markan theology, namely by means of the text as it stands. Indeed, you assume that Mark meant what he said. Then you systematize certain aspects of the messages that Mark conveys to his readers in the individual pericopes as understood within the whole of the gospel. In that way you may, for example, delineate a Markan view on the person of Jesus or on what Christian ethics could be like.[16]

The next element to consider in the model is the Readers/Recipients of the communication of the biblical author. Their cultural and religious backgrounds form decisive presuppositions of how they apprehend what they hear. So a commentator should inform his/her readers of how he/she imagines these readers. In Mark's case, assuming that they are Gentile Christians is not very original, but seems clearly to be the case.[17] Mark also seems to presuppose that they have received some Christian education, and that it is meaningful to quote passages from the Old Testament to them, indeed to allude to such passages (already in 1:2f.). Such presuppositions are especially significant when the heavenly voice in the baptism text (1:11) contains an echo of Psalm 2. It might very well be that they could have caught some of these echoes only after having been instructed in the Christian community. There were presumably differences within the audience when it came to how deep their orientation was in terms of the scriptures, theology, etc., but the author assumes some such general knowledge.

This brings us to the factor of the model that was labeled the Situation. Here the commentator has to give his/her reader some insights into the world in which the communication took place. In our case this is the Situation of the Recipients of Mark. There were things that were self-evident to Mark and to his readers but about which the reader of today knows little or nothing. Nonetheless they form as it were a sounding-board under the music played by Mark in his text.

---

[15] E.g., PESCH, *Markusevangelium 1*, 48–62; JOACHIM GNILKA, *Das Evangelium nach Markus 1* (EKK 2/1), Zürich – Einsiedeln – Köln • Neukirchen-Vluyn 1978, 25–30.

[16] FRANCIS J. MOLONEY does something of this sort in *The Gospel of Mark*, Peabody, Mass. 2002, 352–353, *et passim*. The outlook is fundamental to BAS M. F. VAN IERSEL, *Mark: A Reader-Response Commentary* (JSNTSup 164), Sheffield 1998. Also LARS HARTMAN, "‚Was soll ich tun, damit ich das ewige Leben erbe?' Ein heidenchristlicher Leser vor einigen ethischen Sätzen des Markusevangeliums," in *Eschatologie und Ethik* (FS G. Haufe), ed. CHRISTFRIED BÖTTRICH, Frankfurt am Main 2006, 75–90. [No. 12 in this volume.]

[17] See, e.g., GNILKA, *Das Evangelium nach Markus*, 34; CAMILLE FOCANT, *L'évangile selon Marc* (Commentaire biblique NT 2), Paris 2004, 37.

In addition, there is what we could call the specific Situation, that is, features that belonged to the concrete experience of the Christian addressees of Mark, such as the shadow cast over their existence by persecutions in the past and maybe more to come (cf. Mark 13:11–13). Above it was also mentioned that sometimes redaction critical analyses might give indications about particular features of the specific Situation of a communication.

Of course it is all the more important that a commentator takes into account the specific situation of the NT letters to individual communities with particular problems. It is, for example, of decisive importance to the one who wants to shed light on what Paul was saying to the Romans in Rom 6:1–14 that what seems to be a teaching about baptism is primarily an argument in a situation where Paul's theology of justification is under attack for leading to immorality.[18]

Considering the general Situation, we have seen that the words of the heavenly voice, "You are my son," are the kernel of Mark 1:9–11. Which associations would Gentile Christians get from such a designation? Some commentators find references to Israelite history of religion relevant and cite myths and rituals belonging to the sphere of divine kingship in the Ancient Near East.[19] But what do they say about the conditions of the understanding by Mark's readers? More likely it should have meant something to them that in the Roman empire one also knew to speak of sons of the gods; there were such sons among gods, heroes, rulers, philosophers, and miracle workers.

Here a commentator has to make a choice, although maybe she or he does not always make it consciously. Often the commentators refer to OT passages to shed light on the Markan passage,[20] or may make an excursion into early Judaism, say to Philo or to the Qumran texts,[21] or into Hellenistic history of religion.[22] In practice the commentator may follow the ancient commentary genre, i.e., collect scattered notes to a text which serve other purposes than the interpretation of Mark's message in this text.

## 3. Final Comments

Finally, to the Situation that determined the readers' reception of the textual communication also belongs the way the text was used. As this colors the reception of the Message, a commentator asking what a passage told its readers should have an opinion of how the biblical text has functioned among the readers.[23] As

---

[18] See, e.g., ROBERT JEWETT, *Romans* (Hermeneia), Minneapolis, Minn. 2007, 390–412.

[19] FRIEDRICH HAUCK, *Das Evangelium des Markus* (ThHK 2), Leipzig 1931, 16–17.

[20] E.g., JOEL MARCUS, *Mark 1–8* (AB), New York 1999, 66; ADELA Y. COLLINS, *Mark* (Hermeneia), Minneapolis, Minn. 2007, 147–148.

[21] Thus, e.g., MARCUS, *Mark 1–8*, 66.

[22] See, e.g., ERICH KLOSTERMANN, *Das Markusevangelium* (HNT 3), Tübingen ⁵1971, 10.

[23] It means a particular aspect in the Situation when one suggests that the story of Jesus' baptism at least to some recipients has worked as a cult legend, having Christian baptism in view; thus COLLINS, *Mark*, 147.

to the Gospel of Mark, the present writer is not alone in his belief that the gospel of Mark functioned in the Christian community, in education and in readings at the common worship.[24] This means a particular filter for the reader's/listener's understanding of the message of our Markan passage. Readings carried out at an occasion of worship are open to other semantic dimensions than the merely objective-descriptive ones. In such a context one encounters Mark's citation of the words of the heavenly voice with particular key signatures. There is more of chiaroscuro in the scene than, say, in the one where Herod's daughter says: "Give me the head of John the Baptist on a platter" (Mark 6:25). Regarding the gospel in this manner has consequences in terms of how to view its Purpose – to mention a further factor of the communication model. The purpose then is more to edify than mainly to inform.

Insofar as a commentator should interpret the text, we now, at last, arrive at the message Mark conveys to his readers. Colleagues who have discussed what a commentary is have declared that it should elucidate the message or the meaning of the text for the readers of the commentary.[25] There are, however, many possible ways of understanding such a statement, depending on which interpreter says what to whom in which situation with which purpose. Picking up the somewhat formulaic terms of the interpretation/communication model, we might differentiate between at least the following typical cases. (Message$^1$ is the Message of Sender$^1$ to Recipients$^1$; Message$^2$ is the message the Interpreter takes to be the Message of the Text or of Sender$^1$ to Recipients$^2$; by "rephrasing interpretation" I mean the simpler, non-deepening interpretation I mentioned when defining "interpretation" above.)

1. The Interpreter/Sender$^2$ provides Recipients$^2$ with a rephrasing interpretation of Message$^1$ to Recipients$^1$.

2. The same as 1 above, but presupposing that Message$^1$ is also the Message$^2$ to Recipients$^2$.

3. The same as 1 above but in addition also interpreting Message$^1$ in a deeper or more wide embracing way; still, however, the focus is on Message$^1$ to Recipients$^1$.

4. The same as 3 above, but adding a Message which applies Message$^1$ to Recipients$^2$.

These cases look different in practice, depending on the variables of the model. Thus, which is the task of the Interpreter (more or less academic?, more or less

---

[24] See LARS HARTMAN, "Das Markusevangelium ‚für die *lectio solemnis* im Gottesdienst verfasst'?," in *Geschichte-Tradition-Reflexion* (FS M. Hengel), ed. HUBERT CANCIK ET ALII, Tübingen 1996, 147–171. [Reprinted in HARTMAN, *Text-Centered New Testament Studies* (WUNT 102), Tübingen 1997, 25–51.]

[25] E.g., KIEFFER, "Was heißt das, einen Text zu kommentieren?"

pastoral?), which is the Situation of the Interpretation (academic?, pastoral?), who are its Recipients (scholars?, students?, pastors?, Bible-reading lay-people?), and which is the Purpose (academic training?, Bible study?, preaching?). It is important also to note that some of the possible cases presuppose a particular ideological position, namely that the interpretation given suggests that it represents God's message to Recipients[2]. It should also be pointed out that the differentiation above certainly is more clear-cut than reality. One commentary may in fact represent several combinations of the variables. However, the distinctions may possibly serve as an invitation to reflection, both on the side of the interpreters and among the users of their commentaries, on the central questions: "What am I actually doing when commenting," and "What is going on in this commentary?"[26]

In our Markan example obviously the kernel of the message is that the Jesus whose work the following book is about was God's son equipped with the Spirit. One may be of the opinion that the commentator should only hand over this message to the present day reader without any further explanations; this may be reminiscent of case 1 above, as well as of case 2. Somebody may add that the designation God's son means that Jesus is acting on behalf of God. This represents a small beginning of what was called a deepening interpretation and comes a little nearer to case 3. In the commentaries we thus encounter different degrees of interpretation, from a simple paraphrase using traditional biblical terms, on to "trans-culturations" of the message that require some sort of demythologization in order to make the then-message (Message[1]) understandable to the reader of today.

So we have mustered some aspects of commentaries, asking how they appear when regarded as pieces of communication about texts that basically are themselves acts of communication. The above reflections have had a limited scope, which is due not least to the fact that hermeneutics has largely been left aside; this is so either hermeneutics is taken as a philosophical discussion of the usage of and the understanding of textual signs in general or it is understood as principles of how to interpret and possibly apply biblical texts in new times. This bracketing of philosophical and theological hermeneutics may be regarded as a *religionswissenschaftliche* attitude rather than a theological one, but even so this narrower perspective might stimulate our ways of approaching biblical commentaries. Asking which factors in a textual communication are a commentator's focus may be clarifying both to writers of commentaries and to their readers, and actually even invite them to pose hermeneutical questions: in which sense does a given approach interpret a biblical text – if at all?

---

[26] In my own commentary (see note 9) I have adopted an attitude that very much corresponds to cases 1 and 3, assuming that the main purpose of my commentary is to expose the now-readers (Recipients[2]) to what was the then-message (Message[1]) to the then-readers (Recipients[1]) and its purpose.

## 2. Exegetes – Interpreters?

### 1. Exegeses and Interpretation

All students of theology know that the Greek word *exēgēsis* means "explanation" or "interpretation", and so to them exegesis means biblical interpretation. Accordingly, an exegete is a Bible interpreter. But questions are now and then raised about whether we exegetes deserve our designation. Such misgivings may be heard from different quarters, but, above all, the methodological multiplicity and variety in the field today, including the advance of hermeneutics, make it natural for us to reflect for a moment: are we exegetes interpreters?

In the following paper, dedicated to my friend and exegetical colleague, Professor Karl-Gustav Sandelin, I will try to focus precisely on this issue: how far and in which sense do exegetes interpret when doing exegesis? I will deal with that question by regarding a number of common methodological approaches. What I do may be taken as belonging to hermeneutics, but that certainly does not mean that I discuss hermeneutics, which is a much larger field than the one covered here.

When exegesis was taught in the medieval universities, an interpretation of the Scriptures certainly took place, and it served above all to provide biblical arguments for the dogmatics of the Church.[1]

The Reformation brought no real change in *why* exegesis was used – that is, to bolster dogmatics and ethics – but it did change *how much* it was used, since the dogmatics and ethics of the then new Reformed churches rested in principle on Bible interpretation only. It is only fair to state that the principle of *sola scriptura* was – and is – illusory; this became obvious when *sola scriptura* theologians fought each other with biblical arguments: inherited or newly established presuppositions determined and supplemented the interpreters' understanding of the Scriptures.

Everyone who has looked at the history of our New Testament discipline knows that 18th century Enlightenment brought about the beginning of a change. Some Protestant exegetes began to regard the Bible as a collection of writings which could be investigated in the same manner as other material from the past, by using scientific tools and methods, and without any dogmatic or creedal bias. To these exegetes, exegesis was not interpretation for the needs of the Christian

---

[1] ROBERT M. GRANT 1963, 116–127; WERNER GEORG KÜMMEL 1972, 19–21. [See also WILLIAM BAIRD 1992, XV–XIX.]

community, but scholarship of the same kind as that applied to, say, Plato's dialogues or Plutarch's *Moralia*.[2]

After this beginning, critical and/or historical approaches have gradually been accepted by practically all biblical scholars, although at the Roman Catholic faculties this was not generally the case until this century. Nevertheless, the Catholic Church still expects her exegetes to function within the Church and not to depart from the overall God-centered ideology of the Bible.[3] Even though among Protestant churches the issue is seldom as explicitly articulated, these churches often place similar expectations upon the exegetes at the Protestant faculties. Therefore, today most scholarly exegetes are expected to interpret the Bible in some sense of the word and, in doing so, at least to be conscious of the fact that the majority of their students are being trained in order to interpret the Bible to the Christian community.

Although it is easy to recognize a possible tension between critical scholarship and expectations of Christian Bible interpretation, I will not deal with this problem here. I will, however, take for granted an understanding of interpretation which stays within common scientific borders. As such it should be acceptable both to ordinary literary critics and historians of ideas and to churchmen, although the latter may want to pursue it further beyond scholarly exegesis into the fields of normative application to dogmatics, ethics etc.

## 2. Two Models

I begin by presenting two models, the first of which is one of *communication:*

– In a given Situation a Sender communicates a Message through a Text to a Recipient with a certain Purpose.[4]

Such a model can be applied to both a Festschrift article and to, say, Mark's gospel. In scholarly work on a given document, one can concentrate on particular elements of its communication: for instance, on the text, studying, say, its structure or its grammar, or on the Sender and his/her Situation.[5]

Before combining this communication model with one of text interpretation, my use of the word interpretation should be clarified. I adopt the following definition:

---

[2] [Cf. BAIRD 1992, 3–57.]
[3] Commission 1993, 493–514.
[4] E.g. ELISABETH GÜLICH/WOLFGANG RAIBLE 1977, 21–26.
[5] Of course one can refine this model through differentiating between the Situation of the Sender and that of the Recipient, but in order for the communication to work, these two Situations should have so much in common that to an acceptable extent communication is established, i.e., that the Message gets through and its Purpose is achieved at least to such an extent that the process is not meaningless. Thus, in this case I refrain from differentiating between the two situations mentioned.

– An expression "A" is an interpretation of the expression "B", if "B" can be understood in such a way that its meaning is expressed by "A" in a clearer, more distinct or more complete way.[6]

To this definition two remarks should be added: firstly, it is so softly formulated that it admits that "B" can be understood in more than one way. Secondly, as to "meaning": its denotation is, to say the least, a bit vague.[7] In this connection I will use the term in a rather common sense manner, hoping that this will not cause any unnecessary obscurity. I will, however, make some use of E. D. Hirsch's distinction between "meaning" and "signification", in so far, namely, that "signification" actually takes into account a sort of interpretation that may mean slightly more of a "fusion of the horizons" of the text and of the reader (to use Gadamer's term)[8] than is contained in my definition's wording "clearer, more distinct or more complete way".

For my purpose the communication model should be complemented with one of text *interpretation*:

– In a given Situation an Interpreter interprets a Text as a Sender's Message to a Recipient in a certain Situation with a certain Purpose.[9]

Since exegetes are re-reading older texts, this interpretation model needs to be modified: We differentiate between the original Situation in which the communication took place and the secondary Situation in which the Text is interpreted by persons other than the original recipients and/or interpreters. So, if I designate the original Situations, Interpretations, etc. with the superscript 1, and the secondary ones with the superscript 2, we get:

– In Situation$^2$, Interpreter$^2$ interprets the Text to Recipient$^2$ as the Sender's Message$^1$ to Recipient$^1$ with Purpose$^1$ in Situation$^1$. [See now article no. 1 in this volume.]

This latter variant of the model represents what can be called an historical interpretation. For example: At the end of the 20$^{th}$ century a Finnish academic teacher gives a lecture (Interpreter$^2$ and Situation$^2$) to his students (Recipient$^2$) and interprets a passage from Paul's letter to the Galatians (Recipient$^1$) who were about to accept circumcision as demanded by the Jewish Torah (Situation$^1$); in his lecture the teacher explains how Paul argues when he tries to persuade the Galatians not to do so (Message$^1$ with Purpose$^1$).

My definition characterized interpretation as expressing the meaning of "B" in a clearer, more distinct or more complete way. But the Interpretation presented by Interpreter$^2$ can be more or less penetrating or profound. The extent to which this "more or less" is applicable depends not least on the type of text: a road description does not normally lend itself to any subtler interpretation, whereas an

---

[6] Filosofilexikonet 1988, 551, my translation.
[7] Filosofilexikonet 1988, 362–366, 460–462, 506–507.
[8] HANS-GEORG GADAMER 1979, 258f.
[9] GÖRAN HERMERÉN 1982, 270–273.

autobiography may do so. So also in the example from Galatians: an interpretation may restrict itself to analysing the logical sequence of the argument but may also go further, exposing, for instance, what kind of relationship between human beings and God is implied by Paul's argument. In the second, subtler, interpretation one may talk of an attempt to expose the "signification" of the meaning of Message$^1$.

The problem at issue when we ask about the relationship of Interpretation$^2$ to Message$^1$ is not dissimilar to that encountered when an attempt is made to translate a metaphor from one language into another in which that metaphor does not work: either another metaphor must be found or that which is expressed by the metaphor must be said without recourse to any pictorial language. But in order to do so, the metaphor in the first language must be analysed and a choice made from its several possible meanings. In a similar way, there can be several suggestions as to a possible Interpretation$^2$. For the sake of simplicity I take both the "profound" and the "less profound" Interpretation$^2$ as ways to interpret Message$^1$.

One can imagine a less historical and, say, more existential approach:

– In Situation$^2$, Interpreter$^2$ interprets the Text with its Message$^1$ as having Message$^2$ for Recipient$^2$ with Purpose$^2$.

This describes an attempt to translate the original message (as far as it can be reconstructed) into one which is understandable and relevant to a modern audience, that is, its "signification" to them. Imagine, for example, a modern interpreter interpreting Paul's argument against circumcision just referred to. He/she may claim that as a Message$^2$, the Galatianstext teaches an evangelical freedom from any religious legal rulings either from the Bible or from the Church (whether the "Church" be the Curia of today's Rome or the synod of this or that Protestant church). Or, thinking in the mode of existentialism, he/she may maintain that it is all about the authentic liberty which comes from having made the existential decision of faith.[10]

One may say that both of these interpretations are attempts at a translation and an application of the text's original message, but nevertheless a translation that makes the message so different from a Message$^1$ that it deserves to be described as Message$^2$. But since the promoters of the latter kind of interpretation were convinced that the Bible is about existential issues,[11] they may even claim that such an interpretation does not present a Message$^2$, but what I just called a "profound" Interpretation$^2$ of Message$^1$, representing its "signification". Thus, the relationship between Message$^1$ and Message$^2$ may be a matter of discussion, and it seems that the borderline is not always so sharp between a "profound" Interpretation$^2$ of Message$^1$ and an Interpretation$^2$ which strives for a Message$^2$ of the Text which is relevant in Situation$^2$.

---

[10] RUDOLF BULTMANN 1967, 28ff.
[11] Cf. KARL-GUSTAV SANDELIN 1993, 89–94.

This "existential" or translating approach is similar to, but nonetheless different from, another model which could be described as a pious Bible reading:

- In Situation², Interpreter² interprets the Text to Recipient² as the original Sender's Message to Recipient¹ *and* Recipient² with Purpose¹ in Situation¹ as well as in Situation².

To use the almost classic wording of Krister Stendahl: this means identifying "what the text meant" with "what it means".[12]

If, for a moment, we endeavour to apply the elements of this interpretation model to medieval ways of doing exegesis, we might describe its interpretative work in this way:

- In Situation², Interpreter² interprets to Recipient² the Text of Sender² as Sender¹'s Message² to Recipient² with Purpose² in Situation² which has a spiritual identity with Situation¹.

We should then also bring in a particular application of my definition of interpretation: medieval exegesis applied the principle of Scripture's four senses 1) the historical or literal, 2) the allegorical or Christological, 3) the tropological or moral or anthropological, 4) the anagogical or eschatological. This would then, to a medieval understanding, fulfil the task of expressing the meaning of the text in a "clearer, more distinct or more complete way".

But in order to find out what is hidden in my rewriting of the interpretation model as applied to medieval exegesis, it needs to be elaborated even a little more: In Situation² (the medieval Church) Interpreter² (say, a *doctor biblicus* in Prague) interprets the Text to Recipient² (his students of theology); but the Sender's Message to his Recipients (say, Paul's to the Galatians) becomes an even more original Sender's (the Holy Spirit's) Message² with Purpose² through Interpreter² to Recipient² whose Situation" has a spiritual identity with Situation¹ (the Church being one) in that Interpreter² is a representative of the Church's ministerium which is guided by the Spirit and is in solidarity with Tradition.

After these preliminaries, we come to the main part of this article in which I will compare some common exegetical approaches with the model of historical interpretation, and, in doing so, note how the model's different elements are variously focused. The approaches will be illustrated by features drawn from Matthew's version of the story of Jesus' baptism (Matt 3:13–17). Every exegete knows that the boundaries between some of the approaches are not very sharp; a scholar who uses modern rhetorical criticism may, for example, very well combine this approach with insights from the history of religion. And even exegetes who use tools from literary criticism often (but not always!) pay respect to historical criticism.

---

[12] KRISTER STENDAHL 1962, 420.

## 3. The Situation of the Text as the Focus

a. The *historico-critical* method still dominates biblical studies and covers several different approaches, such as source criticism, form criticism and redaction criticism. These approaches share a common interest in reconstructing the life and thought of Jesus and, not least, of the early Church. Therefore, exegetes who adhere to a historico-critical method also want to find out which ideas are those of the individual New Testament authors and writings. That is, to an essential extent the Situation of the Text is the focus, whereas in other cases the interest of the exegete is in the Author and his thinking.

When considering the Situation, one asks historical questions like: What happened? In our example: *That* Jesus was baptized is generally accepted as being beyond doubt; however, the second half of the story about the descent of the Spirit and the heavenly voice raises questions. In Mark it is a vision experienced by Jesus, whereas Matthew and Luke describe it as something the public sees. Thus, the historical question can be asked: Did Jesus have a vision, or is this element in the story rather a rhetorical means by which the author tells his readers about the greatness of his hero?

As to the history of early Christian ideas: Does Matt 3:13–17, for instance, reflect a self-awareness by Jesus of being a divine messenger, or even a messiah? Or are the Messianic overtones the result of the theological thinking of the early Church?

Should answers to such questions as those raised in the two last paragraphs be called interpretation? While they certainly do not represent an Interpretation[2] of the Message of the Text to its Recipient[1], they can, however, be said to be an Interpretation[2] of the Text taken as a mirror of something more or less belonging to Situation[1]. To use Abrams' definition: the approach is of a mimetic type.[13] But the interpretation hardly considers the communication aspects.

b. The so-called *history of religions* school regarded itself as historico-critical, when its representatives searched for the religio-historical background of different motifs in biblical texts. Thus, in Matt 3:13–17, H. Gressmann could comment on the motif of the divine Spirit's descending "like a dove" by referring to the idea that the dove was a manifestation of the Babylonian goddess Ishtar.[14] That, of course, might indeed seem a bit farfetched as an explanation of the Situation of the text. In addition, the historical basis for Gressmann's suggestion is not too firm. Few exegetes, if any, would call it an (element of an) interpretation of the present text.

However, one is on safer ground when commenting on the feature that Jesus is called the son of God: in this case the history of religions school introduced material we still encounter in the commentaries. Thus they pointed to the cir-

---

[13] MARK ALLAN POWELL 1992a, 5, referring to MEYER H. ABRAMS 1958.
[14] HUGO GRESSMANN 1920/21.

cumstance that in the Old Testament the king and/or the new saviour-king could be called the son of God,[15] and also to the fact that in antiquity in general, mighty rulers could be called sons of a god; in addition, in popular legends wise men also could be held to be sons of this or that god.[16]

Nor is this interpretation in the strict sense of the word. It may illuminate aspects of the prehistory of an expression and, in some cases, point to a possible cultural environment that may determine its reference. In this way it can be regarded as a preliminary step on the way toward an interpretation.

c. *Form-criticism* was also interested in the Situation of the Text, but defined this Situation as one typical of a given literary form (its *Sitz im Leben*, that is, of Israel or of the early Church). It should, however, be noted that this attention paid to the Situation was guided by observations of certain characteristics of the Text. When form-criticism was applied to our example, the somewhat misleading German word *Legende* was used,[17] a literary form that one assumed had the function of edifying or impressing the Recipient through demonstrating the greatness of the hero of the story. The purpose here then was to undergird the Christian proclamation of Jesus.

Actually, form-criticism was more interested in the prehistory of the texts than in interpreting them as we now have them. Thus the Situation, the Message and Purpose are not so much those of a given text, but rather those that the exegete assumed could be deduced from its literary form and placed in a typical situation earlier than that of the Text.

To what degree is this interpretation? Hardly in the full sense of my model of interpretation; however, form-criticism may *contribute* to interpretation by shedding light on the type of situation to which the Text normally belongs, when judging by its form.[18]

d. The *sociological approach* is also interested in the Situation of the Text, asking, for example, about its social preconditions or which sociological patterns it reflects. In our example, one can note, for instance, that Jesus' reception of the Holy Spirit underlines his being holy and pure, something which, later on in the story, creates a particular tension when he confronts the impurity of unclean spirits (4:24; 8:31f.) and also reports that he touches a leper (8:3) or a corpse (9:25), or eats with sinners (9:10).[19]

---

[15] GEORG FOHRER 1969, 349ff.
[16] PETER WÜLFING VON MARTITZ 1969, 337.
[17] RUDOLF BULTMANN 1964, 267f.
[18] But when form-criticism points to conventional structures of a literary form it can contribute more directly to an Interpretation² Take, for example, the pronouncement stories: form-criticism stresses that their kernel is the pronouncement, and accordingly should carry the weight of the Message brought forward by the Interpretation.
[19] DAVID RHOADS 1992, 149.

Although a sociological approach is not interpretation, a deepened knowledge of social patterns in and behind the textual communication certainly advances the possibilities of reaching an historical interpretation.

## 4. The Sender and the Text as the Focus

a. In the *tradition-historical* approach, the individual Text, or elements of it, are regarded as traditions, handed down and edited during a process of transmission. In our example: evidently Matthew edits his source, Mark, when inserting the refusal by John to baptize Jesus. I will consider this particular way of doing tradition-history below under redaction-criticism.

But the tradition-historian also tries to reconstruct earlier forms of the tradition. In our case he may suggest that originally the tradition only said that Jesus was baptized by John in the Jordan. The second element, the vision with the heavenly voice, is taken to be a later addition which, through a Messianic application of two Old Testament passages, turns the baptism into Jesus' installation as the Messiah.[20]

To what extent is this interpretation? It is certainly no interpretation of the present text but an attempt to use it and its reconstructed prehistory as a sort of mirror reflecting elements in the history of early Christian ideas: in our case, the early development of Christology.

b. In *redaction criticism*, Sender and Text are definitely in focus. On the one hand, one studies the Sender's use of his sources. So in our Matthean case, Matthew's editing of Mark may suggest what was Matthew's intention as author, for example, by noticing John's initial refusal to baptize Jesus. Thus, also the Message of the Text is taken into consideration.

But, on the other hand, redaction criticism also particularly looks for how the author's/redactor's changes in wordings and how rearrangements of the material can give insights into his theological interests or bias. Here, the Author's intended Message is sought for. But when one also regards the Message as effected by the Sender's way of moulding the Text of the whole gospel as well as the Situation and Purpose of that Message, the Message appears as more deduced from the Text as it stands.

In our example: the Matthean changes can seem to serve a wish on Matthew's part to present Jesus as superior to John, not least in the sense that he was totally obedient to God and so "fulfilled all righteousness".[21] When this motif returns several times in this Gospel (e.g., 4:10; 5:17; 16:21–23; 26:39), this Christology also appears to be carried by the macro-text.

Is this then interpretation? It is, and as such, it is another example of what Abrams called an "expressive" approach.[22] That is, on the one hand, the text is

---

[20] BULTMANN 1964, 267f.
[21] EDUARD SCHWEIZER 1973, 28–30.
[22] [ABRAMS 1958, 21–26.]

regarded as an expression of the author's ideas: one considers more the intention of the author than the text itself as used as a means of communication. But, on the other hand, the latter aspect is more the focus of attention of that kind of redaction criticism which takes into account the totality of the macro-text's composition.

## 5. The Text as the Focus

This heading may be somewhat misleading because the approaches I am going to deal with here normally couple a text-centered attitude with suggestions concerning Message$^1$ or Message$^2$ of the Text. In the following presentation of text-centered approaches the reader will find that more and more elements of the communication-interpretation model are taken into account. So the pragmatic aspects of the text are also taken into account, i.e., its Situation and the Sender's Purpose with the Recipient.

a. There are several approaches which can be called *semiotic* (or, sometimes, "structuralist"). In these, the Interpreter$^2$ definitely concentrates on the Text, but also in a sense on the Message, and programmatically leaves aside the Sender, Recipient$^1$ etc. One analyses the syntagmatic aspects of the text, distinguishing the phases of the story and their relations. In addition, one asks what actors, actions, time and place signify in their relationships in the ongoing story. Lastly, on the deeper level, one searches for the logical and signifying basic forms which determine the narrative and its contents. Here a focusing of contrasts and oppositions often plays an important role as a help in discovering such deeper structures.

Of course, it is impossible here to perform a semiotic analysis of our Matthean example. But we can easily recognize some features that could be taken into account in a such an analysis. Thus, we first note the phases of the story: initially, John refuses to baptize Jesus; then after a short discussion, he changes his mind and performs the baptism; this earthly event is then complemented by Jesus' vision of the Spirit descending upon him and of a heavenly voice addressing him as his son. In a following discursive analysis we could, amongst other things, consider the roles of the actors: John at first impedes the development, but does so as a prophet who realizes that Jesus is his superior and should not undergo any baptism for the remission of sins. On the other hand, Jesus claims that he must be baptized in order that all righteousness be fulfilled. After the baptism in water (earthly), the Spirit and the voice unite the contraries heaven and earth, and assert that the earthly Jesus is heavenly, or at least an earthly being with a heavenly task. In these latter observations, we have come to the logico-semantic deep level, and a semiotician could pursue these deliberations at length. For example, he/she might suggest that the utterance by Jesus on fulfilling all righteousness places the event in a tension between divine justice and human unrighteousness, a gap which then is bridged by Jesus' symbolic action – or, rather, by submitting himself to John's action in the same way as the one demanded of sinners.

This is certainly interpretation, and one which we, with Abrams, could call "objective"[23]: the text is being taken as a world-in-itself. However, regarding the search for the Message, i.e., a Message$^1$, an outsider may sometimes ask to what extent the results correspond to the original message – something which, in fact, does not disturb the orthodox adherents of this approach. If confronted with our model, they would probably choose to call their exegesis an Interpretation$^2$ of the Text as having this Message$^2$. To take up my definition of interpretation again, a historically minded colleague would doubt that this sort of interpretation expresses the meaning of "B" in a clearer, more distinct or more complete way. There may be different opinions as to whether it has anything to say on the text's "signification", but certainly it is possible to describe it as "signification".

b. The approach using *literary criticism* of various kinds also focuses on the Text and its Message$^1$; but here, in addition, Purpose$^1$ and Situation$^1$ are often considered. Thus, we can encounter discourse analysis in which one studies the interplay of patterns on the textual surface which together contribute to giving the text a meaning of a certain structure. It includes a scrutiny of the roles played by the characters of the story as well as a study of the relationship between the story and the plot.[24]

In our example one might, for instance, note the role which John's refusal plays in the story, and how the information flow puts the focus on the descent of the Spirit and the words of the heavenly voice: the son of God title plays an essential role in the Gospel narrative, and this is confirmed by the highest thinkable authority through the voice from heaven. The main plot of Matthew's Gospel concerns God's plan to save his people through Jesus: In this text he is presented as the son of God, i.e., his representative, and God declares that he is pleased with him.[25] When considering Situation$^1$ and Purpose$^1$, one may refer to the revered status of John in the primitive Christian milieu and to the circumstance that the Text plays a role in a debate between Jews and Christians in which one is anxious to assert the Christian belief that Jesus is the God-sent Messiah – such an assertion may also be essential to strengthen the beliefs of the Christian Jews who seem to have been an important part of Matthew's audience.

Above, I have mentioned some attempts at discovering the intention of an author. However, exegetes have also become aware of "the intentional fallacy" which W. K. Wimsatt and others brought to our attention:[26] It is difficult, sometimes impossible, to scrutinize the mind of the Sender. Those scholars who distinguish between the real author and the implied author avoid this difficulty because the

---

[23] [ABRAMS 1958, 26–29.]
[24] JACK DEAN KINGSBURY 1988a, 2–27, 86.
[25] KINGSBURY 1988a, 50f.; POWELL 1992b, 199.
[26] WILLIAM K. WIMSATT 1954.

implied author is only a construct made on the basis of the text – note this focusing of the text: he may be more or less like the real author. That is, the implied Matthew is the author as he stands forward through his text. He is constructed from what he presupposes, expects, and stresses in his story.[27] Similarly we can distinguish between actual reader, intended reader, and implied reader.[28] Also the implied reader is a construct on the basis of the text.

To literary critics among exegetes it is important to differentiate between the narrated world, the world of narration, and the world of the re-reader. The narrative world (or the narrative Situation) in our example is the one referred to in the story of John and Jesus by the Jordan. The world of narration is the one in which Matthew tells his story to his readers, that is, the Situation of the first readers. Applied to our model of interpretation: In Situation$^2$ (that is, now), Interpreter$^2$ (we) interpret the Text (with its narrative Situation) to Recipient$^2$ (our students) as the Sender's (Matthew's) Message to the first Recipients in their Situation$^1$ (the world of narration) with Purpose$^1$.

This interpreter is anxious not to identify the real world and the narrated world. In our example, the literary critic – as well as, of course, a critical historian – does not take for granted that the event told by Matthew took place some time, somewhere, in this way. But unlike the historian, he/she may refrain from asking essentially historical questions about what happened, if anything, since such answers are not likely to affect the interpretation of the Text.

To my mind it is obvious that this literary criticism approach means interpretation in the sense I defined the term: it expresses the meaning of "B" in a clearer, more distinct or more complete way.

c. The borderline between *text-linguistic* approaches and those of literary critics is not always so sharp. Their point of departure is also the Text, but as a rule the whole communication model is taken into consideration. Thus, to a larger extent than is usual among literary critics, more interest is shown in precisely the communication aspects. As is nowadays well known in the exegetical guild, text-linguistics analyses the syntactic aspect of the text (that is, its detailed structure on the surface), and its semantic aspect (that is, its contents); these then interplay and are subordinated to the pragmatic aspect (that is, Situation$^1$ in which Message$^1$ is supposed to fulfil a certain function with Recipients$^1$). To Situation$^1$ also belong cultural factors which determine the communication between Sender and Recipient$^1$.

In our example, a text-linguistic interpretation may be similar to one made by a literary critic, although – in line with an interest in the pragmatic aspect – more stress might be put on the purpose: in Matthew's gospel Jesus is not only the one who teaches righteousness but also the ultimate example to the audience of a

---

[27] Cf. KINGSBURY 1988a, 30–32. [Cf. SLOMITH RIMMON-KENAN 1997, 86–89; GÉRARD GENETTE 1998, 283–295.]

[28] Cf. KINGSBURY 1981, 36–38; IDEM 1988b, 454–459. [Cf. RIMMON-KENAN *ibid.*; GENETTE *ibid.*]

righteous life.[29] In addition, to non-Christian Jews as well as to Christian ones, the text could undergird the belief that Jesus was the Messiah whom God had promised to send. The text-linguistic approach would also contain a thorough analysis of how the signs on the textual surface indicate how the story is fitted into its larger literary context. I know of no such text linguistic analysis of the whole of Matthew's Gospel, but Hellholm's article marks a beginning.[30]

d. A *rhetorical criticism* approach may more or less take into account the same elements of the communication model. Normally it explicitly focuses on how the Sender influences the Recipient to fulfil a certain (the Sender's) Purpose in his Situation, and all this through his Message embedded in the Text. The Situation is often defined as the rhetorical situation, which is a construct based on the text, and which need not be identical with the actual historical situation. Although "rhetorical situation" is not the same as Situation$^1$ in the model, the regard given to the effect on the reader's situation is common to both the text-linguistic and rhetorical approaches, and in this respect we can regard them as being what Abrams calls a pragmatic type of criticism.[31]

The adverbial phrase "more or less" in the beginning of the previous paragraph indicates that "rhetorical criticism" is a label attached to several approaches. Thus there are rhetorical critics who love to adduce the rhetorical *dispositio*, the rhetorical *genera* etc. referred to in the rhetorical handbooks of Antiquity and compare such patterns with the New Testament texts. In so doing they may pay less attention to the details of the present Text and its Message and Purpose for Recipient$^1$, and rather focus their interest on the Sender, his activity and background. On the other hand, there are those rhetorical critics who think of rhetoric as representing a certain style or type of, say, pictorial or "mythic" language encountered in New Testament texts which had a particular function amongst its Recipients.[32]

The interpretations delivered by these different rhetorical critics deserve to be called interpretations, but in different ways. The approach taking ancient rhetoric as its basis may arrive at results which are less interpretative than the others in the sense of my definition. On the other hand, the language-type approach may be more open to drawing the attention of Recipient$^2$ to the "signification" of Message$^1$ and even give some indications for a Message$^2$.

e. It would hardly be fair not to consider *feministic approaches* – the plural is certainly apt – in this article. However, they actually less represent one or several methodological approaches than rather some particular hermeneutical perspectives. Such include, for instance, a sharpened eye for different kinds of *Vorver-*

---

[29] ULRICH LUZ 1985, 154.
[30] DAVID HELLHOLM 1995.
[31] [ABRAMS 1958, 14–21.]
[32] AMOS N. WILDER 1964; JOHANNES N. VORSTER 1995.

*ständnis*. They relate themselves to the items of my interpretation model in ways that partly differ from other approaches. A feminist certainly takes notice of Situation[1], as well as of Situation[2]. But in addition to the observations made by the ordinary historically oriented exegetes, she draws attention to how often patriarchal patterns colour Situation[1]. However, she also critically scrutinizes Situation[2] in which modern readers, be they scholars or not, without noticing it, are drawn into the patriarchal presuppositions.

In a corresponding manner, a feministic approach may focus both on the Author's Purpose and on Message[1], not to speak of modern Interpreters[2] who uncritically or unknowingly adopt structures degrading to women or those of masculine power. All these investigations also serve a moral duty: the feminist scholar should remind herself and her surroundings that there is a moral aspect to exegesis. The exegete has a moral responsibility for his/her stand *vis-à-vis* the Bible texts and their interpretations.

A feminist approach may end up in an essay of an alternative Message[2] which brings out figures or actions in the text with which a woman may identify. Not least this holds true of such feminists who are willing to make as positive a use as possible of the biblical texts.

I know of no feminist reading of the baptism story. The following reading was made up by me and represents one which might have been made by a "positive" feminist just referred to. When Jesus is baptized he underwent a baptism meant for both men and women. Jesus identifies with the obligation of both men and women and so fulfils all righteousness for humans without any gender difference.

Is this interpretation? In the case of my invented example it may possibly be taken as one which might be covered by my model above of historical interpretation, but in other cases, a feminist interpretation may rather be regarded as one which makes use of the circumstance that texts are capable of several meanings, although the number of possible Messages[2] is certainly larger than that of possible or probable Messages[1].

## 6. The Reader as the Focus

Not least to exegetes of a text-linguistic or rhetorical bent, the Recipient, here called the Reader, plays an important role within the communication model; in this respect these exegetes can also be included among those who perform so-called reader-response criticism.

But there are a few exegetes who do reader-response criticism and who, in doing so, also follow those radical literary critics who stress the role of the reader to such an extent as to maintain that Recipient[2] alone gives the Text a meaning: the Sender's (be he implied or not) intention is of no account, and the historical communication aspect is left aside. The Recipient may be any secondary Recipient, and his/her interpretation of the Text as having a Message[2] or Message[3] is as valid as that of anyone else.

Some exegetes, along with several literary critics, respond like Umberto Eco, when he asserts that the *intentio operis* should be shown respect.[33] Texts do not normally lend themselves to all and sundry readings.[34]

After this rapid survey of some profiles of exegetical approaches, I finally return to where I began – namely exegesis as an academic discipline. My preceding deliberations have taken place under the umbrella of what I called a model of historical interpretation:

– In Situation², Interpreter² interprets the Text to Recipient² as the Sender's Message¹ to Recipient¹ with Purpose¹ in Situation¹.

Exegetes such as Professor Sandelin and myself teach at non-confessional universities, and I think that we would both agree that in that position we should in principle keep to such a model. Labelling interpretation according to this model as "scientific" does not imply any naive claim to objectivity. Most texts are – more or less – open to different understandings.

In my introductory pages I also defined interpretation as:

– An expression "A" is an interpretation of the expression "B", if "B" can be understood in such a way that its meaning is expressed by "A" in a clearer, more distinct or more complete way.

I varied the "clearer, more distinct or more complete way" in claiming that an interpretation can be more or less penetrating or profound, depending not least on which sorts of text are involved. To my mind, most biblical texts invite the interpreter to a "more" penetrating and profound reading, even hinting at their "signification", primarily to Recipient¹.

The interpretative explaining I am hinting at also means that one tries to interpret mythical features of the text, that is, to elucidate what these stood for. However, it is no easy thing to deal with such mytho-poetic language:[35] It seems to belong to the same sphere as metaphors which often elude analysis, not to mention the risk of explanations drifting into platitudes.

But such attempts at analysis mean that we do not treat such *Vorstellungen* merely as items of curiosity in an ideological museum. In our Matthean example, the descent of the Spirit in the form of a dove and the son-proclamation of the heavenly voice are such mytho-poetic features. Even an exegete who wants to keep to the model of historical interpretation can, indeed, should advance beyond a passive analysis of the texts as phenomena which just belong to the past. He/she should also endeavour in pursuing the interpretations into more penetrating and profound ones, even, as I wrote above, hinting at their "signification", although primarily to Recipient¹.

---

[33] UMBERTO ECO 1992, 64f.
[34] E.g. RENÉ KIEFFER 1972, 46, and cf. ERIC DONALD HIRSCH 1967, 1–23.
[35] Cf. WILDER 1964.

When some exegetes began to regard themselves more as historians or scholars of literary criticism than as interpreters in the service of the Church, then interpretation became equal to a "grammatico-historical understanding which attempts to think the author's thought after him" (as someone expressed it). There were those who protested against such a profane approach and maintained that in order to understand biblical writings properly one had to recognize that they were inspired by God. They also wanted to complement the historical-critical attitude with a duty to expose the "moral, religious, and philosophical" meanings of the Bible.[36]

Probably these opponents of old would raise the same objections to my discussion above. My constricted ways of reasoning may be typical of the Swedish scholarly climate. But if they are intellectually reasonable, they might be useful even to theology. For I am convinced that G. K. Chesterton was right when he once had Father Brown explain to an unmasked crook who had disguised himself as a priest: "You attacked reason; that is bad theology".

---

[36] KÜMMEL 1972, 113.

# 3. Interpreting Eschatological Texts

## 1. Preliminaries

The following pages will deal with hermeneutics. It may, however, be rash to discuss such matters in a contribution to a Festschrift dedicated to Professor René Kieffer, since more than many exegetes he has engaged in hermeneutical problems and has dealt with them with philosophical insight. Thus I may be carrying owls to Athens when dedicating this paper to him.

Nevertheless I dare to embark on such an enterprise. Following Mats Furberg I let "hermeneutics" stand for "the theory about interpretation of what is said and expressed in a discourse."[1] Instead of "theory"[2] I will, however, rather speak of "guidelines" or "principles", and I will deal with "texts" instead of "that which is said and expressed in a discourse," which of course has a wider reference.

Such a "theory" or such "guidelines" can concern different textual levels, both text in general, and, on a lower level of generalization, particular kinds of texts including those with a particular kind of contents. Thus, the following will deal with New Testament texts with eschatological contents. Yet many of the guidelines to be discussed can be applied to almost any text.

Furthermore, I will differentiate between two kinds of interpretation, each of which may call for its own hermeneutics. One contains guidelines for what may be termed a *historical interpretation*. In the present writer's view such interpretation is the aim of scholarly exegesis and we encounter a similar kind of interpretation when scholars of other fields, for example history of ideas or church history, interpret their sources.

The other kind of hermeneutics discusses guidelines of what may be called a *topical interpretation*. Such a topical interpretation is, one that shall be applicable or normative, for example, in the present church, and so a topical interpretation may, for example, become the basis or point of departure of formulations of Christian faith. To my mind, scientific scholars of religion may include this kind of hermeneutics in their work, but in so doing they suggest possible topical interpretations which are presented under certain presuppositions regarding, for example, church context, the kind of authority the texts are assumed to possess in the interpretive community, etc.

---

[1] Mats Furberg 1981, 13.
[2] The Swedish word is "lära".

Of course the idea of differentiating between historical and topical interpretation represents a simplification: on the one hand, already the term interpretation may be used in many senses.[3] On the other, the borderline between the two kinds of interpretation is not so sharp, not least because one can mean different things by the verb "understand" which is so commonly used when interpretation is discussed. Often the two verbs are used in such a way that understanding precedes interpretation; thus somebody may be said to have understood the words of a text, but then has to interpret it. However, already in order to understand the words of, say, a sentence in Finnish, we have to be able to interpret what the letters and words stand for and how they function according to usage and grammar; We then interpret their meaning so that we grasp/understand what the sentence is about, so to speak, on the surface. Here interpretation precedes understanding in a certain sense of this term.

I will refrain from any attempts precisely to define how I use the verbs "interpret" and "understand" in the following. Be it enough to state that I use them in a rather unsophisticated way, hoping that the context will make it sufficiently clear what I mean. However, already when it comes to a historical interpretation I want to put more into the verb "understand" than, for example, the circumstance that I "understand" a Greek text if I can translate it into Swedish. The verb will also stand for more than the fact that somebody who "understands" a text can retell its contents using his/her own words; indeed, to understand can also mean to get an idea of deeper, implied nuances of the contents of the text. Linguists and philosophers of language have intensely discussed these matters, often with a high degree of sophistication. With regard to the argument in what follows I want only briefly to state that in my opinion a historical understanding of a text should render justice to its organization on the textual surface, to its contents dimension and to its meta-linguistic function. Text-linguists label these aspects syntactic, semantic, and pragmatic, respectively. Sometimes theologians pay little attention to the pragmatic aspect of the texts, that is, the one that has to do, *inter alia*, with how a given text functioned with which audience, under which circumstances;[4] what was its effect or what was it supposed to effect; was it to inform the addressees, to admonish them, to comfort them or spurn them, etc.? Obviously "understanding" a text in this way comes close to interpretation.[5]

---

[3] See, e.g., GÖRAN HERMERÉN 1982.

[4] [Cf. KIRSTEN MARIE HARTVIGSEN 2012, *passim.*]

[5] The intimations of the preceding paragraph concerning understanding and interpreting may remind of the idea of an empathetic and imaginative entering into the mind of an author that we come across with Schleiermacher and his followers, as well as in the hermeneutical philosophy of Gadamer and others that describes understanding as a fusion of the horizons of the reader and the writer, respectively. The considerations above stand, however, in another philosophical tradition, and there are philosophers who suspect that the ideas about empathy with the inner perception of the author and about fusion of horizons run the risk of leading to uncritical interpretations: see FURBERG 1981 that contains a useful discussion about these matters.

Above I defined the field of the following discussion and thereby not only delimited it to New Testament texts but also to those of eschatological contents. The concept "eschatology/eschatological" is relatively new in the theological vocabulary.[6] In the 20th century it has, however, been used in so many different ways that the usage often is confusing. I will use it in the traditional sense, that is, let it stand for ideas about the ultimate meaning and goal of humans and/or the world.[7]

## 2. Hermeneutics of Eschatology

After these preliminaries we now turn to the hermeneutics of a historical interpretation of eschatological texts of the New Testament. To begin with it might be useful to remind us of the simple fact that our texts are linguistic phenomena. Their authors have written in the language they have shared with their surroundings; they have used normal understandable words and ordinary grammar. They have also used modes of speech recognized by their addressees, and their linguistic usage has verisimilarly not been more peculiar than it could function – if namely their addressees were to be able to understand the text. Thus the authors have cast their texts in linguistic and literary forms that were available in their surroundings and which they and their addressees consciously or unconsciously have learnt to handle. This does not exclude new imagery or originality, but if the authors wanted to tell their contemporary audience something, they must have stayed within the borders of their language.

Such an emphasis on the communication aspect of the texts has some implications for a discussion of what texts mean. Some theorists may namely maintain that in principle the reader alone decides what a text means. If a text is a communication the presuppositions of this communication may restrict the application of such a principle. This problem looks different for different textual genres, but at a historical interpretation the number of possible understandings is limited. In this respect exegetical scholarship works under the same conditions as other disciplines that investigate texts from older times.

The previous contention with regard to literary genre as well as the different communicative functions pertaining to different genres may appear self-evident. When, however, it comes to eschatological texts the situation has been a bit particular. In eschatological Jewish and Christian texts from antiquity we namely often come across so-called apocalyptic features that raise particular problems. Above all some decades ago several exegetes regarded texts of eschatological-apocalyptic contents mainly as speculations on the end; they included calculations of the date of the end, and the people who wrote and read them were supposed to revel in descriptions of heaven and hell, of world-wide catastrophes, of eternal punishments, etc. In the opinion of several scholars Jesus was

---
[6] JEAN CARMIGNAC 1970/71, 367ff.; WERNER GEORG KÜMMEL 1982, 93.
[7] Cf. MEDARD KEHL 1986, 18.

no apocalyptic preacher, that is, apocalyptic of the kind just depicted. Instead he was supposed to have learnt from the Old Testament prophets, who put humans and their history before God; what was at stake with them, and with Jesus, was human confrontation with transcendence. One maintained regarding the so-called apocalyptic Jesus material that Jesus had either not meant it that way, or it had been secondarily added by the early church that had misunderstood the eschatology of Jesus and turned it into apocalyptic. Here the opinion of, for example, the evangelical exegete G. E. Ladd was similar to that of Ernst Käsemann, who was of a radically different theological tendency.[8] Does, however, this not mean that one has made Jesus an exception from the rule that people speak the language of their milieu?

Thus apocalypticism has caused some hermeneutical confusion. One factor behind may possibly be that one has assumed, maybe unconsciously, that those who created and used apocalyptic texts around the beginning of the common era regarded them in the same way as those literalisticly minded Christians who have studied the Book of Daniel, the Book of Revelation, the so-called synoptic apocalypse (Mark 13 par.) etc and so construed an "eschatology." To the mind of several exegetes, among them also the present writer, this is hardly fair to the genre of these texts.

The last line of the preceding paragraph mentioned apocalyptic genre. As a matter of fact, in spite of decades of form criticism, exegetical scholars have only to a small extent put their hands to studies of what is typical of apocalyptic texts as belonging to a genre. However, in recent years things have changed, and new ways of interpreting these texts historically have been launched,[9] and these studies have also included form-critical analyses.[10]

Now, a first simple principle concerning historical interpretation is that one has to respect the literary conventions which determine the linguistic communication, that is, in our case the kind of literature represented by apocalyptic texts in the New Testament age. An apocalypse was a narrative about a revelation granted to a human spokesman; it informed the recipient about heavenly secrets that meant an answer to problems on earth, and, more precisely, an answer with heavenly authority. The revelation could take place in different ways: at a heavenly journey, through a book from heaven, in visions, etc., but the function of the means was to warrant the answer's heavenly authority. The problem in focus was sometimes that political and/or cultural powers attacked or questioned the religion of the author and of his audience. So often questions were raised about goal and meaning of history: God was assumed to have the history in his hand – how could he then allow Syrians, Egyptians or Romans to behave

---

[8] GEORGE ELDON LADD 1979; ERNST KÄSEMANN 1960 and 1962; cf. KLAUS KOCH 1970.

[9] E.g., AMOS N. WILDER 1957/59 and later works; LARS HARTMAN 1975/76; NORMAN PERRIN 1976; KLAUS BERGER 1977; EGON BRANDENBURGER 1984; JOHN J. COLLINS 1984.

[10] See, e.g., COLLINS 1979; DAVID HELLHOLM 1980; IDEM 1986; HARTMAN 1983. [Cf. HELLHOLM 1991; IDEM 1998.]

as they did to God's people? Also people from one's own ranks caused problems: they sided with the enemy, but nonetheless they were successful in everything. The solution was to widen the view, looking forward to a situation when the account was settled. So the message to the addressees was: be not surprised, there may be misery, but hold on, be faithful.

The deliberations of the preceding paragraph make it natural briefly to remind of a couple of linguistic data, which were mentioned in passing above. It is namely often useful to distinguish between different semantic functions of textual utterances: some may have an informative function, others a prescriptive, still others an expressive or a performative function, respectively.[11] The same differentiation can be made between genres. Thus texts belonging to the apocalyptic genre have a typical semantic function when they have eschatological contents, namely a prescriptive, exhortative function and to a certain extent an expressive one.

There are reasons to believe that this was the normal manner of reading this kind of texts. There were people who read them as if they primarily had an informative function. Judging from Josephus' report of the Jewish war the zealots have read the Book of Daniel in that manner (*Jos. Bell.* 6.312f.). In their opinion it predicted how the Roman empire would be overthrown by the kingdom of God as manifested in their victory. The Qumran texts, however, reflect how the people behind these texts have understood the Danielic visions of the great powers and of the evil ruler in another way; they were about Belial and other supernatural or transcendent powers (1QM 1).

Apocalyptic and other texts of eschatological contents presuppose more clearly than many others a mythical world-view and accordingly make use of a massively mythical language. This constitutes a particular difficulty. We do not render justice to this mythical language if we assume that normally it functioned descriptively or informatively. Neither is it fair to it only to register the motifs or concepts to place them in some kind of exhibition-cases of a historical museum of ideas. Thus, for example, 2 Bar 29:8 indicates that there was a Jewish idea that in the days of the Messiah the manna was to be given again, but what did this idea mean, actually? Another "motif:" the first Christians seem to have expected that Jesus was to return from heaven riding on a cloud. If we adopt such a definition of understanding and interpretation as was presented above, such statements are only a first step on the way to a historical interpretation. The motifs and ideas should be understood in their mythical context, and one has to take seriously the expressive and impressionistic style of this language.[12] It is an exegetical task to find out what the expressions stood for and to try to explain

---

[11] [See JOHN R. SEARLE/DANIEL VANDERVEKEN 1985; HARTVIGSEN 2012, 64–67.]

[12] In addition, it may be worthwhile to mention that the "myth" behind this mythical language is not a myth in the sense that it consists of coherent narratives on divine figures etc., but rather is composed of what Heinrich Schlier called mythical fragments which function as elements of a symbolic language (HEINRICH SCHLIER 1967).

what was said in that which was said, To the mind of the present writer such a "demythologizing" less distorts the meaning of the texts than an interpretation that takes as its point of departure that they principally and mainly had a descriptive, informative function.

## 3. The Author and His Text

So far for the principle of respecting genre. My next point also has a general scope and is about respecting the individual author and the individual text. Sometimes one has gathered elements from different Jewish eschatological texts and dealt with them as though they represent a Jewish eschatological doctrine.[13] There was, however, no doctrine concerning the last things among the Jews of antiquity. Not all of them were expecting a Messiah, not even all of them had a hope for a resurrection of the dead. A few biblical scholars and several other Bible readers behave similarly when dealing with the first Christians: they ask for the teaching of the Bible or of the New Testament about the last things and construct an eschatology out of pieces from Mark 13; 1 Cor 15; 1 Thess 4–5, the Book of Revelation etc.

The principle of respecting the individual author does, however, not necessarily mean that one cannot use his text when constructing a "-logy", for example an eschatology of the New Testament. On the one hand, we may namely presuppose that the ideas of an author are not born out of nothing but breathe the atmosphere of his cultural and ideological environment, even if he may be inventive and creative. Thus the eschatological ideas of a New Testament author may be more – or less – similar to those of others, but even texts of one and the same author or redactor may contain ideas or motifs that appear to be inconsistent. Given such a variety, if somebody would try to suggest some kind of New Testament eschatology, then he/she may act in different ways. He/she may take to violence and using the press of a dogmatic conviction squeeze the fragments into a unity. Above such an approach was rejected. Another method could be to leave aside some elements and emphasize others, although in that case it may be difficult to argue for the criteria of selection. One may, however, also rise to a higher abstraction level and ask whether there are general, basic ideas that can form a fundamental structure under a New Testament eschatology. Of course there is a mine under such a formulation, namely: what is basic and important, and important to what? – to the text in which it appears?, to the New Testament author(s) in question?, to the exegete who sets out to construct a New Testament eschatology? In spite of these difficulties I would prefer this last-mentioned way to approach the diversity of the material.

To the mind of the present writer constructing a "-logy" in this manner, be it an eschatology, a Christology or an ecclesiology, is a legitimate task in the work

---

[13] Cf. the title of PAUL VOLZ's classical monograph *Die Eschatologie der jüdischen Gemeinde*, 1934.

to arrive at a historical understanding of New Testament texts. As intimated, however, it is a difficult and delicate task, and the one who puts his/her hands to it must carefully state his/her criteria and be prepared to discuss them.

## 4. A Topical Interpretation

We now proceed to discussing some possible guidelines of a topical interpretation. It is a well-known fact that reading older texts to make them topical was an established custom already with the first Christians. They did so in their use of what was later called the Old Testament, and the practice as well as several interpretations was taken over from the Jewish mother religion. But they also re-read other texts applying them to new situations. This can be concluded from the tradition history of the gospels, and we see it in the fact that the Pauline letters were collected so soon. It is also reflected by the fact that the Book of Revelation was used and read also after the situation under Domitian for which it was written.[14] The particular problem caused by the circumcision propaganda that is dealt with in Galatians, as well as the plea of the letter to Philemon that the runaway Onesimus would be received in a generous way at his return – these issues belonged to the past, but yet early Christians re-read the two letters and did so not because they were awe-inspiring documents left behind by an honored teacher, but because one could read them with regard to the present situation; they contained ideas and principles that could be applied in new situations.[15] We may regard the matter in a similar way when it comes to a topical reading of New Testament eschatological texts.

When I now dare to suggest a few possible guidelines for a topical reading of eschatological texts, we should begin by considering a few critical items, a couple of which we have already touched upon above.

Thus a first critical question is this one: when somebody puts his/her hands to a task like this one, is the reason for it a wish to, so to speak, rescue impossible texts, which actually one ought to disregard? Are they studied only because they belong to the canon of the church and have another importance to the creed of the church than, for example, the sacrificial laws or the lists of greetings in the letters? To my mind it is fair to accept that at least the latter is true: the eschatological texts do play an important role in the Christian thinking, both nowadays and earlier.

The mythical language raises a second critical question. Here it may mean a greater challenge to the interpreter than in the case of a historical interpretation. There are not only the descriptions of underworld and heavens but also the mode of speaking about the Son of Man who "comes" to earth with a court of

---

[14] [Cf. THOMAS WITULSKI 2007b; IDEM 2012: under Hadrian.]
[15] I have even suggested that Paul has anticipated that his letters were to be used in that way – in any case his school did so very soon, See LARS HARTMAN 1986. [Repr. in IDEM 1997, 167–177.]

angels; dead are awaked from their tombs, living people are lifted into the air to meet their Lord, etc.

Amos Wilder has already been mentioned in the foot-notes above. He is unjustly unknown in Europe but made essential contributions to the interpretation of apocalyptic-eschatological texts. He maintained that the language of these texts is of the same kind as that of the expressive lyric poetry. It is useful and necessary that the exegetes analyze it and try to grasp its message, indeed, that they demythologize it, but, as Wilder expresses it, it "must be recognized that every such formulation is a poor surrogate and must always appeal back to the original".[16] To my mind, this "appeal back to the original" may take place in preaching and liturgy, but reflecting Christian theology should take on the not so glamorous task of interpretive analysis that Wilder labeled a poor surrogate and not stay content with reiterating the traditional language.

An anecdote about T. S. Eliot may illustrate the above lines concerning preaching and liturgy: a student once asked the writer what he meant with the line: "Lady, three white leopards sat under a juniper tree." The poet's answer was short: "Lady, three white leopards sat under a juniper tree." Apparently even an analysis by the author himself would mean "a poor surrogate." Nonetheless I do not want to apply the anecdote to the work of the reflecting theologian. This has been argued already above apropos of the historical interpretation.

A third overarching problem was also mentioned in the discussion of the historical interpretation, namely the fact that in some cases several interpretations are possible. As stated there, this problem looks different depending on the genre of the text. In addition, our case is specific in that the texts are re-used.

Thus there are texts that belong to such a literary genre that it is not remarkable if somebody asks their author what he/she has meant, and receives the answer, "Which is your opinion?" Here in principle any interpretation is "correct." Within the limits of their normal usage texts of another type are a little less ambiguous, for example, a biblical psalm. Thus certainly Ps 2:7, 9 ("you are my son … you shall break them [the nations] with a rod of iron") deals with the king of Israel. Christians have understood it as a Christological passage (Matt 3:17; Rev 2:27 etc.), and Jews may dislike this Christian usurpation of the psalm. But both Jews and Christians would certainly find it unfair to use the passage as a scriptural support for, say, an export of weapons to the red Khmers. Less ambiguous are the minutes of a faculty meeting: to understand them as dealing with deep existential problems would certainly mean an over-interpretation.

Umberto Eco has tried to find a way between, on the one hand, a position that gives all power to the reader who can let the text mean just anything, and, on the other, one that invalidates every understanding that is not identical with the original one of the author. The former means focusing on the intention of

---

[16] WILDER 1964, 135.

the reader, the latter on the intention of the author. Instead Eco launches the idea of an "intention of the text" that would play a regulative role.[17]

Eco's idea might be applied in our case. Above I have taken into account that the texts we are now focusing on function in a communication that determines their semantic and socio-cultural functions. This is an aspect to be reckoned among their properties as precisely texts. If these aspects are changed, the conditions of the texts as communication are changed, including the "intentions" that may be typical of them as texts.

If not all interpretations are equally good, there are to my mind good reasons to assume that it is possible to argue for what I have labeled a historical understanding of New Testament texts. As already stated, the problems look different for different genres, but to regard the texts in the perspective of communication can be a regulative factor at a historical interpretation.

To my mind there are reasons in favor of the view that a topical understanding of biblical texts should build on a historical interpretation or take such an interpretation as its point of departure. These reasons are theological, that is, they can be derived from typical features of Christian faith. Such a typical feature is to respect Christianity's historical roots, indeed, it exists and is developed in a dynamic and even organic relationship to its past. The interpretive community, the church in some sense of the word, often claims that it constitutes a unity throughout the ages and therefore reads its Bible in some kind of solidarity with its past. This solidarity may be slavish, respectfully rejecting or anything between these poles. In one form or another, however, we come across the phenomenon in most Christian communities. Because this solidarity with the history particularly means a respect for the early church, its understanding of the texts is particularly important, and this understanding is the object of historical interpretation. If one accepts such a point of departure, there is a limit for what is a good interpretation at a topical re-use of New Testament texts. Nevertheless there exist many interpretations of the same text and still others are possible.

Again we have made an excursion into the fields of general principles of interpretation, but we now proceed to discussing a few possible guidelines for a topical interpretation of eschatological texts in particular. In connecting to the deliberations above concerning constructing a "-logy" I would like to emphasize a few fundamental features that may serve this purpose. We encounter these features on the one hand on the level of the contents of the texts, on the other, on a more general, abstract level.

Beginning with the last-mentioned feature I suggest that one retains the main semantic function of the texts, or, rather, lets them have again the main semantic function that seems to have been theirs in the beginning. That semantic function is one of exhortation and consolation. The history of interpretation contains many examples of how they have been read as meaning description

---

[17] UMBERTO ECO 1992.

and information. Studies and hermeneutic reflections of newer times suggest that there are arguments against such interpretations and that a non-traditional interpretation more agrees with what seems to have been the original semantic function of these texts.

A second overarching principle may be to focus on some ideas that are basic to individual texts and determine the role of the particular motifs. These fundamental ideas can then guide the treatment of other details. To suggest which are such basic thoughts means to step down to the level of the contents, and the following suggestions are inspired by other theologians.[18] They raise further questions, but an attempt at answering them would mean to leave hermeneutics for dogmatics, and so they are left aside here.

One such basic view is to adopt a wide historical perspective. It includes past and present, but also primeval times and future. It takes into account individuals and nations, social contexts, indeed the universe. A typical feature of Christian faith is the conviction that the whole is meaningful or at least has a goal, because one assumes that it all has its origin in God who also constitutes its goal, as he is also the Lord of all. Such a basic view can inspire some questions. Some concern the concept of God: does one, for example, think of him as an acting principle in or behind history? And what about the problem of evil? Furthermore, what is history?: a series of events between which humans try to detect some connections that form meaningful patterns? Is it a small parenthesis within an ultra-short time of the existence of a tiny little planet? Is there an end to what we call history? Does it have a goal and a meaning that are not to be sought beyond it but within it? How valid is the concept of time, both as taken for itself, *per se*, and as connected to questions for goal and meaning? Is the idea of a line of time equally simplified as the three-story world-view? At least some of these questions may present themselves already when somebody wants to produce a topical interpretation of, say, the text on the judgment of the Son of Man.

A second important perspective is Christological. It provides a particular focus for the wide historical outlook. Jesus has a decisive position in the past: this is true of the thought world of the texts and it seems natural that this ought to be so also in the topical interpretation of today. Loyalty with him was at stake in the time of the texts, and this may be so also in that of the present day interpreter. Both the original readers and (most of) the present day topical interpreters confess him to be the Lord of his adherents but also of everything else, at least in principle. Of course this means that the topical interpreter takes a stand in the ongoing Christological discussion, including ideas on Christology from beneath or from above, but also other approaches.[19]

---

[18] See HANS URS VON BALTHASAR 1960; KARL RAHNER 1967; EDWARD SCHILLEBEECKX 1969; KEHL 1986, part 3.

[19] See, e.g. the contribution by Kieffer and others in HARTMAN (ed.) 1995.

A Christological aspect should be decisive when interpreting eschatological texts about the Kingdom of God. On the one hand, one confesses that the Kingdom was realized in the work of Jesus, but on the other hand one prays with him, "may your kingdom come," that is, heeding a hope for a situation in which God's will is realized in a new way. Some generations ago some Christians claimed that the Kingdom of God is established in that humans and human societies more and more conform to God's will. Such was the hope of the so-called Social Gospel tendencies. Others have maintained that only God himself can establish this kingdom. Taking into account the Christological aspect may prevent a topical interpretation of these texts from both a naive optimism and a quietistic passivity. Such a double outlook also fits well to the principal semantic functions of these texts – on which see above.

This Christ also personifies the norm of the ethical responsibility. This is implied when he is pictured as a judge. The responsibility is one in the present and implies a solidarity with the kingdom of God, with anything that realizes God's will. Since it is an authentic responsibility, humans are free to refuse to engage in it. The responsibility for a refusal is, *inter alia*, expressed by the judgment imagery. But the more one focuses on the main semantic functions of these texts, the less they lend themselves to answers to the questions for what the judgment imagery stands for, except for the perspective that present life is confronted with transcendent norms.

A further basic aspect can be expressed by the phrase "God is near." This near-ness is one of time: "soon", "suddenly", "unexpectedly", but we also encounter spatial expressions like: "the Lord comes", "I stand at the door", "he is near." Here Jews and Christians use a cultic language that appears in several religions, for example: "O God, come to my salvation." Already in biblical times this mode of speech was not understood to state that God literally stepped down on the earth, but instead that God was active among humans. What he did when "coming" was, for example, to let the enemy be beaten, to let a sad human be comforted, etc., in other words, the wording presupposes a God who is engaged in humans, not something neutral behind the stage. Finally, this idea of God's nearness and engagement renders a particular nuance to the idea that humans have an ethical responsibility: the transcendent norm is close.

We have now for a while been walking in the borderlands of the exegetical area, since this is where questions about a topical interpretation of eschatological texts belong. This suggests a short final reflection at this border: insofar as scholarly theology shall deliver material to and be useful for Christian doctrinal and ethical reflection on eschatological texts, also other disciplines than the exegetical ones have to be involved, particularly comparative religion and the fields of systematic theology.

So the above pages remind of something that professor Kieffer has represented in a personal manner during his time at the Faculty of Theology at Uppsala University as an exegete, as a philosopher, and as a theologian.

## 4. Bundesideologie in und hinter einigen paulinischen Texten

### 1. Begriffsbestimmung

Es ist nur billig, daß erstens um der Klarheit willen näher angegeben wird, was ich mit dem Wort „Bundesideologie" meine, nicht zuletzt weil ich es nicht ohne Bedenken gewählt habe. Von „Ideologie" wird ja sonst meistens im Zusammenhang mit marxistischer Ideologie u.dgl. gesprochen. Unter marxistischer Ideologie versteht man eine Sammlung von Vorstellungen und Lehren, die zusammen den Marxismus kennzeichnen, und die eine Art marxistischer Dogmatik bilden.

Ein anderer Gebrauch von „Ideologie" kam vor ein paar Jahrzehnten recht oft in exegetischer und religionsgeschichtlicher Forschung in Skandinavien vor, indem u.a. von „Königsideologie" die Rede war.[1] Man verstand darunter eine Sammlung von Vorstellungen, die zusammen ein Muster bildeten, das vielerorts in der Welt der Religionen gefunden wurde z.B. in Krönungsritualen, Jahresfesten, Königspsalmen, aber auch in Schilderungen vom Urmenschen, von Moses, dem kommenden Messias, und anderen. Statt von „Ideologie" sprachen die Vertreter dieser Schule bisweilen von „Mustern", was natürlich von der „pattern"-Rede der angelsächsischen Myth-and Ritual-Schule inspiriert war.[2]

Man könnte sagen, daß mein Gebrauch vom Wort „Bundesideologie" ein Mittelding zwischen den beiden eben angeführten ist, d.h., ich möchte die dogmatischen Assoziationen des ersten vermeiden, und mich nicht auf so weitgehende Anwendungen einlassen, wie die beim anderen mitunter vorkommenden. Unter „Bundesideologie" verstehe ich also eine Sammlung von Vorstellungen, die ein zusammenhängendes Muster bilden, und deren Kerngedanke es ist, daß Gott dadurch, daß er mit den Menschen in Verbindung getreten ist, eine Beziehung errichtet hat, die gegenseitige Gelübde und Verpflichtungen für die Bundespartner, Gott und sein Volk, bedeutet. Dieses Muster ist nicht steif und unveränderlich, aber es taucht dennoch unverkennbar in vielen Texten des AT

---

[1] Siehe SIGMUND MOWINCKEL, *Kongesalmerne i det Gamle Testamente,* Kristiania 1916; GEO WIDENGREN, *Psalm 110 och det sakrala kungadömet i Israel,* Uppsala Univ. Årsskrift 1941: 7,1; IDEM, *Sakrales Königtum im Alten Testament und im Judentum,* Stuttgart 1955; IVAN ENGNELL, *Studies in Divine Kingship in the Ancient Near East,* Uppsala 1943; AAGE BENTZEN, *Det sakrale Kongedømme,* Festschr. hrsg. von der Universität zu Kopenhagen, 1945; HELMER RINGGREN, „König und Messias", in: *ZAW* 64 (1952) 120–147; GÖSTA W. AHLSTRÖM, *Psalm 89,* Lund 1959.

[2] SAMUEL HENRY HOOKE (Hrsg.), *Myth and Ritual,* London 1933; IDEM, *The Labyrinth,* London • New York 1935; IDEM, *Myth, Ritual and Kingship,* Oxford 1958.

und im Judentum auf.³ Es war somit etwas zum religiösen Kulturerbe gehörendes, von dem verschiedene Verfasser des bezüglichen Kulturkreises in ihren Ausdrucksformen und Denkweisen bewußt oder unbewußt geprägt wurden.⁴

Ein derartiges Muster kann in einem Text mehr oder weniger klar hervortreten. Daß es in solchen Texten vorhanden ist, die ausdrücklich vom Bund und dessen Verpflichtungen handeln, ist verständlich. Unter der Textoberfläche findet man das Bundesmuster in prophetischen Scheltreden gegen das Volk wegen des Abfalls⁵ sowie auch in Sündenbekenntnissen.⁶ Es begegnet aber auch in Texten anderer Art, z.B. in Abschnitten von Jub.⁷ oder in Sap. 10–19, welche die Geschichte Gottes mit seinem Volk ins Auge fassen. Hinsichtlich der Sap.-Kapitel können wir als heutige Leser darin eine Bundesideologie erst dann finden, wenn wir bewußt danach suchen. M. E. dürften sie aber ihren ursprünglichen Sitz im Leben im Passahmahl der alexandrinischen Juden haben. In Alexandria scheinen die Juden dabei auch die Bundesgelübde erneuert zu haben.⁸ Behalten wir dieses vor Augen, werden uns die Motive und Züge des Textes klar, und die bundesideologischen Einzelheiten fügen sich zu einem Muster zusammen. Es besteht nämlich eine Beziehung zwischen der (ursprünglichen) Kommunikationssituation eines Textes und Gedankenmustern dieser Art. Die Situation kann das Gedankenmuster bestimmen, und das Muster ist ein Mittel mit dem der Verfasser in die Situation redet.

In diesem Aufsatz werde ich nun Abschnitte aus 1 Thess., Gal. und Röm. erörtern mit dem Versuch, nachzuweisen, wie in verschiedener Weise eine Bundesideologie hinter den Texten liegt, sie prägt und zugleich ihr Problem ist.

## 2. Problemstellung

In der Forschung ist schon vorher die Rolle besprochen worden, die der Gedanke an den Bund, bzw. den neuen Bund, für Paulus spielt. So meint *W. D. Davies*, daß „Paul carried over into his interpretation of the Christian Dispensation the covenantal conception of Judaism";⁹ die Christen haben einen neuen Exodus, eine neue Befreiung, die zum Schließen eines neuen Bundes mit einer neuen, Gehor-

---

³ Siehe z.B. die von ANNIE JAUBERT und KLAUS BALTZER (unten Anm. 7) erörterten Texte. Im folgenden werde ich jedoch öfters als Beispiele Zitate aus dem Deut. anführen. – Das Bundesthema prägt bekanntlich das ganze Werk von WALTHER EICHRODT, *Theologie des Alten Testaments* I–III, Stuttgart • Göttingen ⁴1957–⁵1961.

⁴ Vgl. CHARLES E. OSGOOD/THOMAS A. SEBEOK (Hrsg.), *Psycholinguistics*, Bloomington, In. – London 1965, Kap. 7.

⁵ Siehe z.B. JULIEN HARVEY, *Le plaidoyer prophétique contre Israël après la rupture de l'alliance*, Paris – Brügge • Montreal 1967.

⁶ Siehe HARVEY, a.a.O., I 57ff.

⁷ Kap. I; 21; 22. Siehe zu Kap. I ANNIE JAUBERT, *La notion d'alliance dans le judaïsme aux abords de l'ère chrétienne*, Paris 1963, 106f., und zu Kap. 21: KLAUS BALTZER, *Das Bundesformular* (WMANT 4), Neukirchen 1960, I 42ff.

⁸ Siehe JAUBERT, a.a.O., 358ff.

⁹ WILLIAM DAVID DAVIES, *Paul and Rabbinic Judaism*, London 1955, 259f.

sam verlangenden Torah leitet. Ferner könnte auf den Aufsatz von *W. C. van Unnik* vom neuen Bund im Denken des Paulus hingewiesen werden.[10] Die Frage, ob nicht das in 1977 erschienene Buch von *E. P. Sanders*[11] mir allen Wind aus den Segeln genommen hat, könnte berechtigt sein. Einerseits arbeitet Sanders nämlich etwas heraus, was er ein Muster (pattern) nennt, das er im palästinischen Judentum findet, und das man eben als eine Bundesideologie bezeichnen könnte. Er nennt es ‚covenantal nomism', und ist bestrebt, es in den Texten zu etablieren, – welches ihm weitgehend gelingt, indem er eine „holistische Sicht" anlegt. Wenn er, anderseits, im zweiten Teil seines Werkes entsprechend an Paulus herangeht, kommt er zum Ergebnis, daß das Muster ‚covenantal nomism' bei ihm nicht zu finden ist.

Billigerweise muß herausgestellt werden, wie sich die in diesem Aufsatz benutzte Weise, die Texte anzuschneiden, zu denen der erwähnten Autoren verhält. Es scheint mir, daß sie, trotz der Unterschiede zwischen W. D. Davies, van Unnik und E. P. Sanders, alle eher als Bibeltheologen arbeiten als ich. Davies und van Unnik besprechen und sammeln verschiedene, in den Texten zerstreute, theologische Topoi, und schaffen sozusagen eine Synthese ausserhalb oder über den Texten. Die ‚patterns of religion' von Sanders sind gewiß Versuche, theologische Gesamtauffassungen zu beschreiben, aber er sucht nicht in derselben Weise wie ich nach einem zusammenhängenden Muster in zusammenhängenden Texten – auch wenn er wirklich bestrebt ist, herauszufinden, wie z.B. der Gedankengang des Römerbriefes aufzufassen ist.

Zwei weitere Dinge sollen zu meiner hiesigen Arbeitsweise im Vergleich mit denen der genannten Exegeten angeführt werden. Erstens, meine Berücksichtigung, daß, wenn ein Muster dieser Art in oder hinter einem Text zu finden ist, sein Verfasser im Vergleich mit dem üblichen Gebrauch es umgedeutet oder verändert haben könnte.[12] Ferner: die Bundesideologie oder das von Bundesideen geprägte Gedankenmuster, womit ich rechnen will, umspannt ein weiteres Feld von Vorstellungen als bei ihnen. Dieses Feld umfaßt Motive und Themen, die bereits von einigen Forschern zusammengeführt worden sind, die das Bundesdenken und seine Formen im AT und im Judentum untersucht haben. Für das Judentum seien hier vor allem die Arbeiten von *A. Jaubert* und *K. Baltzer* genannt.[13]

---

[10] WILLEM CORNELIS VAN UNNIK, „La conception paulinienne de la nouvelle alliance", in: ALBERT-LOUIS DESCAMPS u.a., *Littérature et théologie pauliniennes* (Rechbib 5), Brügge – Paris 1960, 109–126. Vgl. auch HENRY A. A. KENNEDY, „The Significance and Range of the Covenant-Conception in the New Testament", in: *Exp.* 8:10 (1915) 385–410; RAYMOND F. COLLINS, *The Berîth-Notion of the Cairo Damascus Covenant and its Comparison with the New Testament* (ETL 39 = BEThL 20), Louvain 1963, 555–594; DENNIS E. H. WHITELEY, *The Theology of St. Paul*, Oxford 1964.

[11] ED P. SANDERS, *Paul and Palestinian Judaism*, London 1977.

[12] Vgl. die sog. ‚Disintegration' der Königsideologie in Volkssitten u.ä. mit welcher gewisse der oben (Anm. 1) genannten Religionsgeschichtler rechneten.

[13] BALTZER, a.a.O.; JAUBERT, a.a.O. (oben Anm. 7).

Wenn ich jetzt das hier zu erörternde Bundesgedankenmuster skizziere, könnte dieses Muster so weitumspannend erscheinen, daß fast alles jüdische Denken in irgendwelchen Texten davon „geprägt" wäre. Sollte dies der Fall sein, wären ja die folgenden Bemerkungen schlechthin ohne jeden Belang. Um aber die relative Kohärenz des Musters einfach aufzuzeigen, wird in der folgenden Skizze durch eingeklammerte Ziffern angegeben, in wievielen von sechzehn explizit von Bundesthemen geprägten Texten[14] das Motiv (oder etwas ähnliches) vorkommt.

Erstens[15] begegnet in diesem Gedankenmuster eine Gruppe von Vorstellungen, die einen grundlegenden „dogmatischen" Teil ausmachen, der *Gott und sein Handeln* betrifft. Gott ist der Schöpfer, der Herrscher der Welt (9), und als solcher ihr Richter (7), gerecht (9), barmherzig (13), ohne Ansehen der Person (2). Aus Barmherzigkeit und Liebe hat er das jüdische Volk erwählt (6) und mit ihm den Bund geschlossen, zuerst mit den Vätern (16), denen er sich offenbart hat (12), und denen er seine Verheißungen gegeben hat (11), bei denen er treu bleibt (10). Während der Geschichte des Volkes hat er es getreu geleitet und vor Gefahren gerettet (14).

Ein *ethischer Abschnitt* dreht sich zum großen Teil um die Bundesverpflichtung der beiden Parteien, d.h. darum was Gott zu tun verheißt, und darum wozu sich Israel verpflichtet, positiv und negativ. Grundlegend ist, daß der Herr der Gott des Judenvolkes sein soll und sie sein Volk sein sollen (10). Er hat sich vor ihnen zu erkennen gegeben – sie kennen ihn (10), eine enge Beziehung, die bisweilen unter dem Bilde von Vater und Söhnen (Kindern) beschrieben wird (6). Wenn das Volk treu im Bunde bleibt (6), oder, mit einem anderen Wort, gerecht ist (7), wird Gott bei ihnen sein, unter ihnen wohnen (3), ihnen Frieden, Sicherheit und gute Verhältnisse verleihen (9), und sie im Land der Verheißung wohnen (15) oder es erben (8) lassen. Das Volk seinerseits verspricht, das Wort oder das Gebot Gottes anzunehmen und ihm zu gehorchen (13). Dabei gehen öfters die Gedanken zum Sinaibund, aber wenn von anderen Bündnissen die Rede ist, z.B. denen mit Noa oder Abraham, verpflichten sich Menschen zu etwas gleichartigem. Im Zusammenhang begegnen oft Wörter wie „Werke", „Taten", „tun" u.dgl. (13). Zu den negativen Pflichten, die das Volk auf sich nimmt, gehört vor allem, daß es sich von Idololatrie aller Art enthalte (12); oft wird vor der sittlichen Verwirrung der Heiden gewarnt (8).

Ein dritter Teil der Bundesideologie nimmt *die Folgen* der Beachtung bzw. Nicht-Beachtung der Bundesgebote durch das Volk, und zwar Segen und Fluch gewahr. Zum Segen gehört Leben in verschiedenen Aspekten; zu Gott Ja zu sagen heißt das Leben wählen (9). Gott behütet sein Volk, gibt ihm Freude und erfolgreiches und gesegnetes Leben (9) im verheißenen Land, ist ihm gnädig und

---

[14] Die Texte sind Ex. 19–34; Lev. 26; Deut. 29–30; Deut. 32; Esr. 9; Neh. 9; Jer. 31; Ez. 36; Dan. 9; Sap. 10–19; Jub. 1; Jub. 21; Jub. 22; CD I–li; Test. Levi 13–18; Test. Juda 18–25.

[15] Die Dreiteilung schließt an BALTZER, a.a.O. an. Sie gibt hier nicht eine obligatorische Folge der Motive an.

vergebend. Falls aber das Volk abfällt, hartnäckig, hartherzig oder lästerlich hochmütig (6) – wie die Ausdrücke gern fallen – wird, dann trifft es der Fluch, der Zorn Gottes, Gericht, Unfrieden, Unglück, Mißwuchs, Exil und Tod (14). Schon die erwähnten Segnungen und Flüche bekommen gern eine eschatologische Farbe: das Land, in dem man wohnen darf, wird ein himmlisches Kanaan, das Reich Gottes, das Gericht und das Exil werden die jenseitigen Strafen. Die Eschatologie kann aber auch in einer anderen Form begegnen: die Gedanken gehen zu einem neuen Bund oder zu einer Zeit der Wiederherstellung (7). Die Abtrünnigen werden sich bekehren (7), Gott wird sein Volk versammeln und die Verheißungen, die Gaben und die Verpflichtungen erneuern. Friede wird walten, Gott wird sie reinigen (3), ihre Sünden vergeben, bei ihnen, ja, in ihnen wohnen, denn er wird ihnen seinen Geist geben (5). So werden sie seine Kinder in Heiligkeit und Gerechtigkeit sein, denn das Gesetz Gottes ist in ihre Herzen geschrieben. Dann ist die Beschneidung nicht nur ein äußeres Zeichen des Bundes, sondern auch die Herzen der Treuen sind beschnitten.

Es unterliegt keinem Zweifel, daß der Gedanke an Gottes Bund mit dem jüdischen Volk, dem anzugehören ein Stolz des Paulus war (Röm. 9,3ff.; 11,1; Phil. 3,5), für ihn eine Rolle spielte. Er nennt die Vorzüge der Juden in Röm. 9,4f.: „ihrer sind die Sohnschaft und die Herrlichkeit und die Bündnisse und die Gesetzgebung und der Kult und die Verheißungen, ihrer sind die Väter …". Und, weil das Hauptproblem des Gal. die Beschneidung, das Bundeszeichen [2,7; 5,6.11; 6,15], ist, ist es nur zu erwarten, dort Erörterungen von den Bündnissen zu finden. Daß ferner die Gedanken des Apostels auch um einen neuen Bund kreisten, geht ja aus 2 Kor. 3 hervor,[16] wo er es, unter Verteidigung seines Apostolats, in den Rahmen eines neuen Bundes einsetzt: er ist mit dem Amt des neuen Bundes betraut, welches dem des Moses im alten Bunde überlegen ist. Durch sein Werk geschieht das von Gott für die Zeit des neuen Bundes Verheißene: in die Herzen der Korinther wird, wohl nicht das Gesetz Gottes, aber ein Christusbrief geschrieben, und zwar mit dem Geist des lebendigen Gottes (3,3). Unten werden wir Passagen erörtern, die uns belehren, daß diese Ideen vom neuen Bund für Paulus nichts zufälliges sind.

Die eben angeführten Stellen erweisen, daß das Bundesdenken sozusagen zum aktiven theologischen Wortschatz des Paulus gehört. Es ist aber auch in seinem, falls wir so sagen dürfen, passiven theologischen Wortschatz zu finden. Davon zeugt die Überlieferung im 1 Kor. von den Einsetzungsworten des Abendmahls. Für einen Mann mit Paulus Respekt vor dem Herrn war es billigerweise von nicht geringer Bedeutung, daß er sich bewußt war, von diesem Herrn eine Tradition mit den Worten: „dieser Kelch ist der neue Bund in meinem Blut" (11,25) zu haben.

Mir dünkt, daß diese Texte uns Grund geben, mit der guten Möglichkeit zu rechnen, daß auch in anderen Texten das Denken des Apostels von Bundesideen

---

[16] Vgl. VAN UNNIK, a.a.O. [Vgl. DAVID HELLHOLM, „Moses as διάκονος of the παλαιὰ διαθήκη – Paul as διάκονος of the καινὴ διαθήκη", in: *ZNW* 99 (2008) 247–289.]

geprägt ist, und daß er so viel von jüdischem Kulturgut in sich gehabt hat, daß eine Bundesideologie in oder hinter Ausdrücken, Gedankenketten und Beweisführungen in seinen Briefen liegt.

### 3. Bundesideologisch gefärbte Texte

(a) M. E. erkennen wir im 1 Thessalonischerbrief die Bundesideologie, oder zu mindest Stücke davon.[17] So sind die folgenden Einzelheiten des Briefes in der Bundesideologie recht wohl zu Hause: Die Thessalonicher sind „von Gott geliebt" und „erwählt" (1,4). Der Herr hat zu ihnen gesprochen (1,5f.8), und sie haben das Wort Gottes entgegengenommen (1,6). Darunter ist zu verstehen, daß sie das getan haben, was von Heiden und Abtrünnigen erwartet war, d.h. sie haben sich von den Götzen zu dem einzigen, lebendigen und wahren Gott bekehrt (1,9).[18] Dazu haben sie das Wort „in Kraft und heiligem Geist" empfangen (1,5) – vgl. Jub. 1,23 „sie werden sich zu mir bekehren ... und ich werde die Vorhaut ihrer Herzen beschneiden ... und ich werde ihnen einen heiligen Geist schaffen."

Im paränetischen Teil des 1 Thess., Kap. 4–5, gibt es mehrere Einzelheiten, die den Gedanken auf die Bundesideologie richten. So will Gott die „Heiligung" (ἁγιασμός, 4,3f.) der Adressaten, er hat sie „gerufen, nicht zur Unreinheit sondern (zu einem Leben) in Heiligung" (4,7). Vgl. Deut. 28,9: (wenn du die Stimme Gottes hörst) „will der Herr dich zu einem Volk erheben, das ihm geheiligt ist."[19] Von der Moral der Thessalonicher heißt es, daß sie „Gott gefallen" soll (4,1 ; vgl. Deut. 6,18), und sie wird der der „Heiden" gegenübergestellt, „die Gott nicht kennen" (4,5). Wir erkennen die exklusive Gotteskenntnis des Gottesvolkes. Wenn aber die Adressaten dies abwiesen (4,8), dann, so wird gesagt, wiesen sie Gott selbst ab, der ihnen seinen Geist gegeben hat. Hier wird auf die Ezechielprophetie der erneuten Bundessegnungen angespielt, zu denen auch die Geistesgabe gehört (Ez. 36,27; 37,14). Aber implizit hört man auch dahinter die klassische Bundesverheißung „ich werde unter ihnen wohnen."[20] Einen anderen Aspekt von diesen Bundessegnungen erkennen wir im folgenden Vers, nach welchem die Thessalonicher „von Gott gelehrt" (θεοδίδακτοι) sind (4,9). Vgl. z.B. Jer. 31,33f.: „ich werde mein Gesetz in ihre Brust legen ... sie werden nicht einander zu belehren brauchen ... denn sie werden alle mich kennen."[21]

Die eschatologische Unterweisung in Kap. 4f. wird damit abgeschlossen, daß die Adressaten eine περιποίησις σωτηρίας (5,9) genannt werden, was vielleicht

---

[17] Vgl. VAN UNNIK, a.a.O., 124.

[18] Vgl. Deut. 30,2. – Zu 1,9 als Ausdruck urchristlicher Missionspredigt siehe BÉDA RIGAUX, *Les Épîtres aux Thessaloniciens*, Paris – Gembloux 1956, z.St.; PETER STUHLMACHER, *Das paulinische Evangelium* I (FRLANT 95), Göttingen 1968, 258ff.

[19] Siehe auch z.B. Deut. 7,6.

[20] Z.B. Ex. 25,8; 29,45; Lev. 26,11; Ez. 37,27.

[21] Siehe auch z.B. Deut. 4,5; Jes. 54,13; vgl. Joh. 6,45. – Vgl. ALBERT-MARIE DÉNIS, *Les thèmes de connaissance dans le document de Damas*, Louvain 1967, 17; 21.

als „ein von Gott gerettetes Eigentum" wiedergegeben werden könnte.[22] Vgl. „ihr werdet mein Eigentum vor allen anderen Völkern sein" (Ex. 19,5).[23] Diese Rettung wird „dem Zorn" gegenübergestellt (vgl. 1,10), und geht darauf aus, daß „wir mit ihm leben werden" (5,10), was an die Hoffnung auf Gottesgemeinschaft und Lebensgabe bundesideologisch geprägter Texte erinnert.[24]

Es unterliegt m.E. keinem Zweifel, daß Paulus in 1 Thess. auf seine heidenchristlichen Adressaten Termini und Vorstellungen anwendet,[25] die er nicht als erster zusammengestellt hat, sondern die schon vor ihm ein zusammenhängendes Muster gebildet haben. Wir können jetzt die Frage beiseite lassen, inwieweit Paulus in dieser Hinsicht Pionier war. Jedenfalls braucht er nicht im 1 Thess. für diese Rede- und Denkweise zu argumentieren. Daß sie doch nicht problemfrei war, wird in 1 Thess. 2,16 angedeutet: die Juden „wollen uns hindern, den Heiden zu predigen, auf daß sie gerettet werden."

(b) Eine Äußerung dieser Spannung begegnet uns im *Galaterbrief.* Es dürfte hier am Platze sein, anschließend an einen für heutige Leser typisch paulinisch gewordenen Ausdruck zu erinnern, nämlich: „Werke". Dieser Ausdruck taucht oft in jüdischen, von Bundesgedanken geprägten Texten auf. Großenteils beruht dies natürlich darauf, daß bereits im AT eben das „tun" der Gebote eine grundlegende Bundespflicht war. Paulus benutzt also eine schon vorhandene religiöse Fachsprache, wenn er von „Werken" usw. spricht, und zwar eine mit bundesideologischen Konnotationen.

Ich gehe jetzt direkt zu Gal. 3, wo Paulus die theologische Beweisführung für sein Evangelium beginnt. In 3,2 fragt er: „empfingt ihr den Geist aus Gesetzeswerken oder aus dem Hören des Glaubens?" M. E. stützt Paulus sich hier auf eine von ihm als unbestreitbar angesehene Tatsache, die gleichzeitig Ausgangsbasis seiner Argumentation ist: Gott hat den Galatern, den vorigen Heiden, seinen Geist gegeben. Im Zusammenhang mit der Bundesideologie ist das etwas merkwürdiges[26] – die Gabe des erneuten Bundes ist Heiden geschenkt worden, und zwar ohne Torah-Observanz ihrerseits. Auch der Glaube der Adressaten gehört zu den unbestrittenen Daten, denn sicherlich hat Paulus von anderen Christen die Redeweise übernommen, daß der Schritt zum Christsein als „glauben", „gläubig werden" beschrieben wird, und daß die Christen „gläubig" hei-

---

[22] Mit einem ungewöhnlichen Gebrauch von περιποίησις; als *nomen actionis* könnte man anderenfalls übersetzen „das Heil zu gewinnen." Siehe RIGAUX, Komm. z.St.
[23] Siehe auch Deut. 7,6; 26,18; Jer. 31,33 usw.
[24] Siehe z.B. Deut. 30,15ff.; Ez. 36,29ff.; äth. Hen. 5,8f.; Jub. 1,16ff.
[25] Von VAN UNNIK, a.a.O., betont. Siehe auch NILS A. DAHL, *Das Volk Gottes,* Oslo 1941, 210f.
[26] Vgl. die These von JACOB JERVELL: „Die meisten Geistaussagen im Neuen Testament sind aus der Konstellation und Konfrontation Kirche – Synagoge zu erklären"; „Das Volk des Geistes", in: *God's Christ and His People* (FS N. A. Dahl), Oslo – Bergen – Tromsø 1977, 87; für Gal. siehe 88f. Zum Geist als Gabe der Endzeit siehe WERNER FOERSTER, „Der Heilige Geist im Spätjudentum", in: *NTS* 8 (1961/62) 134; ERIK SJÖBERG, „πνεῦμα", in: *ThWNT* 6, 1965, 382ff.; PETER SCHÄFER, *Die Vorstellung vom heiligen Geist in der rabbinischen Literatur* (StANT 28), München 1972, 105ff.; 112ff.

ßen.²⁷ Den Glauben und die Geistesgabe gab es also bei den Galatern, davon abgesehen, wie Paulus oder seine Gegner sie verstanden haben. M. E. hat Paulus die Dinge so gesehen, daß Gott selbst, als die Galater gläubig wurden, sie in den neuen oder erneuten Bund aufnahm. Von 3,6 ab zeigt dann der Apostel mit Hilfe der Schrift, wie diese merkwürdige Tatsache möglich sein konnte. Deswegen wendet er sich an Gottes Bund mit Abraham laut dem Bericht in Gen. Abraham wurde wegen seines Glaubens als gerecht – laßt uns es als Ausdruck solider Bundespartnerschaft paraphrasieren²⁸ – angesehen, und so sind die Gläubigen „die Söhne Abrahams" (3,7). Der Gedanke an den mit der Bundesgerechtigkeit verbundenen Segen kommt mit V. 8 hinzu. Die Schrift bezeugt nämlich, daß alle Heiden in Abraham gesegnet sein werden. Diesen Segen verknüpft Paulus mit der Verheißung an Abraham (V. 14), die er als „die Verheißung des Geistes" deutet.²⁹ Die Adressaten haben also an dem den Bundestreuen zukommenden Segen Teil bekommen, als sie den Geist empfingen.

Es ist somit in diesem Zusammenhang kein neues Motiv, das Paulus einführt, wenn er in 3,15ff. vom „Bund" spricht, wenn auch mit der Sinnverschiebung zu „Testament". Diese Verschiebung wird desto natürlicher, als Paulus jetzt auch „das Erbe" diskutiert, das Gott aus seiner „Güte" (κεχάρισται, V. 18) „verspricht", – alles in der Bundesideologie wohl beheimatete Motive. Wenn Paulus so die Empfänger dieses Erbes „Söhne Gottes" (3,26–4,6) nennt, die den Geist Christi im Herzen besitzen, dann erkennen wir wieder die Motive der jüdischen Texte, die die Zeit des erneuten Bundes beschreiben: Gott wohnt unter den Seinigen, reinigt sie und schenkt ihnen den Geist, so daß sie seine Kinder sind.³⁰ Bei Paulus sind aber die Adressaten Söhne Gottes geworden „durch den Glauben in Jesus Christus", denn sie sind getauft (3,26ff.), und unter diesen Bedingungen haben sie den Geist empfangen (4,6).

So weit die Verheißungs- und Segenslinie durch das 3. Kap.: Glaube, Geist, Verheißung, Segen, Erbe, Güte Gottes, Gottessohnschaft. Paulus findet aber auch für den Fluch einen Platz, indem er ihn mit dem Gesetz verknüpft. Das in der Bundesideologie regelmäßig Wiederkehrende ist, daß der Gerechte, d.h. der Gottes Willen tut und das Gesetz hält, gesegnet wird, während der, der es nicht tut, verflucht wird. Hier ist es anders: „alle, welche aus Gesetzeswerken sind, stehen unter einem Fluch, denn es ist geschrieben: ‚Verflucht ist jeder der nicht verharrt bei allem, was im Buch des Gesetzes geschrieben steht, um es zu tun' (Deut. 27,26)" (3,10). Als Schriftbeweis ist wohl das Zitat nicht allzu stark, und man fügt gern als eine stille Voraussetzung des Paulus hinzu, daß eigentlich

---

[27] RUDOLF BULTMANN, „πιστεύω κτλ.", in: *ThWNT* 6, 1965, 209f.

[28] Vgl. z.B. KLAUS BERGER, „Gerechtigkeit", in: *Sacramentum mundi* 2 (1968) 261–267.

[29] Abraham konnte im Judentum als Geistesbegabter angesehen werden – siehe DIETER GEORGI, *Die Gegner des Paulus im 2. Korintherbrief* (WMANT 11), Neukirchen 1964, 78ff.

[30] Vgl. Deut. 14,1; 32,5f.; Jer. 31,20; Jub. 1,24 – siehe van UNNIK, a.a.O., 109f.; JAUBERT, a.a.O., im Register („filiation") a. a. St.; GEORG FOHRER, „υἱός κτλ.", in: *ThWNT* 8, 1969, 352f.; EDUARD LOHSE, *ibid.* 360; FRANK CHARLES FENSHAM, *Father and Son as Terminology for Treaty and Covenant, in Near Eastern Studies ...* (FS W. F. Albright), Baltimore, Md. – London 1971, 121–135.

niemand das Gesetz tut oder tun kann, was also denn der Grund dafür sei, daß alle vom Fluch getroffen werden.[31] Dies mag richtig sein (vgl. Röm. 1,18–3,20), sollte aber doch zusammen mit Phil. 3,6 verstanden werden.[32] Es scheint mir jedoch, daß Paulus von den am Anfang der Argumentation angeführten Tatsachen gedrängt ist: die Heiden haben durch den Glauben, ohne Gesetz, den Geist empfangen, d.h. die Erfüllung der Verheißung, den Segen. Dann geraten diejenigen, die sich zum Gesetz halten, gerade in das Gegenteil des Segens. Dies kombiniert Paulus mit seinem Christusglauben: indem Christus den Fluch des Gesetzes auf sich genommen hat, hat er die Seinigen losgekauft, und durch ihn ist die Erfüllung der Verheißung an die Adressaten gelangt.

Schrittweise verringert Paulus die Bedeutung des Gesetzes: seine Aufgabe wird überwiegend negativ beurteilt, und seine Zeit lief mit der Erfüllung der Verheißung aus (3,19–25). Er verneint im Zusammenhang, daß das Gesetz Leben spenden konnte (V. 21), obwohl Deut. (z.B. Kap. 30) einschärft, daß, wer das Gesetz wählt, Leben und Segen wählt. Noch einmal scheint Paulus indessen von widerstreitenden Fakta gesteuert zu sein[33]: wegen des Glaubens hat Gott den Geist gegeben – also ist Gott mit den Glaubenden verbündet, und der im Bund Bleibende ist gerecht. Dann muß das Übrige, auch die Beurteilung des Gesetzes, sich danach richten. Dahinter liegt m.E. eine von einer Bundesideologie geprägte Grundanschauung: Gott tut, was er versprochen hat, oder besser: was Gott in Christus tut und getan hat, daß er den Glaubenden den Geist verliehen hat, muß alles mit dem Versprochenen übereinstimmen; also gilt es nur herauszufinden wie.

Im folgenden geht es dem Gesetz immer schlimmer. In 4,6f. hat also Paulus beschrieben, wie die Galater jetzt Söhne Gottes sind, die im Geist „Abba" rufen. Hiergegenüber stellt er ihre frühere Lage, als sie „Gott nicht kannten" und „Sklaven unter Göttern, die keine Götter sind, waren" (4,8). Sowohl das Motiv der Gotteserkenntnis des Gottesvolkes wie ihre Konsequenz, daß es nicht Götzen dienen darf, gehören in die Bundesideologie. Danach folgt eine Anwendung: wenn jetzt die Galater Gott erkannt haben, „wie könnt ihr zu den schwachen und armseligen Elementen umkehren (ἐπιστρέφετε)? ... ihr beobachtet Tage und Monate und Zeiten und Jahre!" (4,9f.). Vgl. Deut. 30,10 (Der Herr wird sich freuen) „wenn du seine Gebote und Satzungen hälst ... und zu dem Herrn deinem Gott umkehrst (ἐπιστραφῇς) ...". Die Galater stehen im Begriff, sich zum Gesetz Gottes zu bekehren, was Paulus sich zur Idololatrie zu bekehren nennt!

---

[31] Siehe ALBRECHT OEPKE, *Der Brief des Paulus an die Galater* (ThHK 9), Berlin ²1957, z.St.; FRANZ MUSSNER, *Der Galaterbrief* (HThK 9), Freiburg i. Br. – Basel – Wien 1974, z.St.; RUDOLF BULTMANN, *Theologie des Neuen Testaments*, Tübingen ⁶1968, 263f. Vgl. HEINRICH SCHLIER, *Der Brief an die Galater* (KEK 7), Göttingen ⁴1965, z.St. [HANS DIETER BETZ, *Der Galaterbrief* (Hermeneia), München 1988, 261ff.]

[32] KRISTER STENDAHL, *Paul among Jews and Gentiles,* Philadelphia, Penn. 1976, 80f.

[33] SANDERS betont mehrmals, daß für Paulus die Lösung dem Problem vorangeht (a.a.O., 442ff. u.ö.).

Die Bundesideologie gibt Resonanz unter diesem *tour de force* in der Argumentation des Apostels.

Nach der „Allegorie" über Sara und Hagar, welche für zwei Bündnisse stehen, fängt in der Mitte des 5. Kapitels die Paränese des Briefes an, die in einem eschatologischen Ausblick mündet. Beide sind gut in einer Bundesideologie zu Hause. Auch nach Paulus bringt die Bundesbeziehung Pflichten für die Menschen mit sich, wovon die Tugend- und Lasterkataloge zeugen.[34] Sie enthalten einige Wendungen, die an die Bundesideologie erinnern. So schrieb Ezechiel von der Zeit des erneuten Bundes: „Ich werde meinen Geist in eure Brust kommen lassen und bewirken, daß ihr nach meinen Satzungen wandelt ... So werdet ihr im Land wohnen, das ich euren Vätern gab" (Ez. 36,27f.). Vgl. Paulus im Gal.: „wandelt im Geist" (5,16), „wer solches (d.h. die Werke des Fleisches) tut, wird nicht das Reich Gottes erben" (5,21). Ich erinnere daran, daß auch das Wort „Werk" im bundesideologischen Zusammenhang gewöhnlich ist, und daß „die Werke des Fleisches" solchem entsprechen, das für typisch heidnische Laster gehalten war.

Schließlich können die zwei eschatologischen Möglichkeiten in 6,7ff. den Gedanken in dieselbe Richtung lenken: hier wird vom Verderben (φθορά) und vom ewigen Leben gesprochen. Vgl. Deut. 30,19 „siehe, ich habe dir Leben und Tod, Segen und Fluch vorgelegt. So wähle das Leben ...".

So weit die Bundesideologie in und hinter dem Galaterbrief. Ein darunterliegendes Muster vereint Hauptbegriffe und Themata, wie Bund, Gesetz, Verheißung, Gerechtigkeit, Werke, Segen, Fluch, Geist, Erbe, Gottessohnschaft, Leben, Gotteserkenntnis, Tugend- und Lasterkatalog, Warnungen vor Idolatrie, ewiges Leben und ewiges Verderben. Das Vorhandensein des Musters gibt an die Hand, daß die Argumentation des Apostels nicht *ad hoc*, von einem kühnen Griff nach den Texten von Abraham inspiriert, gemacht ist. Stattdessen webt er seinen Beweis auf dem Boden einer Gesamtauffassung von Gott, seiner Treue, seinen Werken und seinem Verhältnis zu seinem Volk – und von dem Verhältnis des Volkes zu Gott. Paulus scheint diese Gesamtauffassung einigen ihm unerläßlichen Tatsachen gegenüberzustellen, d.h. denen, daß die Galater durch den Glauben an Christus den Geist empfangen haben, und zwar ohne zeremoniell in das jüdische Bundesvolk aufgenommen worden zu sein.

(c) Wir gehen nun zum *Römerbrief* über. Oben wurde schon Röm. 9,4f. angeführt, wo Paulus die Vorzüge seiner Mitjuden aufzählt: „ihrer sind die Sohnschaft und die Herrlichkeit und die Bündnisse und die Gesetzgebung und der Kult und die Verheißungen, ihrer sind die Väter." Zuletzt fügt er hinzu: „aus ihnen ist Christus (oder: der Messias) dem Fleische nach." Das letzte würde kein nicht-christlicher Jude zu den Vorzügen des auserwählten Volkes rechnen. Aber Paulus tut es. Wir sahen, wie er im Gal. von gewissen Tatsachen aus eine Argumentation hervorpreßte, nach welcher Gottes Werk in Christus an den Galatern

---

[34] Vgl. BALTZER, a.a.O., 109f., 130, 133, 154f.

mit der Bundesideologie versöhnt werden sollte. Im Römerbrief geschieht m.E. etwas ähnliches. Laßt uns den Anfang des Briefes von diesem Gesichtspunkt aus betrachten.

Die Kommentare beschreiben oft Röm. 1,18–3,20 als einen negativen Hintergrund zum folgenden. Der Abschnitt soll zeigen, daß man durch nichts anderes als die Glaubensgerechtigkeit gerettet werden kann, die von 3,21 an positiv dargestellt ist.[35] Dies läßt sich sagen, aber es könnte sich lohnen, den Text ergänzend unter Berücksichtigung der Bundesideologie zu lesen.

Dann ahnt man, daß der Zorn Gottes, der nach Röm. 1,18 über alle Gottlosigkeit und Ungerechtigkeit der Menschen vom Himmel offenbart wird,[36] der Zorn des Bundesgottes ist, welcher z.B. nach Deut. 29,22ff. brennt, weil das Volk den Bund verlassen hat, und anderen Göttern dient.[37] Indessen denkt sich Paulus, wie auch viele andere jüdische Verfasser seiner Zeit, daß auch die Heiden vor dem Gott des Bundes verantwortlich sind. Wie Gott sich in einer endgültigen Weise für sein Volk zu erkennen gab, und es deswegen wider besseres Wissen Götzen nicht dienen darf, so hat er sich auch für die Heiden so weit zu erkennen gegeben, daß sie unter Verantwortlichkeit stehen.[38] Die Werke des Schöpfers, die nach 1,20 von seinem Wesen zeugen, werden nicht selten in von Bundesideologie getragenen Texten erwähnt, und wir erkennen davon auch die Verwerfung der Idolatrie (1,23) und der heidnischen Unsittlichkeit (1,24–31). Den Terminus „tun" (ποιεῖν, πράσσειν 1,28.32; 2,1ff.) habe ich oben erwähnt. Wir begegnen ihm sowohl im Reden von den Werken der Heiden als auch im 2. Kapitel vom Wandel der Juden.

Durch die Bundesideologie wird im 2. Kapitel der Kritik des die Bundespflichten nicht vollziehenden Menschen Stütze und Schärfe gegeben. So wird das Gericht Gottes erwähnt (2,3), die Verachtung gegen Gottes Güte und Langmut, die zur Umkehr leiten wollen (2,4). Wie so oft in Fällen, wo Menschen wegen des Abfalls angeklagt werden, wird hier gesagt, daß sie ein hartes und unbußfertiges Herz haben (2,5).[39] Die beiden alternativen Resultate von den Werken des Menschen, d.h. ewiges Leben oder Strafe (2,7–10), werden in Wendun-

---

[35] OTTO MICHEL, *Der Brief an die Römer* (KEK 4), Göttingen [12]1963, 61; JACOB JERVELL, *Gud og hans fiender*, Oslo 1973, 21; ERNST KÄSEMANN, *An die Römer* (HNT 8a), Tübingen 1973, 29; HEINRICH SCHLIER, *Der Römerbrief* (HThK 6), Freiburg i. Br. – Basel – Wien 1977, 48; BULTMANN, *Theologie*, 261ff. [Siehe DAVID HELLHOLM, „Ampflificatio in the Macro-Structure of Romans", in: *Rhetoric and the New Testament* ed. STANLEY. E. PORTER AND THOMAS H. OLBRICHT, Sheffield 1993, 123–151: 135].

[36] Für die Diskussion der viel erörterten γάρ-Verbindung zwischen V. 17 und 18 könnte es von Belang sein, daß bundesideologisch geprägte Texte die δικαιοσύνη und den Zorn Gottes zusammenstellen können – siehe Ex. 34,7 (LXX); Esr. 9,14f.; Dan. 9,16. Vgl. KÄSEMANN, *Komm.*, z.St.

[37] Andere Stellen, wo der göttliche Zorn im Bundeszusammenhang erwähnt ist, sind: Ex. 32,10ff.; Ez. 36,18; Esr. 9,14; Dan. 9,16; äth. Hen. 5,9; 101,3; CD I, 21.

[38] Sap. 13 wird im Zusammenhang oft zitiert. Für palästinisches Judentum siehe DAVIES, a.a.O., 64f.; 116; SANDERS, a.a.O., 88f.; 206ff.; 374f.

[39] Z.B. Deut. 29,19; Ez. 36,26; äth. Hen. 5,4; 100,8. Vgl. KLAUS BERGER, „Hartherzigkeit und Gottes Gesetz. Die Vorgeschichte des antijüdischen Vorwurfs in Mc 10,5", in: *ZNW* 61 (1970) 1–47.

gen ausgedrückt, in denen die Flüche über die Abtrünnigen nach Deut. 28,53 widerhallen. Ohne Ansehen der Person lohnt und straft Gott. Denn, wie in Deut. 28 (V. 1.13.15), soll man nicht nur das Gesetz hören, sondern es auch tun (2,13). Ganz im Rahmen dieses Themas wird so die Erkenntnis des Juden vom Willen Gottes seiner Nichterfüllung gegenübergestellt. Seine Beschneidung, das Zeichen der Bundeszugehörigkeit mit ihrer Verpflichtung zum Gesetz, hat also keine Entsprechung im Leben, und ist somit der Unbeschnittenheit gleichgestellt (2,25ff.). Stattdessen gilt die Beschneidung des Herzens gemäß dem in Deut. 30,6 gezeigten Bild von der Zeit der Wiederherstellung.

Bis hierher hat also Paulus im Rahmen der Bundesideologie den Juden neben den Heiden gestellt. Weder der eine noch der andere ist ein tadelloser Bundespartner. Der Apostel faßt so am Anfang des 3. Kapitels seine bisherige Darstellung zusammen: Was ist aus der Sonderstellung der Juden geworden, die ja in der Bundesideologie so wichtig ist? Die Antwort ist zweifach: einerseits haben die Juden keine sittliche Sonderstellung, denn sowohl Juden als auch Griechen stehen unter der Sünde (3,9). Andererseits haben die Juden den Vorrang, daß „ihnen die Worte Gottes anvertraut worden sind" (3,2). Deut. 6,6 sagt ja: „die Worte, die ich dir heute gebe, sollst du auf dein Herz legen." Aber das haben die Juden nicht getan; sie, oder „einige von ihnen"[40] sind statt dessen untreu, d.h. nicht solide Bundespartner, gewesen (3,3). Gottes Bundestreue[41] (3,3) und Gerechtigkeit (3,5) werden aber nicht dadurch zunichte gemacht. Eine Seite dieser Bundesgerechtigkeit ist der Zorn Gottes über die Ungerechtigkeit (3,5) und sein Gericht über den Sünder (3,7). Die Bezeichnung „Sünder" wird gern in bundesideologisch geprägten Texten von denen gebraucht, die außerhalb des Bundes stehen oder davon abgefallen sind.[42] So lautet der Schluß: „wir haben sowohl Juden als Heiden dafür angeklagt, unter der Sünde zu sein" (3,9).

Bisher hat sich Paulus von 1,18 an innerhalb der Bundesideologie bewegt.[43] Aber er hat das Muster revidiert, indem er nämlich alle Nichtchristen, sowohl Juden als Heiden, unter den göttlichen Zorn gebracht hat, der nach normaler Bundesideologie die Sünder treffen soll, und er hat, obwohl ohne Beweis, dem Gesetz eine nur negative Funktion gegeben: es soll jeden Mund verstopfen (3,19).

---

[40] Für das Verstehen von τινές; gibt es mehrere Vorschläge. Daß die Untreue der „einigen" in der „Ablehnung des Evangeliums gipfelt" (ERNST KÄSEMANN, Komm., z.St.; ähnlich OTTO KUSS, Der Römerbrief I [Regensburg 1957], z.St.) stimmt m.E. gut mit dem paulinischen Gebrauch von der Bundesideologie überein. [Vgl. EDUARD LOHSE, Der Brief an die Römer (KEK 4), Göttingen 2003, z.St.; ROBERT JEWETT, Romans (Hermeneia), Minneapolis, Minn. 2007, z.St.]

[41] Siehe die Komm. von MICHEL, KÄSEMANN, SCHLIER, z.St.

[42] Siehe KARL HEINRICH RENGSTORF, „ἁμαρτωλός", in: ThWNT I, 1933, 328f. Vgl. SANDERS, a.a.O., 111ff.

[43] Daß die „Gottesgerechtigkeit" (1,17) auch einen Platz in der Bundesideologie hat, ist ja von E. Käsemann erwiesen. Siehe ERNST KÄSEMANN, „Zum Verständnis von Römer 3,24–26", in: Exegetische Versuche und Besinnungen I, Göttingen 1960, 96ff. (erstmals in ZNW 43 [1950/51] 150–154); IDEM, Gottesgerechtigkeit bei Paulus (ibid., II, Göttingen 1964), 189f. (erstmals in ZThK 58 [1961] 367–378). Auch PETER STUHLMACHER, Gerechtigkeit Gottes bei Paulus, Göttingen 1965, bes. C III und IV.

Mit 3,21 macht Paulus einen neuen Ansatz: „nun aber ist, ohne Gesetz, Gottes Gerechtigkeit offenbart worden ...". Aber er bleibt innerhalb der Bundesideologie. Jetzt ist jedoch der Augenblick gekommen, in dem er beginnt, die umgedeutete Bundesideologie mit der Ursache dieser Umdeutung zu verbinden, nämlich dem Werk Christi und der Tatsache, daß die Christen, Juden und Heiden, „glauben", und zwar ohne Gesetzesobservanz seitens der Heiden.

Alle waren also unter der Sünde (3,9.19.23). Aber nach 3,25 erwies Gott seine Gerechtigkeit, seine Solidarität als Bundespartner, indem er in göttlicher Geduld die früher begangenen Sünden erließ.[44]

Gerade die Langmut Gottes gegenüber den Sündern ist ein in Bundestexten oft wiederkehrendes Motiv (s. schon 2,4). Dieser Erlaß wird jetzt mit einer Sühne der Sünden zusammengestellt. Gott stellte nämlich Jesus als „ίλαστήριον durch Glauben in seinem Blut auf" (3,25). CD II, 4f. bietet in seiner Ähnlichkeit und Unähnlichkeit eine gute Parallele dar: „Langmut ist bei ihm und reiche Vergebungen, um Sühne zu schaffen für die, die von der Sünde sich abgewandt haben".[45] Auch die Sühne gehört in das Feld der Bundesgedanken.[46] Für Paulus geschieht aber diese Sühne durch Jesu Blut. Noch eine Beziehung zur Bundesideologie ist hier zu spüren; Paulus (und seine Tradition) meint nämlich, daß man beim Herrenmahl „den neuen Bund in meinem Blut" [1 Kor. 11,25] feiert.[47]

Röm. 1,18–3,20 erwies also, daß „es kein Unterschied ist", denn „alle", Juden wie Heiden, „sündigten" (3,23). Jetzt gilt die Gerechtigkeit durch Glauben. So bleibt vom Ruhm des auserwählten Bundesvolkes nichts übrig (3,27), wozu nicht zuletzt der Ruhm wegen des Gesetzes gehörte. Vgl. 2,17ff. und Sir. 39,8: (der Weise) „rühmt sich wegen des Gesetzes des Herrenbundes."

So ist also der Gedanke an Christus und seinen Tod mit der Bundesideologie konfrontiert worden. Wo Paulus nach 1,18–3,20 und nach 3,21–27 angelangt ist, könnte so ausgedrückt werden: „Christus starb für uns, als wir noch Sünder waren ... durch sein Blut jetzt gerechtfertigt, werden wir durch ihn aus dem Zorn gerettet werden" (5,8f.). Daß das aber so „ohne Gesetz" und „durch Glauben" geschieht, sträubt sich gegen die übliche Bundesideologie und hat noch keinen ausreichenden Beweis bekommen. Vor allem das Erstgenannte ist zweifelsohne in den Gedankengang eingeführt worden, um den Heiden Raum zu bereiten (vgl. schon das Thema des Römerbriefes, 1,16f.). Ein gewisses Argument für den Platz der Heiden im Gottesvolk wird indessen in 3,29f. gegeben: „Oder ist Gott allein der Gott der Juden? Nicht auch der der Heiden?" Wir erkennen die Bundesverheißung: „ich werde ihr Gott sein, und sie werden mein Volk sein" (Jer. 31,33).[48] Paulus dehnt also die Gültigkeit dieser Verheißung auf die Heiden aus.

---

[44] Wie der Text syntaktisch zu verstehen ist, ist umstritten. Siehe die *Komm.* z.St.
[45] Übersetzung EDUARD LOHSE, *Die Texte aus Qumran*, Darmstadt 1964.
[46] Siehe KENNEDY, a.a.O., 395ff.; SANDERS, a.a.O., I 57ff. u.ö.
[47] Vgl. MICHEL *Komm.* z.St.; KÄSEMANN, *Komm.* z.St. [Siehe auch DIETER ZELLER, *Der erste Brief an die Korinther* (KEK 5), 372–374.]
[48] Siehe z.B. auch Gen. 17,7; Ex. 6,7; Deut. 29,13; Jos. 24,18.

Den Beweis dafür, daß dies so ohne Gesetzesobservanz geschehen kann, gibt das „unseren Vater Abraham" heranziehende Kapitel 4 (sein προπάτωρ-Titel erinnert an die in bundesideologisch gefärbten Texten gewöhnlichen Hinweise auf die Väter). Daß der Glaube Abrahams ihm zur Gerechtigkeit angerechnet wurde, als er noch unbeschnitten war, wird von Paulus als Argument verwendet (4,10). Bundesideologische Begriffe wie die Verheißungen Gottes an die Väter und das Erbe werden nun umgedeutet, so daß die Gnade das Gesetz ausschließen darf. Dies indessen war nach üblicher Bundesideologie kein notwendiger Schluß. Das Erbe wird ferner des Glaubens wegen, aus Gnade, der *gesamten* Nachkommenschaft Abrahams gegeben, und die Bundesverheißung gilt nun für Juden wie Heiden (4,13–18).

Am Anfang des 5. Kapitels wird dann von der Folge dieses Gerechtwerdens gesprochen. Wir haben Frieden mit Gott, besitzen die Hoffnung, und die Liebe Gottes ist in unsere Herzen ausgegossen durch den uns geschenkten heiligen Geist. Alles ist solches, was gemäß jüdischer Erwartung in die Zeit des erneuten Bundes gehörte.[49]

Ich lege hiermit den Römerbrief beiseite, obgleich er mehr zu unserem Thema zu sagen hätte.[50] Das schon Angeführte mag aber zureichend erwiesen haben, daß irgendwie eine Bundesideologie hinter dem meisten liegt, was Paulus in diesen Kapiteln schreibt. Nicht nur einzelne Wörter und Ausdrücke sind darauf zu beziehen, sondern auch der Gedankengang wird vom Problem hervorgetrieben, die Mitgliedschaft der Heiden im Gottesvolk mit einer Bundesideologie zu vereinen, die einerseits den Verfasser und, vermutlicherweise, die Leser mit einem Referenzsystem versieht, die aber andererseits Paulus sich zu revidieren gezwungen sieht.

## 4. Resumé

Im 2 Kor. konnte Paulus das Amt des neuen Bundes dem des alten gegenüberstellen, und im Galaterbrief konnte er mit zwei, von Isaak und Ismael vorgebildeten Bündnissen argumentieren. Aber er führt dies niemals so aus, daß die Christen in einem neuen Bund stehen, der den alten völlig ausgeschlagen hat. Paulus hält also gewissermaßen den Wiederherstellungsteil der Bundesideologie mit ihren anderen Teilen zusammen, und er scheint vorauszusetzen, daß für das jüdische Volk noch der Bund gültig ist. Aber gleichzeitig ist er genötigt, an dem bundesideologischen Muster Kunstgriffe vorzunehmen, um den auf Christus getauften, „glaubenden" und nicht Torah-gehorsamen Heiden im Gottesvolk Platz zu bereiten. Das tut er in den oben erörterten Kapiteln des Römer-

---

[49] Auch der „Zutritt" (5,2) könnte als Teil einer Bundesideologie angesehen werden – siehe KENNEDY, a.a.O., 405f.

[50] Vgl. z.B. wie die Liste von Widrigkeiten, die nach Röm. 8,35 nicht von der Liebe Christi scheiden können, merkwürdige Anklänge an die Bundesflüche enthält: vgl. Lev. 26,17.25.33.36; Deut. 28,48.53.55.57; 30,7; 32,24f.

briefs. Es wäre aber vorschnell, hieraus die Folge zu ziehen, daß der Römerbrief eine Apologie der Heidenteilnahme am Gottesvolk sei. Kap. 9–11 zeigen, daß es Paulus auch daran lag, die Heiden gegen einen unrechtmäßigen Stolz den „herausgebrochenen Zweigen" (11,17) gegenüber zu warnen.

Dieses Bundesmuster hinter und in diesen Kapiteln zu sehen hat zur Folge, daß die Diskussion darin wie ein Ringen mit Problemen erscheint, die daraus stammen, daß der Verfasser einerseits der Apostel Christi zu den Unbeschnittenen ist[51] und andererseits selbst ein Jude, ja wahrscheinlich eben gewissermaßen ein Torahgehorsamer ist.[52] Er räumt kein neues Gedankenfeld auf, sondern bewegt sich auf der Ebene der befindlichen Bundesideologie. Dann muß er aber gewisse Teile des Feldes in einer neuen Weise bewerten und auch das einschließen, was seine Überzeugung als Christ und Heidenapostel mit sich bringt. Dann handeln diese Kapitel des Römerbriefes mehr von Gott und seinem Volk als vom Einzelnen und seinem Gott.[53]

Gleichzeitig muß auch gesagt werden, daß, wenn die Bundeskategorien Resonanzboden hinter dem Text bilden dürfen, sich zeigt, wie radikal die paulinische Weise war, die Heiden zu akzeptieren. Im Lichte der Bundesideologie scheinen Termini wie „Sünder" und „Gottlose" in grellen Farben. Sagen, daß Gott Sünder oder Gottlose rechtfertigt, heißt sagen, daß er den vom Bunde Abtrünnigen in den dem Bundestreuen zukommenden Status versetzte. Solches erklärt die in Röm. 3,8 und 6,1 spürbaren Angriffe gegen Paulus wegen unmoralischer Verkündigung.

Wir kommen zum Schluß. Wir sind einer Bundesideologie in und hinter drei paulinischen Texten, 1 Thess., Gal. und Röm. nachgegangen. Sie spiegeln drei Stadien und drei Weisen wieder,[54] in denen Paulus mit dieser Ideologie arbeitet. In 1 Thess. waren auf eine zumindest anscheinend unproblematische Weise so viele Termini und Gedanken von der Bundesideologie gefärbt, daß man dahinter eine Betrachtungsweise vermuten muß, nach der die Heidenchristen als Mitglieder des Eigentumsvolkes Gottes betrachtet wurden. Es gab jedoch Schwierigkeiten seitens der Juden „die uns verfolgt haben ... und uns hindern wollen, den Heiden zu predigen, auf daß sie gerettet werden" (2,15f.).

Im Galaterbrief wird das von den Juden laut 1 Thess. Infragegestellte gegen andere Meinungen heftig verteidigt. Paulus muß dafür argumentieren, daß die Heiden ohne Beschneidung dem Gottesvolk zugehören können. Die Bundesideologie gibt den Gegnern Wasser auf ihre Mühle, aber Paulus kann seine Füße gegen den die Erneuerung erblickenden Teil dieser Ideologie anstemmen, wenn er gegen die Gesetzeseiferer polemisiert. So kann er am Ende des Briefes schreiben: „weder die Beschneidung noch die Unbeschnittenheit gilt etwas, vielmehr eine neue Schöpfung. Und alle, die mit dieser Richtschnur übereinstimmen,

---

[51] Vgl. JOHANNES MUNCK, *Paulus und die Heilsgeschichte*, Kopenhagen 1954, 59f.
[52] Vgl. 1 Kor. 9,21 – siehe z.B. DAVIES, a.a.O., 69f.
[53] Siehe STENDAHL, a.a.O., 25ff.
[54] Vgl. DAHL, a.a.O., 254.

Friede über sie und Erbarmen, *und* über das Israel Gottes!" (6,15f.) Es gibt Gründe dafür, daß mit dem ein wenig überraschenden „Israel" hier wirklich „Israel nach dem Fleisch" gemeint ist.[55] Berücksichtigt man indessen die Bedeutung, die die Bundesideologie hinter und in dem Argument des Briefes spielt, und vermutlicherweise in der Briefsituation, nimmt die Überraschung ab, obgleich die Spannung nicht völlig aufgelöst wird.

Im Römerbrief, schließlich, ist die Diskussion ruhiger und mehr systematisch, aber die sachlichen Voraussetzungen die den Gedankengang in den erörterten Abschnitten lenken, sind ähnlich. Deutlicher als im Galaterbrief und mit einer gewissen Variation demgegenüber legt Paulus eine eigene Perspektive auf die Bundesideologie an. Er benutzt sie, wenn er Juden und Heiden unter Gottes Zorn gleichstellt, er strapaziert sie, wenn er dem Gesetz eine andere Rolle gibt, und er bleibt doch in ihr, wenn er das Werk Christi und den Glauben einfügt und die neue Lage zeichnet.

---

[55] MUSSNER, *Komm.* z.St.; vgl. OEPKE, *Komm.* z.St.; SCHLIER, *Komm.* z.St.; DAHL, a.a.O., 212.

# 5. Is the Crucified Christ the Center of a New Testament Theology?[1]

## 1. The Problem of the Center of the New Testament

The reader may rightly sense that the title of this contribution smacks of German. For several of our German colleagues have frequently posed the question, is there a center in the New Testament, *eine Mitte des Neuen Testaments*, or even *eine Mitte der Schrift?*[2] Almost always the response has been, "Yes, there is a center, *viz.*, the cross, or Jesus' death on the cross." Such a response is frequently given by those influenced by the existentialist theology of Professor Bultmann and others, for whom the cross has a central position by virtue of its historical and thus non-mythical character. The cross is a scandal which must not be made less offensive, since it stands for an authentic faith, one without security for its trust in the God who demands faith without reserve.

Exegetes working at faculties which are connected to this or that denomination may find it easier than their colleagues to decide, whether there is a center in NT theology, at least if they accept the theological tenets of the Church in question. But when I understand the title of this paper as an open question, I do so while loyal to my school: a faculty of divinity at a state university, studying theology as *Religionswissenschaft*.

---

[1] A thoroughly revised version of a paper read at a conference arranged June 1987 in Oslo for the faculties of theology at the universities of Greifswald, Rostock, Kiel and of the Scandinavian countries.

[2] See the works of ERNST KÄSEMANN, e.g., *Paulinische Perspektiven*, Tübingen 1972, 61–107; furthermore, e.g., BERTOLD KLAPPERT (ed.), *Diskussion um Kreuz und Auferstehung*, Wuppertal ²1967; WERNER GEORG KÜMMEL, "Das Problem der ‚Mitte des Neuen Testaments'", in: *L'Evangile, hier et aujourd'hui. Melanges offerts au Professeur Franz-J. Leenhardt* (in Genève 1968), 71–85, reprinted in IDEM, *Heilsgeschehen und Geschichte II* (Gesammelte Aufsätze), Marburg 1978, 62–74; ULRICH LUZ, "Theologia crucis als Mitte der Theologie im Neuen Testament," in: *EvTh* 34 (1974) 116–141; WOLFGANG SCHRAGE, "Die Frage nach der Mitte und dem Kanon im Kanon des Neuen Testaments in der neueren Diskussion," in: JOHANNES FRIEDRICH/WOLFGANG PÖHLMANN/PETER STUHLMACHER (eds.), *Rechtfertigung. Festschrift für Ernst Käsemann*, Göttingen 1976, 415–442; SIEGFRIED SCHULZ, *Die Mitte der Schrift. Der Frühkatholizismus im Neuen Testament als Herausforderung an den Protestantismus*, Stuttgart 1976; BERNHARD EHLER, *Die Herrschaft des Gekreuzigten. Ernst Käsemanns Frage nach der Mitte der Schrift*, Berlin – New York 1986, which also contains an extensive bibliography. Cf. FRANZ MUSSNER, "Die Mitte des Evangeliums in neutestamentlicher Sicht," in: *Catholica* 15 (1961) 271–292; RENÉ KIEFFER, *Die Bibel deuten – das Leben deuten. Einführung in die Theologie des Neuen Testaments*, Regensburg 1987, 22f.

Naturally our question immediately leads to another, which should be discussed first, *viz.*, what do we mean by a NT theology?[3] Greater difficulties would have ensued, if the question had pertained to the center of *the* NT theology. In the worldwide exegetical community scholars like Hendrikus Boers have taught us how awkward this would have been.[4] We may, of course, talk of a certain unity of the NT, in so far as the documents which gradually came to compose the NT have several basic ideas in common. But the traditions and writers who are represented in this library hold opinions so diverse that a NT theology may only be achieved in one of three ways. First by harmonizing: Paul with Matthew and James and John. In this case a dogmatic system guides the understanding of the biblical texts while the theological profiles of their authors are blurred,[5] and the risk of wrongfully attributing opinions to them must be accepted. *Or* second, one particular author is allowed to dominate, and his theology understood according to some canon within the canon, which consciously or unconsciously, is determined by the reader's Church affiliation or private views on religious matters.[6] Finally, the road of abstraction may be followed more or less far. Assume, for example that the different NT authors in reality wrestle with humanity's fundamental existential problems,[7] and make their solutions more and more abstract, until you reach a level at which their answers can be reconciled. Thus, Herbert Braun finds that NT theology ultimately concerns our relationship to our neighbour. When the NT tells how a god and a son of a god relate to humankind, this is translated into a view, in which other persons, their existence and their problems, represent external demands on us but also gifts to us. Braun's point of departure is, he maintains, what he finds typical of, and peculiar to the NT as compared with its milieu.[8]

The question, what is NT theology, can also be put in this way: what do you do when you write a NT theology? A member of a *religionswissenschaftlich* faculty could obviously choose to reply in a way reminiscent of the classical History

---

[3] See the material in GEORG STRECKER (ed.), *Das Problem der Theologie des Neuen Testaments* (Wege der Forschung 367), Darmstadt 1975, especially the editor's own introduction. Furthermore HENDRIKUS BOERS, *What Is New Testament Theology? The Rise of Criticism and the Problem of a Theology of the New Testament* (Guides to Biblical Scholarship, N.T. Series), Philadelphia, Penn. 1979, with an annotated bibliography.

[4] See the preceding note.

[5] ALAN RICHARDSON, *An Introduction to the Theology of the New Testament*, New York 1958 comes close to this type of a New Testament theology.

[6] It is clear, for example, that Paul, and a rather Lutheran Paul at that, dominates E. Käsemann's theology.

[7] For example, RUDOLF BULTMANN, *Theologie des Neuen Testaments*, Tübingen [6]1968, especially 586f.

[8] HERBERT BRAUN, "Der Sinn der neutestamentlichen Christologie," in: *ZThK* 54 (1957) 341–377, reprinted in IDEM, *Gesammelte Studien zum Neuen Testament*, Tübingen 1962, 86–99; IDEM, "Die Problematik einer Theologie des Neuen Testaments," *ZThK* 58 (1961) 3–18, reprinted in: *Gesammelte Studien*, 325–341, and in: STRECKER (ed.), *Das Problem* (above, note 3), 405–424.

of Religions School, as represented by e.g., William Wrede.[9] For him NT theology was a presentation of the thought of different early Christian theologians. The task then pertains to the history of ideas and the history of religion. It is only natural that its scholarly context is the study of the religions in Antiquity, of which Christianity is one. The consequence of such a perspective is also that it becomes artificial to limit the study to the canonical NT.

As a rule, however, scholars seek a further objective when constructing a NT theology. They seek to lay the foundation of a reflection upon Christian faith and assign their NT theology a critical function vis-à-vis such a reflection. Whether consciously or not, the exegete's Church affiliation plays a role in this connection (or, in some cases, the exegete's negative attitude towards some denominational or theological point of view.)

One further point of principle concerns the problem of text and context. Our analytical and historical interest may lead us to spend as much energy on reconstructing sources and/or older layers of the texts as on the result of the efforts of the NT authors and redactors. So we are prepared to discuss the theology of, for example, the Logia-source,[10] but can also accept the idea of a theology of Matthew, although it differs from that of the source included in his text. The same holds true of the Gospel of John: many would differentiate neatly between the theology of the original evangelist and that of the final "ecclesiastical redactor",[11] but are nevertheless willing to discuss the theology of the fourth Gospel as we have it today.

The observations of the preceding paragraphs indicate that when we consider the work of authors and redactors it is as true as ever that texts lend themselves to several interpretations. When we think of the first readers/listeners, who encountered the texts without differentiating the sources from the redactor, they can be said to have done the same thing as we, when we write the theology of the same Gospel and forget about its tradition-history. Sources and redaction become attuned to each other, and particular original nuances or references of the former disappear or acquire new meanings.

But as, for example, the completed Gospel of Matthew has a prehistory which led to a situation in which traditions were used, revised and interpreted in a new context, *viz.*, that of the present Gospel of Matthew, so the same Matthew was very soon embodied in a larger context, called the Gospel or the Four-fold Gospel. In other words, what the exegete cherishes as the particular message of Matthew is understood in the light of this context of the fourfold Gospel. With Paul it is the same. An exegete may ask whether Paul changed some of his views,

---

[9] WILLIAM WREDE, *Über Aufgabe und Methode der sogenannten neutestamentlichen Theologie*, Göttingen 1897; pp. 7–80 reprinted in: STRECKER (ed.), *Das Problem* (note 3), 81–154.
[10] E.g., PAUL HOFFMANN, *Studien zur Theologie der Logienquelle* (NTAbh N.F. 8), Münster 1972.
[11] Of course inspired by RUDOLF BULTMANN, *Das Evangelium des Johannes* (KEK 2), Göttingen [10]1941. [Cf. FOLKER SIEGERT, *Das Evangelium des Johannes in seiner ursprünglichen Gestalt* (SIJD 7), Göttingen 2008.]

say those on the Torah, from Galatians to Romans.[12] But once not only the undisputed letters, but also the deutero- and trito-Pauline epistles came to belong to the Pauline letter collection, the readers read the whole as expressing Paul's theology.

We are anxious to separate the historical Paul from the Paul envisaged from Colossians, Ephesians and 2 Thessalonians, not to mention the Pastorals. But those who disseminated the collection gave us a Paul of the Church in the same way as the school of John gave us their John. Indeed, we may even say that in reality this Paul of the Church has been of greater importance throughout the centuries than the Paul we reconstruct from the authentic letters. Thus, there is one Pauline theology made up from the authentic letters and another, derived from the whole Pauline collection of the NT, the origin of which is not only a man but also a re-interpreting tradition and a Pauline school.

Thus, the more we regard the present texts from a reader's point of view, the closer we *can* come to a traditional Christian perspective, leaving aside the historical search for the opinions of individual NT authors or of their sources. I do not say we should do so, but we may do so and adduce some reasons for so doing.

The deliberations of the preceding paragraphs are not simply a few pirouettes on the ice of methodology but sketch a feature of the problematic background for a discussion of a NT theology and its possible center. In what follows, I shall start on a relatively low level of abstraction. Thus, by a "NT theology" I shall refer to the structured world of thought which we can reconstruct from the NT texts with the help of a particular author or a text-producing group. I first pose the question of this paper to the theology of Paul and to that of the fourth Gospel. Secondly I shall, albeit sketchily, widen the perspective and, on a higher level of abstraction, ask our question of a NT theology and its center.

But first one further modification. Often it happens that "the crucified Christ" is understood so broadly as to refer to suffering and death in general. But here I will focus on the crucifixion in the narrow sense of death on the cross as the specific form of Jesus' suffering and death.[13] The more general emphasis would lead us to speak of a "theology of Jesus' suffering and death" rather than a "theology of the cross" (*theologia crucis*).

When we consider the NT writings with this narrower significance of "the crucified Christ" in mind, we find that, although many of them mention Jesus' death on the cross, it is actually only with Paul and John that the cross *per se* is important. In other words, all theologians of the Early Church presumably

---

[12] HANS HÜBNER, *Law in Paul's Thought*, trans. James C. G. Greig, Edinburgh 1984. Cf. ED P. SANDERS, *Paul, the Law, and the Jewish People*, Philadelphia, Penn. 1983; HEIKKI RÄISÄNEN, "Paul's Theological Difficulties with the Law," in: ELIZABETH A. LIVINGSTONE (ed.), *Studia Biblica 1978*, vol. 3: Papers on Paul and Other New Testament Authors (JSNT.S 3), Sheffield 1980, 301–320; reprinted in: IDEM, *The Torah and Christ* (Publications of the Finnish Exegetical Society 45), Helsinki 1986, 3–24.

[13] So does also HEINZ-WOLFGANG KUHN, "Jesus als Gekreuzigter in der frühchristlichen Verkündigung bis zur Mitte des 2. Jahrhunderts," in: *ZThK* 72 (1975) 1–46.

sought an answer to the question of the meaning of Jesus' death, but to judge from our texts, not all have elaborated on the fact that it was on a cross that he died.

## 2. The Crucified Christ in Paul

But with Paul this is the case.[14] In the undisputed letters the motif is first encountered in a polemic against the divisions caused by the devotees of wisdom in Corinth (1 Cor 1–3). Against those who say "I belong to Paul" etc. (1:12), Paul's argument is: Christ is not divided (1:13), which he develops by saying that Paul was not crucified for them nor were they baptized in his name. Indeed, he has only baptized a few of them (1:14–16), since his mission is to preach the Gospel, though not with wisdom of words, lest the cross be made of no effect (1:17). Paul then develops the contrast between wisdom of words and Gospel preaching: the latter is folly to those who perish but the power of God to those who ‚He saved (1:18). For, he says, through this foolish preaching of the crucified Christ, God, in His wisdom, saves the one who believes. A crucified Christ (or a crucified Messiah) is, of course, a stumbling-block to the Jews and a crucified saviour (a *soter* or a *kurios*) a folly to the Greeks, given the associations with crucifixion, the punishment of major, despicable criminals.

In this exercise of God's power the cross represents a principle of folly and weakness, the validity of which is then exemplified. First, it is proved in the social structure of the Corinthian Church, because its members came chiefly from the lower classes. Thus, everything comes from God, so that he who boasts can boast only in the Lord (1:31, quoting Jer 9:24). The next proof of the principle is Paul's own behaviour as an apostle: he refrained from speaking with wisdom and rhetorical elegance in order to know only Christ and Him crucified (2:1–4). Again he states: in human weakness God was powerful.

Furthermore, there is a contrast between Christ's being crucified for the Corinthians and their high esteem for men, which led to the divisions Paul is attacking. His argument about crucifixion and baptism in 1:13 presupposes that in baptism Christ's death was related to the one baptized. Further, in order to prevail, the argument must assume that the consequence of baptism was that the Corinthians became Christ's property (see also 3:23). Then belonging to Christ in that way would be so overwhelming as to invalidate the all too human views that lay behind the divisions. But it is difficult to tell whether this belonging to Christ has anything to do with the crucifixion *per se*. Indirectly the Corinthians detest the shameful death on the cross through their veneration of men, and in

---

[14] See, e.g., KÄSEMANN, *Paulinische Perspektiven* (note 2), 61–107; FRANZ-JOSEF ORTKEMPER, *Das Kreuz in der Verkündigung des Apostels Paulus* (Stuttgarter Bibelstudien 24), Stuttgart ²1968; WOLFGANG SCHRAGE, "Leid, Kreuz und Eschaton. Die Peristasenkataloge als Merkmale paulinischer theologia crucis und Eschatologie," in: *EvTh* 34 (1974) 141–175; PETER STUHLMACHER, "Achtzehn Thesen zur paulinischen Kreuzestheologie," in: *Rechtfertigung* (note 2), 509–525.

other passages Paul expresses the idea that this belonging to Christ implies a life which is determined by the cross (Gal 2:19f.; 5:24; 6:14). But here he does not develop such a thought.

In Galatians too Christ the crucified is contrasted with something more acceptable, less shameful, at least to the Jewish mind, namely circumcision. Paul is horrified at the fact that in obedience to the Law the Galatians can take up circumcision, these people before whose eyes Christ was set forth as crucified (3:1f.). When this proclamation of Christ the crucified was received in faith, the Galatians were endowed with the Spirit, but now they seem to reject it in order to "end with the flesh" (3:3), which I take to denote the concrete fulfilment of the Torah commandment.

In this Galatians passage the crucified Christ is not only contained in the preaching to which people have listened in faith, but also adduced in the argument for the principle of justification by faith which follows. Thus, in 3:13 he cites Deuteronomy 21:23, "Cursed is everyone who hangs on a tree." This implies that "Christ redeemed us from the curse of the Law, becoming a curse for us" (3:13). The conclusion is that, when the curse is taken away, the way is clear for the Gentiles, so that they can inherit Abraham's blessing through faith (3:14).

Towards the end of Galatians the motif of the cross is taken up again. In contrast to the opponents, who "want to show fair in the flesh" (6:12, also 6:13, and cf. 3:3), i.e. through their persuading the Galatians to submit to circumcision, Paul will not glory in anything except in the cross of Christ "through which (or: through whom) the world has been crucified to me and I to the world" (6:14). Here the idea is not so much that of the proclamation of the crucifixion and its salvific consequences as of a continuing relationship to Christ based on this salvation (also 5:24). This relationship is entered through faith and baptism (2:19; 3:20–29), so that now, when we belong to Christ (3:29; 5:24), everything mundane, shame and the works of the Law included, is of no importance – Paul is crucified to the world.

Thus we have seen how in 1 Corinthians the preaching of the folly of the cross was opposed to human wisdom and distinction, and how in Galatians the "for us" of the death on the cross was developed in an exposition of an OT passage on the curse of a hanged person. In Galatians we also noted how the Christ-relationship, established through the application of the consequences of his death in baptism had sequels for the life of the Christian: it became determined by the cross, and conventional values were overthrown.

Since I am examining the position of the cross in a Pauline theology, it may be worthwhile to touch upon another aspect of our motif. Not only is the shameful fact of the crucifixion of importance to Paul, but also the person so executed. He and His cross belong, on the one hand, definitely to human history. On the other, this Christ is also the exalted Lord with whom Christians are united. Nonetheless he is always the crucified one – Paul uses the perfect tense (1 Cor

1:29; 2:2; Gal 3:1). Even the exalted Christ is ever one who has experienced the utmost human misery.

Is then the crucified Christ, understood in the narrow sense I defined above, the center of a NT theology, and, particularly, of a Pauline one? When, as a theologian of the *Religionswissenschaftliche* school, I am confronted by the question and attempt to deal with it in historical terms, I cannot help feeling a little uneasy. For certainly you can speak of things that are important or less important, e.g., in the thinking of Philo or in the theology of Rudolf Bultmann. But a center? One single, indispensable center of a circle? Or am I too rigid? From this unease a new question emerges: why ask for a center at all? Do theologians ask for an exclusive center because, fundamentally, they want to build a bridge between NT theology and Christian preaching and Christian life today? Or are they at least eager to systematize more than is needed for purely historical understanding?

There are more questions. My academic ego – in which there is also a pastor – reminds me that in these passages, in which we surmise a theology of the cross, caution is needed inasmuch as Paul is involved in a keen polemic. In a polemic you are often compelled to mark your profile, but as the opponent has decided the issue, both the counterattack and its target are determined by the position of the other. The cross or rather the crucifixion is only mentioned in Romans 6:6 in connection with baptism: συνεσταυρώθη. From a historical point of view it seems to be a little difficult to answer in the affirmative to the question, whether Christ as crucified, and precisely as crucified, is the center of Pauline theology. *In* the center, yes, but hardly *the* center. That it belongs to the center is proved by the passages we discussed above, but this central area also encompasses the death of Jesus, His resurrection, the problem of Jews and Gentiles, the role of faith, etc.

So far I have posed our question to what we may call the undisputed Paul. I stated above that there is some reason also to deal with the transmitted Paul, whom we encounter in the collection in which the deutero- and trito-Pauline writings are included. Thus, in Col 1:15–20 the author speaks of the divine fullness, which, through the Son, reconciled everything on earth and in heaven with it (or: with Him) and made peace "by the blood of His cross" (v. 20). No issue is made of the fact that the death on the cross was offensive. That it effected reconciliation is of course Pauline, but we do not encounter the cosmic perspective in such a connection in the undisputed letters.

In Col 2:8–15 the author is involved in his controversy with the so-called philosophy. Taking as his point of departure that baptism meant remission of sins, he concludes that this remission also invalidates the demands which certain powers make through "philosophy". In v. 14 this is developed in a complicated image. I paraphrase the unusually entangled sentence: "Canceling our bond which concerned our duties over against the demands, He set it aside, nailing it to the cross." I suggest that the author makes use of two associations with crucifixion. One is that it was a shameful destruction of a despicable criminal; so God did with our guilt. The other intimates how this was done, viz., through Christ's death on the cross, with which the addressees were united in baptism.

The author of Colossians would then attach some importance to the fact that Jesus died precisely on a cross. But he does not use it for a theology of weakness, on the contrary: the crucified Lord is a cosmic victor, in whose victory the audience participates. Insofar as this Paulinist has learned from Paul, the crucified Christ certainly belongs to the center of his thinking, but with different shades of meaning. The shame falls on the powers, while the Christians are victors with Christ.

A short glance at Ephesians draws our attention to 2:16, where the author seems to repeat the thought of Col 1:18–22, applying it to the relationship between Jews and Gentiles: "He reconciled the two to God in one body through the cross." Here the cross "is only the place of the reconciliation, a topos of Christian preaching."[15]

We could wish the material were more reliable, but yet some conclusions can be drawn concerning the motif of the crucified Christ in a Pauline theology built on the whole Corpus Paulinum. In Paul's school they were certain as to the central importance of Christ's death on precisely the cross, and as well, as to the salvific effects of this death. That it was regarded as shameful should be self-evident because of current cultural conventions, but use is rarely made of this fact. Nor does the weakness aspect seem to play any role after First Corinthians, and the thought that the cross should determine the life of the Christian (as crucified to the world) does not occur in the deutero-Pauline letters.

Thus, the crucified Christ is *in* the theological center of the larger collection of Pauline writings, but it is not *the* center. Even if naturally the accents of the historical Paul have not disappeared, they have weakened, on the one hand, through the fact that First Corinthians and Galatians are no longer read in the light of the crises in Corinth and Galatia. On the other hand, they are also attenuated by the fact that now the deutero-Pauline writings belong to the Pauline context.

## 3. The Crucified Christ in John

In the Gospel of John the cross and the crucifixion are not mentioned more frequently than in the Synoptic Gospels. But the fourth Gospel has taken into account the crucifixion *per se* in a way the Synoptics do not.[16] This is done

---

[15] RUDOLF SCHNACKENBURG, *Der Brief an die Epheser* (EKK 10), Zürich – Einsiedeln – Köln • Neukirchen-Vluyn 1982, 117.

[16] See ULRICH B. MÜLLER, "Die Bedeutung des Kreuzestodes Jesu im Johannesevangelium. Erwägungen zur Kreuzestheologie im Neuen Testament," in: *Kerygma und Dogma* 21 (1975) 49–71; PETER VON DER OSTEN-SACKEN, "Leistung und Grenze der johanneischen Kreuzestheologie," in: *EvTh* 36 (1976) 154–176; RUDOLF SCHNACKENBURG, "Paulinische und johanneische Christologie.

through the ambiguous term "lift up", "elevate". "The Son of Man must be lifted up, as Moses lifted up the serpent in the wilderness, that whoever believes in him may have eternal life" (3:14–15). The death on the cross belongs to the divine "must", i.e., to the work the Son had to fulfill. The verb "lift up", refers on the one hand to the concrete lifting up of the criminal at crucifixion. But on the other, its meaning is close to that of the words on the glorification of Jesus: the passion and the death is the "hour" of his glorification 12:13; 13:31f.; 17:1) and the hour of his going to the Father (13:3 etc.). Paradoxically the crucifixion reveals who the crucified Jesus really is and so also who the Father is.

The ambiguity of the term "lift up", "elevate", and the motif of departing, i.e., dying, and so going to the Father, justify us in saying that according to John Jesus dies to (or into) the Father on the cross. But yet the reader is not allowed to stop at such a statement. Mary Magdalene is not permitted to touch or hold Jesus for he has not yet ascended to the Father (20:17). In the sequence of the Johannine story the lifting up on the cross becomes but one element of the ascension to the Father, and the result is a tension between the two modes of reference to going to the Father.

This tension has caused some exegetical debates. The more a scholar (with, e.g., Bultmann) equates crucifixion and lifting up-ascension to the Father,[17] the more it can be claimed that in the humiliation of the incarnate Son the power of God is paradoxically at work. At the other end of the scale there are those who read John in the perspective of the Synoptic texts.

In John the offensiveness of crucifixion is not emphasized. Certainly precisely the crucified Jesus is the King of the Jews (19:19), whose Kingdom is not of this world (18:36). But all through the passion story he is also the unbroken One, who is the master of the situation until the work which the Father sent him to perform is completed (19:30).

Is this crucified Christ the center of a Johannine theology? I am convinced that the answer is: without any doubt he is in the center, but he is not *the* center. On the cross his work reached its culmination and was completed, and in the dialogue with Nicodemus this is presented as the final answer to the question how it is possible to enter the kingdom of God (3:3,5–8): the Son of Man must be "lifted up" (3:14). Moreover the divine revelation, which took place in the Son's incarnation and work debouches in the elevation and glorification in the passion. But nevertheless his death on precisely the cross is not the exclusive center of Johannine theology.

---

Ein Vergleich," in: ULRICH LUZ/HANS WEDER (eds.), *Die Mitte des Neuen Testaments. Einheit und Vielfalt neutestamentlicher Theologie* (FS Eduard Schweizer), Göttingen 1983, 221–237.

[17] BULTMANN, *Das Evangelium des Johannes* (note 11), 324–332, 532f.

## 4. Toward a NT Theology

So far I have stayed on a relatively low level of abstraction, dealing with two easily delimited areas of thought and using the NT authors' own modes of expression. But also an exegete working on a purely academic basis can legitimately try to understand in depth what authors of antiquity are saying. This can be achieved by penetration of modes of expression and concepts, and translation of forms of thinking, mythical language, etc. Of course such an undertaking always runs the risk that the interpreter's imagination brings him so far that the ties to the object of his study and its historical particularity are stretched beyond the breaking-point.

Such considerations bring us for a moment back to Paul and John. I have intimated that the resurrection of Jesus should also belong to the center of a Pauline theology. To one who heeds the opinion that the resurrection of Christ is tantamount to a renewal of the life of the disciples so that they were inspired to adopt the cause of Jesus, the resurrection hardly becomes as important as the offense of the cross. There are, however, other manners of speaking of the resurrection without resorting to neo-orthodox or objectifying language, in which resurrection and ascension are discussed as if they belonged to the same category as a bus ride from the campus into the city. Here the Johannine mode of reference to Jesus' death as an exaltation and a departure to the Father may be taken as a start. Above I reformulated this imagery by saying that Jesus died to (or into) the Father. But, as we noticed, in the fourth Gospel this imagery is combined with another, more narrative one, whereby what is held together in the exaltation language is distributed in a time sequence so that Jesus is first lifted up on the cross, and then ascends to the Father after He has spent three days in the tomb, risen, and appeared to some people. It is feasible to concentrate on the former, the "dying to the Father" language, and do so, not only in a "translated" Johannine, but also in a Pauline theology. Death and renewed transcendent existence with the Supreme Being would then be held together and, thus, cross and death become even more dominant in a Pauline theology, since they are included in his resurrection.

Attempts at such "translation" can be made also for a larger body of material than the texts written by two individual NT writers. Thus, we could try to present early Christian approaches to life, donning the same courage to simplify and generalize as when speaking of the view of life in Ancient Greece, of Buddhism, or of the philosophy of Romanticism – and running the same risks. And, I may add, we should do so, while prepared to discuss other perspectives and other evaluations of the data.

So our search for a NT theology proceeds on a higher level of abstraction, *viz.*, one on which, in principle, use may be made of material from the whole NT. The reason for such an undertaking need not be only a Church interest, but should already be a generally humanistic one, since we learn to be more human through reflection on the humanity of others and their reflections thereon. No doubt such considerations lie behind several expositions of NT theology, not least such as are written by theologians who maintain that the cross is *the* very center of *the* NT theology. But even though I am convinced that the theologian makes too biased a selection of NT motifs who does not render some justice to the motif of the crucified Christ, I do not believe that this motif must be the absolute center, around which must revolve all attempts at a meaningful exposition for our time of early Christian faith as represented by the writings gathered in the NT. A meaningful exposition here means not only one which is intellectually honest but also one that really engages the human subject.

We could as well imagine the construction of a NT theology around the concept of the Kingdom of God. It was central to the proclamation of Jesus; he engaged in this Kingdom through a radical devotion to God and neighbours. From such a center we could also deduce certain principles of Christian ethics. Nonetheless the concept of the Kingdom of God would not be *the* very center but an important idea possibly belonging to the central area.

Or, could we not, with the same reservations, write a NT theology of hope, or one of humanity or human fellowship? Briefly, however much it may be maintained that a particular NT theology is based on the indisputable "center of the NT", I am afraid that the criteria must always remain too subjective to allow us to claim that we have found such an absolute, obligatory center for a NT theology. The world is not so simple, nor the diversified world of the thought of NT writers. This does not mean that we have to surrender to an uninhibited subjectivism. So, like many others, I am convinced that the theme of the crucified Christ, and precisely the crucified one, is important to any NT theology. But how important and in what way these questions must be answered with the help of other criteria, which can differ, depending on the context in which, and the presuppositions from which, a NT theology is devised. That is why we can formulate the theme of this paper as a question, the answer to which is ultimately determined by the one who gives it.

# 6. Two Early Readings of First Corinthians
## Clement of Rome and Third Corinthians

## 1. Introductory Remarks

In one of his treatises St John Chrysostome addresses the duty of observing peace in the Church.[1] He refers in his argument to Paul and says: "although Paul had many and important things to charge against the Corinthians, he charged this against them before everything else," namely their lack of unity. Indeed, Paul had "many and important things" to deal with in his letters to the Christian community in Corinth, and one may say that the picture a reader of later times gets of the community is not a very flattering one. However, the fact that the Apostle had to put his hands to these "many and important things" has given us invaluable glimpses of a Christian community in the Early Church – how much more human and down-to-earth do these "sanctified in Christ Jesus" (1 Cor 1:2) appear to us than, say, the somewhat idealized characters of the Book of Acts! In addition, the shortcomings of the Corinthians forced Paul to react providing precious insights for later generations into his attitudes as a missionary and as a pastor and theologian. If these Christians had not failed in these "many and important things", no Corinthian letters would have made their way into the New Testament of the Church, nor would we have had any Pauline letters to the community to celebrate at this symposium.

In this paper we will encounter two texts that indirectly reflect how Paul's Corinthian correspondence was received and used during the first two centuries CE, that is, in a time when the so-called New Testament step by step became an authoritative collection of writings added to the "Old Testament". The first text, the letter of Clement of Rome, tells us something of how a theologian from the end of the first century used Paul's First letter to the Corinthians as well as which kind of authority it had to him and his addressees. The second text, the so-called Third Corinthians, represents a later stage of the formation of the New Testament, probably during the latter part of the second century.[2] The canon – if we dare to use this term – is still so open that a pseudepigraphic letter written in Paul's name could still find some acceptance – as a matter of fact, Third

---

[1] *Adv. Jud.*, PG 48, 863.
[2] VAHAN HOVHANESSIAN, *Third Corinthians. Reclaiming Paul for Christian Orthodoxy* (Stud. in Bibl. Literature 18), New York etc. 2000, 126–131.

Corinthians was accepted in the canon of the Bible in the Armenian and Syrian Churches.[3]

## 2. First Letter of Clement

Thus, in the middle of the 90'ies Clement wrote to the Corinthians. He did so because there was serious dissension among them – he calls it a *stasis*.[4] There has been some debate as to what was precisely at stake,[5] but it has resulted in that a few people have revolted against the presbyters (47:6) and even removed some of them from their ministry (44:3f.). It is noteworthy that Clement so to speak meddles in the Corinthian affairs. He does not present himself as if he had any authority to interfere with what was going on, but nevertheless he does so and seems to assume that the Church in Corinth would be ready to accept his approaching them in this manner. (As a matter of fact, Clement is never mentioned in the letter, but the sender is "the Church of God which lives in Rome" [1:1]). A testimony from a time only a few decades later also reveals no hard feelings from the Corinthian side, for in the second half of the second century bishop Dionysios of Corinth wrote a letter to Rome, in which he mentions Clement's letter and assures his addressee that it "since long" and "of old custom" is read in the Church of Corinth.[6]

The argument of Clement's letter has two main parts, one that deals with the matter in question in a more general manner and another that is more explicitly directed to the present issue.[7] It is in this second part that Clement explicitly quotes and uses a Pauline text, but the Apostle plays a role already in the first part, in that Paul is introduced as one of the many examples who have suffered because of others' unholy *zêlos* (5:5–7).[8]

In the second part of his letter Clement firstly argues that in the same way as the Old testament priesthood, the institution of presbyters is according to God's will (40:1–44:2). For the sacrifices and other celebrations God has determined particular places and persons, i.e. the priests and the Levites (40). To Clement this becomes an analogy to the apostolic institution of the ministry in the Church (42 and 44). With an eye to the quarrelsome Corinthians he adduces

---

[3] HOVHANESSIAN, *Third Corinthians*, 10–16.

[4] The same designation is used by Hegesippos (Eusebios, *HE* 3.16) and Irenaeus (*HE* 5.6.3).

[5] See ANDREAS LINDEMANN, *Die Klemensbriefe* (HNT 17; Die apostolischen Väter 1), Tübingen 1992, 16f.; HORACIO E. LONA, *Der erste Klemensbrief* (KAV 2), Göttingen 1998, 78–81; ODD MAGNE BAKKE, *"Concord and Peace." A Rhetorical Analysis of the First Letter of Clement with an Emphasis on the Language of Unity and Sedition* (WUNT II/141), Tübingen 2001, 283–290, 324–326.

[6] Eusebios, *HE* 4.23.11.

[7] BAKKE, *Concord*, is of the opinion that the letter follows the rhetorical *genos sumbouleutikon* and regards the two parts as representing the *thesis (quaestio infinita)* and the *hypothesis (quaestio finita)*, respectively.

[8] For the use of Paul and Pauline letters in the letter see ANDREAS LINDEMANN, *Paulus im ältesten Christentum. Das bild des Apostels und die Rezeption der paulinischen Theologie in der frühchristlichen Literatur bis Marcion* (BHTh 58), Tübingen 1979, 177–199. For 47:1–4 see esp. 190–192.

the warning example of the opposition against Moses and Aaron according to Num 17, where it is told how the people were jealous concerning the priesthood of Aaron (43). He concludes: "we therefore do not consider it right to remove these persons from their ministry..." (44:3).

As we have seen, Clement has arrived at this result through an argument based on the Old Testament. It is then confirmed by a combination of Jesus sayings against those who "tear asunder the members of Christ", thereby forgetting that "we are members of one another" (46:7). The Jesus-sayings are harsh: "Woe unto that man. It were better that he were not born than that he should scandalize one of my elect" and "it were better for him to have a millstone hung on him and be thrown into the sea than that he should turn aside one of my elect" (cf. Matt 26:24; Luke 17:2).

Apparently Clement here uses Paul's imagery in 1 Cor 12 of the body and its members. Paul used it at length to illustrate the unity in the body of Christ, which was threatened by the Corinthians' admiration for the spiritual gift of glossolalia. But according to Paul the one Spirit bestowed different gifts, prophecy, gifts of healings, glossolalia etc., and they were given to different members of the church for the service of the whole body.

We could think that Clement should apply the body imagery to the present problem, for example by claiming that the presbyters are a gift of the Spirit as once were the prophets, the teachers, the healers etc. It would have formed a fine ecclesiological-pneumatological argument.[9] But it seems that Clement does not come upon the idea of interpreting Paul's letter as containing a theology of the Church. Rather, his use of the picture may add a rhetorical *pathos*-nuance to his polemic: you are tearing asunder the members of Christ – how gruesome.[10]

When using the body-imagery, Clement did not explicitly refer to Paul. When he does so, he picks up another part of Paul's argument:

> Take up the letter of the blessed apostle Paul ... He wrote to you about himself and Cephas and Apollos, because even then you made yourself partisans. However, that partisanship brought less sin upon you, because you made yourself partisans of apostles of good reputation and of a man approved by them. Now, however, consider who they are who turn you away and have diminished the respect due to your famous love for the brothers. It is a shame, brothers, it is a shame indeed ... (47:1-6)

Thus Clement makes what Paul described as *schismata* (1 Cor 1:10) somewhat less serious by calling them partisanships (*proskliseis*). In addition, he takes to the rhetorical means of *a minore ad maius* argument: the Corinthian "partisanships" in Paul's days were a sin, although connected to honorable personalities

---

[9] For the letter of Clement on the Spirit see, LONA, *Die Apostolischen Väter*, 500–505.
[10] There is another echo of 1 Cor 12 in 48:5, where Clement describes the ideal unity in Christ, in which somebody has faith, another has knowledge, still another has wisdom – cf. 1 Cor 12:8–9. Neither in this case does Clement develop any ecclesiological or pneumatological aspects of the Pauline passage.

– how much more sinful, indeed shameful, is the current action! For – and now he takes to innuendos – you know what sort of mean figures those are who cause this *stasis*! Thus, Clement stays on the practical level, using other arguments than such based on Pauline theology, and we can note that Clement does not make any theological or ecclesiological points out of Paul's forceful question in 1 Cor 1:13, "Is Christ divided?".

To sum up: in Clement's letter Paul encounters the Corinthians again. God's messenger to their community a couple of generations ago is still an authority among them, as represented by his letters. But as an authority he nevertheless seems to be inferior to the Scriptures, i.e., the "Old Testament". Also sayings of the Lord have a more decisive weight. Clement reminds the Corinthians of Paul's strict attitude when dealing with lacking unity, and he makes that attitude relevant to the new situation in Corinth. However, he does not make explicit use of Paul's theological or ecclesiological arguments.

## 3. "Third Corinthians"

Now to the so-called Third Corinthians. The Paul of this letter exchange is a fictitious Paul and so are also the Corinthians involved. It seems that at the time when Third Corinthians was composed, the Corinthian Church had no problems in terms of orthodoxy or unity. Thus, after telling about Clement's letter, Hegesippos reports that "the Church of the Corinthians remained at the right teaching until Primos was the bishop of the Corinthians," that is more or less when Hegesippos was there on his way to Rome and, as he writes, "we rejoiced together in the right teaching."[11] This visit of Hegesippos in Corinth took place in 160 or just before. To this latter part of the second century also belongs the episcopacy of Dionysios, presumably the successor of Primos. (I have already mentioned his letter to Rome, in which he refers to Clement's letter.)

So, the fact that Third Corinthians is connected to Corinth does probably not depend on any particular situation in Corinth. Rather, it may be explained by the circumstance that precisely the Corinthian letters testify to a practice presupposed under this apocryphal correspondence, namely that the Corinthians write to Paul and ask for advice (cf. 1 Cor 7:1). And also, of course the Corinthian letters deliver good examples of how Paul put his hands to moral and doctrinal problems of a Christian community. In addition, one of the questions the fictitious Paul addresses is the one of the resurrection, so thoroughly discussed in 1 Cor 15.

The author is anxious that the letter shall sound Pauline. He uses several turns of phrase from the canonical letters, not least Ephesians, but also from others, First Corinthians included.[12] Such features shall support the claim that also in this letter Paul is an authority. This is all the more important in a situ-

---

[11] Eusebios, *HE* 4.22.2.
[12] HOVHANESSIAN, *Third Corinthians*, 97f.

ation when the development towards the canonicity of the New Testament has come to a stage where Paul's letters are important, although not uncontested, witnesses to "the Apostle".[13] So also "the Corinthians" in this correspondence refer to Paul's teaching them in earlier days. Those under attack in the letter have "overturned the faith of some with corrupted words", and the Corinthians claim that they "have not heard such words from you and the others" (1:2 and 4). But they assure him: "that which we received from you and them, we preserve" (1:5).

"Paul" begins his answer in Third Corinthians by almost quoting himself: "from the beginning I handed down to you what I received from the apostles who were before me…". But what the author introduces in this way does not immediately concern resurrection – as in 1 Cor 15:1f. – but other items questioned by the heretics, namely Christ's being born by the virgin, the use of the prophets etc., matters that actually the real Paul never discussed in his letters.

Thus, in these matters there is no re-reading of Paul and one may wonder why one wanted Paul to state things that were well established, e.g. in the Gospel of Matthew. Or does the author want to save Paul for orthodoxy?[14] Maybe one should note that the Corinthians write: "we received from you *and them*", that is, Paul is joined to the other apostles.

When the author comes to the statements on resurrection, of course he uses First Corinthians. But the issue is changed. In his letter Paul wrote (15:12): "How can some of you say that there is no resurrection?". But here the heretics are said to claim, "there is no resurrection of the flesh" (1:12), which, of course, means placing the accent differently.

The same different accentuation is seen when the Paul of Third Corinthians picks up the real Paul's simile of a seed that is sown and dies, but then "God gives it a body" (1 Cor 15:36–38). The "real" Paul developed this simile by talking of a "spiritual body" (15:44), and stating: "flesh and blood cannot inherit the kingdom of God" (15:59). St. Irenaeus is only one of the Fathers who seemingly would have preferred that Paul had not written so.[15] The author of 3rd Corinthians seems to be of the same opinion. For when he uses the simile of the seed, he writes: "it perishes below and is raised by God's will in a body and clothed" (2:26). This is then explained by biblical examples which demonstrate that this raising is a raising of the flesh. So reference is made to Jonah who returned from Hades without any harm, and from here the author draws an *a minore ad maius* conclusion: "how much more … will he raise you up as he himself was raised up"

---

[13] See HANS FRHR. VON CAMPENHAUSEN, *Die Entstehung der christlichen Bibel* (BHTh 39), Tübingen 1968, 169–172.
[14] This is an important idea in HOVHANESSIAN, *Third Corinthians*.
[15] E.g. *Adv. Haer.* 4.41.4. See HOVHANESSIAN, *Third Corinthians*, 82–87.

(2:31). Finally "Paul" cites the story about the corpse that was thrown upon the bones of Elisha in his tomb and so returned to life (2 Kings 13:20f.).[16]

Thus, this reader of Paul's letter passes over Paul's words on a spiritual body. He makes use of his mentioning a body, but rewrites it so that "body" equals "flesh". So he makes Paul an undisputedly orthodox theologian and sees to it that one does not misread Paul's letters into saying things that the author is persuaded Paul did not mean to say.

## 4. The Principle of Eccleastical Usage

Thus in these two other Corinthian letters we have met two very early instances of ecclesiastical usage of 1 Corinthians. In both cases Paul's authority is taken for granted. In Clement, however, his authority is less than the one of the Old Testament and of sayings of Jesus. Clement does not press any theological or ecclesiological points out of Paul's text. Rather he uses Paul's explicit dismissal of divisions. Clement makes, so to speak, Paul stand on his side in condemning the *stasis* as a person of high moral standard.

The Paul of Third Corinthians is also a man of authority and he is more of a doctrinal and theological authority than in First Clement. But the picture is not totally unambiguous. On the one hand his apostolic authority is used to state things he never touched upon in his real letters, and we may ask ourselves why. Did the author wish to influence persons who respected Paul but maybe less, e.g. Matthew? On the other hand, he makes Paul revise what he wrote on resurrection – was that to impress the same people, or the heretics, or to make him acceptable among the orthodox?

Both our examples of a re-reading meant bringing together the original letter situation and a new one. In Clement's case this was easy: in his opinion the *stasis* of the 90'ies was so similar to the *schismata* of Paul's days that he could have Paul condemn the *stasis*.

The situation of the author of Third Corinthians was more complicated. In order to make Paul address the new situation he had to construct a similar one and place it in the Corinth of the 50'ies. In that way he could make the fictitious Paul deal with it.

But the principle of the ecclesiastical usage was nevertheless the same in both cases: one used the letter situation to assess the new reading situation. This implied transposing the message delivered in the first situation to that of the new one. In our cases such a transposition brought with it an adjustment in the reading of Paul's text. In Clement's letter this meant a slight adjustment, but in Third Corinthians a more far-reaching one.

An exegete might say that the author of Third Corinthians was doing violence to Paul's text in his applying Paul to the new situation. But, honestly, this

---

[16] The manuscript tradition is a little confused at this passage; see HOVHANESSIAN, *Third Corinthians*, 73.

is not the last time ecclesiastical usage of Biblical texts represents a similar attitude.[17] That it is defended by a doctrine that the Church is entitled to do so is a matter we won't discuss now.

## 5. Résumé

The two texts dealt with in this paper, the letter of Clement of Rome to the Corinthians and the apocryphal Third Corinthians, belong to two different stages of the development toward a New Testament canon. In Clement's letter the author argues against a *stasis* that has appeared in the Corinthian Church, but he does not build his argument on Paul, although the apostle is still an authority to the addressees. Instead the principle basis of his arguments is the Old Testament, and in addition he adduces a couple of sayings of Jesus. His references to Paul (some echoes from 1 Cor 12 and a direct reference to the divisions mentioned in 1 Cor 1) function as, as it were, moral arguments but not as theological or ecclesiological ones.

In Third Corinthians Paul is more of a doctrinal authority whom the author uses to attack some heresies of the late second century. He makes Paul emphasize, i.al, the virgin birth and the validity of the Old Testament prophets, items on which there is of course next to nothing in the "real" Paul's letters. But in his treatment of the topic of resurrection the author makes the Paul of Third Corinthians more orthodox than he may appear to be in 1 Cor 15 in that he has him argue for the resurrection of the flesh – cf. 1 Cor 15:59: "flesh and blood cannot inherit the kingdom of God".

Thus the two texts represent two different, early readings of Paul, applying his letters to the Corinthians to new situations. This meant confronting new reading situations with the message that Paul once sent with regard to the then-situation of the Corinthians, a confrontation that implied certain hermeneutical presuppositions in terms of how one could use, re-use, interpret and re-interpret the Biblical texts in the Church.

---

[17] Cf., e.g. HANS-JOSEF KLAUCK, "Der Katechismus der katholischen Kirche. Rückfragen aus exegetischer Sicht", in: EHRENFRIED SCHULZ (ed.), *Ein Katechismus für die Welt* ... (Schriften der katholischen Akademie in Bayern 150), Düsseldorf 1994, 71–82; JACOB KREMER, "Die Interpretation der Bibel in der Kirche", in: *Stimmen der Zeit* 212 (1994) 151–166.

## 7. An Early Example of Jewish Exegesis
### 1 En 10:16–11:2

### 1. The Book of the Watchers

In the first Psalm we learn of the righteous man: 'his delight is in the law of Yahweh and on his law he meditates day and night'. This passage and others of similar contents (e.g. Deut 6:1ff.) describe an essential feature of Jewish religion in ancient times as well as later on. 'Delight' and 'meditation' meant applying the text to the faithful and 'applying' the faithful to the text, in other words, some kind of interpretation that was relevant to the community. In this paper I will deal with one result of such scriptural meditation, and a very old one at that; it may even be the oldest such text that we know of outside the Bible, namely *1 Enoch* 10:16–11:2.[1]

The passage is included in the Enochic Book of the watchers (*1 En* 1–36). The Qumran finds make it probable that this book came into existence *at the latest* towards the end of the third century BCE.[2] Our passage is preserved in Greek, Ethiopic, and in some Aramaic fragments from Qumran.[3]

The few lines that I am going to discuss, describe eschatological salvation. The description consists of a kind of double exposure of the escape of Noah and his family from the deluge. It is the second out of three sections in which the book deals with final salvation, and with the punishment of the evil, that is, of the fallen angels and, to some extent, of wicked men. The first instance is in the introduction (1–5), in which a denouncement speech is directed against wicked people – no angels are in sight[4]: they will receive no mercy, whereas mercy, peace and prosperity are going to be the lot of the righteous.[5] The third instance, in which the fates of the righteous and the evil are envisaged, is in the body of the book, namely in Enoch's dream vision, the second part of which consists of the

---

[1] This paper is an enlarged and revised version of an article in: *SEÅ* 41–42 (1976–77) 87–96; Cf. also Lars Hartman 1979, 142f. [See now George W. E. Nickelsburg 2001 and George W. E. Nickelsburg/James C. VanderKam 2012.]

[2] Jósef Tadeusz Milik (1976: 28) thinks that the author lived around the middle of the third century BCE. He even suggests that 1 En 6–19 is an older work that the author has adopted and included in his book (1976, 28–35). Nickelsburg (1977a, 391) dates 'the *Shemīḥāzā* tradition' (to which our text belongs) to a time around the end of the fourth century BCE.

[3] See for the textual tradition Michael A. Knibb 1978, II, 6–46; Milik 1976, 70ff.

[4] 'He will convict all flesh with regard to all their works of wickedness …' (1:9). 4QEn<sup>c</sup> 1 i. 16 ascertains the 'flesh' (*[b]shr*).

[5] I have discussed *1 En* 1–5 at length in Hartman 1979.

descriptions of his journeys. These take him, *inter alia,* to places of punishment and of reward, such as the accursed valley (27:2f.), the blessed land (26f.), and the garden of righteousness (32).

One of these three sections on eschatological judgement and salvation appears in each of the three main parts of the book: first comes an introductory *māshāl* (1–5); then, on the basis of the Noah story, an intermediate section regards things on earth from a heavenly perspective (6–11); and finally the body of the book (12–36), via the Book of the words of righteousness (14:1), reports what Enoch learns and experiences after having been brought to the heavenly throne room.

I mentioned that our passage belongs to the section of the Book of the watchers that is based on the Noah story. To be more exact, the section (6–11) presupposes and uses Genesis 6–9, beginning with the notice of the fall of the angels and ending with the feature of the covenantmaking after the flood. This is to say that the text represents some kind of interpretation of that passage of Scripture.

Before entering upon a discussion of our text, it might be worthwhile to dwell for a moment upon some possible references of the term 'interpretation of Scripture' which are relevant for our specific theme.

## 2. The Concept of Interpretation of Scripture

Of course, a translation of a biblical text already means an interpretation. This is so with the Septuagint and even more so with the targums; they not only render the Hebrew text in Aramaic but also add interpretative elements, words, sentences and whole paragraphs. The aim, both of the translation and of the interpretative additions (or changes!), is to bridge the gap between the text and its new audience. Some of these interpretative elements have grown out of techniques or represent interpretations which are encountered in the fullblown *midrashim*. Thus there might be an interplay between targum and midrash, although they represent different literary genres.[6]

There is also the interpretation of Scripture that lies behind the more or less allusive usage of biblical passages in many intertestamental texts.[7] They are by no means explicitly presented as scriptural interpretation, but they certainly represent such. One has differentiated between an anthological and a structural use of the Bible in these texts[8]: an anthological use means that biblical passages are brought together because of the topic dealt with, whereas the structural use means that a biblical text forms the thread – which binds echoes from other texts together. In neither of these cases is there any explicit reference to or quo-

---

[6] See ADDISON G. WRIGHT 1967, *passim;* ROGER LE DÉAUT 1969, 411.

[7] See further GÉZA VERMÈS 1961, *passim;* JACOB NEUSNER 1981, 301ff.

[8] DANIEL PATTE 1975, 184f. Here Patte systematizes some of the material in HARTMAN 1966, part 1.

tation of the Bible, only a larger or lesser number of semiquotations from, allusions to, or echoes of biblical passages.

## 3. 1 Enoch 10:16–11:2

Our text may be regarded as belonging to that sort of interpretation of Scripture which retells a biblical text. Jubilees, the Genesis Apocryphon, and the pseudo-Philonic Biblical Antiquities are whole books belonging to the same category. 'This type of text contains elements similar to a targum and to a midrash,' says Prof. Fitzmyer concerning the Genesis Apocryphon,[9] and that holds true also of our 1 Enoch passage. As we will see, this does not exclude other biblical passages being unobtrusively brought in in a manner that reminds of the anthological and the structural methods mentioned above.

It may be instructive to compare briefly the ways in which these texts, which restate or retell the Bible, use the Noah story. As this section of the Genesis Apocryphon manuscript is almost totally destroyed, we have to restrict ourselves to the other three, namely Jubilees, the Biblical Antiquities, and 1 Enoch.

The Biblical Antiquities is, in this case, rather strict and follows the Genesis text in an almost targum-like manner, although the narrative is abbreviated. The fall of the sons of God receives no extra attention, nor does the sinfulness of man. There is one noteworthy addition, however, namely after the divine promise that seedtime and harvest, summer and winter will never cease (Gen 8:21f.). There the author adds, 'but when the years of the world are fulfilled …'; and there follows a passage dealing with the resurrection, the judgement, and the eschatological bliss: 'then will the earth not be without fruit nor barren for its inhabitants. Nobody will be polluted who is justified by me, and there will be another earth and another heaven, an eternal habitation' (3:10).

Jubilees displays more interest than the Biblical Antiquities in the watchers and the evildeeds on earth. The main features of the Genesis narrative are retold, except for the one where the animals are brought into the ark. An addition reports a judgement on the watchers and their offspring, and this is followed by a digression dealing with the general eschatological judgement (5:13–16) and with the possibility of conversion given to Israel (5:17–19). In addition, the passage that relates the Noachian covenant is embellished with special regard to the author's cultic interests, namely the celebration of the Feast of Weeks.

When one puts 1 Enoch 6–11 alongside these sections of the Biblical Antiquities and of Jubilees, both similarities and dissimilarities leap to the eye. Thus, that which the latter book has to say about Enoch and the watchers (4:17–23) gives the impression of being a brief summary of the corresponding parts of the

---

[9] JOSEPH A. FITZMYER 1971, 10. MANFRED R. LEHMANN (1958–59, 251) suggests that the Gen Apocr is 'the oldest prototype of both available to us'. As a matter of fact, I think, *1 En* 6–11 is older.

Book of the watchers, and such might also very well be the case.[10] Furthermore, all of the three books add passages that open an eschatological perspective.

The three texts follow the Genesis text more or less closely. There is no doubt that, of the three, the Enoch section keeps the widest distance from the Genesis narrative. This is due, on the one hand, to the large space taken up by the myth of the watchers, on the other, to the fact that the book reports less details of the flood and of Noah's salvation. As a matter of fact, only the following details from Genesis are explicitly retold: men multiply and get daughters, whom God's sons see and take as wives; the giants are born, and much evil is brought about (Gen 6:1–5, 11); Noah is told of the coming deluge and of his escape (6:13, 17). By this the text, so to speak, takes off from the Genesis narrative: a proclamation of the judgement of the watchers and a divine command that all wrong be destroyed from the earth, are directly followed by our passage on eschatological salvation. The flood and Noah seem to be out of sight, and instead the fate of the righteous people – the audience of the book![11] – comes into the focus. Nevertheless, there can be no doubt that the Genesis text serves as a basis also for this passage.[12]

With these observations in mind we must now take a closer look at our text. Its beginning (10:16) does not represent any special incision in the running text but is directly connected to God's commands to various angels to punish apostate angels and men. Thus, Michael receives four commands: two concerning the evil in Noah's time (to bind Shemīḥāzā and his angels and to destroy the spirits of the giants) and two which deal with what appears to be the *eschaton*, namely our text.[13]

Thus, our passage naturally falls into two parts, each introduced by a divine command to Michael. The first one says, 'destroy iniquity from the face of the earth, and let every deed of wickedness disappear' (10:16),[14] and the second begins in this way: 'and you, cleanse the earth from all impurity and from all wrong ...' (10:20).[15] After each of these commands follows a description of what we may call a new world. The first one depicts the coming bliss and prosperity of the righteous people. Apparently Noah, whose righteousness is already emphasized in Genesis (6:9; 7:1), is regarded as a type of the righteous of later generations,[16] and his escape is taken as prefigurative of their salvation. When the author paints his picture of that salvation, he borrows and reshapes some of

---

[10] MILIK 1976, 24f.

[11] See *1 En* 1:1.

[12] NICKELSBURG (1977a, 388) notes a connection between *1 En* 10:16c–19 and Gen 8:17, 21b, 22; 9:1, 8–20.

[13] See further NICKELSBURG 1977a, 388.

[14] The three first words are retained in 4QEn$^c$ The translation is that of MILIK (1976, 190). Note that in 1 En Michael is to destroy, whereas in Gen God himself acts (but cf. 10:22).

[15] Thus the Greek.

[16] Noah's righteousness is a common topic: see, e.g., Ezk 14:14; Sir 44:17; *Or Sib* 1:148f., 317; *1 En* 67:1; 89:1ff.; Philo, *Praem* 22f. Further VANDERKAM 1980.

the motifs from the latter part of the Noah story. (Which ones he uses and how he uses them I will discuss a little later on).

The first section runs like this:

'Destroy iniquity from the face of the earth and let every deed of wickedness disappear. And let the plant of righteousness appear; and it shall become a blessing, and deeds of righteousness shall be planted forever with joy' (10:16).
'And now all the righteous shall escape and they shall be alive until they beget thousands; and all the days of their[17] youth and of their old age shall be completed in peace' (10:17).
'Then all the earth shall be tilled in righteousness, and it shall all be planted with trees and be filled with blessing' (10:18).
'And all the trees of the earth which they desire shall be planted on it; and they shall plant vines[18] on it, and the vine which will be planted on it shall produce a thousand jars of wine, and of every seed which will be sown on it every single measure shall produce a thousand measures, and each measure of olives shall produce ten baths of oil' (10:19).[19]

The second command to Michael and the ensuing description of the *eschaton* is, in my opinion, remarkable in several respects. First, it seems that the author finds a second meaning in the motif of the flood in the Genesis narrative. Its waters are not only such that destroy the evil and serve as a judgement (10:16), but they are also waters that cleanse. Of course the step is not a long one from destroying all evil from the earth to cleansing it from all evil. Nevertheless, there is a step, and, as far as I know, that step has seldom been taken in ancient Judaism. The only example I have found is in Philo *(Quod det* 170). He presents an allegory concerning the purging of the soul's defilements and begins it by referring to the flood as a means through which the Creator purged the earth by water.[20]

Another remarkable thing in this second half of our passage is that it deals with all mankind and all nations rather than with righteous Jews only. After the cleansing, namely, all the sons of men are said to be righteous and to worship God, and he will never again send a castigation but instead bless men's labour. This vision of worldwide righteousness and harmony in conjunction with a common worship of the only God is, I believe, inspired by or makes use of chapters 8 and 9 of the Noah narrative: after the flood Noah offers burnt offerings (8:20) and is blessed by God together with his sons (9:1) – by whom the

---

[17] The Aramaic (4 Q En<sup>c</sup>) has the second person plural. If original – as MILIK (1976, 191) seems to believe – it means that the real audience of the text, i.e., 'the righteous elect' (1:1) suddenly appear in the text, although the passage otherwise is presented as God's command to Michael.

[18] So the Greek and the Ethiopic. MILIK (1976, 191) suggests an Aramaic reconstruction meaning 'gardens' instead. i.e.. because of the feminine form of the verb behind the ensuing 'will be planted'. But judging from the photography (plate xi) the reading is extremely uncertain.

[19] The translation is largely that in MILIK 1976, 190.

[20] A couple of Christian examples: Ps-Clem., *Hom.* 8:12; Tertullian, *De bapt.* 8 (PL 1209 B); Didym Alex, *de trinii* (PG 39, 697 AB). The cleansing imagery recurs a couple of times in the following text: see 10:20. 22.

world was populated (9:19) – and God promises never again to destroy the living creatures as in the deluge (8:21; 9:11f.).

So our text continues:

'And you, cleanse the earth from all impurity and from all wrong and from all sin and impiety; and remove all the uncleanness which is brought about on the earth' (10:20).
'And all the sons of men shall become righteous, and all the nations shall serve and bless and worship me' (10:21).
'And the whole earth shall be cleansed from all defilement and from all impurity. And I will not send upon them any wrath nor castigation for all generations for ever' (10:22).
'And then I will open the storehouses of blessing which are in heaven, so as to send them down upon the earth, upon the work and upon the toil of the sons of men' (11:1).
'And then truth and peace will be associated together for all the days of eternity and for all the generations of men' (11:2).[21]

*Per se* it is nothing exceptional to have some place for the nations in a picture of the *eschaton*, but it seems to me that this author's non-negative way of dealing with the matter is worthy of notice. It has a certain parallel in the Book of dreams (1 En 90:33)[22]: 'all the beasts of the field, and all the birds of the heaven (i.e., the nations) assembled in that house (i.e., the new Jerusalem), and the Lord of the sheep rejoiced with great joy because they were all good ...' The writer presupposes, however, a subjection of the gentiles under the Jews, for a couple of lines earlier he says (90:30), 'I saw ... all the beasts on the earth and all the birds of the heaven, falling down and doing homage to those sheep and making petition to and obeying them in everything'. Nothing of this sort – which is rather common in various Jewish texts[23] – appears in our portion of text.

If this detail in the text is due to an attitude actually held, two remarks may be appropriate: 1. Certain passages in the Old Testament may point to a similar optimism – or, rather, could be understood in that manner,[24] and 2. this kind of openness towards the Gentiles is even more remarkable, as the preceding description of the evils which the fallen angels taught men so clearly reflects the horror that faithful Jews felt towards certain features of Hellenistic culture.[25]

I have now dwelt on some aspects of the general contents of our passage. One more such aspect should be mentioned, which I have only touched upon in passing, namely that the author's attitude as over against the Genesis story indicates that he reads it in a 'typological' way.[26] Noah is regarded as the 'type' of all the

---

[21] The translation is largely based on the Greek. The Aramaic gives little help, as the identification of the fragments (of 4QEnᵃ) is rather uncertain (MILIK 1976, 163).

[22] MILIK (1976, 44) dates it to 164 BCE.

[23] *Tob* 13:11ff.; *Or Sib* 3:716ff., 772ff.; Cf. PAUL BILLERBECK 1922–28 III, 150ff. and PAUL VOLZ 1934, 358f.

[24] See JOACHIM JEREMIAS 1958, 57ff.

[25] 1 En 7–8. See HARTMAN 1979, 138f., 170. Also NICKELSBURG 1977a, 389.

[26] I refrain from a discussion of 'typology' vs 'allegory' etc; cf. LEONHARD GOPPELT 1969, 251f. (and references); further WALTHER EICHRODT 1956 and GEOFFREY W. H. LAMPE 1957, especially 31ff.

righteous, the flood is seen as prefiguring the judgement, and Noah's escape and behaviour after the flood stand for the eschatological salvation and bliss of the righteous people. As is well known, much of this 'typology' reappears later in both Jewish and Christian texts.[27] Our passage may, however, be the earliest extra-biblical example of it. On the other hand, the writer stands in a biblical tradition, since his way of re-reading the Genesis story is similar to the way in which biblical authors, for example, make David the 'type' of a coming saviour (2 Sam 7; Amos 9:11; Mic 5:1ff.; etc), or present the salvation and return from the exile as a new exodus (Isa 40).

## 4. Interpretative Techniques

I now turn to some details in terms of the writer's interpretative techniques. My deliberations above have already laid bare one such, namely that a text can be understood in several ways at the same time. In our case the two halves of the text represent two ways of interpreting the waters of the flood, namely as waters both of destruction and of cleansing. (It is, by the way, noteworthy that these two halves mostly run parallel[28]). Everyone who has entered into any contact with Jewish scriptural exposition knows that this phenomenon appears constantly in texts such as those produced in Qumran, or by Philo or by the Rabbis.[29] The practice has received a classical expression in the statement of *b Sanhedrin* 34a: 'a Scripture passage has several meanings'.

A further detail worthy of observation is the fact that our passage contains some allusions to or echoes from other Old Testament texts. The author certainly bases his description of the *eschaton* on the Noah story, but he also draws on other Old Testament passages. The principle behind this is the same as that in later times when one could formulate the rule 'Scripture is to be explained by Scripture'.[30] It is at work in the anthological and the structural uses of the Bible referred to above, and also, for instance, in Hillel's *Binyan-ab* rule, according to which details from one Bible text can shed light on one or several other texts with which it has an expression or some contents in common.[31] This is precisely what we come across in *1 Enoch* 10f. It is not difficult to detect which common details connect the Noah story and the 'auxiliary' texts that are visible in the lines of 1 Enoch. Thus, there is an echo in 11:1 from Deuteronomy 28:12, which says: 'Yahweh will open to you his good treasury, the heavens, to give the rain of your land in its season and to bless all the work of your hands'. The link-

---

[27] E.g., *Jub* 6f.; *Mt* 24:37–44; *1 Pt* 3:20f. Cf. PER IVAR LUNDBERG 1942, § 5f.; JEAN DANIÉLOU 1950, 59ff.; ANNIE JAUBERT 1963, 105f. Further JACK P. LEWIS 1968.

[28] Note the two parallel sequences 'destroy evil – righteousness – escape blessed work'/'cleanse from evil – righteousness – no more castigation – blessed work'

[29] Cf. WRIGHT 1967, 63. The phenomenon is also traceable in the LXX; see ISAC LEO SEELIGMANN 1948.

[30] Cf. PATTE 1975, 66f.

[31] See HERMANN L. STRACK/GÜNTHER STEMBERGER 1982, 29.

age is made up by the following motifs: seasonable climate is promised both in Genesis 8:22 and the verse of Deuteronomy; in the Deuteronomic context Yahweh announces that prosperity and blessing will be given to the people if they keep the covenant. This corresponds to the covenant-making of Genesis 9:9ff., to God's blessing of Noah and his sons (9:1) and to the command that they be fruitful and multiply (9:7).

When, in 11:2, it is said that truth and peace will be associated, this is probably inspired by Psalm 85:11ff.: 'steadfast love and faithfulness (*'mt*) will meet, righteousness and peace will kiss each other. Faithfulness (*'mt*) will spring up from the ground ... Yea, Yahweh will give what is good, and your land will yield its increase'. The Psalm also seems to resound in 10:16: the plant of righteousness (and truth: so the Greek) appears. The common motifs are these: crops – and virtues – shoot forth, and heaven bestows its gifts. Furthermore, in the first half of our passage it sounds as if the writer has taken up some details from Isaiah 65:20ff.[32]: 'No more shall there be in it (i.e., the land) ... an old man who does not fill out his days, for the child shall die a hundred years old ... they shall plant vineyards and eat their fruit ... they shall be the offspring of the blessed of Yahweh ...'. Again, the bridge is easy to detect: the Noah narrative and the Isaiah text have several motifs in common, that is those of planting, of blessing and of great age (9:28f.).[33]

Let us now consider what the writer has done with some details in the Noah narrative. Some of these fall naturally into place within the overall typological understanding of the narrative. Thus, the 'blessing' of Noah (Gen 9:1) is transferred to the *eschaton* (10:16, 18; 11:1), and so is the promise that there will be no more destruction (Gen 8:21–1 *En* 10:22); that Noah (and his family) were 'left' (*ysh'r*, 7:23) and 'kept alive' (*lhḥywt*, 6:19f.) becomes the eschatological salvation of the righteous and their 'life' (10:17). Furthermore, the notice that Noah was the first tiller of the earth (*'ysh h'dmh*) and planted a vineyard (9:20) is most probably one reason why the fruitfulness of the *eschaton* is depicted, *inter alia*, in terms of planting vines (10:19). We may also note the following items, some of which I have touched upon already: the information concerning the length of Noah's life (9:28f.) may lie behind the motif of the long life of the righteous (10:17), God's ruling that Noah's family should multiply on earth (9:1,7) has inspired the notice on prolificacy in the *eschaton* (10:17); Noah's sacrificing together with his sons – the fathers of all men (8:20; 9:19) – may lie behind the lines on the worship of the nations (10:21).

Some of these details smack somewhat of 'spiritualizing' or even of allegorizing. This is even more so when Noah's being a tiller of the soil and a vine-planter seem to lie behind the following sentences: 'all the earth shall be tilled in righ-

---

[32] The Noah portion of the Biblical Antiquities also makes use of Isa 65 (v. 17) – see the quotation of Biblical Antiquities above.

[33] Cf. also for 10:18: Amos 9:14f.; Jer 31:5; Ezek 28:26; 34:26ff.

teousness' (10:18), 'let the plant of righteousness appear' (10:16), and 'deeds of righteousness shall be planted for ever with joy' (10:16).[34]

## 5. Theological Message

So much for the interpretative methods. I will, however, not leave this portion of hidden scriptural interpretation without touching upon its contents, although that has to be done in extreme brevity.

The *titulus* of the book mentions its addressees, their situation, and their prospect: 'the elect righteous who will be (living) on the day of tribulation to remove all the enemies, and the righteous will be saved' (1:1).[35] In the interpretative retelling of the Noah narrative we can surmise what their troublesome time was like: warfare, people around them being idolatrous, the pressure of an unJewish culture felt as a threat by those who wanted to stay faithful to the religion of the fathers.[36] These evils had a transcendent origin, that is the watchers, and they meant a rebellion against God. When the archangels plead the cause of suffering men (1 En 9), they ask how God can allow such things (9:11). Actually the classical problem of theodicy is stated.[37] Our text is a part of the divine answer that the evil transcendent powers will be bound and in due course eliminated by stronger transcendent powers, in the last resort by God. Thus, the righteous can hope for a better world that God has already decided to establish – it is approaching.

Seen in this way, our text is an integral part of an answer – in a haggadic form – to a theological and moral problem. As a consequence we may surmise that one should beware of taking it as a self-contained, conclusive description of the *eschaton*.

When 1 *Enoch* 10f. is cited as a typical example of gross, this-worldly expectations in eschatology,[38] this is, in a sense, justified. The promised, radically new conditions of life are certainly meant to prevail on *earth*. That is valid also for the two other descriptions of the eschatological bliss contained in the book. But, on the other hand, the different styles of the three passages already indicate that one misunderstands their messages if one understands them literally. We who, at least some times, prefer abstract terms, should perhaps try to understand the book in the light of its introduction in chapters 1–5. There the writer speaks of the coming bliss in general and abstract terms such as mercy, peace, blessing, etc. In a study, published some years ago, I argued that these chapters are like

---

[34] Cf. Philo, *de agr*, which, from 9 onwards, deals with 'soulhusbandry'. The author makes use of imagery already established in the Old Testament, e.g., in Isa 45:8 and 61:11. Cf. also how Israel is 'planted' according to Exod 15:17; 2 Sam 7:10; Jer 32:41; Amos 9:15; etc. The imagery appears also in 1QS VIII.5; 1QH VI.15 etc.

[35] Cf. the introduction to the Apocalypse of weeks, 1 En 93:2.

[36] 1 En 7f. See Nickelsburg 1977a, 387ff.; Hartman 1979, 137f.

[37] Robert Henry Charles 1963, 213; Nickelsburg 1977a, 387.

[38] Thus, e.g., Volz 1934, 387f.; Emil Schürer 1979, 534.

a key to the rest of the book, and I concluded an attempt at an exegesis of them in this way:

"Thus, the tenor of *1 Enoch* 1–5 could be regarded as an answer to an "asking for a meaning" of the righteous life: in a troubled situation the "elect" are blessed for what they are, viz, righteous and faithful to the covenant, for what they are not, viz, renegades, and for what they, because of God's graceful covenant promises, can expect, something of which they already are the possessors but which God Himself will bring about, a time of full peace and blessing."[39]

It seems to me that the two other descriptions of the new, blessed situation, our text included, paint a similar picture with different dyes, using a more haggadic and mythological language, which has to be understood as such.

With this I come to the end of my discussion of this early example of Jewish exegesis. What we have seen in terms of interpretation and modes of interpretation may raise the question: How and why did this way of using the Bible arise? Such a question becomes all the more exciting when it is motivated by such an ancient witness of Jewish Bible interpretation as the text from the Book of the watchers which has been at the center of our interest in this paper. Of course I cannot go into any discussion of the origins of midrash here.[40] But we can surmise one reason why it arose and why it continued to be a decisive factor in Jewish religion, namely that one was convinced that, in and through the Scriptures, God communicated himself to his people. The moment the receiver of this communication took it as applying to himself, a process of interpretation began. What we have done in this paper is to look beneath the surface of a text that is the result of such an attentive approach to God's word. We can surmise anguish behind it, but also trust and hope – and creative fantasy.

## 6. Excursus:
## A Few Suggestions as to the Construction
## of the Book of the Watchers

The Book of the watchers is probably edited on the basis of older sources and traditions.[41] This does not mean that – as a means of communication – it must be an unorganized patchwork. Therefore, a grasp of the construction of the book is important to understand it.[42]

---

[39] HARTMAN 1979, 138.

[40] See, e.g., SEELIGMANN 1953; FRITZ MAAS 1955; HENRY SLONIMSKY 1956; VERMÈS 1970; GARY PORTON 1979.

[41] MILIK 1976, 25; NICKELSBURG 1981a, 48ff.

[42] The problem of the construction is intensely connected to that of the genre. At a symposium on apocalypticism in 1979, I discussed the problem of apocalyptic genre in a paper, now published (HARTMAN 1983). The question has been thoroughly investigated and essential advancements have been made by my colleague Dr Hellholm (DAVID HELLHOLM 1980 and 1986).

It may be suitable to start a discussion of the book's construction at 14:1, where the Book of the words of righteousness is introduced. This is prepared in the following way: Enoch, being with the angels, is sent to reprimand the fallen watchers (12:3–6). He performs this task (13:1–2), with the result that the latter ask him to write down a petition to God for them (13:4f.). He does so, reads it out, and falls asleep (13:6f.). Then we read: ' ... behold, dreams came down upon me, and visions fell upon me until [I lifted up] my eyelids to the gates of the palace [of Heaven ... ]; and I saw a vision of the wrath of chastisement, [and a voice came and said: "Speak to the sons of heaven to reprimand them." And when I awoke I went] unto them ... And I spoke before them all 'the visions which I had seen in dreams, and I began to speak] in words of truth and vision and reprimand to the heavenly Watchers [ ... ]' (13:8–10).[43]

The cited introduction summarizes that which follows: 14:8–16:4 brings Enoch to the divine throne – this is a 'vision' of the 'palace of heaven', in which he is also ordered to 'reprimand the sons of heaven'. Without any incision such as changes of persons or of situation, 17:1 introduces Enoch's journeys, which bring him to, *inter alia,* 'the prison for the stars ... which have transgressed the commandment of the Lord' (18:15). This is the first 'vision of the wrath of chastisement', and the rest of the book (21–36) contains more such visions.[44]

Chapters 13–36 are joined to the preceding text by 12:1f.: 'Before these things Enoch was hidden ... and his activities had to do with the watchers and his days were with the holy ones'. The lines take account of Genesis 5:24 and, with Genesis, let Enoch's translation occur 'before' Noah and the flood, the topic of chapters 6–11. The effect is that Enoch is available to implement the heavenly watcher's[45] order to reprimand the fallen angels and their offspring (12:3ff.), the fall of whom has been reported in 6ff., and, furthermore, to present the Book of the words of righteousness.

Chapters 6–11,[46] or, rather, 6–8, give the necessary background for 12–36: the crime of the watchers – and its consequences – must be described before[47]

---

[43] Translation MILIK 1976, 195.

[44] As a rule commentators separate chapters 17–36 from chapters 12–16. See, e.g., CHARLES 1913, 199; NICKELSBURG 1981b, 576. Seen from a point of view of literary composition, 13:8–10 speaks in favour of my understanding.

[45] It is only one, see MILIK 1976, 192, and Cf. the Greek and Ethiopic.

[46] One may wonder: does this 'before' also concern Enoch's accusation in 13:3ff. in relation to that which is said in chapters 9 and 10? I am not sure that one should try to order the reported actions against the watchers in a temporal sequence – the author does not seem to be too interested in such a thing.

[47] Seen from a literary point of view the relationship between 6–11 and its context is a bit puzzling. Chapter 6 starts abruptly, without any transitions or explicit indications of what is to follow or who is talking: 'And it happened, when the children of men had multiplied that in those days were born ...'. Two expressions signal a new beginning, viz 'and it happened'. and 'in those days'. The sentence may be said to quote Gen 6:1, and that may possibly also be a signal to the attentive reader. Does it, namely, indicate to him that here begins a retelling of the story of Noah and the flood?

their denouncement and punishment. But what about chapters 9–11, which deal with the angels' bringing the afflicted men's trouble before the ears of God (9) and with the divine commands to the angels with the ensuing description of the salvation (10f.)? I would suggest that the *raison d'être* of chapters 9–11 has to do with the function of the book *vis-à-vis* of its readers, visible in its very beginning (1:1): it is addressed to the righteous, and *it concerns their situation*. Thus, chapters 9–11 are brought in – they concern the righteous addressees.[48]

Something similar holds true for the Book of the words of righteousness (14–36). Within the framework of the reported story, it is directed to the fallen watchers, but the real communication is to the righteous; the punishment and destruction of the powers which are the origin of evil are in *their* interest. Thus, chapters 14–36 not only deal with reprimands and (places of) chastisements of the watchers, but also with the blessed land, the garden of righteousness, and so on.

Finally, in a similar way, the denouncement speech of the introduction (2–5) is directed against the wicked, but it concerns the righteous and therefore tells *about* their coming happiness. (I have already, in the body of this paper, presented my view of chapters 1–5: they are a solemn introduction, giving a definite clue to the book as a whole).

There are many large and small problems which a serious investigation of the construction of *1 Enoch* 1–36 must assess, but this is certainly not the place for such an undertaking. So, these few remarks must suffice for the time being.

---

[48] 1. Cf. HELLHOLM 1986, 53 on 'supplementary visions' which have a similar communicative function in Revelation.

# Part II

The Gospel of Mark

# 8. Grammar and Exegesis
## The Case of Mark 4:11–12

A rather literal translation of Mark 4:11–12 reads:

To you is given the secret of the Kingdom of God. But to those outside it all happens (or, is: τὰ πάντα γένεται) in parables, (12) so that (ἵνα) looking they may look and not see, and hearing they may hear and not understand, in order that (μήποτε) they may not turn again and it be forgiven unto them (ἀφεθῇ αὐτοῖς).

Verse 12 is a hidden quotation of Isa 6:9–10 in a wording that to some extent differs from the Septuagint and is more reminiscent of the Aramaic Targum. Although the origin of the quotation is not mentioned, constructions as 'looking they may look' should nevertheless indicate to a reader who is not well versed in the Septuagint that the sentence has its origin in the Bible.

## 1. Modern Translations

Mark 4:11–12 is often referred to as a *crux interpretum*. Does the Marcan Jesus say that it is determined that some people will not be saved? The difficulties have been dealt with in different ways, and to some extent this uncertainty can already be discerned in how the translations render it. Thus, for example, the Revised Standard Version says: 'so that they may indeed see but not perceive …, lest they should turn again and be forgiven.' La Traduction Oecuménique de la Bible renders the passage in this way: 'pour que, tout en regardant, ils ne voient pas …, de peur qu'ils ne se convertissent et qu'il leur soit pardonné.' The German *Einheitsübersetzung*, finally, chooses this rendering: 'denn sehen sollen sie, sehen, aber nicht erkennen …, damit sie sich nicht bekehren und ihnen nicht vergeben wird.'

Thus the ἵνα at the beginning of v. 12 and the μήποτε introducing its second clause are differently treated: the RSV takes the ἵνα as denoting a consequence, but, as it seems, a consequence behind which there is a purpose. The TOB renders it as being final or telic. The *Einheitsübersetzung*, finally, seems to assume a causal meaning: 'since', 'as', 'because', which has gotten the 'denn' as a result.

As to the μήποτε the three translations take it as final: lest (RSV), de peur que (TOB), damit (*Einheitsübersetzung*).

Thus, the two conjunctions (for the sake of simplicity I use this term also of μήποτε) are rendered thus: 'so that … lest' (RSV), 'pour que … de peur que' (TOB), 'denn … damit' (*Einheitsübersetzung*). That is, there are some slight differences in terms of how the translators have combined consecutive, final and causal aspects.

The commentators mostly take both the ἵνα and the μήποτε as having a final sense.[1] Some, however, understand the ἵνα as being epexegetic, namely as explaining the τὰ πάντα: thus for example Pesch: 'geschieht alles in Gleichnissen, dass sie ‚sehend' …'. Others give it a causal signification, thus for example Lohmeyer: 'weil'.[2] The latter renderings are combined with a particular way of understanding the μήποτε, namely as indicating a reservation or a possibility; thus Pesch 'vielleicht werden sie umkehren',[3] and Lohmeyer, who has Jesus say: 'weil sie sehen, sehen, und sehen nicht … , ob etwa sie umkehren …'.[4]

Two further attempts at interpreting the sentence should be mentioned. The first one does not translate the present text but assesses its prehistory, assuming that behind the ἵνα lies a mistranslation of an Aramaic $d^i$, 'who'. This, of course leaves the difficulty where it is, namely if one does not assume that the reader should be able to translate Mark's Greek back to Aramaic in order to understand it. The other attempt has been advocated by Joachim Jeremias, who suggests that the ἵνα is an abbreviation of ἵνα πληρωθῇ, so that the passage should be translated, or rather paraphrased, in this way: 'in order that what has been written may be fulfilled: that looking they look but do not see …'[5]

The troubles which the passage has caused so many commentators are well represented by C. F. D. Moule in his *Idiom Book of New Testament Greek*, in which he refrains from interpreting the whole phrase – ἵνα and μήποτε alike – as strictly final', because he finds it 'too incongruous with any part of the N.T. period to be plausible'.[6] For does it not sound as if the Marcan Jesus wanted to prevent that certain people ('those outside') turn again and be forgiven?

---

[1] Thus e.g. JOACHIM GNILKA, *Das Evangelium nach Markus* I, Zürich – Einsiedeln – Köln • Neukirchen-Vluyn 1978: "damit … damit"; ROBERT H. GUNDRY, *Mark*, Grand Rapids, Mich. 1992 and JOEL MARCUS, *Mark 1–8*, New York etc. 1999: both "in order that … lest", similarly BEN WITHERINGTON III, *The Gospel of Mark*, Grand Rapids, Mich. – Cambridge (UK) 2001; MORNA D. HOOKER, *The Gospel according to Saint Mark*, London – Peabody, Mass. 1991: "in order that … otherwise". Of the same opinion are, e.g., CRAIG A. EVANS, "The Function of Isaiah 6:9–10 in Mark and John", in: *NT* 24 (1982) 124–138: 132 (after a presentation of different suggestions 127–132); CARL HEINZ PEISKER, "Konsekutives ἵνα in Markus 4,12", in: *ZNW* 59 (1968) 126–127; WALTER BAUER/KURT ALAND/BARBARA ALAND, *Griechisch-deutsches Wörterbuch zu den Schriften des Neuen Testaments*, Berlin – New York [6]1988, s.v. ἵνα.

[2] ERNST LOHMEYER, *Das Evangelium des Markus*, Göttingen [16]1963, ad loc.

[3] RUDOLF PESCH, *Das Markusevangelium* I, Freiburg i. Br. – Basel – Vienna 1976, ad loc. Also DIETER LÜHRMANN, *Das Markusevangelium*, Tübingen 1987, ad loc., referring to PETER LAMPE, "Die markinische Deutung des Gleichnisses vom Sämann Markus 4,10–12", in: *ZNW* 65 (1974) 140–150.

[4] LOHMEYER, ibid.

[5] JOACHIM JEREMIAS, *Die Gleichnisse Jesu*, Göttingen [5]1958, II. A similar solution was already intimated by MARIE-JOSEPH LAGRANGE, *Évangile selon Saint Marc*, Paris 1947, ad loc.

[6] CHARLES F. D. MOULE, *An Idiom Book of New Testament Greek*, Cambridge [2]1960, 143. Similarly LAMPE, art. cit. 140 who finds that grammar speaks in favour of a final reading, but that this causes too great difficulties as to the contents.

I will now discuss the different attempts, one after the other, beginning by the ἵνα. Before going into the grammatical details, I suggest that we assume that the reading is too far-fetched which presupposes that the reader silently completes the text in the way Jeremias suggested: 'in order that (or: so that) what has been written be fulfilled'. As I noted above, Mark does not even help his reader by mentioning that the lines are taken from the Old Testament. The fact that he does so in Mark 1:2 is an indication that there is not enough of an inter-textual echo here to have such an effect on the reader.

## 2. Ancient Grammarians

With respect to the grammar, I have already mentioned that some render the ἵνα by 'so that'.[7] This certainly is a consecutive conjunction, but as soon as it is combined with a final translation of the μήποτε, a nuance of finality is also there. Anyway, it is a well known fact that the Koine widened the use of ἵνα, and that the borderline between the final ἵνα and the consecutive ὥστε was hopelessly blurred.[8]

As to the rendering of ἵνα in introducing a causal clause, the authors who defend it sometimes refer to a couple of grammarians from Antiquity. Accordingly, it is of some interest to consider more closely what these grammarians actually say.[9] (In the following translations, I sometimes paraphrase the technical terms a little in order to make the text easier to understand.) Thus, when Dionysios Thrax (2$^{nd}$ cent. BC) presents the conjunctions (οἱ σύνδεσμοι), he also states the following:

Causal (αἰτιολογικοί) are those conjunctions which are used to explain the cause (αἰτία). They are the following ones: ἵνα, ὄφρα, ὅπως, ἕνεκα, οὕνεκα, διό, διότι,[10] καθ' ὅτι, καθ' ὅσον. (*Ars grammatica* I.1. 93f.)

Apparently Dionysios also regards something planned or wanted for the future, indeed a purpose, as a cause.[11]

In his treatise on the conjunctions Apollonius Dyscolus (2$^{nd}$ cent. AD) can also characterize ἵνα as a 'causal' (αἰτιολογικός) conjunction, but in addition he is more specific:

---

[7] William L. Lane, *The Gospel according to Mark*, Grand Rapids, Mich. 1974, *ad loc.* Cf. RSV and Peisker, *art. cit.*

[8] Friedrich Blass/Albert Debrunner/Friedrich Rehkopf, *Grammatik des neutestamentlichen Griechisch*, Göttingen $^{14}$1976, § 390.2; 391.3; Jerker Blomqvist/Poul Ole Jastrup, *Grekisk/Græsk grammatik*, Copenhagen 1991, § 296.4; Antonius Nicholas Jannaris, *An Historical Greek Grammar*, London 1897, § 1758; Eduard Schwyzer/Albert Debrunner, *Griechische Grammatik ... II: Syntax und syntaktische Stilistik*, Munich 1950, II, 681.

[9] Blass/Debrunner/Rehkopf, *op. cit.* § 456.2, mention that these grammarians assume that ἵνα has a causal meaning, but are a little brief on the matter.

[10] The spiritus asper is in the edition.

[11] In his edition, p. 93, Uhlig has an instructive footnote on Dionysos' use of the term.

ἵνα has two typical usages, one causal (αἰτιολογική), the other final (ἀποτελεστική). For when the reading is the cause: (αἰτία) we say: 'Because I read, I was honoured' (ἵνα ἀναγνῶ ἐτιμήθην), 'Because I slandered, I was punished' (ἵνα λοιδορήσω ἐπεπλήχθην). The same is not imparted in the following examples: 'Give (me what I need) in order to write' (δὸς ἵνα γράψω) ... , 'Theon takes action to be healthy' (διακινεῖ ἵνα ὑγιαίνῃ),[12] 'He is eager that he shall become virtuous' (φιλοπονεῖ ἵνα ἐνάρετος γένηται). For it is evident that in such cases ἵνα is used to signify finality (εἰς ἀποτελεστικόν τι). (*De conj.* 2.1.1, 243.)

A little bit further on, Apollonius returns to the topic:

Concerning the ἵνα and the equivalent conjunctions, one must not overlook the fact that not only are they used to signify finality and causality; they are also followed by specific tenses. Thus, on the one hand, the final use is followed by verbs about something to come, and on the other, the causal goes with past time. For one mentions the cause (αἰτιολογεῖται) for that which has happened. And he who says 'Because I wrote, this happened to me' (ἵνα γράψω ταῦτά μοι ἐγένετο), grants that the writing has already taken place and that he has already executed the 'I wrote' and presented the cause thereof. But what is said in the following way has not yet occurred: 'Give me (the things I need) in order to write' (δὸς ἵνα γράψω), and what has not yet occurred is a final cause: (ἐστιν ἀποτελεστικόν). It thus goes together with some future thing when we think in this way: 'Give me (this or that) in order that at the completion (of the giving) the writing may take place' (δὸς ἵνα ἐν τελειώσει γένηται τὸ γράψαι). (*De conj.* 2.1.1, 244f.)

## 3. Discussion

On the one hand, according to Liddell-Scott-Jones this 'causal' use of ἵνα is not found in the 'literature' (*sub voce*),[13] and Jannaris dates it to the time from the Graeco-Roman period and on.[14] That is, our grammarians are probably dependent on the Greek of their own days, when they construct examples of the 'causal' – in our sense of the word! – usage of ἵνα. Mayser does not, however, mention anything of a causal ἵνα in his grammar of the Ptolemaic papyri. On the other hand, Apollonius limits it to sentences in which the contents of the clause belong to the past, and this, I think, is important in our case. The N.T. grammars which mention a causal use of ἵνα only present examples in present or past tense, that is, such as follow the style of Apollonius, but no examples referring to a future cause. The same holds true of other contributors to the discussion.[15] Accord-

---

[12] In *De constructione* 2.2, 377 Apollonius presents the same examples with slight differences: "Give me the roll of papyrus in order that I write", "Tryphon walks in order to become healthy".

[13] Accordingly, in the grammars it is dealt with only in passing, if at all: SCHWYZER, *op. cit.* II, 674, JANNARIS, *op.cit.*, § 1841. Others, like BLOMQVIST/JASTRUP, *op. cit.*, RAPHAEL KÜHNER/BERNHARD GERTH, *Ausführliche Grammatik der griechischen Sprache. II. Satzlehre I–II*, Hannover – Leipzig 1898, ³1904, and HERBERT WEIR SMYTH, *Greek Grammar* (rev. by G. H. Messing), Cambridge, Mass. 1956 (1966) do not mention it.

[14] JANNARIS, *op. cit.*, § 1741.

[15] See JANNARIS, *op. cit.*, § 1741 and NIGEL TURNER in: JAMES HOPE MOULTON, *A Grammar of New Testament Greek Vol. III*, Edinburgh 1963, 102f. BLASS/DEBRUNNER/REHKOPF, *op. cit.*, are hesitant as to the existence of a causal ἵνα in LXX and the NT, and in any case the examples ad-

ingly, it seems advisable to take Apollonius seriously, when he limits the causal use to past tense, and not to apply it also in clauses dealing with the future. Thus it seems that there are no strong grounds for translating Mark 4:11–12 to read: 'it all happens to them in parables, because looking they look but do not see …'.

Next, we come to the suggestion that the ἵνα is epexegetic, introducing a closer description of the contents of the preceding τὰ πάντα.[16] The points of departure are examples like 1 John 5:3, mentioned in Blaß-Debrunner-Rehkopf (§ 394.3): αὕπη … ἡ ἀγάπη τοῦ θεοῦ, ἵνα τὰς ἐντολὰς αὐτοῦ τηρῶμεν. When it is argued, e.g. by Lampe, that τὰ πάντα 'here has a demonstrative character' (142), it seems to me that this overlooks the point. The demonstrative pronouns and other expressions used in the cases in question are substitutions, that is, through a general or more abstract term they refer to what is described in the ἵνα-clause. Thus, an epexegetic use of ἵνα would here be equal to: '… to those outside it all, namely the fact that looking they look and do not see …, is in parables, in order that they may not turn again'. This is hardly a natural understanding of the Greek.

Thus, as to the ἵνα, I think we are left with the result that the most probable reading is to take it as final or consecutive – which of course is not a very original result. But maybe the alternatives have lost some of their possible strength.

Above, I mentioned that the μήποτε is mostly understood as final, but there is also an attempt to translate it as meaning 'but perhaps (they will turn again)' or something similar. Here, the point of departure is not only the circumstance that clauses expressing a non-explicit fear are introduced by a μή, but also the possibility that a dubitative μή can introduce an indirect question; in the Koine the usage is wider and is also found when a sense of doubt, anxiety or care lies behind. Indeed, the negation can be so weak as to indicate only a supposition.[17] The best, indeed the only, certain N.T. example is 2 Tim 2:25: ἐν πραΰτητι παιδεύοντα τοὺς ἀντιδιατιθεμένους, μήποτε δώῃ αὐτοῖς ὁ θεὸς μετάνοιαν. Here, the caring aspect is still quite clearly implied; but to my judgment, finding a similar nuance in Mark 4:12 is less justified. As Lampe expresses it: 'für Markus verkörpert der μήποτε-Satz Jesu Überlegung und zweifelnde Frage, ob seine Hörer umkehren werden' (144). To my ears the context does not contain enough of such an Überlegung or such a 'zweifelnde Frage' as to suggest this way out of the problems posed by the grammar.

In his Idiom Book Prof. Moule is not willing to put Mark 4:12 'upon the Procrustean bed of Classical grammar' and finds it 'far more reasonable to take

---

duced do not refer to future "causes" (§ 456.2). See also Dirk Christiaan Hesseling/Hubert Pernot, "Neotestamentica: ἵνα = omdat", in: *Neophilologus* 12 (1927) 41–46, whose results were questioned by Hans Windisch, "Die Verstockungsidee in Mc 4:12 und das kausale ἵνα der späteren Koine", in: *ZNW* 26 (1927) 203–209, as well as by Adrianus van Veldhuizen, "OTI-INA (?)" *Nieuwe theologische studiën* (1927) 42–44.

[16] Pesch, *op. cit.*, Lührmann, *op. cit.*, Lampe, *art. cit.*
[17] Blass/Debrunner/Rehkopf, *op. cit.*, § 370,2–3; Lampe, *art. cit.* 143.

both ἵνα and μήποτε as instances of the Semitic blurring of purpose and result'.[18] Here, I want to differ between different approaches of one's research. Thus it is one thing to try to look into the prehistory of the text, maybe even to go back to the words of Jesus; it means something else to try to figure out what the evangelist thought and meant; and it is still another thing to ask how Mark's first readers may have understood the text. When I follow the latter line, I must begin by noticing that there are no signs that Mark's readers thought in a 'Semitic' way; at least Mark has to explain Jewish purity habits to them (7:2–4). His Greek is not 'Semitic', but to some extent it is coloured by the Bible style of the Septuagint. This means that if Mark's readers would understand Mark 4:12 in a way that deviated from the Greek of their day, the usage of ἵνα and μήποτε here should be of a particular Septuagint type. But as a matter of fact, there is no such particular usage. Accordingly, the readers should have been left with the final reading. If what they had learnt in terms of Christian doctrine of God and salvation had brought with it that they blurred purpose and result – to use Moule's words – the problem then becomes how they understood the contents, not how they perceived what they met on the textual surface of Mark 4:11–12.

The interpreters who have tried to avoid the difficulty inherent in the final reading by rendering the ἵνα and μήποτε in other ways, have largely done so by searching for loopholes in the syntax provided by notices in the grammars. Although I certainly have sympathy with their efforts, I am afraid that the support from the grammars dissolves when we are confronted with a text by a person in Antiquity whose natural language was Greek and who, as it seems, would very much have wanted the text to be less thorny. But he does not for a moment seem to consider any of the possibilities that modern commentators have suggested after having scrutinized the grammars.

The person I have in mind is Origen. In his work on the fundamentals of Christian faith, *De principiis*, he also enters upon the philosophical question whether human beings have a free will or not. His basic stand is that this is the case; this also means that no one is predestined to condemnation. Indeed, Origen is of the opinion that in the very last end all shall be saved; this he argues taking 1 Cor 15:28 as his point of departure (God 'will be all in all').

He begins his deliberations in the topic by citing the view of the opponents and continues: "It would be easy to find a convincing argument against this view, if it were not for the fact that it says: 'in order that they may not turn again, and it be not forgiven unto them'" (εἰ μὴ προσέκειτο τὸ μήποτε ἐπιστρέψωσι, καὶ ἀφεθῇ αὐτοῖς; *De principiis* III.16). In addition, a few lines later he paraphrases the saying in this manner: 'Obviously it is said in the Gospel that ... the reason why the Saviour does not speak in plain words is that people shall not turn again and, by so doing, be worthy of the forgiveness of sins' (διὰ τοῦτο σαφῶς μὴ

---

[18] MOULE, *op. cit.*, 142f., referring to ROBERT HATCH KENNETT, *In Our Tongues* 1907, Ch. I.

φθεγγόμενος, ἵνα μὴ ἐπιστρέψωσιν οἱ ἄνθρωποι, καὶ ἐπιστρέψαντες ἀφέσεως ἁμαρτημάτων ἄξιοι γένωνται).

I need not dwell on Origen's suggestions as to how to cut the knot. For in this connection he is a testimony to the fact that although grammars are necessary aids in language studies and in dealings with texts in foreign languages, they cannot replace the experience of the one who has learnt the language from within.

Because I know that Professor Blomqvist, himself a great grammarian, is not of a different opinion as to the role played by grammar, I dare to dedicate the above reflections to him, not least in joyful remembrance of the common sessions in our higher seminars some years ago.

# 9. Markus 6,3a im Lichte einiger griechischer Texte

## 1. Die bisherige Diskussion

Mk 6,3a, „Ist das nicht der Zimmermann, der Sohn der Maria ...", wird in der Literatur unterschiedlich verstanden, auch abgesehen davon, daß keine völlige Einigkeit darüber herrscht, welche Lesart vorzuziehen ist. Mit Nestle-Aland und beispielsweise der Einheitsübersetzung folgen wir jedoch hier dem u.a. in den großen Alexandrinern gegebenen Text, der auch der obigen Übersetzung zugrundeliegt.

Allgemein wird behauptet, daß die Benennung „der Sohn der Maria" merkwürdig ist, da im biblisch-jüdischen Gebiet selten ein Mann als Sohn seiner Mutter identifiziert wird. R. A. Guelich stellt einige Erklärungsvorschläge zusammen:[1] a) die Benennung ist theologisch durch die Jungfrauengeburt motiviert[2]; b) sie bezieht sich auf eine jüdische Polemik, die Jesus als illegitimes Kind verdächtigt[3]; c) die Mutter Jesu war Witwe[4]; d) Markus „hatte kein Interesse" an dem Vater Jesu[5]. Hinzugefügt sei noch der Vorschlag von H. K. McArthur[6], für den die angeführten Deutungen nicht stichhaltig sind: die Wendung sei nicht „formal-genealogical", sondern „informal-descriptive" zu verstehen, d.h. die Nazarener hätten von Jesus als „Mary's boy, from down the street" gesprochen. Das von McArthur herangezogene, biblische und jüdische Material wurde später von Tal Ilan näher analysiert und durch rabbinische Texte komplettiert, die zeigten, daß eine metronymische Benennung eines Mannes gar nicht diffamierend war.[7]

Die bisherige Diskussion hat oft die Benennung aufgrund der angenommenen Situation in Nazareth erwogen: Was meinten die Nazarener? Oder man hat versucht, ihre Traditionsgeschichte zu rekonstruieren: Stecken hier möglicherweise Spuren einer jüdischen Polemik oder frühchristlicher Traditionen,

---

[1] ROBERT A. GUELICH, *Mark 1 – 8:26* (WBC 34A), Dallas, Tex. 1989, 309f.
[2] ERICH KLOSTERMANN, *Das Markusevangelium* (HNT 3), Tübingen ⁴1950, 55; er nimmt jedoch an, daß diese Lesart sekundär ist.
[3] ETHELBERT STAUFFER, „Jeschu Ben Mirjam. Kontroversgeschichtliche Anmerkungen zu Mk 6,3", in: *Neotestamentica et Semitica*, FS M. Black, Edinburgh 1969, 119–128.
[4] U.a. RAYMOND E. BROWN/KARL PAUL DONFRIED/JOSEPH A. FITZMYER/JOHN REUMANN, *Mary in the New Testament*, London 1978, 64.
[5] JOHN DOMINIC CROSSAN, Mark and the Relatives of Jesus, in: *NT* 15 (1973) 81–113.
[6] HARVEY K. MCARTHUR, „Son of Mary", in: *NT* 15 (1973) 38–58.
[7] TAL ILAN, „'Man Born of Woman ...'" (Job 14:1). The Phenomenon of Men Bearing Metronymes at the Time of Jesus, in: *NT* 34 (1992) 23–45.

die sich der Vorstellung von der Jungfrauengeburt annäherten? Außerdem wird danach gefragt, was der Evangelist mit diesem Ausdruck eigentlich sagen wollte.

## 2. Belege aus der hellenistischen Welt

Die folgenden Zeilen stellen demgegenüber den Versuch dar, die Sache aus der Perspektive der heidenchristlichen Leser/Hörer des Markus zu betrachten. Es wird versucht, Belege aus der hellenistischen Welt zu finden, die zeigen, daß ein Mann der Sohn seiner Mutter („X, der Sohn der Z") genannt wurde. Sie könnten als Hinweise auf einen Verstehenshorizont dienen, vor dem die Leser/Hörer den Ausdruck möglicherweise verstanden haben.

(1) In einer ersten, nicht allzu großen Gruppe von Belegen, in denen ein Mann der Sohn seiner Mutter genannt wird, ist die Mutter aus diesem oder jenem Anlaß erwähnenswert. So wird Achilleus „der Sohn der Thetis" genannt[8] – sie war ja eine Seegöttin, während der Vater des Helden ein irdischer König war. Strabo erwähnt in *Geogr.* 17,1,54 „den Sohn der Kandake" (d.h. einer Königin der Äthiopier). Weiterhin kann der Umstand, daß die Mutter eines Mannes aus einer berühmten Familie stammte, Grund dafür gewesen sein, ihn als Sohn seiner Mutter zu benennen: z.B. „Speusippos, Sohn der Potona, der Schwester Platons"[9], oder „Gaios Oktavios Kaipias, denn so hieß der Sohn der Attia, Caesars Nichte".[10] Im unmittelbaren Kontext sagt der Verfasser auch, daß der Sohn, vom Vater verlassen, bei seiner Mutter und ihrem Bruder aufgezogen wurde.[11]

(2) Die in der folgenden Grabinschrift genannte Mutter befindet sich in einer besonderen Lage:

„Poplios Pakonios Hermeias mit dem Beinamen Ethikos aus Rhodos und aus Patara besorgte (das Grab) … damit dort hineingelegt würde (ἀποτεθῆναι) er und seine Frau Oueilia Neike und deren Sohn Tiberios Klaudios Pakonianos Moschos und (ihre) Enkel … Kein anderer darf in das Grab hineingelegt werden. – Ich gestatte, daß über diese hinaus auch hier hineingelegt werden Plotia mit dem Beinamen Pakonia und Mosche, seine (?) Tochter, und die Söhne des Synphoros, Thermos und Prepon und Synphoros, … und Pakonios Euphrosynos, der Freigelassene des Moschos, und Epaphroditos, der Sohn der Oueilia Neike (υἱὸν Οὐειλίας Νείκης) … " (TAM II,1–3, 438; Lykien; Ende des 1. Jh. n. Chr.).

Interessant in diesem Zusammenhang ist Oueilia Neike. Es fällt auf, daß zweimal vorgeschrieben wird, daß sie ins Grab gelegt werden darf, und daß sie auch einen Sohn hat, dessen Vater nicht genannt wird. Doch kann man vermuten, daß es sich um einen Sohn aus der zweiten Ehe handelt, der ihr ins Grab ihrer vorigen Familie folgen darf. Die Relationen zwischen den genannten Personen sind jedoch undurchsichtig, so auch gemäß der Ansicht des Herausgebers.

---

[8] Z.B. Libanius, *Epist.* 125,2.
[9] Philolaos, Frgm. 13.
[10] Dio Cassius, *Hist. Rom.* 45,1,1.
[11] ILAN, „'Man Born of Woman …'" (s. Anm. 7), 29–37, hier: 43f. gibt einige Beispiele für einen ähnlichen Gebrauch in rabbinischen Texten.

(3) In einer anderen, größeren Gruppe von Grab- bzw. Denkmal-Inschriften ist die Mutter eines Sohnes genannt, und es scheint, daß aus irgendeinem nicht genannten Grund sie die Verantwortung für die gesamte Familie trug bzw. sie mit den Brüdern des genannten Sohnes geteilt hat, vermutlich weil sie Witwe war. Einige Beispiele:

„Nana, (Frau) des Menophilos, mit den Kindern Roupheinos und Anteros, ehrte (ἐτείησεν) Menophilos, ihren Sohn (τὸν ἑαυτῆς υἱόν). Zum Gedächtnis" (MAMA 10,150; Phrygien; 215/225 v.Chr.).

Hier werden die Kinder also nicht dem Vater zugeordnet, der wohl nur zur attributiven Näherbestimmung der Mutter namentliche Erwähnung findet und dann auch im Namen des toten Sohnes präsent ist, der den Namen seines Vaters getragen haben dürfte. – Vergleichbares finden wir in dieser Inschrift:

„ ... Arnmias, (Frau) des Hipponeikos, ehrte (ἐτείμησεν) Hipponeikos, ihren Sohn (τὸν ἑαυτῆς υἱόν). Ebenso auch der Bruder Amphilochos" (TAM V/1–2, 431; Lydien; 120 v. Chr.).

(4) In den folgenden Grabinschriften ist der Name des Vaters explizit genannt, es ist aber die Mutter, die das Grabmal errichtet hat und den Sohn als den ihrigen nennt:

„Flavia Sofia, Tochter des P(oplios) Li(kinnios), eines Attikers aus Oios, errichtete (ἀνέθηκεν) (das Denkmal) zu Demeter und Kore (für) ihren Sohn (τὸν ἑαυτῆς) Ti(tos) Fl(avios) Sophokles aus Sounion, (den Sohn) des Konons" (IG II², 3954; Attika; um 100 n. Chr.).

„... Tatia, (Tochter) des Sopatros, ehrte (ἐτείμησεν) Iollas, ihren und Menodoros Sohn (τὸν ἑαυτῆς υἱὸν καὶ Μηνοδώρου), der 8 Jahre alt ein Held wurde (d.h. verschied)" (TAM V/1–2,161; Lydien, 127 v. Chr.).

(5) Der folgende Text eines Denkmals gilt sowohl den Söhnen einer Frau als auch ihrem verstorbenem Vater:

„Mousike (errichtete das Denkmal für) ihren Mann Preimion (τὸν ἄνδρα Π.), ihren Sohn Preimion (τὸν υἱὸν Π.), ihren Sohn Eleutherion (τὸν υἱὸν Ἐ.), die Verstorbenen. Zum Gedächtnis" (IG IX/2, 913; Larissa, Thessalien; röm. Zeit).

(6) In anderen Inschriften werden nur die Mutter und der (tote) Sohn genannt, z.B.:[12]

„Elpis (ehrte hiermit) Philippos, ihren Sohn (τὸν ἑαυτῆς υἱόν). Zum Gedächtnis" (IG IX/2, 949; Larissa, Thessalien; Zeit unbekannt).

„Philoxena (ehrte hiermit) Philoxenos, ihren Sohn (τὸν ἑαυτῆς υἱόν). Zum Gedächtnis. Sei gegrüßt, du edler Held (d.h. du Verstorbener)" (ebd., 958).

„Klaudia Kleodike (ehrte hiermit) Kallippos aus Pisa, ihren Sohn (τὸν ἑαυτῆς υἱόν), olympischen Sieger im Pferderennen. Zum olympischen Zeus" (Peloponnesos, Olympia V, 223; 1. Jh. n. Chr.).

---

[12] Für ähnliche christliche Inschriften s. GARY J. JOHNSON, *Early-Christian Epitaphs from Anatolia* (SBL.TT 35; ECLS 8), Atlanta, Ga. 1995, 68f., 104f.; UTE E. EISEN, *Woman Officeholders in Early Christianity. Epigraphical and Literary Studies*, Collegeville, Minn. 2000, 167–169.

(7) Die folgenden zwei Inschriften sollen zusammengenommen werden:

„Nach Beschluß des Rats des Areopags (ehrte) die Mutter Pompeia Polla (mit diesem Denkmal) ihren Sohn (τὸν ἑαυτῆς υἱόν) Titos Flavios Menandros aus dem Paianiabezirk, den Sohn des Titos Flavios Euthykomas aus dem Paianiabezirk" (IG II²,3985; Attika; Ende 2. Jh. n. Chr.).

Daß die Mutter Pompeia Polla Witwe ist, ergibt sich aus der anderen Inschrift:

„… Nach Beschluß des Rats des Areopags (ehrte) Pompeia Polla, (Tochter) des Philosophen Pompeios Pleistarchos (mit diesem Denkmal) ihren Mann" (ebd., 3984).

## 3. Ergebnis

Es scheint, daß diese Beispiele uns Belege dafür geben, daß die Leser/Hörer des MkEv die Bezeichnung „Sohn der Maria" nicht allzu befremdend fanden. Die oben herangezogenen Texte deuten m.E. auf die naheliegende Möglichkeit hin, daß es in der Umwelt der Leser genügend sprachliche Konventionen gab, um ohne allzuviel Bedenken die Annahme zuzulassen, daß die Bewohner Nazareths in der Erzählung die Benennung „der Sohn der Maria" verwenden konnten, weil Jesu Vater nicht mehr da war, oder sogar schon verstorben war. Schließlich soll unterstrichen werden, daß die oben genannten Beispiele herangezogen wurden, um einen möglichen Referenzrahmen der ersten Generation von Mk-Lesern aufzuweisen; dagegen nicht um eine historische oder traditionsgeschichtliche Erklärung des Ausdrucks „der Sohn der Maria" zu liefern.

# 10. Loving "with Your Whole Heart" — Giving "Her Whole Living"
## An Attempt at Reading Mark 12:41–44 in Its Literary Context

In his Beatitudes Ephraem Syrus writes, "Blessed is he who always has God in mind, for he will be like a heavenly angel, performing his ministry (λειτουργεῖν) to God on earth with fear and love" (*Beatitudines* 10). One may regard the behaviour of the poor widow in Mark 12:41–44 as an illustration of this statement of St. Ephraem: her giving up "her whole living" to God was an expression of love for Him and so a true worship of Him. The following pages will expound this possibility and do so in paying a particular regard to the context of the story.

## 1. General Considerations

When exegetes consider how New Testament texts are related to their context, a double heritage may exert a certain influence, namely one emerging from Church practice, the other depending on some presuppositions taken over from scholarly tradition. As to the first, it is a well known fact that throughout the centuries the Church has to a great extent read the smaller units of the Bible texts one by one, something that of course is most obvious in the case of the gospel narratives. The scholarly part of the heritage is the form-critical view that the gospel tradition consists of pieces that can be compared with pearls which have secondarily been thread on a string. Both elements of the heritage may invite the interpreter by and large to leave the context aside, when it comes to an exposition of a given story, be it in a sermon or in a scholarly commentary.

Redaction criticism of course meant a change. On the one hand its representatives tried to reconstruct earlier compositions or collections of the smaller units of the gospel tradition, on the other, and above all, they focused on how the evangelists/redactors had organized the traditions they took over and what was the theological or pastoral interest behind such editorial work.

The short remarks above can be illustrated by how a couple of commentators have assessed the relation of the story of the widow's offering to its context. Thus, standing in the form-critical tradition Klostermann has only one small remark on the context of our story, namely that it "ihren Platz nur dem Stichwort χήρα [verdankt]"; as a consequence, Klostermann comments on the text only with regards to form, being a so-called "ideal scene"[1]. To Pesch, on the other hand, the story is part of the pre-Markan passion story, which was taken over and edited by Mark. Pesch denies that it was coupled to its context through a catchword connection and is of the opinion that, in the present Gospel of Mark, the story forms a contrast to the preceding warning against the greedy scribes; in addition, he thinks that Mark has understood the widow's behavior as a paradigm of the love for God – something that is effected by the appearance of the keyword *holos* in vv. 30, 33, and 44; indeed, her behavior is said to be a modest sign of the nearness of the Kingdom of God (cf. v. 34 on the scribe)[2].

The discussion of the context of a given text is often rather important to scholars who approach Biblical texts with different methods of literary criticism. So they discuss the "structure" of the context, be it the structure, composition or outline of the whole Gospel or of a more limited part of it[3]. But once one has studied a few different suggestions of such "structures", one realizes that one or two clarifying questions may be in place, namely: to whom does the structure of a given text appear to look in a certain way, and what does this structure mean to whom?

This last question leads us to the so-called reader-response criticism, It is represented by a group of scholars who apply a kind of literary criticism which focuses on the reader, *viz.*, on the readers in the Early Church[4]. As a matter of fact, asking for what a text may have told its first readers has become more and more common among commentators, also such of a more traditional bend[5]. So far, to the present author's knowledge, there are two commentaries on Mark that consistently apply this approach, namely by John Paul Heil and Bas M. F. van Iersel, respectively[6]. They differ in so far as the reader Heil has in mind is a so-called implied reader, that is, whatever the real, historical reader may have been like, this reader is the one made up by Mark's text; this means that, according to Heil, the gospel seems to presuppose, *inter alia*, that the reader recognizes

---

[1] ERICH KLOSTERMANN, *Das Markusevangelium* (HNT 3), Tübingen [4]1959 ([5]1971), 130. The designation "ideal scene" is found in RUDOLF BULTMANN, *Geschichte der synoptischen Tradition*, Göttingen [2]1931 ([6]1964), 32f.

[2] RUDOLF PESCH, *Das Markusevangelium II* (HThK II.2), Freiburg i. Br. – Basel – Vienna 1977, 260–264.

[3] An instructive presentation of different ways of finding structures, outlines etc. in Mark is found in JOHN G. COOK, *The Structure and Persuasive Power of Mark. A Linguistic Approach* (SBL Semeia Studies), Atlanta, Ga. 1985, 15–52. [See now also KIRSTEN MARIE HARTVIGSEN, *Prepare the Way of the Lord* (BZNW 180), Berlin 2012, 99–110.]

[4] In *Let the Reader Understand. Reader-Response Criticism and the Gospel of Mark*, Minneapolis, Minn. 1991, ROBERT M. FOWLER discusses various aspects of such a criticism but does not comment on particular texts.

[5] E.g. DIETER LÜHRMANN, *Das Markusevangelium* (HNT 3), Tübingen 1987; WILFRIED ECKEY, *Das Markusevangelium. Orientierung am Weg Jesu*, Neukirchen-Vluyn 1998.

[6] JOHN PAUL HEIL, *The Gospel of Mark as Model for Action. A Reader-Response Commentary*, New York – Mahvah, N. J. 1992; BAS M. F. VAN IERSEL, *Mark. A Reader-Response Commentary* (JSNT.S 164), Sheffield 1998 (the Dutch original appeared in 1986). [See now in particular HARTVIGSEN, *Prepare the Way*.]

echoes from Scripture, knows about the geography of Palestine, and is relatively well versed in the ideas of Early Judaism, as well as, of course, in early Christian beliefs[7]. van Iersel, on the other hand, is more on the historical side and defines the readers as Gentile Christians, presumably living in Rome; accordingly he wants his exegesis to answer the question what the text told such readers, which may have understood what they heard with presuppositions colored by Hellenistic-Roman culture and slightly seasoned by some Christian education including some knowledge of some O.T. texts[8].

## 2. The Structure of Mark 11:1–12:44. Some Proposals

The following pages will discuss the story of the poor widow's offering with an approach that is rather similar to that of van Iersel, but it will also, and not least, include a rather close study of the context and its structure (although in this respect the suggestions differ considerably from those of van Iersel). So it is time to return to the problem of the context which was touched upon above, notably how literary critics have assessed it. At the same time we should keep in mind the questions intimated above and asking who sees a structure, for whom is it meaningful, how and with which interpretative effects?

Of the scholars just mentioned, van Iersel explicitly claims that he is doing literary criticism. He states that he wants to take seriously that in Mark there is a story-line or, rather, a couple of story-lines to respect when studying the narrative as a whole, But above all he attaches great importance to concentric structures both at micro-and macro-levels[9], claiming that the factors that create a structure of this sort are "the narrated events and the characters involved"[10] and thinks that structures of this kind are somehow recognized by the readers. With regard to our case, he suggests that Mark 11–12 is structured in the following way:

A   preparation of the Temple inspection and entering 11:1–11
   B   cleansing of the Temple and eradication of the fig tree 11:12–25
      C   in discussion with the Temple authorities 11:27–33
         D   parable of the wine growers 12:1–12
      C'   in discussion with other Jewish leaders 12:13–27
   B'   various sayings about scribes 12:28–40

---

[7] HEIL, *op. cit.*, 3–18.
[8] VAN IERSEL, *op. cit.*, 30–57. Sometimes, however, he seems to miss his mark a little and assume rather specialized knowledge about Judaism on the part of the assumed readers; thus, e.g., when he presents the woman with hemorrhage in the light of Jewish rulings (205); these, however, were quite different from the opinions and practice of the non-Jewish world.
[9] VAN IERSEL, *op. cit.*, 68–86.
[10] VAN IERSEL, *op. cit.*, 347.

A' conclusion of the inspection, leaving the temple 12:41–44[11]

The element that joins the A passages is that Jesus observes what is going on in the Temple i.e. a semantic element, or, rather, a particular way of characterizing that element, calling it an inspection. In the same way, the C passages have in common that they are characterized as discussions, notably with Jews in power, the Temple authorities and other Jewish leaders, respectively. The parable on the tenants "forms the turning point in this section"[12]. When commenting on this passage, however, he does not draw any weightier conclusions from the central position of this unit but only notes that it "rounds off the theme of the preceding episode" and "appears to be a mirror story of that which happens to Jesus in the last part of the book"[13], that is, the interpretative consequences of the structure analysis of Mark 11–12 are few.

Quite different is the "structure" which Joanna Dewey detects; she calls it a "rhetorical pattern":

   A  vv.1–9 Public teaching: The parable of the wicked tenants; threat of God's judgment
      B  vv.10–12 Public teaching: Psalm citation; audience reaction
         C  vv.13–17 Public debate: The things of God are to be given to God; audience reaction
            D  vv.18–27 Public debate: The hope in resurrection is real
         C'  vv.28–34 Public debate: The things of God are the commands to love God and neighbor; audience reaction
      B'  vv.35–37 Public teaching: Psalm citation; audience reaction
   A'  vv.38–40 Public teaching: Warning against the scribes; threat of God's judgment[14]

This is not the place to discuss Dewey's suggestions in detail. But with regard to the questions I raised above, one gets the impression that Dr Dewey is the one who has seen the structures and that she is of the opinion that they are intended by Mark himself[15]. For chapter 12 she thinks that Mark has used this composition technique to contrast "Jesus' attack on the Jewish leaders with his defense of himself as a good Jew"[16]. The elements she finds so symmetrically ordered certainly are there, but not everybody would be prepared to see the symmetry.

The grid through which Dr Dewey regards the text makes her keep vv. 41–44 apart from the rest of chapter 12. Instead she combines it with Mark 14:3–9,

---

[11] VAN IERSEL, *loc. cit.* The typographic arrangement of the table has been modified and the misprints have been corrected.
[12] *Loc. cit.*
[13] VAN IERSEL, *op. cit.*, 369.
[14] JOANNA DEWEY, *Markan Public Debate: Literary Technique, Concentric Structure, and Theology in Mark 2:1–3:6* (SBLDS 48), Chico, Calif. 1980, 162.
[15] DEWEY, *op. cit.*, 167.
[16] DEWEY, *op. cit.*, 167.

the story of the woman anointing Jesus at Bethany, and lets them form a frame around the apocalyptic discourse; the two stories have some features in common: in both a woman is praised for her generosity, in both the value of her gift is at stake, the word "poor" appears in both, and both end with an *amen*-saying[17]. Nevertheless, an essential feature of the contents of the story of the widow is that she appears as a contrast to the bad example of the scribes in the preceding pericope[18].

The structures found by Dr Dewey are apparently mainly formed by details on the text's semantic surface, but also by the literary form of the text.

The questions as to who sees a structure and how the latter influences the understanding of a given text are also essential to those text-linguistic scholars who focus on text-structuring markers with special regard to their communicative effect[19]. That is, the point of departure is that out of the many features of a text which may constitute one or several structures, some are more decisive than others *vis-à-vis* of the reader/listener. As a rule they are to be found on the textual surface[20]. Thus one such type of marker can be a meta-communicative expression[21], that is, it tells the receiver something about a given text, or a part of it, instructing him/her about its character, contents etc. Such an expression can, for example, inform the reader of the issue of a debate which constitutes the contents of the text in question. On a lower level the so-called episode-markers are found, which concern time and place of the things told about[22]. Changes in terms of actors also contribute to structuring a text; they may divide, say, an episode at a given time on a given place into sub-units[23].

An analysis following these lines often confirms what many commentators state on more or less intuitive grounds, but can deliver more precise reasons for the suggestions as to how a given text may appear to be structured in the eyes of the receiver. John G. Cook has published a monograph containing a detailed analysis of Mark according to this method. Very much condensed and leaving aside all details in terms of markers on different levels, this is the structure he detects in Mark 11:12–12:44[24]:

---

[17] DEWEY, *op. cit.*, 154.

[18] *Ibid.*

[19] The title of ELISABETH GÜLICH's article is typical: "Ansätze zu einer kommunikationsorientierten Erzähltextanalyse (am Beispiel mündlicher und schriftlicher Erzähltexte)", in: WOLFGANG HAUBRICHS (ed.), *Erzählforschung I* (Beiheft zur Zeitschrift für die Literaturwissenschaft und Linguistik 4), Göttingen 1976, 224–256.

[20] GÜLICH, *op. cit.*, 242.

[21] ELISABETH GÜLICH/WOLFGANG RAIBLE, *Linguistische Textanalyse. Überlegungen zur Gliederung von Texten* (Papiere zur Textlinguistik), Hamburg ²1979, 87; DAVID HELLHOLM, *Das Visionenbuch des Hermas als Apokalypse. Formgeschichtliche und texttheoretische Studien zu einer literarischen Gattung I* (CB.NT 13), Lund 1980, 80–84.

[22] GÜLICH, "Ansätze" (note 19), 242.

[23] GÜLICH, *op. cit.*, 243.

[24] COOK, *op. cit.*, (note 3), 246–257.

11:12–19 The second day
   11:12–14 Cursing of the fig tree
   11:15–19 Temple cleansing, teaching about the Temple
11:20–25 They see the tree withered; teaching about prayer
11:27–12:44 Controversies in the Temple
   11:27–12:34 Questions (note 12:34: "ask")
      11:27–12:12 Debate on authority + parable
         11:27–33 Debate
         12:1–12 Parable
      12:13–17 Debate on tribute to Caesar
      12:18–27 Question about resurrection
      12:28–34 Incident of understanding scribe
   12:35–44 Questions and teaching
      12:35–37 Jesus asks about the Christ
      12:38–40 Jesus' warning against certain scribes
      12:41–44 Episodes by the treasury

Cook does not draw any conclusions from his analysis as to the interpretation of this passage (which might be a bit unfair to demand, as the presentation of his analysis and some theoretical considerations already cover some 350 pages).

Since there are arguments that support the view that structures of this kind do have a communicative effect and accordingly influence how readers tend to conceive the text, I am in favor of approaching our text in this way, not least as it should fit well with a reader-response approach such as the one touched upon above.

There are, however, some details that could be assessed differently from Cook's analysis, and these differences may have consequences for the interpretation. Firstly, the changes in terms of actors could deserve to be observed more closely and so also to suggest another way of apprehending the story-line of these chapters.

Since 10:33 the readers know that the high priests, the scribes, and the elders are going to condemn Jesus to death and deliver him to the Gentiles. Two of these groups are present at the cleansing of the Temple and the following teaching, all three of them raise the question with which authority Jesus acted in this way; but after Jesus' long answer, including the parable on the tenants, they are explicitly said to leave the stage and are not introduced again until 14:2, where they initiate the Passion story proper by their plans to seize Jesus. That is, according to the organization of the story, they do not attend the teaching in 12:13–44. (In the following, I will label this group of the high priests etc. "the enemies".)

From the readers' point of view it is important that the disciples are there all the time; they are their representatives and receive Jesus' teaching on their behalf – in the episodes on prayer and faith (11:20–25) and on the widow's generosity they alone are the audience. However, the readers are actually better oriented than the disciples, because they stand outside the story and know its outcome. In addition, in their situation the things told in chapters 11–12 are not only a prelude to the story of the Passion but also say essential things concerning their Christian existence.

The crowd, lastly, listens to Jesus' teaching on the Temple as a house of prayer (11:18) and also likes his teaching on the Anointed at God's right hand (12:37). But in this part of chapters 11–14 their function is mainly to restrain the enemies' plans to kill Jesus.

So, in terms of the ongoing story of the conflict between Jesus and his enemies the episodes 12:13–34 + 12:35–44 have no connections to the events of the Passion story. They form, as it were, a parenthesis in the plot.

As can be seen from the survey above, Cook is of the opinion that 11:27–12:34 forms a unit, constituted by questions. But it seems to me that the question of 11:28 differs from the ones which introduce the episodes of 12:13–34; it is not even introduced by a meta-phrase characterizing it as a question (although what the enemies "say" is introduced by an interrogative). The concluding phrase in 12:34 ("did not dare to ask any more questions") rather makes those episodes form a unit which takes place after the enemies have left in 12:12.

On the other hand, the issue introduced by the enemies in 11:28 concerns a "this", namely the cleansing of the Temple with the ensuing teaching. But, as Mark constructs his story, this episode can hardly be lifted out of the framing episodes concerning the cursing of the fig tree and the teaching deduced from it; the readers of Mark should recognize this "sandwich technique" and realize that the framing episodes should be seen together with the episode in the center so that they shed light on each other (cf. 3:20–35; 5:21–43; 6:7–30; 15:53–72). That is, as to the story-line, the cleansing and the debate with the enemies, including the parable, stand on the same level. The framing fig tree event is tightly bound to the cleansing episode, although this is clear only to the readers outside the story, not to the enemies within it.

The fact that the issue of a new temple appears at the trial (14:58) reinforces the importance of the teaching of God's house as a house of prayer for all nations. From the readers' point of view it deals with the new conditions which Jesus establishes for the worship of God and how valid this newness is, i.e., which authority Jesus had to establish them. Above, the observations of audience and actors suggested that the episodes after the enemies' leaving the stage, i.e. 12:13–44 (+ chapter 13) form a parenthesis in the plot. So the question presents itself if or how these episodes are related to the preceding block with its center in the teaching on the Temple. This will be considered in what follows.

## 3. A New Proposal

The following episodes are grouped in a three plus three composition of teaching episodes, out of which the three first are introduced by questions[25]. The reader is instructed to regard them precisely as teaching episodes by the high amount of words belonging to the semantic field of teaching (see vv. 14, 19, 32, 35, 38, 43).

With regard to the preceding discussion of markers as to actors etc. it seems that Cook's outline could be revised and that the following one does better justice to the textual markers. With the following discussion in view it has been indicated for every episode which is the topic as appearing in crucial statements by Jesus.

> 11:12–12:12 teaching on new cultic conditions and ensuing debate
> > 11:12–25 on the Temple + framing episodes
> > > 11:12–14 framing episode 1 (fig tree)
> > > 11:15–19 on the Temple; cleansing + teaching (house of prayer)
> > > 11:20–25 framing episode 2; teaching (prayer)
> > 11:27–12:12 on authority behind 11:15–19
> > > 11:27–33 debate on authority
> > > 12:1–12 parable (sending of son; cornerstone)
> 12:13–44 teaching episodes
> > 12:13–34 three teaching episodes begun by questions
> > > 12:13–17 (give to God what is God's)
> > > 12:18–27 (God's power in resurrection; God of the living)
> > > 12:28–34 (love to God and neighbor more than sacrifices)
> > 12:35–44 three teaching pronouncements
> > > 12:35–37 (the Anointed at God's right hand)
> > > 12:38–40 (scribes' ostentation)
> > > 12:41–44 (giving one's whole life to God)

This way of finding a structure suggests that 11:12–12:12 be read as one unit, followed by the teaching episodes in 12:13–44. Now a few details of the first part evidently return in the second one, e.g. the topic of the Temple service and the mentioning of the sacrifices in 12:33. This fact suggests that one considers the possibility that the first part of the composition may shed some light on the six teaching episodes and vice versa.

It is furthermore evident that the first part has two foci, both saying essential things on the Christian existence of the readers, namely the new conditions for man's worship of God and the authority of the one who established those conditions, the latter not being so much a matter of dogmatics as rather something that has to do with the ultimate warrant of their Christian identity. This

---

[25] The Markan passion story is full of similar groups of three: three denials, praying three times in Gethsemane in the presence of three disciples, raise a new temple after three days, phases of three hours at Jesus' execution and death, resurrection after three days.

fact invites us to take this double perspective into account when we consider the mutual relationships between the contents of the two parts. Let it be said immediately, however, that where Christological interpretations are suggested in the following, in most cases they should be regarded as being very tentative – note the many instances of expressions like "might","maybe", etc. With regard to the scope of this article, the treatment of the first five teaching episodes will be rather superficial, whereas more attention will be paid to the story of the widow as read in this context.

Trying such a reading, we can immediately note that the theme of Jesus' authority, raised in 11:27–12:12, is taken up in the teaching pronouncement 12:35–37[26]: the theme of the son, sent by the Lord, killed by those to whom he was sent, and exalted by Him to the position of a cornerstone is further illuminated by the obscure pronouncement on the Anointed at God's right hand. In this case, it seems rather obvious that the interpreter has everything to gain by letting the two passages shed light on each other. The theme concerns both Jesus' resurrection/elevation and his position as the living Lord of the Christian believers.

Are there maybe similar Christological aspects of the cluster of episodes of the basic conflict in 11:27–12:12 that return and are even developed in the following teaching episodes? It seems to me that this is possibly so in the episode on the question of the Pharisees and the Herodians. A crucial feature of the parable was of course the killing of the beloved son of the owner. Now, the episode of the question concerning taxes to Caesar is presented with a mortal shadow hovering over what is told: the readers recognize the questioners from Mark 3:6 – the only other instance where this combination of characters appears in Mark; there they hold counsel how to destroy Jesus; now they are sent by the high priests etc. with the explicit purpose to entrap Jesus. In the parable, the son fulfilled the task of his father and was killed – here one's duty is to give to God what belongs to Him. But what does not belong to Him? "The earth is the Lord's and the fullness thereof, the world and those who dwell therein" (Ps 24:1). Jesus fulfils his Father's will (14:36) through giving his life in service for all (Mark 8:31–33; 10:45; 14:24)[27]. While this reading may be possible, it does not, of course, eliminate the fact that apparently Jesus' answer has a natural relevance to the recipients' situation. It seems that there were ample possibilities for seri-

---

[26] Very often commentators range this episode among those which are constituted by introducing questions. But a reader in Antiquity may rather have heard the question,"How can the scribes,." etc. as representing a kind of rhetorical question to be compared with a not uncommon way of introducing problematic issues among philosophers, e.g.,"How can it be said that the earth is in the middle, and in the middle of what? For the All is infinite and the infinite has neither beginning nor limit…" (Plutarch, *On the Face of the Moon* 925 F); also Philo, *De Decalogo* 101: "How can it be said that the world was created by God in six days, God who does not need any time for his work…?"

[27] Thus ROBERT H. GUNDRY, *Mark. A Commentary on His Apology for the Cross*, Grand Rapids, Mich. 1993, 694.

ous tensions between loyalty to God and what Caesar demanded; at least 13:9–13 suggests such a situation.

Similarly also the answer to the Sadducees might be read in this double perspective. As to what the episode has to say to the readers' situation, there is no need here to develop how they are reminded of the resurrection they expect. But maybe it also could be read as a Christological development of a feature in the parable on the vineyard, namely in its concluding quotation of Ps 118: to speak of the killed son as being elevated by the Lord to a cornerstone, naturally implies some ideas on something beyond death. So this teaching episode develops the idea: the son was elevated through "God's power" (12:24) and those who deny resurrection "are quite wrong" (v. 27).

## 4. The Great Commandment and True Worship

A similar double reading may be possible in the case of the episode on the great commandment. The audience is, except for the scribe, only the disciples. Again, it need not be argued that as the text stands in Mark, the teaching addresses the expected Christian behavior of the readers. But it can also be seen in the light of such a saying of Jesus as "the Son of man has come, not to be served but to serve and to give his life as a ransom for many" (10:45). Certainly there is nothing in Mark that characterizes Jesus' work as led by or driven by his love to God (as in John), but on the other hand there is the nuance of his total engagement, his giving up himself unto death to the Father's will for the good of men (8:31–33; 10:45; 14:24, 36).

These tentative readings of the four first teaching episodes have thus considered whether they not only deal with some fundamentals of Christian existence but also have Christological aspects. We have now seen how the teaching episodes expound some features of the authority of him who launched these new conditions in word and action; in the case of 12:35–37, this was obviously so, in the others it remained a possibility. The Christological motifs which were found can actually be regarded as representing early Christological teaching as it encounters e.g. in Phil 2:7–9, on Christ who humbled himself, obedient unto death, was exalted and given the name over every name.

Above, I argued that the way Mark combines the episodes of 11:12–12:12 justifies that we interpret them as dealing with new conditions for the worship of God. Actually also the topic of these new conditions returns in the teaching episodes, notably such as where the disciples are the audience. So the worship topic is explicitly brought up in the discussion on the great commandment, in that the scribe repeats Jesus' answer and expands on it: love for God and neighbor "is much more than all whole burnt offerings and sacrifices" (12:33). To the disciples – the Christian readers, this intimates that fulfilling the commandments of love for God and neighbor surpasses the Jewish sacrificial system. The fact that the central Jesus-saying in his teaching on the Temple stressed that it should be a house of prayer, which was emphasized by the interpretation of the withered fig-tree, should lead to the conclusion that this surpassing of the sacrificial cult by love had to go hand in hand with a life of prayer in faith (11:22–25).

I would suggest that also the story on the widow's offering can be read in the light of this wider context. The reader-response approach I have chosen means that there is no reason to bring in any considerations of what the Temple treasury was like, which were the Temple courts, where were they situated, what were the offerings for, etc. But in the world of Mark's Gentile-Christian readers there were plenty of temples around, and it was normal that people gave money to these temples. The gifts could be such in general, or a payment for an offering or a sum instead of a certain offering. Consider, for example, the following inscription:

"Those who shall offer a firstling pay to the treasury 1200 for an ox, for a sheep or a goat 300, and for a skin 60." (Inscriptiones antiquae orae septentrionalis (IosPEI) (2) 75, 11–15 (4th–3rd cent., Olbia)

Most important, however: these different gifts of money, as well as other gifts, were ultimately gifts to the god to whom the temple was dedicated. So, in our case, it must have been evident to Mark's readers that it was to God Himself that the widow offered up "her whole living". Reading the episode in the context of the preceding teaching, the readers can again notice that the teaching also this time is given privately to the disciples – they, as well as the readers, enjoy the privilege to be taught what was the real meaning of the episode. It should not have appeared too farfetched to assume that the widow's offering of "her whole living" to God was a radical example of how to love God "with all your heart, and with all your soul, and with all your mind, and with all your strength"[28]. It was of a higher value than any sacrifice.

One may even go a step further. As the texts are now arranged, the teaching because of the withered fig-tree (11:20–24) explains basic features of the new worship conditions; they comprise prayer, but also faith or trust. So the widow's attitude can also be regarded as an expression of a deep trust in God[29]. Also in this respect she illustrated a fundamental feature of the new conditions for the service of God.

Lastly one may ask whether the episode of the widow may be read in a Christological perspective. The answer may be "yes", in so far, namely, as the lines on the great commandment are also read in such a Christological perspective: then

---

[28] As a matter of fact, regarding the widow of 12:41–44 as an example of the attitude demanded in 12:28–34 is represented by some modern commentators: thus PESCH, *op. cit.*, (note 2), 263f.; he regards the ὅλος of vv. 30, 33 and 44 as connecting keywords; also WALTER GRUNDMANN, *Das Evangelium nach Markus* (ThHK 2), Berlin ³1965, 258; EDUARD SCHWEIZER, *Das Evangelium nach Markus* (NTD 1), Göttingen 1967, 248; JOACHIM GNILKA, *Das Evangelium nach Markus* (EKK II:2), Zürich – Einsiedeln – Köln • Neukirchen-Vluyn 1979, 177; JOSEF ERNST, *Das Evangelium nach Markus* (RNT), Regensburg 1981, 365.

[29] Also this thought is represented in some modern commentaries: GRUNDMANN, *op. cit.*, 258; ECKEY, *op. cit.*, (note 5), 325.

giving one's "whole living" was Christ's attitude, not least as proclaimed and described in the second half of Mark's gospel (8:31–33; 10:45; 14:24, 36)[30].

There only remains one teaching pronouncement of the context to be considered, namely the warning against the attitude of the scribes, 12:38–40. The lines can be read as giving an example of how to love oneself more than one's neighbor, and so also as a contrast to the widow's behavior[31]. But regarded in the context of the preceding teaching episodes this contrast may also include the nuance that the behavior of the scribes demonstrated a non-fulfillment of the commandments of love; so also their prayer is empty (v. 40)–cf. the teaching on prayer because of the withered fig-tree.

So these pages have hinted at the possibility of regarding the structure of the composition of Mark 11:12–12:44 in such a way that to its readers its contents dealt with basic conditions of Christian life, including who was the authority behind. This context of the story of the offering of the widow seems to support a reading of the episode as illustrating the same fundamental idea as St. Ephraem formulated in his pronouncement, quoted at the outset of this article: "Blessed is he who always has God in mind, for he will be like a heavenly angel, performing his ministry to God on earth."

---

[30] Actually this reminds of how ELIAN CUVILLIER interprets the story: *L'évangile de Marc*, Paris • Genève 2002, 258, citing LOUIS SIMON, "Le sou de la veuve", in: *Études théologiques et religieuses* 44 (1969) 115–126.

[31] Thus also, e.g., GNILKA, *op. cit.*, (note 28), 175; PESCH, *op. cit.*, (note 2), 263; JOHN R. DONAHUE/DANIEL J. HARRINGTON, *The Gospel of Mark* (Sacra Pagina 2), Collegeville, Minn. 2002, 365.

# 11. Mark 16:1–8: the Ending of a Biography-like Narrative and of a Gospel

## 1. The Problematic Endings of Mark

There is no doubt among today's New Testament exegetes that the Gospel of Mark ends with verse 16:8, or, to put it otherwise, that Mark 16:9–20 is secondary. The same holds true of the other, shorter ending which is found in some manuscripts between vv. 8 and 9. There are exegetes who assume that originally Mark has continued his story after v. 8, but they also admit that this ending is lost for ever.[1] Nevertheless perhaps most Christians unconsciously 'improve' Mark's way of finishing his gospel by adding in their minds the contents of a few selected passages from the other gospels. That is, they behave very much in a way that reminds of how Mark 16:9–20 is composed, in that there the contents of several episodes from Matthew, Luke, John, and Acts are echoed.[2]

This reaction of modern as well as of ancient readers of Mark has probably to do with a feeling that one should not end a narrative in this way. Certainly the presence of, so to speak, a proper ending in the other gospels may inspire such a feeling, but already Mark's text as it stands invites the reader to imagine a continuation – we will soon come back to this.

On the following pages I will first briefly present the difficulties raised by the fact that 16:1–8 forms the finale of a narrative covering a person's career, so containing many features of a biography. Then, in the main part of my paper, I will discuss how 16:1–8 may be taken to be not so much the ending of a biography-like narrative as rather a part of a literary whole which functions as a gospel in the life of the Early Church.

The difficulties caused by Mark 16:1–8 when regarded as the ending of a more or less biographical narrative are well known. As mentioned above, a few commentators even believe that these difficulties are so great that they assume that after 16:8 the evangelist has continued his story, although this continuation is lost. The most conspicuous among these difficulties are the following: is it not strange that people who have received an instruction from heaven do not obey it, and particularly so in the very culmination of the plot of the book? Furthermore, there are the words of Jesus to the disciples on their way to Gethsemane that he

---

[1] E.g. Robert H. Gundry, *Mark. A Commentary on His Apology for the Cross,* Grand Rapids, Mich. 1993, 1009–1012.

[2] For a list of passages see, e.g., Francis J. Moloney, *The Gospel of Mark. A Commentary,* Peabody, Mich. 2002, 357.

will go before them to Galilee (14:28; cf. 16:7): do they not call for a narrative that describes a meeting there? And, finally, the finishing words of 16:8, 'for they were frightened', are exceptionally clumsy as an ending of a book.

Given this situation, the ending of the Gospel of Mark has led to rather lively discussions and to many suggestions from the side of the interpreters, not only assuming that v. 8 was once followed by a more 'satisfactory' ending, but also proposing that the evangelist has revised an earlier version of 16:1–8 and so purposely has given it its present odd shape, not to speak of those who firmly believe that 16:1–8 form the original ending of the gospel.[3]

As a matter of fact it has not been possible to reach any decently ascertained results in the discussions mentioned. Not even the choppy ending, 'for they were frightened', is so convincing a sign that there is something wrong with the text.[4] Thus, once an interpreter of Mark wants to do something more than try to explain how the strange ending of the gospel has come into existence, he/she is left with the text as it stands, that is, finishing with 16:8. Even so, however, one may distinguish, as I do on these pages, between, on the one hand, considering 16:1–8 as above all belonging to a biography-like narrative, and, on the other, as forming a part of a gospel.

Such a distinction calls for some further clarification, because it means taking a particular stand concerning what a gospel is. We will turn to this issue in a moment, but first it may be instructive to note that even when Mark 16:9–20 has been added to 16:8, the result is actually not a smoothly running narrative flow. Thus the statements in vv. 7f. on meeting Jesus in Galilee and on the women's silence are not easily harmonized with vv. 9–20 which mention the appearance to Mary Magdalene and her telling 'those with him', as well as several meetings with Jesus, although none in Galilee.

The situation is not better, when in some manuscripts the so-called shorter ending is inserted between vv. 8 and 9:

(they said nothing to no-one, for they were frightened.) And they reported briefly to those with Peter everything that they had been told. And after this, Jesus himself sent out through them, from east and to west, the holy and imperishable proclamation of the eternal salvation. Amen. (And when he had risen etc., v. 9.)

Actually there is one manuscript with an ending that has eliminated most of the tensions mentioned, namely the Old Latin Codex Bobiensis. It contains only the shorter ending and omits the phrase 'and they said nothing to no-one', thus eliminating the clash between 'they said nothing' and 'they reported'.

---

[3] See, e.g., GUNDRY, *Mark* (note 1), 1009–1021; MOLONEY, *Mark* (note 2), 340f.; RICHARD THOMAS FRANCE, *The Gospel of Mark. A Commentary on the Greek Text* (NIGTC), Grand Rapids, Mich. • Carlisle 2002, 670–676. PAUL L. DANOVE, *The End of Mark's Story: A Methodological Study*, Leiden 1993, is a thorough literary-critical investigation of the passage, based on the text as it stands.

[4] See the survey in PAUL L. DANOVE, *Linguistics and Exegesis in the Gospel of Mark. Application of Case Frame Analysis and Lexicon* (JSTNSS 218), Sheffield 2001, 70f.

Thus, we can note that in this case it seems that the scribal tradition represented in Mark 16:1–20 has rather calmly accepted that the Gospel of Mark reports on the events after the detection of the empty tomb in a narrative flow that is far from smooth. That is, if one has wanted an evenly running narrative on the last phase of a Jesus biography, this has not radically influenced how the secondary endings were written.[5] This may be due to the circumstance that, not very long after the publication of Mark, the other gospels presented more easy-going narratives in this respect. So Mark was allowed to remain a bit odd. It is not impossible that this tolerance has something to do with the function of the gospels as precisely gospels.

So we are brought to the topic what a gospel is. For some time there has been a tendency to refer the gospels to the literary genre of the *bios* (plural *bioi*), i.e. the particular kind of biography which in Antiquity treated famous persons, often philosophical teachers.[6]

When recent commentators discuss the question to which extent the gospels are comparable to the *bioi*, they often express some reserve towards assuming a very close relationship between the two. Thus, e.g., R. T. France states that Mark's book 'represents something distinctive within the field of biographical writing in terms of its subject, its origin, and the use for which it was intended.'[7] He rightly underlines that Mark is 'inspired by the conviction that Jesus of Nazareth was more than just a great man and that he remains alive as the worthy object of devotion' (p. 11). As to the 'use', Frances mentions the opinion that Mark was 'an oral text read aloud probably in meetings of the local church' (p. 9).

In the opinion of the present writer these modifications of the *bios* hypothesis can be carried a few steps further.[8] A literary genre is namely not only characterized by its type of contents, including the organization of these contents, and by its socio-linguistic function. Very often one should also consider the circumstance that texts which are shaped according to the literary conventions of a given genre also make use of a certain style, including a typical phraseology. In the case of Mark it is thus evident that its idiom is not only inspired by the Greek

---

[5] Cf. how the vast majority of the manuscript tradition (the Byzantine text) corrects Mark's original text in 1:2, which says 'Isaiah the prophet'; these manuscripts say 'prophets' instead. I.e., here one has not hesitated to eliminate an odd statement.

[6] See RICHARD A. BURRIDGE, *What are the Gospels? Comparison with Græco-Roman Biography* (MSSNTS 70), Cambridge 1992; CHRISTOPHER BRYAN, *Preface to Mark. Notes on the Gospel in its Literary and Cultural Settings*, New York – Oxford 1993, 32–64; DETLEV DORMEYER, *Das Markusevangelium als Idealbiographie von Jesus Christus, dem Nazarener* (Stuttgarter Bibl. Beiträge 43), Stuttgart 1999; EVE-MARIE BECKER, *Das Markusevangelium im Rahmen antiker Historiographie* (WUNT 194), Tübingen 2006; cf. LARS HARTMAN, "Das Markusevangelium, ‚für die lectio solemnis im Gottesdienst abgefasst'?", in: HUBERT CANCIK/HERMANN LICHTENBERGER/PETER SCHÄFER (eds.), *Geschichte – Tradition – Reflexion*, FS M. Hengel III, Tübingen 1996, 147–171. [See now TOMAS HÄGG, *The Art of Biography in Antiquity*, Cambridge 2012.]

[7] FRANCE, *Mark* (note 3), 6. Similarly, e.g., CAMILLE FOCANT, *L'évangile selon Marc* (Commentaire biblique, NT 2), Paris 2004, 30.

[8] I have discussed the issue more in detail in HARTMAN, "Das Markusevangelium…" (note 6).

Old Testament, but also, and above all, that it reflects the evangelist's intention to write a text that sounds biblical. This intention was certainly matched by the actual use of his gospel. There are reasons to believe that already the traditions Mark took over and used in his narrative were dressed in such biblical clothing and played a role in Christian worship. Thus Colossians 3:16 deals with the worship of the addresses of the epistle, and the line on the indwelling of the word of Christ may very well reflect such a usage of gospel traditions, or – depending on the dating of the letter – of gospel texts.[9]

If this view on the socio-linguistic function of Mark's gospel is right, it has consequences for the way in which the text was received by its readers/listeners.[10] In the eyes – or rather ears – of the worshipers the reading of a passage from Mark belonged to the same category of texts as the readings from the books that later on were called the Old Testament. On the one hand, the gospel was about a man who lived only a generation ago, but, on the other, what was narrated about him belonged to the same atmosphere as the stories about Adam and Eve, Abraham, the manna feeding in the desert, about Elijah, etc. This has probably meant that normally the readers/listeners did not consciously and exactly ask themselves to which extent the things told were 'real' or literally 'true'. What mattered was not, e. g., whether Elijah had actually gone to heaven in a fiery chariot or not, but rather that God cared for his faithful servants and vindicated them in this or that way. Thus, Mark's readers/listeners might very well have received the text on the angel's message to the women in the same vein as when hearing about Enoch's being taken away (Gen 5:24) or about Elijah's assumption (2 Kings 2:11f., 16–18). But being Gentile Christians, their cultural heritage also contained stories from the sphere of religion telling about the exaltation to heaven of heroes like Hercules or of Caesar Augustus. In all these texts they heard of a character who passes from this world into an existence comparable to that of gods, semi-gods or other supra-mundane beings, and this exaltation meant a divine confirmation of how they had represented God/the gods in their lives and expressed a conviction that for ever they belonged to the divine dimension of the world.

Now, it is a basic feature of any worship that there a fusion takes place of past and present, of divine actions in the past and of the present situation of the worshipers. In the case of the readings this means that the contents of the text are made topical to the listeners. Typical is the sentence which the head of the family also in our time is to utter at the Jewish Passover meal at which the story of the Exodus is read: 'This the Lord made for me when I came out of Egypt' (cf. Exod 13:8).

---

[9] Of course we have next to no material on which to base any assumptions as to which passages were read at which occasions and in which sequence. This lack of evidence casts a regrettable shadow over the interesting suggestions by MICHAEL D. GOULDER, e.g. in *The Evangelists' Calendar. A Lectionary Explanation of the Development of Scripture*, London 1978.

[10] In the following I will often use the noun 'readers' in this sense of 'readers/listeners'.

These generic features are important when, as already in the headline of these pages, a distinction is made between a biography-like narrative and a gospel. The text of Mark was not read out as an informative or instructive story, perhaps with exemplary contents, at a gathering of, say, a philosophical school – which was a typical use of a *bios*. The listeners' encounter with the gospel had a more fundamentally existential bearing on their lives.

## 2. The Function of Mark 16:1–8 as a Gospel Ending

Now to an essay at assessing the function of Mark 16:1–8 as the ending of precisely a gospel.[11] A suitable point of departure is that we remind ourselves of the fact that Mark's first audience did not, so to speak, have to wait until they heard Mark's gospel in order to know of Jesus' resurrection. Even if the women kept silent, the gospel of the living Jesus had spread via other media. So the gospel of Mark is presented to an already Christ-believing church. We may very well describe their situation with the early Christian tradition that Paul quotes in Romans 1:4: the addressees already knew

the gospel of his [God's] Son, who regarding the flesh was from the seed of David and who at his resurrection from the dead was installed as God's Son in power regarding the spirit of his holiness.

In what follows I will first consider a few texts in which Jesus somehow refers to circumstances beyond the narrative world, particularly such as reveal that Mark functions as a gospel in the life of a church. Then I will discuss how the ending of Mark is to be connected to preceding passages in the gospel, so functioning as part of a gospel.

Thus, there are a couple of passages of Mark's text in which the narrative world opens out to the world in which the narrative is told; that is, to use the simile of a drama performed on a stage: for a moment Jesus speaks on the stage of something outside the drama, referring to something that rather has to do with the world of the spectators in the theatre. Such is the case in Mark 14:9, where Jesus comments on the action of the woman who anointed him at Bethany: she was to be remembered wherever the gospel was preached. The saying refers to a situation beyond the narrative world in which the scene of Mark 14:3–9 is enacted. So the narrator makes Jesus take for granted not only that a proclamation will take place after the publication of Mark but also, and not least so, that such a proclamation has already been going on for some time between the end of Mark's drama and the situation in the Early Church in which Mark's gospel was read out.

---

[11] To a certain extent the following exegetical discussions pick up and elaborate on things I have written in the second volume of my commentary on Mark, LARS HARTMAN, *Markusevangeliet 8:27–16:20* (KNT 2b), Stockholm 2005. [English trans. *Mark for the Nations. A Text- and Reader-Oriented Commentary*, Eugene, Oreg. 2010.]

This insight makes less dramatic the bewilderment of the reader who looks in vain for a missionary commission in Mark 16. Mark apparently did not think that it was necessary to anchor the preaching of the gospel in a mandate of the risen Lord. His gospel treats the earthly career of a grown up man ending with his execution and burial. That this life also has divine dimensions is indicated in different ways, but these dimensions are apparent to the reader of Mark rather than to people on the stage. So Mark does refer to a commissioning by Jesus of the apostles but places it at the beginning of Jesus' earthly ministry, combining it with their calling. Thus the disciples were called to become 'fishers of men' (1:15) and to be 'sent out to preach' (3:14). That they have taken on this task is obviously presupposed in the readers' situation, but Mark does not feel a need to tell his readers how that came about. It does not seem to be an intrinsic element of Mark's gospel on God's Son (1:1).

We come across something similar in Jesus' order to the three disciples who caught a glimpse of his glory on the mountain: they were not to tell anyone about what they had seen 'until the Son of Man has risen from the dead' (Mark 9:9). To the readers it was clear that sometime that time of silence had come to an end, but to Mark it seems that it was enough to indicate the indirect order – or permission! – to tell about his glory only after his resurrection – *and* death! (9:12). I.e., another case of a statement concerning something outside of the stage and presupposing that the gospel of the risen Lord had been proclaimed to the world long before Mark published the message of the angel in 16:6.

There is a further text in which Mark has Jesus refer to a situation beyond the gospel narrative, namely the parable of the son who was sent to his father's vineyard and was killed by the tenants (Mark 12:1–12). The parable is presented as an indirect answer to the question in Mark 11:28 of Jesus' adversaries with which authority he did 'these things', namely cleansing the Temple and 'teaching' that God's house should be 'a house of prayer for all the nations', whereas his adversaries had made it a den of robbers (11:17). That is, Jesus had proclaimed in word and deed that he was to establish new conditions for men's worship of God. The parable, and, above all, the reference to Psalm 118:22f. at the end explain which was this authority: Jesus was God's 'beloved son' and although he was killed ('the builders rejected' him), God made – was to make – him 'a corner-stone' 'marvelous in our eyes'.

Obviously God's making the rejected stone a corner-stone refers to Jesus' vindication, either one thinks of it as his resurrection, as an exaltation to the Father's right hand or, as one may dare to express it, as dying himself to God. We notice the double time perspective: on the level of the biography-like narrative – on the stage of the drama, as it were – this vindication belongs to the future and remains to be performed, but in the cultic situation of the readers when listening to the gospel, they become the 'we' in whose eyes Jesus is the marvelous corner-stone. That is so because he has performed his task to be rejected by the builders. So on the one hand, the text is on christology, answering a question for Jesus' authority, but on the other, the authority is one to establish new conditions for men's worship of God, that is for those concentrated occasions at which man relates his whole existence to God, turning to him and being met by him. This takes place in prayer, listening, offering, receiving, action, passivity.[12] To readers of this sort the seemingly abrupt ending of Mark's gospel should not be too disturbing, because whatever the angel's message meant, they had heard about the same reality in other texts of the gospel, partly under other wordings, using other imagery, including that of being a corner-stone.[13] The message just confirmed what they knew already.

When Mark 16:1–8 functions as a part of the gospel of God's Son, it does so not least in that the readers naturally connect it with earlier passages of Mark's text. We now turn to some pericopes belonging to this category.

## 3. Earlier Passages in Mark

Obviously Jesus' threefold predictions of his passion, death, and resurrection (8:31; 9;31; 10:34) do not 'land' until the angel has delivered his message in Mark 16:6. It informs the readers that all the elements of the predictions have now come true. Nevertheless there is a difference. The passion and death are carefully narrated. But the resurrection is told of only in a message which explains why the tomb is empty and as a point of departure of the order to tell the disciples to go to Galilee – an order that is not obeyed within Mark's narrative. But, as already claimed, Jesus' predictions of his resurrection probably did not tell the readers anything new of their Lord, and together with 16:1–8 they just meant a confirmation of the gospel they already knew of (cf. 1 Cor 15).

One may wonder why in Mark's narrative no one reacts to the resurrection element of the passion predictions, but, as it seems,[14] only to the idea of suffering. Nor is any astonishment expressed when, on the way to Gethsemane, Jesus tells his disciples that after his resurrection he will go before them to Galilee (Mark 14:28). So it is only in 9:9–13 that anyone is bewildered when Jesus mentions his resurrection, but, although the text is not totally transparent, it seems that the problem is not so much the resurrection as rather its chronology (must not Elijah appear before?) and Jesus' conviction that passion and death must precede it.

Modern Christian readers of Mark may have some preconceived ideas on what resurrection stands for. To the first generation of Christian readers this may not have been so. Thus to them the three predictions of the resurrection were not simply verified by Mark 16:1–8, but their content should have been

---

[12] Cf. MICHAEL SCHMAUS, "Worship", in: KARL RAHNER (ed.), *Encyclopedia of Theology. A Concise Sacramentum Mundi*, London 1977, 1838–1841.

[13] I do not here enter upon the possibility that the corner-stone imagery implies that the living Christ can be compared to a new Temple; see, e.g., MOLONEY, *Mark* (note 2), 234; FOCANT, *Marc* (note 7), 440; MORNA D. HOOKER, *The Gospel according to St. Mark* (BNTC), London: Black 1991, 277.

[14] Possibly 9:32 is an exception.

decisively colored by what Mark's Jesus has taught in the debate with the Sadducees according to Mark 12:18–27.[15] There his argument for the belief that the dead are raised (12:26f.) goes in two steps: first a quotation from Exodus 3:6: 'I am the God of Abraham, the God of Isaac, and the God of Jacob,' then a sentence: 'He is not God of the dead but of the living.' The quotation and the sentence support each other and shed light on each other: The quotation relates the three patriarchs to God: he was their God who gave them his promises and made covenants with them. The relationship to God concerned the whole person of the patriarch in question, including this person's history and its dark and bright sides.

When the quotation is coupled with the sentence, the consequence is that, although certainly everyone of the patriarchs has died, God has not firstly been the God of Abraham, then the God of Isaac, etc. Instead each of them was constituted as a whole human being by his relationship to God. In the sentence it is claimed that this relationship did not come to an end with the person's death, because God is God of the living. Beyond death the relationship remains and still constitutes the human being, so that it can be said that the person is alive, although he has died.

This kind of answer seems to assume that humans are spiritual beings in the sense that they are more than something merely physical. They have a spiritual dimension in that they, as persons, are related to God: he is engaged in them and they relate themselves to him. If death means anything, it is rather a gate into a deeper relationship. The fundamental presupposition under this way of thinking is a belief in God's power (v. 24).

This 'spiritual' aspect of human relationship to God returns when Jesus refutes the opinion that 'when they rise from the dead' physical or biological conditions prevail. Instead 'they are like angels' (Mark 12:25). That is, in the only Markan text in which after-life is really discussed, the rather concrete, almost biological resurrection language is replaced by a more 'spiritual' one.[16]

To the readers the debate with the Sadducees may have demonstrated Jesus' supremacy as a teacher. But more important is probably that here they encounter Jesus' view on what may lie under the words on resurrection in his three predictions of his passion. As he meant that according to God's will he was to suffer and to be killed, so the same powerful will was to carry him farther than to the cross. The fact that in this way the concept of resurrection has been elucidated by using a wholly different language may be a reminder to readers of later times to whom the resurrection language has largely lost its metaphorical function.

---

[15] The following interpretation of the phrase 'the God of Abraham' etc. goes a little further than is usually found in the commentaries. It is found in my Mark commentary, mentioned above, note 11.

[16] FRANÇOIS VOUGA, "Controverse sur la résurrection des morts", in: *Lumière et Vie*, n° 179, vol. 35 (1986) 48–61, stresses the different mode of thinking in this pericope as compared to that which is presupposed by the resurrection imagery and suggests a traditio-historical explanation of the difference.

Mark's readers come across still another imagery of the Beyond in the two passages that refer to the sitting of the Anointed and of the Son of Man on the right side of God (Mark 12:36; 14:62). Mark 16:1–8 should be read also in the light of these two passages. Actually they can be said to express the same conviction about Jesus as is represented by the statements of his resurrection. The same idea is of course expressed in the above quoted Rom 1:4, on Christ being 'installed in glory as the Son of God by his resurrection from the dead'. Firstly, it should be emphasized that the picture of God on his throne in Dan 7:13 and Psalm 110 is precisely a picture. The same holds true of the scene of Phil 2:5–11, when it is described how God has exalted him who died in obedience on the cross and has given him the name above all names. The right side from which the exalted Christ wields a divine power is not a throne hall in a sphere of a certain nebula but everywhere and always where God holds sway.

However, the early Christians as well as their Jewish neighbors, from whose Scriptures the imagery was taken, were strict monotheists. The risen Jesus was not a second, minor god beside the main one. Instead the picture of the Son of Man on the right hand of the Power becomes a way of maintaining that God's creative, life-giving and saving will took shape in Jesus' human life and death in a free and dedicated trust in God. Through God's power the life of this man passed into one in God's dimension.[17] Regarded from the human side, the conviction that in Jesus' life and death God's will and essence took shape has for ever determined their image of God and his will. That is, when the first Christian readers of Mark heard of the angel's message, it could invite them to a reaction like this: 'yes, we know: "Jesus is Lord"' (Phil 2:11; Rom 10:9; 1 Cor 12:3).

We have already touched upon the story of the Transfiguration, Mark 9:2–8. How hard several elements therein may be to understand, nonetheless it contains a couple of features which suggest that we put that story and the ending of the gospel alongside of each other.[18] Thus, one first detail to notice is that the disciples are not allowed to tell anyone of what they 'have seen' until after Jesus' resurrection (9:9). The context emphasizes that this resurrection must be preceded by the passion and violent death of the Son of Man (8:31; 9:12).

But what have these disciples 'seen'? The more a reader thinks of Mark in terms of a biography-like narrative, the more he/she may tend to assume that the vision is an anticipation of either an appearance of the risen Jesus or of the coming of the Son of Man in glory. But in so far as the text functions as a gospel to the readers, the disciples 'see' and hear what is a present reality to the readers.

---

[17] See WALTER KASPER, *Jesus the Christ,* London • New York 1976, 139f.; HERBERT VORGRIMMLER, "Auferstehung (Auferweckung) Jesu Christi", in: *Neues Theologisches Wörterbuch,* Freiburg i. Br. 2000, 72–75.

[18] Although some of the accents in the following discussion stem from the present writer, much of the basic exegetical material is more or less common good. See, e. g., MOLONEY, *Mark* (note 2), 178–182; FRANCE, *Mark* (note 3), 346–360; FOCANT, *Marc* (note 7), 332–343; JOHN R. DONAHUE/DANIEL J. HARRINGTON, *The Gospel of Mark* (Sacra Pagina 2), Collegeville, Minn. 2002, 267–275.

They listen to 'the gospel of Jesus, the Anointed One, the Son of God' (Mark 1:1) and Mark is impressing on them that this divine son-ship was enacted in Jesus' earthly career, and so the narrative on this career begins with a text that puts that which follows under the key-signature that is formed by the proclamation of his son-ship at his baptism by John (1:11). But a necessary element of this enactment was his passion and death; this is emphasized by the statement of the officer which interprets Jesus' death: 'Verily this man was the Son of God' (15:39). On the one hand, in the context of the Transfiguration episode it is an important theme that God wants the Son of Man to suffer and be killed, which will lead to his resurrection (8:31; 9:1). On the other, this suffering Son of Man is also the one of whom and of whose words his followers should not be ashamed, in order that he will not be ashamed of them when appearing in his Father's glory (8:38). In the vision the three disciples learn that the one who shall be killed and be raised according to God's will is God's Son. (Actually this is the first time in Mark's narrative that the disciples get to know this secret.[19]) In addition, they shall 'listen to him', i.e., not least to his words on the necessity of suffering, both such of the Son and such of his followers.

So, when the first passion prediction is followed by the narrative on the vision on the mountain the readers find themselves in a situation that is typical of worship: there past, present and future are fused. The past is Jesus' passion and death, which are topical for them, now, as putting them into a new covenant relationship to God (14:24), but that death also means a passing into an existence in God's dimension, as the elevated Son in glory. So Jesus is their Lord, now (Phil 2:11 etc.). Therefore, on the level of the narrative, this glory of the Son could not be proclaimed until his task as the suffering Son of God had been fulfilled. Before Jesus had died himself to the Father, the fishers of men had no full gospel to preach. But when the text functions as a gospel in the worship of the church, the before and after of the features of the biography-like narrative become less important. So, that Jesus was raised and that he was glorified/elevated refer to the same conviction concerning Jesus. That conviction can also be expressed using the son-image; we encountered it in the tradition cited in Romans 1:4: 'installed as God's Son in power'. But the cultic present also has a future perspective: the Son of Man in his Father's glory (8:38) is the vindicated Son who demands their loyalty and who in the future – or in a beyond – is going to hold them responsible for how faithful they have been.

Mark's gospel is presented as a text through which somehow the recipients encounter the gospel of the Son of God. This Son of God is their Lord in the present, and when the texts from the gospel are read out at their worship, the work and proclamation of this Son something like a generation ago are made topical. That the last scene of the gospel narrative reports of a divine message that this Son is risen becomes less a final episode of his biography than a con-

---

[19] The outbursts of the demons in 3:11; 5:7 are no valid testimonies.

firmation that in his work he was God's Son, that is, God's representative, and, above all, that he is the Son of God also in the present of the readers.

Thus, as read as confirming to the readers that Jesus was alive as God's powerful Son, the Lord of the Christians, the last episode of Mark's gospel becomes the last of a series of passages of the gospel which express the meaning and goal of Jesus death, using the language of resurrection. But in Mark's gospel that meaning and the secret of Jesus' person and work are also expressed by other images, not least the one of his being God's Son. Read as a part of a gospel of 'Jesus, the Anointed, the Son of God' (1:1) these last verses become an important pointer to the readers that Mark's whole text is a gospel to them in their present situation. The Son of God to whom they turned (1:15) when becoming Christians, exercised his power to forgive sins when they were baptized (2:10), he is the one in whom they believe (1:15; 2:5; 5:34, 36 etc.), he is with them with divine power when chaos threatens them (4:38–42; 6:47–52); his power gives life, physically and spiritually (5:21–43; 6:33–44; 8:1–9), and they belong to the 'many' whom he served and for whom he gave up his life as a ransom (10:45) and who have been taken up into the covenant with God he mediated (14:43). But he is also the one to follow in a life inspired by his ethical teaching (9:30–10:31) and colored by his preliminary inauguration of the divine kingship (1:15f.; 4:1–34), a kingship to whose final realization they direct their lives in vigilant prayer (13:33–37).

## 12. „Was soll ich tun, damit ich das ewige Leben erbe?"
Ein heidenchristlicher Leser vor einigen
ethischen Sätzen des Markusevangeliums

### 1. Das Markusevangelium für Heidenchristen

Die Überschrift mit ihrem Zitat aus Mk 10,17 deutet an, wie der folgende Beitrag die Thematik „Eschatologie und Ethik im frühen Christentum" aufgreifen will. Die Frage des Zitates ist eine ethische Frage, und der hinzugefügte Finalsatz bezieht die Ethik auf die Eschatologie, indem das eschatologische Ziel des Fragenden den Ausgangspunkt der Frage darstellt und damit zugleich voraussetzt, dass dies den Inhalt der Antwort bestimmen wird. Der Untertitel der Überschrift gibt zudem an, dass wir uns hier dem Markusevangelium im Hinblick auf die Perspektive seiner Leser [bzw. Hörer] nähern.[1]

Diese Eingrenzungen haben zur Folge, dass wir die Fragen von Eschatologie und Ethik in der Verkündigung Jesu beiseite lassen,[2] ebenso wie auch traditions- und redaktionskritische Erwägungen, die die behandelten Mk-Texte aus einem derartigen Blickwinkel beleuchten könnten.

Den Scheinwerfer auf die Ethik des Markusevangeliums zu richten, ist gewiss nichts Neues,[3] auch nicht, die eschatologischen Akzente dabei herauszuarbeiten.[4] Ein neuer Beitrag zum Thema würde keine Lücke füllen. Doch es könnte vielleicht der Mühe wert sein, einige Nuancen dieser markinischen Ethik im Hinblick auf die Voraussetzung zu beleuchten, dass die ersten Adressaten des Textes Heidenchristen waren, und dass ein solcher Hintergrund sehr wahrscheinlich auch ihr Verständnis der ethischen Aussagen prägte.

Gewiss bewegt man sich mit einer Studie dieser Art auf unsicherem Boden. Zwar gilt die Annahme, dass das Markusevangelium für Heidenchristen ge-

---

[1] [Siehe in diesem Band seite 118 Anm. 10.]

[2] AMOS N. WILDER, *Eschatology and Ethics in the Teaching of Jesus*, rev. ed., New York 1950, bes. 133ff.; JACK T. SANDERS, *Ethics in the New Testament. Change and Development*, London 1975, 1–29; HELMUT MERKLEIN, *Die Gottesherrschaft als Handlungsprinzip. Untersuchung zur Ethik Jesu*, Würzburg ²1981a, 37–42; WOLFGANG SCHRAGE, *Ethik des Neuen Testaments* (NTD.E 4), Göttingen 1982, 33–40; RUDOLF SCHNACKENBURG, *Die sittliche Botschaft des Neuen Testaments* I–II, Völlige Neubearb. (HThK.S 1–2), Freiburg i. Br. – Basel – Wien 1986–1988, I, 31–67, 176–187.

[3] Vgl. SANDERS. *Ethics* (s. oben Anm. 2), 31–36; SCHRAGE, *Ethik* (s. oben Anm. 2), 131–136; SCHNACKENBURG, *Botschaft* II (s. oben Anm. 2), 110–122.

[4] DAN OTTO VIA, *The Ethics of Mark's Gospel – In the Middle of Time*, Philadelphia, Penn. 1985, der auch eine strukturalistisch-narrative Annäherungsweise mit „phenomenological hermeneutics" vereint.

schrieben worden ist, kaum als kontrovers.⁵ Aber wie sieht der ideologische Resonanzboden aus, der ihre Auffassung von den ethischen und eschatologischen Aussagen des Evangeliums zum Klingen bringt?

Wahrscheinlich ist seitens der Leser eine gewisse Kenntnis des christlichen Glaubens vorauszusetzen, einschließlich einigen Wissens über das sogenannte Alte Testament, so dass der Evangelist gezielt z. B. auf den Propheten Jesaja (1,1) hinweisen oder Jesus von der Erfüllung der Schrift (14,49) sprechen lassen konnte.⁶ Weiterhin lässt sich annehmen, dass sie als Christen ihre vorchristliche Lage etwa in der Weise des Epheser-Verfassers charakterisiert hätten: „Einst wart ihr Finsternis, jetzt aber seid ihr durch den Herrn Licht geworden" (Eph. 5,8). Aber wie sah diese „Finsternis" aus, wenn man die Frage nach einem Resonanzboden stellt?

Das Bild von der Moral der Heiden in Röm. 1,18–32 ist traditionell polemisch⁷ und sollte kaum als eine sachliche Beschreibung allgemeiner Moral in der Antike aufgefasst werden. A. D. Nock formuliert es so: „It is in any case a grave error to think of the ordinary man in the Roman Empire as a depraved and cruel fiend, dividing his time between the brothel and intoxication, torturing a slave from time to time when he felt bored and indifferent to the suffering and poverty of others."⁸

Für die begrenzte Aufgabe dieses Beitrags brauchen wir nicht zu versuchen, die Konturen einer Vulgärethik der Kaiserzeit nachzuzeichnen.⁹ Stattdessen genügt es, auf die Studien A. Diehles über dieses schwer zu handhabende Problem hinzuweisen.¹⁰ Er erinnert an die mehr oder weniger unreflektiert übernommene sittliche Praxis von Jedermann, die von den prinzipiellen ethischen Diskussionen der Philosophen und der Philosophenschulen zu unterscheiden ist. Nichtsdestoweniger fand während der Kaiserzeit auf dem Gebiet der Ethik eine gewisse wechselseitige Angleichung der philosophischen Richtungen statt. Auch die Differenzen zwischen Vulgärethik und Philosophie waren durchaus nicht so groß.¹¹ So konnten z. B. die Stoiker die Auffassung vertreten, dass die Menschen aufgrund ihrer Natur zu sittlich korrektem Handeln in der Lage sei-

---

[5] Z.B. Joachim Gnilka, *Das Evangelium nach Markus* (EKK II/1-2), Zürich – Einsiedeln – Köln • Neukirchen-Vluyn 1978–1979, I. 34; Camille Focant, *L'évangile selon Marc* (Commentaire biblique, N. T. 2), Paris 2004, 37. Vgl. Cilliers Breytenbach, *Nachfolge und Zukunftserwartung nach Markus. Eine methodenkritische Studie* (AThANT 71), Zürich 1984, 328.

[6] Vgl. John R. Donahue/Daniel J. Harrington, *The Gospel of Mark* (Sacra pagina 2), Collegeville, Minn. 2002, 35; Focant, *Marc* (s. Anm. 5), 17f.

[7] Ulrich Wilckens, *Der Brief an die Römer* (EKK VI/1), Zürich – Einsiedeln – Köln • Neukirchen-Vluyn 1978, 95–115.

[8] Arthur Darby Nock, *Conversion. The Old and New in Religion from Alexander the Great to Augustine of Hippo*, Oxford 1933, 218.

[9] Albrecht Dihle, „Ethik", in: *RAC* 6 (1966) 646–696: 666.

[10] Albrecht Dihle, „Ethik" (s. Anm. 9), und idem, *Die goldene Regel. Eine Einführung in die Geschichte der antiken und frühchristlichen Vulgärethik* (SAW 7), Göttingen 1962.

[11] Dihle, „Ethik" (s. Anm. 9), 670f.

en, auch wenn ihre δόξα philosopischer Qualität entbehrten.[12] Deshalb wird im Folgenden in einigen Fällen auch besonders auf Epiktet hingewiesen, dessen Aussagen vermutlich mehr als nur einen philosophischen Standpunkt widerspiegeln.

Oben ist schon ein paar Mal das Wort „eschatologisch" verwendet worden. Der Begriff und seine Ableitungen werden bisweilen jedoch mehrdeutig gebraucht;[13] im Folgenden soll deshalb vorzugsweise von „der Herrschaft Gottes" die Rede sein. Auch dieser Ausdruck ist nicht völlig eindeutig, hat aber den Vorteil, dass er ein wesentliches Element aus der Begriffswelt des Markusevangeliums selbst darstellt.

## 2. Die Anwendung des Basileia-Begriffs

So ist es am Platz, in aller Kürze die Anwendung des Basileia-Begriffes im Markusevangelium in den Blick zu nehmen.[14] Er taucht etwa im Zusammenhang von Mk 10,17 auf, wo jedoch die Wendung „das ewige Leben erben" zunächst noch den Ausdruck „in die Herrschaft Gottes kommen" (V. 23.24.25) ersetzt. Am Ende des Gespräches über die Schwierigkeit eines Reichen, in das Reich Gottes zu kommen, kehrt der Terminus „ewiges Leben" dann wieder, nun in Gestalt einer Verheißung an die Nachfolger Jesu und mit Bezug auf die kommende Welt (V. 30). Für die Leser scheinen also hier die beiden Begriffe weithin synonym gebraucht worden zu sein.

In der Perikope vom Reichen (Mk 10,17–31) ist die Herrschaft Gottes offenbar etwas Zukünftiges, worauf sich die Hoffnung des Menschen ausrichten kann – ebenso in 9,1.47; 14,25 und 15,43. Am Anfang des Markus-Berichtes wird diese Herrschaft indessen schon als eine zeitlich und / oder räumlich nahe programmatisch ausgerufen (1,15), wobei ihre Nähe eng mit Person und Werk Jesu verbunden ist. Ihre Nähe wird ebenso in den siegreichen Auseinandersetzungen Jesu mit den Mächten des Bösen sichtbar (3,14 usw.), wenngleich sich das zunächst nur vom Glauben erfassen lässt.

Die Nähe der Gottesherrschaft erweist ihre ethischen Implikationen darin, dass ihre Verkündigung mit einem Ruf zur Umkehr verknüpft ist – einer Umkehr, die sich u.a. in der Nachfolge Jesu realisiert (1,15.20; 8,34; 10,21). So gewinnt die Ethik der Nachfolge im Zeichen der Gottesherrschaft Bedeutung für die Gegenwart: Ein Beispiel dafür ist das, was von dem Reichen in 10,21

---

[12] DIHLE, *Regel* (s. Anm. 10), 94.
[13] S. z.B. GERHARD SAUTER, *Einführung in die Eschatologie. Die Theologie. Einführungen in Gegenstand, Methoden ...*, Darmstadt 1995b, 1–26; VICKY BALABANSKI, *Eschatology in the making. Mark, Matthew and the Didache* (MSSNTS 97), Cambridge 1997, 1–23.
[14] ALOJZIJ M. AMBROŽIČ, *St. Mark's Concept of the Kingdom of God. A Redaction Critical Study of the References to the Kingdom of God in the Second Gospel* (Diss. Würzburg), Würzburg 1970; WERNER H. KELBER, *The Kingdom in Mark. A New Place and a New Time*, Philadelphia, Penn. 1974; HEINRICH BAARLINK, *Die Eschatologie der synoptischen Evangelien* (BWANT VI.20), Stuttgart 1986.

gefordert wird; ebenso auch 9,47 (vom verführenden Auge), 10,14 (von einer Haltung wie der eines Kindes) oder 12,34 (von den Liebesgeboten).

Dabei haftet dem Basileia-Begriff jedoch insofern eine gewisse Mehrdeutigkeit an, als er sowohl für einen Bereich (9,47; 10,15.23–25; 12,34) als auch für etwas, das man annimmt (10,15; vgl. 4,11; 15,43) gebraucht werden kann. Da es aber Jesus ist, der die Gottesherrschaft repräsentiert, lassen sich diese Wendungen auch im Sinne einer Akzeptanz seiner Botschaft verstehen.[15]

So kann man zusammenfassend sagen, dass im Markusevangelium die Gottesherrschaft als etwas Nahegekommenes, von Jesus Ausgerufenes und erst teilweise Verwirklichtes erscheint; als solche hat sie ethische Implikationen für diejenigen, die sie annehmen. Zugleich ist sie etwas Zukünftiges, noch nicht Verwirklichtes, worauf sich die Hoffnung ausrichten kann. Dabei bleibt die Gottesherrschaft auch in der Spannung zwischen Anbruch und Verwirklichung eine einzige, ungeteilte Größe.

### 3. Die Leser/Hörer und die Gottesherrschaftsethik

Nun aber zu den Lesern/[Hörern][16] und ihren Begegnung mit der Gottesherrschaftsethik: Der Gedanke an ein göttliches Herrschen über die Welt war den heidenchristlichen Lesern [bzw. Hörern] des Markus sicher schon aus ihrer vorchristlichen Zeit bekannt. So bestand z.B. – nach Hippolytus – zwischen Chrysippus und Zenon Einigkeit darüber, dass „Gott die ἀρχή von allem sei sowie der reinste Körper, und dass seine πρόνοια alles durchdringe."[17] Bei Plutarch kann man lesen: „Der Kosmos hat einen höchsten Herrscher (ἄρχοντα) und Vorsteher (ἡγεμόνα) über alles, einen Gott mit Sinn und Vernunft (νοῦν καὶ λόγον)."[18] So zu denken war mit großer Wahrscheinlichkeit weit über den Kreis der Philosophen hinaus verbreitet.

Für einen Konvertiten zum Christentum hingegen bedeutete es vermutlich etwas Neues zu erfahren, dass sich der Gott der Basileia-Verkündigung näher für die Moral der Menschen interessiere. E. Schwartz nämlich hat sicher recht mit der Meinung, dass in der Antike „die Ethik neben der Religion als etwas Selbständiges" dastand.[19] Wenn die Adressaten des Markusevangeliums von einem Jesus hörten, der die Nähe der Gottesherrschaft ausrief, war dies jedoch nicht neutral oder nüchtern philosophisch aufzufassen, wie z.B. bei Plutarch: „Es gibt einen einzigen König und Herrscher, Gott, der die Macht über Anfang, Mitte und Ende von Allem hat ... ihn begleitet das Recht (Δίκη), das die das göttliche Gesetz nicht Erfüllenden bestraft, und gemäß dem wir alle von Na-

---

[15] MERKLEIN, *Handlungsprinzip* (s. Anm. 2), 128.
[16] [Siehe in diesem Band seite 118 Anm. 10.]
[17] Chrysippus, *Fragmenta logica* 1029.
[18] *De def. orac.* 425F–426A.
[19] EDUARD SCHWARTZ, *Ethik der Griechen*, hrsg. von W. Richter, Stuttgart 1951, 13. Siehe auch DIHLE, „Ethik" (s. Anm. 9), 672.

tur aus gegenüber allen Menschen handeln."[20] Vielleicht wird der Unterschied zwischen dem markinischen Jesus und Plutarch am besten daran ersichtlich, dass die Botschaft Jesu unmittelbar mit einem Ruf zu Umkehr und Glauben verbunden ist. Sie konfrontiert die Menschen mit einer göttlichen Herrschaft, die keine statische, sondern vielmehr eine virulent aktuelle, sie in ihren Anbruch einbeziehende sein will.

Ein Heidenchrist im Leserkreis des Markus konnte eine solche Umkehr mit dem Schritt eines Adepten etwa des Epictet vergleichen und dabei an so etwas wie den freien Entschluss (*proairesis*) denken – d.h den freien Entschluss, mit dem ein Mensch seine Lebensgestaltung bestimmt. Als Beispiel sei der folgende Dialog angeführt: „Das wirklich Gute ist ein Entschluss einer Art, das wirklich Böse einer anderen Art. – Was ist denn das Äußere? – Es ist Material (ὕλαι) des Entschlusses, um welches es sich dreht, wenn er das eigene Gute oder Böse erreicht. – Wie erreicht man das Gute? – Wenn du nicht das Material bewunderst. Denn wenn du richtig vom Material denkst, macht dies deinen Entschluss gut, aber wenn du verkehrt und falsch denkst, wird der Entschluss böse. Dieses Gesetz hat Gott festgestellt und sagt: Wenn du etwas Gutes wünschst, nimm es von dir selbst. Du sagst: Nein, von einem Anderen. – Nein, von dir selbst."[21]

Doch wenn auch verschiedene Züge einer Konversion im Sinne Epiktets dem Begriff der Umkehr im Sinne des Markus ähneln mögen, so sind doch die Unterschiede gravierend – abgesehen davon, dass der sittliche Hintergrund der Markus-Leser wahrscheinlich weit mehr von einer Vulgärethik als von stoischer Ethik geprägt gewesen sein dürfte. Der wichtigste Unterschied aber besteht natürlich darin, dass für den Markus-Christen Gott, von dessen Basileia Mk 1,15 usw. handelt, der Gott Israels und der Vater Jesu Christi (1,11; 9,7; 14,36) ist. Zu ihm hin umzukehren aber bedeutet etwas anderes als einen Entschluss über den Wert oder Unwert der Dinge bzw. eine richtige Unterscheidung zwischen dem, worüber man verfügen kann und worüber nicht.

In der Markuserzählung wird dieser Schritt – Umkehr und Glaube – narrativ so gestaltet, dass der Bericht über die Berufung der ersten vier Jünger in die Nachfolge unmittelbar auf die programmatische Proklamation der nahen Gottesherrschaft durch Jesus folgt.

Auch Epiktet weiß von einer Nachfolge-Ethik. Er stellt z. B. die Frage: „Wie kann ich in Allem den Göttern folgen (ἑποίμην)? Wie kann ich dem göttlichen Walten (διοικήσει) behagen (εὐαρεστοίην)?"[22] Ein Teil seiner Antwort empfiehlt, „alles so zu wollen, wie es geschieht."[23]

Nachfolge bedeutete *in concreto* neben der Lern- auch eine Lebensgemeinschaft mit dem Lehrer – was den Lesern wohlbekannt sein sollte. So konnte, z.B. Seneca sagen: „Kleanthes hätte nicht ein Abbild von Zenon sein können,

---

[20] *De exilio* 601B; ein Zitat aus Plato, *Leg.* 715 E–716 A.
[21] Epiktet, *Diss.* 1:29.1–4.
[22] Von einer Nachfolge von Gott, bzw. den Göttern s. auch *Diss.* I.12.5; I.20.15.
[23] *Diss.* I.12,8–16.

wenn er nur seine Vorlesungen gehört hätte. Er teilte sein Leben, sah seine Beweggründe (*secreta perspexit*) und beobachtete ihn, um zu sehen, ob er gemäß seinen eigenen Regeln lebte."[24]

Die ethischen Konsequenzen der Nachfolge werden besonders im zweiten Teil des Evangeliums sichtbar – etwa da, wo sich an die erste Leidensankündigung der Nachfolgespruch 8,34 anschließt und den Nachfolger mit Kreuztragen, Selbstverneinung und Lebensgefahr konfrontiert (8,31–38).

Wiederum könnte man an die Belehrungen eines Epiktet denken, welche die Gleichgültigkeit des wahren Stoikers angesichts solcher Bedrohungen herausstellten: „Verbannung, Gefängnis, Tod, Schande, was lehrst du davon? – Ich halte sie für gleichgültig" (ἀδιάφορα, d.h. sie sind der sittlichen Entscheidung des Philosophen entzogen).[25] Eine solche Lebensweise kann auch als eine Nachfolge Gottes bezeichnet werden. In der Fortsetzung des angeführten Textes heißt es nämlich: „Was ist das höchste Ziel? – Dir (meinem Gott) zu folgen."[26]

Die von Epiktet vertretene Haltung war sicherlich nicht die der gewöhnlichen Leute. Aber sie kann uns vielleicht helfen, das besondere Profil des Markus schärfer zu erkennen. Im Markusevangelium stehen alle Leiden und Widrigkeiten im Zusammenhang der Nachfolge Jesu, der Kreuz und Auferstehung entgegengeht. Sowohl Jesu Leiden als auch das der Nachfolger wird im Markusevangelium in einer spannungsvollen Weise dargestellt. Einerseits erscheint es im Sinne allgemein menschlichen Verhaltens als das, was um jeden Preis zu vermeiden ist (8,32 – der Protest des Petrus; 14,50 – die Flucht der Jünger), andererseits steht es unter einem göttlichen „Muss" (8,31; vgl. 14,21; 13,7–23). Jesu Leiden wird dabei vorzugsweise als ein Dienst und als Hingabe für andere (10,45; 14,24) betrachtet und unterliegt demselben „Muss". Aber die Pflicht eines Lebens für andere ist auch Bestandteil der Nachfolge (9,35; 10,43f.). So gilt das Leiden schließlich nur als Durchgang auf dem Weg zur Auferstehung (8,31; 9,31; 10,34) und Rettung (13,13. 20.24–27; vgl. 8,38).

Das „Muss" des Nachfolgeleidens ist wohl kaum als festes Element einer Nachfolge-*Ethik* zu betrachten. Es ist aber an einer solchen Ethik orientiert, die immerhin impliziert, sich als Jünger und später als Christ Jesu und seiner Worte bzw. des Evangeliums nicht zu schämen (8,38). D.h., für die Leser bedeutet Nachfolge / Christsein, sich nicht dessen zu schämen, was Jesus nach dem Markusevangelium gelehrt hat, einschließlich seiner ethischen Aussagen.

Dabei ist für unser Thema von Belang: Das genannte Sich-Nicht-Schämen hat zur Folge, dass auch der in der Hoheit seines Vaters kommende Menschensohn sich dieser seiner Nachfolger nicht schämen wird (8,38), wenn die Gottesherrschaft in Macht kommt (9,1). Hier könnte man dezidiert von einem „eschatologischen" Ausblick sprechen und damit die Art und Weise bezeichnen, in der ein Leben im Zeichen der aktuellen Gottesherrschaft von der zukünftigen

---

[24] *Epist. Lucil.* 6.6.
[25] *Diss.* I.30. S. auch z.B. I.24; I.29.6.
[26] S. auch das oben Angeführte, *Diss.* I.12.8ff.

Gottesherrschaft her motiviert wird.²⁷ Das illustriert auch der Text von dem Reichen: Alles den Armen zu geben und Jesus zu folgen ist ein von Jesus als dem Repräsentanten der Gottesherrschaft im Zeichen ihrer Nähe gefordertes Handeln mit Blick auf das ewige Leben des Fragenden, bzw. auf sein „Eingehen" in die zukünftige Gottesherrschaft.

Will man bei Epiktet von einer eschatologischen Verantwortung sprechen, so ist doch die Stimmungslage eine andere: „Wenn hierunter der Tod mich nimmt, ist es mir genug, dass ich, die Hände zu Gott hebend, ihm sage: die Möglichkeiten, dein Walten zu erkennen und ihm zu folgen habe ich wahrgenommen. Ich habe dich meinerseits nicht entehrt. Siehe, wie ich die Wahrnehmungen (αἰσθήσεσιν), wie ich die Allgemeinvorstellungen (προλήψεσιν) gebraucht habe. Habe ich dich getadelt? ... Ich danke dir für das, was du mir gegeben hast. So lange ich das Deinige benutzt habe, war es mir genug. Nun, nimm es zurück ... ".²⁸

Die Nachfolge Jesus, der gekommen war, um zu dienen, implizierte den Dienst an den Mitmenschen und die gegenseitige Unterordnung als Prinzip. Ein solches Prinzip aber kann nicht in Gestalt einer objektivierenden oder formalisierten Ethik umschrieben werden.²⁹ Angemessener lässt es sich in Gestalt einer Sentenz, die eine zu erstrebende Haltung andeutet, ausdrücken. Aber was ist das für eine Haltung! Vergleichen wir nur was Epiktet in seiner Diatribe über die Freundschaft als allgemeine Einsicht formuliert: „Jedes lebendige Wesen (ζῷον) neigt zu nichts anderem als zu dem, was ihm förderlich ist".³⁰ Umgekehrt drückt Paulus in Röm. 5,7 eine nicht weniger allgemeingültige Haltung aus: Es ist vorstellbar, dass jemand sich für den Guten oder Gerechten hingibt. Zu einer edlen Moral gehörte es nämlich von jeher, „bereit zu sein, für die Freiheit der Stadt zu sterben oder um seinen Eltern und Kindern und Brüdern und der übrigen Familie zu helfen, oder in einem Kampf für Freunde".³¹ Ferner wird dann und wann behauptet, dass es für die Menschen natürlich sei – für die stoischen Philosophen im eigentlichen Sinn des Wortes! – einander zu helfen,³² und es kann geschehen, dass man einen guten König – im Unterschied zum Tyrannen – lobt, weil er „sich abmüht, damit nichts den Untertanen mühselig sei, und er

---

²⁷ CILLIERS BREYTENBACH, *Nachfolge* (s. Anm. 5), 279.
²⁸ *Diss.* IV.10.14.
²⁹ DIHLE, *Regel* (s. Anm. 10), 73.
³⁰ *Diss.* II.22.15.
³¹ Philostratus, *Vit. Apoll.* 7.12. Für andere Beispiele von hellenistischen Freundschaft-Konventionen s. OTTO MICHEL, *Der Brief an die Römer* (KEK 4), Göttingen ¹²1957, 134. Zu φιλία s. SCHWARTZ, *Ethik* (s. Anm. 19), 190f.
³² Siehe Epiktet, *Diss.* III.13.5; Marcus Aurelius 5.16.3 usw. — siehe JÜRGEN KABIERSCH, *Untersuchungen zum Begriff der Philanthropia bei dem Kaiser Julian* (KPS 31), Wiesbaden 1960, 32f.; MAXIMILIAN FORSCHNER, *Die stoische Ethik. Über den Zusammenhang von Natur-, Sprach- und Moralphilosophie im altstoischen System*, Stuttgart 1981, 148f.

setzt sich Gefahren aus, damit sie ohne Furcht leben ...".[33] Bisweilen wird auch gesagt, dass ein idealer Herrscher dieselbe Philanthropie wie Gott üben sollte.[34]

Obwohl also das Gebot des Dienstes für andere nicht ohne Analogien in der Kultur eines markinischen Heidenchristen gewesen sein mag, kann man sich doch vorstellen, wie schroff ihm das (auch ohne eine Ahnung des Nietzschewortes von der „Sklavenmoral") erscheinen musste.

Nun wird im Markusevangelium die Nachfolge als ein Dienen zwar nicht ausdrücklich unter dem Thema der Gottesherrschaft und noch weniger durch explizite Hinweise auf zukünftiges Geschehen dargestellt. Doch der Kontext deutet etwas derartiges an. So findet sich etwa in 10,42f. der Bericht vom Wunsch der Zebedaiden, „in der Herrlichkeit" Jesu die Ehrenplätze neben ihm einnehmen zu dürfen. Sie werden mit der Auskunft beschieden, dass diese Plätze nur „denjenigen zuteil werden, für die es bestimmt ist" (V. 40). Das lässt sich als eine Andeutung der Umkehrung endzeitlicher Erwartungen verstehen, gleich jener Reversion in 10,31 (die Ersten – die Letzten).[35]

Auch die Forderung, alles für die Nachfolge zu verlassen, widerspricht üblichen ethischen Standards. Das Beispiel des Kynikers Diogenes, der seinen Besitz der Polis schenkte, um danach völlig eigentumslos und frei zu leben, dürfte gerade wegen seiner Bizarrerie populär gewesen sein. In einem unter Krates' Namen geschriebenen Brief an die Reichen schreibt der Verfasser: „Wir leben in vollem Frieden, denn Diogenes von Sinope hat uns von allem Übel befreit, und obschon wir nichts besitzen, besitzen wir alles".[36]

Die Komposition von 10,17–31 zeigt, dass die Leser im Prinzip die Worte vom Aufgeben des Besitzes (10,17–22), von der Gefahr des Reichtums (10,23–27) und vom dies- und jenseitigen Lohn (10,28–31) als einen ethischen Unterricht für die Christen im Allgemeinen auffassen konnten – auch wenn sich darin die Lebensverhältnisse urkirchlicher Wandermissionare besonders deutlich widerspiegeln.[37] Die Deutung des Gleichnisses vom Sämann stellt den Lesern dieselbe Gefahr vor: Die Sorgen der Welt und der trügerische Reichtum ersticken allzu leicht die Möglichkeiten der Gottesherrschaft, unter den Menschen Gestalt zu gewinnen (4,19).

So ist für die Leser des Markusevangeliums das Verhalten des Christen zu Besitz und Reichtum im Blick auf die Gottesherrschaft zu betrachten. Bedeutete für die Kyniker das Aufgeben des Besitzes die Freiheit zu individueller Selbstverwirklichung,[38] sodann brachte für die Christen die Nachfolge im Zei-

---

[33] Synesius, *De regno* 6.
[34] KABIERSCH, *Philanthropia* (s. Anm. 32), 9.
[35] BREYTENBACH, *Nachfolge* (s. Anm 5), 276.
[36] *The Epistles of Crates* 7, in: *The Cynic Epistles*. A Study Edition, hrsg. von ABRAHAM J. MALHERBE (SBLSBS 12), Missoula, Mont. 1977, 58. Schon die Tatsache, dass dieser „Brief" aus der Zeit des Prinzipats herrührt, ist ein Zeichen dafür, dass dieses kynische Ideal auch zu dieser Zeit bekannt war.
[37] MERKLEIN, *Handlungsprinzip* (s. Anm. 2), 221.
[38] Vgl. KABIERSCH, *Philanthropia* (s. Anm. 32), 195.

chen der – auch für sie! – nahen Gottesherrschaft vor allem eine Freiheit, die einen solideren Lebensgrund als den materieller Güter bedeutete. Bedenkt man diesen Resonanzboden wahr, dann hört man in der Versicherung von V. 27 auch etwas von der Gegenwart anklingen: „Was bei den Menschen unmöglich ist, ist bei Gott möglich." – Die göttliche Macht, die das Unmögliche ermöglicht, war für die Christen nicht nur etwas, auf das sie sozusagen an der Pforte zum Gottesreich hoffen konnten, sondern sie war vielmehr etwas Aktuelles und in ihrer Gegenwart Wirksames, das doch zugleich auch auf die zukünftige Gottesherrschaft bzw. auf das ewige Leben Bezug nahm.[39]

Mit Recht behauptet z.B. Schrage, dass die ganze Zusammenstellung von ethischen Aussagen in Mk 10,1–31 unter dem Vorzeichen der Nachfolge zu verstehen sei.[40] Zudem ist die Komposition von der Verkündigung der Herrschaft Gottes geprägt;[41] der Begriff kommt ja auch mehrmals auf der Text-Oberfläche vor (V. 14f. 23–25; s. auch 9,47).

## 4. Das Ehescheidungsverbot

In dem Text vom Ehescheidungsverbot (10,2–12), dem wir uns jetzt zuwenden, wird hingegend nicht ausdrücklich vom Reich Gottes gesprochen. Wie konnte dann aus der Sicht des Lesers die vom Kontext her naheliegende Basileia-Perspektive das Verstehen dieses Textes prägen? Das konnte z. B. im Lichte der Antwort Jesu auf die die Sadduzäer-Frage (12,18–27) geschehen: Im zukünftigen Reich, „wenn sie von den Toten auferstehen, [werden] sie weder heiraten noch geheiratet werden". Inwiefern könnte dann das Ehescheidungsverbot für das gegenwärtige Leben im Zeichen der Gottesherrschaft eine Gottesherrschaftsethik darstellen?[42]

Das Gebot wird in Gottes Schöpferwillen verankert. Wenn die Verwirklichung es Gotteswillens als ein Aspekt der Gottesherrschaft betrachtet wird, dann kann dieses Gebot auch mit den Worten an den Reichen verglichen werden. D.h., es geht hier nicht einfach um ein juridisches Gebot, sondern um Strukturen im gegenwärtigen Alltagsleben, die von der teilweise schon gegenwärtigen Gottesherrschaft inspiriert oder getragen werden. Um es mit Dan O. Via auszudrücken: „the permanence of marriage presupposes an ongoing history which is eschatologically revitalized."[43]

Um diese Gedankenlinie weiter zu verfolgen, stellen wir uns die Frage, wie einige Motive des Textes in den Ohren der Markus-Christen geklungen ha-

---

[39] Vgl. SCHRAGE, *Ethik* (s. Anm. 2), 38.
[40] SCHRAGE, *Ethik* (s. Anm. 2), 133f. Siehe auch SCHNACKENBURG, *Botschaft* (s. Anm. 2) II, 119.
[41] Z.B. SCHNACKENBURG, *Botschaft* (s. Anm. 2) I, 150–152, II, 119–121; DETLEV DORMEYER, *Das Markusevangelium als Idealbiographie von Jesus Christus dem Nazarener* (SBB 43), Stuttgart 1999, 233, 247.
[42] Vgl. SCHRAGE, *Ethik* (s. Anm. 2), 93, wo die Gebote bezüglich der Ehe als eschatologisch dargestellt werden.
[43] VIA, *Ethics* (s. Anm. 4), 105.

ben mögen. Ehescheidung galt in ihrer Welt als etwas ganz Normales.[44] Auch dass die Ehe im göttlichen Willen begründet liegt, war für sie nichts Neues. So schreibt z.B. Hierokles: „Was schmückt ein Haus besser als die Zusammengehörigkeit zwischen Mann und Frau?, ... Vom Schicksal sind sie miteinander vereint worden, sie sind von den Göttern der Fortpflanzung, des Herdes und der Ehe geheiligt worden. Sie stehen mit einander im Einklang und tun alles gemeinsam, sowohl körperlich als, und eben vielmehr, auch seelisch."[45]

Hierokles betont die Einheit und die Gemeinschaft der Gatten. Wenn die Deutung des markinischen Jesus eben diese Einheit (dass sie „ein Fleisch" sind) hervorhebt, soll dies – von dem darin anklingenden Hebraismus einmal abgesehen – auch den Heidenchristen als ein bekanntes Motiv erschienen sein. Denn es war in der Umwelt weit verbreitet, von der Einheit und der Gemeinschaft von Mann und Frau in der Ehe zu sprechen.[46] Dass sie ferner „zusammengejocht" seien (vgl. συνέζευξεν, 10,10), lässt geläufige Terminologie anklingen.[47]

Das Hierokles-Zitat sowie die eben genannten geprägten Wendungen spiegeln eine ideale Welt wieder.[48] Wenn Musonius z. B. behauptete, ein Mann sollte sich so strikt zu seiner Frau halten, dass er nicht einmal seiner Sklavin beischläft, wird das von Oepke nüchtern kommentiert: „Er steht in der Antike einzigartig da."[49] Ebenso deutet eine Grabinschrift wie die folgende darauf hin, dass Ehescheidungen an der Tagesordnung waren: „Heutzutage sind so lange Ehen selten, die vom Tod abgeschlossen und nicht von Ehescheidung aufgelöst werden. Denn 41 Jahre dauerte ohne Misshelligkeiten unsere Ehe."[50]

Vor einem derartigen Hintergrund konnte das Gebot Jesu als ein Ruf zum vollen Engagement für den anderen/die andere, bzw. in dem/der anderen aufgefasst werden. So gesehen rückt das Ehescheidungsverbot in die Nähe jenes

---

[44] Siehe z.B. HORST BLANCK, *Einführung in das Privatleben der Griechen und Römer* (Die Altertumswissenschaft. Einführungen ...), Darmstadt 1976, 108f., 122–124.

[45] Zur Redeweise „der Gott/die Göttin/die Götter der Ehe", siehe z.B. Dio Cassius, *Hist.* 79.13.1; Menander Rhetor, Περὶ ἐπιδεικτικῶν, Spengel III 399 und 404; Musonius, *Diss.* 14; Plutarch, *Fragm.* 157, Z. 89.

[46] Siehe HENRY GEORGE LIDDELL/ROBERT SCOTT/HENRY STUART JONES, *A Greek-English Lexicon*, Oxford ⁹1940, und JAMES HOPE MOULTON/GEORGE MILLIGAN, *The Vocabulary of the New Testament Illustrated from the Papyri and Other Non-Literary Sources*, Grand Rapids, Mich. (1930) 1985, s.v. κοινωνία. Ferner, z.B., Plutarch, *Conj. praec.* 140A; Proclus, *In Plat. Tim.* II.14; Hierocles apud Stob., *Anth.* 4.28.17; BGU 1052, 1099; POxy 12.1473; PBabatha 18; [Musonius, *Diss.* 13A und B].

[47] Z.B. Menander, Περὶ ἐπιδεικτικῶν, Spengel III 405; Stobaeus, *Anth.* 2.7.3a; Libanius, *Epist.* 120.1; IG, Attica, II. 12595; MAMA 7.366; IG, Italien, XIV. 607.

[48] Vgl. die Klage von Columella, dass zu seiner Zeit das harmonische Familienleben der alten Tage verschwunden war (*Rust.* 12, praef. 7–8). Vgl. LILIAN PORTEFAIX, *Sisters Rejoice. Paul's Letter to the Philippians and Luke-Acts as Received by First-Century Philippian Women* (CB.NT 20), Stockholm 1988, 15f. [Vgl. DAVID HELLHOLM, „Die Gattung Haustafel im Kolosser- und Epheserbrief" in: PETER MÜLLER (Hrsg.) *Kolosser-Studien* (BThSt 103), Neukirchen-Vluyn 2009, 103–128: 112–114.]

[49] ALBRECHT OEPKE, „Ehe", in: *RAC* 4 (1959) 650–666: 654.

[50] ILS 8393, 27f.

Gebotes, Knecht des anderen zu sein. Von da aus ist es nur ein kurzer Schritt zu Jesu Antwort auf die Frage nach dem wichtigsten Gebot. Für die Leser aber öffnet sich damit auch explizit die Perspektive auf die Gottesherrschaft – hatte doch ihr Herr gelehrt, dass jener Schriftgelehrte, der seine Zusammenstellung von den Geboten der Gottes- und der Nächstenliebe akzeptierte, nicht weit von der Gottesherrschaft entfernt sei (12,34).[51]

## 5. Das Doppelgebot der Liebe

Damit wenden wir uns dieser Belehrung über das Doppelgebot der Liebe zu Gott und dem Nächsten zu (Mk 12,28–34).[52] Angesichts der Einleitung („der Herr, unser Gott ist ein einziger.") empfanden unsere heidenchristlichen Leser natürlich sofort Zustimmung – sie waren ja über die Wahrheit besser informiert als ihre Zeitgenossen, auch wenn die Philosophen häufig von Gott in Singular zu sprechen pflegten. Aber dieser monotheistische Glaube konnte den Christen – wie schon den Juden – in einer Weise teuer zu stehen kommen, die für die Philosophen ausgeschlossen blieb. D.h., diesen einen Gott zu lieben bzw. diese liebende Loyalität zog gelegentlich Verfolgungen bis hin zur Bedrohung des Lebens nach sich (vgl. Mk 4,17; 13,9–13).[53]

Es kann sehr wohl sein, dass unseren heidenchristlichen Lesern auch die Zusammenstellung des Gebotes der Gottesliebe mit dem der Nächstenliebe nicht völlig neu erschien. In der alten Welt war es nämlich nicht ungewöhnlich, in einer kurzen Zusammenfassung die Pflichten des Menschen so zu bündeln, dass man neben die Pflichten gegenüber den Göttern diejenigen gegenüber den Menschen stellte.[54] Ein Beispiel bietet Aelius Aristides:[55] „Frömmigkeit (τὸ εὐσεβές) besteht darin, dass man das wahrnimmt, was gerecht und verordnet gegenüber den Göttern ist; das Gebührende (gegenüber den Menschen: τὸ ὅσιον) besteht darin, dass man das wahrnimmt, was gerecht ist (τὰ δίκαια) gegenüber dem Vaterland, …, seinen Eltern und Wohltätern und Erziehern und den Unterirdischen."[56] Überhaupt kommt das Paar „Frömmigkeit (εὐσέβεια) –

---

[51] Vgl. die Ausführungen von SCHRAGE (Ethik, s. Anm. 1, 95) und MERKLEIN (Handlungsprinzip, s. Anm. 2, 287), die jedoch den Text mit Hinsicht auf die Lehre Jesu, bzw. des Evangelisten, studieren.

[52] Da wir uns hier dem den damaligen Markuslesern bzw. Hörern vorliegenden Text zuwenden, brauchen wir nicht den Umstand zu diskutieren, dass gute Gründe dafür sprechen, dass die Kombination der beiden Gebote nicht vom historischen Jesus herrührt; s. MERKLEIN, Handlungsprinzip (s. Anm. 2), 100–107. Vgl. SCHRAGE, Ethik (s. Anm. 2), 69–72. KLAUS BERGER, Die Gesetzesauslegung Jesu. Ihr historischer Hintergrund im Judentum und im Alten Testament. Teil I: Markus und Parallelen (WMANT 40), Neukirchen-Vluyn 1972, 142–163, bietet eine reiche Darstellung der Traditionsgeschichte des Doppelgebotes dar.

[53] Siehe z.B., FOCANT, Marc (s. Anm. 5), 488–491.

[54] BERGER, Gesetzesauslegung (s. Anm. 52), 143.

[55] In diesem Zusammenhang ist nicht vom Belang, dass der Text wahrscheinlich nicht authentisch ist.

[56] Techn. rhet. 1.12.2.5.

Philanthropie" sehr oft in der Literatur dieser Zeit vor, wenn von den Pflichten des Menschen die Rede ist.[57]

Da also die Kombination der beiden Gebote für die Leser vermutlich nichts Merkwürdiges hatte, schien es ihnen wohl nur ein wenig seltsam, dass man Gott/dem Göttlichen gegenüber nicht nur Ehrfurcht zu erweisen habe, (vor allem durch Teilnahme am offiziellen Kult), sondern dass man ihn/es sogar lieben solle.[58] Gewiss kann Plutarch von etlichen Menschen sagen, dass sie Gefühle wie εὔνοια und φιλία gegen Gott hegten,[59] aber von einer tiefgreifenden und die ganze Person einbeziehenden Loyalität – um Liebe einmal so zu beschreiben – gegenüber Gott/den Göttern ist nur selten, wenn überhaupt, die Rede.[60]

Dass man den Nächsten wie sich selbst lieben solle, gehörte in der antiken Welt gewissermaßen zum Bestand der allgemeinen Ethik.[61] In einer Argumentation, in der er das Naturrecht zu begründen versucht, spricht z.B. Cicero von der natürlichen *benevolentia*, die alle Menschen für einander hegen. Sie fordert den Menschen auf, seinen Nächsten „um nichts weniger als sich selbst liebzuhaben (*diligat*)".[62]

Unter den Philosophen wurde das Verhältnis zwischen den beiden Teilen der Kombination εὐσέβεια und δικαιοσύνη (u.ä.) diskutiert: lagen sie auf derselben Ebene, oder sollte man die εὐσέβεια als einen Aspekt der δικαιοσύνη begreifen?[63] Dabei scheint es jedoch üblich gewesen zu sein, die Götterverehrung und die Pflichten gegenüber Menschen nebeneinander zu stellen, ohne sie

---

[57] Siehe z.B. Appianus, *Libyca* 403.5; Dio Cassius, *Hist.* 30–35.109.1; Didorus Sic., *Bibl. hist.* 3.56.2; Josephus, *C. Ap.* 2.146; Plutarch, *Consol.* 120B, *Quaest. conv.* 614B; vgl. KABIERSCH, *Philanthropia* (s. Anm. 32), 52f. Für andere gewöhnliche Kombinationen ähnlichen Inhalts s. BERGER, *Gesetzesauslegung* (s. Anm. 52), 144.

[58] Man sollte nicht so viel Gewicht darauf legen, dass ἀγαπάω im klassischen Griechisch selten ist (siehe z.B. ETHELBERT STAUFFER, „ἀγαπάω κτλ. B", *ThWNT* 1 (1933) 34–55: 34–38), da es scheint, dass dieses Verb in der Koine größeren Raum eingenommen hat. S. ROBERT JOLY, *Le vocabulaire chrétien de l'amour est-il originel? φιλεῖν et ἀγαπᾶν dans le grec antique*, Brüssel 1968, sowie GREG H. R. HORSLEY, *New Documents illustrating early Christianity. A Review of the Greek inscriptions and papyri published in 1978*, North Ryde, N.S.W. 1983, 15.

[59] *Marcius Coriol.* 38.3.

[60] THOMAS OHM, *Die Liebe zu Gott in den nichtchristlichen Religionen*, München 1950, 166–184.

[61] DIHLE, *Regel* (s. Anm. 10), 117.

[62] Cicero, *De leg.* 1.33f.; vgl. ferner Seneca, *Epist. Morales* 11.88.30: „Humanitas uetat superbum esse aduersus socios, uetat aurum: uerbis, rebus, adfectibus comem se facilemque omnibus praestat: nullum alienum malum putat, bonum autem suum ideo maxime, quod alicui bono futurum est, amat". [„Die Menschenliebe verbietet es, hochmütig zu sein gegenüber den Mitmenschen, verbietet es, geizig zu sein: mit Worten, Taten, Gefühlen erweist sie sich allen als freundlich und zugänglich: kein Unglück empfindet sie als sie nichts angehend, das Gute, das ihr eignet, liebt sie deswegen am meisten, weil es jemandem zugute kommen wird"]. – Text and Übers. in: H. ROSENBACH, *An Lucilius Briefe über Ethik*, Bd. 4, Darmstadt 1984, 314–317.] – Dass diese Gedanken in der stoischen Oikeiosis-Lehre eine wichtige Rolle spielten braucht uns hier nicht zu beschäftigen; siehe DIHLE, *Regel* (s. Anm. 10), 117f.; FORSCHNER, *Ethik* (s. Anm. 32), 144–150.

[63] KLAUS BERGER, *Gesetzesauslegung* (s. Anm. 52), 143–151.

miteinander zu verbinden.[64] Für unsere heidenchristlichen Markus-Leser sollte der abschließende Kommentar des markinischen Jesus die Art und Weise bestimmen, in der sich die Elemente dieser Diskussion zwischen ihm und dem Schriftgelehrten zu einander verhielten: So kennzeichnet Jesus die Zustimmung seines Gesprächpartners durch die Wendung, jener sei nicht fern von der Gottesherrschaft (V. 34). D.h., Gott und den Nächsten zu lieben stellt den eigentlichen Gotteswillen dar,[65] meint ein Leben und Handeln im Zeichen der aktuellen und zukünftigen Gottesherrschaft. Praktisch gesehen bedeutet die Bemerkung des Schriftgelehrten, die Liebe zu Gott und dem Nächsten sei weit mehr als alle Brandopfer und Schlachtopfer (V. 33), dass es εὐσέβεια im Sinne eine Teilnahme am offiziellen Kult der Götter nicht mehr geben darf – zudem würde ja eine solche Teilnahme die Einzigkeit Gott verleugnen.

Weiterhin musste für die Markus-Leser Jesu abschließender Kommentar bedeuten, dass das doppelte Liebesgebot im Zusammenhang mit der übrigen Basileia-Verkündigung zu verstehen sei. So wurden die beiden Liebesgebote unauflöslich miteinander verbunden. Die tiefgreifende Loyalität gegenüber Gott kam zunächste im „ersten Gebot" (V. 30) zum Ausdruck, doch sie schloss nun auch die Loyalität gegenüber jenem von Jesus in Wort und Handeln proklamierten und gelebten Gotteswillen ein.

Wie wir indessen schon in unserer Diskussion des Ehescheidungsverbotes sehen konnten, rief der Gotteswille jene der Basileia angehörenden Menschen zu einer radikalen Zuwendung zum Mitmenschen auf.[66] Genauer betrachtet konnte eine solche Haltung auch als eine Art Nachfolge Jesu charakterisiert werden, der gekommen war „um zu dienen und sein Leben hinzugeben als Lösegeld für viele" (10,45; vgl. 14,24).

## 6. Der Zukunftsaspekt

Zuletzt soll der in unseren Erwägungen häufig erwähnte Zukunftsaspekt des markinischen Gedankens von der Gottesherrschaft berührt werden. Die Nachfolge fand in jener Perspektive statt, dass der in der Herrlichkeit seines Vaters kommende Menschensohn sich seiner Nachfolger nicht schämen solle (8,38). Dieser Aussage folgte unmittelbar die Versicherung, dass einige der dort Stehenden den Tod nicht erleiden würden, bis sie gesehen hätten, dass das Reich Gottes in Macht gekommen sei (9,1). Wenn das Logion möglicherweise auch so verstanden werden kann, als bezöge es sich auf die Verklärung,[67] macht Mk 13,26.30 jedoch klar, dass für die ersten Markus-Leser der Zukunftsaspekt des

---

[64] BERGER, *Gesetzesauslegung* (s. Anm. 52), 145–149; vgl. DIHLE, „Ethik" (s. Anm. 9), 672. — Wenn die ähnliche Kombination in hellenistisch-jüdischem Zusammenhang auftaucht, besteht kein Zweifel, dass die Pflichten gegen Gott übergeordnet sind (siehe BERGER, *ibid.*, 151–165).
[65] Vgl. MERKLEIN, *Handlungsprinzip* (s. Anm. 2), 105.
[66] Vgl. MERKLEIN, *Handlungsprinzip* (s. Anm. 2), 105.
[67] KLAUS BERGER, *Wie kommt das Ende der Welt?*, Stuttgart 1999, 34f. Vgl. BREYTENBACH, *Nachfolge* (s. Anm. 5), 251; GNILKA, *Markus* (s. Anm. 5), II, 27; FOCANT, *Marc* (s. Anm. 5), 331.

Basileia-Gedankens ernst zu nehmen ist. Das bedeutet nicht, dass diese „apokalyptische" Sprache notwendigerweise rational-informativ verstanden werden müsste, anstatt vielmehr eine exhortative, ermahnende semantische Funktion zu haben.[68] Seit wohl die Markus-Leser (wie auch die Thessaloniker) gelernt hatten, Jesus, Gottes Sohn „vom Himmel her zu erwarten" (1 Thess. 1,10), sollte dieser Zukunftsaspekt der Gottesherrschaft die Dringlichkeit der Ethik befördern.

Die volkstümliche Religiosität der Antike kannte allerlei Vorstellungen von jenseitigen Orten für Bestrafung und Belohnung. Für viele waren sie indessen wohl auch nur leere „Mythen". Dieselbe Religiosität mag noch nicht einmal durchgängig mit einem Dasein der Seele jenseits dieses Erdenlebens gerechnet haben, und in dem Falle, dass ein solcher Glaube vorhanden war, enthielt er Vorstellungen sehr unterschiedlicher Art. So zeugen viele Grabinschriften von dem Glauben, die Seele fahre nach dem Tode z.B. auf den Olymp,[69] in den Äther,[70] oder in den Hades/die Unterwelt.[71] Einige von ihnen könnten die Motive jenes „Totengespräches" von Lukian gekannt haben, wo Minos sagt: „Dieser Räuber Sostratus soll in den Pyriphlegethon geworfen, der Tempelräuber von der Chimaera zerrissen ... und seine Leber von den Geiern gefressen werden; ihr aber, ihr Guten, geht eilends zum Elyseischen Gefilde und bewohnt die Inseln der Seligen, zum Lohn für eure guten Taten während des Lebens."[72] Wahrscheinlich nahmen viele Menschen gegenüber diesen Vorstellungen aus der alten Mythologie eine mehr oder weniger skeptische Haltung ein, wenn auch vielleicht nicht eine so spöttische wie Lukian.[73]

Vor einem derartigen Hintergrund tritt die Perspektive der nahen und zukünftigen Gottesherrschaft deutlicher hervor. Sie beinhaltet die Ethik, vor die sich die heidenchristlichen Leser gestellt sahen, als einen ihrer Aspekte, insofern das ganze Leben von der Gottesherrschaft bestimmt war. So wurden die ethischen Forderungen untrennbar mit dem grundlegenden religiösen Glauben verbunden, nicht aber als etwas Eigenständiges betrachtet.[74] Vielmehr lebten die Adressaten unter oder im Zeichen der wirksam nahen Gottesherrschaft, die teils als „Handlungsprinzip" (um Merkleins Ausdruck aufzugreifen) funktionierte, teils für diejenigen eine treibende Kraft darstellte, die sich ihr im Glauben hin-

---

[68] LARS HARTMAN, „The Functions of Some So-Called Apocalyptic Timetables", in: *NTS* 22 (1975/76) 1–14. [Reprinted in: IDEM, *Text-Centered New Testament Studies* (WUNT 102), Tübingen 1997, 107–124.] Vgl. AMOS N. WILDER, *The Language of the Gospel. Early Christian Rhetorics*, New York – Evanston 1964; NORMAN PERRIN, *Jesus and the Language of the Kingdom. Symbol and Metaphor in New Testament Interpretation*, Philadelphia, Penn. 1976, bes. Kap. II; BERGER, *Ende* (s. Anm. 67).

[69] Z.B. SEG 11.384; IG IX.1.882; IGUR III.1329.

[70] Z.B. IG II.12142; II.13009a; XIV.940; SEG 17.172.

[71] Z.B. IGUR 1204; SEG 28.323; 30.268.

[72] *Totengespräche* 24.1.

[73] MARTIN P. NILSSON, *Geschichte der griechischen Religion II. Die hellenistische und römische Zeit* (HAW V.2.2), München ³1974, 520–529, 544–558. Vgl. ERIC ROBERTSON DODDS, *Die Griechen und das Irrationale*, Darmstadt 1970, 127f., 131–140, 257f.

[74] EDUARD SCHWARTZ, *Ethik* (s. Anm. 19), 13.

gaben. Von dieser verborgenen, aber mächtigen Kraft sprechen die Wachstumsgleichnisse in Kap. 4.

Dies bedeutete nicht, die Verantwortlichkeit des Menschen zu verkennen (vgl. 8,38; 9,42–48; 10,21f.; 12,40), denn der markinische Jesus betont ja die Dringlichkeit des Wachens und Aushaltens der unter Druck stehenden Adressaten (4,17–19; 13,13.33–37). Schrage schreibt: „Man kann dem Kommen der Gottesherrschaft entsprechen, auch in seinem Tun. Man kann und darf aus ihr leben und sie weitertragen."[75] So fällt es auch auf, dass der Zukunftsaspekt der Gottesherrschaft den Lesern des Markus überwiegend als etwas Positives erscheint.[76] Dass der in der Macht seines Vaters kommende Menschensohn sich seiner Nachfolger nicht zu schämen braucht, impliziert deren Rettung (13,13.20) und bedeutet, dass die „Auserwählten" künftig in der Gemeinschaft mit dem sie sammelnden Herrn leben dürfen (vgl. 1 Thess. 4,17; Phil. 1,23).

## 7. Zusammenfassung

Zum Schluss stellt sich noch einmal die Frage, wie sich unsere Erwägungen in das Thema „Eschatologie und Ethik" einordnen – vor dem Erfahrungshintergrund der von uns angenommenen heidenchristlichen Leser. Mit einer gewissen Erweiterung des Eschatologie-Begriffes über das traditionelle Verständnis einer „Lehre von den letzten Dingen" hinaus könnte man vielleicht in aller Kürze Folgendes sagen. Wie einst die Jünger Jesu, so waren auch die Leser des Markus in die Nachfolge Christi im Zeichen der nahen und sich im Werk Jesu realisierenden Gottesherrschaft gerufen. Der Gott, an den sie jetzt glaubten, war ihnen näher als die heidnischen Götter und drängte sich ihnen sozusagen auf, in dem Bestreben, ihre ganze Person in Liebe zu sich engagieren zu wollen. Dieses Engagement bedeutete aber gleichzeitig auch, dass die Nachfolge die Pflicht zu radikaler Nächstenliebe in sich trug – so radikal, dass sie als unmöglich erscheinen konnte. Aber diese Unmöglichkeit wurde von der Macht Gottes temperiert, die sich eben in der schon nahen und schon wirksamen Gottesherrschaft manifestierte. Andererseits konnten Menschen den Ruf, sich unter diese Herrschaft zu stellen, ablehnen. Zugleich gab es Texte im Markusevangelium, welche diejenigen, die dem Ruf Folge leisteten, an die Gabe und die damit verbundene Verantwortung erinnerten. Die Nachfolge Jesu stand im Lichte einer Hoffnung, die sich in die versprochene Zukunft hinein und auf das Kommen des jenseitigen Gottesreiches mit der Nähe zu Jesu Christi Gott und Vater erstreckte. D.h. die Leser waren nicht mehr gleich den „anderen, die keine Hoffnung haben" (1 Thess. 4,13).

---

[75] Schrage, *Ethik* (s. Anm. 2), 25.
[76] Focant, *Marc* (s. Anm. 5), 499, in der Erklärung von 13,24–27.

# Part III

Baptism

## 13. "Into the Name of Jesus"
## A Suggestion Concerning the Earliest
## Meaning of the Phrase

### 1. Earlier Research

Apparently the early Church baptized her converts from the very beginning[1] "into the name of Jesus" – or some similar phrase.[2] But what does this phrase mean? The *opinio communis* among New Testament scholars seems to be that the person baptized was dedicated to Jesus, having become his property.[3] But with all respect to the scholars who have discussed the phrase and its variants, I am not entirely convinced that they have done justice to it.

So this paper presents a reassessment of the problem with a consideration of some complementary Jewish material. W. Heitmüller laid the scholarly foundation of the *opinio communis* cited above. For his classical study *Im Namen Jesu* (1903),[4] he was able to use the papyri which made their way to the scholars' desks around the beginning of the twentieth century. In them he found "into the name" used in Graeco-Hellenistic banking terminology, the "name" being that of a person to whose account something was credited. These observations

---

[1] Thus e.g. WILLIAM FREDERICK FLEMINGTON, *The New Testament Doctrine of Baptism*, London 1948, 25ff.; ERICH DINKLER, "Taufe II", *RGG*³, VI (1962), 627ff.; HANS CONZELMANN, *Grundriß der Theologie des Neuen Testaments*, München 1967, 64. Cf. ERNST BARNIKOL, "Das Fehlen der Taufe in den Quellenschriften der Apg.", in: *Wiss. Zschr.* (Halle) VI (1956/57) 593–619, defending the idea that the converts of the earliest period were not baptized.

[2] The phrase has several variants. In addition to εἰς τὸ ὄνομα (Matt 28:19; Acts 8:16, 19:5; 1 Cor 1:13, 15) we also meet ἐν τῷ ὀνόματι (Acts 2:38 – *v.l.* ἐπὶ τ. ὀ. – 10:48) and, presumably, derived from the phrase, εἰς Χριστόν (Gal 3:27; see also Rom 6:3 and 1 Cor 10:2; JAMES D. G. DUNN's reasons for opposing εἰς to εἰς τὸ ὄνομα do not necessarily contradict this view; *Baptism in the Holy Spirit* [SBT II: 15], London 1970, 112, 118, 140f.). There are no examples of the formula mentioning only the name "Jesus", but always "Jesus Christ" (Acts 2:38; 10:48) or "Kurios Jesus" (Acts 8:16; 19:5). In Matt 28:19 the Trinitarian form is used. See further GERHARD DELLING, *Die Zueignung des Heils in der Taufe*, Berlin 1961, 13f.

[3] E.g. JOHANNES LINDBLOM, *Jesu missions- och dopbefallning, Matt. 28:18–20*, Stockholm 1919, 165ff.; ALBRECHT OEPKE, "Βάπτω κτλ.", in: *ThWNT* 1 (1933) 537; SHERMAN E. JOHNSON, "Ad Matt. xxviii. 19", in: *The Interpreter's Bible*, VII, New York – Nashville, Ky. 1951; JOSEF SCHMID, *Das Evangelium nach Matthäus* (RNT I), Regensburg 1956, ad xxviii. 19; RUDOLF BULTMANN, *Theologie des Neuen Testaments*, Tübingen ⁶1968, 42, 140; ERNST HAENCHEN, *Die Apostelgeschichte* (KEK 3), Göttingen ⁶1968, ad ii. 38; DUNN, *op. cit.*, 117f.; HARTWIG THYEN, *Studien zur Sündenvergebung* (FRLANT 96), Göttingen 1970, 147; DINKLER, *op. cit.*, 116f.

[4] WILHELM HEITMÜLLER, „*Im Namen Jesu*" (FRLANT 1:2), Göttingen 1903.

naturally led to the interpretation that Jesus is the heavenly *Kurios* to whose ownership the baptized person was transferred.

Instead of interpretation from Greek parallels, another has been advanced by P. Billerbeck, *inter alios*, with reference to Hebrew-Aramaic usage.[5] It was also adopted by H. Bietenhard in his ὄνομα article in Kittel's *Theologisches Wörterbuch zum Neuen Testament* (1954). Billerbeck tried to explain our formula by the Hebrew-Aramaic expression *l^eshem-l^eshum*, a term often used in the Mishnah and the Talmud. Here, *shem* has not the strict meaning of "name" ; the phrase should rather be translated "with regard to", "with reference to" or "for". But when expounding the meaning of the formula as used in connection with baptism, both Billerbeck and Bietenhard express themselves in terms very similar to those of Heitmüller and his followers.[6]

Ten years ago G. Delling published a study in which he discussed at length the formula "into the name", and suggested another interpretation.[7] He noted that the expression and its variants in the New Testament usually refer to Jesus, and stated that "the person through whom God acts eschatologically is not to be distinguished from the event that God performs through him".[8] Accordingly, Professor Delling ended his book by saying; "Die Taufe ‚auf den (im) Namen' fügt dem Heilsgeschehen ein, das an dem Namen (Jesus) gebunden ist", and gave it the title *Die Zueignung des Heils in der Taufe*.

Heitmüller has been criticized, and rightly so, for having too easily assumed that technical commercial terms (crediting something to a person's account) were used to supply the imagery for the early Church's expression about the relationship between the one baptized and his Lord.[9] His fundamental mistake was the assumption that a word or a formula such as "into the name" carried from one context to another the specific connotation which it acquired in the first. In other words the phrase "into the name of somebody" may lead to the assumption that something has become the property of the person named and this applies in business texts or in contexts where apparently the banking ter-

---

[5] (Hermann L. Strack)/Paul Billerbeck, *Kommentar zum Neuen Testament aus Talmud und Midrash*, I, Munich 1922, 591, 1054f. Joachim Jeremias follows the same line in *Infant Baptism in the First Four Centuries*, London 1960, 29; Joseph Ysebaert, *Greek Baptismal Terminology* (GCP 1), Nijmegen 1962, 50; George R. Beasley-Murray, *Baptism in the New Testament*, London 1962, 90f.; Georg Kretschmar, "Die Geschichte des Taufgottesdienstes in der alten Kirche", in: Karl Ferdinand Müller/Walter Blankenburg (eds.) *Leiturgia* 5, Kassel-Wilhelmshöhe 1970, 18, 32f. This interpretation was first suggested by A. J. H. Wilhelm Brandt, "Onoma en de Doopsformule in het Nieuwe Testament", in: *Theol. Tijdschr.* xxv (1891) 565–610, and by Gustaf Dalman, *Die Worte Jesu*, I, Leipzig 1898, 250f.

[6] See Billerbeck, *Kommentar*, 1, 1005, and Hans Bietenhard, "ὄνομα κτλ.", in: *ThWNT* 5 (1954) 275. Typically enough, Otto Kuss says ("Zur vorpaulinischen Tauflehre im Neuen Testament", originally published in 1951, now reprinted in idem, *Auslegung und Verkündigung*, I, Regensburg 1963, 98): "Es ist nicht von entscheidender Bedeutung ob man die Formel *eis to onoma* aus dem griechischen (...) oder aus dem semitischen (...) Sprachgebrauch ableitet."

[7] Delling, *Die Zueignung des Heils in der Taufe*.

[8] Delling, *op. cit.*, 43.

[9] See e.g. Bietenhard, *op. cit.*, 275, and Delling, *op. cit.*, 32ff.

minology has been used with a transferred meaning. Nevertheless, this does not necessarily imply that "into the name" had the same meaning in an early Christian context. It seems more probable that the phrase itself is more neutral and may have different meanings in different contexts.

The same could be said of Professor Delling's book. Although most (but not all) occurrences of ὄνομα in the New Testament refer to Jesus, the writings of the early Church (such as the Greek Old Testament and, later, the Apostolic Fathers) do not permit the assumption that the noun ὄνομα acquired a specific meaning that applied in all contexts. And likewise, although in some instances "the name of Jesus Christ" may stand for the salvation accomplished by Jesus Christ and/or the message of that salvation (e.g. Acts 8:12, 9:15), this does not provide a semantic basis strong enough for the contention that "baptize into the name of Jesus Christ" meant "by baptism to endow someone with the blessed consequences of the salvation brought about by Jesus Christ".

The acceptance of the opinion of Billerbeck, Bietenhard and others that the formula had its root in the Jewish *lᵉshem* (*lᵉshum*), involves another risk, namely that of finding too precise a grammatical aspect in it. Thus, one may feel compelled to render *lᵉshem* in different ways in our modern languages, distinguishing between a causal and a final usage of the phrase. As an instance of a causal usage scholars often cite *b.Sanhedrin* 99b, "he who studies the Torah for its own sake (לשמה) makes peace in the upper family (i.e. among the angels) and the lower family (i.e. among men)". *m.Pesaḥim* v.2 may provide a final aspect; "The Passover lamb which somebody did not slaughter for its named purpose (שלא לשמו)." Translation of *lᵉshem* into English as "with regard to" may demonstrate the risk of distinguishing too sharply between a final and a causal meaning of the phrase. For example "this article is written 'with regard to' future publication", and "'with regard to' past discussions problems are considered which would have otherwise been omitted". The first case represents a final usage, whereas the second instance is easily understood as having a causal meaning. Without the guidance of the context, it would however be impossible to declare the meaning of the phrase in a third case as final, because the formula could be said to have that meaning in the first example. The English expression may have either a final or a causal meaning, each depending on the context. But in itself the phrase is neutral, and this may be said to apply also to *lᵉshem, lᵉshum*.[10]

Bietenhard seems to have overestimated an alleged "final" denotation of *lᵉshem* in interpreting the phrase "baptized into the name of Jesus" as meaning "dedicated to Jesus". His principal supporting text, already adduced and interpreted in the same manner by Billerbeck,[11] is *m.Zebaḥim* iv.6;

A sacrifice must be offered in the name of six things (i.e. with respect to, having in mind, six things לשם ששה דברים), in the name of the offering (i.e. that one refers it to the cor( rect category), in the name of the offerer, in the name of the Name, in the name of the

---

[10] Cf. e.g. STEPHEN ULLMANN, *Semantics*, Oxford 1962, 64ff.
[11] BILLERBECK, *op. cit.*, 1055.

altar-fires (i.e. that it be a burnt-offering), in the name of the odour, in the name of the sweet savour.

A sacrificial rule such as this, it would seem, cannot justify Billerbeck's conclusion that the baptism in Matt 28:19 means a dedication to the triune God, any more than "in the name of the offerer" of *m.Zebaḥim* iv.6 envisages a dedication to that person. Here the learned rabbinist has brought more content into the formula than both the "finality" (*Zweckbeziehung*) and the sacrificial connotation of the context would allow.[12]

## 2. Jewish Use of the *lᵉshem-* (*lᵉshum-*) formula

At this stage of the discussion we should perhaps remember that what we are trying to discern is how the first Christians who baptized "into the name of Jesus" understood the phrase. But were the Christians who created the formula Greek- or Aramaic-speaking? The Greek seems to have had but little scope for creating such a phrase. The concrete banking term, "transfer a sum to someone's account-name", is far removed from its usage in connection with baptism, and the idea of the heavenly tablets can hardly provide such an imagery.[13] Indeed, it seems more natural to understand it as a literal translation of a Semitic idiom. There are in fact many examples where *lᵉshem* (*lᵉshum*) has apparently been literally rendered into Greek, e.g. *T. Jud.* xiii.4, "he showed me a boundless store of gold in his daughter's behalf" (literally "into the name of his daughter")[14] or Matt 18:20, "where two or three are gathered into my name".[15] (Cf. *ʾAbot* iv.11, "every assembly that is for the sake of Heaven (לשם שמים) will in the end be established".)[16] Thus the phrase seems to have originated in the early Palestinian

---

[12] Cf. JOHANNES LEIPOLDT, *Die urchristliche Taufe im Lichte der Religionsgeschichte*, Leipzig 1928, 34; DELLING, *op. cit.*, 39.

[13] BIETENHARD, *loc. cit.*

[14] Cf. DELLING, *op. cit.*, 37.

[15] Cf. DELLING, *op. cit.*, 43. So also HEITMÜLLER, *op. cit.*, 124f.

[16] This translation phenomenon explains why prepositional phrases with ὄνομα are so numerous in the LXX, although in many cases they must have sounded coarse or difficult to any sensitive Greek ear. (See e.g. BIETENHARD, *op. cit.*, 262; DELLING, *op. cit.*, 27ff.) Nevertheless, as is often the case with cultic or religious language, the group using the holy text obviously adopted its wordings and became accustomed to them. Expressions that might otherwise have seemed odd found a natural place within a kind of technical language, which may or may not have coloured the usage in other areas of life. (Cf. on this problem HENRY S. GEHMAN, "The Hebraic Character of Septuagint Greek", in: *VT* 1 (1951) 90, and CHAIM RABIN, "The Translation Process and the Character of the Septuagint", in: *Textus* VI (1968) 1–26.) Thus, when dealing with NT ὄνομα phrases it is not feasible to derive them directly from the Hebrew OT and from later Semitic usage in first-century Palestine and regard the NT phrases only as direct translations from a Semitic substrate. In addition it seems necessary to take into account the possibility that this translation was promoted by the religious language, including the ὄνομα terms, of the Greek-speaking Jewish communities. To assume, however, that our phrase is inspired solely and directly by a Hellenistic-Jewish usage does not seem to be a viable solution, as the examples of the phrase introduced by εἰς are very rare. (See DELLING, *op. cit.*, 27.)

Church.[17] However, this does not preclude that new nuances of meaning could emerge when the phrase was used in a more Hellenistic environment,[18] and it is hardly permissible to assume that Paul or Luke understood it in the same way as the Palestinians did,[19] although Paul seems to have been bilingual. As we are considering an early period of Palestinian Christianity, these possible new interpretations in a non-Palestine milieu need not present problems.

To sum up: we have seen some difficulties arise from Billerbeck's and Bietenhard's understanding of the formula "into the name of Jesus". Nonetheless, when looking for its earliest meaning, its closest counterpart should be found in a Hebrew-Aramaic *l*ᵉ*shem* used in the early Palestinian Christian community.

An elaborate lexicographical study of the phrase *l*ᵉ*shem*–*l*ᵉ*shum* is not necessary in this paper with its limited purpose. It may be useful, however, to consider some of its usages in the Rabbinic texts.

1. First there are the cases where *l*ᵉ*shem*–*l*ᵉ*shum* appears with one noun qualifying another, both nouns denoting the same person or thing. The person or thing qualified is not always mentioned in the clause, but is at least implicit. For example; *m.Giṭṭin* iv.4, "if a slave were taken captive and they renounced him, if to be a slave (לשם צבד), he remains a slave …"; *m.Kelim* xxx.2, of a plate, "if it

---

[17] Cf. e.g. BULTMANN, *Theologie*, 40, who assumes that the phrase originated in the Hellenistic community.

[18] This does not suggest a theory of a closed Palestine Jewry or Christianity isolated from the Hellenistic world, as if they did not themselves form part of that world. See lately JAN NICHOLAAS SEVENSTER, *Do you know Greek?* (NT.S 19), Leiden 1968; MARTIN HENGEL, *Judentum und Hellenismus* (WUNT 10), Tübingen 1969. Bietenhard does not discuss this possibility of a variety and development of meanings (*op. cit.*, 275). Cf., on the other hand, the more diversified discussion of HEITMÜLLER, *op. cit.*, 115ff.

[19] Delling speaks of a "prepositional" usage of *l*ᵉ*shem* in cases such as the ones cited above, where for example a lamb is offered "as (*l*ᵉ*shem*) a Passover lamb". He admits only as a theoretical possibility that such a "prepositional" *l*ᵉ*shem* was literally translated into Greek, then kept without being understood and finally re-interpreted. This is not the place for a discussion of possible re-interpretations. It is, however, hard to see how a theory of literal translation could be contradicted by a contention that Paul has related εἰς τὸ ὄνομα to the *name* of Jesus and has not understood it as a "preposition" (*op. cit.*, 41). This is hardly proved by 1 Cor 1:13ff. (*op. cit.*, 68), especially as Delling reads this passage on the assumption that Paul consciously distinguished between usages of εἰς τὸ ὄνομα. Are not questions of linguistic usage of a more complex nature and should we not guard against distinctions that depend so much on our own translations? It may prove useful in this context to quote *b.Zebaḥim* 30a. In this passage cultic intentions are discussed and *l*ᵉ*shem* is used as a "preposition" (according to Delling's distinction). But the same text gives the following rule: "it is impossible to pronounce two intentions (תומש יתש – lit. 'two names') simultaneously". There is no hint of a distinction between alleged "prepositional" and "substantial" usages, and it seems that the passage invalidates Delling's argument based on 1 Cor 1.

In addition we may take into consideration *m.ʿAbodah Zarah* iii.7, with its Gemara in *b.ʿAbodah Zarah* 48a. The Mishnah discusses the Asherahs and assumes a case in which "somebody lopped and trimmed (a tree) for idolatry (לשם צבודה זרה)". When the Gemara refers to this clause, however, it replaces *l*ᵉ*shem* with a simple *l*ᵉ. (This is the case in the manuscripts followed by Bomberg-Goldschmidt; the Munich MS, however, reads *l*ᵉ*shem*.) Nor in this case do we seem justified in assuming a "prepositional" usage as consciously delimited from a "substantial" one. Is the passage, perhaps, parallel to the Pauline εἰς τὸ ὄνομα vs. εἰς?

were at the outset fashioned to be a mirror (לשם אספקלריא) ...";  *m.Zebaḥim* i.2, "(sacrifices) slaughtered as a Passover-offering (לשם פסח) or as a sin-offering (לשם חטאת) are invalid". *t.ʿAbodah Zarah* iii.12, "an Israelite circumcises a Gentile in order that he be a proselyte (לשום גר) ... ".[20]

2. There are also similar examples where, instead of a qualifying noun following *lᵉshem*, *lᵉshum*, a suffix is added. The noun and its suffix both refer to the same person or thing. For example; *m.Zebaḥim* i.1, "all sacrifices which have been slaughtered not under their own name (שלא לשמן) are valid ..."; *b.Sanhedrin* 99b, "the one who studies the Torah for its own sake (with respect to its being what it is (לשמה)".[21]

3. In a third group of cases there is no such identity or close relationship between two nouns or pronouns on either side of *lᵉshem–lᵉshum*. The phrase accompanies the verb of the clause, which, although implied, can also be omitted. An example is *m.Zebaḥim* iv.6, "a sacrifice is slaughtered with respect to six things (לשם ששה דברים הזבח נזבח) ...". In the above example of the mirror and the plate (prepared to be a mirror), the two nouns refer to the same thing. The sacrifice of *m.Zebaḥim* iv.6, however, is neither identical with nor qualified as six things, but that which *happens* to the sacrifice happens with respect to six things or aspects. Here are some examples of this usage gathered in three groups;

(a) The action takes place "with respect to" (etc.) things, places, etc. Thus, *y.Yebamot* i.1 discusses whether a man may marry his sister-in-law "on account of (her) money (לשם ממון)"; *b.Yebamot* 24b mentions "somebody who becomes a proselyte (נתייר) because of the royal table (לשום שולחן מלכים)". In *m.Ḥullin* ii.8 the offering is declared invalid "if somebody slaughters (השוחט) out of regard for the mountains (לשם הרים), for the hills, for the seas or for the desert". (The list is even longer in *b.Ḥullin* 40a.) A similar religious context is found in *t.ʿAbodah Zarah* iii.13, which mentions a Samaritan circumcising (מל) "from regard for the mountain of Gerizim (לשם הר גריזים)" (also in *b.ʿAbodah Zarah* 27a). We find another example of a geographic name in *m.Šeqalim* iii.4, "He took the first Terumah (תרם) on behalf of the land of Israel (לשום ארץ ישראל), the second on behalf of the cities near by and the third on behalf of Babylon and on behalf of Media (לשם בבל ולשום מדי) ..." (par. *t.Šeqalim* ii.4).

It should not be overlooked that the implication may often be something more than the "things" or "places" in these examples. Thus the "mountains", "hills" and "seas" of *m.Ḥullin* ii.8 obviously stand for deities or cults, just as the Gerizim of *t.ʿAbodah Zarah* iii.13 symbolizes the Samaritan religion.

---

[20] See also, e.g., *m.Ḥullin* ii.10 (*as* a burnt-offering); *b.Pesaḥim* 38b (loaves saved *as* a Massah), *b.Šabbat* 50a (branches brought together *to be* firewood). Here we may also quote *b.Yebamot* 45b, "somebody buys a slave from a Gentile and he comes to him and receives the proselyte baptism to be a freeman (לשם בן חורין)"; and *m.Nedarim* iv.8 (somebody gives (food) to another *as* a gift).

[21] See also, e.g., *m.Pesaḥim* v.2 (the Passover-sacrifice slaughtered *as such, in its named purpose*).

(b) The action takes place "with respect to" (etc.) things expressed in abstract nouns. Of course, this includes the examples such as the one citing circumcision "with respect to Gerizim". Typically enough, that very text (t.ʿAbodah Zarah iii.13) also speaks of being circumcised "with respect to the covenant (לשום ברית)". Further examples of references to cultic and other religious duties are; m.Bekorot i.7, "they had the intention regarding the religious duty (לשם מתכוויןן מצוה)" (also b.Yebamot 39b); m.ʿAbodah Zarah iii.7, about a stone "renovated for idolatrous worship (לשם צבודה גלולים)"; m.Sukkah i.1, "if somebody makes it (a sukkah) expressly for the Festival (לשם חג) … it is valid".

In m.Nedarim viii.7 there are rules concerning certain vows; "he had the intention (נתכויןן) only regarding marital state (לשום אישות)" and "he had the intention only with regard to eating and drinking (לשום אכילה ושחיה)". In b.Sanhedrin 76a somebody presents his daughter for sexual cohabitation "without having marital state in mind (שלא לשם אישות)". And in y.Yebamot i.1 there is a *dictum* about marrying a widowed sister-in-law "on account of (her) beauty (לשם תואר)".

(c) The action takes place "regarding" (etc.) persons, namely men, as well as beings belonging to the divine sphere who are not engaged as agents in the action described by the verb. First, here are some examples of things done for God, who is mentioned with a circumlocution; ʾAbot ii.2, about labouring with the congregation "for the sake of Heaven (לשם שמים)"; *ibid*. ii.12, "let all your deeds be for the sake of Heaven"; *ibid*. iv.11, "every gathering that is for the sake of Heaven will be established"; and S. Nu. § 136, "there are two kinds of drawing near, one having Heaven in mind, another without having Heaven in mind". Another circumlocution is that in m.Zebahim iv.6, where one has to slaughter a sacrifice "with regard to the Name (לשם השם)". b.Ḥullin 40 was quoted above, dealing with the slaughter "with respect to" mountains, etc. In this list of intentions the archangel Michael also appears as someone "with respect to" whom somebody may (or rather may not) sacrifice. To a similar area of life belongs m.Niddah v.6, which contains a discussion concerning the age at which a person's vows are valid. Youngsters may say; "we know in whose name we have vowed (לשם מי נדרנו) and in whose name we have dedicated (לשם מי הקדשנו)".

Finally, here are a few examples where something is done with respect to men; m.Gittin iii.1, "A letter of divorce which is not written with regard to a (named) woman is not valid (נכתב שלא לשום אשה)";[22] b.Yebamot 24b, "a man who becomes a proselyte (נתגייר) because of a woman (לשום אשה), a woman who becomes a proselyte because of a man …". We can also return to m.Zebahim iv.6, where one has to slaughter with respect to six things and among them also "with respect to the offerer (לשם זובח)".

A passage such as m.Zebahim iv.6 warns against assuming that the usages are sharply delimited, since it incorporates several of them; it comes close to the "identity" cases (the sacrifice has to be a correct sacrifice) and it represents those

---

[22] With a suffix in m.Gittin iii.2 (a letter of divorce, written *for her*; similarly t.Gittin ii.7).

where an act is performed with respect to things (the fires), abstracts (the sweet savour) or persons (the Name, the offerer).

This survey not only seems to prove the inadequacy of the dedicatory interpretation of "into the name", as based on the semitic *l<sup>e</sup>shem–l<sup>e</sup>shum*, but also gives us some idea of how widely the expression could be used. Evidently, the way in which εἰς (τὸ) ὄνομα is used in Matt 10:41f. ("receive a prophet because he is a prophet", etc.) is similar to that under 1 above, whereas Matt 18:20 ("gathered to my name") fits in well with the examples under 3 (c).

## 3. Jesus as the Reference for Baptism

Now for the formula "baptize into the name of Jesus". It is similar in type to the cases quoted above under 3 (c), where an action takes place with respect to someone, whether it be God, Michael or a man. But there is another similarity between many of the examples quoted and our formula, namely that baptism is a rite, and that a considerable number of our examples concern rites too, be it a sacrifice, a "drawing near" or a vow. In these ritual cases the phrase *l<sup>e</sup>shem–l<sup>e</sup>shum* is used to introduce the type, reason or purpose of the rite as well as its intention.[23] Thus, although the *l<sup>e</sup>shem–l<sup>e</sup>shum* phraseology is used in several contexts, we may surmise its almost technical usage in ritual matters.

It seems that the example from *m.Niddah* v.6 (3 (c)) could serve as an analogy to our baptism formula; "we know in whose name we have vowed". The one behind the *shem* is not by what or whom one has promised, but a kind of fundamental reference for the vow. In a similar way "Jesus" could be the fundamental reference for baptism. The phrase then characterized the rite in a fundamental way; it was a "Jesus baptism".

If indeed "baptism into the name of Jesus" *is* parallel to the phrase by which one qualified other rites as to their fundamental reference, their type, reason or purpose, this assumption will affect the interpretation of the formula. Thus, the hypothesis of the "name" referring to some exorcist usage of the name of Jesus at baptism becomes less probable.[24] Further, as has been argued above, the support of the dedicatory interpretation is essentially weakened, and so also is the basis for the contention that the "name" was thought of in terms of "the Name" as a designation for Christ in the same way as "the Name" could stand for "God".[25] Finally, if "into the name" originally introduced the fundamental reference of baptism, then the word "name" in the formula could hardly be understood as representing in itself the salvific event performed by the one men-

---

[23] Cf. JEREMIAS, *Infant Baptism*, 29.

[24] Cf. e.g. BULTMANN, *Theologie*, 42, 139f.; DINKLER, "Taufe II", in: *RGG*³ VI, 629; THYEN, *Sündenvergebung*, 148. See also *Ep. Barn.* 16,17f.

[25] RICHARD N. LONGENECKER, "Some Distinctive Early Christological Motifs", in: *NTS* xiv (1967/68) 533ff.

tioned (Delling).²⁶ On the other hand, taking into account, for example, a parallel such as that concerning vows, just quoted, a definition of the formula like the one presented could open up some new possibilities of understanding early Christian thinking on baptism.

A problem now arises; does the *lᵉshem* parallelism affect the discussion about the name of Jesus actually being mentioned at the ministration of baptism?²⁷ There are some arguments which support a hypothesis to that effect, although they are not very strong.²⁸ An example of the use of *lᵉshem* would perhaps shed some light on the problem.

It seems that when a person presented an offering in the Temple he declared the purpose of it or made clear what kind of offering he was giving – possibly using a *lᵉshem* phrase; e.g. *b.Pesaḥim* 60a, "Behold, I slaughter the Pesaḥ to its name" (לשום), i.e. as a Pesaḥ sacrifice proper, or *b.Zebaḥim* 30a, "it is impossible to pronounce two purposes (שתי שמות) at the same time".²⁹ If the analogy holds good, it is quite possible that a phrase such as "into the name of Jesus" was pronounced at the rite of baptism in order to characterize the rite in terms of its purpose or reference. However, as was the case with the Jewish rites, the phrase also should have been used to characterize the rite when it was related or presented to others. This may have been the case, even if the phrase was not used at the very act of baptism. In other words, it does not much matter whether the formula (or a "name") was actually uttered when a person was dipped in baptism or only when this baptism was mentioned. In both cases the term was primarily used to qualify the rite and distinguish it from other rites.

Therefore, if "into the name of Jesus" was above all a definition, a phrase which mentioned the fundamental reference of Christian baptism which distinguished it from other rites, then it is most probable that the formula especially delimited Christian baptism from that of John.³⁰ It should be noted that the baptism of the early Church was most probably inspired to a great extent by the Baptist movement.³¹ Nevertheless this qualification could hardly only be negative, any more than the explanation concerning a Passover lamb being offered

---

[26] Cf. DELLING, *Zueignung des Heils*.

[27] Thus, e.g., THYEN, *op. cit.*, 148; HANS CONZELMANN, *Geschichte des Urchristentums* (Grundrisse zum Neuen Testament, NTD Ergänz, 5), Göttingen 1969, 36. HANS FRHR VON CAMPENHAUSEN vigorously denies that the name of Jesus was mentioned at baptism ("Taufen auf den Namen Jesu?", in: *VigChr* XXV [1971] 1-16).

[28] See Jas. 2:7; Herm. *Sim.* viii.6,4; Just. *Apol. I* 61,11. Cf. BULTMANN, *Theologie*, 136f.

[29] Cf. also passages such as *m.Zebaḥim* ii.4 and *m.Menaḥot* i.3, where cases are discussed in which the person making the sacrifice and the priest, respectively, perform the rite in silence, i.e. thus raising the question of his intention in relation to what he is actually doing.

[30] Cf. also THYEN, *op. cit.*, 148f.

[31] See, e.g., OSCAR CULLMANN, *Baptism in the New Testament* (SBT 1), London 1950, 9ff.; EDUARD SCHWEIZER, *Church Order in the New Testament* (SBT 32), London 1961, 41; DINKLER, "Taufe II", in: *RGG*³ VI, 628, THYEN, *op. cit.*, 145ff.; CONZELMANN, *Geschichte*, 35. For other opinions, see e.g. NILS A. DAHL, "The Origin of Baptism", in: *NTT* lxi (1955) 36-52; JEREMIAS, *Infant Baptism*, 24; HEINRICH KRAFT, "Die Anfänge der christlichen Taufe", in: *ThZ* xvii (1961) 399-412.

"to the name of Pesaḥ" meant primarily "this is not a sinoffering". Instead it had a positively defining function: "this is a Passover lamb". When transferred to baptism this analogy says that the qualification "into the name of Jesus" was reasonably understood to have a positive content as well as a negatively demarcating meaning. Thus, this understanding of our formula may influence our way of assessing the problem of the earliest Christological thinking of the Church. To open a discussion of these consequences would, however, be outside the sphere of this paper, and must be left for another occasion.

## 14. La formule baptismale dans les Actes des Apôtres
Quelques observations relatives au style de Luc

L'exégète qui se consacre à l'interprétation des Actes des Apôtres ou s'occupe de l'histoire des traditions de ce livre ne peut guère manquer de traiter ce que l'on pourrait nommer la «formule baptismale», c'est-à-dire l'expression «baptiser au nom de Jésus-Christ» qui, avec quelques variantes, se trouve en Ac 2,38; 8,16; 10,48; 19,5. Il en va de même pour qui s'interroge sur l'histoire du baptême dans l'Église primitive.

Une étude de la formule baptismale telle qu'on la trouve dans les Actes, a certainement sa place dans un volume d'hommage offert à un exégète comme le P. Dupont qui a porté tant d'intérêt aux Actes des Apôtres et consacré tant d'efforts à l'interprétation de l'annonce du Seigneur faite par l'Église primitive. Les observations suivantes s'en tiendront cependant à des préliminaires. Concrètement, j'analyserai et je tâcherai de caractériser les trois variantes de la formule, notamment en fonction du style de Luc. Une telle étude pourra, nous l'espérons, se révéler utile pour une recherche plus approfondie qui s'attacherait à l'exégèse des passages des Actes où apparaissent nos formules dans la composition du livre, à la manière dont Luc comprend le baptême, etc. Par ailleurs, il y aurait lieu d'envisager les problèmes historiques relatifs au baptême dans l'Église primitive. Mais ces questions ne seront pas abordées ici.

Nous trouvons donc dans les Actes trois variantes de la formule baptismale qu'on peut étudier sans qu'il soit nécessaire de prendre parti sur la question de savoir s'il s'agit ou non d'une formule rituelle. On lit en effet: «au *[en]* nom de Jésus Christ» (10,48; 2,38 selon B, D, pc), «au *[epi]* nom de Jésus Christ» (2,38 selon la majorité des mss)[1], et «au *[eis]* nom du Seigneur Jésus» (8,16; 19,5). Après avoir examiné la question des prépositions, nous verrons celle des génitifs, c'est-à-dire celle des titres christologiques.

### 1. Les prépositions

Pourquoi donc cette diversité? Peut-on, par exemple, l'expliquer en y voyant les traces de sources ou de traditions différentes auxquelles l'auteur aurait eu recours?

Luc n'est pas seul parmi les auteurs néotestamentaires à utiliser les prépositions *en* et *epi* pour dire «faire quelque chose *au nom de* quelqu'un». Il a pu

---

[1] Voir ci-dessous (p. 157) des raisons pour la leçon *epi*.

en tout cas les rencontrer en Marc². Mais on est tout aussi fondé à penser que la fréquence, dans les Actes, d'expressions composées avec *onoma* vient, pour une bonne part, du désir qu'aurait Luc d'imiter le style des Septante³. Ces «biblicismes» sont particulièrement fréquents dans la première partie du livre des Actes⁴. Aussi n'est-on pas surpris de voir Luc écrire qu'on expulse des démons ou qu'on guérit des malades, etc., «au [en] nom de» Jésus (Lc 10,17; Ac 3,6; 4,7.10: comp. par exemple avec Mc 9,38). De même on est sauvé «au [en] nom de Jésus» (Ac 4,12 comp. avec Ps 53,1/LXX). Luc raconte aussi qu'on parle ou qu'on enseigne «au [epi] nom de» Jésus (Lc 24,47; Ac 4,17 s, etc. comp. par exemple avec Ex 5,23; 33,17). En fait, la construction «*epi tôi onomati*» avec ces verbes est normale chez Luc⁵.

La construction avec *en* ou *epi* est commune dans la Septante. Mais si l'on considère les verbes auxquels se rattache l'expression, on constate qu'il est plus commun d'écrire parler, prophétiser, etc., *epi tôi onomati* que *en tôi onomati*⁶. Dès lors, la manière dont Luc construit l'expression est aussi celle que préfèrent les Septante. Pourtant, ceux-ci ne fournissent pas d'exemples de guérisons ou d'exorcismes opérés «*en [tôi] onomati* ...» qui est la construction préférée par Luc⁷. Les cas qui se rapprochent le plus des Septante sont peut-être ceux où il est dit qu'on prie, loue, bénit, etc., «au [en] nom de Dieu», etc. Il arrive certes que ces verbes soient parfois suivis de la construction avec *epi*, mais plus fréquemment avec *en* du moins si on prend en considération l'ensemble de la Septante⁸. Cependant, personne ne pense que quelqu'un apprend ou imite une langue à partir de données statistiques. Luc non plus. Dès lors, pour porter un jugement sur ses «biblicismes», il ne faut pas accorder trop d'importance à la fréquence relative de telle ou telle construction.

---

[2] Voir Mc 9,37.39; 13,6 (*epi*); 9,38.41; 11,9 (= Ps 118,26) (*en*). Une discussion de ces phrases dans le Nouveau Testament se trouve en G. Delling, *Die Zueignung des Heils in der Taufe*, Berlin 1961, 42–60, 68–96.

[3] Voir Max E. Wilcox, *The Semitisms of Acts*, Oxford 1965, 56–86.

[4] Voir William K. L. Clarke, «The Use of the Septuagint in Acts» in *The Beginnings of Christianity*, II, Londres 1922, 100 ss; Eckhard Plümacher, *Lukas als hellenistischer Schriftsteller. Studien zur Apostelgeschichte* (SUNT 9), Göttingen 1972, 38–50.

[5] Sur 9 cas (ou 10, si en 9,49 il faut lire *epi*) cinq sont de ce type. Quant aux autres, en 9,48 et 21,8 Luc suit Marc. Ac 2,38 est une de nos formules. Le 1,59 est une (autre) imitation des LXX. La leçon de 9,49 est douteuse: la majorité des mss (A C D W 038 0135 Y inclus) lit *epi*, peut-être sous l'influence de la même phrase au verset précédent. Un nombre de mss importants (p. ex. 45,75 Cod. Sin. B *f*1, 13 33) lisent *en*, suivis par Nestle-Aland.

[6] Un calcul donne environ huit cas avec *en* et vingt avec *epi* (dont la majorité en Jr). Les chiffres de cette note, comme ceux des notes suivantes, sont un peu vagues à cause des *variae lectiones* et du doute qu'on peut avoir en classant les verbes.

[7] Sur 11 cas (ou 10, si en 9,49 il faut lire *epi*) six sont de ce type. Parmi les autres Lc 13,35 et 19,38 suivent Q (et Marc) – Ps 118, et Ac 10,48 est une de nos formules; Ac 9,27 («assuré en le nom») est difficile à juger: cf. des passages des LXX où l'on «espère» (Ps 32,21), «dit la vérité» (2 Ch 18,15) ou «parle» (1 R 25,9 etc.) «au nom» de Dieu.

[8] Avec ces verbes environ dix-huit cas avec *en* et cinq avec *epi*.

Donc, abstraction faite des formules baptismales, nous pouvons constater que les constructions *«en»* et *«epi tôi onomati»* utilisées par Luc se retrouvent dans d'autres auteurs chrétiens, notamment Marc. Mais il faut ajouter que Luc en outre cherche manifestement à imiter les Septante. C'est particulièrement perceptible pour la construction *«epi tôi onomati»*.

Il est le seul parmi les auteurs de l'Église primitive à parler en particulier de baptêmes donnés «au nom *[en* ou *epi tôi onomati]* de Jésus, etc. Les Septante ne parlent pas non plus de baptêmes ou d'ablutions «au nom de» quelqu'un. Mais si, élargissant un peu le cercle conceptuel, nous envisageons le baptême en tant que rite, nous trouvons des parallèles dans la Septante, en ce sens qu'elle connaît des actions rituelles faites «au nom de Dieu», etc. Ainsi on peut prier (*epeuchesthai*: Dt 10,8), servir (*leitourgein*: Dt 17,12) ou présenter un sacrifice d'encens (*thymiama prospherein*: Ml 1,11) «au nom *[epi]* de» Dieu. De même, on peut invoquer (*epikaleisthai*: Dt 14,24), ou élever ses mains, (Ps 62,5) en *(en)* son nom.

La manière dont les Septante parlent des rites exécutés «au *[en]* nom de Dieu», etc., a sans doute continué d'avoir cours dans le judaïsme grec[9]. Elle est aussi attestée dans certains textes néotestamentaires: on rend grâce (*eucharistein*: Ep 5,20), on s'agenouille (Ph 2,10) ou on demande (*aitein*: Jn 14,13) au *(en)* nom de quelqu'un; de même on fait des onctions d'huile «au *[en]* nom du Seigneur» (Jc 5,14).

En revanche, il est beaucoup plus difficile de trouver de références attestant avec certitude que dans l'Église primitive on a parlé de rites exécutés «au *[epi]* nom» de Jésus, de Dieu, etc. D'ailleurs, des phrases avec *«epi tôi onomati»* ne se trouvent dans le Nouveau Testament, que dans les évangiles synoptiques et les Actes[10].

En conclusion, l'usage lucanien de l'expression *«epi tôi onomati»* a un certain mais assez minime support chez Marc, un plus solide dans la Septante. Quant à son utilisation en Ac 2,38, dans un contexte rituel, il semble que ce soit un cas unique dans tous les écrits des premières générations chrétiennes: par conséquent, Luc s'inspire des seuls Septante.

Ces remarques peuvent être déterminantes pour choisir, en Ac 2,38, entre les leçons *«en»* (mss B, D, pc) et *«epi»* (les autres mss). *«En»* pourrait en réalité représenter une leçon plus facile et dès lors moins sûre. En écrivant *«en tôi onomati»*, on aura peut-être voulu harmoniser la manière dont parle Pierre en Ac 2,38 avec celle d'Ac 10,48. En tout cas, on ne voit pas pour quelle raison la majorité des manuscrits auraient introduit *«epi»* en 2,38. C'est en effet une tournure

---

[9] Cf. Hans Bietenhard, *«onoma ktl.»*, in *TWNT* V (1954), 270.

[10] Mc 9,37 et 13,6 sont à l'origine de Mt 18,5; 24,5; Lc 9,48; 21,8, Restent dans les évangiles Mc 9,39 (faire un *dynamis;*), Lc 1,59 (nommer; expression des LXX, voir p. ex. Gn 4,17; Dt 3,14) et 24,47 (*kêryssein*) et pour les Actes – sauf 2,38 – 4,17 s; 5,28.40 (tous *lalein* ou *kêryssein*). Pour Lc 9,49 voir note 5.

exceptionnelle chez les autres auteurs néotestamentaires et, autant que je sache, dans la littérature chrétienne des premiers siècles[11].

Examinons maintenant la troisième tournure «*eis to onoma*». Nous constatons d'abord qu'elle apparaît chez Luc dans la formule baptismale seulement (Ac 8,16; 19,5). Les Septante n'ont rien d'équivalent, ni Marc non plus. En dehors des Actes elle se rencontre dans une formule baptismale en Mt 28,19 et, bien qu'indirectement, en 1 Co 1,13.15. Plus tard, elle devient courante dans les formules baptismales des rites de langue grecque[12] et, laissant de côté ce qu'on appelle *Girosprache*[13], il semble même qu'elle ne soit utilisée que dans ce contexte. En dehors de ces cas on ne trouve une tournure semblable qu'en Mt 10,41 s («accueillir un prophète *au nom d'un prophète*») et en Mt 18,20 («s'assembler *en mon nom*»).

Il est temps maintenant d'envisager des questions plus précises au sujet de ces trois locutions. La première est d'ordre historique: la diversité de construction (avec *en, epi, eis*) provient-elle de sources ou de traditions différentes, ou bien même implique-t-elle des conceptions différentes sur le baptême? Ou encore ne faut-il pas plutôt l'attribuer au génie littéraire de Luc?

Il n'est sans doute pas inutile de commencer par noter quelles sont les personnes qui parlent dans les quatre passages où paraît notre formule. En Ac 2,38 c'est Pierre qui, en conclusion de son discours du jour de la Pentecôte, dit: «Que chacun de vous se fasse baptiser au *[epi]* nom de Jésus Christ.» En Ac 10,48, il s'agit encore de Pierre qui donne l'ordre de baptiser Corneille et les siens «au *[en]* nom de Jésus Christ». En Ac 8,16, par ailleurs, c'est Luc lui-même qui raconte à ses lecteurs comment les convertis de Samarie avaient seulement été baptisés «au *[eis]* nom du Seigneur Jésus» sans avoir encore reçu l'effusion de l'Esprit. Enfin, en Ac 19,1–6, c'est Paul qui demande aux Johannites d'Éphèse «en qui *[eis ti]* avez-vous été baptisés?» (v. 3). Et le récit s'achève avec cette notice de Luc lui-même: « Ils reçurent le baptême au *[eis]* nom du Seigneur Jesus» (v. 5).

Les remarques ci-dessus attirent d'emblée l'attention sur un fait: lorsqu'il fait parler Pierre, Luc utilise des tours de phrase qui ont des analogies dans les Septante (avec les prépositions *epi* et *en*). Mais tandis que Pierre s'exprime ainsi en style biblique[14], l'auteur lui-même emploie la tournure «non biblique»:

---

[11] La Peshitta et la Vulgate ont la même préposition dans tous les cas; *b-* et *in* + abl. respectivement. Un tour de phrase comme celui-ci, de Tertullien, est cependant remarquable: *ad singula nomina* in *personas singulas tinguimur* (*Adv. Prax.*, 26).

[12] Voir p. ex. *Did.*, 7,1.3; 9,5; *Herm.*, Vis., III,7; Just., *Dial.*, 39,2 (?); Iren., *Adv. Haer.*, I,21.3; Méthod., *Symp.*, VIII, 8, 191; Épiphan., *Panar.*, LXXVI.54,33; Cyrill. Jer., *Catech. myst.*, III,1; Athan., *Adv. Ar.*, II,42. Ludwig Eisenhofer, *Handbuch der katholischen Liturgik*, II, Fribourg-en-Brisgau ²1941, 261. L'étrangeté de la formule pourrait être la raison du choix fait par Justin de l'expression *epi tou onomatos* dans sa discussion de *Apol.*, I,61.

[13] Wilhelm Heitmüller, „*Im Namen Jesu*" (FRLANT 1.2), Göttingen 1903, a lancé la thèse selon laquelle la formule d'*eis* aurait son origine dans la terminologie des banques, où on payait une somme au nom d'une personne = à son compte. L'évangile de Jean a parfois la construction *pisteuein eis to onoma*, ce qui, bien entendu, est un usage tout à fait différent (Jn 1,12; 2,23; 3,18).

[14] Cf. Ernst Haenchen, *Die Apostelgeschichte* (KEK 3), Göttingen ⁷1977, 188 et l'inventaire des discours d'Ac 2 et 3, dans Plümacher, *Lukas*, (n. 4), 41 ss.

*eis to onoma*. Cette observation concorde bien avec ce que nous savons de la manière lucanienne d'écrire. Comme d'autres historiens de l'époque, Luc a suivi la règle selon laquelle le style des discours rapportés dans un récit devait s'adapter aux habitudes de l'orateur et à la situation évoquée[15]. De toute évidence Luc a considéré Pierre comme une personnalité vénérée de l'Église primitive[16] et qui faisait autorité comme témoin immédiat de la prédication du Christ venue jusqu'aux lecteurs des Actes. Aussi met-il un langage biblique sur les lèvres de Pierre lorsque celui-ci parle du baptême, et plus généralement dans tous ses discours. De fait, l'ensemble des discours rapportés dans la première partie des Actes contient plus d'échos des Septante que les autres parties du livre, ce qui leur donne une allure hiératique et un ton biblique[17].

En revanche, la tournure «*eis to onoma*» semble appartenir à la langue naturelle de Luc. A en juger par les matériaux néotestamentaires (Mt, Paul, les Actes) elle relève, pour ainsi dire, d'une terminologie technique répandue dans l'Église primitive[18], et que Luc a fait sienne en apprenant le parler chrétien. Mais il semble avoir eu un tel sens du style des Septante qu'il a perçu que «*eis to onoma*» ne lui appartenait pas. Cette tournure ressortissait du jargon chrétien de Luc et de ses lecteurs plutôt que du langage de la Bible.

Puisque l'occasion s'en présente, ajoutons par manière de parenthèse que cet emploi lucanien de la formule «*eis to onoma*» a vraisemblablement son origine dans une très ancienne manière chrétienne de parler du baptême. Ailleurs, j'ai suggéré, contrairement aux opinions antérieures, que l'origine de la formule se trouve dans la traduction littérale d'une expression hébraïque ou araméenne semblable à celle que les Juifs employaient pour caractériser, entre autres, des rites comme les sacrifices ou la circoncision[19]. C'est ainsi qu'on dit, par exemple, qu'un Samaritain pratique la circoncision «au nom du mont Gerissin», tandis qu'au contraire une circoncision orthodoxe est faite «au nom de l'alliance» (t. ʿAbodah Zarah 3,13). On peut aussi «s'approcher» (dans le sens cultuel) «au nom du ciel» (S. Nu. § 136). Selon cette terminologie technique, l'expression «au nom …» (hébreu *leshem*) exprime la référence fondamentale du rite. Paul et Matthieu

---

[15] Voir PLÜMACHER, *Lukas* (n. 4), 39; WILLEM CORNELIS VAN UNNIK, «Luke's Second Book and the Rules of Hellenistic Historiography» in JACOB KREMER (éd.), *Les Actes des Apôtres. Traditions, rédaction, théologie* (BEThL 48), Paris – Gembloux – Louvain 1979, 59.

[16] Voir HANS CONZELMANN, *Die Mitte der Zeit. Studien zur Theologie des Lukas* (BHTh 17), Tübingen ⁵1964, 195 ss; WOLFGANG DIETRICH, *Das Petrusbild der lukanischen Schriften* (BWANT 14), Stuttgart 1972, 324 ss; PLÜMACHER, *Lukas* (n. 4), 67 ss.

[17] Voir PLÜMACHER, *Lukas*, (n. 4), 38 ss. Puisque ces traits sont généraux, on ne doit pas les voir comme le résultat d'un essai de Luc pour caractériser la personne de Pierre (PLÜMACHER, *Lukas*, [n. 4], 67).

[18] Il semble que ces passages apportent un appui assez considérable à l'opinion selon laquelle la désignation est à dater des premiers temps de l'Église. Voir GERHARD BARTH, *Die Taufe in frühchristlicher Zeit* (BibTSt 4), Neukirchen-Vluyn 1981, 45 ss, contre HANS F. VON CAMPENHAUSEN, «Taufen auf den Namen Jesu?», in: *VigChr* 25 (1971) 1–16.

[19] Voir LARS HARTMAN, «'Into the Name of Jesus'. A Suggestion Concerning the Earliest Meaning of the Phrase», in: *NTS* 20 (1973–1974) 432–440. Voir ce volume 145–154.

attestent avec Luc que cette formule sémitique a été si étroitement liée à la manière de parler du baptême chrétien que sa traduction, malgré son étrangeté, est entrée dans le langage chrétien grec[20].

Au point où nous sommes arrivés, on peut, semble-t-il, tirer une ou deux conclusions. Les formules baptismales avec *epi* et avec *en* sont à mettre au compte de l'activité littéraire de Luc. Il n'y a pas de raisons *directes* pour estimer qu'elles représentent des traditions particulières ou quelque phase de développement du rite baptismal[21]. Dans ce cas, la recherche relative à la «formule baptismale» de l'Église primitive peut se limiter à l'étude de la tournure avec «*eis*»[22]. Mais, bien entendu, connaître le sens originel d'une locution ne permet pas de présumer que ce sens a été conservé dans l'usage ultérieur qu'on en a fait, donc par Luc.

Pour ce qui est du sens, il me semble qu'il n'y a pas de différence entre les trois locutions employées par Luc dans les formules baptismales[23]. Le texte suivant de Dt 18 (LXX) présente trois traductions de l'expression «parler en le nom de (*b⁽ᵉ⁾shem*) quelqu'un»[24]. «Si un prophète a l'audace de dire en *[epi]* mon nom une parole que je n'ai pas ordonné de dire, et s'il parle au nom *[en onomati]* d'autres dieux, ce prophète mourra [...]. Si ce prophète a parlé au nom *[tôi onomati]* de Yahvé et que sa parole reste sans effet et ne s'accomplit pas, alors Yahvé n'a pas dit cette parole-là» (Dt 18,20.22).

Il n'y a guère ici de différence de sens dans les trois traductions de *b⁽ᵉ⁾shem*[25]. Il me semble donc qu'il en va de même chez Luc. Nous avons pu constater, il est vrai, qu'il préfère construire les verbes parler, proclamer, etc., avec *epi tôi onomati* et qu'il a tendance à employer la tournure *en tôi onomati* avec les verbes qui signifient guérir, etc. Mais il se permet trop de libertés pour que nous puissions en tirer des conclusions sur les nuances que l'emploi de telle ou telle préposition donne au sens de la formule baptismale. Autrement dit, nous estimons que, dans

---

[20] Paul, Matthieu et Luc ne sont pas nécessairement tellement loin l'un de l'autre: Paul peut avoir appris la formule à Antioche, et le premier évangile peut y avoir son origine. Voir RAYMOND E. BROWN/JOHANN P. MEIER, *Antioch and Rome*, Londres 1983, 11–72. Pour les Actes, cf. RICHARD GLOVER, «'Luke the Antiochene' and Acts», in: *NTS* 11 (1964–1965), 97 ss (la citation du titre est d'Eusèbe, *H. E.*, III, 4, 6).

[21] On pourrait avancer une raison *indirecte*, mais pas tellement forte, pour l'antiquité de la construction avec *en* en citant le fait que dans les textes rabbiniques *b⁽ᵉ⁾shem* est parfois employé d'une façon qui rappelle *lšm*; voir p. ex, *m.Sanhedrin*, VII, 6: faire un vœu au nom (*b⁽ᵉ⁾shem*) d'une idole; cf. *m.Niddah*, V, 6: «Nous savons au nom (*l⁽ᵉ⁾shem*) de qui nous avons fait nos vœux.»

[22] HEITMÜLLER, „Im Namen", (n. 13), 90, 127 a-t-il même voulu dire que les formules avec *epi* et *en* représentent une époque plus primitive? Parfois on en a l'impression.

[23] Ainsi plusieurs auteurs, p. ex. HEITMÜLLER „Im Namen", (n. 13), 121 – «im wesentlichen synonym», HANS CONZELMANN, *Die Apostelgeschichte* (HNT 7), Göttingen ²1972, 36 (*en* = *epi*), JÜRGEN ROLOFF, *Die Apostelgeschichte* (NTD 5), Göttingen 1981, 62. Cf. DELLING, *Zueignung*, (n. 2), 91 ss et aussi FREDERICK FYVIE BRUCE, *The Acts of the Apostles*, Londres ²1952, 98, 187.

[24] *B⁽ᵉ⁾shem* est aussi l'expression régulière derrière les phrases avec *epi* et *en tôi onomati* dans les LXX.

[25] Je veux souligner que cet avis se base sur le texte grec et son contexte, pas sur la lecture du TM avec son *b⁽ᵉ⁾shem* répété. Car quand un texte a quitté la table du traducteur, son sens – ou ses sens – dépend d'autres facteurs que ses réflexions privées en traduisant le texte original.

ce cas, le style de Luc est davantage tributaire de son goût pour un ton solennel et de l'usage courant que d'un choix sémantique conscient.

## 2. Les génitifs

En ce qui concerne le «nom» évoqué dans les locutions étudiées, il faut évidemment le comprendre dans sa référence au génitif qui le suit et à la lumière du contexte. Mais c'est une question que nous n'aborderons pas ici.

Passons donc aux génitifs qui déterminent ce «nom». Rappelons les quatre locutions:

2,38: «au *[epi]* nom de Jésus Christ»
10,48: «au *[en]* nom de Jésus Christ»
8,16: «au *[eis]* nom du Seigneur Jésus»
19,5: « au *[eis]* nom du Seigneur Jésus»[26].

Dans les deux cas où il se montre plus « biblique» en utilisant *epi* et *en* plutôt que *eis*, l'auteur dit «Jésus Christ» et «le Seigneur Jésus» dans les deux locutions de facture plus lucanienne. On peut à nouveau se demander si cette différence provient des sources ou des traditions. Ou encore si Luc a choisi l'appellation «Christ» dans une perspective juive, et celle de *Kyrios* en songeant davantage à ses lecteurs hellénistes[27].

L'appellation «Jésus Christ» est peu fréquente dans Ac: huit fois (plus trois avec en outre le titre de *Kyrios*)[28]. Mais la manière dont Luc l'utilise concorde avec ce que nous avons noté plus haut à propos de ses méthodes littéraires. Luc a évidemment estimé que la dénomination «Jésus Christ» convenait mieux dans la bouche de judéo-chrétiens s'adressant à des Juifs[29]: c'est donc ainsi qu'il fait parler Pierre lorsque ses auditeurs appartiennent à ce milieu (2,38; 3,6; 4,10; 9,34; 10,36.48; 11,17 avec *Kyrios*). Cette appellation se trouve aussi en 15,26 [avec *Kyrios hêmôn*] dans la lettre que l'Église de Jérusalem adresse aux «frères d'ori-

---

[26] Le codex D lit dans tous les quatre passages (sauf en 19,5 où l'article manque) *tou kyriou Iêsou Christou*. Cf. CARLO M. MARTINI, «La tradition textuelle des Actes des Apôtres et les tendances de l'Église ancienne» in: *Les Actes*, (n. 15), 31 (cohérences des variantes de D), et MAX E. WILCOX, «Luke and the Bezan Text of Acts», *ibid.*, 447-455 (plus de style lucanien en D qu'en B; pour *kyrios*, voir 449).

[27] Les questions sont posées par DELLING, *Zueignung*, (n. 2), 85 ss.

[28] 2,38; 3,6; 4,10; 8,12; 9,34; 10,36.48; 16,18; 11,17 (*kyrios J. Ch.*) ; 15,26 (*kyrios hêmôn J. Ch.*); 28,31 (*kyrios J. Ch.*).

[29] Les exégètes se contentent en règle générale de constater que «*Christos*» est employé dans la perspective de «Verheissung und Erfüllung». Voir CONZELMANN, *Mitte* (n. 16), 151; GERHARD SCHNEIDER, *Die Apostelgeschichte*, I (HThK 5/I), Fribourg-Bâle-Vienne 1980, 333; ULRICH WILCKENS, *Die Missionsreden der Apostelgeschichte* (WMANT 5), Neukirchen ²1974, 157. Wilckens discute cependant explicitement la combinaison *I. Ch.*, ainsi que le fait DELLING, *Zueignung* (n. 2), 88. Ma suggestion correspond, dans une certaine mesure, à l'avis de JOHN COCHRANE O'NEILL, *The Theology of Acts*, Londres 1961, 15: Luc utilise des titres christologiques pour donner à sa présentation *«an archaic and scriptural ring»*.

gine païenne qui sont à Antioche, en Syrie et en Cilicie» (Ac 15,23). Et puisque Luc considère les Samaritains comme membres du peuple de Dieu auquel les agrège l'accueil de la Parole[30], il dit que Philippe proclame le Christ, c'est-à-dire le Messie, dans le pays des Samaritains (8,5) auxquels il annonce «la Bonne Nouvelle [...] du nom de Jésus Christ» (8,12). Et à la fin du livre (28,31), on lit que, durant les deux années de sa captivité à Rome, Paul enseignait «ce qui concerne le Seigneur Jésus Christ». Une telle appellation qui inclut les trois titres correspond bien à la situation, puisque l'apôtre s'adresse à «tous», c'est-à-dire aux Juifs aussi bien qu'aux païens[31]. Seul 16,18 ne cadre pas avec les autres exemples: là, en effet, Paul chasse l'esprit de divination d'une femme de Philippes, en lui ordonnant de sortir d'elle «au nom de Jésus Christ». Mais peut-être s'agit-il dans ce cas d'une formule stéréotypée car on la lit aussi en 3,6 et en 4,10 où elle est également utilisée pour opérer des guérisons.

Ces observations *n'excluent* pas que l'appellation «Jésus Christ», en 2,38 et en 10,48 puisse provenir d'une sorte de tradition ou d'un usage judéo-chrétien auquel se conformerait Luc. Mais la manière dont il distribue ce titre tout au long de son récit ne favorise guère une telle hypothèse[32].

Venons-en à l'autre titre (baptiser au nom du) «Seigneur Jésus». *Kyrios*, employé seul, est très commun dans les Actes. Ce terme désigne parfois Dieu, souvent Jésus, parfois l'un ou l'autre sans qu'on puisse déterminer à coup sûr lequel. La combinaison «le Seigneur Jésus» est plus rare: treize exemples plus quatre avec soit *hemôn* soit *Christos*[33].

Si nous examinons encore une fois comment cette appellation est distribuée entre l'auteur et ceux qu'il met en scène, nous pouvons synthétiser nos observations de la manière suivante. Quand c'est lui qui parle, Luc dit «le Seigneur Jésus» (4,33 ; 8,16; 11,20; 19,5.13.17)[34]. Paul fait de même lorsqu'il s'adresse au geôlier de la prison de Philippes (16,31), aux anciens d'Éphèse (20,21.24.35)[35] et aux frères de Césarée (21,13). Pierre parle du «Seigneur Jésus» aux «frères» (1,21)[36], puis

---

[30] JACOB JERVELL, *Luke and the People of God*, Minneapolis, Minn. 1972, 113 ss.

[31] JACQUES DUPONT, «La conclusion des Actes et son rapport à l'ensemble de l'ouvrage de Luc», in JACOB KREMER (éd.), in: *Les Actes*, (n. 15), 377 ss.

[32] La combinaison christologique «Jésus Christ» est bien sûr traditionnelle. Voir p. ex. WILCKENS, *Missionsreden*, (n. 29), 157; on la trouve dans diverses traditions néotestamentaires. Étant donné l'usage lucanien que nous avons vu plus haut, cette «traditionalité» ne justifie pourtant guère une idée qu'Ac 2,38 et 10,48 représenteraient une tradition liturgique. Peut-être faut-il souligner que je ne nie pas la possibilité de sources. Mais il me semble que les détails que je discute ici s'expliquent sans qu'on introduise un facteur si incertain dans la discussion. Voir l'étude classique de JACQUES DUPONT, *Les Sources du livre des Actes. État de la question*, Bruges 1960. Pour les discussions plus récentes, voir p. ex. CONZELMANN, *Apostelgeschichte*, (n. 23), 4 ss; SCHNEIDER, *Apostelgeschichte* (n. 29), 82 ss. Un bon aperçu bref dans ALFONS WEISER, *Die Apostelgeschichte. Kapitel 1–12* (ÖTK 5/I), Gütersloh • Würzburg 1981, 36 ss.

[33] 1,21; 4,33; 7,59; 8,16; 11,20; 15,11; 16,31; 19,5.13.17; 20,24.35; 21,13 ; *ho kyrios J. Ch.*: 11,17 et 28,31; *ho kyrios hêmôn J.* (plusieurs mss ajoutent *Ch*: 20,21; *ho kyrios hêmôn J. Ch.*: 15,26).

[34] 28,31 y ajoute Christos. Cf. DELLING, *Zueignung* (n. 2), 87 ss.

[35] Avec hêmôn.

[36] 11,17 y ajoute Christos.

«aux apôtres et aux anciens» (15,11). Enfin, tandis qu'on le lapide, Étienne invoque le «Seigneur Jésus» (7,59).

Il me semble que pour Luc «le Seigneur Jésus» soit une manière dont les chrétiens parlent entre eux. Ce n'est certes pas la seule mais toutefois une manière naturelle, que ce soit à Jérusalem, à Milet ou à Éphèse, et également lorsque Luc s'adresse à ses lecteurs chrétiens. Le cas de 16,31 est à part où Paul, à Philippes, dit à son geôlier, un païen: «Crois au Seigneur Jésus.» Mais cela peut s'expliquer par le fait qu'il s'agit là de croire: en effet, quand Luc présente Jésus comme objet de la foi, il l'appelle normalement *Kyrios*[37].

Ce que nous avons constaté au sujet des titres christologiques donnés à celui dont le «nom» est invoqué dans la formule baptismale des Actes s'harmonise bien avec les observations faites plus haut à propos des prépositions qui expriment cette invocation. Là nous avons pu confirmer la remarque de Delling selon laquelle *eis to onoma* serait «die ihm [à Luc] geläufige Taufformel[38]». Nous pouvons maintenant avancer quelque chose de semblable à propos de la dernière partie de la formule: selon Luc, les chrétiens, quand ils sont entre eux, disent «le Seigneur Jésus».

En conclusion, la formule *eis to onoma tou kyriou Iêsou* représente la tradition que Luc a reçue et qui est en vigueur dans son milieu. En l'utilisant, il ne fait pas œuvre d'homme de lettre comme lorsqu'il écrit *epi (en) tôi onomati Iêsou Christou*. Pour une étude plus approfondie des questions historiques qui se posent, il faudrait envisager l'origine certainement sémitique de la tournure *eis to onoma*, ainsi que la formule «le Seigneur Jésus» dans sa relation avec la confession de foi primitive «*Kyrios Iesous*» (Rm 10,9; 1 Co 12,3; 2 Co 4,5; Ph 2,11; Col 2,6). Mais ceci nous entraînerait trop loin. Notre but sera atteint si ces réflexions contribuent à clarifier quelque peu, voire à simplifier le problème posé par le fait que Luc donne trois «formules baptismales» différentes.

---

[37] JACQUES DUPONT, «Jésus, Messie et Seigneur dans la foi des premiers chrétiens», dans: IDEM, *Études sur les Actes des Apôtres* (LD 45), Paris 1967, 382 ss. Ac 24,24 (Félix écoute Paul parler de la foi *eis Christon Jêsoun*) n'est guère une exception, car la pistis n'y désigne pas une foi de Félix, mais plutôt le contenu de la foi chrétienne.

[38] DELLING, *Zueignung* (n. 2), 94.

# 15. Early Baptism – Early Christology

Rites are normally assumed to mean something. This "something" may be intimated in a cult foundation myth, expressed by ritual texts, or merely implied in the rite's cultural and religious contexts. Often, however, the rite, as such, is more stable than its interpretation. This means that the ritual (actions and, in some cases, texts) has inherent possibilities, which may allow new perceptions of the rite. One example is the understanding of baptism among certain clergy in the Church of Sweden, who regard baptism as mainly the sacrament of God's prevenient grace, expressing in action an idea of God as the God of unconditional and merciful love. Their view probably derives from the role of this church as a *Volkskirche* and is also, presumably, influenced by Swedish theologians such as G. Aulén and A. Nygren.[1] But, compared to the early church and classical theology, this view represents a different emphasis.

## 1. The Baptismal Formula "in(to) the name of Jesus"

In this paper I shall seek the early interrelation between the rite of baptism and Christology[2] by concentrating on a single detail – the fact that from the very beginning baptism seems to have been performed "into the name of Jesus the Lord" or "in the name of Jesus the Messiah." It is my contention that understood in a partly new and, I hope, more correct manner, these formulas indicate some features of early christological thinking.

There are good reasons to assume that the formula "(baptize) into the name of the Lord Jesus" represents the oldest layer of baptismal traditions. As is well known, the formula is commonly explained as meaning that the person baptized was dedicated to the *kyrios* Jesus. This understanding of the formula was

---

[1] See, e.g., GUSTAF AULÉN, *The Faith of the Christian Church,* Philadelphia, Penn. 1960, in which the chapter on baptism (§ 44) is titled "The Sacrament of Prevenient Grace." See also ANDERS NYGREN, *Agape and Eros,* Philadelphia, Penn. 1953.

[2] Actually the constellation baptism – Christology has received relatively little attention in New Testament scholarship, at least as compared with the vast amount of literature dealing with baptism and the even more substantial quantity of writings on Christology. One exception is PETR POKORNÝ, "Christologie et Baptême a l'époque du Christianisme primitif," *NTS* 27 (1980/81) 368–380; edited Ger. version in IDEM, *Die Entstehung der Christologie. Voraussetzungen einer Theologie des Neuen Testaments,* Berlin 1985, 148–156. See also my "La formule baptismale dans les Actes des Apôtres: Quêlques observations relatives au style de Luc," *A cause de l'évangile. Études sur les Synoptiques et les Actes offertes au P. Jacques Dupont* (LD 123), Paris 1985, 727–738. [In this volume nr. 14, pp. 155–163.]

supported from two different sides, both of which refer to modes of speech found in the world of the early church. W. Heitmüller assumed that the phrase "into the name (εἰς τὸ ὄνομα) of the Lord Jesus" indicated that the person baptized became the Lord's property in the same way a sum of money paid "into the name" of the owner of a bank account became the property of this person.[3] A similar understanding of the formula was advanced by, among others, P. Billerbeck who found an analogy in a mishnaic sacrifice-ruling which stated that a sacrifice had to be offered "into the name of the Name," that is, of God (*m.Zebaḥim* 4:6). By analogy, the baptismal formula should mean the baptized person was dedicated to the Lord in the same way an offering was dedicated to a given deity.[4] Irrespective of which background is accepted, the christological idea becomes one according to which Jesus is regarded as a powerful heavenly king or master who owns his subjects or, possibly, one whose powerful name can be invoked as protection.

Over against this explanation of the formula, I have suggested that although Billerbeck was correct when he adduced the sacrificial rule as a parallel to the baptismal formula, it ought to be differently assessed. In fact, the quoted rule is only one of several that represent a manner of speaking of different rites in Hebrew and Aramaic (*lᵉshem, lᵉshum*).[5] The "name" "into" which the rite was performed indicated a fundamental reference of the rite; thus it also, indirectly, separated the rite from other similar rites which were performed "into" other "names." Thus someone might circumcise "into the name of the mountain of Gerizim" (*t.ʿAbodah Zarah* 3:13), that is, within the religious system of Samaritan Judaism. Furthermore, someone could slaughter into the name of the mountains, the hills, the seas, or the desert (*m.Ḥullin* 2:8; cf. Deut 12:2); or one might gather (i.e., for a religious service) into the name of Heaven (God; *ʾAbot* 4:11), sacrifice into the name of the archangel Michael (*b.Ḥullin* 40a), or vow and sanctify to the name of one's god (*m.Niddah* 5:6).

I suggest that when the phrase "into the name ..." was used in connection with Christian baptism, it was the result of a literal translation of a Semitic turn of phrase from the Aramaic-speaking early church. As in the examples above from rabbinic literature, it should have indicated the fundamental reference of the rite concerned. It also distinguished Christian baptism from other baptisms, probably especially the one of John the Baptist. How the phrase has spread can only be surmised, but maybe the so-called Hellenists first used the queer Greek form – for queer it is – and then took it with them when they had to leave Jerusalem. There are traces of it in Paul (1 Cor 1:13); Luke reports it in Acts (8:16;

---

[3] WILHELM HEITMÜLLER, "*Im Namen Jesu*" (FRLANT 1:2), Göttingen 1903.

[4] HERMANN L. STRACK/PAUL BILLERBECK, *Kommentar zum Neuen Testament aus Talmud und Midrasch I*, Munich 1922, 591, 1054–55.

[5] LARS HARTMAN, "'Into the Name of Jesus': A Suggestion concerning the Earliest Meaning of the Phrase," *NTS* 20 (1973/74) 432–440; [In this volume nr. 13, pp. 145–154]; IDEM, "Baptism 'Into the Name of Jesus' and Early Christology: Some Tentative Considerations," *ST* 28 (1974) 21–48. See also IDEM, "ὄνομα," *EWNT* 2: 1268–77.

19:5); and Matthew uses it, although changed, so that the "name" is that of the triune God (28:19).

It should be mentioned that sometimes the rabbinic texts use the preposition "in" ($b^e$) with the "name," but with no recognizable difference in meaning.[6] Luke also, however, uses different prepositions (εἰς, ἐν, ἐπί) indiscriminately.[7] Thus, it is not improbable that another phrase was also used early, namely, "*in* the name …," represented in Acts 10:48 (cf. 1 Cor 6:11).

Now, leaving aside for a moment the christological titles used in the formulas, let us further consider what may have been implied when baptism was performed with Jesus as a fundamental reference of the rite – "into" his "name." When a sacrifice was slaughtered "into the name of the mountains," this meant not that it was offered to the mountains but that, via an allusion to passages such as Deut 12:2, it belonged to pagan idolatry.[8] When, furthermore, a gathering was taken seriously which took place "into the name of Heaven" (*'Abot* 4:6), or when all one's doings should be "into the name of Heaven" (*'Abot* 2:12), the name-phrase indicates basic aspects of what was happening.

In all these examples the statements concern actions which, depending on the presuppositions, can be understood in different ways. A sacrifice could take place within the referential framework of traditional Judaism, but also so that "the altar was filled with [offerings] which were unclean according to the Laws" (2 Macc 6:5). So also circumcision could be judged differently, although a Samaritan circumcision and one "into the name of the covenant" (thus the rabbis according to *t.'Abodah Zarah* 3:13) both took place as fulfillments of the Torah. Similarly one could assess in different ways both "gatherings" and different "approaches" (i.e., when one approached God in sacrifice or prayer).[9]

The examples concerning vows and gatherings are especially instructive when one reflects on baptism, because in none of them is anything being done

---

[6] Thus vows can be said to be made "into the name of" God (as above, *m.Niddah* 5:6), but with the same meaning an idolater is reported to vow "in" his god's name (*m.Sanhedrin* 7:6).

[7] At least as far as the meaning of the preposition is concerned. But I suggest that Luke differentiates between the manners of speech that he ascribes to his characters: thus he makes Peter speak more "biblically," using ἐν τῷ ὀνόματι. See HARTMAN, "La formule baptismale."

[8] The Gemara of the passage (*b.Hullin* 40a) includes stars and planets and Michael among those, "to the name" of whom one must not sacrifice. The added "names" no more indicate primarily receivers of the sacrifices than do the ones in the Mishna, but, rather, point to a wider framework of the cult, namely, the astral religiosity which was widespread. The passage may also contain echoes from Deut 4:19; 17:3, etc. That Michael occurs in the list is explained by the fact that angels and archangels often became associated with stars and planets, which were also members of the celestial host. In addition, it may indicate a sort of syncretism in which the heavenly host was more revered than rabbinic orthodoxy liked, and may lead our associations to incantations in which not least angelic names appear. See PHILIP S. ALEXANDER, "Incantations and Books of Magic," in EMIL SCHÜRER, *The History of the Jewish People in the Age of Jesus Christ*, rev. ed., 3:1, Edinburgh 1986, 342–379: 347–348, 350–351. The Jewish incantations mentioned by Alexander seem to belong to roughly the same era as *b.Hullin* 40. Of course, the Gemara does not refer directly to sacrifices actually offered in the Temple, which had been ruined long ago.

[9] Hebrew קרב (*Sipre Num.* 136).

to God or with respect to Him so to speak as taken for Himself. Rather the reference is to the religious fundamentals that depend on God's relation to human beings. Gathering to the name of God (heaven) does not mean to gather to God, but means, rather, to gather to prayers, readings, applications of Scripture and so forth, all of which relate to and are marked by God and by what God means to human beings, not least through what He does and has done to them. Furthermore, what may be missing in the case of vows given by certain young people is that they do not realize this framework of their vows, despite their assertion, "We know into whose name we have vowed" (*m.Niddah* 5:6).

Thus, the formula "(baptize) into the name (of the Lord Jesus)" does not refer only to the person of Jesus as the basic reference of baptism – as the gatherings of ʾAbot 2 do not refer only to God *per se* (or the gatherings of Matt 18:20 refer only to Christ *per se*). Instead the basic reference and presuppositions are what the one named means in his relation to human beings. How exactly people thought of this relation when they began to baptize into the name of Jesus (or however he was named), we do not know. But there are a few aspects to be considered. First, it is highly probable that the baptism of the early church was taken over from John the Baptist.[10] The high esteem in which the Baptist was held in the early church supports the assumption that she did not simply take over an insulated mode of action, namely, dipping people into water. Baptism's essential presuppositions, meanings, and implications must have been of decisive importance: in the light of an imminent eschatological crisis people had to repent, and when the repentant underwent baptism, past sins were forgiven. This all meant preparing a people for God, who was soon to establish the kingdom of God.[11] In addition, somehow God's Spirit would play a role in this coming drama.

In all probability, the adopted Johannine baptism was, from the beginning, Christianized by being performed into the name of Jesus.[12] To my mind, the Aramaic origin of the formula points to its early date. By analogy this "Jesus" (still irrespective of any "titles") did not refer only to a Jesus *per se*, but also and not least to what he meant to people, especially the baptized. His importance must then depend on his position and on what he had done of relevance to human beings. These aspects must have colored the understanding of the meaning of the adopted baptism, the eschatological expectation, the forgiveness of the penitent, the preparation of a people for God, the ideas concerning the Spirit.

With this, we have touched upon a second factor of importance for our issue. John's baptism was taken over when the disciples were convinced that Jesus had risen from the dead. This conviction not only indicated certain ideas about

---

[10] For the arguments see, e.g., GERHARD BARTH, *Die Taufe in frühchristlicher Zeit*, Neukirchen-Vluyn 1981, 23–43. [2nd ed., 2002, 20–54.]

[11] BARTH, *ibid.*, 27, 34ff. [2nd ed., 23f.; 30–33] has observed that the fact that people passively received John's baptism indicates that forgiveness was given in the rite in a "sacramental" manner.

[12] This is what RUDOLF BULTMANN maintains, *Theologie des Neuen Testaments* (Neue theologische Grundrisse), Tübingen ⁶1968, 41–42.

Jesus and what had happened to him (of course, expressed with the linguistic and conceptual means of the time – what else!) but also had consequences for humankind and for how the situation should be assessed. A belief that Jesus had risen implied a belief that a new phase in history had begun – that the fully realized kingdom, the nearness of which Jesus had preached, was even closer at hand.[13]

We now proceed to consider some consequences of the combination of these factors, the Christian baptism as a Christianized Johannine one, its being performed "into the name" of Jesus, and the conviction that Jesus had risen, which implied a conclusion concerning the nearness of the eschaton. I leave aside at first the christological titles used with the name of Jesus, in order then to discuss the possible implications of making "the Lord" and "the Messiah," respectively, the fundamental references of baptism.

To start baptizing with John's baptism into the name of Jesus, who had risen and so introduced a decisive phase of the last times, presupposes a preceding proclamation of a necessary conversion. But if the conversion resulted in a baptism into Jesus' name, this proclamation ought to have said something about this Jesus. One statement must have been that Jesus' resurrection meant a landmark in the last events. But baptizing into his name must have presupposed more, namely, that he was of decisive importance to the person baptized. It is hard not to assume that he was presented as one who meant salvation in the approaching judgment, which John foresaw. But why were those baptized into the name of Jesus not to be judged? Not only because they had repented, left a sinful life behind, and turned to a righteous one, but also because they had turned to Jesus and accepted that he was this sort of portal figure into the eschaton.

But there was also forgiveness. In the Christianized baptism this must have been connected with the basic reference of the rite – Jesus. This might have been done in several ways. One way could have consisted of a reference to the earthly Jesus' acceptance of sinners in word and action, which, moreover, Jesus had maintained was actually God's acceptance of them. Another way could have been a presentation of the glorified Jesus as a graceful heavenly Lord who pardoned the repentant sinner (this is a picture intimated in Acts; see, e.g., 5:31; 13:37–39). Yet another might have interpreted his death as a death "for our sins," as the pre-Pauline formula says (1 Cor 15:3; 2 Cor 5:21; Gal 1:4) or "for us" (with some variant pronouns, e.g., Rom 8:32; 14:15; 1 Cor 11:24).

Lastly there was John's prospect of a coming baptism in Spirit. This feature had a natural place within the framework of contemporary Jewish eschatological expectations,[14] and although it is impossible to be certain as to the Baptist's meaning in this respect, it is still clear that somehow he expected that in the ap-

---

[13] This aspect is stressed by KARL MARTIN FISCHER, *Das Urchristentum* (Kirchengeschichte in Einzeldarstellungen I/1), Berlin 1985, 62–63; see also, e.g., BULTMANN, *Theologie*, 39ff.; and POKORNÝ, *Christologie*, chap. 3.

[14] See, e.g., 1QS 4:19–23; *Jub.* 1:22–25. See also Ezek 36:22–32.

proaching crisis God's Spirit would be at work, probably as a cleansing force, but very possibly also as an aspect of God's active presence among His people. The early Christians maintained that, in contrast to the Baptist's flock, God's Spirit was at work among them (Acts 19:3).[15] It was only to be expected that this was regarded as a consequence of the new phase of the last times which was introduced by Jesus' resurrection.

## 2. The Use of Christological Titles

This seems to be as far as the simple phrase "into the name" takes us as referring to Jesus when John's baptism was adopted after Easter. But in all the instances we possess of the formula, a title is joined with the name Jesus. There are good reasons for the view that "the Lord" *(kyrios)* was a very early component. It is known to Luke together with the fixed "into the name" phrase,[16] and so might have belonged to it when imported to the environment where he learned it later on. Taken by itself, *kyrios* (as well as the Aramaic *mara*) can differ in meaning, and may denote any authoritative figure – from an ordinary "sir" to a Greek (or Aramaic) equivalent to the divine name.[17] In order to be able to function as a fundamental reference of a cultic action, Jesus as *kyrios* must, however, be placed somewhere at the latter end of the range. To quote Fitzmyer: "It at least implies that Early Christians regarded Jesus as sharing in some sense the transcendence of Yahweh, that he was somehow on a par with him."[18] As a matter of fact, the close connection between baptism and the *kyrios*-title may well represent a third early usage of the title, to be added to the two between which biblical scholarship has differentiated: (1) its use in the prayer *marana tha*, "come, our Lord," and (2) its use in the acclamation "Lord (is) Jesus." The first one is assumed to reflect the eschatological expectations of the earliest period and so to be slightly earlier than the acclamation, which is possibly derived from it.[19] If we take the Johannine background of Christian baptism seriously and also understand the interpretative formula "into the name ..." as I have argued, it intimates some possible connotations of the *kyrios*-title as used in the baptismal formula.

Thus, the "Lord" should be a subject of the proclamation which led to baptism. Probably it envisaged Jesus as the risen Lord who had inaugurated the last phase of the eschaton, and whose coming was near (cf. *marana tha*: "come, our Lord"). But he was already in the present a transcendent authority. The same high position he had might also imply a demand that he be obeyed. Conversion should in some sense mean a change in a person's attitude to him, say accepting

---

[15] E.g., FISCHER, *Urchristentum*, 64.

[16] The detailed arguments are in HARTMAN, "La formule baptismale."

[17] JOSEPH A. FITZMYER, "The Semitic Background of the New Testament Kyrios-Title," in: IDEM, *A Wandering Aramean* (SBLMS 25), Missoula, Mont. 1979, 115–142.

[18] *Ibid.*, 130.

[19] See POKORNÝ, *Christologie*, 62–63.

him as the coming Savior and – why not – paying heed to his moral will. Furthermore, the forgiveness given in baptism should somehow be dependent on him, and he should be the one to trust when facing the imminent crisis.

Finally, the Spirit: the same circles as those in which the baptism was performed knew that during his earthly life Jesus had worked in the power of the Spirit (Matt 12:28/Luke 11:20; Mark 1:10 par.[20]). There do not seem to be any obvious connections between the Christians' possession of the Spirit and their being baptized with reference to Jesus as their Lord. The later interpretations differ: Paul maintains that the Spirit is given because of belief (Gal 3:2), but can also state in a somewhat confusing manner that "the Lord *is* the Spirit, and where the Spirit *of* the Lord is, is freedom" (2 Cor 3:17, italics added). Luke makes Peter proclaim that the glorified Lord has received the Spirit and poured it out (Acts 2:33ff.). John makes Jesus promise that he will return, specifically, in the Paraclete's coming, which however is also given by the Father (John 14:16ff.). In some way or another, all of these solutions relate the risen Lord with the Spirit to the work of which John the Baptist's baptism looked forward.

There are also grounds to assume that another early christological title was joined to a name-formula used about baptism – Christ, the Messiah. It is natural to infer that such a formula was used in Jewish-Christian circles. In this case the formula seems to have been "*in* the name." We observed above that a name-formula with "in" could be used in the same way as "into the name." In Acts it is used by Peter in 10:48, and 1 Cor 6:11 also suggests that it has existed as a formula. If this is so, then in this case the fundamental presupposition of baptism has been that the risen Jesus was the Messiah. Here too we do not simply stand before a dogmatic statement concerning Jesus as a person for himself; it also and not least tells us something of Jesus' significance to the one baptized. The context of a Christianized Johannine baptism implies some nuances in the connotations of the Messiah title that are not otherwise visible, for example, when one only regards the so-called identification-statements ("he is the Messiah": Acts 9:22; 17:3; Mark 8:29, etc.), which are sometimes held to belong to the earliest layer.[21] We should, however, remember that it is hard to find any criteria as to how to date a formula like this one. If we do not take Luke's witness of a very early usage for granted – and that might be a little too optimistic! – we are left with the argument adduced for the dating of the usage of the Messiah-title: that an early date is indicated by the fact that, as far back as with Paul, "Christ" has become a mere name.[22]

That Jesus the Messiah is the fundamental frame of reference of baptism thus presupposes that certain events have played a part in the preceding proclamation. It seems next to inevitable that the proclamation somehow must have touched

---

[20] LEANDER E. KECK has demonstrated the early Palestinian origin of the feature in the narrative of Jesus' baptism, "The Spirit and the Dove," *NTS* 17 (1970/71), 41–67.
[21] POKORNÝ, *Christologie* 66, referring to H. von Campenhausen and R. N. Longenecker.
[22] So, rightly, POKORNÝ, *Christologie*, 66.

upon the past of this Jesus, since in both biblical and Jewish language the designation normally referred to an earthly figure, although one sent by God and/or acting on God's behalf. Giving such attention to the earthly career of Jesus must have meant that Jesus' passion and death must also be assessed. Paul was certainly right when he stated: "A crucified Messiah is a stumbling-block to the Jews" (1 Cor 1:23). We need not enter a detailed discussion of how far a Messiah-title as used by the early church had any roots in Jesus' understanding of himself. That he had a unique consciousness of having a divine mission is hardly disputable, nor that he meant that this was in accordance with God's promises to His people. But apparently he avoided an identification with messianic figures such as, for example, the one given in *Pss. Sol.* 17 of the expected ruler. Thus the very early usage in the church of the title "Messiah" would be more easily understandable if it had a certain counterpart in Jesus' own life. To the heritage from Jesus belonged also his personal understanding of his mission as being for the good of others, which seems to have brought with it a conviction that he was to suffer and die.[23] Then Luke's clearance of the messianic way would have its roots in Jesus' appearance, when he made the risen Jesus teach that "Messiah had to suffer these things and so enter his glory" (Luke 24:26). Luke certainly also had some predecessors in the church who similarly understood Jesus' passion and death. The explanation which adduced the model of the suffering servant of Deutero-Isaiah would also be linked with the historical Jesus, when the death of the Messiah was interpreted as one "for" (ὑπέρ) others.[24]

Thus, when the proclamation that preceded a baptism "in the name of Jesus, the Messiah," presented him as the Messiah, the preaching must have depicted him as one who during his life had acted on God's commission according to God's promises. Somehow his passion and death were fitted into this picture. Above all, however, the eschatological role of the Messiah must have been in focus. To repent in the perspective of the imminent end also meant to join the people who gathered around this ruler of the new age. But baptism's reference to Jesus the Messiah ought also to have something to do with a forward-looking eschatological expectation, that is, we should seek a coming eschatological role of Jesus the Messiah. Such a one is provided by a Son of man Christology, and it seems reasonable to assume that the traditional messianic figure was complemented with features of the Son of man. There are reasons which favor the opinion that such a combination had its roots in Jesus' own appearance.[25] Notwithstanding, Paul's eschatological picture in 1 Thess 4:14 contains features from a Son of man scenario, in which the Christians expect to be "brought for-

---

[23] E.g., TRAUGOTT HOLTZ, *Jesus aus Nazareth*, Berlin 1979, 86–94; GRAHAM N. STANTON, *The Gospels and Jesus* (Oxford Bible Series), Oxford 1989, 223–224. HEINZ SCHÜRMANN has coined the expression of Jesus' "Proexistenz" for others; see, e.g., the essays in IDEM, *Jesu ureigener Tod. Exegetische Besinnungen und Ausblick*, Freiburg 1975.

[24] See, e.g., LEONHARD GOPPELT, *Theologie des Neuen Testaments*, Göttingen ³1981, 240–247, 420–421.

[25] E.g., HOLTZ, *Jesus*, 89–90.

ward together with" their Lord by God (note the allusion to Dan 7:13).[26] In other words, this kind of Messiah was one to hope for and to join when the last crisis of the world occurred and the kingdom was finally realized.

In the baptism in the name of Jesus the Messiah, sins were forgiven. Insofar as the title referred to the historical Jesus, it is hard to avoid the conclusion that reference was made to his attitude over against sinners in word and action, in which in a preparatory but real way the kingdom of God made its powers known. Now, after his resurrection, the messianic people enjoyed the eschatological gift of the remission of their sins in his name. It also implied a lack of fear of the approaching judgment.

Lastly, the gift of the Spirit, again. It was an established view that the Messiah was to be equipped with God's Spirit, although this was not regarded as typical of him.[27] The conviction that the same Spirit was at work in the community may have given support to the view that its Spirit-anointed ruler now fulfilled John's prophecy in an anticipatory way.

So much for the reflections on the possible relationship between the rite of baptism in the early church and its Christology, as expressed in the fact that the rite was performed with Jesus, the Lord and the Messiah, as its basic reference.[28] These deliberations have necessarily been rather tentative, but the formulas are there, and it seems more likely than not that they meant something. How far I have hit the truth when searching for this meaning is a wholly different question.

---

[26] I have discussed the passage in LARS HARTMAN, *Prophecy Interpreted* (CB.NT 1), Lund: Gleerup 1966, 185ff.

[27] E.g., Isa 11:2; *Pss. Sol.* 17:37; PETER SCHÄFER, *Die Vorstellung vom heiligen Geist in der rabbinischen Literatur* (SANT 28), Munich 1972.

[28] [See DAVID HELLHOLM, "Vorgeformte Tauftraditionen und deren Benutzung in den Paulusbriefen", DAVID HELLHOLM ET ALII (eds.), *Ablution, Initiation, and Baptism*, Vol. I (BZNW 176/I), Berlin – New York 2011, 415–495: esp. 439–452.]

# 16. Usages – Some Notes on the Baptismal Name-Formulae[1]

In 1903 Wilhelm Heitmüller published an impressive study of 347 pages, „*Im Namen Jesu*".[2] The amount of pages of that volume is an indication that a discussion of the topic mentioned in the above headline can cover wide fields. The following considerations have, however, a limited scope and are precisely "notes." They will mainly focus on the linguistic surface of the texts referred to, and will accordingly deal less with the contents and the exegesis of the passages in question.

## 1. The Formulae

In the New Testament the baptismal name-formula appears in the following forms:

- "into the name of the Lord Jesus" (εἰς τὸ ὄνομα τοῦ κυρίου Ἰησοῦ): Acts 8:16; 19:5
- "in the name of Jesus Christ" (ἐν τῷ ὀνόματι Ἰησοῦ Χριστοῦ): Acts 10:48
- "because of the name of Jesus Christ" (ἐπὶ τῷ ὀνόματι Ἰησοῦ Χριστοῦ): Acts 2:38[3]
- "into the name of the Father and the Son and the Holy Spirit" (εἰς τὸ ὄνομα τοῦ πατρὸς καὶ τοῦ υἱοῦ καὶ τοῦ ἁγίου πνεύματος): Matt 28:19

The first formula is echoed in 1 Cor 1:13, "into the name of Paul" (εἰς τὸ ὄνομα Παύλου) and in 1 Cor 1:15, "into my name" (εἰς τὸ ἐμὸν ὄνομα). The sentence in 1 Cor 6:11 reminds of the second formula: "(you were washed ..., you were justified) in the name of Jesus Christ the Lord" (ἐν τῷ ὀνόματι τοῦ κυρίου Ἰησοῦ Χριστοῦ). Also Rom 6:3 should be taken into account, ("we were baptized into Christ Jesus" [εἰς Χριστὸν Ἰησοῦν]), as well as Gal 3:27, ("you were baptized into Christ [εἰς Χριστόν]"), and 1 Cor 10:2, ("baptized into Moses").

In *Did.* 9:5 baptism takes place "into the name of the Lord" (εἰς τὸ ὄνομα τοῦ κυρίου), and so also in Hermas, *Vis.* 3.7.3. In *Did.* 7:1 the same formula is used as in Matt 28:19.

---

[1] To a large extent the deliberations of 2.1. below make use of material and discussions advanced in a few earlier works of mine, especially LARS HARTMAN, "'Into the Name of Jesus.' A Suggestion concerning the Earliest Meaning of the Phrase" [In this volume nr. 13, pp. 145–154], and '*Into the Name of the Lord Jesus. Baptism in the Early Church*, especially 37–50.

[2] WILHELM HEITMÜLLER, „*Im Namen Jesu.*" *Eine religionsgeschichtliche Untersuchung zum Neuen Testament.*

[3] The codices Vaticanus and Bezae and some minuscules read ἐν, a reading often encountered in the patristic texts.

The "into the name" construction in Matt 18:20 is similar to the one in the baptismal contexts in that the sentence concerns worship: two or three persons gather "into the name" of Jesus. The phrase also occurs in Matt 10:41-42, where, however, the usage is different: it is about being received "into the name" of a prophet and "into the name" of a righteous person, respectively, that is, "as being" or "because he/she is" a prophet etc. Otherwise the phrase does not appear in the New Testament in this more or less prepositional usage. Unlike the other two "name"-phrases the one with "into" neither appears in the Greek OT, nor in other Greek Jewish texts. (There are some constructions in which the verb + "into the name" etc. functions in another way and which therefore need not be taken into account here; see for example "utter blasphemies against — 'into' — his name," 2 Macc 8:4, and "believe into the name of …," e.g., John 1:12.)

In contrast, the phrase "in the name of …" is common in the New Testament and is used with verbs of different meanings, e.g., Matt 23:39 (come in the name of the Lord; quoting Ps 118:26); Mark 9:38 (receive a child in my name); John 10:25 (works done in the name of my Father); 1 Cor 5:4 (judge in the name of Jesus the Lord); Phil 2:10 (kneeling in the name of Jesus).

Also the phrase "because of the name of …" is rather common in the New Testament, although not so frequent as the "in"-construction: for example, Matt 18:5 (receive a child because of my name); Matt 24:5 (many appear because of my name); Mark 9:39 (perform a mighty deed because of my name); Mark 13:6 (many come because of my name, saying …); Acts 4:17 (speak because of this name).

The constructions "in the name of … " and "because of the name of …" represent a relatively established early Christian usage, and no doubt they have been taken over, directly or indirectly, from the Greek Old Testament. There are a few examples of them in Jewish pseudepigrapha, but in comparison with the Greek texts we still have at our disposal from Early Judaism these two formulae are much more common in the New Testament.[4]

On the other hand, as already mentioned, the "into the name" construction does not appear in the Greek Old Testament, and is a bit peculiar also as regarded within a wider framework of Greek literature — it mainly appears in documents using banking terminology and there refers to the "name" of the person who disposes an account in a bank.[5] We will return to this problem below.

---

[4] "In the name": *Joseph and Aseneth* 9:1; 15:7; *Testament of Solomon* 67 and 115; *Prayer of Joseph*. fragm. 190. "Because of the name": *1 Enoch* 10:2; *Testament of Asher* 2:4.

[5] The classic study is HEITMÜLLER, *"Im Namen Jesu"*.

## 2. Different Communication Situations

### 2.1. The Enigmatic Beginning

Very early in the history of the church the Christians have apparently practiced a rite of initiation that meant that neophytes entered the church via accepting ("believing") the message about Christ and undergoing a rite of immersion.[6] The similarities between the baptism of John and this Christian baptism suggest that the first Christians have taken over John's baptism and, so to speak, have christianized it; this ought to have taken place during a short, formative period under the influence of experiences and convictions that are reflected in the resurrection traditions. When Paul was baptized some five years after the end of Jesus' earthly career,[7] this was a sign that at least by then baptism was an established Christian rite of initiation.

What has happened in this early phase of the history of the Christian church is hidden behind the oldest traditions. However, to these traditions belong the name-formulae connected to baptism, and it is a common scholarly opinion that at least the "into the name of ..." phrase is very old.[8] The "in the name of ..." construction appears in 1 Cor 6:11, where the whole sentence can represent tradition taken over by Paul.[9]

There are various scholarly suggestions as to the linguistic and cultural background of the formula/the formulae, and they have led to different assumptions concerning which were the meaning and the interpretation of baptism and of the person of Jesus in this hidden phase of early Christianity.[10] Thus Wilhelm Heitmüller built his argument on what baptism meant on the fact, already mentioned, that the "into the name" phrase was common in banking documents; there it was used referring to the procedure that a sum of money was transferred to somebody whose "name" was the name over a bank account.[11] He concluded

---

[6] See HARTMAN, *Into the Name of the Lord Jesus*, 29–35; GERHARD BARTH, *Die Taufe in frühchristlicher Zeit*, 9–39. Further references can be found in both of these books. In my book just mentioned I had the opportunity to refer very often to the first edition of Barth's study, and to do so in agreeing with him.

[7] For a Pauline chronology see HELMUT KOESTER, *Introduction to the New Testament II*, 99–106. [2nd ed., 109–113.]

[8] See already HEITMÜLLER, *"Im Namen Jesu"*, 120, etc.

[9] E.g., FERDINAND HAHN, "Taufe und Rechtfertigung. Ein Beitrag zur paulinischen Theologie in ihrer Vor- und Nachgeschichte", 105f.; UDO SCHNELLE, *Gerechtigkeit und Christusgegenwart. Vorpaulinische und paulinische Tauftheologie*, 39–42.

[10] JENS SCHRÖTER's contribution in [DAVID HELLHOLM ET ALII (eds.) *Ablution Initiation and Baptism*, Vol I. 557–586: 563–567], "Die Taufe in der Apostelgeschichte", has an excursus, "Zur Bedeutung der präpositionalen Taufformulierungen", which contains a sober discussion of the debate. Schröter discusses more in detail the history of religions aspects of Heitmüller's ideas than I do on these pages. [Cf. also FRIEDRICH AVEMARIE, *Die Tauferzählungen der Apostelgeschichte*, 26–43.]

[11] Passages of such contents are also adduced to explain 1 Cor 1:13 in PETER ARZT-GRABNER ET ALII, *Papyrologische Kommentare zum Neuen Testament: 1. Korinther*, 70–72.

that to Greek speaking Christians baptism meant that the person baptized became the property of the Lord Jesus like a sum of money paid to a person's bank account. In addition Heitmüller assumed that this manner of speaking about baptism was embedded in a belief in the magical power of names, not least those of divine figures.

Heitmüller's understanding has been widely accepted,[12] but it has also been criticized, not least on linguistic grounds. Thus it has been doubted how far it is justified to insulate the adverbial expression "into the name" from verbs denoting payments, debts, etc. and then combine it with a verb belonging to a totally different semantic field but still let the prepositional phrase retain the associations with banking practice.[13] In addition, one has noted, in order to function as imagery the usage should presuppose that in the linguistic milieu — the communication situation — there existed a convention according to which a deity was compared to a rich person who was the owner of his/her adherents like money on his/her banking account. Certainly one could claim that Israel was God's "heritage," his flock, etc., but the step is long from that imagery to that of the banking-language.[14]

So another suggestion has been launched as to how to explain the "into the name" phrase as used concerning baptism. The scholars in question assume that the phrase is a literal translation of a Hebrew expression $l^e shem$ (or its Aramaic equivalent $l^e shum$). Thus the communication situation is supposed to be an early Hebrew/Aramaic speaking community, whose terminology has been literally translated into Greek. Normally the expression means "with regard to ...," "having in mind ..." and the like.

The following Mishnah passage has played an important role for the scholars who have defended this interpretation:[15]

An offering must be slaughtered into the name of (with regard to) six things: into the name of the offering (which offering category?), into the name of the offerer (who presents the offering?), into the name of the Name (the offering is to Almighty God, nobody else), into the name of the altar-fire (be conscious of its being a burnt offering), into the name of the fragrance, into the name of the pleasure (both: bear in mind that the offering shall please God) (*m.Zebaḥim* 4:6).

---

[12] E.g. RUDOLF BULTMANN, *Theologie des Neuen Testaments*, 42; JOSEPH A. FITZMYER, *Romans*, 430.

[13] The criticism is well developed in the new edition of Barth's study, referred to above.

[14] HEITMÜLLER refers to the seal-image to support his interpretation ("*Im Namen*", 150f., 171, 175, etc.), but it seems to the present writer that the connections between sealing and transferring to a bank account are not obvious enough. Cf. the article "Seal and Baptism" by KARL OLAV SANDNES in [DAVID HELLHOLM ET ALII (eds.), *Ablution, Initiation, and Baptism*, Vol. II, 1441–1481].

[15] (HERMANN L. STRACK)/PAUL BILLERBECK, *Kommentar zum Neuen Testament aus Talmud und Midrasch* I, 591, 1005; HANS BIETENHARD, "ὄνομα", 275. The idea had earlier been launched by A. J. H. WILHELM BRANDT, "Onoma en de Doopsformule in het Nieuwe Testament," and GUSTAF DALMAN, *Die Worte Jesu I*.

In the interpretation of the scholars who take this passage as a point of departure for their understanding of baptism in the early church, the "into the name" formula meant that the sacrifice in question was presented to God. They then assumed that the formula indicated something similar when used about baptism: the person baptized was given to Jesus and became his property. Consequently, the result is very much the same as Heitmüller's.

There seems, however, to have existed a usage of the "into the name" phrase about ritual matters that suggests that God, "into" whose "name" the rite was performed, plays another role than to receive something — or somebody — to be his property. It may be instructive briefly to consider the saying of R. Jose (around 150 CE) that follows immediately after the lines quoted above: "Even if somebody in his heart were not mindful of one 'name' of all these, the offering is valid." This demonstrates that the "name" nuance of the noun "name" is very weak and that the l$^e$shem also here has a vaguer meaning of "with respect to," "having in mind," etc.[16] Thus to be mindful of God (in *m.Zebaḥim* 4 "the Name") when performing the rite, did not so much focus on God as being the receiver of the sacrifice as rather the fundamental referent of the rite, the one who stands for a meaningful presupposition of the cultic act.

This is further illustrated by the following examples of the phrase as used about rituals. *m.Niddah* 5:6 deals with the validity of religious vows: young people may be too rash in giving vows, although they say, "We know into whose name (l$^e$shem mi) we have vowed."

In the Tosephta tractate on idolatry it is stated apropos of circumcision as practiced by the Samaritans that it is performed "into the name of Mount Gerizim" (*t.ʿAbodah Zarah* 3:13). Here the Gerizim stands for the religious system that forms the basic ideological frame of the rite. Furthermore, when *m.Ḥullin* 2:8 discusses how to apply the biblical rules for slaughter (for food), the possible case is introduced that if somebody slaughters "into the name of mountains or into the name of hills or into the name of seas or into the name of wildernesses, his slaughter is invalid," i.e., the slaughter is assumed to take place under the presupposition of idolatry (cf. Deut 12:2).

Such a key to a rite is radically different from what is ruled, for example, in *m.ʾAbot* 4:11: "R. Johanan the Sandal Maker (around 140 CE) said: 'Every assembly that is into the name of heaven (i.e., God) will be established in the end, the one that is not into the name of heaven will not be established in the end'." A statement in S. Num. § 136 makes a similar distinction: "There are two ways of drawing near (that is, to one's god in worship), one into the name of heaven, one not into the name of heaven."

---

[16] I would suggest that this is also what the phrase means in the first line of the following magic amulet from late antiquity and said to have been found south of Bethlehem: "With regard to (to the name of, l$^e$shem) Marten daughter of Qoriel. [Period added by L.H.] I adjure against Marten daughter of Qoriel. In the name of (b$^e$shem) Agirat, my lady, ... I destroy ..." (JOSEPH NAVEH/SHAUL SHAKED, *Amulets and Magic Bowls*, 78f.).

In order to strengthen the relevance of this rabbinic material for an assessment of the original meaning of the "into the name" phrase as a characterization of early Christian baptism one may have wanted to find it represented in other early Jewish texts, indeed earlier than the passages so far cited. Particularly it would have been an advantage if the Qumran material could provide us with something similar. This is, however, not so,[17] and the only relatively certain example locating the usage in the first century CE is Matt 18:20 (gathering into Jesus' name); however, it is a Jewish-Christian one and thus of some importance.

A couple of further details should be mentioned in this context: It is often maintained that the three prepositional expressions as such mean the same thing;[18] if there are any differences in their respective contents, these should be sought in the genitives added to the "name" and in the nuances effected by the context. So, as so often is the case with established phrases in ritual contexts, the phrase should be capable of several applications.[19] Another aspect of this flexibility is that the expression can be varied: this was so in the rabbinic material too: people may, e.g., vow "into the name of" God (see above), but it can also be stated that an idolator vows "*in* the name of" his god (*m.Sanhedrin* 7:6).[20] Such variations may be analogous to the variety of prepositions in our formulae as well as with the cases where Paul seems to replace an "into the name" with a mere "into" (Rom 6:3; Gal 3:27).

We now turn to the formula "in the name of Jesus (etc.)" as used in connection with baptism. As intimated above this use may be traditional and as such belong to the same early period as the "into the name" formula. If this is so, it means using a phrase with biblical roots. In the Old Testament it is used with several meanings. Thus one may, for example, walk in the name of the Lord (Micah 4:5), but in our context it is of interest to note that the formula is also used as characterizing ritual actions.[21] Thus one may praise God rejoicing in his name (Ps 89:13, 17), one prays in God's name and invokes (in) it (1 Kgs 18:24) as well as Baal's prophets do "in the name of" their god (1 Kgs 18:24). Furthermore, one may swear by ("in") God's name (Deut 6:13), bless and curse in it (Deut 10:8, 2 Kgs 2:24, respectively). Likewise Elijah builds an altar in the name of the Lord (1 Kgs 18:3). We also come across the formula in the deutero-canonical writings: see Sir 47:18; 50:20.

---

[17] I would not be prepared to regard 1Q20 XXI.2 as an example: "praise (the verb is *halal* piel) (into) God's name."

[18] E.g. CHARLES F. D. MOULE, *An Idiom Book of New Testament Greek*, 50.

[19] Rightly emphasized by BARTH, *Die Taufe in frühchristlicher Zeit*, 52f. See also HARTMAN, "'Into the Name of Jesus'", 436f.

[20] Similarly the *lᵉshem* of *m.ʿAbodah Zarah* 3:6 is taken up in the Gemara as a simple *lᵉ* (*b. ʿAbodah Zarah* 48a). In this context it may also be worthwhile to note that the translators of the Peshitta do not bother to try to imitate the into" (*eis*) in e.g. Matt 28:19 and 1 Cor 1:13 but have "in (*bᵉ*) the name" instead. Similarly the Vulgate says *in nomine*.

[21] BIETENHARD, "ὄνομα", 259f.,

Thus the "in the name"-formula is part of a religious language also in early Judaism, and so appears also in the Qumran texts: "All" boast in God's name (4Q292, fragm. 3), the priests bless in God's name (11Q14, 1.1 and 3) as do also the angels (*Songs of the Sabbath Sacrifice*, 4Q403, 1.9 and 12). Another, also biblical usage is represented by *Temple Scroll* 61.3: the prophets spoke in God's name (cf., e.g., Deut 18:20; Jer 11:21; 14:14; 23:25).

Above we have encountered other instances of the formula in the rabbinic material, where it could be used more or less as a synonym of "into the name," as well as a couple of passages from the pseudepigrapha (*Joseph and Aseneth, Testament of Solomon*, and *Prayer of Joseph*).[22]

The meaning of the phrase is also in this case rather vague, but when used in the characterization of a rite the one behind the "name" is of basic importance for the rite and its meaning.

## 2.2. Outside the New Testament

The purpose of the following few paragraphs is to give the present-day exegete an idea of what the linguistic soil was like in which our formulae appeared. In other words, we will look for possible different communication presuppositions in terms of linguistic usage after the enigmatic beginning.

When Heitmüller elaborated the linguistic basis for his contention, he claimed that such a transferred usage was "hellenistische Umgangssprache."[23] Very briefly I now present some examples that show different possibilities of using the three prepositional phrases. Unlike the aim of Heitmüller but also going farther than I have done in earlier studies of the topic,[24] this means taking into regard that the formulae can get different nuances of meaning not only because of their vagueness but also because of differences between reading contexts: it is, for example, not self-evident that the original meaning discussed above, Paul's individual understanding, and, e.g., the reading of some Gentile-Christian Corinthians were identical. An essential part of the presuppositions of such differences should be the various linguistic associations of those who used the formulae or encountered them in a communication.[25]

### 2.2.1. "Into the Name ..."

It was mentioned above that this construction is not found in the Septuagint. So we now ask for a possible communication situation in which the question may arise how to understand the "into the name" formula in relation to exist-

---

[22] Cf. also *1 Enoch* 50:2: the righteous ones will be victorious in God's name.
[23] HEITMÜLLER, *"Im Namen Jesu"*, 102.
[24] Particularly in the works mentioned in footnote 2.
[25] [Cf. DAVID HELLHOLM, "Vorgeformte Tauftraditionen und deren Benutzung in den Paulusbriefen", in: DAVID HELLHOLM ET ALII (eds.), *Ablution, Initiation, and Baptism*, Vol. I (BZNW 176/I), 415–495: 418f.]

ing Greek usage. A search in the collections of papyri and ostraca[26] reveals that there is a great number of examples in those texts of the banking usage mentioned above. This usage includes instances where the phrase does not refer to a concrete banking account or an official register of real estate, but also passages where the phrase has a more general meaning of "to be the property of ..." or the like. In general, however, also in these cases the contents concern economical matters.

A few examples may be enough. A typical topic is dealt with in P.Meyer 8.13 (151 CE): a man orders that "it all" be registered "into the name" of his wife. BGU 15.2495 (3$^{rd}$ cent. CE) is a testament in favor of ("into the name") of two persons. P.Mert. I 8,8–9 (3–4 CE) is also typical: the named person is officially registered as the one who shall cultivate a piece of public land. A similar topic is dealt with in P.Lond. 3.908 (139 CE) about a fortune transferred to be the property of the person mentioned.[27]

BGU 15.2495 (3$^{rd}$ cent. CE) concerns a contract made "into the name" of somebody and P.Lond. 2.180 (228 CE) refers to a certain amount of wheat that has been measured out "into the name" of a priest. We come across a slightly different usage in P.Mert. 1.23 (2$^{nd}$ cent. CE), where it is prescribed that a person shall deliver "this letter," and if he wants to do certain negotiations "into the name" of the sender, he may do so, although, if he would prefer so, he may as well do it "into your (own) name." The meaning of the phrase seems to come close to "on my (your) behalf," "being commissioned by me."

It should, however, be noted that the phrase "into the name" is not exclusively bound to economical language.[28] Some texts represent a not uncommon terminology when they tell that people name children, places, etc. "into the name" of a person. Thus according to Pausanias somebody gave a city its name "into the name" of his daughter (*Fragment* 407, line 107), and Diodorus Siculus mentions that somebody was called Hermes "into the name" of the planet (*Bibliotheca historica* 6.5.2). So also the founders of Thebae are said to have named the city "into the name of their father" (Cephalion, *Fragment* 6). In examples like these the meaning of the expression might contain a nuance of "with respect to" or even "to the honor of."

Already Heitmüller mentioned an exception to the circumstance that the "into the name" phrase was not represented in the Greek literary language of

---

[26] I have used the CD *Greek Documentary Texts*, compiled by The Packard Humanities Institute. For other Greek literature I have used the CD *Thesaurus Linguae Graecae*, ed. University of California at Irvine.

[27] These two texts are also quoted in ARZT-GRABNER ET. AL., *Papyrologische Kommentare*, 71. A rich material is found in the ὄνομα-article in FRIEDRICH PREISIGKE, *Wörterbuch der griechischen Papyrusurkunden*.

[28] The following Plutarch passage is a weak witness to the non-monopoly of the economical associations: Damon seemed to "slink away into the name of music" to conceal his power as a sophist (*Pericles* 4). It should rather be classed in the same category as the above-mentioned John 1:18 ("believe into the name ...") etc.

New Testament times, namely Herodianus, *History* 2.2.10 and 2.13.2, where the phrase is used in connection with the verb "to swear."[29] There are a few more examples that suggest that to a Greek ear of the times the "into the name" phrase was not automatically associated with transferring goods of economical value. Thus according to Aelianus a person writes to another that either he is serious (σπουδάζεις) "about (into) my name" or he is making sport (*Epistulae* 8.1), and an inscription from the Aegean Islands (IG 12.7, 409) deals with persons who have "served" their native city in many offices personally (on their own costs) and "into the name of" their children. The meaning of the passage may not be too lucid — they may have rendered the service "on the children's behalf" — but anyway the inscription can serve as another sign that the adverbial phrase "into the name" was not necessarily bound to economical language or to imagery inspired by such terminology.

One further detail should not be forgotten, namely that at this stage of the development of the Greek language the usage of the preposition εἰς as referring to direction was weakened and could come close to ἐν.[30] This circumstance may be related to the fact that in the Peshitta translation of the formula the preposition used is $b^e$-, and similarly Jerome uses *in*+ablative in the Vulgate.

Thus, if we assume a communication situation in which people are not acquainted with a Christian usage colored by the Hebrew-Aramaic idiom as also represented by Matt 18:20, the persons in question might feel a bit bewildered. They might vaguely come to think of banking terminology, but other associations could be possible. They might even suspect that in this context the use of the Greek "into the name" phrase represented "a particular Christian usage."[31] Insofar as the communication situation also contained a use of a baptismal "in the name …" formula it may have colored the understanding of the "into the name" phrase (cf. 1 Cor 1:13–15 and 6:11).

### 2.2.2. "In the Name …" and "Because of the Name …"

As already mentioned, the phrase "in the name …" is common in the Septuagint, both with and without the definite article. Thus the examples from the Old Testament mentioned above under 2.2.1. are topical also when we focus on Greek texts, although the Septuagint uses both ἐν and ἐπί + dative to translate $b^eshem$. This means that to Greek speaking Christians there existed a collection of texts that formed a sounding-board under the communication when they used and/ or encountered turns of phrase concerning baptism as being a rite performed "in the name of" Jesus Christ (etc.).

---

[29] HEITMÜLLER, *"Im Namen Jesu"*, 101. Heitmüller notes that others have referred to Herodianus before him.

[30] See FRIEDRICH BLASS/ALBERT DEBRUNNER/FRIEDRICH REHKOPF, *Grammatik des neutestamentlichen Griechisch*, § 206.

[31] UDO SCHNELLE, "Taufe", 665.

One may ask whether this sounding-board has been the only one, and, as a matter of fact, it seems that there are no good analogies in the profane literature to this religious/ritual usage.[32] There are, however, some papyri that represent the same category as the texts we encountered above which dealt with economical matters like registration of property, delivery of crops, etc. Thus one example is P.Col. 8.209 (3rd cent. CE) according to which some fields are cultivated by a man "in his name," and another is P.Oslo 107 (2nd cent. CE), which states that a certain cottage that is registered as a woman's heritage must not be (unlawfully) disposed "in her name." Similarly P.Oxy. 45.3242 (185–187 CE) concerns some fields that have been registered "in the name of my forefathers."

Thus, if in this case somebody's ear was not used to catch the biblically inspired idiom but stayed with "profane" associations, he/she might have found the usage a bit peculiar.[33]

Lastly, as to the third phrase, ἐπὶ τῷ ὀνόματι, we noted above that it only appears in Acts 2:38, and that there are no echoes of it in traditional material. Rather it may be assessed as representing Luke's tendency to take to biblical turns of phrase, that is, to give his Greek a flavor of the Greek style of the LXX.[34] Here also Luke's choice of preposition may have been influenced by the ἐπί component of the verb in the Joel quotation in v. 21.[35]

The deliberations so far concerning different possible "sounding-boards" under the production and reception of the baptismal name-phrases may bring to mind some suggestions concerning the linguistic usage of Greek speaking Jews in antiquity, namely that it represents a so-called diglossia, that is, persons using a certain language are able to use different linguistic codes or registers that exist beside each other. The term was introduced by C. A. Ferguson,[36] and J. M. Watt has analyzed the phenomenon in Luke and Acts, thereby noting how Luke switches between two registers of *koine*, one semitizing and one more standard Greek.[37] G. Walser has applied these insights in a broader study of the Greek

---

[32] JAMES HOPE MOULTON/GEORGE MILLIGAN, *The Vocabulary of the Greek Testament Illustrated from the Papyri and Other Non-Literary Sources*, 451; WALTER BAUER ET ALII, *Griechisch-deutsches Wörterbuch zu den Schriften des Neuen Testaments und der frühchristlichen Literatur*, 1160. —The wording of a magical papyrus may be inspired by Jewish usage: "Come, O Lord ..., save me and this boy unharmed, in the name (ἐν ὀνόματι) of the most high god, SAMAS PHRĒTH" *Papyri graecae magicae I*, ed. KARL PREISENDANZ, 5.45, 182f. [See HANS DIETER BETZ (ed.), *The Greek Magical Papyri in Translation*, Chicago, Ill. – London: University of Chicago Press 1986, 102]. See also the exorcism "in the name of" a certain spirit, quoted in footnote 16 above.

[33] A "normal" Christian usage appears in a great number of somewhat later papyri: contracts and similar documents begin by "in the name of God ..." and similar phrases. The custom is continued in documents written by Muslims.

[34] HARTMAN, *Into the Name of the Lord Jesus*, 38.

[35] HANS CONZELMANN, *Die Apostelgeschichte*, 36; JOSEPH A. FITZMYER, *The Acts of the Apostles*, 264: a "Lucan composition."

[36] CHARLES A. FERGUSON, "Diglossia".

[37] JONATHAN M. WATT, *Code-Switching in Luke and Acts*.

of the ancient synagogue[38] and concludes that "the speech community of the ancient synagogue was polyglossic, i.e., there existed several varieties of Greek side by side" (note his broadening of the diglossia concept!).[39] It seems to the present writer that the usage of the baptismal name-formulae can be taken as an example of such polyglossia among the early Christians — they used formulae and phrases about baptism that were different from the phraseology of everyday language. One may compare this usage with their way of taking over the biblical concept of "flesh": in normal Greek it meant meat etc., and a Greek-speaking person who converted to Judaism or Christianity had to learn that in the context of their new religion the word sometimes had a quite different meaning.

## 2.3. Some Christian Greek Texts after the New Testament

We now turn to a type of communication situation in which Christian writers in the patristic era represent what becomes an established usage in terms of the baptismal formulae.

### 2.3.1. "Into the Name ..."

The textual material for a discussion of the usage of the baptismal formulae after the New Testament is rich *and* poor. It is rich in so far as there are many passages that quote or allude to a baptismal formula, but it is poor in other respects. On the one hand practically only one formula appears, namely the one characterizing baptism as one "into the name of" the Trinity, on the other, the formula is taken for granted to such an extent that the writers do not seem to think that they need to explain what it means.

As to the predominance of the "into the name of" the Trinity, in the *Didache* it still appears together with a shorter formula. The longer formula appears in 7:1 and 7:3, that is, in the instruction concerning how baptism shall be performed. On the other hand, in 9:5 we hear the echo of a shorter formula when it is stated who are allowed to share the Eucharist, namely those who are "baptized into the name of the Lord." We may assume that the longer formula is used at the baptismal rite, whereas the other can function as a short characterization of Christian baptism.

One might regard Hermas *Vis.* 3.7.3 in a similar manner: the interpreter of the vision characterizes a certain group of possible converts: they have heard the word and "want to be baptized into the name of the Lord."

The longer form is used at the rite of baptism according to the First Apology of Justin Martyr. He reports that those who are "born anew" "receive the washing with water in the name (ἐπ' ὀνόματος) of God the Father and the Lord of the All and of our Savior Jesus Christ and of the Holy Spirit" (*Apology* I. 61.3).

---

[38] GEORG WALSER, *The Greek of the Ancient Synagogue. An Investigation on the Greek of the Septuagint, Pseudepigrapha and the New Testament*.
[39] WALSER, *The Greek of the Ancient Synagogue*, 183.

We may note that Justin, turning to outsiders, uses a less awkward preposition than "into."

This tendency in terms of the use of our prepositional phrases becomes the norm in the texts of the ecclesiastical writers of the following centuries. The fact that according to Matt 28:19 the risen Jesus has ordered that baptism should be performed "into the name of" the Three Persons has apparently had the effect that this is how one expresses oneself. As mentioned above, the formula seems to be so established that the fathers normally do not care to explain what they think it means. One exception is when John Chrysostom more or less in passing says that in principle it is not the baptizer who baptizes but the Father, the Son and the Holy Spirit "whose name is called upon by the one who is baptized when he/she answers "I believe" (*Catechesis ultima* 170). Quite often, however, the formula is used as an argument in defending or exposing the Trinitarian dogmas (e.g., Epiphanius, *Ancoratus* 7.1; 81.2: Eusebius, *Contra Marcellum* 1.1.9).

With regard to the deliberations above on the meaning of the "into the name" formula in the earliest church we may state that at least at a relatively quick reading of the passages where it appears in the patristic texts there seems to be no clear examples of an understanding of the formula that implies an imagery that compares the one baptized with a sum of money or with a piece of land that is transferred to a new owner.

So this baptismal formula is also the most common context in which the "into the name" construction appears. Some figures can illustrate the distribution: the ecclesiastical writers included in the CD-Rom Thesaurus Linguae Graecae quote or refer to the baptismal formula of Matt 28 about 140 times, to the name-phrases of Matt 10 ("into the name of a prophet") and Matt 18 ("gather into my name") some 20 times, and a little more seldom to "into the name" phrases in connection with baptism in First Corinthians and Acts.[40] Remains a small number of passages, say around a dozen, in which "into the name of ..." occurs; it is there combined with verbs like "swear," "talk nonsense," "prophecy," "seal" (thus Epiphanius, *Panarion* 1.192), "exorcise" (thus *Fragmentum alchemicum* 299.3r). Ignatius of Antioch praises the churches that have received him "into the name of Jesus Christ," not as a mere passer – by (Rom 9:3; cf. Matt 18:5, receive a child "in — ἐπί — my name"). There are also some cases where an author uses "into the name" when telling that one names a house or a temple after a person — cf. the "profane" examples of, e.g., Pausanias, quoted above.[41] There

---

[40] The around 40 passages containing the phrase "believe into the name ..." of course represent another category of adverbial phrases.

[41] The texts of Epiphanius may represent a particular case. HEITMÜLLER (*"Im Namen Jesu"*, 108f.) intimates that when quoting Epiphanius he does so taking him as a representative of the patristic literature — which then is said to support his particular views on the "into the name" phrase and its background. Searchings on the *Thesaurus Linguae Graecae* CD show that this is hardly a fair assessment of Epiphanius' style, which actually is a bit peculiar (see JOHANNES QUASTEN, *Patrology III*, 385f.). His style includes a richer use of "into the name" phrases than with other writers. These phrases seem, however, rather inspired by a kind of biblical style than by banking language.

*Usages – Some Notes on the Baptismal Name-Formulae* 187

are also some examples in which a writer repeats "into the name" using instead a simple "into" (e.g., John the Damascene, *Expositio fidei* 82; Basilius, *Prologus* 8,31.688).

The dominating use of the "into the name" phrase in the trinitarian baptismal formula does not render much support to an assumption that the fathers understood the formula in the light of the banking terminology, of which we saw a few examples under 2.2.1. above.[42] The relatively few instances of a use with other verbs do it even less.[43]

### 2.3.2. "In the Name ..." and "Because of the Name ..."

As to these two formulae we can be brief. The fact that they are well established phrases in the Septuagint and often appear in New Testament texts determines their usage in the texts of the fathers. The two phrases seem to be more or less synonymous and a further reason to deal with them together is the text-critical situation in Acts 2:38: beside the best reading with ἐπί there is namely a variant reading with ἐν, and it has a relatively good manuscript support.[44] Both readings are represented in the writings of the fathers.

The two phrases are very common in the patristic material, although it is particularly true in the case of "in the name." There is no need to go into detail, but "in the name" of somebody one speaks or prophecies, performs miracles, comes, or blesses; two more examples chosen at random from a vast material: in Jesus' name one drinks poison without being harmed (Papias, fragment 11.2) and is delivered from this evil age (Epiphanius, *Panarion* 2.36). On the other hand it was noted above that the two phrases appear rather seldom in "profane" texts.

Concerning the three prepositional expressions it was pointed out under 2.3.1. that in the texts of the fathers a dominating position was held by "into the name," more precisely in the form encountered in Matt 28:19. Consequently, in spite of the frequent use of the two phrases with ἐν and ἐπί, especially the for-

---

Thus, e.g., when Epiphanius writes that a temple was built "into" God's name (*Panarion* 1.373), the expression is found in 2 Sam 7:13, where the Hebrew text says "to my name" (*lishmi*), whereas the LXX uses plain dative; similarly when he reports that certain saints, particularly the Virgin Mary, were revered and that offerings were brought "into" their "name," the style reminds of, e.g., Mal 1:11 (*Ancoratus* 13.8; *Panarion* 1.159 etc,). Epiphanius also uses "into the name" when reporting on books as being ascribed to or written by certain persons; thus John's gospel is "into the name of John" (*Panarion* 2.275) and similar turns of phrase are used about books ascribed to Moses (*Panarion* 1.209), Eve (*Panarion* 1.278), Seth (*Panarion* 1.284), or Philip (*Panarion* 1.292).

[42] See the beginning of the preceding footnote.

[43] This should also hold true of a few passages that mention "into the name" of the Divinity: Epiphanius, *Ancoratus* 8.8; *Panarion* 1.231 (but according to *Ancoratus* 22.6 "we receive the seal" "*in* the name" of the three Persons); John Chrysostom, *Catechesis ad illuminandos* 2.22: one receives the seal whereby the minister says "So and so is anointed into the name of the Father, the Son and the Holy Spirit." Cf. HEITMÜLLER, who claims that the sealing rite supports his idea that the into the name phrase is rooted in banking language ("*Im Namen Jesu*", 150f., 171, 175, etc.).

[44] The variant reading is supported by Codices Vaticanus and Bezae and by a few minuscules.

mer, there are few passages in which baptism is characterized by one of these two expressions. In most of the cases it seems that the phrase appears in the text because the writer refers to or comments on a New Testament passage which makes use of the ἐν or ἐπί phrase.[45] In some of these cases the author raises the question whether the shorter formula means anything else than the "normal" one, *viz.*, the Matt 28 form. Thus, e.g., Basilius claims that the reference to the Lord in the shorter form is no problem, "for at the rebirth the Son does the same work as the Father and the Spirit" (*Adv. Eunomium* 29.720).

There are, however, some instances where an author refers to baptism as performed "in the name" without any connection to a specific New Testament passage. Thus Epiphanius mentions baptism "in" the name of the Trinity (*Panarion*, 3.299) and Cyrillus can write about baptism in general as one "in" Christ's name (*Catechesis* 17.21). Furthermore, Didymus Caecus, *De trinitate* 39.733 (probably spurious) deals with some non-orthodox Christians who baptize "in" the name of the three Persons; the text reminds of Matt 28:19 (which, as we remember uses "into"), and this is a sign that the three prepositional expressions were regarded as more or less synonymous.[46]

## 3. Conclusion

In the introduction to these "notes" it was stressed that they were precisely "notes" and that they would not deal much with the contents of the passages where the formulae appeared. The reader can by now state that this has been true, both as to the biblical texts and those from post-New Testament Christian authors. If, on the other hand, the above deliberations could to some extent be termed lexicographical, they still are "notes" and leave lots of material and aspects without consideration.

A couple of terms have, however, played a certain role in the above discussion, namely (linguistic) usage and communication situation. These concepts cover linguistic aspects that are interrelated in a way that can be a challenge to the student of the texts concerned. Thus we have been able to note how the different name-formulae appear in several usages, partly very different from each other. We have also noted how our phrases are used in different communication situations; this is true for the Christian texts, but also for the comparative material. So the interpreter of a given text has to come to grips with the interrelationship of usage and communication situation. In other words, the context of a given document calls for attention, both the literal context (the co-text) and the

---

[45] Thus with "in the name": Epiphanius, *Panarion* 1.202; John Chrysostom, *Hom. in Acta* 60.63; *Hom. in 2 Cor* 61.458; 61.608; Cyrillus, *Catechesis* 3.4; 17.30; Theodoretus, *Explanatio in Canticum Canticorum* 81.204. "Because of the name": John Chrysostom, *Hom. in Acta* 60.65; Procopius Gazaeus, *Comm. in Is* 2244.

[46] There are other indications to this effect: thus Basilius quotes Matt 28:19 and then repeats its contents in writing "in the name of the Trinity" (*Adv. Eunomium* 29.720).

social one. To get an idea of the more precise meaning of a given passage, in our case one containing a baptismal name-formula, we have to analyze carefully the literal unit with its linguistic, rhetorical etc. properties, but also, and not least, try to get an idea of cultural, theological, ecclesiastical and pastoral preconditions of the text. So it may be appropriate at the end of a discussion like this one to remind us of the need to combine investigation of vocabulary and grammar with the texts themselves with their manifold aspects as textual communication.

# Part IV

Hellenistic Contexts

# 17. *Psychē* – "Soul"?
## Reading the Septuagint as a Greek Text[1]

### 1. How do the Words נפשׁ and ψυχή Relate to Each Other?

It is well known that the Hebrew נפשׁ (*næphæsh*), which is often translated with "soul", covers a wide area of reference, and even when "soul" is an acceptable translation, there is a risk that the translation invites the reader to associations that are different from those implied by the Hebrew original. A similar problem concerns the translators of the Septuagint (hence LXX) who as a rule have translated *næphæsh* with ψυχή. How apt is their rendering?

This question has played an important role in the scholarly discussion of the LXX usage of ψυχή. It has often taken place in the light of more over-arching opinions on LXX as a translation of the Hebrew Bible. The Old Testament introduction that was required reading in the elementary exegetical studies of the present writer in the 1950' had the following to say about the matter: the LXX means "a transfer into a new sphere, a spiritualizing of the original and down-to-earth Old Testament…"[2] Although the writer, Professor Ivan Engnell, did not discuss the soul concept in that context, he did express himself in other places in such a way that it is evident that he would be prepared to regard the translation of נפשׁ into ψυχή as an example of this "spiritualizing."[3] A similar opinion of the LXX usage of ψυχή is/was relatively commonly held by Old Testament scholars.[4] However, some 40 years ago D. Lys and N. P. Bratsiotis launched radically different ideas.[5] The former claimed that "Psyche had for the LXX translators a Hebrew more than a Greek content",[6] and Bratsiotis maintained that the LXX translators consciously had chosen a "pre-Platonic" usage of ψυχή and thus in an excellent manner had actually done justice to the biblical–Hebrew נפשׁ. In

---

[1] Some paragraphs of the first part of this article represent a development of an excursus in the present writer's commentary on the Gospel of Mark in Swedish. It has now also appeared in English translation as *Mark for the Nations. A Text-and Reader-Oriented Commentary* (Pickwick Publications), Eugene, Oreg. 2010, 329–333.

[2] Ivan Engnell, *Gamla testamentet. En traditionshistorisk inledning I*, Stockholm 1945, 31.

[3] Idem, "Själ. I. GT", *Svenskt Bibliskt Uppslagsverk II*, Stockholm ²1963, 964–969: 964.

[4] See, e.g., the examples in Nikolaus Pan Bratsiotis, "נפשׁ ΨΥΧΗ. Ein Beitrag zur Erforschung der Sprache und der Theologie der Septuaginta", in: *Volume de congrès Genève 1965* (VT.S 15), Leiden 1966, 58–89: 59.

[5] Daniel Lys, "The Israelite Soul according to the LXX", *VT* 6 (1965) 181–228. For Bratsiotis see the preceding footnote.

[6] Lys, *op. cit.*, 216.

his article on נפש in *Theologisches Wörterbuch zum Alten Testament* H. Seebass reports on the ideas of Lys and Bratsiotis and comments on them in this way:

> Da die griech[ische] Sprachentwicklung jedoch zum platonisch–nachplatonischen Gebrauch geführt hat, wird man die Übersetzung der LXX insofern bemerkenswert einstufen müssen, als sie in der lingua franca mit einem Gegengewicht biblischer Tradition aufwartete.[7]

These last-mentioned positions also take their point of departure in the Hebrew Old Testament and its anthropology, including its multifarious usage of נפש.[8] The question thus can be raised whether the translators of the LXX have preserved the view of the original or distorted it. One can, however, view the situation from another angle, namely from the side of the Jews to whom the LXX was = the Scripture.[9] If for a moment we assume that Bratsiotis' view of the attitude of the translators is correct, we may ask: did the readers get the point of the translators? Did they, so to speak, bracket what Bratsiotis labels Platonic and post-Platonic usage and let instead the way in which Homer, Aeschylus, Euripides etc., used the word ψυχή guide their understanding of the Bible in this respect? I admit that this may mean to parody Bratsiotis' view and, above all, that it does not take into account the conditions, so difficult to grasp, of understanding words in the light of their literary, social, and cultural context; in addition, the problem may be even more complicated when classics are involved — and the Bible belonged to that category. But even if Philo and the author of the Book of Wisdom would be considered as confused thinkers, writing about the soul in next to Middle-Platonic terms,[10] both of them studied the Bible diligently, and did so in its LXX form. In other words, at least these two LXX readers were not guided by the alleged intention of the translators concerning how to understand what the LXX said about the human soul. Philo and the author of Wisdom were, however, not alone in their ways of using the word "soul", on the contrary. Thus a Jewish tomb inscription says: "The tomb hides my body, but the soul is close to the holy ones (εἰς ὁσίους ἔπετε)."[11] This reflects a view on the human soul that hardly is "biblical" — if we follow the opinion of Seebass, referred to above, according to which the "soul" language of LXX was a biblical counterweight to the usage of the time.

---

[7] HORST SEEBASS, "נפש", *ThWAT* 5 (1986) 531–555: 537.

[8] A survey of the meanings of נפש is found in HANS WALTER WOLFF, *Anthropologie des Alten Testaments*, Berlin ³1977. 20–32.

[9] In the introduction to JOHAN LUST/ERIK EYNIKEL/KATRIN HAUSPIE, *A Greek-English Lexicon of the Septuagint I–II*, Stuttgart 1992–1996. p. x, different approaches to problems concerning translations as precisely translations are listed, but not this one.

[10] DAVID WINSTON, *The Wisdom of Solomon* (AncB 43), Garden City, N.Y. 1979, 25–32.

[11] *Corpus Inscr. Jud.* 1510.

## 2. The Word ψυχή in koine Greek

On the following pages an attempt will be made to investigate the usage of the LXX of ψυχή and to consider what the term may have meant to a Greek-speaking Jew who encountered the text in Hellenistic-Roman times in a Greek-speaking environment. However, as has already been intimated, it is a vain enterprise to seek for a typically "Greek" manner of speaking about the soul. The philosophers differed from each other in their descriptions of it, be it Plato, Aristotle, or the later philosophical schools like Stoics, Epicureans and middle-Platonists. Yet some features appear over and over again, and as a rule they are also represented among what could be termed more general, popular ideas in late antiquity. Although it is difficult to get a firm grip of these ideas, they will be the comparative material for the discussion of the following pages. Thus, when I try to sketch what ψυχή may stand for in this usage, I leave aside the philosophical discussions of the soul. Part of the material I glean from Dihle's articles on ψυχή in *Theologisches Wörterbuch zum Neuen Testament*.[12]

Thus it was a common belief that the soul was the inaccessible kernel of the human being, the seat of thinking, will, and feelings, indeed something that constituted the person as a living being.

So when somebody states that a letter ought to be an image of the soul, this means that it should reflect the essence or the personality of the sender.[13] Furthermore, according to Epictetus the true and consistent Cynic philosopher should be able to provide moral advice "with the whole of his soul", that is, with full conviction and with a basis in his real self.[14] A tomb inscription refers to the community of a married couple: their souls (ψυχαί) were united in the concrete way of life (βιότοις) and bodily (σώμασιν); here the soul stands for the kernel of the personality.[15] This is why "my soul" can replace "I", "I myself", or "my inner being." One example is the (non-Christian) rhetor Libanius, who solemnly utters: "my soul, praise and magnify the Lord (fragm. 90: Εὐλόγει μεγαλύνουσα, ψυχή μου, τὸν δεσπότην)."

Often the soul stands for a part of the human that is held to be nobler and much more important than the body. The two can even be contrasted, and thus according to an inscription a professional athlete "was admired for the strength of his body but his character was praised, because he took care of his soul."[16] The way of thinking is similar in a tomb inscription after an Ethiopian who is said to have had a black body but a white soul.[17]

---

[12] ALBRECHT DIHLE, "ψυχή im Griechischen", *ThWNT* 9 (1973), 605–614, and "Judentum", ibid., 630–633.

[13] Pseudo-Demetrius, *De elocutione* 227.

[14] *Diatribes* 3.22.18.

[15] Peloponnesos *IG* V.2.268. 33.

[16] The inscription is from Afrodisias in Asia Minor: WANKEL/BÖRKER/MERKELBACH 1a, 11.

[17] The inscription is Egyptian: BERTRAND, *Inscr. métriques* 26.

Thus the soul was regarded as a particular part of the human person rather than as an aspect of the human as a psycho-somatic unity. This is also presupposed when, for example, Artemidorus in his book on dreams reports how the soul leaves the body and goes elsewhere, while the body is asleep.[18]

This leads us to the great number of texts that deal with the soul after death, when it is liberated — often this is a point — from the body. Thus already Xenophon reports in his book on the education of Cyrus (Cyropaedia 8.17.19): he [i.e. Cyrus] had not been convinced about the opinion that "the soul only lives as long as it exists in a mortal body, whereas it is dead when it has been separated from it." The wording implies that not all shared this opinion, but in a tomb inscription from a later time we read: "The body is dissolved for ever, but the soul rose as a newly initiated [into a mystery rite] to the Olympus."[19] Another tomb inscription: "O, Lyxinus, the ether now possesses your soul but the earth your body which fire has consumed."[20] The existence of the soul after death is described in another way in the following Roman tomb inscription written in Greek (it refers to two persons); "The fire has consumed our flesh, and the earth that nourishes everything covers our bones, but our god-sent souls have departed on the voyage under earth that is the fate of all."[21] Thus it was a common belief that the soul had a life after death, but the opinion that death meant the definitive end of the life/the soul of a human being may have been as prevalent.

Among the older Greek authors like Homer, Sophocles, etc. we come across a usage according to which one speaks of a "soul" and means a person. It is rare in later times, but has not totally disappeared. Thus, for example, Epictetus gives the advice: "Take care that those who serve at a dinner are not more numerous than those who are served, for it is wrong that many souls serve a few guests [literally: a few sofas]."[22]

However, very often "soul" is equal to "life." To quote Xenophon's book on Cyrus' education again: Cyrus asked a certain Tigranes how much he would be prepared to pay to release his captivated wife and received the answer: "I would give my soul in payment" (Cyropaedia 3.1.36). In a later text the novel writer Achilles Tatius has a character say: "This man had plans against my soul, but Artemis saved me."[23]

## 3. The Word ψυχή in the Septuagint

In the light of the above material I will now discuss how the LXX uses ψυχή asking what the word may have meant to Jews who did not have a Hebrew-

---

[18] E.g., *Oneirokritios.* V.43.
[19] *SEG* 11.384.
[20] *SEG* 17.172.
[21] *IGRom* 1204.
[22] *Gnomologium* 21.
[23] *Leucippe* 8.3.1.

biblical basis under their reading. I will assume that their associations to the word could be determined by the Greek that was the common language in their culture, although modified under the influence of diaspora Jewish texts, the LXX included.

For the purpose of this article I confine myself to considering the passages where ψυχή appears in Genesis and the Psalms, complementing them with a few other LXX passages. This does not mean that I quote all of the instances in the book of Genesis and in the Psalms (around 40 and around 140, respectively), but they make up the material investigated. The following pages contain an attempt to present the different "meanings" in which the word is used in these texts ("meanings" is put within quotation marks, since often several meanings are possible). The circumstance that the noun is much more frequent in the Psalms than in Genesis is certainly due to the fact that expressions like "my soul praises you" represent a hymn style that is typical of the genre.

In many LXX passages the Greek speaking reader comes across the common Greek use of ψυχή in the sense of "life," for example in Gen 19:17 about Lot: "save your soul/your life", Ps 6:5: "Turn around, Lord, save my soul/my life", Ps 25:9: "Do not destroy my soul/my life with the wicked ones, my life with the men of blood." Sometimes, however, passages representing this usage of ψυχή may have sounded a bit strange or at least compressed; thus in Gen 9:4: "you shall not eat flesh with the blood of the soul/the life (ἐν αἵματι ψυχῆς)." With some imagination one may understand the genitive as one of quality, although used in a way that is rare in ordinary Greek;[24] an example is Sophocles', *Oidipus Rex* 533: τόλμης πρόσωπον; literally "the countenance of audacity", that is, "(with) an audacious countenance." We encounter the same kind of construction in Luke 16:9 ὁ μαμωνᾶς τῆς ἀδικίας, "the mammon of injustice", "the unjust mammon."

A variety of this way of speaking of "soul" is to use the noun in a somewhat wider sense referring to living beings in general.[25] The relatively common Greek phrase "every soul" (πᾶσα ψυχή) means "all", "everybody." Yet, when we come across it in Gen 12:5 it presumably stands for the whole lot, man and beast, that Abram brought with him when departing for the land of Canaan. The idea that animals have a soul, at least in some sense of the word, should not be too difficult to accept for anyone to whom "soul" also means "life."[26] Yet the text of Gen 1:20 may have sounded a little odd, although not totally incomprehensible, when it says that the waters brought forth reptiles with (of) living souls (ἑρπετὰ ψυχῶν ζωσῶν)." This is developed in the following verse according to which God "made every soul of reptile animals (πᾶσαν ψυχὴν ζῴων ἑρπετῶν)", that is, all the reptiles. In v. 24 this is followed by the statement that God ordered the earth to

---

[24] EDUARD SCHWYZER/ALBERT DEBRUNNER, *Griechische Grammatik II: Syntax und syntaktische Stilistik* (HAW), Munich 1950, 122.

[25] Cf. MARGUERITE HARL, *La Bible d'Alexandrie. La Genèse*, Paris 1986, 60f.

[26] See, e.g., Isocrates, *Ad Nicoclem* 12; Josephus, *Jewish War* 1.632; Dio Chrysostom, *Fragm.* 459.

bring forth "living soul according to kinds" (ψυχὴν ζῶσαν κατὰ γένος)", four-footed, reptiles etc.; "every soul" has the same reference in Gen 2:19, according to which "every soul", that is, all animals, receives their names. In between, in 2:7, the human has also become "a living soul (εἰς ψυχὴν ζῶσαν)." As already mentioned, the text presumably represents a way of using "soul" that may have been vaguely understandable to a Greek speaking reader, but the constructions would nonetheless have sounded exotic.

While a Greek speaking reader of Ps 6:5, quoted above, may have assumed that ψυχή stood for "me", "(my) life", the word is used with a slightly different nuance a couple of lines earlier: "my soul was very much troubled" (v. 4). However, our reader has certainly not thought it was remarkable that the LXX has ψυχή denote the seat or the subject of humans' thoughts and feelings. One could imagine, though, that, as to the Psalms, the reader in question may have thought that this "soul" usage was a little overloaded. A few more examples: Gen 42:21: "we did not respect the anguish (θλῖψιν) of his soul", Ps 9:24: "the sinner boasts of the desires of his soul", Ps 34:9: "my soul will rejoice in the Lord", Ps 68:21: "my soul expected disgrace." Although Ps 43:26 may have been understandable when saying "our soul was abased to the dust", the wording may have sounded a little rough. One may, however, consider rendering the "soul" of the latter clauses by "I" and "we", respectively; so, for example, "I was abased to the dust" is not so strange. We will deal with this possibility below.

Probably the reader of Ps 104:18 assumed that the verse was about Joseph's feelings, when the text said: "they abased his feet with bonds, his soul went through iron (σίδηρον διῆλθεν)." When John Chrysostom quotes this passage in a context where he deals with Joseph's exemplary morals, he does not seem to find the phrase to be in need of explanation.[27] But another commentator among the church fathers, whose text is ascribed to Chrysostom, but wrongly so, is obviously of the opinion that the wording is not so clear and writes: "For after he had been accused of adultery, he was imprisoned, and of course they immediately put fetters of iron on him. For thus says Symmachus: 'his soul came to iron.' This is the same as: he was in danger of being killed. Or else he [the author] called the hardness and the strength of the affliction iron."[28]

As we have seen, in Greek phrases like "with all his soul", "soul" can stand for the person as involved in or committed to something. Isa 58:10 may remind of this usage: "If of (all) your soul (ἐκ ψυχῆς σου) you give bread to the one who is hungry"; this also holds true of Ezra 25:6: "you rejoiced (malignantly) of (all) your soul over the land of Israel", and also 1 Macc 8:27; "The Romans will fight together with them of (all their) soul."[29]

---

[27] *In epist. ad Ephes.* 62.71.
[28] *In Ps 101–107*, PG 55. 656, 65.
[29] See also Deut 6:5: "You shall love the Lord, your God, of all your mind (A: heart) and of all your soul and of all your might."

Rather close to this usage is the one in passages where ψυχή stands for the human as a reflecting person and/or as a being with religious commitment. Gen 23:8 deals with the attitude of the Hittites to Abraham: "If you are of the opinion of your soul (ἔχετε τῇ ψυχῇ) that I may bury my wife." Gen 49:6 may possibly represent the same usage: "may my soul not go into their council." We move in a similar field of associations in Ps 68:11: "I bent down my soul in fast", and in the passages where the praying person "lifts" his/her soul to God (Ps 24:1; 85:4; 142:8).

In this context Ps 68:33 can be adduced as a reminder that the "soul"-terminology often is so vague that it seems to be unrealistic to try to establish precise meanings of the word. This holds true both of the Old Testament passages and of other Greek material. Thus Ps 68:33 says: "Seek God, and your soul will live." On the one hand we may imagine a reader in antiquity who would think that "your soul" just is a solemn manner of saying "you", on the other such a reader might assume that "your soul" is a nobler part of the person to be held apart from the body. (We will soon discuss some instances of this usage.)

In Ps 18:8 the LXX says of the law of God that it "turns (ἐπιστρέφων) the soul", which may sound a little bewildering to a modern reader to whose mind the same Law is "reviving the soul" (Ps 19:8, RSV). However, one may very well translate the Greek phrase by "reproves the soul", like, for example, in Plutarch's note on Pompey that he reproved (ἐπέστρεψε) people who offended Cato."[30] In another example Plutarch uses "soul" in a similar manner with another verb (although belonging to the same semantic field): "a proof of a cultivated and disciplined (πεπαιδευμένης) soul."[31] We may ask whether here the "soul" again is thought of as the religiously committed self or whether the line is to be understood as referring to the god-given soul which is disciplined.

It was noted above that "your (2nd plural) soul" can be equal to "you", and that this usage is found also outside the LXX. We should take into account that the phrase can be used in such a manner in almost all cases in which somebody's "soul" thinks, feels, wants, praises, etc. and thus more or less becomes a circumlocution of a pronoun, possibly implying an additional nuance that the person in question is deeply engaged in his/her thought, prayer, etc. A few examples: Gen 27:4 about Jacob: "that my soul/I may bless you before I die": Ps 10:1: "How can you say to my soul/me…?"; Ps 24:13: "his soul/he will dwell among the good (or: live in good circumstances)"; Ps 40:5: "have mercy upon me, heal my soul/me, for I have sinned against you"; Ps 65:16: "hear … how much he has done to my soul/me."[32]

---

[30] *Cato minor* 14.2. Similarly John Chrysostom *Comm. in Job* 173: the friend would ἐπιστρέψαι τὴν ψυχὴν αὐτοῦ.

[31] Plutarch, *Lucullus* 29.6. Also, e.g., Libanius, *Decl.* 1.1.128 about people "who neither discipline (παιδεύοντας) the soul nor exercise the body."

[32] It is easy to read Ps 68:1 in a similar way: "Save me, O God, water has come to my soul, I have been stuck in deep mire, and there is nothing to stand on."

The reader who has not learnt that according to the Old Testament the soul is not a specific part of the human, even less a nobler element of it, may read some passages of the LXX as meaning precisely something to that effect. (I do not now take the Book of Wisdom into account, where this soul concept is evidently represented.) We have already come across some passages where such a reading is conceivable, and here are a few more: Ps 10:5: "He who loves unrighteousness hates his soul"; somebody could also understand this line as saying that the person involved hates his own life. Furthermore Ps 119:5f.: "I live among Kedar's tents, my soul lives very much as a foreigner (πολλὰ παρῴκησεν)." We come across a differentiation between the body and the (nobler) soul in Job 7:15 (ms A): "you will separate my soul from my body", and one may also find a similar idea in Job 33:17f.: "he saved his body from (becoming) a corpse, and he spared his soul from death." In 2 Macc 6:30 such a differentiation is easily made: when the martyr is tortured he says: "Tormented (in this way) I endure the hard pains in my body, but in my soul I suffer them gladly because of the awe of him" (see also 2 Macc 7:37).[33]

One may in this context ask how a reader understood Ps 23:4 concerning the one who has a pure heart and is allowed to ascend to the hill of the Lord: οὐκ ἔλαβεν ἐπὶ ματαίῳ τὴν ψυχὴν αὐτοῦ, literally: "he did not take his soul in vain." The adverbial phrase is not so difficult to understand, because the construction is not uncommon and the preposition introduces manner or circumstances; see, for example, Rom 4:18, ἐπ' ἐλπίδι, or P.Oxy. 2.237, ἐπὶ φθόνῳ. Or something happens "with regard to" or "for" something, as, for example, in 1 Thess 4:5; Eph 2:10 ("for good works"). As to Ps 23:4, however, is somebody careless with regard to his/her soul like a lion that does not care about the life/the soul of the deer (Dio Chrysostom, *Oratio* 62.7)? Although the somewhat rough text still offers some resistance, it seems that Didymus Caecus in his comments suggests how a reader would naturally understand the line: He understands the verb as meaning "get", "receive" and explains that the human has not got her soul in order to devote herself to vain things.[34] This means that the reader of the LXX psalm could understand the line as referring to the soul as something nobler than the body.

Another shade of meaning that we also recognize from common Greek usage is that "soul" means "person", "human being." This is the case in Gen 46:15: "all souls, sons and daughters (numbered) thirty–three"; the chapter contains more examples of the same construction, and the usage is similar in Exod 16:16: "according to the number of souls/persons."

A particular usage appears in the passages where "soul" means something like a spirit or ghost. Thus Lev 19:28 rules "you shall not make any cuttings in your body on account of a soul." This usage is well documented in Homer and

---

[33] The differentiation comes close to a contrast in *Wis* 9:15: "The perishable body presses down the soul."

[34] *Comm. in Psalmos* 67.

other older texts, but Lucian's the *Lover of Lies* is a younger text, in which we encounter a person who wants to convince other people "that there are spirits (δαίμονας) and that ghosts (φαντάσματα) and dead people's souls (νεκρῶν ψυχάς) walk about the earth and appear to whom they want" (29).

Lastly we arrive in passages that deal with the soul beyond life on earth. In Wis 2:2f. the author opposes people who deny that the soul is alive after death; the wicked say: "Our breath (πνοή) is a smoke and reason (λόγος) a spark … and when it is put out, the body turns to ashes, and the spirit (πνεῦμα) is dissolved as thin air." A few verses later on; "they have no hope for reward for holiness and they do not take into account any reward for blameless souls (ψυχῶν)" (v. 22). In 3:1f the author has more to say to the theme: "The souls of the righteous are in the hands of God, and no torment shall touch them. In the eyes of the fools they are held to have died."

The Book of Wisdom is directly written in Greek, and thus its terminology is not dependent on an underlying Hebrew text. But whoever thought in a manner similar to that of the writer of the Book of Wisdom probably read LXX passages like the following in a particular way: Ps 21:30: "before him all who have descended into the earth shall fall down; also my soul is alive to him"; Ps 29:4: "Lord, you brought my soul up from Hades, you saved it from those who descend into the pit (the tomb)"; Ps 33:22f.: "Those who hate the righteous will prove wrong. The Lord will deliver the souls of his servants"; Ps 48:16: "God will deliver my soul from the hand of Hades when he grasps me"; Ps 68:33: "The poor will see and rejoice; seek God, and your soul will live." See also Ps 88:49; 114:8, and of course Job 7:15, ms. A, 33:17f., and 2 Macc 6:30, which were quoted above.

## 4. Conclusions

So this paper represents an attempt to read the LXX as a Greek text and to do so without asking how well or badly the translators have treated the Hebrew original (whatever that was like). This manner of approaching the text from the angle of the readers of antiquity is not so common, even if the reader of the above pages can recognize most of the lexicographical data and viewpoints from the studies of Lys and Bratsiotis to which I referred in the beginning or from the Septuagint lexicon of Lust–Eynikel–Hauspie. Looking back at our deliberations the following considerations may, however, be appropriate:

Sometimes the Greek-speaking reader of Hellenistic–Roman times has probably found the text to be strange. Such an assumption is by no means anything remarkable: rightly its language has often been characterized as translation Greek.[35] But considering the particular noun ψυχή we can note that as a rule it is not used in a way that is against Greek usage. Thus we have seen that Bratsiotis' assumption that the translators have chosen a "pre–Platonic" usage of

---

[35] See, e.g., LUST ET ALII, *Greek–English Lexicon*, viiif..

the word verisimilarly says nothing about how the contemporary readers understood the text. To them the Greek of their own time ought to have sufficed for a meaningful reading, or, to express it in terms of our traditional horizon: it is a translation that presupposes a Koine Greek vocabulary.[36] Yet the high frequency of phrases like "my soul will rejoice" may have made a particular, sometimes solemn, impression and may have contributed to a feeling with the readers that the text was special. The above pages have only dealt with one single noun, but the study does not contradict a more overarching opinion that a normal Greek vocabulary would have been sufficient to enable a reader to use the text. However, it should be pointed out that this issue has been the object of some debate.[37]

In the preceding paragraph I used the adverb "as a rule", and there are good reasons so to do, since the tendency of the translators to translate the text literally has now and then got the result that stretches the usage a bit, and this holds true also for ψυχή. In such cases the readers may have felt a little doubtful of the meaning. Regarding a couple of such passages we have seen how the readings and comments of one or two church fathers have confirmed the impression that the text may have appeared to be somewhat obscure.

So, when contemporary Greek usage allowed the readers to find the LXX use of ψυχή meaningful — and it mostly did —, this means that there was nothing to prevent the readers from letting certain passages tell something about the "soul" that surpassed what the Hebrew original meant, indeed even something quite different. Particularly this is true of instances where the LXX reader can find support for the view that the soul is a part of the human being that is contrasted with the body or at least is nobler than it. This means that what G. Bertram once wrote about the text of the LXX may get a wider bearing: "Die Septuaginta gehört mehr in die Geschichte der Auslegung des Alten Testaments als in die des alttestamentlichen Textes."[38]

---

[36] E.g., LUST etc., *loc. cit.*

[37] See EMIL SCHÜRER, *The History of the Jewish People in the Age of Jesus Christ (175 BC – AD 135)*, rev. and ed. by GÉZA VERMÉS/FERGUS MILLAR/MARTIN GOODMAN, III.1, Edinburgh 1986, 478.

[38] GEORG BERTRAM, "Das Problem der Umschrift und die religionsgeschichtliche Erforschung der Septuaginta", in: PAUL VOLZ/FRIEDRICH STUMMER/JOHANNES HEMPEL (eds.), *Werden und Wesen des Alten Testaments* (BZAW 66), Giessen 1936, 97–109: 109.

# 18. "...with the Overseers and Servants"
## The Opening of Paul's Letter to the Philippians, when Considered in the Light of Certain Letter Conventions of the Time

The words in the opening of the Philippians, quoted in the headline above, could be compared to a very small 'pebble in a shoe': no big problem, but nonetheless a bit irritating. In the following pages I will first briefly describe why this might seem to be the case; then, secondly, I would like to point out some common conventions in Antiquity for introducing official letters. Consideration in this regard seems to have been overlooked. Thereupon I would like to present a few reflections which such a comparison could inspire. To some extent they elaborate matters said before by others; however, I suggest that the material presented below can help clarify in some degree the positions and responsibilities of these Philippian 'overseers and servants'.

## 1. The Problem

The opening of Philippians is of the normal Pauline type:[1]

Paul and Timothy, servants of Christ Jesus, to all the holy ones in Christ Jesus who are at Philippi with the overseers and servants. Grace to you and peace from God our father and the Lord Jesus Christ. (Phil 1:1)

This letter introduction recalls the normal opening of a then contemporary Greek letter. This is well known to anyone acquainted with letters from Greek Antiquity, among whom is of course Professor Strömholm, the learned *polyhistor, nunc septuagenarius*, to whom this paper is dedicated.

The common letter opening followed the formula: A [says] to B [that he shall] be well (Greek *chaírein*). Paul adapts the formula in this way: Paul to NN. Grace (Greek *cháris*) from the Lord (or similarly) [be with you]. But Paul's mention of the overseers and servants goes beyond his usual formula. This is the only occasion in Paul's letters that any officials – or whatever we choose to call them – are mentioned in a letter introduction, and such does not happen either in other letters of the New Testament nor in other letters from the first Christian generations. Is there any particular reason why Paul mentions these people in this very

---

[1] [See, e.g., Franz Schnider/Werner Stenger, *Studien zum Neutestamentlichen Briefformular*, (NTTS 11), Leiden 1987, 3–41.]

context? There are several answers suggested to this question, none, however, generally accepted.

Furthermore, what do the nouns "overseers" and "servants" actually mean?[2] In terms of lexicography they are not complicated. "Overseer" renders the Greek *epískopos* (plural *epískopoi*). When it appears in Christian literature a couple of generations or so after Philippians, say in the epistles of Ignatius of Antioch (from around 107), the word naturally stands for "bishop". In this early text (from sometime in the fifties CE) such a translation would, however, be misleading. Later on a bishop was *the* leader of a church, for example of the one in Antioch, and in that function was also the head of the ministers of the lower orders, that is, of the presbyters and the deacons. But here the *epískopoi* evidently form a group with common tasks, to be compared with the people in some sort of leading position whom Paul mentions in other letters: "those who are over you" (*proïstámenoi*, literally: "those standing before you"; 1 Thess 5:12; also Rom 12:8), and those who are in charge of "steering" (*kybernêseis*, 1 Cor 12:28).

Neither are any problems raised by the Greek behind "servant"; *diákonos* (plural *diákonoi*) simply means "servant". Soon it became the official designation of those in the ministry of the ordained deacons. In Rom 16:1 Paul recommends a "sister Phoebe," who is a "servant" (*diákonos*) of the church at Cenchreae, the sea-port of Corinth; she may have had a function similar to the servants of our Philippians opening. Nothing is known of their tasks, and the rather common idea that they were involved in aid to the poor and ill stands on a rather unstable ground.[3] In 1 Corinthians Paul summons his addressees to respect and obey "Stephanas and his house" who "have put themselves to the service (*diakonía*) of the holy ones" (16:15). Here also Rom 12:7f. should be mentioned, in which Paul admonishes those whom he says are particular divine "gifts" to the church: among them are not only "those who are over you" (the *proïstámenoi*, mentioned above), but also those who have "service" (*diakonía*) as their task, and "sharing" (or "giving").

Thus, as far as lexicography is concerned, the terms are not problematic. But what do these persons do? Of course one has sought for analogies in the surrounding world and found other overseers – *epískopoi*. Epigraphic material from the period informs us that the designation was by no means uncommon:

---

[2] [See now RICHARD S. ASCOUGH, "Voluntary Associations and the Formation of Pauline Christian Communities: Overcoming the Objections" in: ALEXANDER GUTSFELD/DIETRICH-ALEX KOCH (eds.), *Vereine, Synagogen und Gemeinden im kaiserzeitlichen Kleinasien* (STAC 25), Tübingen 2006, 149–183, esp. 162–169: "Leadership and Officials"; DIETRICH-ALEX KOCH, "Die Einmaligkeit des Anfangs und die Fortdauer der Institution. Neutestamentliche Beobachtungen zum Problem der Gemeindeleitung", in: IDEM, *Hellenistisches Christentum. Schriftverständnis – Ekklesiologie – Geschichte* (NTOA 65), Göttingen 2008, 197–210.]

[3] [Cf. ROBERT JEWETT, *Romans* (Hermeneia), Minneapolis, Minn. 2007, 941–948: "Leader of the Congregation" (944).]

it was, for example, used for village leaders in Southern Syria[4] and it appears in texts from Rhodes, where it is used of municipal officials and of temple officials at an Apollo temple.[5] In one of the so-called Socratic letters (from the time of the Empire) the writer, "Aristippos," mentions the *epískopoi* of Cyrene (in Northern Africa), that is, the leaders of the city.[6] Also in the Egyptian papyri finds from Antiquity we encounter several *epískopoi* who apparently are supervisors in certain areas of public life on a local level.

On the other hand, the search for analogies has also pointed to other designations, actually more common than *epískopos*, for people in leading positions in cities, communities or associations. Thus, maybe the most common designation for such persons was *árchontes*, "leaders", and so there were "leaders" in charge of a great number of cities, but also of some Jewish Diaspora communities[7] and of certain associations for the worship of this or that god or goddess.[8] Other designations were, for example, "overseers" (*éphoroi*), and "managers" (*prostátai*). That the terminology was somewhat fluid is illustrated by "Aristippos"' letter which I quoted in the preceding paragraph: he also refers to the *epískopoi* as the *árchontes*.

However, of all these comparisons, it must be said that they tell us next to nothing more than that the *epískopoi* of Phil 1:1 had some sort of leading responsibility. But the type of responsibility is not indicated by the word used.

Something similar holds true of the "servants". Among city officials there appear no *diákonoi*, but the designation is used for an official in a cultic association in Troizen (NE Peloponnesos[9]). A Jewish inscription from Northern Syria mentions a certain Nemias, a *diákonos* who probably has "served" in the worship as a *chazzan* – the text is not totally lucid.[10] The *chazzan* had certain duties in the synagogue worship; such a function of the "servant" (the *hypêrétes*, a synonym to *diákonos*) is intimated in Luke's story of Jesus' appearance in the synagogue of Nazareth (Luke 4:20), where obviously "the servant" has asked Jesus to

---

[4] HENRY I. MACADAM, "Epigraphy and Village Life in Southern Syria during the Roman and Early Byzantine Periods", *Berytos* 31 (1983) 103–115: 107.

[5] JAMES HOPE MOULTON/GEORGE MILLIGAN, *The Vocabulary of the Greek Testament Illustrated form the Papyri and Other Non-Literary Sources*, Grand Rapids, Mich. (1930) 1985, ad voc.

[6] LISELOTTE KÖHLER (ed.), Die Briefe des Sokrates und der Sokratiker, *Philologus Suppl.* 20/2, Leipzig 1928, 27.

[7] EMIL SCHÜRER, *The History of the Jewish People in the Age of Jesus Christ (175 BC – AD 135)*. A new English version revised and edited by GÉZA VERMÈS/FERGUS MILLAR/MARTIN GOODMAN. Vol III. Part I, Edinburgh 1986, 92f., SHIMON APPLEBAUM, "The Organization of the Jewish Communities in the Diaspora", in: *The Jewish People in the First Century I* (ed. SHEMUEL SAFRAI/MENAHEM STERN etc.) (Compendia Rerum Iudaicarum ad Novum Testamentum I), Assen 1974, 464–503: 491.

[8] ERICH ZIEBARTH, *Das griechische Vereinswesen*, Leipzig 1896, 147; [Cf. ULRIKE EGELHAAF-GAISER/ALFRED SCHÄFER (eds.), *Religiöse Vereine in der römischen Antike. Untersuchungen zu Organisation, Ritual und Raumordnung* (STAC 13), Tübingen 2002].

[9] ZIEBARTH, *Vereinswesen*, 153

[10] JEAN-BAPTISTE FREY, *Corpus inscriptionum Iudaicarum II* (Sussidi allo studio delle antichità cristiane 1,3.) Rome 1952, 805.

recite the reading from the prophets. A Jewish "servant" could also have other tasks in the community, but the material is scarce.[11] A "servant" in this sense of the word also appears in a Roman epitaph; here again *hypêrétês* is used.[12] So also the Jewish historian Josephus from the 1st century CE reports that every Jewish city should have a leading group of seven, assisted by two "servants" (*hypêrétai*; *Antiquities* IV.214).

On the other hand, there also seems to have existed a manner of speaking of "service" when referring in a more general way to fulfilling functions in the area of religion. Thus Josephus quotes a letter from Antiochus III (3rd cent. BCE) in which he orders that the Jews who were settled in certain areas of Asia Minor would receive support for their religious functionaries: "sufficient means shall be given to those serving [*hypêretoúsin*] their needs" (Josephus, *Antiquities* XII.152;[13] this interpretation is, however, not totally certain). We may surmise a similar wider usage in Paul's reference to the "service" (*diakonía*) of Stephanas in 1 Cor 16:15.

Thus, lexicography only tells us that the "servants" had some kind of subordinate position; they may have been subordinate to the "overseers", but not necessarily so. Their "service" may as well have been one to the community and included a wide area of duties. There are also (Jewish) cases in which "servant" was a designation of such an importance that it was natural to add it to a person's name engraved on tomb stones and other memorials.

## 2. An Overlooked Parallel

It could be useful to note here a type of comparative material which, much to the present writer's surprise, the commentators of Philippians do not seem to have noticed. There is namely a well established letter convention in Antiquity pertaining to letters from an authority to a community or from one community to another. The community in question is very often a city; but also other communities were possible addressees and/or senders of such letters, as, for example, the Jewish community in Alexandria or the adherents of a certain god in a particular area. The following few examples show the stability of the convention as well as some variations, partly depending on local terminology and on differences in organization.

"Trajan, the father of the fatherland to the Areopagus council and to the council of the fifty and to the people of the Athenians, greetings." (Inscript. Graec., ed. minor IV, 1102; concerning a gift to the city)

---

[11] SAMUEL KRAUS, *Synagogale Altertümer*, Berlin – Vienna 1922, 121–131; APPLEBAUM, "Organization", 496

[12] JEAN-BAPTISTE FREY, *Corpus inscriptionum Iudaicarum I* (Sussidi allo studio delle antichità cristiane 1,3.) Rome 1932, 172.

[13] APPLEBAUM, "Organization", 468f.

The Roman senate "to the leaders (*árchontes*), council, people of the Epidaureans, greetings." (Inscript. Graec. IV.2, Epidauros, 89; concerning the appointment of priests)

"Tiberius Caesar, son of the divine Augustus, … to the overseers (*ephóroi*) and city of the Gytheians, greetings." (Suppl. Epigr. Graec. 11,922; a response to the city's wish to worship Tiberius' father as a god, Tiberius himself being "content with more moderate and human honours")

"Claudius Caesar Germanicus … father of the fatherland, to the leaders (*árchontes*), council, the whole people of the Jerusalem inhabitants and to the whole nation of the Jews, greetings." (Josephus, *Antiquities* XX.11; concerning the Jews being allowed to handle the high priest's vestments)

In these examples an authoritative individual or a group of leaders addresses cities. In the last example, also a larger group of recipients than that of a city is in view.

Here is an example of another kind of group being addressed, namely people adhering to a mystery cult:

Marcus Aurelius and Lucius Verus "to the gathering (*súnodos*) of the artists (*technítai*) and initiates of Dionysos" (presumably of the Smyrna region; Inscript. Graec. 3177)

Also the following letter is addressed to the adherents of a particular religion: the Second Book of the Maccabees cites a letter from the Jewish authorities of Jerusalem to the Jews of Alexandria; it is probably a forgery, but follows the same pattern as the above examples. The letter tells the Alexandrian Jews to celebrate the Feast of the Purification of the Temple and also contains some arguments from the Bible for the celebration which have a certain admonishing accent.

"Those in Judea and the senate and Judas to Aristoboulos, teacher of king Ptolemy and belonging to the stock of the anointed priests, and to the Jews in Egypt, greetings and good health" (2 Macc 1:10f.)

In the above examples the leader(s) and/or the city council are mentioned first. But, as in the case of Philippians, the people may be mentioned before the officials:

"The rulers (*kósmoi*) and city of the Polyrhenians to the people and council of the Teians, greetings." (Inscript. Graec. II.xxiii, Crete 3.2; concerning Dionysos worship in connection with asylum agreements).

As to the construction of the letter opening, the above examples demonstrate that the normal arrangement of those addressed is to put them in a row, with or without an "and" to connect them. But in Philippians the officials are not only mentioned after the community, they are addressed as being "together with" it. Here is an example which recalls the beginning of Philippians:

"Philammon to Pates, son of Tsnous, and to Pachrates and to the soldiers together with them, greetings and good health." (Pap. Graec. Louvre inv. 10593; on the movement of a troop of soldiers)

Thus it seems quite evident that the opening of Phil 1:1 rather closely follows the convention of how to begin official letters to a community. A possible implication of Paul's adopting this convention of addressing is of course that the *epískopoi* and *diákonoi* were regarded, both by Paul and by the Philippians, as some kind of officials comparable to the officials addressed in the kind of letters I have quoted.

## 3. Is the Comparison Valid?

Adducing these examples to shed light on Phil 1:1 may, however, seem somewhat unsuitable in the mind of a New Testament exegete. The letters they introduce deal with practical, often economical or political matters, whereas Paul's letter should rather be called a letter of admonition, and as such should be compared to such letters written by philosophers of the time.[14] Such letters were mostly addressed to individuals, although there are also such directed to collective addressees, even cities.[15] But a quick scanning of the material[16] suggests that in such cases the officials were not addressed together with the people of the city in question. (Actually, in the collections of philosophers' letters the opening is mostly left out and the addressee only briefly indicated, e.g. "to his brother"; "to the Athenians".)

Certainly the message of Philippians is not of the same kind as that in which, for example, the Polyrhenians confirm how they aim to follow the asylum agreements with the Teians. But, albeit Philippians can very well be comparable to philosophers' letters of admonition, it is reasonable to assume that it has functioned as a public letter *vis-à-vis* the Philippians;[17] therefore I can see no reason why not the officials addressed in the opening are addressed precisely as officials.

## 4. Institutionalization?

The introduction of the officials in the letter opening brings us to the question of the organization structures of the early church. As a matter of fact it seems to me that the appearance of the *epískopoi* and *diákonoi* in Phil 1:1 confirms what has been indicated by exegetes who have approached the early Christian texts with a sociological point of departure.[18]

---

[14] E.g. TROELS ENGBERG-PEDERSEN, "Stoicism in Philippians, in: IDEM (ed.), *Paul in his Hellenistic Context*, Minneapolis, Minn. 1995; JONAS HOLMSTRAND, *Markers and Meaning in Paul. An Analysis of 1 Thessalonians, Philippians and Galatians* (CB.NT 28), Stockholm, 140f.

[15] KLAUS BERGER, "Hellenistische Gattungen im Neuen Testament", in: *Aufstieg und Niedergang der römischen Welt II*, 25,2, Berlin 1984, 1031–1432: 1338.

[16] CARL LUDWIG KAYSER (ed.), "Apollonii Epistulae", in: *Flavii Philostrati opera I*, Leipzig 1870 • Hildesheim 1964, 345–368; RUDOLPH HERCHER (ed.), Anacharsidis epistulae, in: *Epistolographi Graeci*, Paris 1873 • Amsterdam 1965, 345–368.

[17] KLAUS BERGER, *Formgeschichte des Neuen Testaments*, Heidelberg 1984, 216f.

[18] For the following presentation I owe much to BENGT HOLMBERG, *Paul and Power. The Structure of Authority in the Primitive Church as Reflected in the Pauline Epistles* (CB.NT 11), Stockholm 1978, chapter 3.

It has happened that those who have treated the history of the Early Church have assumed that the first Christian generation was a non-organized, charismatic movement, far from institutionalism; in addition it was assumed that they were so eagerly expecting the end of this age that the idea of organizing did not occur to them. When, in the Deutero-Pauline Pastoral letters (1, 2 Timothy, Titus) the beginnings of an ordained ministry can be surmised, this was regarded as the result of a "Catholizing" tendency.

On the one hand, it is certainly true that one gets the impression that the early Christian communities were charismatic groups, something which is indicated by the important role that "prophets" seem to have played in them (Rom 12:6; 1 Cor 12:18; 1 Thess 5:20). As another sign of the charismatic and non-institutionalized attitudes and tendencies, one may adduce the ecstatic glossolalia at the worship of the Corinthian Christians, which became so prominent that Paul had to intervene (1 Cor 12–14). Furthermore, the different ways of designating the "officers" may also intimate a certain looseness in terms of institutionalization.

But, on the other hand, there were people in the early Christian communities who were explicitly called leaders, and who were apparently known as such both by the letter-writing apostle and by the recipient community. I have referred to such leaders above and the Philippians opening is also evidence to this.

One factor behind the existence of these leaders may have been the natural tendency of any group that a leading stratum emerges in it. This common tendency should have been combined with practical social facts: personal engagement and capacity, also such a simple thing as the circumstance that someone was the owner and thus the host in a home that was big enough to house the gatherings of the Christian community of the place.

Paul may not have formally elected and/or installed people to be in charge in the Christian communities (cf. the Deutero-Pauline 2 Tim 1:6 and Acts 14:23, which report that he did). Nevertheless it is probable that he has not simply passively noted what was going on in terms of leadership, instruction, forms of worship, social care etc., but rather has been active in the matters.

The parallel between the *epískopoi* and *diákonoi*, on the one hand, and the *árchontes*, the council etc. of secular communities – or of this or that religious association – on the other, has hardly anything to say in terms of how the *epískopoi* and *diákonoi* got their offices, nor for how long they had them. They could have been chosen for a given period or may have had the office for life time, something which seems to be the case in the younger Deuteropauline epistles (1 Tim 3; 5:17–20). It is also probable that those who were paid for being teachers (Gal 6:6) were supposed to serve for more than a short period of time.

We should, however, not assume that the development of the community organization in the first generation went at the same pace and contained the same elements in the same order in all places, and we should be prepared to take into account the possibility that there was a variety in these respects also among the churches that were founded by Paul or influenced by him. The Christian groups of both Corinth and Philippi had their origin in Pauline mission and thus can be supposed to have received similar guidelines in terms of community life (worship, everyday ethics, instruction of new converts etc.); nonetheless they need not have had identical organizations.

## 5. The Neglecting of the *Diákonoi*

Because of the discussions of institutionalism and leadership the *epískopoi* in Phil 1:1 have been in the focus of the debate, whereas less attention has been paid to the *diákonoi*. But the observation that Phil 1:1 follows a letter convention can also have some implications as to how to understand the appearance of the *diákonoi* in the opening.

Above, I remarked that lexicography intimates that the Philippian *diákonoi* had a subordinate position as compared to the *epískopoi*. In some (Jewish) texts, however, the designation appears to have been quite honorable; and, in addition there are indications of a wider usage of the "service" concept both in Jewish and Early Christian contexts.

The relatively honored Jewish "servants" I just mentioned belonged to a constellation of persons in charge of the worship: the head of the synagogue (*archisynágôgos*) and the "servant" (Hebrew *hazzan*), whereas the secular affairs of the community were taken care of by others (*árchontes*, elders etc.). The existence of such a pair may have been of some importance in the ways the Early Christian communities organized themselves.[19] But if so, the Christians have filled the offices with new content.[20]

As a matter of fact it seems to be exceptional that subordinate people are addressed together with the leaders in the epistolary opening of official letters. I have found no non-Christian example in which "servants" (*diákonoi* or *hypêrétai*) are mentioned together with the leaders, council etc., addressed, nor any clear cases with any other people in "serving" positions.

Here, however, is an example that may vaguely remind of the Philippian combination:

"Aurelius Isidorus, the governor (*epítropos*) of the lower Thebais to Apolinarius, the commander (*stratêgós*) of Panopolis, and to those in charge (*epeíktai*) of preparing the ships (*ploiopoiía*)". (Papyri from Panopolis, Chester Beatty Libr. 2.10.271)

But when one realizes that the letter deals with exactly the preparation of ships, the mentioning of "those in charge" who are under the *stratêgós* is natural. This can remind us of what we noted before, namely that the officials mentioned in a letter opening are such as are responsible for the matter dealt with in the letter.

---

[19] Hermann Wolfgang Beyer, "διάκονος", in: *ThWNT* 2, 1935, 91f.
[20] Beyer, "διάκονος", 91.

So the inclusion of the Philippian servants in the opening may indicate that they have a more important position than one may initially imagine.

## 6. Possible Tasks of the Philippian Officials as Surmised from the Letter

My discussion so far is admittedly a bit inconclusive. But possibly one further step may help us to co-ordinate the different features into a decently meaningful picture of which these officials are a part.

When the leaders were mentioned in the openings of the public letters, this had to do with their position as executives; they were responsible for the implementation of the matters dealt with in the letter. Likewise then, when we find that convention echoed in Phil 1:1, it would indicate that the *epískopoi* and the *diákonoi* were supposed to see to it that the contents of Paul's letter was somehow implemented.

Therefore I would like to turn to Paul's letter itself, looking for possible matters the handling of which may have been the task of the *epískopoi* and the *diákonoi*.

Such an inventory is not so particularly easy. A scholar of literary criticism might consider an "implied reader"; but, although my approach may be influenced by this kind of analysis, I will read the text with slightly less sophistication. I will look for passages where Paul directly addresses the readers and hearers, not least with admonitions, but furthermore for words which seem to be *indirectly* admonishing. As far as the "theological" contents are concerned, they seem to be there to serve as arguments for Paul's admonitions, more precisely his admonitions to stand firm under adversity.[21] That is, if the *epískopoi* and the *diákonoi* were to be involved in implementing Paul's message, their task would less be that of a teacher in theology than that of being a moral support and a guardian.

The background of many of the admonitions of Philippians is obviously that the community is suffering from persecutions of some kind (1:29: "it has been granted to you ... to suffer for Christ's sake"). Against this background they are summoned to "walk worthily of the gospel", "to stand firm in one spirit for the faith of the gospel" and not to be frightened (1:27–29; also 4:6). They shall imitate the example of Epaphroditus, one of their own, who is now with Paul; he "nearly died for the work of Christ, risking his life" together with Paul (2:30). But not least should they imitate Paul himself (3:17; 4:9), who is imprisoned because of the gospel (1:12–26) but nevertheless rejoices and is full of hope (1:18; 2:17). Such should also be the attitude of the Philippians (2:18; 3:1). Above all, however, they should, as Paul, imitate Christ: he was obedient unto death and suffered willingly (2:5–11; 3:10). So the Philippians must also be obedient and work out

---

[21] HOLMSTRAND, *Markers*, 139–144, 219

their salvation (2:12); they must not be like those who are "enemies of the cross of Christ" (3:18). On the contrary, they shall be "blameless, children of God in the midst of a perverse generation, shining as lights in the world, keeping to the word of life" (2:15f.), i.e. the word that Paul has preached for them and, I would say, the one that is now proclaimed by officials in the community and that these have learnt from Paul and others (see 1 Cor 12:28 and Gal 6:6, which testify to such a work).

The pressure of the persecution may also explain why Paul so often summons the Philippians to unity, for it is well known that pressure from outside on a group may often be fertile ground for internal grumbling and division. So they shall be "of the same mind, having the same love, being in full accord and of one mind" (2:5; also 1:27; 4:2f.).

Now, it is a common feature that persecutions or other pressures from outside put particular responsibility on the leaders of a community. Judaism in Paul's days had bitter experiences of this. So Philo reports what happened when Petronius, the governor of Syria, had been ordered by Caligula to introduce a colossal statue of him into the Temple of Jerusalem. Petronius realized how serious a blow this would be to Jewish religious feelings and foresaw that the result could be a violent uprising. So firstly he tried – but without success – to reconcile the Jewish authorities – "the priests and the *árchontes*" – to what seemed to be inevitable (Philo, *Legatio* 222). In a later phase masses of Jews protested, and then "the council of the elders" (the *gerousía*) pleaded their case before the governor (229). Similarly, the leading men (the *dynatoí*) of the Jews in Caesarea presented their complaints to the procurator Florus for his contempt of Jewish religion; instead of listening to them he put them into jail (Josephus, *War* II.292).

Also spiritual and social pressure was all too well known to the Jews of Paul's time. On the other hand, there were some members of their community who were tempted to compromise, to slacken in their observance of the inherited rules and to conform to the majority. So the leaders of what later came to be called normative Judaism began stressing very strongly to their fellow Jews their obligation to firmness and loyalty, to fidelity to God's law. This is a constant theme in Jewish literature produced in Hellenistic-Roman times.

It is no surprise that we encounter a similar anxiety to defend one's religious identity among the early Christians. Such a defence, and such a pastoral care of their fellow-Christians, was here also obviously regarded as belonging to the duties of the people in leading positions. Thus the "leaders" ("those who stand in the front", the *proïstámenoi*) of the Thessalonian Christians "instruct and warn" (*nouthetein*) them; among the Galatians there are such as "instruct them in the word", with whom they shall "share all good things" (i.e., they shall give them their living) (Gal 6:6). In Rom 12:7f. Paul refers to people in a responsible position who teach and admonish, and 1 Cor 12:28 mentions among others also prophets, who reveal people's hidden thought and who admonish (14:24f.), and teachers. To a slightly later period belongs the Acts of the Apostles, in which

Paul is reported to give a farewell speech in which he exhorts the elders of Ephesus whom "the Holy Spirit has made into overseers (*epískopoi*) of the flock": they shall take heed to themselves and to the flock, for wolves will come in among them and in their midst there will "arise men who speak perverse things to draw away disciples after them" (Acts 20:28–30).

It seems to me that this look into some of the basic motifs of Philippians suggests a reason why the *epískopoi* and *diákonoi* are addressed together with the community. This idea is not new[22] but has not earlier been connected to the convention of official letters, which implied that the officials mentioned in the letter opening are supposed to have a particular responsibility for the implementation of the letter's message. That this letter is one of admonition does not weaken the force of this convention; on the contrary, parallel material both from contemporary Judaism and from Early Christianity confirms that precisely the officials of a group were expected to take on a particular responsibility when the group was put under pressure.

As I intimated in the beginning of this paper, I dare not claim that these reflections indisputably answer the questions raised by the occurrence of the *epískopoi* and *diákonoi* in the opening of Philippians. No doubt, some of my colleagues in the exegetical guild may still feel that there is a pebble in their exegetical shoe; others may think that the material I have adduced and discussed has at least eased the irritation a little.

Anyway, I would like to finish these pages by stating that it has been a joy and honor to compose them having in mind Professor Strömholm, who in so many contexts has taken on the responsibilities of leadership, including the duty to stand up in situations of crisis.

---

[22] See ERNST LOHMEYER, *Die Briefe an die Philipper, an die Kolosser und an Philemon* (KEK 9), Göttingen ¹³1930 (1964), 11f.

# 19. "He Spoke of the Temple of His Body" (John 2:13–22)

This contribution to the *Festschrift* for Professor Ottosson deals with ideas bearing on temples by reason of his reputation as an archaeologist with a special interest in temple archaeology. May these pages be regarded as a respectful tribute to "the man in the ditch"[1] from a colleague in a neighboring discipline.

One may deal with the Johannine story of Jesus' cleansing of the temple in John (2:13–22) in many ways, questioning, e.g., its history of tradition,[2] its historicity,[3] the message of the evangelist,[4] etc. In what follows I shall pose a rather plain question, *viz.*, what would the temple imagery suggest to the audience of the gospel, when the evangelist used it of Jesus in this text?[5]

One need not doubt as to the message of John 2:13–22. The body of Jesus is a temple which replaces the one in Jerusalem; this circumstance is closely connected with his death and resurrection and can only be understood in the light thereof.[6] But this imagery leads us to ask what ideas and associations a Johannine audience of the Early Church may have had concerning temples.

---

[1] The quotation is from MAGNUS OTTOSSON, *Temple and Cult Places in Palestine* (Acta Univ. Ups., Boreas 12), Uppsala 1980, 9.

[2] See, e.g., CARL J. BJERKELUND, "En tradisjons- og redaksjonshistorisk analyse af perikopen om tempelrenselsen", *NTT* 69 (1968) 206–216; ROBERT TOMSON FORTNA, *The Gospel of Signs. A Reconstruction of the Narrative Source Underlying the Fourth Gospel* (MSSNTS 11), Cambridge 1970, 144–147; FRANS SCHNIDER/WERNER STENGER, *Johannes und die Synoptiker: Vergleich ihrer Parallelen*, Munich 1971, 26–53. esp. 37–53; JÜRGEN BECKER, *Das Evangelium nach Johannes* (ÖTK 4), Gütersloh 1979, 121ff.

[3] VICTOR EPPSTEIN, "The Historicity of the Gospel Account on the Cleansing of the Temple", *ZNW* 55 (1964) 42–58; ÉTIENNE TROCMÉ, "L'expulsion des marchands du Temple", *NTS* 15 (1968/69) 1–22. Cf. BECKER, *Comm.*, 124; ERNST HAENCHEN, *Das Johannesevangelium*, Tübingen 1980, 205–210.

[4] By "the evangelist" I simply refer to the man who published the Fourth Gospel, and do not now, as, e.g., Bultmann, differentiate between the evangelist who was responsible for an earlier version and an ecclesiastical redactor who revised and edited it: RUDOLF BULTMANN, *Das Evangelium nach Johannes* (KEK II), Göttingen 1941 ([10]1960).

[5] For a similar reader- (and text-)oriented perspective see BIRGER OLSSON, *Structure and Meaning in the Fourth Gospel. A Text-Linguistic Analysis of John 2:1–11 and 4:1–42* (CB.NT 6), Lund 1974, 1.2. It is also found in RENÉ KIEFFER, *Johannesevangeliet* (KNT 4 A, B), Uppsala 1987–88.

[6] E.g., RUDOLF SCHNACKENBURG, *Das Johannesevangelium* (HThK 4) I, Freiburg i. Br. – Basel – Vienna 1965, 370; KIEFFER, *Comm.*, 72f.

## 1. Temples and their Functions

I shall begin by presenting some aspects of temples and of their functions, which are widely encountered in the religious world, and which are featured in common handbooks on the phenomenology of religion.[7] These concepts will be illustrated by examples from the world of the Fourth Gospel, especially as represented by diaspora Judaism. Then I turn to John's gospel in search of passages outside 2:13–22 which express in other terms the thoughts about Christ which seem to be suggested by the temple imagery.

Turning first to the temple ideas, one which is very widespread is that, in some sense or another, a temple is the dwelling place of one or several gods.[8] It is the presupposition behind the Jewish polemical story about Bel and the dragon, according to which food was presented to Bel in his temple, which he (the idol) was told to consume at night. And when Philo, e.g., in *Cher.* 98–101, argues that the soul shall be as beautiful a dwelling (ἐνδιαίτημα οἶκος) as possible to God, he describes it with features from such temples as were found everywhere in the cities of his day.[9]

In the preceding paragraph I wrote that a god "in some sense or another" dwelt in his temple. The idea is by no means always conceived in a concrete manner, but, not least in Greek religion,[10] we find modes of thinking similar to those encountered in the OT.[11] There, on the one hand, the temple is God's abode, although he cannot be seen there (see, e.g., 1 Kgs 8:13). But, on the other hand, even if God is in his temple, his throne is in heaven (Ps 11:4). Otherwise it is said that his "glory" or his "name" dwells there (1 Kgs 8:11, 29; Exod 40:34). It is this "glory" that, according to Josephus, left the temple when its destruction by the Romans was imminent:

> At the feast which is called Pentecost, when the priests were going by night ... to perform their customary holy service, they said that, in the first place, they noticed a quaking and a noise, and after that they heard a manifold (ἀθρόας) cry: "Let us remove hence." (*Bell.* VI.299)[12]

An important aspect of the idea of temples as divine dwellings is that a temple is set apart and consecrated (a *temenos*) to be a place where man meets the divine

---

[7] GERHARD VAN DER LEEUW, *Phänomenologie der Religion*, Tübingen 1956; KURT GOLDAMMER, *Die Formenwelt des Religiösen*, Stuttgart 1960; GEO WIDENGREN, *Religionens värld*, Stockholm ³1971. [IDEM, *Religionsphänomenologie* (DGL), Berlin 1969.]

[8] GOLDAMMER, *op. cit.*, 194; WIDENGREN, *op. cit.*, 196; [*op. cit.*, 347]; JOHANN MAIER, *Geschichte der jüdischen Religion*, Berlin – New York 1972, 30f.; WALTER BURKERT, *Griechische Religion der archaischen und klassischen Epoche* (RM 15), Stuttgart 1977, 147f.

[9] See also *Somn.* 149, 215; *Virt.* 188.

[10] WILLIAM BREDE KRISTENSEN, *The Meaning of Religion*, Haag 1960, 375.

[11] BARUCH A. LEVINE, "On the Presence of God in Biblical Religion", in *Religions in Antiquity. Essays in Memory of E. R. Goodenough* (SHR; Suppl. Numen 14), Leiden 1968, 71–87; IDEM, "Biblical Temple", in *The Encyclopedia of Religion* II (1987) 202–217, esp. 211ff.

[12] Cf. Ezra 11:23.

sphere.¹³ We come across this thought in Solomon's prayer at the consecration of the temple according to 1 Kgs 8:27ff.:

> But will God indeed dwell on the earth? Behold, heaven and the heaven of heavens do not contain you; how much less this house which I have built. Yet turn to the prayer of your servant and to his supplication ... that your eyes may be open toward this house.

Another believer expressed similar ideas in this way:

> My soul will be sent to the heavenly thrones of Zeus-Oromasdes ... I undertook to make this holy place a common throne room of all the gods ... I have set up these divine images of Zeus-Oromasdes and of Artagnes-Heracles-Ares, and also of my all-nourishing homeland Commagene; and from the same stone, throned likewise among the gracious daemons, I have consecrated the features of my own form, and thus admitted a new Tyche to share in the ancient honors of the great gods, ... who were my leaders in a good beginning and have been the source of universal blessings for my whole kingdom.¹⁴

Thus, Antiochus I of Commagene, who has ordered this inscription, takes it for granted that the worship before the images of the temple really "honors" the gods, himself included, but, on the other hand, it is also self-evident that they are enthroned in heaven, being there the source of all earthly blessings.

So temples are normally thought of as cult-places.¹⁵ To Philo this is natural, both when he touches upon temples in general (*Immut.* 8: εὔχεσθαι καὶ θύειν *Ebr.* 66: εὐχὰς καὶ θυσίας καὶ πᾶσαν τὴν περὶ τὸ ἱερὸν ἁγιστείαν),¹⁶ and when he deals with the Jerusalem temple. Of the worship in the latter he says, e.g., in *Spec. Leg.* I.67:

> One should not check the forwardness of men who pay their tribute to piety (εὐσέβειαν) and desire by means of sacrifices either to give thanks for the blessings that befall them or ask for pardon and forgiveness of sins.¹⁷

The large number of Jews who lived far away from their temple participated indirectly both in the sacrifices to God and in the blessings which sprang from the cult. So they did through the temple tax, which Philo calls the "ransom" (λύτρα; *Spec. Leg.* I.77). He says that they gladly paid it, because they would thereby find "release from slavery or healing of diseases and the enjoyment of liberty fully secured and also complete preservation from danger."¹⁸ Later on (152) we are told that this gift was brought as "thank-offerings (χαριστηρίους) to God by those whose life in all its aspects is blessed by his beneficence."

Accordingly man brings himself and his whole life into the cult and thus relates them to the god he encounters there. Sin-offering and confession of sins

---

¹³ GOLDAMMER, *op. cit.*, 190; WIDENGREN, *op. cit.*, 196f.; [*op. cit.*, 347–351].

¹⁴ The inscription is from Commagene and is dated to some time between 50 and 35 BC. The text is in WILHELM DITTENBERGER, *Orientis Graeci Inscriptiones Selectae*, Leipzig 1903–1905, 383. (Trans. in FREDERICK C. GRANT, *Hellenistic Religions*, Indianapolis, Ind. – New York 1953, 21ff.).

¹⁵ VAN DER LEEUW, *op. cit.*, 446; GOLDAMMER, *op. cit.*, 191; WIDENGREN, *op. cit.*, 196–199 [*op. cit.*, 347–353].

¹⁶ See also *Somn.* I.215.

¹⁷ Trans., largely, Colson. See also, e.g., *Vit. Mos.* II.174.

¹⁸ Trans. Colson.

mean that he avows that his trespasses are precisely trespasses of the norms for which his god stands, on whom his life depends. The disturbed harmony with fundamental patterns is restored, when the god hears the prayer and accepts the offering which represents the donor. Similarly, e.g., a thank-offering for the harvest means that man realizes that his and his society's life depend on the grace of the god behind wind and weather and fertility.

We should notice the double direction in worship: from god to man and from man to god. In the temple the two directions meet. The god hears, regards, gives, answers, meets[19] – the invocation "come" is universal. Man comes, gives, prays, asks, gives thanks.

The encounter of god and man in the temple can also mean that man asks for enlightenment or guidance, and that his god reveals himself to him, gives oracles or instruction. So temples are also the sites of divine revelation, often such as has life-giving consequences.[20] Thus we hear of several oracle sanctuaries, and the temples of the healer god Asclepius contained particular precincts where suppliants could sleep, in order, hopefully, to see Asclepius appear in a dream, giving healing instructions.[21]

Within Judaism, gathered as it was around God's revelation in the Scriptures, the motif of the temple as a place for God's revelation was not salient, but did exist. When, e.g., in Sir 24:10 it is said that Wisdom was given rest on Sion, this is reminiscent of how Isis, who shares several features with Wisdom,[22] finds rest in her house.[23] Furthermore, the Bible told the Jew of John's times that the tables of the covenant were once kept in the ark in the Holy of Holies. It also seems that the *Sanhedrin* met in the temple area for its interpretation and application of God's Law.[24] Thus the idea that the temple is the place of divine revelation lies behind the story of the announcement of John's birth in Luke 1:11–22.[25] Josephus reports something similar about John Hyrcanus, the high priest:

A surprising thing is told of this high priest Hyrcanus: God came to talk to him. They say that on the very day on which his sons fought with (Antiochus) Cyzicenus, the high priest offered incense, alone in the temple, and heard a voice that his sons just had overcome Antiochus. (*Ant.* XIII.10.3)[26]

---

[19] GOLDAMMER, *op. cit.*, 190f.

[20] E.g., GOLDAMMER, *op. cit.*, 191; MAIER, *op. cit.*, 31, 123f.

[21] Cf. ERNST LUDWIG EHRLICH, *Die Kultsymbolik im Alten Testament und im nachbiblischen Judentum* (SyR 3), Stuttgart 1959, 20 (on incubation).

[22] BURTON LEE MACK, *Logos und Sophia. Untersuchungen zur Weisheitstheologie im Hellenistischen Judentum* (StUNT 10), Göttingen 1973, 30–42.

[23] MACK, *op. cit.*, 41.

[24] *m.Sanhedrin* XI.2. See further EMIL SCHÜRER, *The History of the Jewish People in the Age of Jesus Christ (175 BC – AD 135)*, rev. ed. by GÉZA VERMÈS/FERGUS MILLAR/MATTHEW BLACK, II, Edinburgh 1979, 223ff.

[25] HEINZ SCHÜRMANN, *Das Lukasevangelium* (HThK 3), Freiburg i. Br. – Basel – Vienna 1969, 32.

[26] More material in (HERMANN STRACK)/PAUL BILLERBECK, *Kommentar zum Neuen Testament aus Talmud und Midrasch* II, Munich 1924, 78.

One further aspect to be mentioned is that, particularly large, temples become meeting-places of great numbers of people who worship and adhere to the same god or gods.[27] Luke knew the normal appearance of the scene at great sacrificial feasts, when he reported how a large crowd gathered when the priests at the Jupiter temple of Lystra arranged for a sacrifice to Barnabas and Paul (Acts 14:11–13). Philo tells us rather solemnly about the masses of Jews who gathered from everywhere to the Jerusalem temple:

> Countless multitudes from countless cities come, some over land, others over sea, from east and west and north and south at every feast. They take the temple for their port as a general haven and safe refuge from the bustle and great turmoil of life ... Friendships are formed between those who hitherto knew not each other, and the sacrifices and libations are the occasion of reciprocity of feeling and constitute the surest pledge that all are of one mind. (*Spec. Leg.* I.69–70, trans. Colson.)

Philo thus connects the role of the temple as a socially gathering and uniting institution with the worship which took place in it. Such an attitude is common. It is the same in Greek religion, where the cult concerns the human community, be it the *polis*, the family or the amphictyony.[28] The circumstance that religious worship is not a matter of private concern is a dominant factor in the widespread suspicion of Jewish (and, later, Christian) cultic separatism, clearly reflected in Philo's report on the Jewish embassy to Caligula.

I now leave aside other temple aspects, such as their function as places of asylum, and the fact that they are often considered as representing heaven or cosmos.[29] I do so despite the fact that the Logos Christology, so important to the Fourth Gospel, certainly has a cosmic perspective. Nor do I take into account Jewish ideas of a heavenly temple or the existence of Jewish expectations of a new temple in the age of salvation.[30] For in both cases it can be argued that the temple imagery is the same anyway. Thus I now return to John 2.

## 2. Temple Imagery in John

We need not linger on the expression "his body". It stands for the person of Jesus who was executed and glorified.[31] Accordingly the text envisages the situation after the "three days" of 2:20, which was also the situation of the readers, when Jesus, to use Johannine terms, had gone to the Father (13:1; 14:28; 16:10; 20:17 etc.) One can reasonably understand the quotation of Ps 69:10 (2:17) in the

---

[27] GOLDAMMER, *op. cit.*, 195.
[28] BURKERT, *op. cit.*, 383ff.
[29] See, e.g., RAPHAEL PATAI, *Man and Temple*, London 1947, chapters 3–4; GEO WIDENGREN, "Aspetti simbolici dei templi e luoghi di culto del Vicino Oriente antico", *Numen* 7 (1960) 1–25; PETER SCHÄFER, "Tempel und Schöpfung", *Kairos* 16 (1974) 122–133.
[30] See, e.g., BERTIL GÄRTNER, *The Temple and the Community in Qumran and the New Testament* (MSSNTS 1), Cambridge 1965. Nor do I take into account that, according to Philo, the first man (Gen 2:7) was "a house or a holy temple for the reasonable soul" (*Opif.* 137).
[31] See, e.g., GÄRTNER, *op. cit.*, 120; SCHNIDER/STENGER, *op. cit.*, 52.

same light: out of zeal for the house of the Father, i.e., a zeal that a new temple be erected among men, Jesus was to be consumed, indeed, killed.[32] Actually his "going away" was necessary in order that this temple be built (cf. 16:7).

Temples were dwelling-places of gods. Was – and is – Jesus God's dwelling-place according to John? When putting the question so bluntly we should remember that both Jews and Greeks were wont to speak rather subtly of the dwelling of gods among men. Thus we should not expect our evangelist to be simplistic, when he uses other expressions, the sense of which approaches a "yes" to our question. In 14:10 we are told: "I am in the Father and the Father is in me" (also 10:38). In a sense he is the place where man meets God: "he who has seen me has seen the Father" (14:9); "nobody comes to the Father but by me" (14:6).[33] When (6:69) Jesus is called "the holy one of God", this places him in the same category as a temple, a place set apart for holy, divine purposes (also 10:36). Many expositors have seen an allusion to the OT-Jewish motif of God's glory dwelling in the Tabernacle or the Temple:[34] "the Logos ... dwelt – or: pitched its tent – ἐσκήνωσεν – among us, and we beheld its glory, as of an only begotten from the Father". In some of his deeds one "beheld" this glory: at the wedding (2:11), and at the tomb of Lazarus (11:40).

We have touched upon the role of temples as cult sites. In 4:21ff. the old cult sites are invalidated: neither on Mount Gerizim nor in Jerusalem shall God be worshipped. In the farewell discourse Jesus' death and resurrection introduce a new cultic situation: "hitherto you have not asked anything in my name" (16:24); but hereafter: "if you ask anything of the Father in my name, he will give it to you" (16:23; also 14:13f.; 15:16).

We hear nothing of any sacrifices or offerings on the part of the Christians, or rather of the disciples, who are often the personages with whom the reader can identify.[35] On the one hand the verb "worship" (προσκυνεῖν) of 4:21ff. seems to represent the whole of the cultic attitude, i.e. that in worship the believer relates his whole existence to his god. On the other hand this attitude takes other expressions in John, in which Jesus plays the same role as the cult place. Thus we may regard some phrases, according to which man "comes": he comes to the light (with his deeds, 3:20f.), to the Father through the Son (14:6), to the Son (who does not cast out the one who comes, 6:35f.), to drink the life-giving water (from the temple well?, 7:37f.;[36] cf. 4:11). We can also regard some passages where "faith" is mentioned: "he who does not believe in the Son will not see life, and the wrath of God rests upon him" (3:36), furthermore the story of the officer who

---

[32] BULTMANN, *Comm.*, 87; SCHNACKENBURG, *Comm.* I, 362; SCHNIDER/STENGER, *op. cit.*, 50. Cf. C. KINGSLEY BARRETT, *The Gospel according to St. John*, London ²1978, 199.

[33] SCHNIDER/STENGER, *op. cit.*, 52.

[34] E.g., SCHNACKENBURG, *Comm.* I, 244f.; RAYMOND E. BROWN, *The Gospel according to John* (AncB) I, Garden City 1966, 32ff.; BARRETT, *Comm.*, 165. Cf. BULTMANN, *Comm.*, 43; SCHNIDER/STENGER, *op. cit.*, 52.

[35] E.g., SCHNACKENBURG, *Comm.* I, 234–237

[36] See SCHNACKENBURG, *Comm.* II (1971), 215f.

believed with his whole house (4:53), and the admonition to the disciples not to be troubled: "believe in God, believe also in me" (14:1).

There are also some other turns of phrases which express the attitude that the believer's whole life is carried by the God-relationship, but now not connected to a temple-worship: "remain in me ... for apart from me you can do nothing" (15:4f.). So the one who presents an offering in John is Jesus, who consecrates himself (as a sacrifice) "for the sake of" the disciples (17:19), who lays down his life for the sheep (10:11; see also 15:11), and who dies "not only for the nation, but to gather into one the scattered children of God" (11:52).

The Christian of the Johannine community could have his sins forgiven, although no longer through sin-offerings, but through the mediation of those who, by the power of the Spirit, continued and applied the work of the Son (20:23; cf. 7:38; 16:7).

Temples were also places at which divine revelation was given. That Jesus reveals God is, of course, essential in John: "no one has ever seen God – an only-begotten god (or: son) has made him known" (1:18). In him God addressed man: "the word which you hear is not mine but the Father's who sent me" (14:24; also 3:34; 7:17; 8:26). In his deeds God himself was at work: "the Son can do nothing of his own accord but only what he sees the Father doing" (5:19; also 5:30; 8:26). And as the divine revelation in a temple may mean life, so does God's revelation in Christ: "the Son gives life to whom he will" (5:21,24 etc.)

Finally, temples became meeting-places, where the common worship united the participants. That people who worship the same god are thus unified is, of course, a motif also encountered in John, and explicitly connected to the role of Jesus: one flock and one shepherd, after also "other sheep" have been brought to him (10:16); Jesus died "to gather into one the scattered children of God" (11:52). Lastly, we should cite 17:22: "they shall be one, as we are one".

This survey should not be understood as if I were of the opinion that the phrase "he spoke of the temple of his body" contained an imagery which was only made explicit in such passages as those I have cited. But I believe that in its position at the beginning of the Johannine gospel the narrative of the cleansing of the temple brought associations to an early Christian audience, which, as the reading proceeded, they could easily specify and expand in a way reminding of the one I have suggested.

When the Johannine audience heard this passage, the Jerusalem temple was no longer standing. Some Jews dreamt about its restoration. Others, and notably they who developed the so-called formative Judaism, maintained that the study and observance of the Torah now had to replace the temple service.[37]

---

[37] See, *inter alia*, *b.Sanhedrin* 44b, 99b. Further JACOB NEUSNER, "Torah and Israel's National Salvation in the Talmud of Babylonia", in IDEM, *Major Trends in Formative Judaism. Society and Symbol in Political Crisis*, Chico, Calif. 1983, 93–106, 95f.; SCHÜRER, *op. cit.*, I, 523ff.

If the Johannine community had any relationship to Jews, as is likely, these were probably cool.[38] In addition, in these relationships the Jews were presumably the stronger and the more powerful part. If such Jews and Johannine Christians may have been agreed that the time of the temple worship had passed, nevertheless the latter maintained that "the law was given through Moses; grace and truth came through Jesus Christ" (1:17). Their understanding of the confrontation in our John passage was also likely to be colored by some decades of debate about God's Law, including its rules on the Sabbath (John 5) and (probably also) *kosher*.[39] These had resulted in a growing gulf between Johannine Christianity and its mother religion. When the Johannine Christians believed that they "in" Christ had a new temple, this meant totally new conditions of man's relationship to God, which were established through the work of Jesus, and which were realized and experienced in their own time through the Spirit-Paraclete (7:39; 14:16ff.; 16:7-14). Thus they encountered God and he them, thus they had life from him, as branches from the vine (15:1-11).

There are reasons to believe that this opinion on the temple and its worship – and on the Torah – did not exclude moral principles and cult ceremonies (see 3:5; 6:53ff.; 21:9), nor leaders of the religious community and its worship (see 17:20; 20:22f.; 21:15-19). But this is not the place to discuss such matters. It suffices if I have managed to indicate that John's first story of Jesus' appearance in Jerusalem contains Christological intimations which are likely to have been more telling to people in Antiquity than we may first imagine. For they knew better than we what a temple was.

---

[38] RAYMOND E. BROWN, *The Community of the Beloved Disciple*, New York – Toronto 1979, 40ff., 66ff.

[39] See SEVERINO PANCARO, *The Law in the Fourth Gospel*, Leiden 1975; J. LOUIS MARTYN, *History and Theology in the Fourth Gospel*, Nashville, Ky. 1979; WAYNE MEEKS, "Breaking Away: Three New Testament Pictures of Christianity's Separation from the Jewish Communities", in: JACOB NEUSNER/ERNST FRERICHS (eds.), *To See Ourselves as Others See Us*, Chico, Calif. 1985, 94-104; PER JARLE BEKKEN, "Apropos jødedommens mangfold i det første århundrede: Observasjoner til debatten om jødisk kultus hos Filo, i Acta og Johannesevangeliet", *TTK* 59 (1988) 161-173: 168ff.

## 20. Humble and Confident
## On the So-Called Philosophers in Colossians

### 1. Introductory Remarks

"May no one take you captive through his philosophy" (Col 2:8). The thinking and morality of this "philosophy", which is the main reason why the Letter to the Colossians was written,[1] are discussed in every commentary on the Epistle, in every text-book on New Testament Introduction, and, of course, in several other studies. But no agreement is in sight, nor does the present writer expect his treatment of the issue to have any such result. Nevertheless I shall propose a reconstruction of its ideology and relate it to the circumstance that the representatives of the "philosophy" evidently constitute a minority among the Christians in Colossae,[2] albeit a minority which seems to exert so great a pressure on the majority that it appears to be a "mighty minority".

These "philosophers" – which, for the sake of brevity, I shall call them in what follows – represent a minority; this may be inferred from a few details in Colossians. But apparently they do not form a minority in the usual sociological sense of the term; they certainly see themselves as a group, but do not lack power, are not regarded with contempt by the majority, and are not insulated or placed on a socially or culturally inferior level.[3]

I shall proceed as follows: firstly, I briefly collect those details in Colossians which indicate the philosophers' minority status. Then I attempt to describe their ideology, and thirdly, consider how, according to the Letter, this "mighty minority" is related to the majority, in order, finally, to examine the other side of the relationship, *viz.* how the author depicts the attitudes of the majority to the minority, on the one hand considering their present attitude, which he thinks is unwarranted, and, on the other, the one he wants them to adopt.

---

[1] I am of the opinion that the Colossians was written by a member of the Pauline school. I have argued this opinion in my commentary, *Kolosserbrevet* (Kommentar till Nya Testamentet 12, Uppsala 1986), 200–201. I agree with W. Schenk who maintains that the purpose of the letter is more parenetic than is usually assumed; see WOLFGANG SCHENK, 'Der Kolosserbrief in der neueren Forschung (1945–1985)', *ANRW* II, 25:4, Berlin – New York 1987, 3327–64: 3350.

[2] When writing "Colossae", here and in the following, I am conscious of the fact that not only the author is a pseudo-Paul, but that it is also quite possible that Colossae is a pseudo-addressee. See, e.g., SCHENK, *op. cit.*, 3334–35.

[3] See, e.g., ARNOLD M. ROSE, "Minorities", in: *International Encyclopedia of the Social Sciences* 9–10 (1968) 365–370.

## 2. The Representatives of the Philosophy as a Minority

The glimpses of the ideas of the philosophers indicate that they do not represent any of the contemporary thought systems, which we normally label philosophies, like Stoicism, Middle Platonism etc. On the contrary, they seem to exist on a local or possibly regional basis (cf. 4:15 and 2:1, on Laodicea).

The "somebody" of 2:8,16 and the "no one" of 2:4,18 suggest that the philosophers were not a large group, but actually a minority from a numerical point of view. They were, however, influential enough to worry the author and so numerous as to form a group which shared some cultic observances; whatever "festival, new moon, sabbaths" (2:16) denote, the enumeration implies something more than mere individual calculation. The same should hold true of the "service of the angels" (2:18), whatever this service may have meant. The rulings of 2:21, "do not handle, do not taste, do not touch" are characterized by the author as "rules and teachings of men", but can *per se* support the self-consciousness of the group.

## 3. The Philosophy

Of course the author does not give us an objective, full and balanced picture of the phenomenon against which he warns his addressees. They knew what he had in mind, we do not. We can assume that he chose those features against which he wanted to direct his polemic, but we do not know how important they were to the representatives of the philosophy. Nor do we notice when he picks up slogans or turns of phrase typical for the group; the addressees would have heard the quotation marks and caught possible nuances of irony or parody – we do not.[4]

My attempt to reconstruct the philosophy takes as its point of departure a couple of methodological considerations. I have divided the material in Colossians pertaining to the philosophy into three categories. In one I gather statements, items etc. which *certainly or almost certainly* tell us something about it. These are features which the author explicitly ascribes to it, and about which I assume that he is sure that the addressees cannot simply state that he lies or is wrong; if so, his argument would fail.

In a second group I bring together those features which *probably* refer to the philosophy. Thus, the writer's argument occasionally presupposes that the contents pertain to aspects of the philosophy. In other cases we can draw the conclusion *e silentio* that they should be taken into account. Thus, for example, if they had had a polytheistic faith, it is fair to assume that the author would have selected some weapons from the arsenal with which his tradition could provide

---

[4] [Cf. HANS HÜBNER, *An Philemon, An die Kolosser, An die Epheser* (HNT 12), Tübingen 1997, 94–97; ROBIN McL. WILSON, *Colossians and Philemon* (ICC), London 2005, 35–58.]

him. Accordingly, I infer that the philosophers were monotheists in a sense of the word that the author could accept.

In a third group I gather those features which *possibly* characterize the philosophers. A glance at the commentaries on Colossians reveals a host of suggestions as to such features, often deduced from passages which are thought to allude to views held by the group.

In consequence of my manner of sifting the material on the philosophy I do not take into account the features of the third group until towards the end, in order then to see whether they naturally fit the pattern established on other, more reliable grounds.

Another presupposition of my discussion is that if we do not find a philosophy already known, in which the features of the philosophy can be discerned (and we do not), then, nevertheless, the reconstruction should be simple, combining features from as few other known philosophies as possible. This differentiates me from some colleagues, e.g. Martin Dibelius, according to whom the philosophy comprised elements from Iranian religion, Gnosticism, Judaism, astrology and, in addition, an otherwise unknown mystery cult.[5]

And now for my attempt to reconstruct the philosophy. First, then, features which *explicitly* apply to the philosophy: it represents some kind of wisdom (2:23), and its adherents apparently propagate their ideas with considerable energy and conviction; they are said to deceive with "persuasion through probabilities" (πιθανολογία, 2:4)[6] and to "take people captive" (2:8). They "condemn" and "disqualify" those who do not follow their rules for behavior (2:16,18). The nuances chosen by the writer indicate that they are very self-confident; he also accuses them of being "puffed up" (2:18).

Furthermore, the philosophy confronts people with regulations concerning what food and drink is allowed and what is not (2:16,21); it also requires observance of "festival, new moon and sabbaths" (2:16). Keeping their rules means "severe treatment of the body" (2:23) and "humility" (ταπεινοφροσύνη; 2:18,23). The word hardly has its ordinary Christian meaning (thus, though, in 3:12), nor the normal "secular" one, *viz.* "mean-spiritedness", etc. Rather it seems to stand for self-abasement or asceticism.[7] The author also mentions "worship of angels" (2:18) and "self-imposed piety" (ἐθελοθρησκία; 2:23), whatever these details mean.

Finally, the representative of the philosophy is said to "enter what he has seen" (2:18; ἃ ἑόρακεν ἐμβατεύων). The term is capable of several meanings and may refer to involvement in one's visions, to come into that which one has seen

---

[5] Martin Dibelius, *An die Kolosser, Epheser, an Philemon* (HNT 12), Tübingen, 3rd ed., rev. by Heinrich Greeven 1953. For a survey of the suggestions see Frederick Fyvie Bruce, "Colossian Problems, Part 3: The Colossian Heresy", *BS* 141 (1984) 195–208.

[6] The noun has in itself no negative nuance of meaning, but denotes an argument based (only on) probabilities; thus Plato, *Theaet.* 162 E, opposes it to ἀπόδειξις.

[7] E.g., Eduard Schweizer, *Der Brief an die Kolosser* (EKK 12); Zürich – Einsiedeln – Köln • Neukirchen-Vluyn 1976, 122.

(as Joshua entered the promised land, Josh 19:49), or to "things one saw when entering", say, things shown to the initiate in a mystery cult; but in connection with a certain type of visions one also entered the divine Throne Hall with the heavenly court (cf., e.g., 2 Cor 12:2; Rev 4:1f.).

Certainly rules concerning food, calendar and sabbath were important to the Jews, but the author does not connect them with Judaism. If they were derived from any form of Judaism otherwise known to us, they would probably also have included the rule for which generations of Jews had been prepared to give their lives, *viz.* circumcision. In 2:11,13, baptism is characterized as a spiritual circumcision, and sometimes this has been taken as a hint that the philosophy circumcised its members. But had the philosophy practised circumcision and required it of its adherents, then the author would most probably have polemicized against it. The rite was largely held to be repulsive and when the author's master, Paul, encountered Jewish demands that converted former Gentiles be circumcised, his polemics became almost choleric.[8]

Even if the people who maintained seemingly Jewish rules were not Jews, we need not go far to find another group who observed them. It was not sociologically delimited, but the behavioral pattern was with some variations well represented in the world of Early Christianity, *viz.*, the so-called God-fearers, who, without becoming Jewish proselytes, adopted some features of Jewish practice and belief, such as monotheism, keeping the Sabbath and observing some of the food laws. But they were not circumcised and their social relationships with the Jews could be anything from close to fairly loose.[9]

It seems, however, that even if the said practice belonged to the God-fearers, it was not argued on purely Jewish grounds. Instead we can surmise other underlying reasons. These may also lie behind the other features mentioned, *viz.*, the asceticism, the worship of angels, and the "seeing" of 2:18. Here we may as well add the details in Colossians which are *probably* pertinent to the philosophy. Thus, it claims to represent tradition (2:8). The writer argues that this tradition is (only) human (cf. 2:22); he may have spoken in contempt, but would presumably have expressed himself otherwise if the philosophy had meant that the traditions were of heavenly origin.

---

[8] The same position as that of the present writer is taken by PETER T. O'BRIEN, *Colossians, Philemon* (WBC 44), Waco, Tex. 1982, 115. Others regard it as a possibility that the philosophy practised circumcision as a part of a mystery cult (not as a fulfillment of the Mosaic commandment); thus JOACHIM GNILKA, *Der Kolosserbrief* (HThK X:1), Freiburg etc. 1980, 133, referring to Ewald, Lohse, Lohmeyer, Masson. SCHENK, *op. cit.*, 3350–53, argues that the philosophy was in fact a kind of Judaism.

[9] For a balanced discussion of this problem, recently somewhat hotly debated, see SHAYE J. D. COHEN, "Crossing the Boundaries and Becoming a Jew", *HThR* 82 (1989) 13–33. [See now DIETRICH-ALEX KOCH, "Proselyten und Gottesfürchtige als Hörer der Reden von Apostelgeschichte 2,14–39 und 13,16–41" and "The God-fearers between facts and fiction. Two theosebeis-inscriptions from Aphrodisias and the bearing for the New Testament", in: IDEM, *Hellenistisches Christentum. Schriftverständnis – Ekklesiologie – Geschichte* (NTOA 65), Göttingen 2008, 250–271 and 272–298.]

Furthermore, the rules are somehow connected with "the rulers and powers" (ἀρχαὶ καὶ ἐξουσίαι; 2:10,15), for when according to 2:14 the document containing the duties (the χειρόγραφον) was erased by being crucified, this meant a triumph over these "rulers and powers". This leads to the conclusion: "accordingly, nobody shall condemn you in matters of food and drink or concerning festival, new moon or sabbaths" (2:16). In 1:16 it is emphasized that the same rulers and powers are inferior to Christ, in that they owe their existence to him. The two nouns are often coupled (e.g., Luke 12:11; 20:20) and refer in, e.g., Eph 6:12 to cosmic, angelic powers (cf. 1 Cor 15:24).

Here, I suggest, we glimpse a second principal component in the philosophy, *viz.* an ideology which belongs to the so-called astral religion.[10] It is well known to scholars that in antiquity, e.g., the planets were held to be divine beings, that rainfalls, seasons etc. were thought to be governed by cosmic powers, and that, as the position of the sun affected the seasons, so human lives and destinies were influenced by stars and planets.

Jews and Christians were not alien to these views.[11] Thus, e.g., Philo meant that the universe was filled by God's different powers (δυνάμεις), e.g., the one through which everything came into being and was upheld, or the one through which he judged. Philo can also speak of spirits in the air who are "subordinate governors under the ruler of the All, so to speak the ears and eyes of the Great King which see and hear everything. Other philosophers call them spirits (δαίμονες), but the sacred word is wont to call them messengers (ἄγγελοι)" (*de somn.* 1:140–141). A fellow Jew, Paul, appears to have regarded things in a similar way. Thus, I find it permissible, slightly to paraphrase Rom 8:38f. as follows: "I am convinced that neither life nor death, neither angels (ἄγγελοι) nor rulers (ἀρχαί), neither anything present or coming, nor any powers (δυνάμεις), neither stars in their rising (ὕψωμα) nor such in decline (βάθος), indeed nothing created will be able to separate us from God's love in Christ Jesus our Lord."[12] One might even suppose that Paul's student who wrote Colossians had learnt from him of Christ's superiority to angels and powers and then adopted it in his own manner when polemicizing against the philosophy.

No doubt the rulers and powers to which Colossians refers belong to the cosmic potentates mentioned. But here is a crucial point: what is the connection

---

[10] See, *inter alia*, FRANZ CUMONT, "Le mysticisme astral dans l'antiquité", *Académie Royale de Belgique: Bull. de la classe des lettres* 1909, 256–286; HUGO GRESSMANN, *Die hellenistische Gestirnreligion* (Beih. zur "Alten Orient" 1925:5), Leipzig 1925; ANDRÉ-JEAN FESTUGIÈRE, *La révélation d'Hermès Trismégiste* I; *L'astrologie et les sciences occultes* (Études bibliques), Paris 1944, 1–186; MARTIN P. NILSSON, *Geschichte der griechischen Religion* II (HAW V.2.2), Munich ³1974, 268–281, 598–601.

[11] See, e.g., JAMES H. CHARLESWORTH, "Jewish Interest in Astrology during the Hellenistic and Roman Period", *ANRW* II.20.2, Berlin – New York 1987, 926–950.

[12] See, e.g., HANS LIETZMANN, *An die Römer* (HNT 8), Tübingen ⁵1971, 88–89; HEINRICH SCHLIER, *Der Römerbrief* (HTK 6), Freiburg etc. 1977, 280–281. A somewhat similar view is expressed in Plutarch, *de fato* 572 F–574 C (although the text is probably a pseudepigraph).

between, on the one hand, such rulers and powers and, on the other, the rules advanced by the philosophy?

In the case of "festival, new moon and sabbaths" it is not too difficult to find a connection. The calendar was of course closely linked with that which was observed in the heaven. Although to a Jew the straightforward commandment was a sufficient argument for keeping the Sabbath and other festivals, he could also support his practice by referring to heavenly phenomena and to speculations on the number seven.[13]

Correct insight into calendar calculation and astronomy was a gift bestowed on particularly wise people. This is maintained by the author of *Astronomica* I.25–32:

Deeper knowledge of heaven was first granted to earth by the gift of the gods. For who, if the gods wished to conceal it, would have guilefully stolen the secret of the skies, by which all things are ruled? (28) Who of but human understanding, would have essayed so great a task as to wish against heaven's wish to appear as god himself, (32) to reveal paths on high and paths beneath the bottom of the earth and stars obedient to appointed orbits through the void?[14]

The author of the Book of Wisdom is of a similar opinion, inasmuch as he maintains that the wisdom given from God also comprised knowledge of

the construction of the world and of the effects of the elements, the beginning, the end and the midst of the times, the changes of the position of the sun ... , and the changes of the seasons, the course of the years and the positions of the stars. (Wis 7:17f.).

There are several testimonies among the ancient astrologers to the effect that in their view their study meant moving in the heavenly world, indeed, communing with divine beings. Thus, Seneca the older has this passage in his *Suasoriae*, referring to the views of the astrologers:

the stars are available to us and we can mingle with the gods (*pateant nobis sidera et interesse numninibus liceat*; 4.1).

Ptolemy, the mathematician from the 2$^{nd}$ century CE, expressed himself in this manner:

I know that I am mortal and born for a day, but when I follow the dense crowd of the stars in their orbits, my feet no longer touch the earth, but together with Zeus himself I satisfy myself with ambrosia, the godly food. (*Ant. Palatina* IX.577)

A context of this kind could be a suitable ideological framework when the author of Colossians states that the philosopher not only devotes himself to wisdom but also "enters upon that which he has seen" (2:18).

Such an attitude and such a "seeing" may be reflected in the following passage of the *Astronomica* II.115–123:

---

[13] See Aristoboulos in Eus., *Praep. evang.* 13.12.13, and Philo, *de decal.* 158-161.

[14] Trans. George Patrick Goold[, in LCL 1977]. Traditionally, the author is named Manilius, but the treatise is usually held to be pseudepigraphous. [See *Der Neue Pauly*, Vol. 7, Stuttgart – Weimar 1999, s.v. Manilius III. Dichter, 819–821.]

Who could know heaven save by heaven's gift and discover God save one who shares himself in the divine *(pars ipse deorum est)*? (117) Who could discern and compass in his narrow mind the vastness of this vaulted infinite, the dances of the stars, the blazing dome of heaven, and the planets' everlasting war against the signs ... (121) had not nature endowed our minds with divine vision *(ni sanctos animis oculos natura dedisset)*, had turned to herself a kindred intelligence, and had prescribed so great a science (trans. G. P. Goold).

It is befitting one who would approach the dwellings of the gods to observe purity, and asceticism may serve this purpose. So thought also Vettius Valens, an astrologer from the 2nd century CE:

> when I arrived at the divine and awe-inspiring vision of the heavens I also wanted to cleanse my life from all evil and from every pollution and to take into consideration that my soul is immortal (τὴν ψυχὴν ἀθάνατον προλῆψαι [sic!]). Therefore also the divine seemed to commune (προσομιλεῖν) with me. (*Anthol.* VI.1.16)

Another example comes from Cleomedes, who attacked the way in which Epicuros dealt with astrology and burst out: Epicuros has been

> blinder than a mole, and no wonder, because, by Jove, it is not the affair of pleasure-loving people to find the true essence of things, but this should be done by those who have a virtuous character and put nothing before virtue and do not love "the healthy condition of the body".[15]

If the representatives of the philosophy heeded ideas like those mentioned in the preceding paragraph, the other rules they have defended also fit into the picture. These concerned not only pure and impure food but also some mortification and asceticism. They involved "severe treatment of the body" (ἀφειδία τοῦ σώματος) and ταπεινοφροσύνη (Col 2:18, 13). If we should hear a nuance of "humility" in the latter term, the writer may put it within invisible quotation-marks: "humility – indeed!".

The writer of Colossians does not think highly of this asceticism: he describes it as "without reason puffed up by a carnal mind" (2:18) and "a self-imposed piety" (ἐθελοθρησκία). When he characterizes it as a "worship of angels", this may be deprecatory (2:18), intimating that the rulers and powers are degraded to messengers in a way reminiscent of Philo.

We saw that the philosophy has cited authorities to support its teachings. This is also a common feature among the representatives of astral religion, e.g. Vettius Valens (*Anthol.* VI.1.8f.) who speaks of "the old kings and rulers who cared for these things", quoting Nechepso, the more or less mythical Egyptian priest who, together with a certain Petosiris was also an authority on astrology. Actually, Vettius Valens' major work is largely made up of material from older authorities as befits its title, *Anthologiae*. The same holds true of the *Libri Matheseos* by Firmicus Maternus.

---

[15] Cleomedes, *de motu* II,1,86–87. It is difficult to date Cleomedes, but he is later than Poseidonios, to whom he often refers. The words within quotation-marks are from Epic. *fragm.* 668. – See further HERMANN STRATHMANN, *Geschichte der frühchristlichen Askese* I (Leipzig 1914), 310–317.

The conviction that one's ideology is of old and noble descent can inspire confidence; it can be further supported by the claim that one's belief and practice are closely related to the world of the divine. One lives in accordance with great cosmic patterns. In contrast the common simple people are regarded with contempt. This accounts for what we hear of the philosophy's judgment and dismissal of all others (2:16,18).

It remains to discuss material in Colossians which *possibly* represents the ideology of the philosophy. "Fullness" – "Pleroma" (πλήρωμα) – occurs twice in the Letter (1:19; 2:9), and was widely used by contemporary religious thinkers as a way of referring to the universal Deity. It appears in 2:9f. in a passage where the author maintains that by their union with Christ in baptism the addressees are united with the Pleroma. The passage *per se* is not a necessary link in the argument, but would function well in it, if the author indirectly said: you do not attain union with the Pleroma in the manner prescribed by the philosophy. In other words, the philosophy may well have claimed that it mediated a union with the divine All.[16]

In the passages quoted above as illustrations of the concepts of astral religion we also encountered turns of phrase which refer to the close communion between the divine and the astrologer. Here is a further example from *Astronomica*. The unknown author writes (IV.407):

man must sacrifice himself in order that God be in him *(impendendus homo est, deus esse ut possit in ipso)*.

Maybe the philosophers' wisdom also brought them into union with the Divine, when their life and speculations followed divine rules and complied with divine principles, and asceticism subdued the bad influence of the body.[17]

A couple of times we encounter the term "the elements of the world" (τὰ στοιχεῖα τοῦ κόσμου 2:8,20), on which according to the writer the teachings of the philosophy depend (and not on Christ; 2:8). Almost all commentators regard this as tantamount to a technical term of the philosophy and try to find a reference for it in the culture and religion of the Roman Period.[18] Moreover it

---

[16] In addition the writer claims (2:10): "in him (i.e., Christ) – and in no one else (σωματικῶς) – dwells the divine Pleroma, and you are filled in (or: through) him, the head of every ruler and power". – Sometimes the author's way of referring to a body of cosmic dimensions (1:18,24; 2:17,19) has been incorporated into the attempts to reconstruct the ideas of the philosophy. This assumes an underlying idea of the cosmos as being the body of the God of All. The idea might well be used for the author's cosmic Christology, but does not mean that the philosophy taught that, say, cosmos was the body of the Pleroma. Thus, I prefer not to take any of these features into consideration. See further EDUARD SCHWEIZER, σῶμα etc., *ThWNT* 7, 1024–91, 1035–36. [See also GEORGE H. VAN KOOTEN, *Cosmic Christology in Paul and the Pauline School* (WUNT 171), Tübingen 2003, 9–58, 110–146.]

[17] Another example is from Firmicus Maternus, *Err. prof. rel.* II.30,1: *oportet eum qui cotidie de diis vel cum diis loquitur, animum suum ita formare atque instruere, ut ad imitationem divinitatis semper accedat ...* (2) *Esto pudicus integer sobrius, parvo victu, parvis opibus contentus* .... Further material in CUMONT, *op. cit.*, 271–273.

[18] See the survey in O'BRIEN, *Colossians*, 129–132.

is inferred that these "elements of the world" and "the rulers and powers" are similar phenomena. Then, in 2:15 the author could as well have said that God disarmed and triumphed over the "elements" instead of, as now, over the "rulers and powers". This would be so, if either the elements are assumed to be the four (or five) elements, or stars, or cosmic powers which represent fundamental cosmic principles. It seems to me that the expression in 2:8 can as well be translated "according to cosmic fundamental principles". This takes into account both the context in Colossians and contemporary usage. If such a translation is accepted, there is still a relationship between "elements" and "rulers and powers", but the former do not belong to the same class of phenomena as the latter; instead rulers and powers are authoritative "according to cosmic fundamental principles" and for this very reason their rules should be upheld. In other words, either the elements are part of the doctrine of the philosophy or they are not, whatever is said about them at most complements what we already know, *viz.* that "rulers and powers" belong there.[19]

In fact, however, it seems to me that the writer has not picked up a technical term from the philosophy, but has instead taken Paul to his help. Paul uses the term in Gal 4:3 (cf. Gal 4:9), a letter which obviously also in other respects has provided the author with phrases and ideas, although he fills them with slightly different, or even quite different contents.[20] If this is so, the restriction I put forward in the preceding paragraph is even more justified.

A further detail which may shed light on the philosophy is the mention of a "circumcision not made by hands" (2:11), which stands for baptism and is contrasted to the pre-Christian life of the addressees when they "were dead because of the un-circumcision of (their) flesh" (2:13). It has been suggested that this implies that the philosophers practised circumcision, either because they were Jewish or for another reason. Above I have argued against such an assumption.[21]

I am even more doubtful concerning the suggestion that "do not touch" in 2:21 means sexual abstinence (cf. 1 Cor 7:1 and 1 Tim 4:3). The context does not favor such an understanding. For the following clause is best understood as referring to all the regulations of 2:21 ("do not handle, do not taste, do not touch"), characterizing them as concerned with objects that "perish with use"; this can hardly be maintained of women (as, e.g., of beans, which, e.g., the Neopythagoreans did not eat!).

Above, I quoted 2:18, "entering that which one has seen" and also briefly mentioned that it could refer to the initiate's entry into the shrine when he is

---

[19] In addition, there are good reasons to assume that the phrase actually has a vague reference. Only a few generations after Colossians, Clement of Alexandria understands it in two ways in his same book. Thus, in *Strom.* 1:11 he quotes Col 2:8 in support of a polemic against philosophers who think that the "elements" are gods, whereas in 6:8 he refers to the same passage to prove that a certain philosophy only devotes itself to "elementary" matters.

[20] See ED P. SANDERS, 'Literary Dependence in Colossians', *JBL* 85 (1966) 28–45.

[21] See above and note 8.

shown pictures or symbols.²² Was the philosophy involved in some sort of mystery cult, and is an affirmative answer supported by the use of μυστήριον in 1:26f. and 2:2? The suggestion was inspired by the History of Religion school's enthusiasm over the discovery of "influences" here and there and is nowadays rejected by the commentators.²³ The indications are vague and the obscure 2:18 might as well refer to phenomena seen in the context of astronomy and astrology without any linkage to a mystery cult.²⁴

Thus, only one feature of my third group seems to fit smoothly into the picture composed of the details from the first two collections, *viz.*, the mention of the Pleroma.

I shall now give a rough outline of the philosophy. I thereby also take into account that it almost certainly regarded its ideology as Christian, or to express myself more cautiously: their ideology was compatible with that held by people who regarded themselves as adherents to the religion which once was preached by Paul, but it should be refined and completed.

As a background we should recall various aspects of the cultural climate in the days of the Roman Empire, aspects which are more or less the same as those typical of the Hellenistic Age.

Official state religion and the *polis*-religion seem largely to have lost their ability to provide the citizens with the existential frames of reference which they desired. The syncretism which was a typical feature of the age meant a confusing ethnic and cultural pluralism in which many religions, philosophies and cults offered their solutions, also such as involved magic, mantics and astrology. Many individuals seem to have felt insecure and sought for meaning, structure, stability, perhaps for atonement with Tyche, or for support by powers stronger than destiny. Such support could be provided by joining this or that kind of association, by participating in higher wisdom, performing certain rites or following a particular way of life.

In such an environment Christianity spread, indeed at a remarkable speed, and its cultural climate determined the context of the Christian group which is called a philosophy in Colossians. In all probability, like so many Christians, they confessed Jesus as Lord, κύριος Ἰησοῦς. But in which sense? There were

---

[22] See DIBELIUS, *Briefe*, 35.

[23] E.g. BORNKAMM, μυστήριον, *ThWNT* 4,827–828; O'BRIEN, *Colossians*, 83–84.

[24] The vague phrase of 2:23, "in no honor" has been brought into the discussion of the philosophy. Here too those who think that it constituted something of a mystical association try to fit the expression into their suggested reconstruction; thus, they assume that the words echo a proclamation at the initiation to the effect that it was in honor of the initiand (e.g., EDUARD LOHSE, *Die Briefe an die Kolosser und an Philemon* (KEK IX/2), Göttingen 1968, 185f.; GNILKA, *Kolosserbrief*, 161). This is not impossible either, but the phrase is not *per se* a technical term at all. The main reason for assuming an external influence here is the rough construction of the sentence, which leads some interpreters to infer that the writer is using a series of technical terms of the philosophy, known by the addressees. This is, however, rather shaky ground for a reconstruction, and, in any case, the turn of phrase is so vague that it seems to me that attempts to find hidden allusions therein must remain pure conjecture.

many κύριοι; already Paul could agree to that (1 Cor 8:5f.), and this group was obviously of another opinion than Paul, than his pupil Epaphras (presumably) [1:7;4:12], and, of course, than the writer of Colossians, all of whom held that the κύριος position of Jesus was far superior to that of other κύριοι, cosmic rulers, stars, elementary powers. The philosophy may have conceded that Jesus Christ, as living in one way or another, was one of the κύριοι, but he was of less importance than certain others.

In order to be in harmony with the Pleroma, the Highest Being, who was in, over, under, behind and beyond everything, one must, according to the philosophy, ensure that one was reconciled (cf. 1:20,22) with the rulers and powers who reigned in the universe. The observance of certain calendar rules brought a certain contact with such lofty beings, already because rites of the new moon and living in a seven day cycle involved conformity to cosmic patterns, i.e. practices of so-called Godfearers, but they were adopted for non-Jewish or, rather, more-than-Jewish reasons.

It was, however, mandatory that people who wanted to live in harmony with the divine beings of the pure space did not pollute themselves – although we do not know what the philosophy regarded as polluting. But certainly the body was regarded with suspicion; it drew humans towards the earth and thus had to be subdued. Some forms of abstinence may have been the same as that of the Godfearers, and, as a matter of fact, here and there a Jew like Philo expresses himself in the same manner as his colleagues among, for example, the Stoics. Thus he can contrast hope (which causes the mind to depend on God) to desire, which causes the mind to "depend on the body, which nature created as a receptacle and a place of pleasures" (*de post.* 26). Indeed, he may maintain that the body is a polluted prison-house, from which man should try to escape, "its jailers being pleasures and lusts" (*migr.* 9).

In these matters the representatives of the philosophy apparently regarded Epaphras and his followers as unduly frivolous; they did not care about the calendar and they ate and drank and dealt with profane things and/or persons in such a way as to reject any possibility of reconciliation with the Fullness of the All. They themselves were freed to behold deep secrets and to be filled by heavenly light, whether their sessions dealt with horoscopes, astronomical observations and speculations or with other deep matters. In any case they were granted participation in extraordinary wisdom.

## 4. The Philosophers' Attitude to the Majority

The conviction that one is infinitely more enlightened than the common people promotes either an attitude which involves a withdrawal into splendid isolation or of one of missionary zeal. Apparently the adherents of the philosophy took the second path. They devoted considerable energy to persuading others to join their group: they tried to "talk them over to them" (παραλογίζεσθαι; 2:4), indeed, spiritually to abduct them (συλαγωγεῖν; 2:8). In their propaganda they seem to combine practical issues and theoretical principles. Thus, they present the others with their rules – δόγματα; 2:14,20 – and seem rigid in their assessment of those who do not follow them: they "judge" (κρίνειν; 2:16) and "disqualify" (παραβραβεύειν; 2:18) them. The practical rules were intimately connected with the ideology, an important topic of which seems to have been the insight into and good relationship with the Pleroma (cf. 1:19f.; 2:9). However, this knowledge of how to behave, and this contact with the Ultimate Fullness also seem to have resulted in arrogance (cf. 2:18, being puffed up).

In response to this attitude of the minority, the author, on the one hand, claims that Christ is superior to the authorities of the philosophy, they owe their existence to him (1:16), in him, personally, dwells the Pleroma (2:9), in his death and victorious resurrection the rulers and powers were put to shame and the rules which they authorized were nullified (2:14). Secondly, he denigrates the teachings and practices of the philosophy: the philosophers use πιθανολογία (2:4), i.e., unfair arguments to convince people,[25] their teaching consists only of shadows (2:17), "empty erring" (2:8), human and worldly inventions (2:8,23), it is not worthy of being called wisdom (2:23), and has no honor to it; instead of being an asceticism it rather indulges the flesh (2:23). In the Greek text the final phrase even sounds scornful with its alliterations and taking into account the itacism it goes in transcription: *ouk en timi tini pros plismonin tis sarkos.*[26]

## 5. The Majority as Confronted by the Minority

Apparently the majority has been impressed by the minority. They regarded them as a "mighty minority". Judging from how the writer urges them to behave, they felt uncertain: was that which they had learnt of Christian belief and life not accurate or sufficient? Was their hope for the future vain? Did they not "know" enough? Thus, the author exhorts and encourages them, sometimes through praising them for virtues in which he presumably fears they are lacking. So, I hear the impact of the minority's pressure on the majority in passages like the following: provided that they keep to the old Gospel (1:5,23) and do not surrender to the philosophy, they have a firm hope of a heavenly heritage (1:5,12); thus, for a positive relationship to "heaven" they do not need the philosophy. If they faithfully hold on to what they have learnt from Epaphras concerning Christ, they have real and sufficient "knowledge" and understanding (1:6,9f.), indeed, of God's "mystery" (1:27; 2:2), i.e., the philosophy cannot offer anything better or more valid in these respects – on the contrary. This is so because they are baptized into the reign of the victor (1:13,16,20,22; 2:11–15), their Lord, Jesus Christ, and he is superior to the lords of the philosophers, *viz.* that which was

---

[25] See above, note 6.
[26] Cf. HEINRICH LAUSBERG, *Handbuch der literarischen Rhetorik* (Munich 1960), 661–671 (§434).

held against the philosophy as I described it above, is also something that bolsters up the majority. In Christ they really meet the Pleroma (1:19; 2:9) and he, and no powers or potentates, is the Judge to whom they are responsible (1:22).

Rebuking the vociferous minority the writer also admonishes those among the majority who are tempted to align with the "wise", and maintains: already in this world you belong to a larger community, for the Gospel you have taken to yourselves prospers "in the whole world" (1:6), indeed, it is proclaimed "to every creature under heaven" (1:23). So the writer attempts to make the majority and the minority realize that, in a mundane perspective, the minority really is a minority, no matter how impressive it may sound.

Yet the small but apparently mighty minority in Colossae appears to have been convinced that it had found the Truth in a chaotic world, and that it belonged to a large, meaningful context in the contemporary world, in history, and, not least, in the heavenly realm. In what seems to have been a sturdy self-confidence, they obviously attempted to cozen the other Christians in Colossae and persuade them to realize the truth and so to leave their un-spiritual religion – so apparently the philosophers – in favor of the real thing. Of course they could not know that the future was not to belong to them but to the others, those more simpleminded Christians.

# 21. The Human Desire to Converse with the Divine
## Dio of Prusa and Philo of Alexandria on Images of God

## 1. What Does the Title Imply?

The "and" of the title opposes the names of two philosophers. There is a risk in concocting such "and"-topics or "and"-titles. It may be unclear for what purpose the two items are combined. Does, for example, the "and" imply a relationship to be discussed – "Jesus and Paul", for example? Or is it a simply additive "and", intimating that the items so apposed are dealt with one after the other – the period of Domitian "and" that of Nerva, for example? The "and" may also indicate that the parties are compared. This might be the case in the latter example, but not necessarily so. But if it is, one may ask, is the comparison justified in scholarly terms? It is not self-evident that this would be true, for example, of a treatment of a topic such as "Socrates 'and' Jesus".

When the title of this article says "Dio and Philo", I am not suggesting that there is any direct or semidirect relationship between the two. But both of them were philosophers living in the time of the Roman Empire (Philo *ca.* 10 BCE – 45 CE; Dio *ca.* 40 CE – after 112 CE; as so often, the dates are uncertain[1]). Both had breathed the same philosophical air – Philo perhaps one with a slightly more Middle Platonic gust,[2] and Dio a more Stoic breeze which turned to Cynicism.[3] But we shall find that, although Philo was a Jew and Dio a "Gentile", they had much in common in their thinking of the Divine, and also when it came to reflecting on how human beings relate to their God/their gods.

In this paper I shall discuss one aspect of this relationship, namely the role played by the human desire to come close to the being(s) they worship. To Dio such a desire is met by the use of idols, and Philo deals with it in the context of his comments upon the commandments concerning monotheism and idola-

---

[1] For Dio see CHRISTOPHER P. JONES, *The Roman World of Dio Chrysostomus*, Cambridge, Mass. 1978, 140.

[2] See DAVID T. RUNIA, *Philo of Alexandria and the* Timaeus *of Plato* (Philosophia antiqua), Leiden 1986, esp. 505–519. According to Runia, Philo certainly stands in a Platonic tradition, but nevertheless "he is doing his own thing" (p. 519). Here Runia opposes JOHN M. DILLON, *The Middle Platonists: A Study of Platonism 80 BC to AD 220*, London 1977, 143 etc.

[3] On Dio and Stoicism see HERMANN BINDER, *Dio Chrysostomus und Posidonius: Quellenuntersuchungen zur Theologie des Dio von Prusa*, Diss. Tübingen – Borna-Leipzig 1905; *Dion Chrysostomos. Sämtliche Reden*. Eingeleitet, übersetzt und erläutert von WINFRIED ELLIGER, Zürich – Stuttgart 1967, xxix–xxxi (also underlining Dio's eclecticism).

try. I shall proceed as follows. After a brief presentation of the texts on which I shall focus, I outline the thoughts of each concerning the Divine. Thereafter I consider the reasons adduced by Dio in defence of the cult of the Zeus statue at Olympia, and Philo's arguments for opposing idolatry. Then follows a brief discussion of how the two philosophers deal with the human desire to be close to the Divine, mentioned above. Actually the attitude in question can be described as a variety of "being religious and living through the eyes", as the title of this Bergman Festschrift says.

## 2. Texts to Be Considered

Three texts will serve as points of departure. Two are by Philo and actually belong together, namely the section of *De decalogo* (hence *Dec.*) where he discusses the commandments on monotheism and idolatry (52–81), and the passages of *De specialibus Legibus* (hence *Spec. leg.*) which develop the same topics (I,12–50).

The third text is Dio's Twelfth speech, the Olympic one, particularly the section in which he makes Pheidias explain why he made the great Zeus statue at Olympia. The speech can be read from the point of view of aesthetics-does Dio present something of a theory of art in this text?[4] But both the themesetting passages in the beginning of the speech (25f.) and its epilogue (84f.) assure us that a central topic thereof is man's conception of God and its relationship to images of God/gods like the Zeus statue. The speech has been dated to 101 CE[5] and thus belongs to the late phase of Dio's life, after Nerva had revoked his banishment by Domitian. This means that the speech belongs to a period in which we can expect his thought to be more coloured by CynicStoic thinking than in his earlier life.[6]

## 3. Main Features of the Divine

For the purpose of this study it suffices to sketch only a few main features of the ideas on the Divine held by Dio and Philo, respectively.

### 3.1. *Dio's Ways of Conceiving the Devine*

To begin with Dio, his ways of conceiving the Divine are highly reminiscent of that of the Stoics.[7] Now and then he refers to the gods in the plural, counting as such also the stars and planets (e.g., XII.34). But actually all these gods can be

---

[4] See ELLIGER, *Dion Chrysostomos. Sämtliche Reden*, xxxviiif.
[5] Thus JONES, *The Roman World*, 138, although with some hesitation. HANS VON ARNIM, *Leben und Werke des Dio von Prusa*, Berlin 1898, p. 463, suggests the year 105, and so does ELLIGER, *Dion Chrysostomos. Sämtliche Reden*, xxxvii.
[6] See footnote 3, above. [HANS-JOSEF KLAUCK/BALBINA BÄBLER, *Dion von Prusa, Olympische Rede oder über die Erste Erkenntnis Gottes* (SAPERE II), Darmstadt 2000.]
[7] VON ARNIM, *Leben und Werke*, 476.

taken together as one divine power (XXXI.11), whose "king and ruler and lord and father" is Zeus (XII.22, 75), who can also be called "the supreme and most perfect being" (XII.54; τὴν ἄκραν καὶ τελειοτάτην φύσιν). As such he is invisible in the same manner as mind and intelligence, indeed, he is the "intelligence and rationality" (φρόνησις καὶ λόγος, XII.59), the ruler of the all (πάντων ἡγεμών; XII.27). The conception of him is innate to the whole human race (XII.27) and Dio is violent in his polemics against "certain men" (i.e., the Epicureans) whose only god is Pleasure (XII.36) and who maintain that

> the all has no purpose or intelligence or lord (τὰ ξύμπαντα φάσκοντες ἀγνώμονα καὶ ἄφρονα καὶ ἀδέσποτα), with no ruler or steward or overseer, wandering at random and swept along, no master now taking care of the all[8] nor earlier having created it (XII.37).

Nature obeys his command, both plants and animals (XII.35), and he is the immortal parent (γονεύς) of mankind (XII.42), their "common father, saviour, and guardian" (κοινὸν ἀνθρώπων καὶ πατέρα καὶ σωτῆρα καὶ φύλακα; XII.74). He is called a father, assumes "Pheidias", "because of his solicitide for us and his kindness" (XII.75), and he is gracious to men when they pray (ibid.), he is "peaceable and altogether gentle" (XII.74).[9]

When men experience all the generous gifts of God, for example, how the seasons are perfectly arranged for the sake of "our well-being (σωτηρία)", they cannot but admire and love him (XII.32).

## 3.2. Philo on Monotheism and Idolatry

Turning to Philo, we cannot of course do justice to his idea of God in a page or two[10] – the writings of this theologian, apologete, and expositor of the Bible contain a rich and complicated material, which, in addition, is not always easily interpreted. But for our purpose we can be content to consider a few main features of his thoughts of God, above all such as appear in the two texts on monotheism and idolatry with which we are here concerned.

As a faithful Jew, Philo is positive that there is only one God. There are indeed those who claim that the sun and the moon and the other stars are "gods with absolute power" (θεοὺς αὐτοκράτορας; *Spec. leg.* I.13). But according to Philo they are only officials or servants of the one supreme God (*Dec.* 61; *Spec. leg.* I.14). He is "the highest beginning and principle of everything that is" (ἀρχὴ δ'ἀρίστη πάντων ... τῶν ὄντων; *Dec.* 52). As our mind (νοῦς) is an invisible ruler within us, so "the mind of the universe, utterly great and perfect, is of course

---

[8] On God's protection see also XII.29.

[9] These features of mildness attributed to Zeus correspond to the Cynic ideal of a king; see ELLIGER, *Dion Chrysostomos. Sämtliche Reden*, xxxviii.

[10] On Philo's concept of God see BINDER, *Dio Chrysostomus*, 74–87; HARRY A. WOLFSON, *Philo: Foundations of Religious Philosophy in Judaism. Christianity, and Islam*, Cambridge Mass. 1947, vol. II., 73–164; SAMUEL SANDMEL, *Philo of Alexandria: An Introduction*, New York – Oxford 1979, 89–101; RONALD WILLIAMSON, *Jews in the Hellenistic World: Philo* (Cambridge Commentaries on Writings of the Jewish and Christian World 200 BC to AD 200 1/2), Cambridge etc. 1989, 74–102.

the king of kings, who is not seen by those whom he sees" (*Spec. leg.* I.18). To say that at some earlier time God did not exist (οὐκ ὄντα) or that he came into being (γενόμενον) and is not eternal (μὴ διαιωνίζοντα) is not allowed (θεμιτόν; *Dec.* 58). So Philo attacks those who "suppose that there is no invisible and conceptual cause (νοητὸν αἴτιον) outside things perceived" (*Dec.* 59). Instead he is really the maker of the universe (ὁ ποιητὴς τῶν ὅλων), so that Philo, like so many others, also knows to call his God "the father of all" (*Dec.* 32.64; *Spec. leg.* I.14 etc.).

It is well known that the idea of Zeus' *logos* which sustained all, was held by many Stoic philosophers. It is not elaborated by Dio, but his comments on Zeus as the mind of the universe (its φρόνησις and λόγος, XII.59) should be understood as representing such an idea. But to Philo the *logos* concept is important: he maintains that the *logos* and other intermediate beings are spiritual powers through which God is active in the world. In this context we need not, however, dwell on the *logos*- concept of our two authors.

Although Philo can state that God is better than the good and the beautiful (*De opificio* 8), and cannot be categorised or defined (*Quod Deus sit immutabilis* 55), he can nevertheless list divine epithets which describe him as generous and saving in a way reminiscent of what we encountered in Dio. Thus *Dec.* ends by saying:

It is proper to ascribe the general safety of everything to the great king, to him who is the guardian of peace and who always, richly and abundantly, supplies the blessings of peace to all people everywhere (*Dec.* 178).

There is a similar list in *Spec. leg.* I.209:

God is good (ἀγαθός) and the maker and begetter (γεννητής) of the all, and the protector (προνοητικός) of what he has begotten, he is a saviour (σωτήρ) and a benefactor (εὐεργέτης) is full (ἀνάπλεως) of blessedness and all happiness. Each of these (attributes) is to be revered and praised ...

To anyone who is but slightly acquainted with Philo and contemporary philosophers it will come as no surprise that the preceding paragraphs reveal several similarities between Dio's and Philo's concepts of God. We need not discuss whether Philo knew that his arguments did not pertain to philosophers of Dio's type when he attacked the idolaters as in *Dec.* and *Spec. leg.* Passages of such contents were probably meant as apology and polemics rather than as a serious discussion between philosophers.

## 4. Cult Sites and Images of the Divine

In the texts I have chosen for this study each of the two philosophers discusses a typical feature of contemporary religion, namely that the cult sites contained images of the gods who were worshipped there. Dio abides by the practice; he is conscious of the fact that it can be questioned, not least by those who accept the same ideas of the Divine as he does, and so he defends and explains the practice.

Philo, on the other hand, is also loyal, but to the traditions of a minority religion, *viz.* monotheistic Judaism with its strict prohibition of idols. So he too defends and explains the practice to which he adheres.

## 4.1. *Dio's Defence of the Cultic Practice of Idols*

Dio first praises Pheidias for the charming image he has wrought (XII.59) but then raises the question: "did you create the proper shape and the form worthy of the divine nature, when you used (not only) beautiful material but also (*the shape of) a man* ... ?" (52). The earlier, less perfect pictures did not, in their diversity, bind or restrict men's concepts of the Divine, but now the overwhelming impression conveyed by this marvellous statue may result in too precise an idea of the unfathomable. Could it perhaps tempt people to believe that it was possible "through mortal art to portray the supreme and most perfect being (τὴν ἄκραν καὶ τελειοτάτην φύσιν)" (54). To Dio it obviously goes without saying that the statue is not the god, nor that Zeus is manlike.

In what follows Dio makes Pheidias his mouth-piece. As a first step in his answer, "Pheidias" takes the human mind as an example. No painter or sculptor can represent mind and intelligence (νοῦν καὶ φρόνησιν; XII.59). But when the mind and intelligence in and behind the universe manifest themselves and people know that God underlies these manifestations, they take refuge in him, attributing to him a body as a vessel of this φρόνησις and this λόγος. Then, when trying to conceptualise that which is invisible and unportrayable, they see fit to think of it in a human body, so that the picture actually functions as a "symbol" (συμβόλου δύναμις.) (XII.59).

"Pheidias" also rejects the idea that it would suffice to look towards the heavens, where man actually sees gods, i.e. the heavenly bodies, although from afar. Precisely this great distance causes a problem. For "all" humans have a strong yearning (ἰσχυρὸς ἔρως) to honour and worship the Divine from close at hand "approaching and touching them, giving them sacrifices and crowns" (XII.60). Actually the humans are like children who stretch out their hands to their parents; they love the gods and "desire to be with them and converse (ὁμιλεῖν) with them" (61). This human need is met by a statue like the one made by Pheidias. So, also the Zeus statue expresses the divine properties which the worshippers ascribe to the Divine; it shows a god who is peaceable, gentle, mild, and majestic; he stands forth as the father, saviour and guardian of all (74f.).

Thus Dio defends the daring attempt to depict the invisible, to represent the Divine in human shape. The gist of his argument is that humans insatiably yearn to have the Divine nearby, to have something close and concrete as a vessel for the Divine with which they would converse, to have a visible and tangible symbol of that towards which their worship is addressed.

Dio's treatment of the cult of the gods is consistent with his justification of the use of idols.[11] Advancing to the idol, sacrificing before it, and adorning it with wreaths are all expressions of the human need to worship the deity "from close at hand" (ἐγγύθεν) (60). In the epilogue Dio lets Zeus himself approve of the celebrations in Olympia, the sacrifices and, above all, the games, in which the participants "pay respect to the inherited customs (ἔθη λαβοῦσα)".[12]

Through the cultic practices humans offer their thanks to God. But Dio stresses that what matters is the right intention of the worshipper; if somebody offers but a little incense or only touches the image, his gift is of no less worth than that of anyone else, provided it is offered with the right intention (διάνοια; XXXI.15). Offerings are accompanied by prayers (XI.59; XL.28), but – as a Stoic! – Dio maintains that praying to the gods that this or that evil will not occur is of no use (VIII.28f.; XVI.7f.):

that is as if someone went out in the rain without a cloak and prayed concerning every drop that he may escape it, for annoying things happen more often than rain-drops fall (XVI.8).

It may be more than conventional words, when after his return from his exile Dio states that he dared to oppose Domitian, not in madness or stupidity but trusting the strength and help which come from the gods (XLV.1); and the polemics against the Epicureans mentioned above, together with other features of his deliberations in the Olympic speech may justify H. von Arnim's verdict that Dio was a pious man.[13] But his piety is Stoic: it is characterised by reverence, gratitude, and even love, for the unfathomable divine being, from whom humans should accept whatever befalls. The worship of images, sacrifices, processions etc. are forms in which this religion is duly expressed.

## 4.2. Philo's Contemplation instead of Idolatry

In his exposition of the commandment against idolatry Philo relies to a large extent on classical arguments which already appear in the Bible. Thus he ridicules the idol makers who offer prayers and sacrifices to their own creations (*Dec.* 72): as the craftsman is superior to the craft, should we not rather worship the sculptor instead? (*Dec.* 69f.). And why should we worship "our brothers", he asks, referring to the heavenly bodies, which have the same father as mankind (*Dec.* 64). In contrast to Dio, who claims that the human imagination and reason need the support of images despite the risk of acquiring unduly precise ideas of the Divine, Philo is consistent: he regards such a practice as deceptive: poets and sculptors spread illusions (*Spec. leg.* I.28f.), they destroy the soul's correct notion (ὑπόληψις) of the ever living god (*Dec.* 67), namely through their concretisations (*Dec.* 70). We should instead

---
[11] Wilhelm Schmid, "Dion (18)", *PRE* 5 (1905), col. 848–877: col. 864.
[12] See also III.52.
[13] von Arnim, *Leben und Werke*, col. 477f.

with our thinking pass beyond the whole visible realm to honour the immaterial, the invisible one, who is perceived only through the understanding (διανοίᾳ) (*Spec. leg.* I.20).

We remember that an essential element of Dio's argument was the human desire to approach the gods and converse with them. Philo knows of a similar human desire. He finds it expressed in Moses' prayer in Exod 33:13: "reveal yourself to me" (*Spec. leg.* I.40f.). The request is worthy of praise, it is said, but it cannot be granted to a creature (I.43). The more advanced (like Moses) may, however, "not by sight but by mind" (46) discern, not God, but God's powers (some of which are equated with "ideas;" 47). They are enjoined to "let the unsleeping eyes of the mind contemplate the cosmos (κόσμος) and what is therein" (49). Indeed, this contemplation can enable the individual to be "carried into the heights possessed by some God-sent inspiration of the soul" (*Spec. leg.* III.1). This Philonic mode of approaching God has often – and rightly so – been characterised as a kind of mysticism.[14] Philo apparently describes the same kind of relationship to God when he explains how Abraham, the wise man, "drew near" to God (Gen 18:22f.): "only to a truly unchanging soul is there access (πρόσοδος) to the unchanging God, and the soul of such a disposition really stands near to the divine power" (*De posteritate Caini* 27).[15]

The rational and mystical elements of Philo's religion are, however, also combined with expressions of human love of God.[16] So Philo, on the basis of Deut 30:19f., can say that "Moses defines living in accordance with God as loving him" (*De posteritate Caini* 69).

To Philo it is but a short step from the idea of human love of God to prayer, both being inspired by God's generosity: "as the work most appropriate to God is to be a benefactor, so that of creation is to give thanks" (*De plantatione* 130). In principle temples and sacrifices are inadequate means for such worship (*ibid.* 126), but nevertheless Philo accepts them wholeheartedly. Once he even went to Jerusalem himself "to offer prayers and sacrifices" (*De providentia*, fragm. 2, 64), and in *Spec. leg.* I.68f. he writes with warmth about the crowds of worshippers around the Temple. The Temple "made by hands" (as distinguished from the cosmic temple[17], *Spec. leg.* I.55) was there

because one should not repress men's desires when they would pay tribute to piety and wish through sacrifices either to give thanks for the blessings which have befallen them or to ask pardon for their sins (*Spec. leg.* I.67).[18]

In other words, Philo explains the existence of the Temple with reasons which are similar to those used by Dio to account for the erection of the Zeus image!

---

[14] WILLIAMSON, *Jews*, 71f.
[15] Similarly *De Cherubim* 19f.
[16] WILLIAMSON, *Jews*, 69.
[17] On Philo's idea of the cosmos as God's temple see URSULA FRÜCHTEL, *Die kosmologischen Vorstellungen bei Philo von Alexandrien* (Arbeiten zur Literatur und Geschichte des hellenistischen Judentums 2; Leiden 1968), 70–115.
[18] But because God is one, there must be only one temple (*loc. cit.*).

Like Dio, Philo too stresses the necessity for the worshipper to be reverent and reminds him:

> my friend, God does not rejoice in sacrifices, even if somebody offers hecatombs, for all things are his possessions ..., but he rejoices in good, loving inclinations and in men who practise holiness, from whom he accepts (were it only) meal or barley and the cheapest things, adjudging them very precious rather than the costly offerings (*Spec. leg.* I.271).

So we may also here note some similarities between the two philosophers: both regard sacrifices etc. as in principle unnecessary, but individuals need the outward ceremonies to express their religion, not least their gratitude, and God gladly accepts them, provided that the worshippers are well meaning; then the simplest gift is as meritorious as anything. So Dio in principle regards even the idols as superfluous, and to Philo the same may be said of the Temple. But in Dio's case the statue and in Philo's the Temple meet piety's needs, not to mention that in Dio, Zeus approves of the cult and that to Philo God's indisputable commands exclude the possibility of discussion.

There is one great difference between these material and external means which serve the human wish to converse with the Divine, namely that for the people whom Dio has in mind there were temples and idols everywhere, not only at Olympia, whereas, as Philo stresses, to the Jews there was only one Temple and no images. In addition, to most Jews this Temple was far distant.[19]

Thus it would seem that the Jews had at their disposal fewer external, tangible forms of outward expression of their religious beliefs. When, with his rational and mystical approach, Philo encounters this human desire to "see God", this is wholly internal and spiritual. Prayer was, however, already something slightly more concrete[20]. In *De plantatione* 130, quoted above, Philo defined it as "to give thanks" (εὐχαριστεῖν). Indeed, prayer is a major virtue:

> each of the virtues is holy, but thanksgiving (εὐχαριστία) pre-eminently so. But it is not possible genuinely to thank God through the means most people think sufficient, namely through sites (κατασκευῶν), votive offerings, and sacrifices – for not even the whole world would be an adequate temple in his honour – but (it can only be done) through hymns of praise, not those which a loud voice sings, but those which the invisible and most pure mind (νοῦς) lets sound and resound (*De plantatione* 126).

Here Philo's wording echoes, on the one hand, the situation of the Diaspora Jew, far away from the Temple of Jerusalem, on the other, his tendency to abstract spirituality and/or mysticism.

A few more points should be made in the above quotation from *De plantatione:* Prayer was rarely regarded as a virtue in contemporary religion and philosophy; accordingly Philo's attitude shows the importance of prayer to him – and to other Diaspora Jews. Furthermore, "thanksgiving" covers several kinds

---

[19] Philo even sees a point in this difficulty: overcoming it was a sign of the quality of one's religious disposition (*Spec. leg.* I.68).
[20] On Philo on prayer see WOLFSON, *Philo,* II, 237–248.

of prayer, not least that represented by the blessings of God, the *berakhoth*.[21] Finally, contrary to normal Greek custom,[22] Philo thinks highly of silent prayer, although he also recognises spoken prayer: they pray

> sometimes with the organs of speech, sometimes without the tongue or the mouth, when within the soul, and appreciable by the intellect alone, they make their confessions and invocations, which one ear only can apprehend, the ear of God, because human hearing cannot attain the perception of such (*Spec. leg.* I.272).

There was one further, even more concrete means whereby Jews could express their loyalty to and love for their God and even somehow come close to him, namely in their compliance with God's law, In *Spec. leg.* I.300 Philo says that this was a way of manifesting love for God:

> This is to love him as a benefactor ... to walk in all such ways as lead to his pleasure, to serve him, not half-heartedly, but with the whole soul filled with a will to love God, and to cleave to his commandments and to honour what is right.

Indeed, living according to God's commandments could even actualise God's presence: "God, who fills all things is close; accordingly let us refrain from evil-doing, in respect for him who sees us and is near ..." (*De gigantibus* 47).[23]

So the Jews who in their everyday life sought to converse with the Divine or be close to their God could satisfy this wish in action through prayer and through living according to God's law. Certainly Dio's followers had the same possibilities in their religions, but not least the Jewish way of life was regarded as so extraordinary, both by the Jews themselves and by their neighbours, that it is not too far-fetched to suggest that this became the foremost means whereby they expressed their loyalty to God and love for him, and also felt close to him.

## 5. Conclusion

Thus, this study of two philosophers from the Roman Empire has confronted us with two religious thinkers from two different religions (one of them would even say, two radically opposed religions). Both of them deal with what they regard as a basic human need, namely to be close to their god, and each in so doing takes his religious tradition for granted. Despite their differences of belief, they reached similar conclusions, because they had much of the basic philosophic theology in common and agreed on the presupposition that humans want to be close to the Divine.

To a New Testament scholar such as the present writer observations like those herein presented are a reminder of the cultural and religious climate in which the mission of the Early Church met with remarkable success. Perhaps

---

[21] WOLFSON, *Philo*, II, 241. – Cf. how *Oracula Sibyllina* IV.25f. praises the Jews for "blessing the great God before eating and drinking".

[22] WOLFSON, *Philo*, II, 252.

[23] Philo moves in the same direction in *De mutatione nominum* 216f. a propos of Gen 46:30 ("before you", i.e. God).

one reason for this success was the Christian message that human desire to come close to the Divine was met by the unfathomable God's coming close to them in a real man, Jesus of Nazareth.[24]

---

[24] See ARTHUR DARBY NOCK's classic *Conversion: The Old and the New in Religion from Alexander the Great to Augustine of Hippo*, Oxford 1933, 209–211, etc.

## 22. Hellenistic Elements in Apocalyptic Texts

### 1. Introductory Remarks

Let us rejoice and exult and give him the glory, for the marriage of the Lamb has come and his bride has made herself ready (Rev 19:7).

A person familiar with the History of Religions may see fit to associate the contents of this quotation with the concept of the *hieros gamos*, in which one of the partners is a divine bull or ram, represented by the king. Those of us who studied at Uppsala University in the 1950's will easily do so, as we were trained in the so-called patternistic school and became well versed in sacral kingship and New Year Festivals.[1] For comparison we may adduce the following extract of an inscription from around 264 BCE found at Mendes in Ptolemaic Egypt:

Hail to Horus ... the gods adore him and the goddesses revere him in his shape as the living ram ... (The queen) is the mistress of grace, mild in love ... beloved by the ram.[2]

Here we envisage a holy wedding between a ram and its bride, connected to Egyptian royal ideology from Hellenistic times. When we encounter it in the Book of Revelation, the motif could certainly be labelled a Hellenistic element in an apocalyptic text. By "Hellenistic" I mean such things as are typical of the time and the milieu, in which Greek culture, *sensu lato*, from Alexander onward, was confronted with the views and ways of thinking of the East. I shall use the term rather loosely, also adducing examples from what is otherwise called the Roman Age.[3] By "apocalyptic" texts I shall denote narrative texts in which a human messenger, prophet or the like, often through extraordinary means (e.g. heavenly journeys), receives revelations of heavenly secrets which provide a solution to earthly problems. Often these problems are such as raise questions concerning the meaning or the goal of human life and history – theologians often call them eschatological. As a rule, the message of the texts has the semantic function to exhort or strengthen the addressees.[4]

---

[1] See, e.g., GEO WIDENGREN, *Religionens värld* (Uppsala: Almquist & Wiksell 1945). [IDEM, *Religionsphänomenologie* (DG), Berlin 1969.]

[2] HERMAN DE MEULENAERE, "History of the Town", *Mendes II*, ed. EMMA SWAN HALL/BERNARD V. BOTHMER; Warminster 1976, 72–177, 174f.

[3] On the term see HANS DIETER BETZ, "Hellenism", *ABD* 3. 127–135, esp. 127. On its vagueness see, e.g., MARTIN HENGEL, *The 'Hellenization' of Judaea in the First Century after Christ*, London • Philadelphia, Penn. 1989, 1–6.

[4] On the apocalyptic genre see JOHN J. COLLINS, "Introduction; Towards a Morphology of a Genre", *Apocalypse: the Morphology of a Genre (Semeia* 14), ed. JOHN J. COLLINS; Missoula, Mont. 1979, 1–20; LARS HARTMAN, "Survey of the Problem of Apocalyptic Genre," *Apocalypticism in the Mediter-*

The quotation above from the Book of Revelation could be taken as an example of "Hellenistic elements in apocalyptic texts".[5] But how to continue? Should I search for more motifs of this kind, listing traces of ideas concerning the Ages of History, of astrological concepts, of belief in the four (or five) divine elements (earth, water, fire, air (ether)), etc.? Or should I make an attempt reminiscent of Professor H. D. Betz's article of 1966 where he sought out long, far-reaching rootlets under the motif of the angel of the waters in Rev 16:5; thus he emphasised that apocalyptic texts must be studied within the framework of the general Hellenistic History of Religion.[6]

Should I adopt a similar approach to, say, the world conflagration or the heavenly journeys? Or the heavenly books?

I shall do nothing of the sort, but rather take as my point of departure some more general aspects of the essence of Hellenism: we read of them in common presentations of the cultural and religious history of the age. Examples from apocalyptic texts will illustrate how Judaism and Christianity related themselves to Hellenism as far as these aspects are concerned. It may even be that there is a purpose in seeking the presence of these aspects just in apocalyptic texts, since these belong to a genre which normally has a function in situations which are critical to author and readers. Thus there may be more sensitive soundings than in many other texts.[7]

---

ranean World and the Near East, ed. DAVID HELLHOLM, Tübingen 1979, 329–343; [Repr. in IDEM, Text-Centered New Testament Studies (WUNT 102), Tübingen 1997, 89–105]; DAVID HELLHOLM, "The Problem of Apocalyptic Genre and the Apocalypse of John," Semeia 36 (1986) 13–64; IDEM, "Methodological Reflections on the Problem of Definition of Generic Texts," Mysteries and Revelations. Apocalyptic Studies Since the Uppsala Colloquium (JSP Suppl. Ser 9), ed. JOHN J. COLLINS/JAMES H. CHARLESWORTH, Sheffield, 1991, 135–163.

[5] Note, accordingly, that I shall not deal with the question of the origin of Jewish apocalyptic, e.g., in Iran or in prophetism or in wisdom traditions or in combinations thereof. It is surveyed in DAGFINN RIAN, "Den religionshistoriske bakgrunn for Jødisk apokalyptikk," Fremtiden i Guds Hender, ed. Collegium Judaicum, Oslo ²1978, 14–30. For a useful general perspective on apocalypticism, see TORD OLSSON, "The Apocalyptic Activity. The Case of Jāmāsp Nāmag," Apocalypticism in the Mediterranean World and the Near East, ed. DAVID HELLHOLM, Tübingen 1979, 21–49: 21–31.

[6] The paper was originally HANS DIETER BETZ' lecture for "habilitation" in Mainz 1966; it was printed as "Zum Problem des religionsgeschichtlichen Verständnisses der Apokalyptik," ZThK 63 (1966) 391–409 (ET, "On the Problem of the Religio-Historical Understanding of Apocalypticism," Apocalypticism (JTC 6), ed. ROBERT W. FUNK 1969, 134–156. It received a moderating answer in ADELA YARBRO COLLINS, "The History-of-Religions Approach to Apocalypticism and the 'Angel of the Waters' (Rev 16:4–7)," CBQ 39 (1977) 367–381. – Another example is MATTHIAS DELCOR's following of the motif of the great beast: "Mythologie et apocalyptique," Apocalypses et théologie de l'espérance (LD 95), Paris 1977, 143–177.

[7] Two well-established opinions will be confirmed. On the one hand, PHILIPP VIELHAUER maintains, referring to MARTIN HENGEL's now classical study, Judentum und Hellenismus (see note 8): "die Apokalyptik ist ein Erzeugnis der hellenistischen Zeit, in der mannigfache Kultureinflüsse in Palästina sich kreuzen"; for this reason, he writes, the questions of the origin of its structural elements and its motifs lead in all directions in the Near East (Geschichte der urchristlichen Literatur, Berlin – New York 1975, 492f.). On the other: "Die Apokalyptik ist aber auch in einem anderen Sinne ein Produkt des Hellenismus: Sie ist eine jüdische Reaktion auf die vordringende hellenistische Kultur und will

We should take into account that the relationships between the said factors were complicated. The reference to "Hellenistic elements in apocalyptic texts" may suggest that these elements are present as clearly determinable entities. But this is seldom so. They are more or less integrated, and this "more or less" means different things with different motifs, with different texts, and at different times.

## 2. Syncretism

The textbooks always tell us that syncretism was a typical feature of Hellenistic culture and religion. The term may be a little difficult to define exactly, but there was, if I may say so, a militant syncretism which prompted at least an essential number of Jews to offer violent resistance. The most evident example is of course the attempt by Antiochus Epiphanes to combine the cult in the Temple of Jerusalem and the Zeus cult.[8] The reactions as we encounter them in the Book of Daniel are well known: the awe-inspiring image of the Cloud-gatherer is denounced as the abomination of desolation (11:31; cf. 9:17; also the text on the statue Dan 2).[9]

We have learnt – and rightly so – that the Judaism of those days was a religion not so much of doctrine as of practice. But there was a point where practice was indissolubly joined to a doctrine, *viz.* monotheism. When a cult questioned this doctrine it was sharply rejected.

Cultic reverence of the sovereign is easily joined to syncretism. It was practised at several times and at several places in the Hellenistic kingdoms, not least in Egypt, where it was an old tradition.[10] In the Hellenistic Age the cult of the sovereign also performed the political function of binding the different parts of the kingdom together, without suppressing the local cults. Caligula's attempt to have a statue of himself raised in the Jerusalem Temple may be seen in such a political light. It has been suggested that this attempt has left its traces in Mark 13:14 (on the abomination of desolation, standing at a place where it should not). Some kind of a cult of the sovereign, presumably of Domitian,[11] also lies behind the picture of the beast in Rev, bearing the number 666 (Rev 13). This political understanding is supported by the circumstance that the beast is associated with

---

durch Rückgriff auf höhere Weisheit und Offenbarung das Selbstbewusstsein des Judentums stärken" (*ibid.*, 493).

[8] Martin Hengel, *Judaism and Hellenism I-II*, Philadelphia, Penn. 1974, 294–295. The German original is *Judentum und Hellenismus, Studien zu ihrer Begegnung unter besonderer Berücksichtigung Palästinas bis zur Mitte des 2. Jh.s v. Chr.* (WUNT 10), Tübingen ²1973. In what follows I shall refer to it as Hengel, *JH*.

[9] In the Book of Revelation a similar attitude is to be surmised, in that the Zeus altar at Pergamon is characterized as the Throne of Satan (Rev 2:13).

[10] Robert Turcan, "Le culte impérial au III$^e$ siècle," *ANRW* II.16.2 (1978) 996–1084.

[11] Even if an older Nero tradition lies behind. [Cf. Thomas Witulski, *Die Johannesoffenbarung und Kaiser Hadrian. Studien zur Datierung der neutestamentlichen Apokalypse* (FRLANT 221), Göttingen 2007; idem, *Apk 11 und der Bar Kokha-Aufstand. Eine zeitgeschichtliche Interpretation* (WUNT 337), Tübingen 2012.]

political power. In the Apocalypse of Elijah, however, it is totally transformed into an Anti-Christ concept.

In the cases so far mentioned, the tendency to syncretism provoked resistance. In other cases one may wonder whether the term syncretism is relevant: the visionary in the Book of Revelation does not shudder when prophesying about the lamb and its bride. Certainly we can think of the imagery as representing a cultural mixture but the elements have been totally Christianised. We might even call this assimilation of features from another religion, a tamed syncretism.

## 3. Judaism as a Hellenistic Religion

Not least Professor Hengel has emphasised that Judaism, both inside and outside Palestine, was actually thoroughly Hellenistic. Most of the material cited in what follows is mentioned in Professor Hengel's publications.[12]

Thus, the Judaism behind the early apocalyptic texts was part and parcel of the Hellenistic culture, some expressions of which it tried vehemently to resist. We have already surmised that the Jews fought actually not against Hellenism *per se* but rather against features thereof which were felt to threaten the Jewish religious identity. The borderline was difficult to draw, and different circles drew it differently. Thus, the so-called *hasidim* drew it in other places than did, e.g., the Tobiads or those Jerusalemitic circles which established a gymnasium for their youth.

Let us, for example, consider how Daniel is presented in the book which bears his name. God, it says, gave him "knowledge and skill in all letters and wisdom" (1:17); his non-Jewish neighbours concede that he was "a man in whom is the spirit of holy gods" (5:11). Thus, he was ranked among those wise men who were highly respected in Hellenistic culture; this was a way of preserving the heritage of the old Hellas. But in Hellenistic times not only the rational followers of Aristotle belonged to the group of wise men. The same Hellenistic culture had a tendency to revere cool rationality less than wisdom which had been revealed from the gods and preferably those of exotic origin. Thus, Daniel can be assigned to the same group as Brahmans, magi and Egyptian wise priests, being an Oriental sage of the Hellenistic type who gives advice to Chaldeans. But simultaneously this Daniel is on his guard against everything which may violate his Jewishness: he is anxious not to be defiled by the food or wine served at the king's table (1:8); furthermore, monotheism is strictly defended (e.g., 2:28, 47; 3:26 etc.), and Daniel prays facing Jerusalem (6:10). A man of such stature is the hero of a book written at a time when Palestinian Judaism entered a decisive struggle against the Seleucidic attempts forcibly to Hellenize the Jews.

---

[12] See note 8. But presumably he could draw on WILHELM BOUSSET/HUGO GRESSMANN, *Die Religion des Judentums im späthellenistischen Zeitalter* (HNT 21), Tübingen ⁴1966.

## 4. The Non-Rational Acquisition of Knowledge

In the non-Jewish world Hellenism meant strengthening a tendency which was not new, *viz.*, that traditional religion was perceived as powerless. Philosophers had long been critical of the classical Greek religion, which was now supplemented by magic, mantics, astrology, mystery religions, religious associations, and, in due course by Christianity and gnosticism. (Not that e.g. magic had not been practised earlier, but it seems that its role increased in Hellenistic times.)

Several kinds of revelatory literature were at home in this religious atmosphere. Thus we encounter the Sibylline Oracles, of which the later Jewish and Christian with the same designation are an imitation.[13] Furthermore, there the Potter's Oracles were produced, and there Lucian could write a parody of an apocalypse, *viz.*, *Icaromenippos*.[14]

The tendency to revere age-old, exotic wisdom led the authors of such Hellenistic non-Jewish literature to publish it under a pseudonym, giving their works the names of more renowned authorities. Thus, Enoch, Ezra, Baruch, and Abraham, who are all presented as authors of apocalypses, are joined with Axiochus, the 5$^{th}$ century Greek whose name is given to a pseudoplatonic dialogue, furthermore, with Hystaspes, the Zoroastrian whose name is attached to a collection of oracles. The group also includes the Egyptian king Nechepso, who with the priest Petosiris is said to be the author of some mystic-religious texts of astrological content. All of them claim to mediate profound wisdom and knowledge through revelations. The fact that Judaism was a religion of the Book encouraged similar phenomena in Judaism.

Thus, already the literary genre of the apocalypse can be regarded as representing a Hellenistic element. Jews and Christians were convinced that God had revealed vital truths to Moses and to the prophets. But in their own time questions appeared which, according to some, the wisdom of the wise and the diligence of the lawyers were not capable of answering, although both of these groups really did their best to face up to the new times with openness and firmness. Dreams, visions, and trances offered new, extraordinary ways to knowledge and orientation. The apocalyptic texts were such literature as gave access to them.

So, we can also consider how revelation is mediated in these texts. Not only the prophet of the Apocalypse of Abraham is overwhelmed by the divine voice, and not only Daniel has visions in the night. Ennus of Apamea in Syria also has dreams in which he sees the future in a trance, and the author of the Egyptian Potter's Oracle is filled by a divine spirit when he presents his prophecies to the

---

[13] Note how the author of *Or Sib* 4 stands out against the common horizon when emphasizing that his message is from the real god and not from the false Phoebos, whom humans wrongly call a god (*Or Sib* 4:4ff.).

[14] [Cf. DAVID HELLHOLM, "Lucian's Icaromenippos as a Parody of an Apocalypse and 2 Corinthians 12,2–4 as a Report about a Heavenly Journey", in: DAVID C. BIENERT ET ALII (eds.), *Paulus und die antike Welt. Beiträge zur zeit- und religionsgeschichtlichen Erforschung des paulinischen Christentums* (FRLANT 222), Göttingen 2008, 56–82.]

king, "after he has been driven out of his senses" (ἐξεστ[ηκότως] ... τῶν φρενῶν; fragm 1,1,14–15).[15]

There were also other ways of mediating such supra-mundane knowledge. One was the heavenly journey, another that the person who received the revelation was allowed to gaze into the opened heavens.[16] Enoch went to heaven according to the Book of the Watchers (*1 En* 1–36), and John of the NT Apocalypse saw the heavens opened. But Nechepso and Poimandres too went to heaven to receive information, and heavenly journeys are also made in the *Apocalypse of Abraham* (15; on the wing of a dove), in the *Romance of Alexander* and in the *Icaromenippos*, just mentioned (3).[17]

It would be far from me, here to speak of "influences" in the sense that these examples represent simple cultural loans from outside, like today's pop-corn, Coke, or lawn-tennis. Instead we do well to remember that there is beneath the world-view common to most people in Antiquity or at least a way of talking of the heavenly regions which was universally understood. In addition the heritage of Jews and Christians contained several motifs and ideas which easily lent themselves to features of this kind. Thus, in our texts we often hear echoes from Biblical passages as the accounts of Moses on Sinai or in the land of Moab, of Isaiah in the Temple or of Ezekiel's vision of the Divine Majesty.

Sometimes the mediators receive a heavenly book, containing the secrets which the author should reveal in the present critical situation. This holds true of Enoch, John and Hermas. Certainly there is, e.g., the Biblical motif of Moses' tablets, but we should not forget the Egyptian Book of the Dead or the significantly later letters in which Asclepios gave advice on how to cure certain infirmities. In all these instances the issue is to bridge the gap between the world of the gods and that of human beings so that a message from the former could be read by the latter, among whom the situation was so serious as to require divine solutions.[18]

## 5. Astral Religion

The phenomenon mentioned in the headline is, as is well known, a manner of describing a general attitude to the stars, planets, etc., regarding them as divine members of the enormous celestial world, who influenced life on earth. Astral

---

[15] HENGEL, *JH* I, 216. Also JOHN S. HANSON, "Dreams and Visions in the Graeco-Roman World and Early Christianity," *ANRW* II.23.2. (1980) 1395–1427.

[16] See ALAN F. SEGAL, "Heavenly Ascent in Hellenistic Judaism, Early Christianity and their Environment," *ANRW* II.23.2 (1980) 1333–1394. MARTHA HIMMELFARB, *Ascent to Heaven in Jewish and Christian Apocalypses*, Oxford – New York 1993, discusses the texts mentioned in the title but does not really deal with any parallels.

[17] Apuleius' journey through the elements at his initiation into the Isis-mysteries (*Metam.* 11,23,8) is certainly for his own advantage only, but presumably mediated some divine insights.

[18] We may under this theme also mention the motif that statues of gods speak. On Rev 13:5 see Plut., *Coriol.* 37, 232 A, HELGE ALMQUIST, *Plutarch und das Neue Testament* (ASNU 15), Lund • Copenhagen 1946, 140.

religion played a role in almost every kind of religious thinking in Hellenistic and Roman times.

One aspect of the astral religion was astrology. It had an important place in the unstable world of Hellenism. In the celestial regions security and order, light and purity held sway, so different from the conditions in the sublunary world. Among Jews the attitudes to astrology were not unambiguous.[19] It seems to have been rather common that Jews were convinced, on the one hand, that stars and planets were divine beings, which controlled events on earth but, on the other, that they were reserved *vis-à-vis* astrology when it threatened to infringe on the monotheism of their fathers.

The following quotation from *Jubilees* 12:16–18 is typical of this contradiction; Abraham is introduced as an astrologer[20] but is immediately made to correct himself:

> And in the sixth week, in its fifth year, Abram sat up during the night on the first of the seventh month,[21] so that he might observe the stars from evening until daybreak so that he might see what the nature of the year would be with respect to rain. And he was sitting alone and making observations. And a word came into his heart, saying: 'All of the signs of the stars and the signs of the sun and the moon are in the hand of the Lord. Why am I seeking? If he desires, he will make it rain morning and evening and if he desires, he will not send (it) down; and everything is in his hand.[22]

The discovery of horoscopes at Qumran reflects a slightly more positive attitude,[23] as of course, does the *Treatise of Shem*,[24] which is a so-called calendoscope, i.e., a text which describes the characteristics of the year depending on the sign of the Zodiac in which it begins.

The power of the heavenly deities is resolutely tamed in *1 En* 17f., where Enoch during his heavenly journey is allowed to see

> the cornerstone of the earth, the four winds (spirits) who bear the earth and the firmament of heaven and they stand between earth and heaven. I saw the winds (spirits) of heaven who turn and bend the wheel of the sun and all the stars. (*1 En* 18:1–4)[25]

Similarly, in the Book of Parables Enoch learns about several heavenly secrets, *inter alia*, about the angels of snow, of frost, of mist, of dew, and of rain; these are in charge, but the Most High has given them certain rules to follow (*1 En* 60:17–23).[26]

---

[19] See JAMES H. CHARLESWORTH, "Jewish Interest in Astrology during the Hellenistic and Roman Period," *ANRW* II.20.2 (1987) 926–950; Dan 8 has such an astral background. See also HENGEL, *JH* I, 239.

[20] Ps.-Eupol., fragm. 1: Abraham taught the Egyptians astrology, but Enoch (*ibid.*) was the one who discovered it.

[21] I.e., the First of Tishri, the beginning of the new year.

[22] Intr. and trans. ORVAL S. WINTERMUTE, *OTP* II, [35–142: 81].

[23] See HENGEL, *JH* I, 236ff.

[24] [Intr. and trans. JAMES H. CHARLESWORTH, *OTP* I, 473–486.]

[25] I follow the Greek of the Gizeh fragment.

[26] Cf. how Philo describes the service of the heavenly bodies, which they perform "according to ordinances and laws, which God laid down to be unalterable in the All" (*de Opif.* 61).

On the other hand, the questioning of astrology in *Jubilees* has several polemical counterparts in passages in our apocalypses. Thus, in *1 En* 8:3 astrology is counted among the gruesome secrets which the fallen angels teach human beings: thus Barakiel instructs them therein, and so does Kokiel who teaches them concerning the signs (of the stars) etc.

In the *Apocalypse of Abraham* (chapter 7) Abraham directs an argument against his father, Terah, proving that fire, water, earth, sun, moon and stars are not gods.[27]

But again, knowledge of astrology or astronomy – they were rarely sharply differentiated – could be used only if they did not run counter to monotheism; thus Enoch's journey in the cosmos, according to *1 En* 33–36 and even more so the whole of the astronomical book (*1 En* 72–82) indicate an author who is well versed in contemporary astronomical science and in the latter instance, also in meteorology.

The astronomical knowledge exposed in *1 En* 72–82 is, so to speak, deployed in the service of the Most High God, insofar as the scientific apparatus is apparently there in order to deliver the basis for the assessment of a problem which lies on the heart of the writer. For the vision of the heavenly secrets authorises a particular solution of the calendar problem, which caused much controversy among the Jews of the time. Here divine authority is made to support a solar calendar to be used instead of the traditional lunar calendar. So we read towards the end of the book:

Blessed are all the righteous ones; blessed are those who walk on the road of righteousness and have no sin like the sinners in the calculation of the days in which the sun goes its course in the sky. (*1 En* 82:4)[28]

Here, in *1 En* we encounter "Hellenistic elements" which consist of the author's understanding of contemporary astrological and astronomic theories. But it is an understanding taken into the service of the Most High God.

Two other aspects of astral religion, *viz.* determinism and a way of conceptualizing the fate of righteous souls after death, will be treated below.

## 6. An Individual Perspective

*A. Magic etc.*
I mentioned before that the religion of the *polis* was, so to speak, supplemented by magic, astrology, etc. This also increased the importance of the individual's own

---

[27] See also, e.g., *Or Sib* 3:228: the Jews do not – in contrast to the Chaldeans – believe in astrology.
[28] This uncertainty in terms of the calendar had a counterpart in the non-Jewish environment, in which an embarrassing confusion in these matters prevailed during Hellenistic times. Unanimity was not reached until the Romans introduced the Julian calendar in 46 BCE. See ELIAS JOSEPH BICKERMAN, *Chronology of the Ancient World*, Ithaca, N.Y. ²1980, 31, 44–47.

life and decisions.[29] Individuals ascertain their fate through diverse incantations, magic or mantic practice, e.g. observation of how a pendulum swings over a plate with inscribed letters,[30] and horoscopes are personal.

Among the Jews the attitudes were not totally unambiguous in these matters – we have already noted something similar apropos of the astrology. All are not so straightforward as the author of the Book of the Watchers, who enumerates secrets which the fallen angels taught mankind:

> Semiaza taught them incantation and the cutting of roots, Armaros the resolving of incantations, Barakiel astrology, Kokiel concerning the signs (of the stars), Sathiel the observation of the stars; Seriel the course of the moon (1 En 8:3f.)

The *Second Book of Enoch* represents a similar stand, in that Enoch is allowed to see a horrible place of punishment which is prepared for those who practise

> witchcraft, enchantments, divinations, trafficking with demons ... (2 En 10:4)[31]

On the other hand, Josephus reports that Jews were renowned as skilful exorcists,[32] and Goodenough gathered examples of Jewish magic.[33] But in the apocalyptic texts which I have scrutinised, I have only found repudiation of these practices. This may not be pure chance: it might very well be that the authors of the apocalypses were more eager to recognise activities which threatened their religious identity.

*B. Associations, Groups*

There were other aspects of the tendency to focus on individuals, *viz.* the inclination to gather in more or less closed associations, the members of which could feel privileged as compared with the general public.

The apocalypses are commonly assumed to have been produced by conventicles and to reflect their attitudes.[34] I am afraid this reflects a formcritical axiom which, to my mind, should not be accepted so easily, *viz.* that a type of literature presupposes a certain type of community as its *Sitz im Leben*. But even if this is so, there is no doubt that the apocalypses often address themselves to or ascertain the existence of a group, the righteous, the elect, etc., in which the addressees are to be found.

---

[29] HENGEL, *JH* I, 195, refers to PAUL WENDLAND, *Die hellenistisch-römische Kultur*, Tübingen 1912, 45ff. As to the Jews, see HENGEL, *ibid.*; BENEDIKT OTZEN, *Den antike jødedom*, Copenhagen 1984, 64, 80, 88, 179. Cf. LUTHER H. MARTIN, "The Anti-Individualistic Ideology of Hellenistic Culture," *Numen* 41 (1994) 117–140, who claims that the assessment of the period in this respect has been unduly influenced by a modern individualism from the preceding century. He admits, however, that the socio-political transformations that characterized Hellenistic culture challenged traditional collective bases for identity.

[30] Ammianus Marcellinus, *Res gestae* 29.1.25ff. Ammianus lived in the 4th century CE, but the practice he describes is certainly older.

[31] Intr. and trans. FRANCIS IAN ANDERSEN, in *OTP* I, [91–213: 118].

[32] Jos., *Ant.* VIII.45–49.

[33] ERWIN R. GOODENOUGH, *Jewish Symbols in the Greco-Roman World* II, New York 1953, 155–295. Further literature, HENGEL *JH* II, note 851.

[34] VIELHAUER, *Geschichte* (note 7), 493.

Our texts do not represent a uniform position in this case either. On the one hand, "the righteous" regard themselves as a minority, which in the Diaspora almost becomes equal to: "we Jews in contrast to the others, the non-Jews". Thus, in this milieu the Jewish community functioned in some respects as a mystery association. But in Palestine where the Jews were a majority, the righteous and the elect may feel at a disadvantage to the rich and the powerful who represented a "modern", better adjusted group in terms of those ways of life which intrude upon established religious practice. Such might have been the situation during the first wave of Hellenism. But step by step the representatives of the minority establish their position and at last constitute the so-called normative Judaism.

But these "righteous" bring with them an ideology concerning the people of God; the covenants and the promises are for the people of God, the Jewish nation. This is the principal view still represented in Ben Sirach and also largely in the Tannaitic Literature.[35]

On the other hand, it seems that at least the First Book of Enoch in all its parts assumes that the minority, "the righteous" and "elect", sees itself as the real people of God.[36] The woes against the apostates are not only intended to strengthen the righteous but also to induce the apostates to join the group which represents the real people of God.

## C. Individual Responsibility

In consequence of the focusing of the demands on God's people and its good standing within the covenant individual responsibility was accentuated. When the environment is pluralistic, it is essential that the individual take the right stand in terms of morale and choose the behaviour of the right group with which to conform.[37] Thus also the deeds of the individual are observed from heaven:

Know that your deeds shall be inspected among the angels in heaven and from the sun, from the moon and from the stars (1 En 100:10)[38]

Compare, e.g., the passage in Plautus' *Rudens* (*prol.* 9ff.) according to which the stars on Jupiter's behalf observe the evil deeds of mankind.[39]

The same idea, although with another imagery:

You sinners, even if you say, Our sins shall not be investigated or written down, yet all your sins are being written down every day ... (1 En 104:7)[40]

This derives from OT ideas concerning the book in which God writes (Exod 32:32) and passages such as Ps 56:8, "you have kept count of my tossing; put my

---

[35] EMIL SCHÜRER, *The History of the Jewish People in the Age of Jesus Christ* I-III.2, rev. ed.; ed. by GÉZA VERMÈS/FERGUS MILLAR/MATTHEW BLACK; Edinburgh 1973-87, II, 494, 544ff.; ED P. SANDERS, *Paul and Palestinian Judaism*, London 1977, 237f., 341-346.
[36] SANDERS, *Paul*, 361f.
[37] HENGEL, *JH* I, 195.
[38] Cf. Philo, *de Somn.* I.140 on spirits in the air (angels) who are "viceroys of the Ruler of the universe, ears and eyes, so to speak, of the great king, beholding and hearing all things".
[39] HENGEL *JH* I, 201; II, 134f.
[40] See also *1 En* 90:20; 98:7; 103:2ff.; *4 Ez* 4:35f.; *2 Bar* 24:1; Rev 20:12.

tears in your bottle! Are they not in our book?". Of course Dan 7:10 is in the same tradition: "the court sat in judgement, and the books were opened".

This increased tendency to focus on the individual and on personal responsibility also contains an eschatological aspect which appears in the references to what to expect after death and even further beyond. Still, according to the author of the Book of Siracides (14:12, 16f.), the dead have a shadowy existence in Sheol. Moreover, in the Book of the Watchers, during his journey through the different regions of the universe Enoch is allowed to see the realm of the dead beyond the seas in the North-West. We find a counterpart in Greece, including the Orphic ideas of the Elysian fields. In this realm of the dead Enoch sees a bright, pleasant region which is meant for the spirits of the righteous, and a dark, gruesome one, which is prepared for the souls of the sinners. In these places the souls of the two groups are to be housed till the Judgement (*1 En* 22). In other contexts the sinners can expect to come to a cruel fire, e.g. in *Or Sib* 4:43: "then he will send the wicked down to darkness and fire".[41] This idea of the judgement of the souls also has its parallels in Orphicism, with Plato, in mystery religions and in Hellenistic popular religion.[42] Furthermore the thought of a separation between body and soul in death, which is now evident, is of course Greek. Compare also *Jub* 23:30: "the bones rest in the earth, but the souls of the righteous rejoice."[43]

Sometimes, but not always, such thoughts are connected with a belief in the resurrection of the individual. In Dan 12:2f. and *1 En* 104:2 (at least) the righteous are raised, and "shall shine like the heavenly luminaries" (*1 En* 104:2; similarly Dan 12:2f.). This astral feature is worthy of notice, for it might very well, as Martin Hengel says, be "a Jewish version of 'astral immortality', which was uncommonly widespread in the Hellenistic period, in both philosophy and poetry as in popular belief".[44]

## 7. The Large Hellenistic World

The tendency to focus on the individual is connected with a feeling, and a fear, that he might disappear into too large a collective. In its turn this fear may be regarded as a pendant to the insecurity and anxiety inherent in the Hellenistic world, overwhelmingly large as it was, politically and culturally.

---

[41] Also, *inter alia*, *1 En* 91:9.
[42] HENGEL, *JH* I, 198; II, 132, note 585.
[43] Also *1 En* 103:3.
[44] HENGEL, *JH* I, 197. He also quotes Aristophanes, *The Peace*, 832ff., where we encounter the idea that after death humans become stars. See his references in II, 131, note 579. It should, however, be pointed out that these Hellenistic elements and these early explicit expressions of a belief in the resurrection of the dead appear in a text which is to give comfort and hope in the situation in which Antiochus IV Epiphanes attempted to force a Hellenization upon the Jews (HANS C. C. CAVALLIN, *Life After Death* (CB.NT 7:1), Lund 1974, 24, 26).

## A. Administration

Firstly, a detail at which we may smile somewhat sardonically at a time when vivid discussions are in progress concerning the relationships of the Nordic countries to the European union, which, we are told, is a monster of bureaucracy. The Hellenistic kingdoms had an effective administration, Ptolemies and Seleucids each in their own ways, and the succeeding Romans were no less so. The administrative efficiency was not least experienced when it came to taxes and customs.[45]

As the secular kingdoms were well organised, so was the divine administration of the world. Philo explicitly uses this analogy and places angels in the world who are the subordinate governors of the Ruler of All (ὕπαρχοι τοῦ πανηγεμόνος; de Somn 1.140) So we can also regard it as a Hellenistic element that, e.g., the *Apocalypse of Zephaniah*[46] fills the cosmos with angels to whom all kinds of tasks are assigned by God, or, when toward the end of the astronomical Book of Enoch, a list is given of the powers who govern the heavenly regions, the seasons and the weather (*1 En* 82:7–20). The angel of the waters in Rev 16:5 also belongs to this administrative staff of God.[47]

Nor are these motifs to be regarded as wholly new or radically alien to Judaism. The idea of the Lord of Hosts and the image of the Supreme Being as a king having a court and servants belong to the spiritual heritage of both Jews and Christians, irrespective of whether or not Ptolemies and Seleucids organised an effective administration of their kingdoms. But now they did, and this may have contributed to the fact that the imagery was further developed. (The belief in the existence of angels is another presupposition, but this is hardly a Hellenistic feature.)

## B. The Economical Development

Another external aspect of Hellenism concerned economics and the social structure.[48] The Egypt of the Ptolemies was an economic super-power, chiefly by reason of its trade in grain. As a Ptolemaic province Palestine became economically important, primarily through the transit trade, *inter alia* with spices from the East. So the country acquired a strong upper class, consisting of the priestly nobility and the big land-owners, who were responsible for this economic rise. The social differences increased, although we can hardly speak of an oppression of the less privileged. Notwithstanding, the differences existed,[49] and were also

---

[45] SCHÜRER, *History* I, 372ff.

[46] [Intr. and transl. ORVAL S. WINTERMUTE, *OTP* I, 497–516.]

[47] This passage was the point of departure of H. D. Betz' extensive investigation, mentioned in note 6, above.

[48] HENGEL, *JH* I, 35–55.

[49] See further, e.g., SEÁN FREYNE, *Galilee from Alexander the Great to Hadrian 323 BCE to 135 CE*, Wilmington, Del. • Notre Dame, Ind. 1980; GILDAS HAMEL, *Poverty and Charity in Roman Palestine, First Three Centuries C. E.*, Berkeley – Los Angeles – Oxford 1989, esp. chapter 3 and 4, and cf. for a useful reminder on Josephus JOHN DOMINIC CROSSAN, *The Historical Jesus. The Life of a Mediterranean Jewish Peasant*, San Francisco 1991, 92–102.

connected with religion, insofar as this upper class tended to be more culturally open-minded and to practise their Judaism less strictly. The heritage from the prophets made it easy to identify, on the one hand, being rich and being wicked, and, on the other, being poor and being righteous.[50] Read in this context the following lines of *1 En* imply a Hellenistic element:

> Those who gather gold and silver will quickly be destroyed. Woe unto you, you rich, because you have put your trust in your wealth. You will have to leave your riches, for you have not remembered the Most High in the days of your wealth. (*1 En* 94:7f.)

More existential questions of whether a righteous life is actually meaningful can be surmised from the following lines:

> You righteous souls, do not fear; be hopeful, you souls who died in righteousness. Be not sad because your souls have gone down to Hades in sorrow and your body of flesh was not paid according to your piety during the days of your life. For your days were the time of the sinners, of men accursed on earth. When you die, the sinners say: "The righteous have died according to their fate, and what have they gained from their deeds? They died in the same way as we. See now, how they die in grief and darkness and what have they more than we?" ... I say unto you, you sinners, you have satiated yourselves with food and drink, you have impoverished people and gained property and seen god days. (*1 En* 102:4–7, 9)[51]

## C. *The Cosmic Law*

The perspective was larger and wider than before. Certainly the God of the Jews had all power in heaven and on earth, even though it was not recognised by all. He was the Creator of all and He ruled and sustained the universe. This became a common motif in the polemic against the idolatry of the environment, and was of course inspired by a heritage like the polemic of Isa 40. It is also encountered in *Or Sib* 4:10–14:

> He is not to be seen from earth ... he sees all at once but is seen by nobody. His are the dark night and the day, the sun, the stars and the moon and the fish-filled sea ...[52]

So God's power had a cosmic perspective. But this power had long also been associated with His Law. In wisdom circles the thoughts were developed that God creates with His word or His Law/Torah, and therefore this word also constitutes a fundamental law of the whole creation.[53] The idea has a counterpart, particularly in Stoicism, where, e.g., it can be said in Cleanthes' hymn to Zeus:[54]

> You, oh Zeus, be praised ... with your law you govern everything ... The order of the heavens beg your word, when it moves around the earth ... nor is anything done upon earth without you, neither in the firmament nor in the sea, except for what the sinners do in their folly.

---

[50] Stressed by GEORGE W. E. NICKELSBURG, "The Apocalyptic Message of 1 Enoch 92 – 105," *CBQ* 39 (1977b) 309–328. [IDEM, *1 Enoch 1* (Hermeneia), Minneapolis, Minn. 2001, 416–535.]

[51] By and large, I have here followed the Chester Beatty text.

[52] See also, e.g., *Jub* 21:3ff.; *1 En* 46:7; 99:7.

[53] The first example is in Siracides; see HENGEL *JH* I, 159ff.

[54] [See JOHAN CARL THOM, *Cleantes Hymn to Zeus. Text, Translation, and Commentary* (STAC 33), Tübingen 2005: Text 34–39; Trans. 40–41; Comm. 43–163.]

The picture is similar in the Book of the Watchers:[55]

> Consider everything that happens in the sky – it does not deviate from its ways ... Behold the summer and the winter how the whole earth is filled with water and clouds and dew ... All his work prospers and obeys him, and it does not change, but everything is done in the way in which God has ordered it ... But as for you, you have not stood fast and have not done according to his commandments ... (from 1 En 2–5).

Inversely the righteous can feel sure that in their Torah obedience they live in accordance with a cosmic rule. Indeed, one who is guided by God's law is the real world citizen.[56] Without claiming that these Jews borrowed their ideas from Stoicism, we can state that in this respect the latter would presumably have had little difficulty in following the thoughts of the visionary behind 1 En 1–5.[57]

## 8. The View of History

I have repeatedly called attention to the larger universe in which people found themselves during the Hellenistic Era. Certainly mighty kingdoms like Egypt and Babylon play significant and gruesome roles in the OT, and certainly the Gentiles rebel against the Lord and His Anointed, according to Psalm 2. But the perspective around history becomes wider, indeed our authors tend to embrace a totality of history, from the decisive final age – often that of the author and of his audience – through the end.[58] The vision of the statue with clay feet in Dan 2, crushed by a stone from heaven thrown by no human hand, has the same significance as the vision in Dan 7 of the four beasts which are replaced by the Son of Man, viz. the final establishment of God's Kingdom. In both cases the final phases of history are summarised in an overall view, and end in a divine rule. Such summarising, schematising images of history are, as we know, common in apocalyptic literature.[59] Scholars find no strictly Hellenistic counterparts to these periodizations in jubilees, year-weeks, ten ages or twelve etc., but refer more generally to a possible influence from Iranian apocalypticism, where an interest in periodization existed.[60]

---

[55] I have analysed the text in detail in *Asking for a Meaning* (CB.NT 12), Lund 1979.

[56] Thus explicitly Philo, *de Opif.* 3.

[57] Not least so in Philo's version; see, e.g., *de Opif.* 3. See PEDER BORGEN, "Philo of Alexandria," *Jewish Writings of the Second Temple Period*, ed. M. E. STONE; Assen • Philadelphia, Penn. 1984, 233–282: 271.

[58] See the deliberations in DAVID SYME RUSSELL, *The Method and Message of Jewish Apocalyptic*, Philadelphia, Penn. 1964, 217–224.

[59] E.g., *Or Sib* 4; *2 Bar*; *Apc Abr*. A full presentation in Russell, *Method*, 224–228. In the younger texts the span is sometimes from the origin of the world to the end. (As my reader may have noted, I do not in this paper differentiate earlier from later apocalypses. Hengel holds together what he calls early *hasidic* apocalypticism, including Dan and the oldest parts of 1 En (*JH* I, 189f.).

[60] See RUSSELL, *Method*, 228f. Furthermore, JOHN J. COLLINS, "Persian Apocalypses," *Apocalypse: The Morphology of a Genre* (Semeia 14), ed. JOHN J. COLLINS; Missoula, Mont. 1979, 207–217. [GEO WIDENGREN, "Les quatre âges du monde", in: GEO WIDENGREN/ANDERS HULTGÅRD/MARC PHILONENKO, *Apocalyptique iranienne et dualisme qoumrânien* (Rech. Intert. 2), Paris 1995, 23–62;

In such overall presentations of history the imagery is sometimes inspired by Hellenistic mythology. To trace possible paths along which such motifs have wandered is a task in itself and, furthermore, often an enterprise with small chance of arriving at accurate results. This is, for example, true of the statue in Dan 2. The roots of the underlying concepts are long and winding: there are the ideas of the history of the world as a great man, found in astrology, Orphicism and hermetism, and the four metals which follow each other from bad to worse are known from Hesiod and others.[61] The picture of the four beasts in Dan 7 also has its counterparts in the surrounding world.[62]

It is also a common feature in these overarching views of history that everything deteriorates, and that cosmic catastrophes occur, e.g. *Or Sib* 4:173ff.:

There will be a conflagration over the whole world, a mighty sign with sword and trumpet at the rising of the sun. The whole world will hear a bellowing noise and a mighty sound. He will burn the whole earth and will destroy the whole race of men.[63]

Similarly in the Potter's Oracle:

When the sun and the moon grow dark in the constellation of the ram, the places of Egypt and Syria will undergo great distress and death; persecution and rebellion will come upon the rulers of those places. And hosts will engage in battle and wreak conflagrations ...[64]

Periodizations and schematizations like these have often prompted scholars to maintain that the apocalyptic texts contain traces of a deterministic view, which, in its turn is taken to be a Hellenistic element. The text-books commonly remind the reader that the goddess of Fate, Tyche, attracts an increased following in this time and that belief in her goes well together with the determinism associated with astrology. Furthermore, one may quote Dan 2, "a great God has made known to the king what shall be hereafter" (2:45).[65] Certainly also the literary technique that an author, allegedly from ancient times, predicts "what shall be" can strengthen the impression that things so foretold are predetermined. For the reader, of course, recognises them, either he has heard of them from, e.g., the Old Testament or they belong to the events of his own generation.

But it is more important that in Jewish and Christian texts this overall view of history implies that history has a meaningful goal and that the road towards this goal is marked out by God.[66] One may very well establish some similarities

---

ANDERS HULTGÅRD, "Persian Apocalypticism", in: JOHN J. COLLINS (ed.), *The Encyclopedia of Apocalypticism*, Vol. I, New York 1998, 39–83.]

[61] HENGEL, *JH* I, 183.
[62] HENGEL, *ibid.*
[63] Further examples: *Apc El* 28:12; 31:9ff. (WOLFGANG SCHRAGE compares this passage with the Potter's Oracle – see his translation in *JSHRZ* V.3, 216); 32:14ff. HENGEL, *JH* I, 184 also refers to the Demotic Chronicle. [Cf. DAVID HELLHOLM, "Religion und Gewalt in der Apokalyptik", in: FRIEDRICH SCHWEITZER (ed.), *Religion, Politik und Gewalt*, Gütersloh 2006, 413–438.]
[64] HENGEL, *JH* I, 185; II, 125, note 520. [*CCAG* 7 (1908) 129–151: 132].
[65] The phrase is echoed in Rev 1:2f., 19, as well as in Mark 13:4.
[66] Also *1 En* 16:1 which makes use of the term "the great eon" (ὁ αἰὼν ὁ μέγας 16:1; 18:16; 21:6), presupposes that God has an all-embracing plan for history.

between these ideas and those on the great secular kingdom having its origin in Babylonian and Greek conceptions of cycles of the world; cosmos revolves like planets do in their courses. Iranian religion may have exerted an influence on Jewish theologians in the second century BCE.[67] Nevertheless, all this is integrated with a view of history which presupposes a struggle for the faith in, and faithfulness to God's covenant, as it was understood well before Daniel. The wicked king attacks precisely "the holy covenant" according to Dan (11:28, 30) and he destroys "the prince of the covenant" (Onias III, the high priest; Dan 11:22).

I think this covenant ideology is an overarching paradigm which determined the view of history, the eschatology, and the thought pattern of the individual works, including the periodization.[68] We might term it a macro-structure on a higher level than the macro-structure of the individual literary work. The covenant is at stake: God has promised support and salvation, the people have vowed to live according to the words of the covenant. Hellenism caused questions to be asked about both sides of this covenant relationship. Members of the chosen people joined alien powers, the actions of which became attacks on the heart of the covenant relation, the cult of the Temple. So here was "a time of tribulation such as never has been from the day humans came into being" (Dan 12:1). How could one bear it? Or why should one, after all? We have surmised the question whether it was worthwhile to be righteous: the sinners do well and "we die as they do" (cf. 1 En 102:6). Did God actually keep His promises? The answer was: yes, in the long run God is faithful to His promises; the history which seemed to be overwhelmingly wicked and hopelessly out of joint, was in its totality in God's hand.

## 9. A Final Glance at the Small World

Finally let us briefly consider a quotation which, simple as it is, brings us down to the so-called grass-roots, and which illustrates the problems underlying the examples of Hellenistic elements on which I have touched in these pages. The passage points to the confusion which many felt facing the new and powerful culture.

In the Book of the Watchers, the story of the Fall of the angels in Gen 6 is developed and embellished; *inter alia* the text tells the reader what Azazel taught the humans. He instructed them, it is said, how

to make swords and knives and shields and breastplates. (1 En 8:1)

---

[67] See ANDERS HULTGÅRD, "Das Judentum in der hellenistisch-römischen Zeit und die iranische Religion – ein religionsgeschichtliches Problem," *ANRW* II.19.1 (1979), 512–590, esp. 532ff., 570ff. [See now KLAUS KOCH, "Weltgeschichte und Gottesreich im Danielbuch und die iranischen Parallelen", in: IDEM, *Die Reiche der Welt und der kommende Menschensohn. Studien zum Danielbuch. Gesammelte Aufsätze 2*, Neukirchen-Vluyn 1995, 46–65; IDEM, *Daniel* (BKAT XII), Neukirchen-Vluyn 1994, 131–138.]

[68] Cf. HELMER RINGGREN, "Apokalyptik," *RGG* I (3rd ed.; 1957) 463–466; HENGEL, *JH* I, 194; HARTMAN, *Asking*, 123–138.

This view of the origin of weapons hints at the attitude of people who are tired of all the wars, the extensive campaigns, the huge armies and the terrifying military techniques of the superpowers.

But Azazel also taught them to use

> bracelets, decorations, antimony, ornamentation, the beautifying of the eyelids, all kinds of precious stones. and all colouring tinctures and alchemy, and how to change their appearance. (1 En 8:1)[69]

Here the small world seems to be as confusing as the big one which we just considered. Not that the women among the righteous were unfamiliar with jewellery and the like (cf., e.g., Judith's outfit as described in Judith 10:3–4). But here, it seems, alien and even terrifying customs were impressed upon God's elect.

The reaction of the righteous in this distressing situation is intimated in the immediate context:

And the people cried and their voice reached unto heaven. (1 En 8:4)

In my opinion this is also the content of these apocalyptic texts: in them we surmise a similar cry, and because people believed that their voice reached to heaven, they were also able to cope with the Hellenistic elements, indeed, even to adopt some of them.

So what is the upshot of these deliberations? From a particular angle we might state that Judaism was affected by alien, forceful, cultural currents, struggled against them and managed to preserve its identity until the so-called normative Judaism had come into being. But this is too simplistic a picture. At the same time this Judaism was intensely coloured and marked by the culture by which it was beset, strangely or ironically enough. This picture appears to be even more complicated when we realise that the situation looked different in different texts and at different times. That which we have seen – although only in scraps and glimpses – resembles a biological process in an organism in which several processes are occurring simultaneously, at different speeds, in different directions, sometimes reversing, sometimes in interaction, sometimes in opposition to each other, sometimes in isolation from each other. Nevertheless, the totality develops in one direction, but it takes some time to perceive which. Our apocalypticists firmly believed that there is a purpose in the world's course and tried to convince their audience that this was so. In spite of everything.

---

[69] The last phrase is linguistically obscure.

## 23. The Book of Revelation
### A Document for its Time as John Sees it

What is the "communication situation" of Revelation,[1] and what does the author convey to his addressees in this situation? In the following discussion of these questions I shall let John characterise the situation. Another theologian of John's time *would* perhaps describe it otherwise, and could, for example, be much less horrified by the Nicolaitans,[2] and when we as historians try to reconstruct the historical situation, the upshot *could* be quite different from the picture John paints.

### 1. Similarities in Apocalyptic Texts

Two Jewish sisters of the Book of Revelation, *Fourth Ezra* and *Second Baruch*, and, if I may say so, one cousin, the *Fourth Sibylline Oracle*, all belong to the same time as Revelation.[3] They resemble Revelation in several respects, and I shall begin by pointing to three such similarities.

First, the *divine authorisation* of the author is made clear. This happens both in *4 Ezra*, and in *2 Baruch*.[4] When, in *2 Baruch*, the coming things are about to be revealed, the prophet is allowed to see into the open heaven (22:1). That is, there shall be no doubt as to the divine origin of the message. As to the *Sibylline oracle*, it stresses in its beginning that it does not come from the false Apollo but from the real god (4-22).

So, the Book of Revelation is authorised as a revelation from Christ, given by God (1:1). The divine authority behind Revelation is specified in the inaugural visions of the one like a son of man (1:9-20). When further revelation is to be

---

[1] My approach thus differs from that of, e.g., JOHN T. KIRBY (1988) dealing with "the rhetorical situations" of Rev 1-3. Rather "communication situation" to me has the same meaning as the "Kommunikationssituation" of which text-linguistic scholars as ELISABETH GÜLICH/WOLFGANG RAIBLE speak (1977, 26f., 38-41). DAVID E. AUNE (1990) argues that the author "consciously employed the forms of the royal or imperial edict as part of his strategy to emphasize the fact that Christ is the true king in contrast to the Roman emperor" (204). This does not, however, answer the question which is the literary function of the messages as regarded within the literary composition of Rev.
[2] Cf. HANS-JOSEF KLAUCK 1992; HEIKKI RÄISÄNEN 1995. [NIKOLAUS WALTER 2002.]
[3] See PIERRE-MAURICE BOGAERT 1980 for a comparison of the "sisters" with each other.
[4] HARTMUT STEGEMANN rightly stresses how crucial the authority behind the message is in apocalyptic texts (1983, 505-507, 526f.).

given, John is granted a vision of the heavenly throne-room, in which the scroll of history is given to the Lamb to be unsealed (4–5).[5]

Secondly, in the beginning of all four books *the addressees and their situation* are envisaged.[6] Thus, both *4 Ezra* and *2 Baruch* state that they concern the Jews whose city has been destroyed (3:1). As *4 Ezra* puts it: "Why has Israel been given over to the Gentiles as a reproach, why has the people whom you loved been given to godless tribes and the Law of our fathers been made of no effect and why do the written covenants no longer exist?" (4:23).[7]

In the beginning of the Sibylline oracle we encounter a macarism of the Jews. Their pious ways of life are lauded and contrasted to those of others, who sneer at them and falsely attribute wicked and evil deeds to them (24–39). Such is *their* situation.

Correspondingly, Revelation is addressed to the seven churches, and their situation is depicted in the seven messages. This manner of understanding the role of the messages in relation to the rest of the Book of Revelation is by no means common among the commentators.[8] Nevertheless it seems to me that comparative material supports this understanding. It will be important for the rest of this paper.

Thirdly, in the beginning of these documents there is an *indication of the divine message* which will be directed to the audience in their situation. Thus, in *4 Ezra* (4:26): "The age is hastening swiftly to its end". In the beginning of *2 Baruch*, the mourning Jews are assured that the new Jerusalem will replace the one which is now destroyed (4). And on its first page the *Fourth Sibylline Oracle* has a brief preview of the judgement, which will mean punishment for the wicked but blessing for the righteous (4:41–47).

Such previews have their counterparts in Revelation. Thus in 1:3, "The time is near"; 1:7, "Behold he comes with the clouds … and all tribes on earth will mourn because of him". And in the seven messages: "To the victorious I shall give to eat from the tree of life" (2:7), or: "if you do not awake, I shall come as a thief" (3:3).[9]

---

[5] See LARS HARTMAN 1980, 140–142; [repr. in HARTMAN 1997, nr 7, 125–149]; DAVID HELLHOLM 1986, 45; [IDEM 1990, 109–146: esp 120; IDEM 2009, 226–253: esp. 246–249].

[6] In HARTMAN 1980, 143f., I argued that this holds true for Rev and also adduced some further examples from Jewish apocalyptic texts. [Repr. in IDEM 1997, 125–149.]

[7] The translation is largely that by BRUCE M. METZGER, "The Fourth Book of Ezra", in: JAMES H. CHARLESWORTH, *OTP* I, 517–559: 530.

[8] It also differs from the understanding of WIARD POPKES 1983.

[9] Both Rev 1:3 and 1:7 have rather salient positions in the introduction of Rev. Thus, 1:3 delivers the reason for the macarism of those who keep the things written in the following prophetic writing, and 1:7 is the prophetic "motto" of the book (thus WILHELM BOUSSET 1906, 189 and others; in HARTMAN 1980, 137f. I have discussed the function of 1:7, also adducing examples from other apocalyptic writings).

## 2. The Situation Behind Rev 2–3

Let us now regard the situation of the church more in detail as it appears in the introductory seven messages. After the author of Canon Muratori several interpreters of the messages have rightly maintained that the seven churches represent the whole church.[10] So, for example, although the church in Smyrna is praised, these Christians should also be as eager as the Ephesians not to leave their first love (2:4).

The descriptions of the churches are made from a divine point of view, which is emphasized by the chain of transmission in 1:1–2: from God to Christ, to the angel, to John, to the readers.[11] The speaker demands that the audience respect his superiority and his right to judge the quality of their religion. He "knows" what is under the surface of the life of the church, and this knowledge lies behind his praise and blame and behind his descriptions of the situation. Thus Christ appreciates the good standing of some: the Ephesians have refused to accept false apostles, and they hate the work of the Nicolaitans (2:2, 6); the Christians in Pergamon "keep" Christ's "name" and do not deny their faith, living as they are where "Satan's throne is" (2:13).

But Christ also "knows" things to blame. "I know your works: you are neither cold nor hot" (3:15); "I know your works: you are said to live but you are dead" (3:1).

The references in the seven messages to the religious situation can be gathered under three headings: heresies, oppression and lacking zeal.[12]

In their reconstruction of the *heresies* several commentators assume that they were some sort of early Gnostics.[13] But the only thing of which we can be relatively certain, is that they are accused of fornication and of eating meat from sacrifices. Either the fornication is illicit sexual behaviour[14] or it is a metaphor for syncretism.[15] The reference to Balaam as a sort of characterisation of their

---

[10] E.g., HEINRICH KRAFT 1974, 49; ULRICH B. MÜLLER 1984, 90. [Cf. already Victor of Petua, *Comm. in Apoc.* I, 7 (ad 1,20): quia quod uni dicit, omnibus dicit...; Text and trans. in NILS A. DAHL 2000, 153 note 22].

[11] See, i.a., BOUSSET 1906, 181; EDUARD LOHSE 1971, 11; DAVID HELLHOLM 1980, 45; [IDEM 1990, 120].

[12] On the social context of Rev see, e.g., ADELA YARBRO COLLINS 1984, 84–107; ELISABETH SCHÜSSLER FIORENZA 1985, 192–199; JAN A. DU RAND 1990, 354–357. The latter two deal with the "rhetorical situation". Cf. also LEONARD L. THOMPSON 1990, 186–197.

[13] ROBERT HENRY CHARLES 1920 I, 63; LOHSE 1971, 30; PHILIPP VIELHAUER 1975, 502f.; HANS-MARTIN SCHENKE/KARL MARTIN FISCHER 1978–1979 II, 297; MÜLLER 1984, 96–99; SCHÜSSLER FIORENZA 1985, 116–126; CHARLES HOMER GIBLIN 1991, 53.

[14] MÜLLER 1984, 113; SCHÜSSLER FIORENZA 1985, 116 and DUANE F. WATSON 1992, 1106f. assume both a literal and a metaphorical meaning.

[15] ERNST LOHMEYER 1953, 31; GEORGE BRADFORD CAIRD 1966; KRAFT 1974, 65 (but cf. his assessment of Jezebel, 69, which takes up the idea of THEODOR ZAHN [1924–1926 II, 606, 612] that Jezebel be the wife of the angel/bishop of Thyatira); GEORGE R. BEASLEY-MURRAY 1978, 86; COLLINS 1984, 88; ELISABETH SCHÜSSLER FIORENZA 1991, 14, 56; RÄISÄNEN 1995, 156–158.

so-called teaching could even suggest that it stands for mixed marriages.[16] It seems to me that what worries John is not one or several types of doctrinal heresy but rather a practice which differs from the one he demands.[17] The issue is how to behave in the areas where normal behaviour of the surrounding world and Christian behaviour meet: what is Christian and what is not?[18] The Nicolaitans regard themselves as Christians as do those who censure them, so gaining John's approval.

Secondly, the situation was marked by some kind of *oppression*. The classical view is that the churches were severely persecuted, so that being a Christian actually brought real and mortal danger.[19] In other words, the situation is understood as one in which the civil authorities applied the practice described a generation later in Pliny's correspondence with Trajan.[20]

But the evidence for such a persecution in Domitian's time (which I take to be the time of Revelation[21]) is weak,[22] and it might very well be that the adversities in the times of Revelation are of the same kind as those we glimpse in 1 Peter, namely there are sporadic local outbursts of oppression, but by and large the problems are such as depend on the Christians' being a minority, under suspicion from their environment and sometimes harassed, but only sometimes violently so.[23] To keep Christ's name (2:3, 13; 3:8) and not to deny it (2:13; 3:8) brings toil and the need for endurance. Antipas has been killed (2:13), but this seems to be an exception.

However, in accordance with his eschatological-apocalyptic conviction and perspective John foresees worse difficulties of quite other dimensions.[24] In my opinion, they do not belong to the present situation, but they cast their shadow over it, and remind the addressees of its gravity.

Thirdly, some features of the situation can be gathered under the designation *lacking zeal*. We could also call them tendencies to assimilation or to compromise.[25] Some in Pergamon and Thyatira eat meat from sacrifices (2:14,20).

---

[16] Thus JOSEPHINE MASSINGBERDE FORD 1975, 398.

[17] Thus LOHMEYER 1953, 31; COLIN J. HEMER 1986, 91–94. Cf. RÄISÄNEN 1995, 161f. (they represent a perspective "on the relation between faith and culture" different from John's).

[18] Cf. SCHÜSSLER FIORENZA 1991, 132–134.

[19] BOUSSET 1906, 133f.; CHARLES 1920 I, xciv–xcvi; SCHENKE/FISCHER 1978–1979 II, 294–298; MÜLLER 1984, 41f.

[20] BOUSSET 1906, 133; MÜLLER 1984, 259.

[21] ALAN J. P. GARROW has, however, made a good effort to challenge this common opinion (1994, 91–97), but still I tend to accept the common dating. [Cf. THOMAS WITULSKI 2007b; IDEM 2012: under Hadrian.]

[22] Several commentators have pointed to this circumstance (e.g. PIERRE PRIGENT 1974–1975, I) but lately it has been energetically argued by THOMPSON (1990, 95–115).

[23] Cf. PRIGENT 1981, 37; SCHÜSSLER FIORENZA 1985, 147, 195; THOMPSON 1990, 172–174; KLAUCK 1992, 162–164. For 1 Peter see NORBERT BROX 1979, 24–30; FRANÇOIS BOVON 1993.

[24] COLLINS 1984, 111–115; SCHÜSSLER FIORENZA 1985, 193f. For the apocalyptic-eschatological frame of reference see MICHAEL DOUGLAS GOULDER 1995.

[25] CHARLES 1920 I, 68–72; MÜLLER 1984, 103, 136f. RÄISÄNEN 1995, 153, 156. Cf. SCHÜSSLER FIORENZA 1985, 195f.

The Christians of Sardis are summoned to strengthen what is about to die (3:2) and should remember what they once received and heard (3:3). Among the Laodiceans John finds most fault: they are lukewarm.[26] Oh that they were hot or cold (3:15f.)! The Christians in Pergamon (2:14), Thyatira (2:20) and Sardis (3:4) are accused of lax sexual ethics. As stated above, I tend to assume a metaphorical understanding of the fornication of which they are accused, thinking of syncretism or of mixed marriages. But we should remember that the society was anything but Victorian in its view of sex, and Paul's Corinthian correspondence also bears evidence that the church was not untouched by this circumstance.

To my mind, both the so-called heretical tendencies and the lack of zeal point to a situation, typical of the second and third generation of many highly idealistic or charismatic minority movements:[27] some hold on to the ideals of the beginning and get into trouble, others tend to assimilate to the majority, to compromise, sometimes without much reflection, sometimes with some sort of argument to defend or to support their practice.[28] As I read Revelation, it is this sort of deradicalised Christianity John criticises.[29] So he summons them to repent (2:5,16; 3:3,19), to wake up (3:2), and to return to what they have left (2:5; 3:3). To the praised communities he says: be faithful (2:10), hold fast what you have so that no one may seize your crown (2:25; 3:11).

Towards the end of the book the same message returns: "The one who conquers will inherit these things" (that is, the new heaven and the new earth, and the new Jerusalem) but for "cowards, faithless, murderers, fornicators, sorcerers, idolaters and all liars, their lot is in the lake burning with fire and sulphur" (21:7f.).[30] The imperatives directed to the wicked in 22:11 are half ironic:[31] "May the unrighteous continue to act unrighteously and the impure continue to pollute himself". But the faithful are exhorted: "may the righteous still act righteously and the holy keep being holy".

Thus I believe that the situation John presents is one of a certain pressure, and contains tendencies to assimilation and compromise which he vehemently dislikes. Christ calls for attention ("repent") and action ("hold on"). Chapters 4–22 then deepen the perspective of this situation and present the ultimate mo-

---

[26] HEMER (1986, 186–191) takes the expression to mean ineffectiveness instead; nevertheless, the difference from the above understanding does not seem to be too great.

[27] Cf. THOMPSON 1990, 193–195.

[28] The fact that according to John "Jezebel" and the Nicolaitans "teach" (2:20) or have a "teaching" (2:14f., 24) should correspond to such a defense.

[29] In a not un-similar direction move SCHÜSSLER FIORENZA 1985, 55; 1991, 132–135; RÄISÄNEN 1995; KLAUCK 1992. Cf. THOMPSON 1990, 195.

[30] It is important to realize that 21:5–8 is the most embedded text in the book as regarded from the point of view of the communicative levels, i.e., the point where the writer is commanded to write down the words of the Supreme Being Itself. This indicates that it contains the most central message of the book. See HELLHOLM 1986, 44f.

[31] MÜLLER 1984, 369.

tivation for the attention and action called for; they place the situation and the attitude called for into an eschatological framework.[32]

The main parts of the two Jewish sisters of Revelation, *4 Ezra* and *2 Baruch*, relate to their situations in a similar manner. Thus, *2 Baruch* connects its descriptions of the apocalyptic horrors with the present day in this way: "If you prepare your minds to sow in them the fruits of the Law, he shall protect you in the time in which the Mighty One shall shake the entire creation" (32:1). The end of the book says, "Remember Zion and the Law (84:8) ... Zion has been taken away from us, and we have nothing now apart from the Mighty One and his Law. Therefore, if we direct and dispose our hearts, we shall receive everything which we lost... The Most High ... has shown to us that which comes and has not concealed from us what will happen at the end. Therefore, before his judgment... let us prepare ourselves that we may possess and not be possessed" (85:3–9).[33]

Similarly, when the catastrophes of the last age have been foretold by the Sibyl, she calls: "Stretch out your hands to heaven and ask for forgiveness for your former deeds ... then God will grant conversion and not destroy" (166ff.). To the righteous she says: "But all who are pious will live again on earth ... Oh, most blessed the man who then will be on earth" (187,192).

So also the Book of Revelation sheds an eschatological light on the present situation and demands repentance and steadfastness in this perspective.

Finally, let me pick up one feature of this larger perspective in which the main part of Revelation places the situation which is revealed and characterized in the seven messages.

Already in 1:5, when Christ salutes the seven churches, he presents himself as the "ruler of the kings on earth". This is not empty rhetoric, but represents a deep conviction on John's side. The idea of the kingdom of God and/or of Christ lies like a *basso ostinato* under that which the writer has to convey.[34] Not least it plays an important role in the hymns which are inserted as interpretative resting places in the main part of the book.[35] Mostly they have a bearing on the addressees and their situation. That is, the horrifying visions of what is to come have these hymns as a counterpoint. From a heavenly point of view, they remind the righteous of where they belong. That God is the king stands in a vehement contrast to the religion and morality of the times, both among the blamed Christians and in the pagan society. But already now they belong to his rule, not to that of the world. The contrast is not eliminated until after the fall

---

[32] Cf. GOULDER 1995. – In his analysis of the hierarchic structure of the partial texts of Rev. HELLHOLM has demonstrated how 1:9–3:22 are on the same level as 4:1–22:5 (1986, 47f.).

[33] Trans. ALBERTUS F. J. KLIJN, "2 (Syriac Apocalypse of) Baruch" in: JAMES H. CHARLESWORTH, *OTP* I, 615–652.

[34] LOHSE 1971, 116; PRIGENT 1980; MÜLLER 1984, 54f.; M. EUGENE BORING 1986; SCHÜSSLER FIORENZA 1991, 119–124.

[35] JAN LAMBRECHT 1980, 99f.; SCHÜSSLER FIORENZA 1985, 171f.

of Babylon, when a voice like the sound of many waters proclaims: "Alleluia, the Lord, our God, the Almighty, has taken power" (19:6).

The contrast is dramatised by the pride and blasphemous behaviour of the beasts and of Babylon. Using traditional motifs the seer interprets tendencies of his time.[36] The worship of the empire and the emperor, wide spread in Western Asia Minor,[37] were already a denial of the fact that God was the ruler. John foresaw a development into a situation which meant vehement and violent blasphemy. So in his visions he expected much worse confrontations,[38] in view of which he apparently felt anxious about God's servants. What will the lukewarm Christians do, and what about those who already compromise with paganism? How firmly would they be able to behave in accordance with their real status, as servants of the only Ruler?

So the idea of God's kingdom, on the one hand, gives an ontological perspective to the situation of Revelation; the reality is greater and awfully more powerful than the compromisers realise; God is the ruler of the kings on earth, and it is dangerous not to live up to your being his servant. The blasphemous tendencies of the mundane authorities to demand honour and respect which belong only to God, will according to the divine revelation increase to an inescapable violent clash, in which it will be visible who really is the ruler of all.

But to the ontologically determined perspective comes one of temporal categories. The prophecy sheds light on the present times in referring to what is going to happen: it will "show to his servants that which must happen soon" (1:1). The present situation is pregnant with eschatology, although not all realise it, not even among the Christians. But to the author it is a question of life and death so to do.

I have read the Revelation on the author's conditions, and have let him define the situation of the church he addresses. It may very well be that the real situation could be described and assessed differently.[39]

What John regards as compromises with paganism, *could* be similar to the attitude which Paul accepts in 1 Corinthians 8. In a pagan's house Christians may eat whatever is set before them. But if somebody says, "this is sacrificial meat," then they should not eat it, not because of the idol, but for the sake of the weak brother's conscience. That which I (and I think with John) have called "lacking zeal" and compromise, others may have been prepared to characterise as honourable realism and good and sober Christian respect for life realities.[40] But now the prophet has had his say. According to the same Paul, the task of a prophet was to call his audience into account and to disclose the secrets of their

---

[36] COLLINS 1984, 145–152; HEINZ GIESEN 1990.
[37] See PRIGENT 1974–1975 II, and lately KLAUCK 1992. [See now THOMAS WITULSKI 2007a.]
[38] See PRIGENT 1974–1975, III.
[39] RÄISÄNEN 1995; cf. SCHÜSSLER FIORENZA 1991, 56f.
[40] Cf. PAUL W. WALASKAY 1983, 66f. *et passim* as quoted with approval by RÄISÄNEN, 1995, 164f. (on Luke). KLAUCK characterizes the Nicolaitans as "ein nachpaulinisches Christentum mit manchen Zügen, die zur späteren Gnosis hin tendieren" (1992, 169).

heart so that they realise that God is among them. Thus Revelation became a document *for* its time; John understood this time in a particular way and had a particular message for it, expressed by literary means *of* his time.

# 24. Universal Reconciliation (Col 1:20)[1]

## 1. Preliminary Remark

It is commonly held that Col 1:15–20 is a hymn which the author – who in the opinion of many is not Paul[2] – has used for his letter. A review of the suggestions concerning the original form of the "hymn"[3] reveals an impressive amount of scholarly ingenuity, but there seems to be depressingly little which is certain about these suggestions, as, of course, the exegetical results become less certain the more they are based on literary reconstructions which are necessarily hypothetical.[4] Such a statement is not to deny the legitimacy of this kind of traditio-historical and redactio-critical research. The latter can suggest valuable insights

---

[1] This is a thoroughly revised version of a paper delivered in October 1981 at the Swedish Theological Institute in Jerusalem. It is dedicated to Professor Harald Riesenfeld, Uppsala, at the occasion of his 70th birthday, February 8, 1983, as a token of gratitude to him as a teacher, who, being himself an expert in the Biblical languages and in the history of religions, has always been eager to convey to his students a due respect for such facts.

[2] In the following I am going to assume that the writer of Col is not Paul personally, but somebody close to him. EDUARD SCHWEIZER's suggestion that Timothy has wielded the pen seems rather attractive (*Der Brief an die Kolosser* [EKK 12], Zürich – Einsiedeln – Köln ²1981, 26).

[3] There is a need for further research as to the criteria for isolating hymns, formulas etc. in older texts, including the vast Jewish pseudepigraphic literature. ETHELBERT STAUFFER pointed to some criteria in his *New Testament Theology*, London 1955, 338f. See further HANS CONZELMANN/ANDREAS LINDEMANN, *Arbeitsbuch zum Neuen Testament* (UTB 52), Tübingen ⁶1982, § 12 (+ lit.). Cf. KLAUS BERGER, *Exegese des Neuen Testaments* (UTB 658), Heidelberg ²1984, 115. [Cf. PHILIPP VIELHAUER, *Geschichte der urchristlichen Literatur* (DGL), Berlin 1975, 10–14; GEORG STRECKER, *Literaturgeschichte des Neuen Testaments* (UTB 1682), Göttingen 1992, 95–106.]

[4] JEAN-NOËL ALETTI, *Colossiens 1,15–20* (AnBib 91), Rome 1981, 21ff. gives a good survey of the vast amount of suggestions. In JOACHIM GNILKA's commentary (*Der Kolosserbrief* [HThK 10/1]), Freiburg i. Br. – Basel – Wien 1980, 53ff.) one finds a presentation of the more significant attempts at a reconstruction. See also PIERRE BENOIT, "L'hymne christologique de Col 1,15–20. Jugement critique sur l'état des recherches", in: JACOB NEUSNER (ed.), *Christianity, Judaism and Other Graeco-Roman Cults*, I (= FS M. Smith) (SJLA 12), Leiden 1975, 226–263, esp. 245ff. – JOHN COCHRANE O'NEILL, "The Source of the Christology in Colossians", in: *NTS* 26 (1980) 87–100 suggests that the author actually quoted different fragments of Jewish traditions; this means a concentration on the author-side of the textual communication, which has the same advantages and drawbacks as the "hymn"-hypotheses. HARALD RIESENFELD has often expressed his doubts concerning the latter hypotheses, so already in "Allt är skapat i Kristus", in: *FS R. Prenter*, ed. by GUSTAF WINGREN/ANNA MARIE AAGAARD, Copenhagen 1967, 54–64, esp. 54f. [Cf. GEORGE H. VAN KOOTEN, *Cosmic Christology in Paul and the Pauline School* (WUNT 171), Tübingen 2003, 100–129.]

As to v. 20, the words "and through him to reconcile all things unto him" are regarded by some as an addition; the whole phrase "making peace through the blood of his cross" is deleted by some, whereas others content themselves with leaving out "through the blood of his cross"; finally, "whether on earth or in heaven" is deemed an embellishment by some (see GNILKA, *Kol*, 53ff.).

into early Christian ideas and issues behind the ones we encounter more overtly in the NT texts themselves.

On the following pages, however, I will try to shed some light on the text of Col 1:20 as it stands,[5] assuming that its author believed his shaping of the text to be reasonable and that (at least some of) his readers would understand his intent.[6] For this purpose I will adduce some material from contemporary Judaism, not least Philo, which, I think, represents ways of thinking that may have played a role in the author's conception and for the readers' understanding of the passage.

## 2. Different Problems

Col 1:20 presents us with several problems, some of which are the following: How is one to deal with εἰς αὐτόν, the adverbial phrase connected to ἀποκαταλλάξαι? As normally (ἀπο)καταλλάξαι is followed by a dative or by πρός, the εἰς is a bit peculiar. In addition, one must ask to whom does this αὐτόν refer. Is it God, the actor behind the following εἰρηνοποιήσας, or is it the Son, "in" whom everything is held together according to v. 17? Closely related to the problem of εἰς αὐτόν is the question of the partners of the reconciliation: Are they to be understood as "all things" among themselves, earthly things to heavenly ones, all things to God, or all things to the Son, or is it that the actual partners are not mentioned in the text?[7]

## 3. Background to the Idea of Universal Reconciliation

This, in turn, leads to the question, what is the relevant background to the idea of the universal reconciliation? Here I only mention some suggestions which have been given: E. Lohmeyer referred to the Jewish Day of Atonement,[8] E. Käsemann pointed to Virgil's 4th eclogue as representative of Hellenistic-Roman expectations that cosmic peace belonged to the conditions to be established in

---

[5] I prefer the more difficult reading which includes a second δι' αὐτοῦ. – Although 1:15–20 stands out as a literary unit, stylistically seen, I take the stand that, although the author of Col may have taken over this "hymn" in changing it, adding or leaving out things, it is sound method to approach the whole text of Col as a consistent literary work. Such a stand means assuming that the readers were able to get the writer's message without needing any insights into his doings when writing. So I do not adduce reworkings of an original as explanation of the contents; such a stand is also relevant for an assessment of the suggestion of P. Benoit that the ἀποκαταλλάσσειν of 1:20 is brought into the text as an afterthought under the influence of its appearance in 1:22 (BENOIT, "L'hymne", 256ff.).

[6] Thus also THOMAS EVAN POLLARD, "Colossians 1:12–20. A Reconsideration", in: *NTS* 27 (1981) 572–575, who concentrates on the existing text, that being "the exegete's primary concern" (573).

[7] Cf., e.g., ALETTI, *Colossiens*, 21ff., who favors the last possibility.

8 ERNST LOHMEYER, *Die Briefe an die Philipper, an die Kolosser und an Philemon* (KEK 9), Göttingen [14]1974, *ad loc.*

the golden age.⁹ S. Lyonnet quoted Philo's *Spec. Leg.* (II,190ff.) as a witness of a Jewish Rosh ha-Shanah tradition taken up in Col, which stressed God's role as the peace-maker of the universe.¹⁰ E. Schweizer, using Lyonnet's suggestion, pointed to a widely spread conviction in Antiquity that the world was continuously threatened by a struggle among its elements; one response to this threat can be seen in the way Philo presented God as the real peace-maker, and in a similar but christianized way, as expressed by the author of the original hymn in Col 1.¹¹

## 3.1. Linguistic Issues

Before entering into this discussion of the contents of Col 1:20 and its background, we should deal with the more linguistic issues. Thus, we first have to ask the question: To – or unto – whom are all things reconciled? Several versions suggest that the referent is God, rendering the text "reconcile all things to (unto) himself".¹² Presumably the translators have been inspired by 2 Cor 5:19 ("God in Christ was reconciling the world to himself"). But there the Greek says precisely "himself" (ἑαυτῷ). My contention is that one should take seriously the fact that, from v. 15 on, the prepositions ἐν, διά, and εἰς appear in a solemn series, all of them connected with a "him". That is, the "to him" of v. 20 links up with the preceding "in him" ("all fullness was pleased to dwell") and with "through him" ("reconcile all things"). This indicates that the linguistic sequence suggested to a reader or listener that the εἰς αὐτόν of v. 20 referred to the Son.¹³

Next, we take up the awkward εἰς. In vv. 15-20 the three prepositions ἐν, διά and εἰς appear in two parallel sequences. It is likely that this parallelism has caused ἀποκαταλλάσσειν to be followed by an εἰς. As I have already mentioned, the one to whom one is reconciled is normally put in dative or after a πρός. So some want a translation which is as awkward as the Greek, e.g., "unto him", "auf ihn hin",¹⁴ "pour lui".¹⁵ But perhaps the εἰς is not so terribly awkward. εἰς and πρός were used similarly in the Greek of those days, and often in what seems

---

⁹ ERNST KÄSEMANN, "Eine urchristliche Taufliturgie", in: IDEM, *Exegetische Versuche und Besinnungen*, I, Göttingen ⁶1970, 34–51: 37 (first publ. in 1949).

¹⁰ STANISLAS LYONNET, "L'hymne christologique de l'épître aux Colossiens et la fête juive du Nouvel An", in: *RSR* 48 (1960) 93–100.

¹¹ EDUARD SCHWEIZER, "Das hellenistische Weltbild als Produkt der Weltangst", in: IDEM, *Neotestamentica*, Zürich – Stuttgart 1963, 15–27; IDEM, "Versöhnung des Alls. Kol 1,20", in: GEORG STRECKER (ed.), *Jesus Christus in Historie und Theologie* (= FS H. Conzelmann), Tübingen 1975, 487–501; IDEM, *Kol, ad loc.* and 100ff..

¹² E.g., AV, RSV, and the Swedish translation of 1981.

¹³ [Differently ROBERT McL. WILSON, *Colossians and Philemon* (ICC), London – New York 2005, 123 and 154.]

¹⁴ [Thus HANS HÜBNER, *An Philemon, An die Kolosser, An die Epheser* (HNT 12), Tübingen 1997, 54 and 63.]

¹⁵ [Cf. *Nouveau Testament* (TOB): par lui et pour lui.]

to be totally indiscriminate ways.[16] Thus, given the context, I think that there are sufficient linguistic arguments for translating "reconcile all things to him". Nonetheless one should be prepared to hear a slight accent of direction in the expression, of a movement towards an aim, as in v. 16c: "All things are created ... unto him".

Thus I end up with a translation like this one: "(He who is the beginning, the first-born from the dead, for in him all fullness was pleased to dwell) and through him to reconcile all things to him, whether on earth or in heaven, making peace by the blood of his cross".

## 3.2. "All things" (τὰ πάντα)

Before assessing the history of religions background of our text, we must briefly consider that to which the "all things" reconciled may refer. The expression (τὰ πάντα) occurs four times in vv. 15–20:" All things were created through him and to him" (v. 16 bis), "all things are held together in him" (v. 17). In v. 16 the concept is specified: "All things in heaven and on earth, visible and invisible, thrones, dominations, sovereignties, powers" (θρόνοι, κυριότητες, ἀρχαί, ἐξουσίαι). The same perspective returns at the end of v. 20: "whether on earth or in heaven". We need not now enter upon a discussion of the Colossian heresy, nor of the terminology used for these thrones, sovereignties etc.[17] Let us only note that the author shares a view widely held in Antiquity, viz., that man belonged to a cosmos that was alive, filled and swayed by all sorts of living powers. Elements like fire and water, the seasons, the sun, moon and stars, gods, demons, angels, etc. all were powers that had to be more or less controlled or subdued, be it through a mighty god (Zeus or Isis or Yahweh) or by magic. Jews and Christians of course shared this outlook. Philo argues, e.g., that the stars are divine beings which function as the supreme god's lieutenants (Spec. Leg., I, 13ff.), and Paul, like Philo, believes "there is no god but the One, even if there are so-called gods, either in the sky or on the earth, as there are many gods and many lords" (1 Cor 8:4f.).[18]

Behind the designations of the thrones, sovereignties etc. of Col 1 we should expect as little of systematic thinking and consistent terminology as one finds in other texts which reflect this kind of mythological thinking.[19] It is enough for our purpose to state that the author sees his addressees as belonging to a cosmos

---

[16] FRIEDRICH BLASS/ALBERT DEBRUNNER/FRIEDRICH REHKOPF, Grammatik des Neutestamentlichen Griechisch, Göttingen [16]1984, § 402,2.4; 196,2; CHARLES F. D. MOULE, An Idiom-Book of New Testament Greek, Cambridge 1971 (= [2]1959), 54, 67f.

[17] An illuminating investigation that points to the remaining difficulties is PIERRE BENOIT, "Angélologie et démonologie pauliniennes. Réflexions sur la nomenclature des Puissances célestes et sur l' origine du mal angélique chez S. Paul", in: Foi et Culture à la lumière de la Bible, Torino 1981, 217–233.

[18] Cf. also Rom 8:38f. and, less confident, Jude 8f. See for the general outlook RAPHAEL PATAI, Man and Temple, London 1947, chap. 1.

[19] BENOIT, "Angélologie"; GNILKA, Kol, 65; ALETTI, Colossiens, 61.

in which there are spiritual elements that demand their respect: They should not touch this, not taste that, etc. (2:16ff.). He argues that the respect demanded should not be payed, because these thrones, principalities etc. have all been subdued under Christ, indeed they owe there existence to him.

## 3.3. Cultic Connotations

We now proceed to consider some further factors in the contemporary religious background of Col 1:20. E. Lohmeyer and E. Schweizer, each in his own way, have drawn attention to the cultic connotations of the phraseology of v. 20: To talk of reconciliation and peacemaking through blood could hardly cause but cultic associations.[20] Furthermore, it is a general phenomenon in religion that man's worship concerns his whole world, heaven and earth.[21] The gods or the powers whom he worships reign over the universe he lives in, however small or large it may be. This has, of course, to do with the fact that he *is* dependent on the universe involved. In an agricultural environment, for example, his life hangs on the crops, which in their turn, depend on the powers who command the seasons and the climate, be they benevolent or angry.

Not only do the rites of the worship envisage man's whole world, but the cult sites themselves also lead his thoughts to the universe; they or their equipment represent the cosmos in one or another way. Let me mention a couple of examples, chosen at random: Plutarch reports that "Numa is said to have built the temple of Vesta in circular form ... copying not the figure of the earth as being Vesta but of the whole universe" (Numa, II). According to Josephus, the three parts of the Jerusalem Temple corresponded to the three parts of the world, sea, land, and heaven (*Ant*, III. 7,7).[22]

The last example indicates that the Jews were no exception when it came to putting their worship in a universal perspective. So Philo, like several of his fellow-Jews,[23] understood the details that composed the high priest's vestment as symbolizing the universe and its elements:

"The high priest of the Jews makes prayers and gives thanks not only on behalf of the whole human race but also for the parts of nature, earth, water, air, fire. For he holds the world to be, as in very truth it is, his country, and in its behalf he is wont to propitiate the Ruler (ἐξευμενίζεσθαι τὸν ἡγεμόνα) with supplication and intercession, beseeching him to make his creature a partaker of his kindly and merciful nature" (*Spec. Leg.*, I, 97).[24]

---

[20] Although SCHWEIZER, "Versöhnung", 492f. mentions the cultic perspective, its importance is diminished by his concentration on a reconstructed hymn without the words "through the blood of his cross".

[21] See, e.g., GERARDUS VAN DER LEEUW, *Phänomenologie der Religion*, Tübingen ³1970, 439ff.; SIGMUND MOWINCKEL, "Kultus", in: *RGG*³ IV, 120–126: 124.

[22] See further PATAI, *Man*, chaps. 3 and 4; GEO WIDENGREN, "Aspetti simbolici dei templi e luoghi di culto del Vicino Oriente antico", in: *Numen* 7 (1960) 1–25; PETER SCHÄFER, "Tempel und Schöpfung", in: *Kairos* 16 (1974) 122–133.

[23] E.g., *Wis*. 19:29; Josephus, *Ant*, III. 7,7.

[24] Here and elsewhere in this paper I largely follow the English trans. of the Loeb edition.

A passage from the Life of Moses presents the cosmic powers as more actively involved in the rites of worship, and yet man's sins are also taken into account. After an interpretation of the priestly garment similar to the one of *Spec. Leg.*, I, 97, Philo describes the high priest's entering to offer "the ancestral prayers and sacrifices" and goes on to state that "the whole universe" enters with him "to plead his cause, that sins be remembered no more and good gifts showered in rich abundance" (πρός τε ἀμνηστίαν ἁμαρτημάτων καὶ χορηγίαν ἀφθονωτάτων ἀγαθῶν) (*Vit. Mos.*, II, 133f.).

The author of Col 1:20, as well, seems to stand within a similarly wideembracing sphere of cultic ideas. Somehow the death of Jesus is comparable to the sacrifices that established a good relationship between God and creation, and then, as in Philo, both man's sins and the lawful behavior of the whole universe are taken into account. He does not, however, work out these associations like, e.g., the author of Hebrews, and he is also less explicit than, for instance, the fourth evangelist who makes Jesus die as a paschal lamb. Although other NT texts speak of Jesus as dying on behalf of (ὑπέρ) others, it is difficult to trace that kind of thinking in our passage.[25] Two details may run counter to such associations, *viz.*, on the one hand, the stress on the divine activity (which is more marked than, e.g., the divine δεῖ behind the ὑπέρ of Jesus' death in Mark). Furthermore the "reconcile to him", i.e., to the Son, blurs a picture of a sacrifice offered to propitiate the wrath of God.

## 3.4. Wisdom – Christology

We are brought one step further when we consider that Col 1:15–20 is permeated by so-called Wisdom-Christology.[26] As is well known, the central idea of such a Christology is that God's wisdom or Word (λόγος)[27] or the Divine Reason was in Jesus, so that in his work and words God communicated himself to man; so he did also in the death of Jesus. Another aspect of this Wisdom-Christology concerns creation, and so our author writes that "all things are created through him and all things hold together in him". Philo and others in the Jewish Wisdom-tradition said exactly the same thing about the divine Logos or Wisdom.[28]

What has been said in the preceding paragraph is commonplace in the commentaries to our passage. But it may be worthwhile to note that Philo also presented the Logos as a mediator in cultic terms. Thus, very often he gives an allegoric interpretation of the high priest as symbolizing the Logos. This is the case, e.g., in *Quis rer*, 205f.: The Logos "both pleads with the immortal as suppliant for afflicted mortality and acts as ambassador of the ruler to the subject ...". To God

---

[25] Cf. GNILKA, *Kol, ad loc.*, who thinks that such ideas are not represented in the original hymn, though very well in its revised Colossian form.

[26] See lately ALETTI, *Colossiens*, 141ff. (+lit.).

[27] For my purpose I do not find it necessary to differentiate between the two concepts. See BURTON LEE MACK, *Logos und Sophia* (StUNT 10), Göttingen 1973, 96ff., 133ff. *et passim*.

[28] E.g., *Sir* 43:26; Philo, *Cher*, 36, 127; cf. *Wis.* 9:9; 7:12. See MACK, *Logos*, 71f., 144ff.

the Logos pledges "the creature that It should never altogether rebel against the rein and choose disorder rather than order". Over against the creation it warrants its "hopes that the merciful God will never forget his own work. For I am the harbinger of peace (says the Logos) to creation from that God whose will is to bring wars to an end, who is ever the guardian of peace".[29] We note that here also the motif of God as the peacemaker appears in connection with that of the mediating function of the Logos.

Thus, although our Col-text does not specifically mention the Logos, its idea of the Son's role as the mediator of creation seems to reflect a Logos (Wisdom) Christology, and such a Christology is also compatible, with the motif that through him God has reconciled the whole universe, making peace through the blood on his cross.

The motif of God as the peacemaker is worthy of some further considerations. Thus, E. Schweizer has stressed – as already mentioned – that a passage like the one from Quis rer reflects a Philonic, indeed Jewish, answer to a worldview according to which the world threatened to break down in the struggle among its elements: through his Logos God warrants the stability and peace of the world.[30] This aspect of the universal perspective certainly is important to Philo, and, as a matter of fact, the passage belongs to an extended discussion of the principle of a universal ἰσότης, beginning at Quis rer, 141.[31] In Col, however, the accents may be different. This will be further discussed below.

Another Philonic passage has played a role in the discussion concerning God's peacemaking in Col 1:20, viz., *Spec. Leg.*, II, 188ff. Lyonnet quoted it as a basis for his suggestion that the New Year celebrations could shed light on our Col-verse, and Schweizer has used it as another witness of Philo's manner of dealing with the *Brüchigkeit der Welt*.[32] In this text Philo comments on the *shophar* blasts of the Rosh ha-Shanah and first interprets them as a remembrance of the Sinai revelation. Then he remarks that "the trumpet is the instrument used in war" and finds symbolism in this as well:

"There is another war not of human agency when nature is at strife in herself, when her pans make onslaught one on another and her law-abiding sense of equality (ἰσότης) is vanquished by the greed for inequality ... the forces of nature use drought, rainstorms, violent moisture-laden winds, scorching sun-rays, intense cold accompanied by snow, with the regular harmonious alternations of the yearly seasons turned into disharmony, a state of things in my opinion due to the impiety which does not gain a gradual hold but comes rushing with the force of a torrent among those whom these things befall. And therefore the law instituted this feast figured by that instrument of war the trumpet ... to be as a thank-offering to God the peace-maker (εἰρηνοποιός) and peace-keeper

---

[29] See also, e.g., *Plant.*, 8–10; *Agr*, 50ff.

[30] SCHWEIZER, "Versöhnung".

[31] Philo is, by the way, eager to demonstrate that the principle in question has its origin with Moses, not with Heraclit (214).

[32] LYONNET, "L'hymne"; SCHWEIZER, "Versöhnung"; IDEM, *Kol, ad loc.* See also GNILKA, *Kol, ad loc.*

(εἰρηνοφύλαξ), who destroys faction both in cities and in the various parts of the universe and creates plenty and fertility and abundance of other good things and leaves the havoc of fruits without a single spark to be rekindled".

There are good reasons to assume that *Spec. Leg.*, II, 188ff. contains several echoes from the Jewish New Year feast, although it is very difficult to discern more precisely their outlines.[33] The idea of God's role as the supreme warranter of peace is, however, by no means confined to this New Year text and envisages more than the ἰσότης of the universe. In the ending of *Decal* (178), for example, Philo explains why there are no punishments coupled to the commandments of the decalogue in that he assigns the punishments of sinners to God's assessor (πάρεδρος) Justice (δίκη):

"But it benefits the Great King that the general safety of the universe should be ascribed to him, that he should be the guardian of peace (εἰρηνοφυλακῶν) and supply richly and abundantly the good things of peace, all of them to all persons in every place and at every time. For indeed God is the Prince of Peace (πρύτανις εἰρήνης) while his subalterns are the leaders in war".

Texts like these seem to presuppose that, somehow, universe and man stand together under moral obligation, and while the universe, in the form of planets, elements etc. always is loyal, man ist not. This brings us to a further aspect of Philo's view on cosmos, man and God, *viz.*, that of the right Logos (ὀρθὸς λόγος) as a rule. This may be of some interest to him who, like me, has taken Col 1:20 as saying "reconcile to him" = the Son who has been presented in Logos terms. So in *Opif*, 3 we read:

"The world is in harmony with the Law and the Law with the world ... the man who observes the Law is constituted thereby a loyal citizen of the world, regulating his doings by the purpose and will of Nature, in accordance with which the entire world itself also is administered".[34]

The true world-citizen, the moral man, follows the same constitution as the whole world, namely nature's right Logos (*Opif*, 143). So also the repentant soul is said to be reconciled with the right Logos (*Quod det*, 149; it finds καταλλαγή).

I have quoted Philo as a representative of a way of thinking which to a certain extent has the same basic perspective on the universe as has the author of Col 1:15–20. Both see themselves surrounded by a living cosmos, both believe in the One and Only God, the supreme peace-maker, both seem to assume that worship of that God has a universal bearing, both are convinced that God's Word or Wisdom is a supreme mediator between God and the world, in the "beginning" as well as when it comes to the relationship between God and creation in the present. Both seem to believe that God's Word represents a code by which

---

[33] See LYONNET, "L'hymne"; LARS HARTMAN, *Asking for a Meaning* (CB.NT 12), Lund 1979, 103ff. (+lit.).

[34] See also, e.g., *Migr*, 130; *Vit. Mos.*, II,48. These ideas, of course, have Stoic counterparts; see JOHANNES VON ARNIM, *Stoicorum Veterum Fragmenta* I, Leipzig 1903, 262; Diogenes Laertius, VI, 63; VII, 87.

"the all", man included, must live. There are, of course, also differences between Philo and our author, the principal one being that the latter was convinced that God's Logos or Wisdom had been incarnate in Jesus. Another difference is that Philo is a philosopher, although as such he does not forget his religion. He reflects on the threatened ἰσότης of the universe, but does not sharply distinguish the question of the relationships of the elements to God and his Logos from that of man's place before God. This holds true when he pictures the high priest's service and the mediation of the Logos, as well as when he discusses the peace: Note, e.g., how, in the passage on the New Year celebration, Philo assumes that the disturbance in the climate is due to man's ἀνομία. In so linking man together with "the all" he is not too different from our Christian author.[35] But to the philosopher Philo the peace between the universal powers seems to belong to the world of theories to a larger extent than do the problems caused by the thrones, sovereignties etc. which lie behind Col 1. So a decisive difference seems to be that while Philo envisages a peace which is warranted in eternity by God the creator, the Christian author, on the other hand, thinks that through Jesus' death and resurrection a change has taken place in the universe, and that a peace is established through Jesus that was not previously there.

The reason why one investigates the background of a text is to clarify the contents of the text. Accordingly I will now try to develop a few aspects of Col 1:20 in the light of the suggestions of the preceding pages.[36]

## 4. The Content of Col 1:15–20

One important aspect of all Logos or Wisdom speculation[37] is the notion of a mediation between a transcendent God and a world that is dependent on him. This mediation is seen from man's point of view, through which, on the one hand, man finds an active and divine reason or purpose behind that which exists and happens. On the other hand, man can become aquainted with this mediating divine reason, he can take part of it so that he is drawn into the divine sphere. The Wisdom, being "a breath of the power of God", "passes into holy souls and makes them friends of God" (*Wisd* 7:25.27). Thus Logos or Wisdom speculation implies the idea of divine self-communication, of revelation, of salvation through revelation, etc.

---

[35] If I read SCHWEIZER right ("Versöhnung"), he understands Philo differently.
[36] There are certainly others, which, however, I leave aside, not least those pertaining to the exaltation/ vindication motifs in early Christologies, often connected with a Son-Christology – see MARTIN HENGEL, *Der Sohn Gottes*, Tübingen ²1977, 93ff.
[37] For the following see MACK, *Logos*, 184f.

Now Col 1:15–20 presupposes that the absolute Being in, under and behind everything, the "Fullness",[38] communicated itself[39] according to its creative will. So it did and so it does in creation, but also in the person of Jesus, in his life, and, not least, in his death and resurrection – in the wording of v. 20: God made peace "through the blood of his cross". That Jesus died through crucifixion, the *mors turpissima*, was a gruesome fact that must necessarily have been a *scandalon* to man in Antiquity,[40] and it must have influenced the Christian reflection on its meaning.

To regard the person of Jesus in this way requires the conviction that his person and career represented a total dedication to God and his will, for otherwise he could hardly be identified with the divine Logos or Wisdom. There are indications that the historical Jesus meant that God wanted him to live and die for others.[41] Paul also thought that this attitude was typical of Jesus (see, e.g., Rom 15:3; 2 Cor 8:9), and the author of Col seems to be of a similar opinion. The way in which the apostolic mission is presented in Col 1:24 is a sign of that view of his, and so is the catalogue of virtues in 3:12ff.

This being so, we may imagine what, in the eyes of our author, was an essential feature of God's Logos, made manifest in Jesus. One might dare say that the divine Logos or Wisdom, or, using a less technical expression, the active principle in and behind the all, appeared also as a principle of total dedication to God and to fellowmen. This was what real manhood should be, and this was a manifestation of what the Fullness was like. According to our writer that was the reason why Jesus' death was not the end; for a death in such a spirit became a death unto God. Thus his death was also a birth, as the author of Col says: *Because* the fullness dwelt in him and reconciled all things, he is the firstborn from the dead (1:18).

At this point we should also note that the Logos-Wisdom categories invite us to regard God as the ultimate subject behind the work of the Logos/Wisdom. It was the εὐδοκία of the Fullness to reconcile and make peace through his death. Thus, on the one hand, Jesus was a man who dedicated himself to God and fellowmen, on the other the reconciliation that was so achieved was the work of the Fullness. It seems that the second view includes the first one without eliminating the acts of will that belong to such a commitment of self.[42] The Logos/Wisdom categories thus serve to underline that the principle made manifest in

---

[38] Cf. Philo, *Leg. All.*, III, 4: "God fills and penetrates all things" (πάντα πεπλήρωκεν ὁ θεός). Also, e.g., *Som*, II,221. See JOSEF ERNST, *Pleroma und Pleroma Christi* (BU 5), Regensburg 1970, esp. chaps. 2 and 3. Further lit. in ALETTI, *Colossiens*, 77.

[39] Cf. the role played by the knowledge of God in, e.g., 1:9f.; 2:2f.; 3:10.

[40] See MARTIN HENGEL, *Crucifixion*, London 1977.

[41] See lately MARTIN HENGEL, *The Atonement*, London 1981, 71ff. with references, and, not least, HEINZ SCHÜRMANN, *Jesu ureigener Tod*, Freiburg i. Br. – Basel – Wien ²1976.

[42] For further discussion, which rather belongs to the field of systematic theology, see, e.g., JOHN MACQUARRIE, *Principles of Christian Theology*, London ²1977, 290ff., 311ff. [Cf. HANS HÜBNER, *An Philemon, An die Kolosser, An die Epheser* (HNT 12), Tübingen 1997, 63.]

Jesus' person and work is really divine and that it really becomes a means of divine self-communication.

Now the Christ-event also meant that the principle that was made manifest became the rule of the universe in a way it had not been before. Our author is namely of the opinion that the Christ-event brought with it a change in the position of the all, to be compared to the change of the situation of the addressees ("you too …"; v. 21). This raises a couple of questions. Does the author mean that, e.g., the actual situation of the planets has been changed through Christ? And how can he see the realities around himself and believe that all things are reconciled with this Logos, are pacified and brought into harmony with this principle?[43]

Of course, to answer such questions, one must employ some guesswork. Still, as to the first question asked, we should again remind ourselves of the common view that, e.g., the planets were living creatures, belonging to the same world as man. Further, in the writer's mode of thinking (the Logos categories included) the focus is on man, so that even when talking of the all, he talks of the all as related to man. Accordingly, an answer to the question concerning the planets could be: Yes, the Christ event has changed their situation in so far as, if anyone is afraid of them or of their ability to influence his destiny, he should know that the real power and the deepest divine principle of the world is the one he is ruled by, Christ's.[44] The "peace" is not one between two equal parts, but one forcefully brought about by a triumphant victor (cf. Col 2:15).

In suggesting an answer to the second question, concerning how realistic our author is, we may once more consider his focus, which is on man and on man's relationship to God. He seems to talk of cosmos and its different powers and principles only to say that God's active purpose, made incarnate in Christ, is stronger than they, and that, fundamentally, they are to yield to this purpose. In its turn this is said in order that the addressees realize that they should be ruled by Christ, not by any other principle, tendency or power, although such demand to be respected.

Thus, facing the gruesome realities of evil, our author has not solved the problem of the earthquake in Lisbon. We should also note, however, that the Logos/Wisdom aspects in Col 1:20 also imply a nuance of hope. The revelation of God's Logos indicates a pattern of love that already prevails in those circumstances when God's reign holds sway among men and elsewhere in creation. But one also expects that this pattern, somehow, will prevail throughout. This dimension of hope is indicated by the nuance of direction in the εἰς αὐτόν of 1:15–20: "All things are created unto him", and "all things are reconciled to/ unto him". The possible tension between the two renderings is minimized when

---

[43] Cf. Gnilka, *Kol*, *ad loc.*

[44] Cf. how Paul, in his triumphant "not any power or height or depth … can separate us from the love of God in Christ Jesus our Lord" (Rom 8:38f.), may very well refer to astrology (thus Hans Lietzmann, *An die Römer* [HNT 8], Tübingen ⁵1971, *ad loc.*).

that with which one is reconciled is also described as a purpose, such as we have done with the Logos. The divine purpose, through which all things came into being (v. 16), still is there as the purpose that is a gravitation point of all things. In the present, man looks forward, waiting for the fulfilment of this purpose. But the pattern of love and divine generosity is also a task: "Put on, as the elect of God and beloved, sincere compassion, kindness, humility ... and over all these put on love" (3:12ff.).

The preceding pages represent an attempt to deal with Col 1:20 not primarily as the upshot of a revision of another text (which it might very well be!), but as a text that in its present shape makes use of and for its understanding presupposes ideas from its cultural environment. It seems to me that the Philonic ways of thinking of the Logos represent such ideas. They are certainly not the only ones behind our text, but I hope I have shown that they or similar opinions probably belong to the background of Col's motif of the reconciliation of the all, *viz.*, a background, the knowledge of which can promote our understanding of the text.

## 25. Code and Context
### A Few Reflections on the Paraenesis of Col 3:6–4:1

During the last decade or so, New Testament scholarly discussions have revealed a renewed interest in the so-called household codes, especially the two NT texts which deserve this designation, *viz.* Col 3:18–4:1 and Eph 5:22–6:9.[1] One reason is, of course, that the feminist movement has increased the embarrassment many exegetes have felt regarding the admonitions that wives be submissive.[2] Another is that new suggestions have been made in terms of background material, *viz.* the so-called household management traditions, and, as a matter of fact, these have also been used when it has come to grappling with the hermeneutic problems posed by the texts. In this paper some of these new insights will be combined with older suggestions concerning the possible role played by the Decalogue[3] in the context of the Colossian household code. In addition, this will be carried out with respect to the argument of Colossians. I find it natural to dedicate this article to Professor Ellis, as it touches upon a field of research on which he has done so much significant work, *viz.* the investigation of the use of the OT in early Christian history and traditions.[4]

### 1. History of Research

It has been a widely spread opinion that the household code of Col 3:18–4:1 is a textual unit that was formulated before Col was written. Its style is different from that of the surrounding paraenesis, and if one should withdraw it, the text would flow smoothly all the same. If, then, the passage is a loan, from where has it been borrowed? Furthermore, what, if anything, does that tell us about the history of

---

[1] Other texts referred to as household codes are: 1 Pet 2:18–3:7 (which does not deal with the whole household). 1 Tim 2:8–15; Titus 2:1–10; *Did.* 4:9–11; *Barn* 19:5–7; *1 Clem* 21:6–9; Pol. *Phil.* 4:2–6:3 are no real household codes. [See further literature below in note 40.]

[2] E.g., DAVID L. BALCH, "Early Christian Criticism of Patriarchal Authority: 1 Peter 2:11–3:12". *UnSemQuartRev* 39 (1984) 161–173.

[3] Contemporary Jews counted the commandments of the Decalogue in such a way that the one against making graven images became number two, and the one on honoring one's parents number five, the last of the first table. In this paper I will follow this way of counting. The Decalogue has been drawn into the discussion of the household code by ROBERT M. GRANT, "The Decalogue in Early Christianity", *HThR* 40 (1947) 1–17, and PETER STUHLMACHER, "Christliche Verantwortung bei Paulus und seinen Schülern", *EvTh* 28 (1968) 165–186, esp. 177–178.

[4] E.g., E. EARLE ELLIS, *Paul's Use of the Old Testament*, Edinburgh 1957; IDEM, *Prophecy and Hermeneutic in Early Christianity. New Testament Essays* (WUNT 18), Tübingen 1978, chaps. 9–17.

the Early Church and about its relationship to the surrounding world? Finally, how does the household code function within the framework of the letter, and what is its function with regard to the situation of the addressees?[5]

The questions of the preceding paragraph have received different answers among NT scholars.[6] Thus, Martin Dibelius held (1913)[7] that behind the "Haustafeln" lay a "schema", which was originally Stoic and visible in the way such philosophers organized their discussions of what was "fitting" (*kathēkon*) "towards the gods, one's parents, one's brothers, one's country, and towards foreigners" (Epict. *Diss.* 2.17.31). He saw the Church's adoption of this pattern as a sign that it was on the way to abandoning the eschatological perspective which was thought to characterize its attitude from the beginning, and was adjusting itself to a life in this world.

Fifteen years later Karl Weidinger elaborated Dibelius' ideas, presenting more material from the philosophers as well as from Judaism.[8] "Hellenistic Judaism"[9] had also used the "schema", and he thought that it was possibly the milieu from which the Christians got it. But, in addition, the Christians assumed not only the "schema" but also the very texts themselves, at least in the case of the code of Col 3:18–4:1. They merely Christianized the code by adding "in the Lord" at suitable places.

Dibelius' and Weidinger's ideas dominated the understanding of the household codes for several decades. In 1972, however, J. E. Crouch went through the material again.[10] He too assumed an "Hellenistic" origin of the codes, and thought that "Hellenistic Judaism" had had a decisive influence.[11] However, he criticized Dibelius and Weidinger for simplifying the problem of the role played by the

---

[5] One could use different terms for these two "functions". In another context I have distinguished between a literary (or illocutionary) and sociolinguistic function (LARS HARTMAN, "Survey of the Problem of Apocalyptic Genre", in *Apocalypticism in the Mediterranean World and the Near East*, ed. by DAVID HELLHOLM, Proceedings of the International Colloquium on Apocalypticism, Uppsala, August 12–17, 1979, Tübingen 1983, 329–343, §§ 3.3.1 and 3.3.2.), but I here follow the terminology of D. Hellholm, preferring "(text-) internal" and "(text-) external" (DAVID HELLHOLM, "The Apocalyptic Genre: The case of the Apocalypse of John", in: *IDEM New Testament and Textlinguistics. A Theoretical Approach to Early Christian Narrative*, Tübingen forthcoming, § 3.3.3.2).

[6] For a discussion of the scholarly debate see JAMES E. CROUCH, *The Origin and Intention of the Colossian Haustafel* (FRLANT 109), Göttingen 1972, chap. 1, and DAVID L. BALCH, *Let Wives be Submissive: The Domestic Code in 1 Peter*, SBL Monogr. Ser. 26, Chico, Calif. 1981, chap. 1.

[7] MARTIN DIBELIUS, *An die Kolosser, Epheser, an Philemon* (HNT 12), ed. by HEINRICH GREEVEN, Tübingen ³1953, 48–50.

[8] KARL WEIDINGER, *Die Haustafeln. Ein Stück urchristlicher Paränese* (UNT 14), Leipzig 1928.

[9] Although I use this traditional expression (because the cited authors do so), the quotation marks are there to mark that I would rather replace it by "Greek speaking, largely non-Palestinian Judaism" or something similar.

[10] CROUCH, *Origin and Intention*.

[11] ERNST LOHMEYER *Die Briefe an die Philipper, an die Kolosser und an Philemon* (KEK 9), by WERNER SCHMAUCH, Göttingen ⁹1953; (the 8th ed., the first one written by Lohmeyer, appeared in 1930) also held the opinion that Col 3:18–4:1 was a pre-Colossian unit, but regarded it as being of purely Jewish origin. In so doing, he did not ask so much for the provenance of a "schema" as for the root system of the ideas.

eschatological expectations. Weidinger was also accused of being too quick to generalize, both in terms of the pre-Christian Stoic-Cynic *and* Jewish material, as well as when it came to the Christian codes.

Others have claimed that the household codes had a purely Christian origin. Thus, H. Rengstorf has derived them from an early Christian interest in the *oikos*.[12] A partly similar opinion concerning the origin is held by David Schroeder.[13] He finds the roots of the *form* in OT apodictic law *and* in Stoic lists of the stations in life. But "the content is drawn from the OT, Judaic tradition, although with the addition of certain Greek (what is fitting) and Christian *(agapē)* concepts. The basic ethical conception of the NT codes – that without belonging to the world as such, one has responsibilities within the structure of society – takes us back to the teaching and example of Jesus himself."

The second half of the 1970's brought a new stage in research on the codes: instead of having parallels in the *kathēkon*-lists, the "stations" addressed in the codes, as well as some of the advice found in them, were seen as having clearer parallels in the philosophical treatises from Plato and Aristotle onwards, which dealt with household management, *oikonomia* or *oikonomos*.[14] Regarding the NT household codes in the light of this tradition led to new suggestions of what the Church was actually doing with its household codes. D. Lührmann saw therein a latent claim of the Christians that the Christian house was a model for society.[15] D. C. Balch concluded, having especially 1 Pet in mind, that "the code has an apologetic function in the historical context: the paraenesis is given in light of outside criticism", *viz*. from persons who "were alienated and threatened by some of their slaves and wives who had converted to the new, despised religion, so they were accusing the converts of impiety, immorality, and insubordination".[16] K. Müller seems to suggest something similar: the early Christians lived in a society, in which some people, including some women, questioned the age-old subordination system of the "house", whereas others wanted to hold on to or to reinforce the good old authoritative pattern. In such a situation "the oldest household code

---

[12] KARL HEINRICH RENGSTORF, "Die neutestamentlichen Mahnungen an die Frau, sich dem Manne unterzuordnen", in *Verbum Dei manet in aeternum: Festschrift O. Schmitz*, ed. by WILHELM FOERSTER, Witten 1953, 131–145.

[13] DAVID SCHROEDER, "Lists, ethical", *IDBSup*. 1976, 546–547. His unpublished Hamburg dissertation from 1959 dealt with the household codes, their origin and their theological meaning. It has not been available to me.

[14] DIETER LÜHRMANN, "Wo man nicht mehr Sklave oder Freier ist", *Wort und Dienst*, NF 13 (1975), 58–83; IDEM, "Neutestamentliche Haustafeln und antike Ökonomie", *NTS* 27 (1980/81) 83–97; KLAUS THRAEDE, "Ärger mit der Freiheit", in *"Freunde in Christus werden …"*, ed. by GERTA SCHARFFENORTH/ KLAUS THRAEDE, Gelnhausen – Berlin • Stein 1977, 31–182; IDEM, "Zum historischen Hintergrund der ‚Haustafeln' des NT", in: *Pietas Festschrift für B. Kötting*, ed. by ERNST DASSMANN/K. SUSO FRANK — JAC, Erg. bd. 8, 1980, Munich 1980, 359–368; BALCH, *Wives Be Submissive*, after a Yale dissertation in 1974; KARLHEINZ MÜLLER, "Die Haustafel des Kolosserbriefes und das antike Frauenthema", in: *Die Frau im Urchristentum*, ed. by GERHARD DAUTZENBERG/HULMUT MERKLEIN/KARLHEINZ MÜLLER (QD 95), Freiburg i. Br. – Basel – Vienna 1983, 263–319, esp. 284–290.

[15] LÜHRMANN, *NTS* 27 (1980/81) 86.

[16] BALCH, *Wives Be Submissive*, 109.

of the NT demonstrates ... a highly respectable early Christian decision in favor of a middle course of social morality".[17]

## 2. The Text in Its Context

After this short review of some answers to the questions raised in the beginning of this paper,[18] let us turn to the text itself, first considering its context in the literary sense of the word.

As I see it, Col has a more hortatory character than one often assumes. This is seen not least from the fact that the author reverts to the second person when summoning the addressees.[19] The Christologically loaded passages of 1:13–20 and 2:9–15 serve as bases for admonition; in 1:21–23 this is indicated indirectly, whereas 2:16–23 is directly addressed to the believers. To concentrate on the second instance, this part of the letter begins with 1:24–2:5. It functions as a *captatio benevolentiae* which is partly realized by tying bonds of affection between "Paul"[20] and the addressees. Then, an introductory exhortation follows in 2:6–8: "walk in him ... as you were taught ... See to it that nobody carries you away captive ... according to the principles of the world *(ta stoicheia tou kosmou)*, not according to Christ". This leads *(hoti)* directly into the Christological basis, 2:9–15, which is applied in the following admonition of 2:16–23: "thus *(oun)*, nobody must judge you in terms of food or drink ... If you died with Christ from the principles of the world, why do you allow rules to be laid on you: do not touch ...". The whole section of 1:24–2:23 becomes the background against which positive ethical teaching is given in 3:1–4:6. In a sense 2:6–7 ("walk in him as you were taught") becomes specified in 3:1–4, and the life with Christ (3:1, 3) and the heavenly mind (3:2) are placed over against the human and this-worldly rules (2:8, 14, 16, 20–23) and the earthly mind (3:2), for which the "philosophers" stand.

3:1–4 opens up the general Christologically determined perspective for the ethics. Then, in 3:5–4:6 more particular instructions follow. Regarded in this way, the paraenesis in 3:1–4:6 is not only a section added to the theological parts of the letter, but rather something that has been prepared for almost from the beginning of the letter (cf. "knowledge of his will", 1:9).

We need not discuss the details of how the instruction of 3:5–4:6 is construed,[21] but only state that 3:5–17 is largely made up of catalogues of vices and virtues with a tendency of grouping them by fives. 3:16 deals with worship, and 3:17 is

---

[17] MÜLLER, "Die Haustafel", 290.

[18] Müller's article contains a broader and slightly peppered review of the research. The strictly literary and form-critical questions have largely been left aside here. I deal with them in my contribution to the Festschrift for H. C. Kee: ["Some Unorthodox Thoughts on the Household Code Form", repr. in LARS HARTMAN, *Text-Centered New Testament Studies* (WUNT 102), Tübingen 1997, 179–194].

[19] See 1:9–12, 21–23, 2:4, 6–8, 10, 16, 18, 20.

[20] I assume that the author is a member of Paul's school.

[21] See, e.g. the literature referred to and the discussion in JOACHIM GNILKA, *Der Kolosserbrief* (HThK 10:1), Freiburg i. Br. – Basel – Vienna 1980, *ad loc.*

often understood as a summarizing conclusion: "whatever you do in word and deed, do it all in the name of Lord Jesus, thanking God the Father through him". However, since the following household code starts without any connecting conjunction or particle, and because of the seven occurrences of "the Lord" in the code, 3:17 also becomes a bridge to the household code; indeed, it might very well be regarded as its introduction.[22]

As already mentioned, however, the code appears like an island in its context. The shift in style is one factor contributing to this effect, *viz.* the direct address, "You wives", etc., and the shape of the admonitions (address + imperative + motivation). Furthermore, it is tightly held together by its reference to the household.

After the household code, the style in 4:2 is once again more similar to that in 3:5-17, and these admonitions have a concluding character inasmuch as they contain several echoes from the preceding text. Such observations would seemingly confirm Lohmeyer's opinion *(ad loc.)* that "one could hardly surmise that there were a gap if this passage were blotted out".

Of course one could assume, then, as does Lohmeyer, that there must have been something in the Colossians' situation that demanded the insertion of this text. This might very well be so, but that does not make it unnecessary to consider the possibility I mentioned at the outset, *viz.* that the Decalogue might have something to do with this parenetic section, the household code included.

## 3. The Decalogue as a Structuring Factor

As a matter of fact, the Decalogue is a structuring factor in several ethical catalogues.[23] Mark 7:21-22 is a Christian example: fornication, theft, murder, adultery, coveting, wickedness, deceit, licentiousness, evil eye, slander, pride, foolishness. The parallel text in Matt 15:19 brings the text even closer to the OT: murder, adultery, fornication, theft, false witness, slander. 1 Tim 1:8-10 is another NT instance:[24] "lawless and disobedient, ungodly and sinners, unholy and profane, murderers of fathers and murderers of mothers, manslayers, fornicators, sodomites, kidnappers, liars, perjurers …" There are echoes of the Decalogue in Jew-

---

[22] As a matter of fact the three cases of *kai* introducing a main clause in vv. 15-17 are a little strange: cf. WALTER BUJARD, *Stilanalytische Untersuchungen zum Kolosserbrief als Beitrag zur Methodik von Sprachvergleichen* (SUNT 11), Göttingen 1973, 42. GNILKA, *Kolosserbrief*, 198, concludes that they are to be explained through the assumption that "in 3:15-17 Einzelmahnungen zusammengestellt sind". It would, however, fit well with my suggestions below, if v. 15 begins a reinterpretation of the sabbath-commandment (sabbath-rest-peace). The idea that v. 17 introduces the household instruction, which covers "everything" a man could be, is supported by, e.g. Seneca, *ep.* 94.1, in which he describes what is contained in a household management treatise: *eam partem philosophiae, quae dat propria cuique personae praecepta…!*

[23] KLAUS BERGER, *Gesetzesauslegung Jesu I*, Neukirchen 1972, 272-273.

[24] See GRANT, *HThR* 40 (1947) 7. Cf. ANTON VÖGTLE, *Die Tugend- und Lasterkataloge exegetisch, religions- und formgeschichtlich untersucht* (NTAbh 16, 4-5), Münster 1936, 16: SIEGFRIED WIBBING, *Die Tugend- und Lasterkataloge im NT und ihre Traditionsgeschichte unter besonderer Berücksichtigung der Qumran-Texte* (BZNW 25), Berlin 1959, 83.

ish, non-Palestinian texts as well, e.g. *Sib. Or.* 4.24–39: "love the great god (in contrast to worshiping idols, 25–30), ... no murder, ... no dishonest gain, ... no desire for another's spouse or for abuse of a male ..." Similarly in the beginning of the ethical admonitions of Pseudo-Phocylides (3–21): "do not commit adultery, homosexuality, treachery, nor stain your hands with blood; do not become rich unjustly ... be content with what you have and abstain from what is another's, do not tell lies ..., honor God foremost, and afterward your parents, ... flee false witness ... , do not commit perjury, ... do not steal seeds, ... give the laborer his pay."[25] In passing we may note that the order between the commandments is not always the same, and there are more examples of this than Mark 15:19.[26]

With the examples of the preceding paragraph in mind one is immediately prepared to endorse Gnilka's supposition in his commentary on Colossians[27] that the two vice catalogues of Col 3:5 and 8 are dependent on the Decalogue: "fornication, impurity, passion, evil desire, and covetousness, which is idolatry", and: "anger, wrath, malice, slander, foul talk". I would also add the beginning of v. 9: "do not lie to (or, about) one another". Counting (with, e.g., Philo) the image-commandment as the second one, and taking hatred and murder as equal (Matt 5:21–22, 1 John 3:15), we see that numbers 2, 6, 7, 8, 9 and 10 of the Decalogue have counterparts in Col 3:5–9.[28] The application and interpretation of the commandments, visible in the lists of Col 3, have several parallels in Jewish texts.[29]

As a contrast, 3:10–4:1 presents the life of the New Man. The description of this New Man begins with the characteristic "neither Greek nor Jew". I find it natural to combine this detail with the abundant epithets applied to the addressees in the subsequent verse, "God's elect, holy and beloved". Commentators state that the author here transfers classical designations of God's people to the addressees.[30] However, in this context it is appropriate to remember that Israel's election and holiness was closely connected with the covenant and the Law (e.g. Exod 19:5–6; Lev 19; Deut 4:37–40)," and that the covenant and the Divine Revelation were expressions of God's love for His people (e.g., Deut 4:37; 7:8). In Col 3, however, God's elect are those in the New Man, in whom there is neither Greek

---

[25] BERGER, *Gesetzesauslegung Jesu*, 374, is not prepared to hear any echos from the Decalogue here, but cf. MAX KÜCHLER, *Frühjüdische Weisheitstraditionen* (OBO 26), Freiburg (CH) • Göttingen 1979, 277–279. [Cf. WALTER T. WILSON, *The Sentence of Pseudo-Phocylides* (CEJL), Berlin – New York 2005, 73–83.]

[26] BERGER, *Gesetzesauslegung Jesu*, 275–276.

[27] GNILKA, *Kolosserbrief*, 185.

[28] The *blasphēmia* of v. 8 should hardly be taken as based on the commandment against taking the Name in vain.

[29] See BERGER, *Gesetzesauslegung Jesu*, chap. 4. There are indications to the effect that the Decalogue had a central place in the synagogue worship in the times of the Early Church. That this position of the Decalogue changed is often assumed to have taken place because of the Christian usage of the Decalogue. See GRANT, *HThR* 40 (1947).

[30] E.g. EDVIN LARSSON, *Christus als Vorbild* (ASNU 23), Lund 1962, 210; EDUARD LOHSE, *Die Briefe an die Kolosser und an Philemon* (KEK 9:2), Göttingen [14]1968, *ad loc.*; EDUARD SCHWEIZER, *Der Brief an die Kolosser* (EKK 12), Neukirchen-Vluyn 1976, *ad loc.*

nor Jew. But, precisely as in the case of Israel, the election is bound up with duties, with "putting on" a particular sort of life.

Certainly the "put on" of 3:12 is the positive counterpart to the "put off" of 3:5. But one cannot put the virtues of vv 12–14 in a one-to-one contrast to the vices of 3:5–9. i.e., as precise positive instructions implied in the prohibitions as they have been re-phrased and interpreted in the vice lists. Many Christians are used to reading the Decalogue in such a way, and may therefore be too ready to hear echoes from the Decalogue also behind the positive admonitions. Thus, e.g., Lutherans learn in Luther's classical small catechism that the commandment against false testimony means: "We should fear and love God, and so we should not tell lies about our neighbor, nor betray, slander, or defame him, but should apologize for him, speak well of him, and interpret charitably all that he does". In the Office of Instruction of the Episcopal Church we hear of the duties towards one's neighbor as brought forward by the tenth commandment: "Not to covet nor desire other men's goods; But to learn and labor truly to earn mine own living, And to do my duty in that state of life unto which it shall please God to call me".

When Philo comments on the Decalogue, there is not much of this sort of discovery of implicitly commanded virtues, but in the catalogue I just cited from Pseudo-Phocylides we come across a similar tendency to add a "but" to the prohibitions: "do not become rich unjustly, *but* live from honorable means, ... do not tell lies, *but* always speak the truth" (5, 7) (*alla* and *de*, respectively).

In Col 3 the virtues are not, as we noted, directly related to the individual items of the vice lists, but nonetheless one could say that they counter the transgressions of the commandments concerning murder, stealth, false witness and covetousness as the author of Col has interpreted them. Like his master, Paul, and following Jesus, he also regards love as the all-embracing commandment (3:14; Matt 5:43–48; Mark 12:28–33; Rom 13:8–10, etc.).

So far we have traced nothing from the first five commandments (except for idolatry in 3:5), including the one concerning parents. Nor has the one on adultery, such as the author interpreted it, been given any positive counterpart in 3:12–17. It seems to me that this lack is met in the household code of 3:18–4:1. But before delineating this let me point to the possibility that even the Sabbath commandment lies behind a piece of the paraenesis in Col 3.

The author certainly has nothing but contempt for the "philosophers'" ceremonial rules concerning "a feast, a new moon or a sabbath" (2:16). But there are traces of Jewish speculations on the Sabbath and its deeper meaning, which, in my opinion, a writer who held the sort of cosmic wisdom-Christology we encounter in Col could use for an interpretation of the Sabbath commandment. Thus, Philo explains the meaning of "sabbath" as "rest" (*anapausis*; see *Abr.* 28). He finds this very fitting, for number seven "is always free from factions and war and quarrelling and is of all numbers the most peaceful". Indeed, as a matter of fact, to real lovers of wisdom the whole of life is a feast, for they always strive for "a life free from war and peaceful" (*Spec. leg.* 2.45). Furthermore, to Philo, but even more to Aristobulos, the number seven is something like a basic principle to the All which becomes manifest in the celebration of the seventh day.[31] To a philosophically minded Christian interpreter of the Sabbath commandment this might become a point of departure for a reference to the "peace of Christ" with this followed by some advice that Christ's word should dwell among the addressees and that they should teach each other and praise God. The study and the teaching of the Scriptures are, as is well known, of central importance to Philo when he describes the Sabbath,[32] and to his fellow Jews as well. The picture Philo gives of prayers, singing, and instruction at the Sabbath worship of the Therapeuts[33] is not too distant from Col 3:16.[34]

Whether there be any intimations of the fourth commandment behind 3:15–16 or not, to anyone who has felt that the commandment concerning parents should not be left out of consideration, and that the one on adultery should also be addressed with positive admonitions, this feeling of something lacking would be satisfied in the household code, 3:18–4:1. But did anybody – author and/or reader – feel that lack and then regard 3:18–4:1 as complying with it?

It may be of some importance to an answer to that question that, e.g., Philo understood the fifth commandment as covering the laws which "deal with the relations of old to young, rulers to subjects, benefactors to benefited, slaves to masters" (*Decal.* 165).[35] He also saw parents and masters as, in some respects, being gods to the other members of the house (*Decal.* 107–120; *Spec. leg.* 2.225–227), which gives an extra echo to the references to "the Lord" in the household code: being obedient "pleases the Lord" (3:20), and the slaves are to serve as it were to the Lord (3:23). That is, if 3:20–4:1 somehow represents the fifth commandment, it does so in a way that was found in contemporary Judaism. Also in favor of a positive answer to my question, there is the fact that, when the author of Eph uses Col 3:20,[36] he finds it natural to insert an explicit quotation of the fifth commandment (Eph 6:2–3).[37]

Philo did not include the relationship between wife and husband in that which was covered by the fifth commandment. Nonetheless, it is undeniable that

---

[31] MARTIN HENGEL, *Judaism and Hellenism I*, Philadelphia, Penn. 1974, 166–169.

[32] *Decal.* 98, 100; *Spec. Leg.* 2.62; *Prob.* 82; cf. Euseb. *Praep. ev.* 8.7, 12–13.

[33] *Vit. Cont.* 29, 75–80.

[34] A scholar who is more fanciful than I might even be prepared to combine 3:17, about doing everything in the name of the Lord Jesus, with the commandment concerning God's name. I would be hesitant, though, and prefer seeing the verse as introducing the code, which covers "everything" one does as an individual; see note 22 above.

[35] Similarly in *Spec. Leg.* 2.226–227. Cf. CROUCH, *Origin and Intention*, 78–79, who criticizes Schroeder's thesis concerning the role of the Decalogue. *Sib. Or.* 2.278, also includes servants who turn against their masters among those who transgress this commandment.

[36] Cf. HELMUT MERKLEIN, "Eph 4,1–5,20 als Rezeption von Kol 3,1–17 (zugleich ein Beitrag zur Problematik des Epheserbriefes)", in: *Kontinuität und Einheit, Festschrift für F. Mussner*, Freiburg 1981b, 194–210.

[37] Some modern authors are positive in finding the Decalogue in the background, see note 3 above.

it provides the positive instruction that would give the other side of the coin also in the case of the adultery commandment. On the other hand we have to realize that the contents certainly have some parallels in the surrounding world, but not, as far as I know,[38] in connection with an explanation of the prohibition of adultery. Accordingly, we should either assume that our text represents an innovation in terms of Decalogue interpretation, or that the code derives its contents from reasons other than the author's wish to reinterpret and apply two commandments of the Decalogue.

It is possible that the alternatives are too harshly stated in the preceding paragraph. At least it may seem so, if we supplement our discussion of the contents with some literary and form-critical observations. There are good reasons to assume that the code is a pre-Colossian unit, or, rather, that it is written in accordance with traditional turns of phrase.[39] Its coherence and the difference in style as compared to the context have been mentioned above, and its coherence is not only stylistic, but also caused by the thought pattern of the "house". Accordingly, I would suggest that the author does not draw upon a ready made development of the commandments about honoring parents and not committing adultery. Rather, when composing this paraenesis with all its echoes of and interpretative applications of the Decalogue, he used this (partly pre-formulated?) code which was structured according to the role system of the "house". Thus, in the Col-context it came to fulfill the function of applying parts of the Decalogue to God's elected and beloved people, in whom there was neither Greek nor Jew.[40]

I have argued above that the paraenesis of 3:1–4:1 is not merely added to a "theological" part of the letter, but rather that Col as a whole has a more exhortatory character than is often realized. But the echoes of the Decalogue, of the Law in some sense of the word, is something also met with in Paul (Rom 13:8–10).[41] Our author had, however, not simply learned from his master that letters to Christian communities should have a paraenesis. The phenomenon was not exclusively Pauline – in the NT 1 Pet, Jas and Heb follow a similar line. It is often held that most of the *material* that is parenetic in a form-critical sense has a non-Christian origin, *viz.* in Judaism and popular Philosophy.[42] Our deliberations above have not falsified that opinion. I would, however, suggest that the

---

[38] Such a well informed author as BERGER (*Gesetzesauslegung Jesu*) does not refer to any interpretation of that kind either.

[39] [Cf. ERNEST BEST, "The Haustafel, in Ephesians (Eph. 5.22–6.9)", in: IDEM, *Essays on Ephesians*, Edinburgh 1997, 189–203: esp. 196f.; IDEM, *Ephesians* (ICC), Edinburgh 1997a, 519–527: esp. 521; GERHARD SELLIN, *Der Brief an die Epheser* (KEK 8), Göttingen 2008, 424–471; DAVID HELLHOLM, "Die Gattung Haustafel im Kolosser- und Epheserbrief", in: PETER MÜLLER (ed.), *Kolosser-Studien* (BThSt 103), Neukirchen-Vluyn 2009, 103–128: esp. 103–112.]

[40] If CROUCH *Origin and Intention*, 79, and BALCH, *Wives Be Submissive*, 53, cite Schroeder's theses correctly, the latter binds the code to the Decalogue in a way that is quite different from my approach.

[41] Cf. STUHLMACHER, *EvTh* 28 (1968) 169–171.

[42] PHILIPP VIELHAUER, *Geschichte der urchristlichen Literatur* (DLB), Berlin – New York 1975, 53–55.

*practice* of admonishing one's addressees to hold on to the morals they had learnt is a tradition from Judaism. Thus, the Epistle of Baruch (*2 Bar* 78–86) is an example of a "letter" which should be read in the assemblies of the addressees (86), and in chapter 84 the author instructs them in different ways to keep faithfully to the Law. This invites us to conclude that the author of Col followed a convention not only when he concluded his letter with a paraenesis, but also when he did so by using material that to such a large extent was interpretation and application of the Law, in this case, the Decalogue.[43]

## 4. Conclusions

It is now time to return to the questions I asked at the outset. Concerning the question of origin, it seems that we must reckon with a rather developed root-system behind both the household code of Col and the preceding paraenesis. *Per se* the code and the other paraenesis can have different roots. The tradition behind the preceding paraenesis appears to have a Christian *Sitz* before its appearance in Col – the echoes of Jesus' teaching indicate this. But its interpretations of the Decalogue are ultimately inspired by Judaism. The list-form is widely used in Jewish as well as in other Hellenistic circles.[44] On the one hand the household code is also to be related to the Decalogue, but indirectly, although its parallel in Eph explicitly quotes the fifth commandment in relation to a part of it. On the other hand, it regards people in their standard positions in society, i.e. in the "house". This thought pattern of the "house" organizes the code, but it is so general and natural in antiquity that one can hardly use it when asking more particularly for a milieu of origin. The manner of expression in the code reminds one of the so-called apodictic law, and indicates an OT-Jewish inspiration at the very bottom. But this does not necessarily mean that it was directly taken from there. On the contrary, the fact that the addressees have been "taught" (2:7) should indicate that the author makes use of traditions, though not necessarily very fixed ones, which were taught as being based on divine law and not human tradition (cf. 2:8, 22).

Does the presence of the "house" pattern tell us anything particular about the development of the Church, when seen generally? I doubt this – thinking in terms of the "house" was next to inevitable (cf. e.g., Matt 10:35) – and the connection with the Decalogue is only one more sign of the fact that in a way Gentile Christian churches were also Jewish-Christian.[45]

---

[43] See STUHLMACHER, *EvTh* 28 (1968) 177–178. [IRENE TAATZ, *Frühjüdische Briefe* (NTOA 16), Freiburg (CH) • Göttingen 1991, 59–76; HANS-JOSEF KLAUCK, *Ancient Letters and the New Testament*, Waco, Tex. 2006, 272–278; MATTHIAS HENZE, *Jewish Apocalypticism in the Late First Century Israel* (TSAJ 142), Tübingen 2011, 350–371.]

[44] See EHRHARD KAMLAH, *Die Form der katalogischen Paränese im NT* (WUNT 7), Tübingen 1964, 2: III–IV.

[45] HELMUT KOESTER, "*Gnomai diaphoroi*. The Origin and Nature of Diversification in the History of Early Christianity", in: *JAMES MCCONKEY ROBINSON/HELMUT KOESTER. Trajectories through Early Christianity*, Philadelphia, Penn. 1971, 114–157: 115.

Most of that which has been said in the preceding paragraphs concerns the author's side of the letter's communication: his producing a text is allowed to testify about *his* ways of thinking and *his* background. But we should also ask for the function of the code and of its parenetic context within Col, and, as well, for their function in relationship to the addressees and their situation. As to the first question, I have already intimated an answer: the paraenesis is there as a God-given contrast to the precepts advanced by this-worldly "philosophy", and it has been prepared for at least from 2:6 onwards *(peripateite)*. The catalogues of vices and virtues in relation to one's fellowmen stand over against "humility", angelic service, visions (2:18, 23). The worship of 3:16 is different from the observance of feasts, new moon and sabbath (2:16), and the household code, in its practical worldliness,[46] is quite different from "do not touch," etc., of 2:23.[47]

Scholars have suggested several solutions to the problem of the external function of the paraenesis, and especially of the household code. I have mentioned some of them above. One such function is implied by the contrast to the "philosophical" rules I just pointed to. Are there also any attempts to temper some sort of emancipation on the part of women and slaves? There are no signs *in* the letter that the author was disturbed because the women of the Colossian community were caught up in the liberal tendencies of some circles. Also, if the sister church in Laodicea met in a house owned by a woman, Nympha, which is rather probable,[48] nothing in the text indicates that this circumstance called for any remarks. Thus, the Decalogue and "house" structures seem to be sufficient reasons for the wife-husband admonition, the contents of which seems to be what was rather normal in the sort of Jewish circles[49] that have been the original seedbed of both the Decalogue reinterpretation and the wisdom-Christology. But that which is said concerning slaves breaks the frames of style and proportion, as most commentators note. Already A. Deissmann assumed that this reflected the social structure of the church.[50] The situation of house slaves was not to be compared with slavery of more modern times,[51] but possibly the Christian view of masters and slaves as brethren in Christ can have caused problems.[52]

---

[46] SCHWEIZER *(Brief an die Kolosser)* makes a lot of this "gute und nüchterne Weltlichkeit", 161.

[47] Of course I cannot pretend to know, any more than anyone else, what these rules of the "philosophy" actually aimed at.

[48] See the commentaries for a discussion of the MSS evidence and of the linguistic problem. I take 4:15 as saying "Nympha ... in her house", regarding this to be the *lectio difficilior*.

[49] Philo, Josephus and Pseudo-Phocylides agree to a large extent in these matters of morality. See further CROUCH, *Origin and Intention*, chaps, 5, 6.

[50] ADOLF DEISSMANN, *Paul: A Study in Social and Religious History*, London ²1926, 243.

[51] S. SCOTT BARTHCHY, *Mallon crēsai. First Century Slavery and 1 Corinthians 7.21* (SBLDS 11), Missoula, Mont. 1973, chap. 2 and ROLAND GAYER, *Die Stellung des Sklaven in der paulinischen Gemeinden in der Antike*, Europ. Hochschulschr., 23;78, Bern – Frankfurt 1976. [J. ALBERT HARRILL, *Slaves in the New Testament. Literary, Social, and Moral Dimensions*, Minneapolis, Minn. 2006.]

[52] See FREDERICK FYVIE BRUCE, *The Epistle to the Colossians, to Philemon, and to the Ephesians* (NICNT), Grand Rapids, Mich. 1984, *ad loc.*

For the rest, even the circumstance that the whole paraenesis seems to be making extensive use of traditional material can be regarded in two ways. On the one hand, being standard exhortations and having the Decalogue as a point of departure, the paraenesis does not tell us very much about its particular external function. On the other hand, the very fact of its "standard" character might be a point: the "philosophy" seems to have claimed that the "standard" was not enough and that, instead, the perfect should stand in a good relationship also to other powers besides the Lord Jesus and hold to loftier and more particular rules than the standard ones. Against this the author has argued: the Lord Jesus was good enough, and so was the sort of life in him that they had learnt.

# Bibliography

## Texts and Editions

Greek texts are quoted according to the CD *Thesaurus Linguae Graecae*, compiled 1999, ed. University of California, Irvine, and *Greek Documentary Texts*, compiled 1991–1996 by The Packard Humanities Institute.

ANDERSEN, FRANCIS IAN
    1983    "2 (Slavonic Apocalypse of) Enoch" in: *Old Testament Pseudepigrapha* I, Garden City, N.Y.: Doubleday, 91–213.

VON ARNIM, JOHANNES
    1903    *Stoicorum Veterum Fragmenta*, I, Leipzig: Teubner.

CHARLES, ROBERT HENRY
    1913    (Ed.) *The apocrypha and pseudepigrapha of the Old Testament in English. With introductions and critical and explanatory notes to the several books. II. Pseudepigrapha.* Oxford: Clarendon.

CHARLESWORTH, JAMES H.
    1983    "Treatise of Shem", in: *Old Testament Pseudepigrapha* I, Garden City, N.Y.: Doubleday, 473–486.

DITTENBERGER, WILHELM
    1903–1905    *Orientis Graeci Inscriptiones Selectae*, Leipzig: Hirzel.

ELLIGER, WINFRIED
    1967    *Dion Chrysostomos. Sämtliche Reden*, Zürich – Stuttgart: Artemis Verlag.

FREY, JEAN-BAPTISTE
    1932    *Corpus inscriptionum Iudaicarum I* (Sussidi allo studio delle antichità cristiane 1,3.) Rome: Pontificio Istituto di Archeologia Cristiana.
    1952    *Corpus inscriptionum Iudaicarum II* (Sussidi allo studio delle antichità cristiane 1,3.) Rome: Pontificio Istituto di Archeologia Cristiana.

GOOLD, GEORGE PATRICK
    1977    Manilius, *Astronomica* I, in: LCL.

HERCHER, RUDOLPH
    1965    (Ed.) Anacharsidis epistulae, in: *Epistolographi Graeci*, Paris: Didot 1873 • Amsterdam: Hakkert 1965.

KAYSER, CARL LUDWIG
    1964    (ed.), Apollonii Epistulae, in: *Flavii Philostrati opera I*, Leipzig: Teubner 1870 • Hildesheim: Olms 1964.

KLAUCK, HANS-JOSEF/BÄBLER, BALBINA
2000     Dion von Prusa, *Olympische Rede oder über die Erste Erkenntnis Gottes* (SAPERE II), Darmstadt: Wissenschaftliche Buchgesellschaft.

KLIJN, ALBERTUS F. J.
1983     "2 (Syriac Apocalypse of) Baruch", in: *Old Testament Pseudepigrapha* I, Garden City, N.Y.: Doubleday, 615–652.

KNIBB, MICHAEL A.
1978     *The Ethiopic Book of Enoch. A new edition in the light of the Aramaic Dead Sea fragments. I–II. Introduction, translation and commentary.* Oxford: Clarendon.

KÖHLER, LISELOTTE
1928     *Die Briefe des Sokrates und der Sokratiker* (Philologus Suppl. 20/2), Leipzig: Dieterich.

LOHSE, EDUARD
1964     *Die Texte aus Qumran*, Darmstadt: Wissenschaftliche Buchgesellschaft.

METZGER, BRUCE M.
1983     "The Fourth Book of Ezra", in: *Old Testament Pseudepigrapha* I, Garden City, N.Y.: Doubleday, 517–530.

NAVEH, JOSEPH/SHAKED, SHAUL
1985     *Amulets and Magic Bowls. Aramaic Incantations of Late Antiquity*, Leiden: Magnes Press • Jerusalem: Hebrew University.

PREISENDANZ, KARL
$^2$1973     (Ed.), *Papyri Graecae Magicae. Die Griechischen Zauberpapyri I*, Stuttgart: Teubner.

THOM, JOHAN CARL
2005     *Cleantes Hymn to Zeus. Text, Translation, and Commentary* (STAC 33), Tübingen: Mohr Siebeck.

WINTERMUTE, ORVAL S.
1983     "Apocalypse of Zephaniah", in: *Old Testament Pseudepigrapha* I, Garden City, N.Y.: Doubleday, 497–516.
1985     "Jubilees", in: *Old Testament Pseudepigrapha* II, Garden City, N.Y.: Doubleday, 35–142.

## Literature

ABRAMS, MEYER H.
1958     *The Mirror and the Lamp: Romantic Theory and the Critical Tradition.* New York: W. W. Norton and Co.

AHLSTRÖM, GÖSTA W.
1959     *Psalm 89*, Lund: Gleerup.

ALETTI, JEAN-NOËL
1981     *Colossiens 1,15–20* (AnBib 91), Rome: Biblical Institute Press.

ALEXANDER, PHILIP S.
- 1986 "Incantations and Books of Magic," in: EMIL SCHÜRER, *The History of the Jewish People in the Age of Jesus Christ*, rev. ed., 3:1 Edinburgh: T. & T. Clark.

ALMQUIST, HELGE
- 1946 *Plutarch und das Neue Testament* (ASNU 15), Lund: Gleerup • Copenhagen: Munksgaard.

AMBROŽIČ, ALOJZIJ M.
- 1970 *St. Mark's Concept of the Kingdom of God. A Redaction Critical Study of the References to the Kingdom of God in the Second Gospel* (Diss. Würzburg).

APPLEBAUM, SHIMON
- 1974 "The Organization of the Jewish Communities in the Diaspora", in: SHEMUEL SAFRAI/MENAHEM STERN ET ALII (eds.) *The Jewish People in the First Century I*, (Compendia Rerum Iudaicarum ad Novum Testamentum I), Assen: Van Gorcum 1974, 464–503.

VON ARNIM, HANS
- 1898 *Leben und Werke des Dio von Prusa*, Berlin: Weidmannsche Buchhandlung.

ARZT-GRABNER, PETER/KRITZER, RUTH ELISABETH/PAPATHOMAS, AMPHILO-CHIOS/WINTER, FRANZ (EDS.)
- 2006 *1. Korinther* (Papyrologische Kommentare zum Neuen Testament 2), Göttingen: Vandenhoeck & Ruprecht.

ASCOUGH, RICHARD S.
- 2006 "Voluntary Associations and the Formation of Pauline Christian Communities: Overcoming the Objections" in: ALEXANDER GUTSFELD/DIETRICH-ALEX KOCH (eds.), *Vereine, Synagogen und Gemeinden im kaiserzeitlichen Kleinasien* (STAC 25), Tübingen: Mohr Siebeck, 149–183.

AULÉN, GUSTAF
- 1960 *The Faith of the Christian Church* (trans. Eric H. Wahlström); Philadelphia, Penn.: Muhlenberg.

AUNE, DAVID E.
- 1990 "The Form and Function of the Proclamations to the Seven Churches (Revelation 2–3)", in: *NTS* 36, 182–204.

AVEMARIE, FRIEDRICH
- 2002 *Die Tauferzählungen der Apostelgeschichte Theologie und Geschichte* (WUNT 139), Tübingen: Mohr Siebeck.

BAARLINK, HEINRICH
- 1986 *Die Eschatologie der synoptischen Evangelien* (BWANT 120), Stuttgart: Kohlhammer.

BAIRD, WILLIAM
    1992    History of New Testament Research. Volume One: From Deism to Tübingen, Minneapolis, Minn.: Fortress Press.

BAKKE, ODD MAGNE
    2001    "Concord and Peace." A Rhetorical Analysis of the First Letter of Clement with an Emphasis on the Language of Unity and Sedition (WUNT 2/141), Tübingen: Mohr Siebeck 2001.

BALABANSKI, VICKY
    1997    Eschatology in the making. Mark, Matthew and the Didache (MSSNTS 97), Cambridge: Cambridge University Press.

BALCH, DAVID L.
    1981    Let Wives be Submissive: The Domestic Code in 1 Peter (SBLMS 26), Atlanta, Ga.: Scholars Press.
    1984    "Early Christian Criticism of Patriarchal Authority: 1 Peter 2:11–3:12", in: USQR 39, 161–173.

VON BALTHASAR, HANS URS
    1960    "Eschatologie", in: JOHANNES FEINER ET ALII (eds.), Fragen der Theologie heute, Einsiedeln – Zürich – Köln: Benziger, 402–422.

BALTZER, KLAUS
    1960    Das Bundesformular (WMANT 4), Neukirchen-Vluyn: Neukirchener.

BARNIKOL, ERNST
    1956/57    "Das Fehlen der Taufe in den Quellenschriften der Apg.", in: WZ 6, 593–619.

BARRETT, C. KINGSLEY
    [2]1978    The Gospel according to St. John, London: SPCK.

BARTH, GERHARD
    1981    Die Taufe in frühchristlicher Zeit (BibTSt 4), Neukirchen-Vluyn: Neukirchener.
    [2]2002    Die Taufe in frühchristlicher Zeit, Revised ed., Neukirchen-Vluyn: Neukirchener.

BARTHCHY, S. SCOTT
    1973    Mallon crēsai. First Century Slavery and 1 Corinthians 7.21 (SBLDS 11), Missoula, Mont.: Scholars Press (Repr. 1985).

BAUER, WALTER/ALAND, KURT/ALAND, BARBARA
    [6]1988    Griechisch-deutsches Wörterbuch zu den Schriften des Neuen Testaments, Berlin – New York: de Gruyter.

BEASLEY-MURRAY, GEORGE R.
    1962    Baptism in the New Testament, London: Macmillan.
    [2]1978    The Book of Revelation (NCB), London: Oliphants.

BECKER, EVE-MARIE
    2006    *Das Markusevangelium im Rahmen antiker Historiographie* (WUNT 194), Tübingen: Mohr Siebeck.

BECKER, JÜRGEN
    1979    *Das Evangelium nach Johannes* (ÖTK 4), Gütersloh: Gütersloher.

BEKKEN, PER JARLE
    1988    "Apropos jødedommens mangfold i det første århundrede: Observasjoner til debatten om jødisk kultus hos Filo, i Acta og Johannesevangeliet" in: *TTK* 59, 161–173.

BENOIT, PIERRE
    1975    "L'hymne christologique de Col 1,15–20. Jugement critique sur l'état des recherches", in: JACOB NEUSNER (ed.), *Christianity, Judaism and Other Graeco-Roman Cults* I (= FS M. Smith) (SJLA 12), Leiden: Brill, 226–263.
    1981    "Angélologie et démonologie pauliniennes. Réflexions sur la nomenclature des Puissances célestes et sur l'origine du mal angélique chez S. Paul", in: *Foi et Culture à la lumière de la Bible*, Torino: Editrice Elle di ci, 217–233.

BENTZEN, AAGE
    1945    *Det sakrale Kongedømme*. Copenhagen: Bianco Lunos.

BERGER, KLAUS
    1968    "Gerechtigkeit" in: *Sacramentum mundi* 2, Freiburg i. Br.: Herder, 261–267.
    1970    "Hartherzigkeit und Gottes Gesetz. Die Vorgeschichte des antijüdischen Vorwurfs in Mc 10,5", in: *ZNW* 61, 1–47.
    1972    *Die Gesetzesauslegung Jesu. Ihr historischer Hintergrund im Judentum und im Alten Testament*. Teil I: Markus und Parallelen (WMANT 40), Neukirchen-Vluyn: Neukirchener.
    1984a    Hellenistische Gattungen im Neuen Testament, in: *Aufstieg und Niedergang der römischen Welt II*, 25,2, Berlin: de Gruyter, 1031–1432.
    1984b    *Formgeschichte des Neuen Testaments*, Heidelberg: Quelle & Mayer.
    $^{1,\,2}$1984    *Exegese des Neuen Testaments* (UTB 658), Heidelberg: Quelle & Mayer.
    1999    *Wie kommt das Ende der Welt?*, Stuttgart: Quell.

BERTRAM, GEORG
    1936    "Das Problem der Umschrift und die religionsgeschichtliche Erforschung der Septuaginta", in: PAUL VOLZ/FRIEDRICH STUMMER/JOHANNES HEMPEL (eds.), *Werden und Wesen des Alten Testaments* (BZAW 66), Giessen: Töpelmann, 97–109.

BEST, ERNEST
    1997    "The Haustafel, in Ephesians (Eph. 5.22–6.9)", in: IDEM, *Essays on Ephesians*, Edinburgh: T. & T. Clark, 189–203.
    1997a    *Ephesians* (ICC), Edinburgh: T. & T. Clark.

BETZ, HANS DIETER
    1966    "Zum Problem des religionsgeschichtlichen Verständnisses der Apokalyptik", in: *ZThK* 63, 391–409 (Eng. Trans., "On the Problem of the Religio-Historical Understanding of Apocalypticism", in: ROBERT W. FUNK (ed.) *Apocalypticism*, in: *JTC* 6, 134–156.
    1986    (Ed.), *The Greek Magical Papyri in Translation*, Chicago, Ill. – London: University of Chicago Press.
    1988    *Der Galaterbrief* (Hermeneia), München: Kaiser.
    1992    "Hellenism", in: *ABD* 3, 127–135.

BEYER, HERMANN WOLFGANG
    1935    "διάκονος", in: *ThWNT* 2, 88–93.

BICKERMAN, ELIAS JOSPEH
    ²1980    *Chronology of the Ancient World*, Ithaca, N.Y.: Cornell University Press, 31, 44–47.

BIETENHARD, HANS
    1954    "ὄνομα κτλ.", in: *ThWNT* 5, 242–283.

BILLERBECK, see STRACK, HERMANN L./BILLERBECK, PAUL

BINDER, HERMANN
    1905    *Dio Chrysostomus und Posidonius: Quellenuntersuchungen zur Theologie des Dio von Prusa*, Diss. Tübingen, Borna-Leipzig: Noske.

BJERKELUND, CARL J.
    1968    "En tradisjons- og redaksjonshistorisk analyse af perikopen om tempelrenselsen", in: *NTT* 69, 206–216.

BLANCK, HORST
    1976    *Einführung in das Privatleben der Griechen und Römer* (Die Altertumswissenschaft. Einführungen...), Darmstadt: Wissenschaftliche Buchgesellschaft.

BLASS, FRIEDRICH/DEBRUNNER, ALBERT/REHKOPF, FRIEDRICH
    ¹⁴1976    *Grammatik des neutestamentlichen Griechisch*, Göttingen: Vandenhoeck & Ruprecht.
    ¹⁶1984    *Grammatik des neutestamentlichen Griechisch*, Göttingen: Vandenhoeck & Ruprecht.

BLOMQVIST, JERKER/JASTRUP, POUL OLE
    1991    *Grekisk/Græsk grammatik*, Copenhagen: Akademisk Forlag.

BOERS, HENDRIKUS
    1979    *What Is New Testament Theology? The Rise of Criticism and the Problem of a Theology of the New Testament* (GBS), Philadelphia, Penn.: Fortress.

BOGAERT, PIERRE-MAURICE
    1980    "Les apocalypses contemporaines de Baruch, d'Esdras et de Jean", in: JAN LAMBRECHT (ed.), *L'Apocalypse johannique et l'apocalyptique dans le Nouveau Testament* (BEThL 53), Paris – Gembloux: Duculot • Leuven: Leuven University Press, 47–68.

BORGEN, PEDER
- 1984 "Philo of Alexandria," in: MICHAEL E. STONE (ed.), *Jewish Writings of the Second Temple Period*, Assen: van Gorcum • Philadelphia, Penn.: Fortress, 233–282.

BORING, M. EUGENE
- 1986 "The Theology of the Book of Revelation: 'The Lord our God the Almighty Reigns'", in: *Interp* 40, 257–269.

BORNKAMM, GÜNTHER
- 1942 "μυστήριον", in: *ThWNT* 4, 809–834.

BOUSSET, WILHELM
- ⁶1906 *Die Offenbarung Johannis* (KEK 16), Göttingen: Vandenhoeck & Ruprecht.

BOUSSET, WILHELM/GRESSMANN, HUGO
- ⁴1966 *Die Religion des Judentums im späthellenistischen Zeitalter*, Tübingen: J. C. B. Mohr (Paul Siebeck).

BOVON, FRANÇOIS
- 1993 "Foi chrétienne et religion populaire dans la première Épître de Pierre", in: IDEM, *Révélations et écritures. Nouveau Testament et littérature apocryphe chrétienne*, Recueil d'articles, Genève: Labor et Fides.

BRANDENBURGER, EGON
- 1984 *Markus 13 und die Apokalyptik* (FRLANT 134), Göttingen: Vandenhoeck & Ruprecht.

BRANDT, A. J. H. WILHELM
- 1891 "Onoma en de Doopsformule in het Nieuwe Testament," in: *ThT* 25, 565–610.

BRATSIOTIS, NIKOLAUS PAN
- 1966 "נפש ΨΥΧΗ. Ein Beitrag zur Erforschung der Sprache und der Theologie der Septuaginta", in: *Volume de congrès Genève 1965* (VT.S 15), Leiden: Brill, 58–89.

BRAUN, HERBERT
- 1957 "Der Sinn der neutestamentlichen Christologie," in: *ZThK* 54, 341–377; reprinted in: IDEM, *Gesammelte Studien zum Neuen Testament*, Tübingen: J. C. B. Mohr (Paul Siebeck) 1962, 86–99. [²1967.]
- 1961 "Die Problematik einer Theologie des Neuen Testaments," in: *ZThK* 58, 3–18; reprinted in *Gesammelte Studien*, 325–341, and in: GEORG STRECKER (ed.), *Das Problem der Theologie des Neuen Testaments* (1975), 405–424.
- 1966 *Qumran und das Neue Testament* I & II, Tübingen: J. C. B. Mohr (Paul Siebeck).

BREYTENBACH, CILLIERS
- 1984 *Nachfolge und Zukunftserwartung nach Markus. Eine methodenkritische Studie* (AThANT 71), Zürich: Theologischer Verlag.

BROWN, RAYMOND E.
  1966   *The Gospel according to John* (AncB) I, Garden City, N.Y.: Doubleday.
  1979   *The Community of the Beloved Disciple*, New York – Toronto: Paulist Press.

BROWN, RAYMOND E./DONFRIED, KARL PAUL/FITZMYER, JOSEPH A./REUMANN, JOHN
  1978   *Mary in the New Testament*, London: Chapman.

BROWN, RAYMOND E./MEIER, JOHN P.
  1983   *Antioch and Rome*, London: Chapman.

BROX, NORBERT
  1979   *Der erste Petrusbrief* (EKK 21), Zürich – Einsiedeln – Köln: Benziger • Neukirchen-Vluyn: Neukirchener.

BRUCE, FREDERICK FYVIE
  ²1952  *The Acts of the Apostles*, London: Tyndale Press.
  1984   "Colossian Problems, Part 3: The Colossian Heresy", in: *BSac* 141, 195–208.
  1984   *The Epistle to the Colossians, to Philemon, and to the Ephesians* (NICNT), Grand Rapids, Mich.: Eerdmans.

BRYAN, CHRISTOPHER
  1993   *Preface to Mark. Notes on the Gospel in its Literary and Cultural Settings*, New York – Oxford: Oxford University Press.

BUJARD, WALTER
  1973   *Stilanalytische Untersuchungen zum Kolosserbrief als Beitrag zur Methodik von Sprachvergleichen* (SUNT 11), Göttingen: Vandenhoeck & Ruprecht.

BULTMANN, RUDOLF
  ¹⁰1960 *Das Evangelium nach Johannes* (KEK 2), Göttingen: Vandenhoeck & Ruprecht (1941).
  ², ⁶1964 *Die Geschichte der synoptischen Tradition*, Göttingen: Vandenhoeck & Ruprecht.
  1965   "πιστεύω κτλ.", in: *ThWNT* 6, 174–182, 197–230.
  ⁵1967  "Neues Testament und Mythologie", in: HANS-WERNER BARTSCH (ed.), *Kerygma Lind Mythos*, Hamburg-Bergstedt: Herbert Reich, 15–48.
  ⁴, ⁶1968 *Theologie des Neuen Testaments*, Tübingen: J. C. B. Mohr (Paul Siebeck).

BURKERT, WALTER
  1977   *Griechische Religion der archaischen und klassischen Epoche* (RM 15), Stuttgart: Kohlhammer.

BURRIDGE, RICHARD A.
  1992   *What are the Gospels? Comparison with Græco-Roman Biography* (MSSNTS 70), Cambridge: Cambridge University Press.

CAIRD, GEORGE BRADFORD
  1966   *The Revelation of St. John the Divine* (BNTC), London: Black.

VON CAMPENHAUSEN, HANS FRHR
- 1968   *Die Entstehung der christlichen Bibel* (BHTh 39), Tübingen: J. C. B. Mohr (Paul Siebeck).
- 1971   "Taufen auf den Namen Jesu?", in: *VigChr* 25, 1–16.

CARMIGNAC, JEAN
- 1970/71   "Les dangers de l'eschatologie", in: *NTS* 17, 365–390.

CAVALLIN, HANS C. C.
- 1974   *Life After Death. Paul's Argument for the Resurrection of the Dead in I Cor 15* (CB.NT 7:1), Lund: Gleerup.

CHARLES, ROBERT HENRY
- 1920   *The Revelation of St. John* I–II (ICC), Edinburgh: T. & T. Clark.
- 1963   *Eschatology. The doctrine of a future life in Israel, Judaism and Christianity,* New York: Schocken.

CHARLESWORTH, JAMES H.
- 1987   "Jewish Interest in Astrology during the Hellenistic and Roman Period", in: *ANRW* II.20.2, Berlin – New York: de Gruyter, 926–950.

CLARKE, WILLIAM K. L.
- 1922   "The Use of the Septuagint in Acts" in: FREDERICK JOHN FOAKES-JACKSON/KIRSOPP LAKE (eds.), *The Beginnings of Christianity* II, London: Macmillan.

COHEN, SHAYE J. D.
- 1989   "Crossing the Boundaries and Becoming a Jew", in: *HThR* 82, 13–33.

COLLINS, ADELA YARBRO
- 1977   "The History-of-Religions Approach to Apocalypticism and the 'Angel of the Waters' (Rev 16:4–7)", in: *CBQ* 39, 367–381.
- 1984   *Crisis and Catharsis: The Power of the Apocalypse*, Philadelphia, Penn.: Westminster.
- 2007   *Mark. A Commentary* (Hermeneia), Minneapolis, Minn.: Fortress.

COLLINS, JOHN J.
- 1979a   (Ed.): *Apocalypse: The Morphology of a Genre* (Semeia 14), Missoula, Mont.: Scholars Press.
- 1979b   "Introduction; Towards a Morphology of a Genre", in: JOHN J. COLLINS (ed.), *Apocalypse: the Morphology of a Genre*, 1–20.
- 1979c   "Persian Apocalypses," in: JOHN J. COLLINS (ed.), *Apocalypse: The Morphology of a Genre*, 207–217.
- 1984   *The Apocalyptic Imagination. An Introduction to the Jewish Matrix of Christianity,* New York: Crossroad.

COLLINS, RAYMOND F.
- 1963   *The Berîth-Notion of the Cairo Damascus Covenant and its Comparison with the New Testament* (ETL 39 = BEThL 20), Louvain: Publications Universitaires de Louvain.

COMMISSION BIBLIQUE PONTIFICALE
　　1993　"L'interprétation de la Bible dans l'Église", in: *Biblica* 74, 451–528.

CONZELMANN, HANS
　　⁵1964　*Die Mitte der Zeit. Studien zur Theologie des Lukas* (BHTh 17), Tübingen: J. C. B. Mohr (Paul Siebeck).
　　1967　*Grundriß der Theologie des Neuen Testaments*, München: Kaiser.
　　1969　*Geschichte des Urchristentums* (Grundriße zum N.T., NTD Ergänz, 5); Göttingen: Vandenhoeck & Ruprecht.
　　²1972　*Die Apostelgeschichte* (HNT 7), Tübingen: J. C. B. Mohr (Paul Siebeck).

CONZELMANN, HANS/LINDEMANN, ANDREAS
　　⁶1982　*Arbeitsbuch zum Neuen Testament* (UTB 52), Tübingen: Mohr Siebeck.

COOK, JOHN G.
　　1985　*The Structure and Persuasive Power of Mark. A Linguistic Approach* (SBL Semeia Studies), Atlanta, Ga.: Society of Biblical Literature.

CROSSAN, JOHN DOMINIC
　　1973　"Mark and the Relatives of Jesus", in: *NT* 15, 81–113.
　　1991　*The Historical Jesus. The Life of a Mediterranean Jewish Peasant*, San Francisco, Calif.: Harper.

CROUCH, JAMES E.
　　1972　*The Origin and Intention of the Colossian Haustafel* (FRLANT 109), Göttingen: Vandenhoeck & Ruprecht.

CULLMANN, OSCAR
　　1950　*Baptism in the New Testament* (SBT 1), London: SCM Press.

CUMONT, FRANZ VALERY MARIE
　　1909　"Le mysticisme astral dans l'antiquité", in: *Académie Royale de Belgique: Bull. de la classe des lettres*, 256–286.

CUVILLIER, ELIAN
　　2002　*L'évangile de Marc*, Paris: Bayard • Genève: Labor et Fides.

DAHL, NILS A.
　　1941　*Das Volk Gottes. Eine Untersuchung zum Kirchenbewusstsein des Urchristentums* (SNVAO.HF 2), Oslo: Jacob Dubwad.
　　1955　"The Origin of Baptism", in: *NTT* 61, 36–52.
　　2000　"Welche Ordnung der Paulusbriefe wird vom Muratorischen Kanon vorausgesetzt?", in: *Studies in Ephesians* (WUNT 131), Tübingen: Mohr Siebeck, 147–163.

DALMAN, GUSTAF
　　1898　*Die Worte Jesu I. Einleitung und wichtige Begriffe*, Leipzig: Hinrichs.

DANIÉLOU, JEAN
　　1950　*Sacramentum futuri. Études sur les origines de la typologie biblique* (ETH), Paris: Beauchesne.

DANOVE, PAUL L.
   1993   *The End of Mark's Story: A Methodological Study,* Leiden: Brill.
   2001   *Linguistics and Exegesis in the Gospel of Mark. Application of Case Frame Analysis and Lexicon* (JSTN.S 218), Sheffield: Sheffield Academic Press.

DAVIES, WILLIAM DAVID
   1955   *Paul and Rabbinic Judaism,* London: SPCK.

LE DÉAUT, ROGER
   1969   "A propos d'une définition du midrash", in: *Bib.* 50, 395–413.

DEISSMANN, ADOLF
   [2]1926   *Paul: A Study in Social and Religious History,* London: Doran.

DELCOR, MATTHIAS
   1977   "Mythologie et apocalyptique", in: *Apocalypses et théologie de l'espérance* (LD 95), Paris: Cerf, 143–177.

DELLING, GERHARD
   1961   *Die Zueignung des Heils in der Taufe,* Berlin: Evangelische Verlagsanstalt.

DÉNIS, ALBERT-MARIE
   1967   *Les thèmes de connaissance dans le document de Damas* (StHell 15), Louvain: Publications universitaires de Louvain.

DEWEY, JOANNA
   1980   *Markan Public Debate: Literary Technique, Concentric Structure, and Theology in Mark 2:1–3:6* (SBLDS 48), Chico, Calif.: Scholars Press.

DIBELIUS, MARTIN/GREEVEN, HEINRICH
   [3]1953   *An die Kolosser, Epheser, an Philemon* (HNT 12), Tübingen: J. C. B. Mohr (Paul Siebeck).

DIETRICH, WOLFGANG
   1972   *Das Petrusbild der lukanischen Schriften* (BWANT 14), Stuttgart: Kohlhammer.

DIHLE, ALBRECHT
   1962   *Die goldene Regel. Eine Einführung in die Geschichte der antiken und frühchristlichen Vulgärethik* (SAW 7), Göttingen: Vandenhoeck & Ruprecht.
   1966   "Ethik", in: *RAC* 6, 646–696.
   1973   "ψυχή im Griechischen", in: *ThWNT* 9, 605–614.

DILLON, JOHN M.
   1977   *The Middle Platonists: A Study of Platonism 80 BC to AD 220,* London: Duckworth.

DINKLER, ERICH
   1962   "Taufe II", in: *RGG*[3], VI, 627ff.

DODDS, ERIC ROBERTSON
   1970   *Die Griechen und das Irrationale,* Darmstadt: Wissenschaftliche Buchgesellschaft.

DONAHUE, JOHN R./HARRINGTON, DANIEL J.
2002   *The Gospel of Mark* (Sacra Pagina 2), Collegeville, Minn.: Liturgical Press.

DORMEYER, DETLEV
1999   *Das Markusevangelium als Idealbiographie von Jesus Christus, dem Nazarener* (SBB 43), Stuttgart: Katholisches Bibelwerk.

DU RAND, JAN A.
1990   "A Socio-psychological View of the Effect of the Language (parole) of the Apocalypse of John", in: *Neotest.* 24, 351–365.

DUNN, JAMES D. G.
1970   *Baptism in the Holy Spirit* (SBT II: 15), London: SCM Press.

DUPONT, JACQUES
1960   *Les Sources du livre des Actes. État de la question*, Bruges: Desclée de Brouwer.
1967   "Jésus, Messie et Seigneur dans la foi des premiers chrétiens", in: IDEM, *Études sur les Actes des Apôtres*, (LD 45), Paris: Cerf, 367–390.
1979   "La conclusion des Actes et son rapport à l'ensemble de l'ouvrage de Luc", in: JACOB KREMER (ed.), *Les Actes des Apôtres. Traditions, rédaction, théologie* (BEThL 48), Paris – Gembloux: Ducolot • Louvain: Leuven University Press, 359–404.

ECKEY, WILFRIED
1998   *Das Markusevangelium. Orientierung am Weg Jesu*, Neukirchen-Vluyn: Neukirchener.

ECO, UMBERTO
1992   "Overinterpreting texts", in: UMBERTO ECO ET ALII, *Interpretation and Overinterpretation*, ed. Stefan Collini, Cambridge: Cambridge University Press, 45–66.

EGELHAAF-GAISER, ULRIKE/SCHÄFER, ALFRED
2002   (Eds.), *Religiöse Vereine in der römischen Antike. Untersuchungen zu Organisation, Ritual und Raumordnung* (STAC 13), Tübingen: Mohr Siebeck.

EHLER, BERNHARD
1986   *Die Herrschaft des Gekreuzigten. Ernst Käsemanns Frage nach der Mitte der Schrift*, Berlin – New York: de Gruyter.

EHRLICH, ERNST LUDWIG
1959   *Die Kultsymbolik im Alten Testament und im nachbiblischen Judentum* (SyR 3), Stuttgart: Hiersemann.

EICHRODT, WALTHER
1956   "Ist die typologische Exegese sachgemässe Exegese?", in: *ThLZ* 81, 641–654.
⁴1957–⁵1961  *Theologie des Alten Testaments* I–III, Stuttgart: Klotz • Göttingen: Vandenhoeck & Ruprecht.

EISEN, UTE E.
   2000   *Women Officeholders in Early Christianity. Epigraphical and Literary Studies*, Collegeville, Minn.: Glazier, 167–169.

EISENHOFER, LUDWIG
   ²1941   *Handbuch der katholischen Liturgik*, II, Fribourg-en-Brisgau: Herder.

ELLIS, E. EARLE
   1957   *Paul's Use of the Old Testament*, Edinburgh: T. & T. Clark.
   1978   *Prophecy and Hermeneutic in Early Christianity. New Testament Essays* (WUNT 18), Tübingen: Mohr Siebeck.

ENGBERG-PEDERSEN, TROELS
   1995   "Stoicism in Philippians", in: TROELS ENGBERG-PEDERSEN (ed.), *Paul in his Hellenistic Context*, Minneapolis, Minn.: Fortress, 256–290.

ENGNELL, IVAN
   1943   *Studies in Divine Kingship in the Ancient Near East*, Uppsala: Almqvist & Wiksell.
   1945   *Gamla testamentet. En traditionshistorisk inledning I*, Stockholm, SKDB.
   ²1963   "Själ. I. GT", *Svenskt Bibliskt Uppslagsverk II*, Stockholm: Nordiska uppslagsböcker, 964–969.

EPPSTEIN, VICTOR
   1964   "The Historicity of the Gospel Account on the Cleansing of the Temple", in: *ZNW* 55, 42–58.

ERNST, JOSEF
   1970   *Pleroma und Pleroma Christi. Geschichte und Deutung eines Begriffs der paulinsichen Antilegomena* (BU 5), Regensburg: Pustet.
   1981   *Das Evangelium nach Markus* (RNT), Regensburg: Pustet.

EVANS, CRAIG A.
   1982   "The Function of Isaiah 6:9–10 in Mark and John", in: *NT* 24, 124–138.

FENSHAM, FRANK CHARLES
   1971   "Father and Son as Terminology for Treaty and Covenant", in: *Near Eastern Studies* (FS W. F. Albright), Baltimore, Md. – London: John Hopkins, 121–135.

FERGUSON, CHARLES A.
   1959   "Diglossia", in: *Word* 16, 325–340.

FESTUGIÈRE, ANDRÉ-JEAN
   1944   *La révélation d'Hermès Trismégiste I; L'astrologie et les sciences occultes* (Études bibliques), Paris: Lecoffre.

FILOSOFILEXIKONET
   1988   Stockholm: Forum.

FISCHER, KARL MARTIN
   1985   *Das Urchristentum* (Kirchengeschichte in Einzeldarstellungen I/1), Berlin: Evangelische Verlagsanstalt.

FITZMYER, JOSEPH A.
²1971   *The Genesis Apocryphon of Qumran Cave 1. A Commentary* (BibOr 18 A), Rome: Biblical Institute.
1979   "The Semitic Background of the New Testament Kyrios-Title," IDEM, *A Wandering Aramean* (SBLMS 25), Missoula, Mont.: Scholars Press, 115–142.
1993   *Romans* (AncB 33), New York etc.: Doubleday.
1998   *The Acts of the Apostles* (AncB 41), New York etc.: Doubleday.

FLEMINGTON, WILLIAM FREDERICK
1948   *The New Testament Doctrine of Baptism*, London: SPCK.

FOCANT, CAMILLE
2004   *L'évangile selon Marc* (Commentaire biblique NT 2), Paris: Cerf.

FOERSTER, WERNER
1961f.   "Der Heilige Geist im Spätjudentum", in: *NTS* 8, 134.

FOHRER, GEORG
1969   "υἱός", B. Altes Testament, in: *ThWNT* 8, 340–354.

FORSCHNER, MAXIMILIAN
1981   *Die stoische Ethik. Über den Zusammenhang von Natur-, Sprach- und Moralphilosophie im altstoischen System*, Stuttgart: Klett-Cotta.

FORTNA, ROBERT TOMSON
1970   *The Gospel of Signs. A Reconstruction of the Narrative Source Underlying the Fourth Gospel* (MSSNTS 11), Cambridge: Cambridge University Press.

FRANCE, RICHARD THOMAS
2002   *The Gospel of Mark. A Commentary on the Greek Text* (NIGTC); Grand Rapids, Mich.: Eerdmans • Carlisle: Paternoster.

FREYNE, SEÁN
1980   *Galilee from Alexander the Great to Hadrian 323 BCE to 135 CE*, Wilmington, Del.: Glazier • Notre Dame, Ind.: University of Notre Dame Press.

FRÜCHTEL, URSULA
1968   *Die kosmologischen Vorstellungen bei Philo von Alexandrien* (ALGHJ 2), Leiden: Brill.

FURBERG, MATS
1981   *Verstehen och förstå. Funderingar kring ett tema hos Dilthey, Heidegger och Gadamer*, Lund: Doxa.

GADAMER, HANS-GEORG
²1979   *Truth and Method*. Trans. from the 2nd German edition by W. Glen-Doepel. Eds. John Cumming and Garret Barden, London: Sheed and Ward.

GÄRTNER, BERTIL
1965   *The Temple and the Community in Qumran and the New Testament* (MSSNTS 1), Cambridge: Cambridge University Press.

GARROW, ALAN J. P.
1994   "What is and What is to Come". The serialized story in the Book of Revelation (unpublished thesis for the degree of Master of Philosophy, Wycliffe Hall, Oxford, October 1994).

GAYER, ROLAND
1976   Die Stellung des Sklaven in der paulinischen Gemeinden in der Antike (EHS.T 23; 78), Bern – Frankfurt am Main: Peter Lang.

GEHMAN, HENRY S.
1951   "The Hebraic Character of Septuagint Greek" in: VT 1, 90.

GENETTE, GÉRARD
²1998   Die Erzählung (UTB Wissenschaft), München: Wilhelm Fink.

GEORGI, DIETER
1964   Die Gegner des Paulus im 2. Korintherbrief (WMANT 11), Neukirchen-Vluyn: Neukirchener.

GIBLIN, CHARLES HOMER
1991   The Book of Revelation. The Open Book of Prophecy (Good News Studies 34), Collegeville, Minn.: Liturgical Press.

GIESEN, HEINZ
1990   "Symbole und mythische Aussagen in der Johannes-Apokalypse und ihre theologische Bedeutung", in: KARL KERTELGE, (ed.), Metaphorik und Mythos im Neuen Testament (QD 126), Freiburg i. Br. – Basel – Wien: Herder, 255–277.

GLOVER, RICHARD
1964–1965   "'Luke the Antiochene' and Acts", in: NTS 11, 97–106.

GNILKA, JOACHIM
1978   Das Evangelium nach Markus 1 (EKK 2/1), Zürich – Einsiedeln – Köln: Benziger • Neukirchen-Vluyn: Neukirchener.
1979   Das Evangelium nach Markus 2 (EKK 2/2), Zürich – Einsiedeln – Köln: Benziger • Neukirchen-Vluyn: Neukirchener.
1980   Der Kolosserbrief (HThK X:1), Freiburg i. Br. – Basel – Wien: Herder.

GOLDAMMER, KURT
1960   Die Formenwelt des Religiösen: Grundriss der systematischen Religionswissenschaft, Stuttgart: Kröner.

GOODENOUGH, ERWIN R.
1953   Jewish Symbols in the Greco-Roman World II, New York: Pantheon.

GOPPELT, LEONHARD
1969   "τύπος κτλ.", in: ThWNT 8, 246–260.
³1981   Theologie des Neuen Testaments, Göttingen: Vandenhoeck & Ruprecht.

GORMAN, FRANK H., JR.
2003 "Commenting on Commentary: Reflections on a Genre," in: TIMOTHY J. SANDOVAL/CARLEEN MANDOLFO (eds.), Relating to the Text, London – New York: Clark, 100–119.

GOULDER, MICHAEL D.
1978 The Evangelists' Calendar. A Lectionary Explanation of the Development of Scripture, London: SPCK.
1995 "The Phasing of the Future" in: TORD FORNBERG/DAVID HELLHOLM (eds.), Texts and Contexts. Biblical Texts in Their Textual and Situational Contexts. Essays in Honor of Lars Hartman, Oslo – Copenhagen – Stockholm – Boston, Mass.: Scandinavian University Press, 391–408.

GRANT, FREDERICK C.
1953 Hellenistic Religions: The Age of Syncretism, Indianapolis, Ind. – New York: MacMillan.

GRANT, ROBERT M.
1947 "The Decalogue in Early Christianity", in: HThR 40, 1–17.
²1963 A Short History of the Interpretation of the Bible, New York: MacMillan.

GRESSMANN, HUGO
1920f. "Die Sage von der Taufe Jesu und die vorderorientalische Taubengöttin", in: Archiv für Religionswissenschaft 20:1–40, 323–359.
1925 Die hellenistische Gestirnreligion (BAO 5), Leipzig: Hinrichs.

GRUNDMANN, WALTER
³1965 Das Evangelium nach Markus (ThHK 2), Berlin: Evangelische Verlagsanstalt.

GUELICH, ROBERT A.
1989 Mark 1 – 8:26 (WBC 34A), Dallas, Tex.: Word.

GÜLICH, ELISABETH
1976 "Ansätze zu einer kommunikationsorientierten Erzähltextanalyse (am Beispiel mündlicher und schriftlicher Erzähltexte)", in: WOLFGANG HAUBRICHS (ed.), Erzählforschung I (Beiheft zur Zeitschrift für die Literaturwissenschaft und Linguistik 4), Göttingen: Vandenhoeck & Ruprecht, 224–256.

GÜLICH, ELISABETH/RAIBLE, WOLFGANG
1977 Linguistische Textmodelle. Grundlagen und Möglichkeiten (UTB 130) München: Wilhelm Fink.

GÜLICH, ELISABETH/RAIBLE, WOLFGANG
²1979 "Überlegungen zu einer makrostrukturellen Textanalyse", in: ELISABETH GÜLICH/KLAUS HEGER/WOLFGANG RAIBLE (eds.), Linguistische Textanalyse. Überlegungen zur Gliederung von Texten (Papiere zur Textlinguistik 8), Hamburg: Buske, 73–126.

GUNDRY, ROBERT H.
    1993    *Mark. A Commentary on His Apology for the Cross*, Grand Rapids, Mich: Eerdmans.

HÄGG, TOMAS
    2012    *The Art of Biography in Antiquity*, Cambridge: Cambridge University Press.

HAENCHEN, ERNST
    [6-7]1968    *Die Apostelgeschichte* (KEK 3), Göttingen: Vandenhoeck & Ruprecht.
    1980    *Das Johannesevangelium*, Tübingen: J. C. B. Mohr (Paul Siebeck).

HAHN, FERDINAND
    1976    "Taufe und Rechtfertigung. Ein Beitrag zur paulinischen Theologie in ihrer Vor- und Nachgeschichte", in: JOHANNES FRIEDRICH/WOLFGANG PÖHLMANN/PETER STUHLMACHER (eds.), *Rechtfertigung. Festschrift für Ernst Käsemann*, Tübingen: J. C. B. Mohr (Paul Siebeck) • Göttingen: Vandenhoeck & Ruprecht, 95–124.

HALL, BASIL
    1963    "Biblical Scholarship: Editions and Commentaries," in: *Cambridge History of the Bible* 3, Cambridge: Cambridge University Press, 38–93.

HAMEL, GILDAS H.
    1989    *Poverty and Charity in Roman Palestine, First Three Centuries C. E.*, Berkeley – Los Angeles – Oxford: University of California Press.

HANSON, JOHN S.
    1980    "Dreams and Visions in the Graeco-Roman World and Early Christianity," in: *ANRW* II.23.2. Berlin: de Gruyter, 1395–1427.

HARL, MARGUERITE
    1986    *La Bible d'Alexandrie. La Genèse*, Paris: Cerf, 60f.

HARRILL, J. ALBERT
    2006    *Slaves in the New Testament. Literary, Social, and Moral Dimensions*, Minneapolis, Minn.: Fortress.

HARTMAN, LARS
    1966    *Prophecy interpreted. The formation of some Jewish apocalyptic texts and of the eschatological discourse Mark 13 par.* (CB.NT 1), Lund: Gleerup.
    1973/74    "'Into the Name of Jesus.' A Suggestion concerning the Earliest Meaning of the Phrase" in: *NTS* 20, 432–444. In this volume nr. 13, 145–154.
    1974    "Baptism 'Into the Name of Jesus' and Early Christology: Some Tentative Considerations", in: *StTh* 28, 21–48.
    1975/76    "The Functions of Some So–called Apocalyptic Time–Tables", in: *NTS* 22, 1–14. Reprinted in HARTMAN 1997a, 107–124.
    1979    *Asking for a meaning. A study of 1 Enoch 1–5* (CB.NT 12), Lund: Gleerup.
    1980    "Form and Message. A Preliminary Discussion of 'Partial Texts' in Rev 1–3 and 22,6ff.", in: JAN LAMBRECHT (ed.), *L'Apocalypse johannique et l'apocalyptique dans le Nouveau Testament* (BEThL 53), Paris – Gem-

bloux: Duculot • Leuven: Leuven University Press, 129-149. Reprinted in: HARTMAN 1997a, 125-149.
1981 "ὄνομα," in: *EWNT* 2, Stuttgart: Kohlhammer, 1268-77.
1983 "Survey of the Problem of Apocalyptic Genre", in: DAVID HELLHOLM (ed.), *Apocalypticism in the Mediterranean World and the Near East, Proceedings of the International Colloquium on Apocalypticism, Uppsala August 12-17, 1979*, Tübingen: J. C. B. Mohr (Paul Siebeck), 329-343.
1985 "La formule baptismale dans les Actes des Apôtres: Quêlques observations relatives au style de Luc," in: *A cause de l'évangile. Études sur les Synoptiques et les Actes offertes au P. Jacques Dupont* (LD 123), Paris: Éditions du Cerf, 727-738. In this volume nr. 14, pp. 155-163.
1986 "On Reading Others' Letters", in: GEORGE NICKELSBURG/GEORGE MACRAE (eds.), *Christians Among Jews and Gentiles. Essays in Honor of Krister Stendahl*, Philadelphia, Penn.: Fortress, 137-146. Reprinted in HARTMAN 1997a, 167-177.
1986 *Kolosserbrevet* (KNT 12), Uppsala: EFS-förlaget.
²1989 "Survey of the problem of apocalyptic genre", in: DAVID HELLHOLM (ed.), *Apocalypticism in the Mediterranean World and the Near East. Proceedings of the international colloquium on Apocalypticism, Uppsala August 12-17, 1979*, Tübingen: J. C. B. Mohr (Paul Siebeck), 329-343. Reprinted in HARTMAN 1997a, 89-105.
1995 (Ed.): *Jesustolkningar idag. Tio teologer om kristologi*, Stockholm: Verbum.
1996 "Das Markusevangelium ,für die *lectio solemnis* im Gottesdienst verfasst'?", in: HUBERT CANCIC/HERMANN LICHTENBERGER/PETER SCHÄFER (eds.) *Geschichte-Tradition-Reflexion*, Tübingen: Mohr Siebeck, 147-171. Reprinted in HARTMAN 1997a, 25-51.
1997a *Text-Centered New Testament Studies. Text-Theoretical Essays on Early Jewish and Early Christian Literature*, ed. DAVID HELLHOLM (WUNT 102), Tübingen: Mohr Siebeck.
1997b *Into the Name of the Lord Jesus. Baptism in the Early Church*, Edinburgh: T. & T. Clark 1997.
2004 *Markusevangeliet 1-2* (Kommentar till Nya Testamentet 2a), Stockholm: EFS-förlaget/Verbum. An English revised version 2010.
2005 *Markusevangeliet 8:27-16:20* (Kommentar till Nya Testamentet 2b), Stockholm: EFS-förlaget/Verbum. An English revised version 2010.
2006 ",Was soll ich tun, damit ich das ewige Leben erbe?' Ein heidenchristlicher Leser vor einigen ethischen Sätzen des Markusevangeliums," in: *Eschatologie und Ethik.* (FS G. Haufe); ed. CHRISTFRIED BÖTTRICH; Frankfurt am Main: Peter Lang, 75-90. In this volume nr. 12, pp. 127-133.
2010 *Mark for the Nations. A Text- and Reader-oriented Commentary* (Pickwick Publications), Wipf and Stock Publishers, Eugene, Oreg. 2010.

HARTVIGSEN, KIRSTEN MARIE
2012 *Prepare the Way of the Lord. Towards a Cognitive Poetic Analysis of Audience Involvement with Characters and Events in the Markan World* (BZNW 180), Berlin - Boston: de Gruyter.

HARVEY, JULIEN
    1967    *Le playdoyer prophétique contre Israël après la rupture de l'alliance,* Paris – Brügge: Desclée de Brouwer • Montreal: Bellarmin.

HAUCK, FRIEDRICH
    1931    *Das Evangelium des Markus* (ThHK 2), Leipzig: Deichert, 16–17.

HEIL, JOHN PAUL
    1992    *The Gospel of Mark as Model for Action. A Reader-Response Commentary,* New York – Mahvah, N. J.: Paulist Press.

HEITMÜLLER, WILHELM
    1903    ‚*Im Namen Jesu.*‛ *Eine religionsgeschichtliche Untersuchung zum Neuen Testament* (FRLANT 1.2), Göttingen: Vandenhoeck & Ruprecht.

HELLHOLM, DAVID
    1980    *Das Visionenbuch des Hermas als Apokalypse.* Formgeschichtliche und texttheoretische Studien zu einer literarischen Gattung I: Methodologische Vorüberlegungen und makrostrukturelle Textanalyse (CB.NT 13:1), Lund: Gleerup.
    1982    "The problem of apocalyptic genre and the Apocalypse of John", in: KENT H. RICHARDS (ed.), *Society of Biblical Literature 1982 seminar papers.* Chico, Calif.: Scholars Press, 157–198.
    1986    "The Problem of Apocalyptic Genre and the Apocalypse of John", in: *Semeia* 36, 13–64.
    1991    "Methodological Reflections on the Problem of Definition of Generic Texts", in: JOHN J. COLLINS/JAMES H. CHARLESWORTH (eds.), *Mysteries and Revelations, Apocalyptic Studies since the Uppsala Colloquium* (JSPE.S 9), Sheffield: JSOT Press, 135–163.
    1993    "Ampflificatio in the Macro-Structure of Romans", in: *Rhetoric and the New Testament,* STANLEY E. PORTER/THOMAS H. OLBRICHT (eds.), Sheffield: JSOT Press, 123–151.
    1995    "Substitutionelle Gliedermerkmale und die Komposition des Matthäusevangeliums" in: TORD FORNBERG/DAVID HELLHOLM (eds.), *Texts and Contexts. Biblical Texts in Their Textual and Situational Contexts.* Essays in Honor of Lars Hartman, Oslo – Copenhagen – Stockholm – Boston, Mass.: Scandinavian University Press, 11–76.
    1998    "The 'Revelation-Schema' and Its Adaptation in the Coptic Gnostic Apocalypse of Peter", in: *SEÅ* 63, 233–248.
    1998    "Beatitudes and Their Illocutionary Function", in: ADELA YARBRO COLLINS (ed.), *Ancient and Modern Perspectives on the Bible and Culture:* Essays in Honor of Hans Dieter Betz (Scholars Press Homage Series 22), Atlanta, Ga.: Scholars Press, 286–344.
    1990    "The Visions He Saw or: To Encode the Future in Writing. An Analysis of the Prologue of John's Apocalyptic Letter", in: THEODORE W. JENNINGS, JR. (ed.), *Text and Logos. The Humanistic Interpretation of the New Testament* (Scholars Press Homage Series), Atlanta, Ga.: Scholars Press, 109–146.

2006 "Religion und Gewalt in der Apokalyptik", in: FRIEDRICH SCHWEITZER (ed.), *Religion, Politik und Gewalt* (Veröffentlichungen der Wissenschaftlichen Gesellschaft für Theologie 29), Gütersloh: Gütersloher Verlagshaus, 413–438.

2008a "Moses as διάκονος of the παλαιὰ διαθήκη – Paul as διάκονος of the καινὴ διαθήκη", in: *ZNW* 99, 247–289.

2008b "Lucian's Icaromenippos as a Parody of an Apocalypse and 2 Corinthians 12,2–4 as a Report about a Heavenly Journey", in: DAVID C. BIENERT/ JOACHIM JESKA/THOMAS WITULSKI (eds.), *Paulus und die antike Welt. Beiträge zur zeit- und religionsgeschichtlichen Erforschung des paulinischen Christentums* (FRLANT 222), Göttingen: Vandenhoeck & Ruprecht, 56–82.

2009 "Die Gattung Haustafel im Kolosser- und Epheserbrief", in: PETER MÜLLER (ed.) *Kolosser-Studien* (BThSt 103), Neukirchen-Vluyn: Neukirchener, 103–128.

2011 "Vorgeformte Tauftraditionen und deren Benutzung in den Paulusbriefen", in: DAVID HELLHOLM ET ALII (eds.), *Ablution, Initiation, and Baptism*, Vol. I (BZNW 176/I), Berlin – New York: de Gruyter, 415–495.

forthcom. "The Apocalyptic Genre: The case of the Apocalypse of John", in: IDEM *New Testament and Textlinguistics. A Theoretical Approach to Early Christian Narrative*, Tübingen: Mohr Siebeck forthcoming, § 3.3.3.2.

HEMER, COLIN J.
1986 *The Letters to the Seven Churches of Asia in Their Local Setting* (JSNT.S 11), Sheffield: JSOT Press.

HENGEL, MARTIN
1969 *Judentum und Hellenismus* (WUNT 10), Tübingen: J. C. B. Mohr (Paul Siebeck).
²1973 *Judentum und Hellenismus, Studien zu ihrer Begegnung unter besonderer Berücksichtigung Palästinas bis zur Mitte des 2. Jh.s v. Chr.* (WUNT 10), Tübingen: J. C. B. Mohr (Paul Siebeck).
1974 *Judaism and Hellenism I*, Philadelphia, Penn.: Fortress.
²1977 *Der Sohn Gottes*, Tübingen: J. C. B. Mohr (Paul Siebeck).
1977 *Crucifixion: In the Ancient World and the Folly of the Message of the Cross*, London: SCM Press • Philadelphia, Penn.: Fortress.
1981 *The Atonement: The Origins of the Doctrine in the New Testament*, London: SCM Press.
1989 *The 'Hellenization' of Judaea in the First Century after Christ*, London: SCM Press • Philadelphia, Penn.: Trinity 1989, 1–6.

HENZE, MATTHIAS
2011 *Jewish Apocalypticism in the Late First Century Israel* (TSAJ 142), Tübingen: Mohr Siebeck.

HERMERÉN, GÖRAN
1982 "Tolkningstyper och tolkningskriterier", in: *Tolkning och tolkningsteorier*, (Kungl. Vitterhets Historie och Antikvitets Akademien, Konferenser 7), Stockholm: Almqvist & Wiksell International, 269–292.

HESSELING, DIRK CHRISTIAAN/PERNOT HUBERT
 1927 "Neotestamentica: ἵνα = omdat", in: *Neophilologus* 12, 41–46.

HIMMELFARB, MARTHA
 1993 *Ascent to Heaven in Jewish and Christian Apocalypses*, Oxford – New York: Oxford University Press.

HIRSCH, ERIC DONALD
 1967 *Validity in Interpretation*, New Haven, Conn: Yale University Press.

HOFFMANN, PAUL
 1972 *Studien zur Theologie der Logienquelle* (NTA.NF. 8), Münster: Aschendorff.

HOLMBERG, BENGT
 1978 *Paul and Power. The Structure of Authority in the Primitive Church as Reflected in the Pauline Epistles* (CB.NT 11), Lund: Gleerup. Reprinted: Philadelphia, Penn.: Fortress 1980.

HOLMSTRAND, JONAS
 1997 *Markers and Meaning in Paul. An Analysis of 1 Thessalonians, Philippians and Galatians* (CB.NT 28), Stockholm: Almqvist & Wiksell.

HOLTZ, TRAUGOTT
 1979 *Jesus aus Nazareth,* Berlin: Union.

HOOKE, SAMUEL HENRY
 1933 (Ed.), *Myth and Ritual,* London: Oxford University Press.
 1935 (Ed.) *The Labyrinth,* London: SPCK • New York: Macmillan.
 1958 *Myth, Ritual and Kingship,* Oxford: Oxford University Press.

HOOKER, MORNA D.
 1991 *The Gospel according to Saint Mark* (BNTC), London: Black • Peabody, Mass.: Hendrikson.

HORSLEY, GREG H. R.
 1983 *New Documents illustrating early Christianity. A Review of the Greek inscriptions and papyri published in 1978*, North Ryde, N.S.W.: Ancient History Documentary Research Centre, Macquarie University.

HOVHANESSIAN, VAHAN
 2000 *Third Corinthians. Reclaiming Paul for Christian Orthodoxy* (Studies in Biblical Literature 18), New York: Peter Lang.

HÜBNER, HANS
 1984 *Law in Paul's Thought*, trans. James C. G. Greig, Edinburgh: Clark.
 1997 *An Philemon, An die Kolosser, An die Epheser* (HNT 12), Tübingen: Mohr Siebeck.

HULTGÅRD, ANDERS
 1979 "Das Judentum in der hellenistisch-römischen Zeit und die iranische Religion – ein religionsgeschichtliches Problem," in: *ANRW* II.19.1, Berlin: de Gruyter, 512–590.

1998 "Persian Apocalypticism", in: JOHN J. COLLINS (ed.), *The Encyclopedia of Apocalypticism*, Vol. I, New York: Continuum, 39–83.

VAN IERSEL, BAS M. F.
1998 *Mark: A Reader-Response Commentary* (JSNTSup 164), Sheffield: Sheffield Academic Press.

ILAN, TAL
1992 "'Man Born of Woman…' (Job 14:1). The Phenomenon of Men Bearing Metronymes at the Time of Jesus", in: *NT* 34, 23–45.

JANNARIS, ANTONIUS NICHOLAS
1897 *An Historical Greek Grammar*, London: Macmillan.

JAUBERT, ANNIE
1963 *La notion d'alliance dans le Judaïsme aux abords de l'ère chrétienne* (PatSor 6), Paris: Seuil.

JEREMIAS, JOACHIM
1958 *Jesus' promise to the nations. The Franz Delitzsch lectures for 1953* (SBT 24), London: SCM Press.
⁵1958 *Die Gleichnisse Jesu*, Göttingen: Vandenhoeck & Ruprecht.
1960 *Infant Baptism in the First Four Centuries*, London: SCM Press.

JERVELL, JACOB
1972 *Luke and the People of God*, Minneapolis, Minn.: Augsburg.
1973 *Gud og hans fiender*, Oslo – Bergen – Tromsø: Universitetsforlaget.
1977 "Das Volk des Geistes", in: JACOB JERVELL/WAYNE MEEKS (eds.), *God's Christ and His People*. (FS N. A. Dahl), Oslo – Bergen – Tromsø: Universitetsforlaget, 87–106.

JEWETT, ROBERT
2007 *Romans* (Hermeneia), Minneapolis, Minn.: Fortress.

JOHNSON, GARY J.
1995 *Early-Christian Epitaphs from Anatolia* (SBL.TT 35; ECLS 8), Atlanta, Ga.: Scholars Press.

JOHNSON, SHERMAN E.
1951 "Ad Matt. xxviii. 19", in: *The Interpreter's Bible* VII, New York – Nashville, Ky.: Abingdon Press.

JOLY, S. ROBERT
1968 *Le vocabulaire chrétien de l'amour est-il originel? φιλεῖν et ἀγαπᾶν dans le grec antique*, Brussels: Presses Universitaires de Bruxelles.

JONES, CHRISTOPHER P.
1978 *The Roman World of Dio Chrysostomus*, Cambridge, Mass.: Harvard University Press.

JONES, DOUGLAS RAWLINSON
1963 "Commentaries: a Historical Note", in: *Cambridge History of the Bible* 3, 531–535.

KABIERSCH, JÜRGEN
- 1960 *Untersuchungen zum Begriff der Philanthropia bei dem Kaiser Julian* (KPS 31), Wiesbaden: Harrassowitz.

KÄSEMANN, ERNST
- 1960 "Eine urchristliche Taufliturgie", in: IDEM, *Exegetische Versuche und Besinnungen*, I, Göttingen: Vandenhoeck & Ruprecht, 34–51 (first published in: FS R. Bultmann, Stuttgart: Kohlhammer 1949, 133–148).
- 1960 "Zum Verständnis von Römer 3,24–26", in: *ibid.* I, Göttingen: Vandenhoeck & Ruprecht, 96–100, (first published in: *ZNW* 43 [1950/51] 150–154).
- 1964 "Die Anfänge christlicher Theologie", in: IDEM, *Exegetische Versuche und Besinnungen* II, Göttingen: Vandenhoeck & Ruprecht, 82–104, (first published in: *ZThK* 57 [1960] 162–185).
- 1964 "Zum Thema der urchristlichen Apokalyptik", in: *ibid.*, II, Göttingen: Vandenhoeck & Ruprecht, 105–131, (first published in: *ZThK* 59 [1962] 257–284).
- 1964 *Gottesgerechtigkeit bei Paulus*, in: *ibid.*, II, Göttingen: Vandenhoeck & Ruprecht, 181–193, (first published in: *ZThK* 58, 367–378).
- 1972 *Paulinische Perspektiven*, Tübingen: J. C. B. Mohr (Paul Siebeck).
- 1973 *An die Römer* (HNT 8a), Tübingen: J. C. B. Mohr (Paul Siebeck).

KALVERKÄMPER, HARTWIG
- 1998 "Körpersprache", in: *HWR* 4, 1339–1371.

KAMLAH, EHRHARD
- 1964 *Die Form der katalogischen Paränese im NT* (WUNT 7), Tübingen: J. C. B. Mohr (Paul Siebeck).

KASPER, WALTER
- 1976 *Jesus the Christ,* London: Burns & Oates • New York: Paulist Press.

KECK, LEANDER E.
- 1970/71 "The Spirit and the Dove", in: *NTS* 17, 41–67.

KEHL, MEDARD
- 1986 *Eschatologie*, Würzburg: Echter.

KELBER, WERNER H.
- 1974 *The Kingdom in Mark. A New Place and a New Time*, Philadelphia, Penn.: Fortress.

KENNEDY, HENRY AGNUS ALEXANDER
- 1915 "The Significance and Range of the Covenant-Conception in the New Testament", in: *Exp.* 8:10, 385–410.

KENNETT, ROBERT HATCH
- 1907 *In Our Tongues: Some Thoughts of the English Bible,* London: Edward Arnold.

KIEFFER, RENÉ
- 1972 *Essai de méthodologie néo-testamentaire* (CB.NT 4), Lund: Gleerup.
- 1976 "Was heißt das, einen Text zu kommentieren?", in: *BZ* 20, 212–216.

1987     *Die Bibel deuten – das Leben deuten. Einführung in die Theologie des Neuen Testaments*, Regensburg: Pustet.
1987–88     *Johannesevangeliet* (KNT 4 A, B), Uppsala: EFS-Förlaget.

KINGSBURY, JACK DEAN
1981     *Jesus Christ in Matthew, Mark and Luke* (Proclamation Commentaries), Philadelphia, Penn.: Fortress.
²1988a     *Matthew As Story*, Philadelphia, Penn.: Fortress.
1988b     "Reflections on 'the Reader' of Matthew's Gospel", in: *NTS* 34, 442–460.

KIRBY, JOHN T.
1988     "The Rhetorical Situations of Revelation 1–3", in: *NTS* 34, 197–207.

KLAPPERT, BERTOLD
²1967     (ed.), *Diskussion um Kreuz und Auferstehung*, Wuppertal: Aussaat.

KLAUCK, HANS-JOSEF
1992     "Das Sendschreiben nach Pergamon und der Kaiserkult in der Johannesoffenbarung", in: *Bib* 73, 153–182.
1994     "Der Katechismus der katholischen Kirche. Rückfragen aus exegetischer Sicht", in: EHRENFRIED SCHULZ (ed.), *Ein Katechismus für die Welt: Informationen und Anfragen* (Schriften der katholischen Akademie in Bayern 150), Düsseldorf: Patmos, 71–82.
2006     *Ancient Letters and the New Testament*, Waco, Tex.: Baylor.

KLAUCK, HANS-JOSEF/BÄBLER, BALBINA
2000     *Dion von Prusa, Olympische Rede oder über die Erste Erkenntnis Gottes* (SAPERE II), Darmstadt: Wissenschaftliche Buchgesellschaft.

KLOSTERMANN, ERICH
⁵1971     *Das Markusevangelium* (HNT 3), Tübingen: J. C. B. Mohr (Paul Siebeck).

KNIBB, MICHAEL A.
1978     *The Ethiopic Book of Enoch. A new edition in the light of the Aramaic Dead Sea fragments. I–II. Introduction, translation and commentary*. Oxford: Clarendon.

KOCH, DIETRICH-ALEX
2008     "Die Einmaligkeit des Anfangs und die Fortdauer der Institution. Neutestamentliche Beobachtungen zum Problem der Gemeindeleitung", in: IDEM, *Hellenistisches Christentum. Schriftverständnis – Ekklesiologie – Geschichte* (NTOA 65), Göttingen: Vandenhoeck & Ruprecht, 197–210.
2008a     "Proselyten und Gottesfürchtige als Hörer der Reden von Apostelgeschichte 2,14–39 und 13,16–41", in: IDEM, *Hellenistisches Christentum*, 250–271.
2008b     "The God-fearers between facts and fiction". Two theosebeis-inscriptions from Aphrodisias and the bearing for the New Testament", in: IDEM, *Hellenistisches Christentum*, 272–298.

KOCH, KLAUS
1970     *Ratlos vor der Apokalyptik*, Gütersloh: Gütersloher.
1994     *Daniel* (BKAT XII), Neukirchen-Vluyn: Neukirchener.

1995 "Weltgeschichte und Gottesreich im Danielbuch und die iranischen Parallelen", in: IDEM, *Die Reiche der Welt und der kommende Menschensohn. Studien zum Danielbuch* (Gesammelte Aufsätze 2), Neukirchen-Vluyn: Neukirchener, 46–65.

KOESTER, HELMUT
1971 "*Gnomai diaphoroi*. The Origin and Nature of Diversification in the History of Early Christianity", in: JAMES MCCONKEY ROBINSON/HELMUT KOESTER. *Trajectories through Early Christianity*, Philadelphia, Penn.: Fortress, 114–157.
1982 *Introduction to the New Testament II: History and Literature of Early Christianity*, Philadelphia, Penn. – Berlin – New York: Fortress. [2$^{nd}$ ed., Berlin – New York: de Gruyter 2000].

VAN KOOTEN, GEORGE H.
2003 *Cosmic Christology in Paul and the Pauline School* (WUNT 171), Tübingen: Mohr Siebeck.

KRAFT, HEINRICH
1961 "Die Anfänge der christlichen Taufe", in: *ThZ* 17, 399–412.
1974 *Die Offenbarung des Johannes* (HNT 16a), Tübingen: J. C. B. Mohr (Paul Siebeck).

KRAUS, SAMUEL
1922 *Synagogale Altertümer*, Berlin – Wien: Harz.

KREMER, JACOB
1994 "Die Interpretation der Bibel in der Kirche", in: *Stimmen der Zeit* 212, 151–166.

KRETSCHMAR, GEORG
1970 "Die Geschichte des Taufgottesdienstes in der alten Kirche", in: KARL FERDINAND MÜLLER/WALTER BLANKENBURG (eds.) *Leiturgia* 5, Kassel-Wilhelmshöhe: Stauda.

KRISTENSEN, WILLIAM BREDE
1960 *The Meaning of Religion*, Den Haag: Martinus Nijhoff.

KÜCHLER, MAX
1979 *Frühjüdische Weisheitstraditionen* (OBO 26), Freiburg (CH): Universitätsverlag • Göttingen: Vandenhoeck & Ruprecht.

KÜHNER, RAPHAEL/GERTH, BERNHARD
²1898 *Ausführliche Grammatik der griechischen Sprache. II. Satzlehre I–II*, Hannover – Leipzig: Hahnsche Buchhandlung.
³1904 *Ausführliche Grammatik der griechischen Sprache. II. Satzlehre I–II*, Hannover – Leipzig: Hahnsche Buchhandlung.

KÜMMEL, WERNER GEORG
1968 "Das Problem der ‚Mitte des Neuen Testaments'", in: *L'Évangile, hier et aujourd'hui. Mélanges offerts au Professeur Franz-J. Leenhardt,* Genève:

Labor et fides, 71–85. Reprinted in: IDEM, *Heilsgeschechen und Geschichte II* (Gesammelte Aufsätze), Marburg: Elwert, 62–74.

1972     *The New Testament: The History of the Investigation of Its Problems*, trans. S. M. Gilmore/H. C. Kee. Nashville, Ky. – New York: SCM Press.

1982     "Ein Jahrhundert Erforschung der Eschatologie des Neuen Testaments", in: *ThLZ* 107, 81–96.

KUHN, HEINZ-WOLFGANG

1975     "Jesus als Gekreuzigter in der frühchristlichen Verkündigung bis zur Mitte des 2. Jahrhunderts", in: *ZThK* 72, 1–46.

KUSS, OTTO

1957     *Der Römerbrief* I, Regensburg: Pustet.

1963     "Zur vorpaulinischen Tauflehre im Neuen Testament", originally published in 1951; reprinted in: IDEM, *Auslegung und Verkündigung*, I, Regensburg: Pustet.

LADD, GEORGE ELDON

1979     *The Presence of the Future*, London: SPCK.

LAGRANGE, MARIE-JOSEPH

1947     *Évangile selon Saint Marc*, Paris: Gabalda.

LAMBRECHT, JAN

1980     "A Structuration of Revelation 4,1–22,5", in: JAN LAMBRECHT (ed.), *L'Apocalypse johannique et l'apocalyptique dans le Nouveau Testament* (BEThL 53), Paris – Gembloux: Duculot • Leuven: Leuven University Press, 77–104.

LAMPE, GEOFFREY WILLIAM HUGO

1957     "The reasonableness of typology", in: GEOFFREY W. H. LAMPE/KENNETH J. WOOLCOMBE (eds.), *Essays on typology* (SBT 22) London: SCM Press.

LAMPE, PETER

1974     "Die markinische Deutung des Gleichnisses vom Sämann Markus 4,10–12", in: *ZNW* 65, 140–150.

LANE, WILLIAM L.

1974     *The Gospel according to Mark*, Grand Rapids, Mich.: Eerdmans.

LARSSON, EDVIN

1962     *Christus als Vorbild* (ASNU 23), Lund: Gleerup.

LAUSBERG, HEINRICH

1960     *Handbuch der literarischen Rhetorik* I, München: Hueber.

VAN DER LEEUW, GERHARD

$^3$1970     *Phänomenologie der Religion*, Tübingen: J. C. B. Mohr (Paul Siebeck). [First ed. 1956.]

LEHMANN, MANFRED R.

1958–59     "1Q Genesis Apocryphon in the light of targumim and midrashim", in: *RdQ* 1, 249–263.

LEIPOLDT, JOHANNES
    1928    *Die urchristliche Taufe im Lichte der Religionsgeschichte*, Leipzig: Dörffling & Franke.

LEVINE, BARUCH A.
    1968    "On the Presence of God in Biblical Religion", in: *Religions in Antiquity. Essays in Memory of E. R. Goodenough* (SHR; Suppl. Numen 14), Leiden: Brill 1968, 71–87.
    1987    "Biblical Temple", in: *The Encyclopedia of Religion* II, New York: MacMillan, 202–217.

LEWIS, JACK P.
    1968    *A study of the interpretation of Noah and the flood in Jewish and Christian literature*, Leiden: Brill.

LIDDELL, HENRY GEORGE/SCOTT, ROBERT/JONES HENRY STUART
    [9]1940    *A Greek-English Lexicon*, Oxford: Clarendon Press.

LIETZMANN, HANS
    [5]1971    *An die Römer* (HNT 8), Tübingen: J. C. B. Mohr (Paul Siebeck).

LINDBLOM, JOHANNES
    1919    *Jesu missions- och dopbefallning, Matt. 28:18–20. Tillika en studie över det kristna dopets ursprung*, Stockholm: Svenska kyrkans diakonistyrelse.

LINDEMANN, ANDREAS
    1979    *Paulus im ältesten Christentum. Das Bild des Apostels und die Rezeption der paulinischen Theologie in der frühchristlichen Literatur bis Marcion* (BHTh 58), Tübingen: J. C. B. Mohr (Paul Siebeck).
    1992    *Die Clemensbriefe* (HNT 17; Die apostolischen Väter 1), Tübingen: Mohr Siebeck.

LOHFINK, GERHARD
    1974    "Kommentar als Gattung," in: *BibLeb* 5, 1–16.

LOHMEYER, ERNST
    [13]1964    *Die Briefe an die Philipper, an die Kolosser und an Philemon* (KEK 9), Göttingen: Vandenhoeck & Ruprecht ([8]1930).
    [9]1953a    *Die Briefe an die Philipper, an die Kolosser und an Philemon* (KEK 9), by W. SCHMAUCH, Göttingen: Vandenhoeck & Ruprecht.
    [2]1953b    *Die Offenbarung des Johannes* (HNT 16), Tübingen: J. C. B. Mohr (Paul Siebeck).
    [16]1963    *Das Evangelium des Markus* (KEK 1/2), Göttingen: Vandenhoeck & Ruprecht.
    [14]1974    *Die Briefe an die Philipper, an die Kolosser und an Philemon* (KEK 9), Göttingen: Vandenhoeck & Ruprecht.

LOHSE, EDUARD
    [14]1968    *Die Briefe an die Kolosser und an Philemon* (KEK IX/2), Göttingen: Vandenhoeck & Ruprecht.
    1971    *Die Offenbarung des Johannes* (NTD 11), Göttingen: Vandenhoeck & Ruprecht.

2003    *Der Brief an die Römer* (KEK 4), Göttingen: Vandenhoeck & Ruprecht.

LONA, HORACIO E.
1998    *Der erste Clemensbrief* (KAV 2), Göttingen: Vandenhoeck & Ruprecht.

LONGENECKER RICHARD N.
1968    "Some Distinctive Early Christological Motifs", in: *NTS* 14, 526–545.

LÜHRMANN, DIETER
1975    "Wo man nicht mehr Sklave oder Freier ist", in: *Wort und Dienst NF* 13, 58–83.
1980/81    "Neutestamentliche Haustafeln und antike Ökonomie", in: *NTS* 27, 83–97.
1987    *Das Markusevangelium* (HNT 3), Tübingen: Mohr Siebeck.

LUNDBERG, PER IVAR
1942    *La typologie baptismale dans l'ancienne église* (ASNU 10), Leipzig: Alfred Lorentz.

LUST JOHAN/EYNIKEL ERIK/HAUSPIE, KATRIN
1992–1996    *A Greek-English Lexicon of the Septuagint I–II*, Stuttgart: Deutsche Bibelgesellschaft.

LUZ, ULRICH
1974    "Theologia crucis als Mitte der Theologie im Neuen Testament", in: *EvTh* 34, 116–141.
1985    *Das Evangelium nach Matthäus (Mt 1–7)* (EKK 1/1), Zürich – Einsiedeln – Köln: Benziger • Neukirchen-Vluyn: Neukirchener. [²2002.]

LYONNET, STANISLAS
1960    "L'hymne christologique de l'épître aux Colossiens et la fête juive du Nouvel An", in: *RSR* 48, 93–100.

LYS, DANIEL
1965    "The Israelite Soul according to the LXX", in: *VT* 6, 181–228.

MAAS, FRITZ
1955    "Von den Ursprüngen der rabbinischen Schriftauslegung", in: *ZThK* 52, 129–161.

MACADAM, HENRY I.
1983    "Epigraphy and Village Life in Southern Syria during the Roman and Early Byzantine Periods", in: *Berytos* 31, 103–115.

MACK, BURTON LEE
1970    *Logos und Sophia. Untersuchungen zur Weisheitstheologie im Hellenistischen Judentum* (StUNT 10), Göttingen: Vandenhoeck & Ruprecht.

MACQUARRIE, JOHN
²1977    *Principles of Christian Theology*, London: SCM Press.

MAIER, JOHANN
1972    *Geschichte der jüdischen Religion*, Berlin – New York: de Gruyter.

MALHERBE, ABRAHAM J.
  1977    (Ed.) "The Epistles of Crates 7", in: *The Cynic Epistles. A Study Edition* (SBLSBS 12), Missoula, Mont.: Society of Biblical Literature. [Reprinted Atlanta, Ga.: Scholars Press 1986.]

MARCUS, JOEL
  1966    *Mark 1–8* (AncB), New York: Doubleday.

MARTIN, LUTHER H.
  1994    "The Anti-Individualistic Ideology of Hellenistic Culture", in: *Numen* 41, 117–140.

MARTIN, WALLACE
  1986    *Recent Theories of Narrative,* Ithaca, N.Y. – London: Cornell University Press.

MARTINI, CARLO M.
  1979    "La tradition textuelle des Actes des Apôtres et les tendances de l'Église ancienne", in: JACOB KREMER (ed.), *Les Actes des Apôtres. Traditions, rédaction, théologie* (BEThL 48), Paris – Gembloux: Duculot • Louvain: Leuven University Press, 21–35.

MARTYN, J. LOUIS
  1979    *History and Theology in the Fourth Gospel*, Nashville, Ky.: Abingdon.

MASSINGBERDE FORD, JOSEPHINE
  1975    *Revelation* (AncB 38), Garden City, N.Y.: Doubleday.

MCARTHUR, HARVEY K.
  1973    "Son of Mary", in: *NT* 15, 38–58.

MEEKS, WAYNE
  1985    "Breaking Away: Three New Testament Pictures of Christianity's Separation from the Jewish Communities", in: JACOB NEUSNER/ERNST FRERICHS (eds.), *To See Ourselves as Others See Us*, Chico, Calif.: Society of Biblical Literature, 94–104.

MERKLEIN, HELMUT
  $^2$1981    *Die Gottesherrschaft als Handlungsprinzip. Untersuchung zur Ethik Jesu*, Würzburg: Echter.
  1981a    "Eph 4,1–5,20 als Rezeption von Kol 3,1–17 (zugleich ein Beitrag zur Problematik des Epheserbriefes)", in: *Kontinuität und Einheit, Festschrift für F. Mussner*, Freiburg i. Br.: Herder, 194–210.

DE MEULENAERE, HERMAN
  1976    "History of the Town", in: *Mendes II* (EMMA SWAN HALL/BERNARD V. BOTHMER eds.), Warminster: Aris & Phillips, 72–177.

MICHEL, OTTO
  $^{11}$1957    *Der Brief an die Römer* (KEK 4), Göttingen: Vandenhoeck & Ruprecht.
  $^{12}$1963    *Der Brief an die Römer* (KEK 4), Göttingen: Vandenhoeck & Ruprecht.

MILIK, JÓZEF TADEUSZ
　1976　(Ed.) *The books of Enoch. Aramaic fragments of Qumrân cave 4*, Oxford: Clarendon.

MOLONEY, FRANCIS J.
　2002　*The Gospel of Mark. A Commentary*, Peabody, Mass.: Hendrickson.

MOULE, CHARLES F. D.
　²1959　*An Idiom Book of New Testament Greek*, Cambridge: Cambridge University Press. [Reprinted 1960 and 1971.]

MOULTON, JAMES HOPE/MILLIGAN, GEORGE
　²1985　*The Vocabulary of the Greek Testament Illustrated from the Papyri and Other Non-Literary Sources*, Grand Rapids, Mich.: Eerdmans 1985. [First edition 1930.]

MOWINCKEL, SIGMUND
　1916　*Kongesalmerne i det Gamle Testamente*, Kristiania: Aschehoug & Company (W. Nygaard).
　1960　"Kultus", in: *RGG*³ IV, 120–126.

MÜLLER, KARLHEINZ
　1983　"Die Haustafel des Kolosserbriefes und das antike Frauenthema", in: JOSEF BLANK/GERHARD DAUTZENBERG/HELMUT MERKLEIN/KARLHEINZ MÜLLER (eds.), *Die Frau im Urchristentum* (QD 95), Freiburg i. Br. – Basel – Wien: Herder, 263–319.

MÜLLER, ULRICH B.
　1975　"Die Bedeutung des Kreuzestodes Jesu im Johannesevangelium. Erwägungen zur Kreuzestheologie im Neuen Testament," in: *Kerygma und Dogma* 21, 49–71.
　1984　*Die Offenbarung des Johannes* (ÖTK 19), Gütersloh: Mohn • Würzburg: Echter.

MUNCK, JOHANNES
　1954　*Paulus und die Heilsgeschichte*, Copenhagen: Munksgaard.

MUSSNER, FRANZ
　1961　"Die Mitte des Evangeliums in neutestamentlicher Sicht," in: *Catholica* 15, 271–292.
　1974　*Der Galaterbrief* (HThK 9), Freiburg i. Br. – Basel – Wien: Herder.

NAVEH, JOSEPH/SHAKED, SHAUL
　1985　*Amulets and Magic Bowls. Aramaic Incantations of Late Antiquity*, Leiden: Magnes Press • Jerusalem: Hebrew University.

NEUSNER, JACOB
　1981　*Judaism. The evidence of the Mishnah*. Chicago, Ill.: Chicago University Press.
　1983　"Torah and Israel's National Salvation in the Talmud of Babylonia", in: IDEM, *Major Trends in Formative Judaism. Society and Symbol in Political Crisis*, Chico, Calif.: Society of Biblical Literature, 93–106.

NICKELSBURG, GEORGE W. E.
1977 "Apocalyptic and myth in 1 Enoch 6-11", in: *JBL* 96, 383-405.
1977 "The Apocalyptic Message of 1 Enoch 92 - 105", in: *CBQ* 39, 309-328.
1981 *Jewish literature between the Bible and the Mishnah. A historical and literary introduction*, London: SCM Press.
1981a "Enoch, Levi, and Peter: recipients of revelation in Upper Galilee", in: *JBL* 100, 575-600.
2001 *1 Enoch 1. A Commentary on the Book of 1 Enoch Chapters 1-36; 81-108* (Hermeneia), Minneapolis, Minn.: Fortress.

NICKELSBURG, GEORGE, W. E./VANDERKAM, JAMES C.
2012 *1 Enoch 2. A Commentary on the Book of 1 Enoch Chapters 37-82* (Hermeneia), Minneapolis, Minn.: Fortress.

NILSSON, MARTIN P.
³1974 *Geschichte der griechischen Religion II. Die hellenistische und römische Zeit* (HAW V.2.2), München: Beck.

NOCK, ARTHUR DARBY
1933 *Conversion. The Old and New in Religion from Alexander the Great to Augustine of Hippo*, Oxford: Oxford University Press.

NYGREN, ANDERS
1953 *Agape and Eros* (trans. Philip S. Watson), Philadelphia, Penn.: Westminster.

O'BRIEN, PETER T.
1982 *Colossians, Philemon* (WBC 44), Waco, Tex.: Word.

OEPKE, ALBRECHT
1933 "Βάπτω κτλ.", in: *ThWNT* 1, 527-544.
²1957 *Der Brief des Paulus an die Galater* (ThHK 9), Berlin: Evangelische Verlagsanstalt.
1959 "Ehe", in: *RAC* 4, 650-666.

OHM, THOMAS
1950 *Die Liebe zu Gott in den nichtchristlichen Religionen*, München: Erich Wewel Verlag.

OLSSON, BIRGER
1974 *Structure and Meaning in the Fourth Gospel. A Text-Linguistic Analysis of John 2:1-11 and 4:1-42* (CB.NT 6), Lund: Gleerup.

OLSSON, TORD
1979 "The Apocalyptic Activity. The Case of Jāmāsp Nāmag," in: DAVID HELLHOLM (ed.) *Apocalypticism in the Mediterranean World and the Near East*, Tübingen: J. C. B. Mohr (Paul Siebeck), 21-49.

O'NEILL, JOHN COCHRANE
1961 *The Theology of Acts*, London: SPCK.
1980 "The Source of the Christology in Colossians", in: *NTS* 26, 87-100.

ORTKEMPER, FRANZ-JOSEF
²1968 *Das Kreuz in der Verkündigung des Apostels Paulus* (SBS 24), Stuttgart: Katholisches Bibelwerk.

OSGOOD, CHARLES E./SEBEOK, THOMAS A.
1965 (Eds.) *Psycholinguistics: A Survey of Theory and Research Problems*, Bloomington, In. - London: Indiana University Press.

VON DER OSTEN-SACKEN, PETER
1976 "Leistung und Grenze der johanneischen Kreuzestheologie," in: *EvTh* 36, 154-176.

OTTOSSON, MAGNUS
1980 *Temple and Cult Places in Palestine* (AUU.Boreas: Uppsala Studies in Ancient Mediterranean and near Eastern Civilizations 12), Uppsala: Uppsala University.

OTZEN, BENEDIKT
1984 *Den antike jødedom: politisk udvikling og religiøse strømninger fra Aleksander den Store til Kejser Hadrian*, Copenhagen: Gad.

PANCARO, SEVERINO
1975 *The Law in the Fourth Gospel*, Leiden: Brill.

PATAI, RAPHAEL
1947 *Man and Temple in Ancient Jewish Myth and Ritual*, New York - London - Paris: Nelson.

PATTE, DANIEL
1975 *Early Jewish hermeneutic in Palestine* (SBLDS 22), Missoula, Mont.: Society Biblical Literature.

PEISKER, CARL HEINZ
1968 "Konsekutives ἵνα in Markus 4,12", in: *ZNW* 59, 126-127.

PERRIN, NORMAN
1976 *Jesus and the Language of the Kingdom. Symbol and Metaphor in New Testament Interpretation*, Philadelphia, Penn.: Fortress.

PESCH, RUDOLF
1976 *Das Markusevangelium I* (HThK 2/1), Freiburg i. Br. - Basel - Wien: Herder.
1977 *Das Markusevangelium II* (HThK 2/2), Freiburg i. Br. - Basel - Wien: Herder.

PLÜMACHER, ECKHARD
1972 *Lukas als hellenistischer Schriftsteller. Studien zur Apostelgeschichte* (SUNT 9), Göttingen: Vandenhoeck & Ruprecht.

POKORNÝ, PETR
1980-1981 "Christologie et Baptême a l'époque du Christianisme primitif", in: *NTS* 27, 368-380; edited German version in: IDEM, *Die Entstehung der Christo-*

*logie. Voraussetzungen einer Theologie des Neuen Testaments,* Berlin: Calwer 1985, 148–156.

POLLARD, THOMAS EVAN
1981 "Colossians 1:12–20. A Reconsideration", in: *NTS* 27, 572–575.

POPKES, WIARD
1983 "Die Funktion der Sendschreiben in der Johannes-Apokalypse. Zugleich ein Beitrag zur Spätgeschichte der neutestamentlichen Gleichnisse", in: *ZNW* 74, 90–107.

PORTEFAIX, LILIAN
1988 *Sisters Rejoice. Paul's Letter to the Philippians and Luke-Acts as Received by First-Century Philippian Women* (CB.NT 20), Stockholm: Almqvist & Wiksell.

PORTON, GARY
1979 "Midrash. Palestinian Jews and the Hebrew Bible in the Greco-Roman period", in: WOLFGANG HAASE (ed.), *Principat 19.2. Religion (Judentum: Allgemeines; Palästinisches Judentum).* (Aufstieg und Niedergang der römischen Welt 2), Berlin: de Gruyter, 103–258.

POWELL, MARK ALLAN
1992a *The Bible and Modern Literary Criticism. A Critical Assessment and Annotated Bibliography,* New York etc.: Greenwood Press.
1992b "The Plot and Subplots of Matthew's Gospel", in: *NTS* 38, 187–204.

PREISIGKE, FRIEDRICH
1925–1971 *Wörterbuch der griechischen Papyrusurkunden mit Einschluss der griechischen Inschiften, Aufschriften, Ostraka, Mumienschilder usw. aus Ägypten,* ed. EMIL KIESSLING, vol. 1–4 and suppl., Berlin – Marburg: Selbstverlag.

PRIGENT, PIERRE
1974 "Au temps de l'Apocalypse, I", in: *RHPhR,* 54 455–483.
1975a "Au temps de l'Apocalypse, II", in: *RHPhR* 55, 215–235.
1975b "Au temps de l'Apocalypse, III", in: *RHPhR* 55, 344–363.
1980 "Le temps et le Royaume dans l'Apocalypse", in: JAN LAMBRECHT (ed.), *L'Apocalypse johannique et l'apocalyptique dans le Nouveau Testament* (BEThL 53), Paris – Gembloux: Duculot • Leuven: Leuven University Press, 231–245.
1981 *L'Apocalypse de St. Jean* (CNT 14) Lausanne – Paris: Delachaux & Niestlé.

QUASTEN, JOHANNES
1960 *Patrology III: The Golden Age of Greek Patristic Literature,* Utrecht: Spectrum • Westminster, Md.: Newman.

RABIN, CHAIM
1968 "The Translation Process and the Character of the Septuagint", in: *Textus* VI, 1–26.

RÄISÄNEN, HEIKKI
 1978 "Paul's Theological Difficulties with the Law," in: ELISABETH. A. LIVINGSTONE (ed.), *Studia Biblica*, vol. 3: Papers on Paul and Other New Testament Authors (*JSNT.S* 3); Sheffield: JSOT Press, 301-320; reprinted in: IDEM, *The Torah and Christ* (Publications of the Finnish Exegetical Society 45), Helsinki: Finnish Exegetical Society, 3-24.
 1995 "The Clash Between Christian Styles of Life in the Book of Revelation", in: DAVID HELLHOLM ET ALII, Mighty Minorities? *Minorities in Early Christianity - Position and Strategies*. Essays in honour of J. Jervell, in: *StTh* 49, 151-166. [Also in: Oslo - Copenhagen - Stockholm - Boston, Mass.: Scandinavian University Press.]

RAHNER, KARL
 1967 "Eschatologie", in: *Sacramentum mundi* 1, 1183-1192.

RENGSTORF, KARL HEINRICH
 1933 "ἁμαρτωλός", in: *ThWNT* 1, 328f.
 1953 "Die neutestamentlichen Mahnungen an die Frau, sich dem Manne unterzuordnen", in: WERNER FOERSTER (ed.) *Verbum Dei manet in aeternum: Festschrift O. Schmitz*, Witten: Luther Verlag, 131-145.

RHOADS, DAVID
 1992 "Social Criticism: Crossing Boundaries", in: JANICE CAPEL ANDERSON/ STEPHEN D. MOORE (eds.), *Mark & Method: New Approaches in Biblical Studies*, Minneapolis, Minn: Fortress, 135-161.

RIAN, DAGFINN
 [2]1978 "Den religionshistoriske bakgrunn for Jødisk apokalyptikk", in: *Fremtiden i Guds Hender* (ed. Collegium Judaicum), Oslo: Skrivestua, 14-30.

RICHARDSON, ALAN
 1958 *An Introduction to the Theology of the New Testament*, New York: Harper.

RIESENFELD, HARALD
 1967 "Allt är skapat i Kristus", in: GUSTAF WINGREN/ANNA MARIE AAGAARD (eds.), *FS R. Prenter*, Copenhagen: Gyldendal, 54-64.

RIGAUX, BÉDA
 1956 *Les Épîtres aux Thessaloniciens*, Paris: Gabalda • Gembloux: Duculot.

RIMMON-KENAN, SHLOMITH
 1983 *Narrative Fiction: Contemporary Poetics*, London - New York: Methuen 1983.
 1997 *Narrative Fiction: Contemporary Poetics* (New Accents), London - New York: Routledge.

RINGGREN, HELMER
 1952 "König und Messias", in: *ZAW* 64, 120-147.
 [3]1957 "Apokalyptik", in: *RGG*³ I, 463-466.

ROSE, ARNOLD M.
1968   "Minorities", *International Encyclopedia of the Social Sciences* 9-10, 365-370.

RUNIA, DAVID T.
1986   *Philo of Alexandria and the* Timaeus *of Plato* (Philosophia antiqua), Leiden: Brill.

RUSSELL, DAVID SYME
1964   *The Method and Message of Jewish Apocalyptic,* Philadelphia, Penn.: Westminster.

SANDELIN, KARL-GUSTAV
1993   "Kommentar till förståelsemodellen", in: KARL-GUSTAV SANDELIN/GUN LUNDELL/FREDRIC CLEVE (eds.), *Texten - tolkaren - talet. Fyra hermeneutiska modeller* (Studier utgivna av Institutionen för systematisk teologi vid Åbo Akademi 24), Åbo: Åbo Akademi, 89-94.

SANDERS, ED P.
1966   "Literary Dependence in Colossians", in: *JBL* 85, 28-45.
1977   *Paul and Palestinian Judaism,* London: SCM Press.
1983   *Paul, the Law, and the Jewish People,* Philadelphia, Penn.: Fortress.

SANDERS, JACK T.
1975   *Ethics in the New Testament. Change and Development,* London: SCM Press.

SANDMEL, SAMUEL
1979   *Philo of Alexandria: An Introduction,* New York – Oxford: Oxford University Press.

SANDNES, KARL OLAV
2011   "Seal and Baptism in Early Christianity", in: DAVID HELLHOLM ET ALII (eds.), *Ablution, Initiation, and Baptism,* Vol. II, (BZNW 176/II), Berlin – New York: de Gruyter, 1441-1481.

SAUTER, GERHARD
1995a  *The Question of Meaning: A Theological and Philosophical Orientation,* Grand Rapids, Mich. – Cambridge (UK): Eerdmans.
1995b  *Einführung in die Eschatologie* (= Die Theologie. Einführungen in Gegenstand, Methoden und Ergebnisse ihrer Disziplinen und Nachbarwissenschaften), Darmstadt: Wissenschaftliche Buchgesellschaft.

SCHÄFER, PETER
1972   *Die Vorstellung vom heiligen Geist in der rabbinischen Literatur* (StANT 28), München: Kösel.
1974   "Tempel und Schöpfung", in: *Kairos* 16, 122-133.

SCHENK, WOLFGANG
1980   "Was ist ein Kommentar?", in: *BZ* 24, 1-20.
1987   "Der Kolosserbrief in der neueren Forschung (1945-1985)", in: *ANRW* II, 25:4, Berlin – New York: de Gruyter, 3327-3364.

SCHENKE, HANS-MARTIN/FISCHER, KARL MARTIN
1978-1979   Einleitung in die Schriften des Neuen Testaments I-II, Gütersloh, Güterslo-her.

SCHILLEBEECKX, EDWARD
1969   "Einige hermeneutische Überlegungen zur Eschatologie", in: Concilium 5, 18-25.

SCHLIER, HEINRICH
⁴1965   Der Brief an die Galater (KEK 7), Göttingen: Vandenhoeck & Ruprecht.
²1967   "Das Neue Testament und der Mythus", in: IDEM, Besinnung auf das Neue Testament. Exegetische Aufsätze und Vorträge II, Freiburg i. Br. – Basel – Wien: Herder, 83-96.
1977   Der Römerbrief (HThK 6), Freiburg i. Br. – Basel – Wien: Herder.

SCHMAUS, MICHAEL
1977   "Worship", in: KARL RAHNER (ed.), Encyclopedia of Theology. A Concise Sacramentum Mundi, London: Burns & Oates, 1838-1841.

SCHMID, JOSEF
1956   Das Evangelium nach Matthäus (RNT I); Regensburg: Pustet.

SCHMID, WILHELM
1905   "Dion (18)", in PRE 5, 848-877.

SCHNACKENBURG, RUDOLF
1965   Das Johannesevangelium (HThK 4) I, Freiburg i. Br. – Basel – Wien: Herder.
1982   Der Brief an die Epheser (EKK 10), Zürich – Einsiedeln – Köln: Benziger • Neukirchen-Vluyn: Neukirchener.
1983   "Paulinische und johanneische Christologie. Ein Vergleich", in: ULRICH LUZ/HANS WEDER (eds.), Die Mitte des Neuen Testaments. Einheit und Vielfalt neutestamentlicher Theologie (FS E. Schweizer), Göttingen: Vandenhoeck & Ruprecht, 221-237.
1986-1988   Die sittliche Botschaft des Neuen Testaments I-II, Völlige Neubearbeitung (HThK.S 1-2), Freiburg i. Br. – Basel – Wien: Herder.

SCHNEIDER, GERHARD
1980   Die Apostelgeschichte I (HThK 5/1), Freiburg i. Br. – Basel – Wien: Herder.

SCHNELLE, UDO
1983   Gerechtigkeit und Christusgegenwart. Vorpaulinische und paulinische Tauftheologie (GTA 24), Göttingen: Vandenhoeck & Ruprecht.
2001   "Taufe II. Neues Testament", in: TRE 32, 663-674.

SCHNIDER, FRANZ/STENGER, WERNER
1971   Johannes und die Synoptiker: Vergleich ihrer Parallelen, München: Kösel.
1987   Studien zum Neutestamentlichen Briefformular (NTTS 11), Leiden: Brill.

SCHRAGE, WOLFGANG
1974   "Leid, Kreuz und Eschaton. Die Peristasenkataloge als Merkmale paulinischer theologia crucis und Eschatologie", in: EvTh 34, 141-175.

1976 "Die Frage nach der Mitte und dem Kanon im Kanon des Neuen Testaments in der neueren Diskussion", in: JOHANNES FRIEDRICH/WOLFGANG PÖHLMANN/PETER STUHLMACHER (eds.), *Rechtfertigung. FS für Ernst Käsemann* Tübingen: J. C. B. Mohr (Paul Siebeck) • Göttingen: Vandenhoeck & Ruprecht, 415–442.

1982 *Ethik des Neuen Testaments* (NTD.E 4), Göttingen: Vandenhoeck & Ruprecht, 33–40.

SCHROEDER, DAVID

1976 "Lists, ethical", in: *IDBSup.*, New York – Nashville, Ky.: Abingdon, 546–547.

SCHÜRER, EMIL

1973 *The History of the Jewish People in the Age of Jesus Christ*, ed. by GÉZA VERMÈS/FERGUS MILLAR/MATTHEW BLACK; Edinburgh: Clark 1973–87.

1979 *The History of the Jewish People in the Age of Jesus Christ (175 BC – AD 135).* A new English version, revised and edited by GÉZA VERMÈS/FERGUS MILLAR/MATTHEW BLACK. II. Edinburgh: Clark.

1986 *The History of the Jewish People in the Age of Jesus Christ (175 BC – AD 135).* A new English version revised and edited by GÉZA VERMÈS/FERGUS MILLAR/MARTIN GOODMAN. Vol III, Part 1, Edinburgh: Clark.

SCHÜRMANN, HEINZ

1969 *Das Lukasevangelium* (HThK 3), Freiburg i. Br. – Basel – Wien: Herder.

1975 *Jesu ureigener Tod. Exegetische Besinnungen und Ausblick,* Freiburg i. Br. – Basel – Wien: Herder.

²1976 *Jesu ureigener Tod. Exegetische Besinnungen und Ausblick*, Freiburg i. Br. – Basel – Wien: Herder.

SCHÜSSLER FIORENZA, ELISABETH

1985 *The Book of Revelation – Justice and Judgment*, Philadelphia, Penn: Fortress.

1991 *Revelation, Vision of a Just World* (Proclamation Commentaries), Minneapolis, Minn.: Fortress.

SCHULZ, SIEGFRIED

1976 *Die Mitte der Schrift. Der Frühkatholizismus im Neuen Testament als Herausforderung an den Protestantismus,* Stuttgart: Kreuz.

SCHWARTZ, EDUARD

1951 *Ethik der Griechen*, WOLFGANG RICHTER (ed.), Stuttgart: Koehler.

SCHWEIZER, EDUARD

1961 *Church Order in the New Testament* (SBT 32), London: SCM Press.

1963 "Das hellenistische Weltbild als Produkt der Weltangst", in: IDEM, *Neotestamentica*, Zürich – Stuttgart: Zwingli, 15–27.

1964 "σῶμα κτλ.", in: *ThWNT* 7, 1024–91.

1967 *Das Evangelium nach Markus* (NTD 1), Göttingen: Vandenhoeck & Ruprecht.

1973 *Das Evangelium nach Matthäus* (NTD 2), Göttingen: Vandenhoeck & Ruprecht.

1975 "Versöhnung des Alls. Kol 1,20", in: GEORG STRECKER (ed.), *Jesus Christus in Historie und Theologie* (FS H. Conzelmann), Tübingen: J. C. B. Mohr (Paul Siebeck), 487–501.

1976 *Der Brief an die Kolosser* (EKK 12); Zürich: Benziger • Neukirchen-Vluyn: Neukirchener.

²1981 *Der Brief an die Kolosser* (EKK 12), Zürich – Einsiedeln – Köln: Benziger • Neukirchen-Vluyn: Neukirchener.

SCHWYZER, EDUARD/DEBRUNNER, ALBERT

1950 *Griechische Grammatik II: Syntax und syntaktische Stilistik* (HAW), München: Beck.

SEARLE, JOHN R./VANDERVEKEN, DANIEL

1985 *Foundations of Illocutionary Logic*, Cambridge: Cambridge University Press.

SEEBASS, HORST

1986 "נפשׁ", in: *ThWAT* 5, 531–555.

SEELIGMANN, ISAC LEO

1948 *The Septuagint version of Isaiah. A discussion of its problems* (MEOI 9), Leiden: Brill.

1953 *Voraussetzungen der Midraschexegese* (VT.S 1), Leiden: Brill, 150–181.

SEGAL, ALAN F.

1980 "Heavenly Ascent in Hellenistic Judaism, Early Christianity and their Environment", in: *ANRW* II.23.2, Berlin: de Gruyter, 1333–1394.

SELLIN, GERHARD

2008 *Der Brief an die Epheser* (KEK 8), Göttingen: Vandenhoeck & Ruprecht.

SEVENSTER, JAN NICOLAAS

1968 *Do you know Greek?* (NT.S 19), Leiden: Brill.

SIEGERT, FOLKER

2008 *Das Evangelium des Johannes in seiner ursprünglichen Gestalt* (SIJD 7), Göttingen: Vandenhoeck & Ruprecht.

SIMON, LOUIS

1969 "Le sou de la veuve", in: *ETR* 44, 115–126.

SJÖBERG, ERIK

1959 "πνεῦμα", in: *ThWNT* 6, 373–387.

SLONIMSKY, HENRY

1956 "The philosophy implicit in the Midrash", in: *HUCA* 27, 235–290.

SMALLEY, BERYL

1969 "The Bible in the Medieval Schools", in: *Cambridge History of the Bible* 2, Cambridge: Cambridge University Press, 197–220.

SMYTH, HERBERT WEIR

1956 *Greek Grammar* (rev. by G. H. Messing), Cambridge, Mass.: Harvard University Press. [Reprint 1966.]

STANTON, GRAHAM N.
  1989   *The Gospels and Jesus* (Oxford Bible Series), Oxford: Oxford University Press.

STAUFFER, ETHELBERT
  1933   "ἀγαπάω κτλ. B", in: *ThWNT* 1, 34–55.
  1955   *New Testament Theology*, London: Macmillan.
  1969   "Jeschu Ben Mirjam. Kontroversgeschichtliche Anmerkungen zu Mk 6,3", in: *Neotestamentica et Semitica* (FS M. Black), Edinburgh: T. & T. Clark, 119–128.

STEGEMANN, HARTMUT
  1983   "Die Bedeutung der Qumranfunde für die Erforschung der Apokalyptik", in: DAVID HELLHOLM (ed.), *Apocalypticism in the Mediterranean World and the Near East, Proceedings of the International Colloquium on Apocalypticism, Uppsala August 12–17, 1979*, Tübingen: J. C. B. Mohr (Paul Siebeck), 495–530. [2nd ed. enlarged by Supplementary Bibliography 1989].

STENDAHL, KRISTER
  1962   "Biblical Theology, Contemporary", in: *The Interpreter's Dictionary* 1, 418–432.
  1976   *Paul among Jews and Gentiles,* Philadelphia, Penn.: Fortress.

(STRACK, HERMANN L.)/BILLERBECK PAUL
  1922–28   *Kommentar zum Neuen Testament aus Talmud und Midrasch I–IV*, München: Beck.
  1922   *Kommentar zum Neuen Testament aus Talmud und Midrasch I: Das Evangelium nach Matthäus*, München: Beck.
  1924   *Kommentar zum Neuen Testament aus Talmud und Midrasch II: Das Evangelium nach Markus, Lukas und Johannes*, München: Beck.

STRACK HERMANN L./STEMBERGER, GÜNTHER
  $^7$1982   *Einleitung in Talmud und Midrasch*, München: Beck.

STRATHMANN, H.
  1914   *Geschichte der frühchristlichen Askese* I, Leipzig: Deichert.

STRECKER, GEORG
  1975   (Ed.), *Das Problem der Theologie des Neuen Testaments* (Wege der Forschung 367), Darmstadt: Wissenschaftliche Buchgesellschaft.
  1992   *Literaturgeschichte des Neuen Testaments* (UTB 1682), Göttingen: Vandenhoeck & Ruprecht.

STUHLMACHER, PETER
  1965   *Gerechtigkeit Gottes bei Paulus*, Göttingen: Vandenhoeck & Ruprecht.
  1968   "Christliche Verantwortung bei Paulus und seinen Schülern", in: *EvTh* 28, 165–186.
  1968   *Das paulinische Evangelium* I (FRLANT 95), Göttingen: Vandenhoeck & Ruprecht.
  1976   "Achtzehn Thesen zur paulinischen Kreuzestheologie", in: JOHANNES FRIEDRICH/WOLFGANG PÖHLMANN/PETER STUHLMACHER (eds.), *Rechtfer-*

*tigung.* (FS E. Käsemann), Tübingen: J. C. B. Mohr (Paul Siebeck) • Göttingen: Vandenhoeck & Ruprecht, 509–525.

TAATZ, IRENE
1991   *Frühjüdische Briefe* (NTOA 16), Freiburg (CH): Universitätsverlag • Göttingen: Vandenhoeck & Ruprecht.

THOM, JOHAN CARL
2005   *Cleantes Hymn to Zeus. Text, Translation, and Commentary* (STAC 33), Tübingen: Mohr Siebeck.

THOMPSON, LEONARD L.
1990   *The Book of Revelation. Apocalypse and Empire*, New York: Oxford University Press.

THRAEDE, KLAUS
1977   "Ärger mit der Freiheit", in: GERTA SCHARFFENORTH/KLAUS THRAEDE (eds.), *"Freunde in Christus werden ..."*, Gelnhausen – Berlin: Burckhardthaus • Stein (Mittelfranken): Laetare-Verlag, 31–182;
1980   "Zum historischen Hintergrund der ‚Haustafeln' des NT", in: ERNST DASSMANN/K. SUSO FRANK (eds.), *Pietas FS B. Kötting* (JAC, Erg. Band 8), Münster: Aschendorff, 359–368.

THYEN, HARTWIG
1970   *Studien zur Sündenvergebung* (FRLANT 96); Göttingen: Vandenhoeck & Ruprecht.

TROCMÉ, ÉTIENNE
1968/69  "L'expulsion des marchands du Temple", in: *NTS* 15, 1–22.

TURCAN, ROBERT
1978   "Le culte impérial au III<sup>e</sup> siècle", in: *ANRW* II.16.2, Berlin: de Gruyter, 996–1084.

TURNER, NIGEL
1963   In: JAMES H. MOULTON, *A Grammar of New Testament Greek*, Vol. III, Edinburgh: T. & T. Clark.

ULLMANN, STEPHEN
1962   *Semantics. An Introduction to the Science of Meaning*, Oxford: Blackwell.

VAN UNNIK, WILLEM CORNELIS
1960   "La conception paulinienne de la nouvelle alliance", in: ALBERT DESCAMPS ET ALII (eds.), *Littérature et théologie pauliniennes* (Rechbib 5), Brügge – Paris: Desclée de Brouwer, 109–126.
1979   "Luke's Second Book and the Rules of Hellenistic Historiography", in: JACOB KREMER (ed.), *Les Actes des Apôtres. Traditions, rédaction, théologie* (BEThL 48), Paris – Gembloux: Ducolot • Louvain: Leuven University Press.

VanderKam, James C.
  1980    "The righteousness of Noah", in: John J. Collins/George W. E. Nickelsburg (eds.), *Ideal figures in ancient Judaism. Profiles and paradigms* (SBLSCS 12) Chico, Calif.: Scholars Press, 13–32.

van Veldhuizen, Adrianus
  1927    "OTI-INA (?)", in: *NThS* 10, 42–44.

Vermès, Géza
  1961    *Scripture and tradition in Judaism. Haggadic studies* (StPB 4), Leiden: Brill.
  1970    "Bible and midrash: early Old Testament exegesis", in: Peter R. Ackroyd/Christopher F. Evans (eds.), *The Cambridge history of the Bible. I. From the beginnings to Jerome,* Cambridge: Cambridge University Press.

Via, Dan Otto
  1985    *The Ethics of Mark's Gospel – In the Middle of Time,* Philadelphia, Penn.: Augsburg Fortress.

Vielhauer, Philipp
  1975    *Geschichte der urchristlichen Literatur* (DGL), Berlin – New York: de Gruyter.

Vögtle, Anton
  1936    *Die Tugend- und Lasterkataloge exegetisch, religions- und formgeschichtlich untersucht* (NTAbh 16, 4–5), Münster: Aaschendorff.

Volz, Paul
  ²1934   *Die Eschatologie der jüdischen Gemeinde im neutestamentlichen Zeitalter nach den Quellen der rabbinischen, apokalyptischen und apokryphen Literatur,* Tübingen: J. C. B. Mohr (Paul Siebeck).

Vorgrimmler, Herbert
  2000    "Auferstehung (Auferweckung) Jesu Christi", in: *Neues Theologisches Wörterbuch,* Freiburg i. Br.: Herder, 72–75.

Vorster, Johannes N.
  1995    "Why opt for a rhetorical approach?", in: *Neotest.* 29(2), 393–418.

Vouga, François
  1986    "Controverse sur la résurrection des morts", in: *Lumière et Vie* 35 (179), 48–61.

Walaskay, Paul W.
  1983    *"And so we came to Rome". The Political Perspective of St. Luke* (MSSNTS 49), Cambridge: Cambridge University Press.

Walser, Georg
  2001    *The Greek of the Ancient Synagogue. An Investigation on the Greek of the Septuagint, Pseudepigrapha and the New Testament* (Studia Graeca et Latina Lundensia 8), Stockholm: Almqvist & Wiksell.

WALTER, NIKOLAUS
    2002    "Nikolaus, Proselyt aus Antiochien, und die Nikolaiten in Ephesus und Pergamon", in: *ZNW* 93, 200–226.

WATSON, DUANE F.
    1992    "Nicolaitans", in: *AncBD* IV, New York – London – Toronto – Sydney – Auckland: Doubleday, 1106–1107.

WATT, JONATHAN M.
    1997    *Code-Switching in Luke and Acts* (Berkeley Insights in Linguistics and Semiotics 31), New York etc.: Peter Lang.

WEIDINGER, KARL
    1928    *Die Haustafeln. Ein Stück urchristlicher Paränese* (UNT 14), Leipzig: Hinrichs.

WEISER, ALFONS
    1981    *Die Apostelgeschichte. Kapitel 1–12* (ÖTK 5/1), Gütersloh: Gütersloher • Würzburg: Echter.

WENDLAND, PAUL
    1912    *Die hellenistisch-römische Kultur*, Tübingen: J. C. B. Mohr (Paul Siebeck).

WHITELEY, DENNIS EDWARD HUGH
    1964    *The Theology of St. Paul*, Oxford: Blackwell.

WIBBING, SIEGFRIED
    1959    *Die Tugend- und Lasterkataloge im NT und ihre Traditionsgeschichte unter besonderer Berücksichtigung der Qumran-Texte* (BZNW 25), Berlin: de Gruyter.

WIDENGREN, GEO
    1941    *Psalm 110 och det sakrala kungadömet i Israel* (Uppsala Univ. Årsskrift 17,1).
    1945    *Religionens värld*, Uppsala: Almquist & Wiksell.
    1960    "Aspetti simbolici dei templi e luoghi di culto del Vicino Oriente antico", in: *Numen* 7, 1–25.
    1969    *Religionsphänomenologie* (DGL), Berlin: de Gruyter.
    [3]1971    *Religionens värld*, Stockholm: Almqvist & Wiksell.
    1995    "Les quatre âges du monde", in: GEO WIDENGREN/ANDERS HULTGÅRD/ MARC PHILONENKO, *Apocalyptique iranienne et dualisme qoumrânien* (Rech. Intert. 2), Paris: Maisonneuve, 24–62.

WILCKENS, ULRICH
    [2]1974    *Die Missionsreden der Apostelgeschichte* (WMANT 5), Neukirchen-Vluyn: Neukirchener.
    1978    *Der Brief an die Römer* (EKK VI/1), Zürich – Einsiedeln – Köln: Benziger • Neukirchen-Vluyn: Neukirchener.

WILCOX, MAX E.
    1965    *The Semitisms of Acts*, Oxford: Clarendon.

1979 "Luke and the Bezan Text of Acts", in: JACOB KREMER (ed.), *Les Actes des Apôtres. Traditions, rédaction, théologie* (BEThL 48), Paris – Gembloux: Doculot • Louvain: Leuven University Press, 447–455.

WILDER, AMOS N.
1950 *Eschatology and Ethics in the Teaching of Jesus*, rev. ed., New York: Harper.
1958/59 "Eschatological Imagery and Earthly Circumstance", in: *NTS* 5, 229–245.
1964 *The Language of the Gospel. Early Christian Rhetoric*, New York – Evanston: Harper & Row.

WILLIAMSON, RONALD
1989 *Jews in the Hellenistic World: Philo* (Cambridge Commentaries on Writings of the Jewish and Christian World 200 BC to AD 200 1/2), Cambridge etc.: Cambridge University Press.

WILSON, ROBERT McL.
2005 *Colossians and Philemon* (ICC), London: T. & T. Clark.

WILSON, WALTER T.
2005 *The Sentence of Pseudo-Phocylides* (CEJL), Berlin – New York: de Gruyter.

WIMSATT, WILLIAM K.
1954 "The Intentional Fallacy", in: *The Verbal Icon: Studies in the Meaning of Poetry*, Lexington, Ky.: University of Kentucky Press, 3–20.

WINDISCH, HANS
1927 "Die Verstockungsidee in Mc 4:12 und das kausale ἵνα der späteren Koine", in: *ZNW* 26, 203–209.

WINSTON, DAVID
1979 *The Wisdom of Solomon* (AncB 43), Garden City, N.Y.: Doubleday.

WITHERINGTON, BEN III
2001 *The Gospel of Mark*, Grand Rapids, Mich. – Cambridge (UK): Eerdmans.

WITULSKI, THOMAS
2007a *Kaiserkult in Kleinasien. Die Entwicklung der kultisch-religiösen Kaiserverehrung in der römischen Provinz Asia von Augustus bis Antoninus Pius* (NTOA 63), Göttingen: Vandenhoeck & Ruprecht • Fribourg: Academic Press.
2007b *Die Johannesoffenbarung und Kaiser Hadrian. Studien zur Datierung der neutestamentlichen Apokalypse* (FRLANT 221), Göttingen: Vandenhoeck & Ruprecht.
2012 *Apk 11 und der Bar Kokhba-Aufstand. Eine zeitgeschichtliche Interpretation* (WUNT II/337), Tübingen: Mohr Siebeck.

WOLFF, HANS WALTER
³1977 *Anthropologie des Alten Testaments*, Berlin: Evangelische Verlagsanstalt.

WOLFSON, HARRY A.
1947 *Philo: Foundations of Religious Philosophy in Judaism. Christianity, and Islam*, vol. II., Cambridge, Mass.: Harvard University Press.

WREDE, WILLIAM
  1897    Über Aufgabe und Methode der sogenannten neutestamentlichen Theologie, Göttingen: Vandenhoeck & Ruprecht; reprinted in: GEORG STRECKER (ed.), Das Problem der Theologie des Neuen Testaments (1975), 81-154.

WRIGHT, ADDISON G.
  1967    The literary genre midrash, Staten Island, N.Y.: Alba.

WÜLFING VON MARTITZ, PETER
  1969    "υἱός im Griechischen", in: ThWNT 8, 335-340.

YSEBAERT, JOSEPH
  1962    Greek Baptismal Terminology. Its Origin and Early Development (GCP 1), Nijmegen: Dekker & Van de Vegt.

ZAHN, THEODOR
  1924-1926    Die Offenbarung des Johannes I-II (KNT 18), Leipzig – Erlangen: Deichert.

ZELLER, DIETER
  2010    Der erste Brief an die Korinther (KEK 5), Göttingen: Vandenhoeck & Ruprecht.

ZIEBARTH, ERICH
  1896    Das griechische Vereinswesen, Leipzig: Hirzel.

# Selected Bibliography — Lars Hartman

## 1963

*Testimonium linguae* (CNT 19), Lund: Gleerup, and Copenhagen: Munksgaard 1963.
"Davids son. Apropå Acta 13,16–41," in: *Svensk Exegetisk Årsbok* 28–29 (1963–64) 117–134.
Review of K. Aland, *Synopsis Quattuor Evangeliorum*, *Svensk Exegetisk Årsbok* 28–29 (1963–64) 156–157.

## 1964

Commentaries in *Kommentar till evangelieboken. Högmässotexterna* 1–3, Uppsala: Svensk Pastoraltidskrift 1964.

## 1966

*Prophecy Interpreted* (CB.NT 1), Lund: Gleerup 1966.
Commentaries in *Kommentar till evangelieboken. Aftonsångstexterna*, Uppsala: Svensk Pastoraltidskrift 1966.
Review of B. de Solages, *Synopse Grecque des évangiles* and P. Benoit and M.-E. Boismard, *La synopse des quatre évangiles en Français avec parallèles des apocryphes et des Pères* 1, in: *Svensk Exegetisk Årsbok* 31 (1966) 133–135.

## 1967

"Antikrists mirakler," in: *Religion och Bibel* 26 (1967) 37–63.
Summary of L. Hartman, *Prophecy Interpreted*, in: *Svensk Exegetisk Årsbok* 32 (1967) 148–152.
Review of J. Jeremias, *Abba*, and E. Schweizer, *Das Evangelium nach Markus*, in: *Svensk Exegetisk Årsbok* 32 (1967) 152–154.
Review of P. Borgen, *Bread from Heaven*, in: *Svensk Exegetisk Årsbok* 32 (1967) 154–156.

## 1968

Review of J. Lambrecht, *Die Redaktion der Markus-Apokalypse*, in *Biblica* 49 (1968) 130–133.

## 1969

"Ny Testamentlig isagogik," in: Birger Gerhardsson (ed.), *En bok om Nya Testamentet*, Lund: Gleerup 1969, 11–132. Later editions: 2nd ed. 1970, 3rd ed. 1976, 4th ed. 1982, 5th ed. 1989.

Review of R. Pesch, *Naherwartungen. Tradition und Redation in Mk 13*, in: *Biblica* 50 (1969) 576-580.

## 1970

(Ed.), *Ur Nya Testamentet*, Lund: Gleerup 1970.
"'Såsom det är skrivet.' Några reflexioner över citat som kommunikationsmedel i Matteusevangeliet," in: *Svensk Exegetisk Årsbok* 35 (1970) 33-43.

## 1971

"Dopet till 'Jesu namn' och tidig kristologi," in: *Svensk Exegetisk Årsbok* 36 (1971) 136-163.
Review of R. Walker, *Die Heilsgeschichte im ersten Evangelium*, in: *Svensk Exegetisk Årsbok* 36 (1971) 179-180.
Review of Chr. Burchard, *Der dreizehnte Zeuge*, in: *Svensk Exegetisk Årsbok* 36 (1971) 180-181.
Review of G. Delling, *Studien zum Neuen Testament und zum hellenistischen Judentum*, in: *Svensk Exegetisk Årsbok* 36 (1971) 182-183.

## 1972

"Dop, ande och barnaskap," in: *Svensk Exegetisk Årsbok* 37-38 (1972-73) 88-106.
"Scriptural Exegesis in the Gospel of Matthew and the Problem of Communication," in: MARCEL DIDIER (ed.), *L'évangile selon Matthieu: Rédaction et théologie* (BEThL 29), Gembloux: Duculot 1972, 131-152.

## 1973

"Texten," in: BIRGER GERHARDSSON (ed.), *En bok om Nya Testamentet* (3rd ed.), Lund: Liber • Oslo: Universitetsforlaget 1973, 107-127.

## 1974

"Some remarks on 1 Cor. 2:1-5," in: *Svensk Exegetisk Årsbok* 39 (1974) 109-120.
"'Into the Name of Jesus': A suggestion concerning the earliest meaning of the phrase" in: *New Testament Studies* 20 (1974) 432-440. [In this volume 145-154.]
"Baptism 'Into the Name of Jesus' and Early Christianity," in: *Studia Theologica* 28 (1974) 21-48.
Review of B. Mack, *Logos und Sophia*, in: *Svensk Exegetisk Årsbok* 39 (1974) 174-176.
Review of H.-W. Kuhn, *Ältere Sammlungen im Markus-evangelium*, in: *Svensk Exegetisk Årsbok* 39 (1974) 188-189.
Review of J. Jervell, *Luke and the People of God*, in: *Svensk Exegetisk Årsbok* 39 (1974) 190-191.
Review of W. Trilling, *Untersuchungen zum zweiten Thessalonischerbrief*, in: *Svensk Exegetisk Årsbok* 39 (1974) 199-200.

## 1975

"Bibelvetenskap" (with Helmer Ringgren), in: *Religionsvetenskap. En introduktion*, Uppsala: Teologiska institutionen 1975, 42–56. 2nd ed. 1978, 43–57.

"The Functions of Some So-Called Apocalyptic Timetables," in: *New Testament Studies* 22 (1975) 1–14. [Reprinted in Hartman 1997, 107–124].

*Handikapp lidande skuld i ljuset av Nya Testamentet*, Diakoniaktuellt nr 4, 1975.

Review of M. Müller, *Messias og "Menneskesøn" i Daniels Bog, Første Enoksbog og Fjerde Ezrabog*, in: *Svensk Exegetisk Årsbok* 40 (1975) 129–121.

## 1976

"'Comfort of the Scriptures' – An Early Jewish Interpretation of Noah's Salvation, 1 En 10:16–11:2," in: *Svensk Exegetisk Årsbok* 41–42 (1976–77) 87–96.

"New Testament Exegesis," in: *Faculty of Theology at Uppsala University, Uppsala University 500 years* 1 (AUU). Uppsala: Uppsala University 1976, 51–65.

"Taufe, Geist und Sohnschaft," in: ALBERT FUCHS (ed.), *Jesus in der Verkündigung der Kirche* (Studien zum Neuen Testament in seiner Umwelt A 1; Linz: privately printed 1976) 89–109.

## 1978

"Enhet och mångfald i urkyrkan och dess förhållande till judendomen," in: *Religion och Bibel* 37 (1978) 3–13.

"Till frågan om evangeliernas litterära genre," in: *Annales Academiae R. Scientiarum Upsaliensis* 21 (1978) 5–22 [Translated and published as "Some Reflections on the Problem of the Literary Genre of the Gospels" in Hartman 1997, 3–23].

Review of H. Conzelmann and A. Lindemann, *Arbeitsbuch zum Neuen Testament*, in: *Svensk Exegetisk Årsbok* 43 (1978) 126–128.

Review of G. Strecker (ed.), *Das Problem der Theologie des Neuen Testaments*, in: *Svensk Exegetisk Årsbok* 43 (1978) 138–140.

Review of H. Kraft, *Die Offenbarung des Johannes*, in: *Svensk Exegetisk Årsbok* 43 (1978) 168–169.

## 1979

*Asking for a Meaning. A Study of 1 Enoch 1–5* (CB.NT 12), Lund: Gleerup 1979.

"Att förstå en nytestamentlig text. Undersökningsmetoder och tolkningsresultat," in: *Svensk Exegetisk Årsbok* 44 (1979) 115–121.

## 1980

"Bundesideologie in und hinter einigen paulinischen Texten," in: SIGFRED PEDERSEN (ed.), *Die paulinische Literatur und Theologie* (Teologiske studier 7), Århus: Aros • Göttingen: Vandenhoeck & Ruprecht 1980, 103–18. [In this volume 41–56.]

"Lär oss att bedja," in: *Bibeln – lär oss att bedja*, Stockholm: Svenska bibelsällskapet 1980, 19–30.

"*Hierosolyma/Ierousalem*," in: HORST BALZ/GERHARD SCHNEIDER (eds.), *Exegetisches Wörterbuch zum Neuen Testament* 2 (1980) 432–439.

"Form and Message. A Preliminary Discussion of 'Partial Texts' in Rev 1–3 and 22,6ff.," in: JAN LAMBRECHT (ed.), *L'Apocalypse johannique et l'Apocalyptique dans le Nouveau Testament* (BEThL 53), Paris – Gembloux: Ducolot • Leuven: Leuven University 1980, 129–49 [Reprinted in Hartman 1997, 125–149].

Review of K. Aland, *Novum Testamentum Graece* (26th ed.), in: *Svensk Exegetisk Årsbok* 45 (1980) 143–145.

Review of W. O. Walker (ed.), *The Relationships among the Gospels*, in: *Svensk Exegetisk Årsbok* 45 (1980) 146–147.

## 1981

"Nya Testamentet i ny översättning," in: *Signum* 8 (1981) 232–235.

"*onoma, onomazo*," in: HORST BALZ/GERHARD SCHNEIDER (eds.), *Exegetisches Wörterbuch zum Neuen Testament* 2 (1981) 1268–1277.

Review of J. Jeremias, *Die Sprache des Lukasevangeliums*, in: *Svensk Exegetisk Årsbok* 46 (1981) 183–184.

Review of H. Köster, *Einführung in das Neue Testament*, in: *Svensk Exegetisk Årsbok* 46 (1981) 179–180.

## 1982

"Situationen inom den nytestamentliga exegetiken," in: *Svensk teologisk kvartalskrift* 58 (1982) 109–116.

"Your Will be done on Earth as it is in Heaven," in: *Africa Theological Journal* 11 (1982) 209–218.

## 1983

"1 Co 14,1–25: Argument and Some Problems," in: LORENZO DE LORENZI (ed.), *Charisma und Agape* (1 Ko 12–14), Rome: Benedictina 1983, 149–169 [Reprinted in Hartman 1997, 211–233].

"Zur Hermeneutik neutestamentlicher eschatologischer Texte," in: HANS-JÜRGEN ZOBEL (ed.), *Hermeneutik eschatologischer biblischer Texte*, Greifswald: Ernst-Moritz-Arndt-Universität 1983, 30–48.

"Survey of the Problem of Apocalyptic Genre", in: DAVID HELLHOLM (ed.), *Apocalypticism in the Mediterranean World and the Near East*, Tübingen: J. C. B. Mohr (Paul Siebeck) 1983 (= 2nd ed. 1989), 329–343 [Reprinted in Hartman 1997, 89–105].

"An early example of Jewish exegesis: 1 Enoch 10:10–11:2," in: *Neotest.* 17 (1983) 16–27. [In this volume 77–88.]

"Att förstå en nytestamentlig text," in: RENÉ KIEFFER/BIRGER OLSSON (eds.), *Exegetik idag* (Religio 11), Lund: Teologiska institutionen 1983, 7–13.

"Den apokalyptiska genrens problem," in: RENÉ KIEFFER /BIRGER OLSSON (eds.), *Exegetik idag* (Religio 11), Lund: Teologiska institutionen 1983, 66–82.

## 1984

"Hermeneutics of New Testament eschatological texts," in: *Harvard Theological Studies* 40 (1984) 4–15.

"An Attempt at a Text-Centered Exegesis of John 21," in: *Studia Theologica* 38 (1984) 29–45 [Reprinted in Hartman 1997, 69–87].

Review of J. Kiilunen *et alii*, (eds.), *Glaube und Gerechtigkeit*, in: *Teologinen aikakauskirja* 3 (1984) 216–218.

## 1985

*Kolosserbrevet* (Kommentar till Nya Testamentet 12), Uppsala: EFS-förlaget 1985.

"En framtid och ett hopp," in: *KISA-rapport* nr 25 (1985).

"La formule baptismale dans les Actes des Apôtres: Quelques observations relatives au style de Luc", in: François Refoulé (ed.), *À cause de l'évangile. Mélanges offerts à Dom Jacques Dupont* (LeDiv 123), Paris: Cerf 1985, 727–738. [In this volume 155–163.]

"Universal Reconciliation (Col 1,20)," in: Albert Fuchs (ed.), *Studien zum Neuen Testament und seiner Umwelt* 10, Linz: Plöchl 1985, 109–121. [In this volume 273–284.]

## 1986

"'Kroppsligen', 'personligen' eller vad? Till Kol 2:9," in: *Svensk Exegetisk Årsbok* 51–52 (1986–87) 72–79.

"Theological Education in Sweden," in: *Canadian Theological Society Newsletter* 6:1 (1986) 7–8.

"On Reading Others' Letters," in: George Nickelsburg/George MacRae (eds.), *Christians Among Jews and Gentiles. Essays in Honor of Krister Stendahl*, Philadelphia, Penn.: Fortress 1986, 137–146; also in: *Harward Theological Review* 79 (1986) 137–146. [Reprinted in Hartman 1997, 167–177].

'*Att sammanföra de krafter som finns...*' *Uppsala Exegetiska Sällskap 1936–1986*, Uppsala: Uppsala Exegetiska Sällskap 1986.

Review of Michal Quesnel, *Baptisés dans l'Esprit*, in: *Theologische Literaturzeitung* 111 (1986) 431–432.

## 1987

"Guds ord och människors förståelser," in: *Signum* 13 (1987) 130–132.

"I Faderns och Sonens och den Helige Andes namn...," in: *Kateket-nytt* 1987:1, 5–8.

Co-author of the report *Läroansvar i kyrkan – teologisk belysning*, Stockholm: Civildepartementet DsC 1987:13.

"Vad säger Sibyllan? Byggnad och budskap i de sibyllinska oraklens fjärde bok," in: Peter Wilhelm Bøckman/Roald E. Kristiansen (eds.), *Context: Essays in Honour of Peder Johan Borgen*, Trondheim: Tapir 1987, 621–674 [Translated and published as "'Teste Sibylla'. Construction and Message in the Fourth Book of the Sibylline Oracles", in: Hartman 1997, 151–164.]

"Johannine Jesus – Belief and Monotheism," in: LARS HARTMAN/BIRGER OLSSON (eds.), *Apsects of the Johannine Literature* (CB.NT 18), Stockholm: Almqvist & Wiksell 1987, 85-99.

"Code and Context: A Few Reflections on the Parenesis of Col 3:6-4:1," in: GERALD F. HAWTHORNE/OTTO BETZ (eds.), *Tradition and Interpretation in the New Testament. Essays in Honor of E. Earle Ellis*, Grand Rapids, Mich.: Eerdmans • Tübingen: Mohr 1987, 237-247. [In this volume 285-296.]

## 1988

"Some Unorthodox Thoughts on the 'Household-Code Form,'" in: JACOB NEUSNER ET ALII (eds.), *The Social World of Formative Christianity and Judaism. Essays in Tribute to Howard Clark Kee*, Philadelphia, Penn.: Fortress 1988, 219-232 [Reprinted in Hartman 1997, 179-194].

Review of H. Räisänen, *The Torah and Christ*, in: *Teologinen aikakauskirja* 93 (1988) 149-150.

Review of J. Kremer, *Die Geschichte einer Auferstehung*, in: *Svensk Exegetisk Årsbok* 53 (1988) 127-129.

Review of H. Cancik (ed.), *Markus-Philologie*, in: *Svensk Exegetisk Årsbok* 53 (1988) 124-126.

Review of M. J. J. Menken, *Numerical Literary Techniques in John*, in: *Svensk Exegetisk Årsbok* 53 (1988) 126-127.

## 1989

"'He spoke of the Temple of His Body' (Jn 2:13-22)," in: *Svensk Exegetisk Årsbok* 54 (1989) 70-79. [In this volume 215-222.]

"Varför i allvärlden? En judisk apokalyps för 2000 år sedan," in: ERLAND JANSSON (ed.), *Meningar om livets mening i asiatiska kulturer* (Skrifter utgivna av Sällskapet för asienstudier 4). Uppsala 1989, 78-87.

"Minikommentar till Kol," in: LARS HARTMAN ET ALII, *Minikommentar till 1 Kor 1-4, 12-15, Fil 2, Kol*, Uppsala: Teologiska institutionen 1989, 27-37.

## 1990

"Tolkning och tillämpning av två bud" (with Anders Jeffner), in: *KISA-rapport* 1990:3, 35-45.

"The Eschatology of 2 Thessalonians as Included in a Communication," in: RAYMOND COLLINS (ed.), *The Thessalonian Correspondence* (BEThL 87), Leuven: Leuven University and Peeters Press 1990, 470-485 [Reprinted in Hartman 1997, 283-300].

"En okänd filosof i urkristendomen," in: *Kungliga Vitterhets Historie och Antikvitets Akademiens Årsbok* 1990, Stockholm: Vitterhets Akademien 1990, 141-148.

"Skepp, fårflock, byggnad ... Kyrkvisioner i Bibeln", in: *Kyrkligt Magasin* 1990:6, 39-48.

Review of G. Delling, *Die Bewältigung der Diasporasituation durch das hellenistische Judentum*, in: *Svensk Exegetisk Årsbok* 55 (1990) 119-120.

Review of J. Collins, *The Apocalyptic Imagination*, in: *Svensk Exegetisk Årsbok* 55 (1990) 120-121.

Review of E. Brandenburger, *Markus 13 und die Apokalyptik*, in: *Svensk Exegetisk Årsbok* 55 (1990) 140-142.

### 1991

"Is the Crucified Christ the Center of a New Testament Theology?" in: THEODORE W. JENNINGS, JR. (ed.), *Text and Logos*. Essays in Honor of Hendrikus Boers (Scholars Press Homage Series), Atlanta, Ga.: Scholars Press 1991, 175-188. [In this volume 57-67.]

### 1992

*Auf dem Namen des Herrn Jesus. Die Taufe in den neutestamentlichen Schriften* (SBS 148), Stuttgart: Katholisches Bibelwerk 1992.

"Reading Luke 17,20-37," in: FRANS VAN SEGBROECK ET ALII (eds.), *The Four Gospels 1992. FS Frans Neirynck* (BEThL 100), Leuven: University and Peeters 1992, 1663-75 [Reprinted in Hartman 1997, 53-67].

"Baptism," in: *The Anchor Bible Dictionary* 1, New York: Doubleday 1992, 583-594.

"Scandinavian School, NT Studies," in: *The Anchor Bible Dictionary* 5, New York: Doubleday 1992, 1002-4.

### 1993

*Till Herrens Jesus namn* (Tro & Tanke 1993:4), Uppsala: Svenska Kyrkans forskningsråd 1993.

"Early Baptism - Early Christology," in: ABRAHAM J. MALHERBE/WAYNE A. MEEKS (eds.), *The Future of Christology. Essays in Honor of Leander E. Keck*, Minneapolis, Minn.: Augsburg Fortress 1993, 191-201. [In this volume 165-173.]

"Från 'patternism' till bildspråk," in: *Svensk Exegetisk Årsbok* 58 (1993) 51-58.

"Frötallar och ropande eldtungor. Om bilder i predikan," in: Tro & Tanke 1993:8, Uppsala: Svenska Kyrkans forskningsråd 1993, 47-66.

Review of H.-Fr. Weiß, *Der Brief an die Hebräer*, in: *Theologische Literaturzeitung* 118 (1993) 33-35.

"Galatians 3:15-4:11 as Part of a Theological Argument on a Practical Issue," in: JAN LAMBRECHT (ed.), *The Truth of the Gospel (Galatians 1:1-4:11)* (Monographic Series of "Benedictina" Biblical-Ecumenical Section 12), Rome: Benedictina 1993, 127-158. [Reprinted in Hartman 1997, 253-282.]

### 1994

"Obligatory Baptism - but Why? On Baptism in the Didache and in the Shepherd of Hermas," in: *Svensk Exegetisk Årsbok* 59 (1994) 127-143.

"Tre läsningar av uttågsberättelsen. En nutida exeget, en alexandrinsk jude, en fornkyrklig biskop," in: Tro & Tanke 1994:5, Uppsala: Svenska kyrkans forskningsråd 1994, 39-53.

"Dop och ande - nio frågor," in: REIDAR HVALVIK/HANS KVALBEIN (eds.), *Ad Acta*. FS Edvin Larsson; Oslo: Verbum 1994, 86-108.

"Kommentarer och hermeneutiska överväganden," in: *Kyrkan och homosexualiteten* (Svenska kyrkans utredningar 1994:8), Stockholm 1994, 130-137.

Review of F. Neirynck et alii, The Gospel of Mark. A Cumulative Bibliography 1950-1990, in: *Svensk Exegetisk Årsbok* 59 (1994) 179-181.

## 1995

"Vad är evangelierna för sorts texter?" in: *Om tolkning IV. Myt - historia - verklighet* (Tro & Tanke 1995:3), 51-64.

"Humble and Confident. On the So-Called Philosophers in Colossians," in: DAVID HELLHOLM ET ALII (eds.), *Mighty Minorities?* (FS Jacob Jervell), Oslo: Scandinavian University Press 1995, 25-39. [= *Studia Theologica* 49 (1995).] [In this volume 223-235.]

"Att tolka eskatologiska texter," in: *Svensk Exegetisk Årsbok* 60 (1995) 23-38. [In this volume 29-39.]

"Guiding the Knowing Vessel of your Heart. On Bible Usage and Jewish Identity in Alexandrian Judaism," in: PEDER BORGEN/SØREN GIVERSEN (eds.), *The New Testament and Hellenistic Judaism,* Århus: Århus University 1995, 19-36.

## 1996

"Qumran och den intertestamentala litteraturen," in: TRYGGVE KRONHOLM/BIRGER OLSSON (eds.), *Qumranlitteraturen. Fynden och forskningsresultaten* (Kungliga Vitterhets Historie och Antikvitets Akademien. Konferenser 35), Stockholm: Vitterhets Akademien 1996, 111-119.

"Das Markusevangelium, ‚für die lectio sollemnis im Gottesdienst abgefasst‘?" in: HUBERT CANCIK ET ALII (eds.), *Geschichte - Tradition - Reflexion,* FS Martin Hengel, Tübingen: Mohr Siebeck 1996, 147-171. [Reprinted in Hartman 1997, 25-51.]

"Hellenistic Elements in Apocalyptic Texts", in: GUNNLAUGUR A. JÓNSSON/EINAR SIGURBJÖRNSSON/PÉTUR PÉTURSSON (eds.), *The New Testament in Its Hellenistic Context* (Ritröð Guðfræðistofnunar/Studia Theologica Islandica 10), Reykjavík: Guðfræðistofnun Háskóla Íslands 1996, 113-133. [In this volume 247-263.]

Review of K. Jeppesen et alii (eds.), In the Last Days. On Jewish and Christian Apocalyptic and its Period (Århus: Århus University 1994), in: *Svensk Exegetisk Årsbok* 61 (1996) 136-137.

Review of F. Bovon, *Révélations et écritures. Nouveau Testament et littérature apocryphe chrétienne. Receuil d'articles* (Le Monde de la Bible 26), Genève: Labor et Fides 1993, in: *Svensk Exegetisk Årsbok* 61 (1996) 149-150.

## 1997

*'Into the Name of Jesus'. Baptism in the Early Church,* Edinburgh: T. & T. Clark 1997.

*Text-Centered New Testament Studies. Text-Theoretical Essays on Early Jewish and Early Christian Literature,* DAVID HELLHOLM (ed.) (Wissenschaftliche Untersuchungen zum Neuen Testament 102), Tübingen: Mohr Siebeck 1997.

## 1998

"The Human Desire to Converse with the Divine. Dio of Prusa and Philo of Alexandria on Images of God," in: PETER SCHALK (ed.), *Being Religious and Living through the Eyes*

(FS Jan Bergman; Acta Universitatis Upsaliensis. Historia Religionum 14), Uppsala: Uppsala University 1998, 163-171. [In this volume 237-246.]

"'Mitt hjärtas tröst' - 'inte efter eget sinne'. Några funderingar kring bibeltolkning och tolkningsgemenskap," in: PER BLOCK (ed.), *Om tolkning V. Bibeln som auktoritet* (Tro & Tanke 1998:1; Uppsala 1998) 147-162.

"Inte sörja som de andra. Reflektioner kring familjeriter i tidig kristen tid, särskilt sådana kring dödsfall," in: *Svensk Exegetisk Årsbok* 63 (1998) 249-280.

"How Revolutionary are the Qumran Findings?" in: *Theology & Life* 20-21 (1998) 157-170.

### 1999

"The Book of Revelation: a Document for its Time as John sees it," in: ELIAS V. OIKONOMOU ET ALII (eds.), *1900th Anniversary of St. John's Apocalypse. Proceedings of the International and Interdisciplinary Symposium* (Athens - Patmos; 17-26 September 1995) (Athens: Monastery of St John 1999) 205-215. [In this volume 265-272.]

"Text and Context. How Texts Get New Meanings," in: *Theology & Life* 22 (1999) 149-162. Also in: *McGilvary Journal of Theology* 1/2002, 50-62.

"Gamla testamentet i Nya: Gamla texter i nytt ljus," in: TRYGGVE KRONHOLM/ANDERS PILTZ (eds.), *Bibeltolkning och bibelbruk i västerlandets kulturella historia* (Kungliga Vitterhets Historie och Antikvitets Akademien. Konferenser 45), Stockholm: Vitterhets Akademien 1999, 31-43.

"Att läsa andras brev, korinthiernas till exempel," in: *Kungliga Vitterhets Historie och Antikvitets Akademiens Årsbok* 1999, Stockholm: Vitterhets Akademien 1999, 184-190.

### 2000

*För tid och evighet. Bibeln och kristet framtidshopp,* Uppsala: Ordbruket 2000.

"Exegetes - Interpreters?" in: KARL-JOHAN ILLMAN/TORE AHLBÄCK/SVEN-OLAV BACK/ RISTO NURMELA (eds.), *A Bouquet of Wisdom.* FS Karl-Gustav Sandelin (Religionsvetenskapliga skrifter 48), Åbo: Åbo Akademi 2000, 79-98. [In this volume 13-27.]

### 2001

"Att läsa Bibeln retoriskt - problem och möjligheter," in: KURT JOHANNESSON (ed.), *Vetenskap och retorik,* Stockholm: Natur och Kultur 2001, 75-87.

"Nils Alstrup Dahl om Efeserbrevet." Review article on Nils Alstrup Dahl, *Studies in Ephesians* (eds. DAVID HELLHOLM ET ALII; Tübingen: Mohr Siebeck 2000), in: *Norsk Teologisk Tidsskrift* 102 (2001) 67-74.

"'... with the overseers and servants'. The Opening of Paul's Letter to the Philippians, when Considered in the Light of Certain Letter Conventions of the Time," in: OLLE MATSSON ET ALII (eds.), *Libens merito.* FS Stig Strömholm (Acta Academiae Regiae Scientiarum Upsaliensis 21), Uppsala: Uppsala University 2001, 169-178. [In this volume 203-213.]

"Overseers and Servants - for What? Philippians 1:1-11 as Read with Regard to the Implied Readers of Philippians," in: GEORG GALITIS ET ALII (eds.), *Per me il vivere è Cristo (Filippesi 1,1-3,21)* (Serie Monografica di Benedictina, Sezione Biblico. Ecumenica 14), Rome: Benedictina 2001, 13-43.

## 2002

"Do Exegetes Interpret?" in: DAG PRAWITZ (ed.), *Meaning and Interpretation. Conference Held in Stockholm, September 24-26 1998* (Kungliga Vitterhets Historie och Antikvitets Akademien. Konferenser 55), Stockholm: Vitterhets Akademien 2002, 213-229.

"Text and Context. How texts get new meanings," in: *McGilvary Journal of Theology* 2002:1, 50-62.

"'I en dröm om natten fick han befallning ...' Något om drömmars funktion i Nya testamentet," in: PETER SÖDERGÅRD/ERIK WALLRUP (eds.), *Drömmarna och Gud. Essäer om att möta Gud i drömmen*, Stockholm: Axel och Margaret Ax:son Johnsons Stiftelse för allmännyttiga ändamål 2002, 29-40.

"Verkligt men bildligt," review of R. Kieffer, *Evangeliernas Jesus. Myt och verklighet* (Örebro: Libris 2001), in: *Signum* 28 (2002) 57-59.

"Ett slutackord - N. A. Dahl om Efeserbrevet," in: *Svensk Exegetisk Årsbok* 67 (2002) 176-179.

## 2003

"Grammar and Exegesis. The Case of Mark 4:11-12," in: ANDERS PILTZ ET ALII (eds.), *For Particular Reasons*, FS Jerker Blomqvist, Lund: Nordic Academic Press 2003, 133-141. [In this volume 91-97.]

## 2004

*Markusevangeliet 1:1-8:26* (Kommentar till Nya testamentet 2a), Stockholm: EFS-förlaget/Verbum 2004.

"Mk 6,3a im Lichte einiger griechischer Texte," in: *Zeitschrift für die neutestamentliche Wissenschaft* 95 (2004) 276-279.

"Tell What the Lord has Done. Notes from a Class on Mark 5:1-20," in: *Theology & Life* 27 (2004) 75-91.

Review of T. Fornberg, *Det trovärdiga vittnet. En bok om Nya testamentet* (Skellefteå: Artos 2004), in: *Signum* 30:9 (2004) 68-69.

## 2005

*Markusevangeliet 8:27-16:20* (Kommentar till Nya testamentet 2b), Stockholm: EFS-förlaget/Verbum 2005.

"*Psychē* – 'själ'? Att läsa Septuaginta som grekisk text," in: *Svensk Exegetisk Årsbok* 70 (2005) (FS Stig Norin) 89-99. [In this volume 193-202].

## 2006

"'Det är skrivet' – Markusevangeliets läsares bibel," in: TROELS ENGBERG-PEDERSEN ET ALII (eds.), *Kanon. Bibelens tilblivelse og normative status* (FS Mogens Müller; Forum for Bibelsk Eksegese 15), Copenhagen: Museum Tusculanum 2006, 81-91.

",Was soll ich tun, damit ich das ewige Leben erbe?' Ein heidenchristlicher Leser vor einigen ethischen Sätzen des Markusevangeliums," in: CHRISTFRIED BÖTTRICH (ed.), *Eschatologie und Ethik im frühen Christentum*. FS Günter Haufe (Greifswalder theologische Forschungen 11), Frankfurt am Main: Peter Lang 2006, 75–90. [In this volume 127–141.]

"Loving 'with Your Whole Heart' – Giving 'Her Whole Living'. An Attempt at Reading Mark 12:41–44 in its Literary Context," in: IOANNIS GALANIS ET ALII (eds.), *Diakonia – Leitourgia – Charisma. Patristic and Contemporary Exegesis of the New Testament.* FS Georg Galitis [Geórgios Galítis], Athens: En Plo 2006, 261–273. [In this volume 103–114.]

"Om vikten av att exegeter besinnar vad de vill förklara. En fallstudie ut från Mark 1:40–45," in: LARS HARTMAN ET ALII (eds.), *Vad, hur och varför. Reflektioner om bibelvetenskap*, FS Inger Ljung (Acta Universitatis Upsaliensis/Uppsala Studies in Faiths and Ideologies 17), Uppsala: Uppsala Universitet 2006, 161–168.

Review of I. Peres, *Griechische Grabinschriften und neutestamentliche Eschatologie* (Wissenschaftliche Untersuchungen zum Neuen Testament 157; Tübingen: Mohr Siebeck 2003), in: *Svensk Exegetisk Årsbok* 71 (2006) 272–274.

## 2007

"Tolkningars villkor. En närmare blick på några tolkningar av Paulus' brev till Filemon," in: LARS HARTMAN ET ALII (eds.), *När religiösa texter blir besvärliga. Hermeneutisk-etiska frågor inför religiösa texter* (Kungliga Vitterhets Historie och Antikvitets Akademien. Konferenser 64), Stockholm: Vitterhets Akademien 2007, 46–64.

"Mark 16:1–8: The Ending of a Biography-like Narrative and of a Gospel," in: *Theology & Life* 30 (2007) 31–47. [In this volume 115–125.]

Review of E. Broadhead, *Mark. Readings: A New Biblical Commentary* (Sheffield: Sheffield Academic Press 2001), in: *Svensk Exegetisk Årsbok* 72 (2007) 226–228.

## 2008

"Biblioteket i Qumran," in: ERIK CARLQUIST/HARRY JÄRV (eds.), *Mänsklighetens minne*, Helsingfors: Schildt 2008, 154–181.

## 2009

"A Commentary: A Communication about a Communication," in: *Novum Testamentum* 51 (2009) 389–400. [In this volume 3–12.]

"Two Early Readings of First Corinthians: Clement of Rome and Third Corinthians," in: CONSTANTINE J. BELEZOS (ed.), *Saint Paul and Corinth. 1950 Years since the Writing of the Epistles to the Corinthians*. Athens: Psichogios Publications S. A. 2009, 613–622. [In this volume 69–75.]

Review of A. Y. Collins, *Mark. A Commentary* (Hermeneia), Minneapolis, Minn.: Fortress 2007, in: *Svensk Exegetisk Årsbok* 74 (2009) 207–210.

"Harald Riesenfeld in memoriam," in: *Svensk Exegetisk Årsbok* 74 (2009) 181–186.

## 2010

*Mark for the Nations. A Text- and Reader-Oriented Commentary*, Eugene, Oreg.: Pickwick Publications 2010.

## 2011

"Usages – Some Notes on the Baptismal Name-Formula", in: DAVID HELLHOLM ET ALII (eds.), *Ablution, Initiation, and Baptism/Waschungen, Initiation und Taufe. Late Antiquity, Early Judaism, and Early Christianity/Spätantike, Frühes Judentum und Frühes Christentum* (BZNW 176/I), Berlin – New York: de Gruyter 2011, 397–413. [In this volume 175–189.]

# Acknowledgements

1. "Commentary: A Communication about a Communication", in: *Novum Testamentum* 51 (2009) 389–400.
2. "Exegetes – Interpreters", in: Karl-Johan Illman/Tore Ahlbäck/Sven-Olav Back/Risto Nurmela (eds.), *A Bouquet of Wisdom. Essays in Honour of Karl-Gustav Sandelin* (Religionsvetenskapliga skrifter 48), Åbo: Åbo Akademi 2000, 79–98.
3. "Att tolka eskatologiska texter", in: *Svensk Exegetisk Årsbok* 60 (1995) 23–38 (Translated for this volume as Interpreting Eschatological Texts.
4. "Bundesideologie in und hinter einigen paulinischen Texten", in: Sigfred Pedersen (ed.), *Die Paulinische Literatur und Theologie/The Pauline Literature and Theology* (Teologiske Studier 7), Århus: Aros • Göttingen: Vandenhoeck & Ruprecht 1980, 103–118.
5. "Is the Crucified Christ the Center of a New Testament Theology?", in: Theodore W. Jennings, Jr. (ed.), *Text and Logos. The Humanistic Interpretation of the New Testament. Festschrift Hendrikus W. Boers* (Scholars Press Homage Series), Atlanta, Ga: Scholars Press 1990, 175–188.
6. "Two Early Readings of First Corinthians: Clement of Rome and Third Corinthians", in: Constantine J. Belezos (ed.), *Saint Paul and Corinth. 1950 Years since the Writing of the Epistles to the Corinthians,* Athens: Psichogios Publications S. A. 2009, 613–622.
7. "An Early Example of Jewish Exegesis: 1 Enoch 10:16–11:2", in: *Neotestamentica* 17 (1983) 16–27.
8. "Grammar and Exegesis: The Case of Mark 4:11–12", in: Anders Piltz et alii (eds.), *For Particular Reasons. Studies in Honour of Jerker Blomqvist,* Lund: Nordic Academic Press 2003, 133–141.
9. "Mk 6,3 im Lichte einiger griechischer Texte", in: *Zeitschrift für die Neutestamentliche Wissenschaft* 95 (2004) 276–279.
10. "Loving 'with Your Hole Heart' – Giving 'Her Whole Living'. An Attempt at Reading Mark 12:41–44 in Its Literary Context", in: Ioannis Galanis et alii (eds.), *Diakonia – Leitourgia – Charisma. Patristic and Contemporary Exegesis of the New Testament. Festschrift Georg Galitis,* Levadeia: Holy Metropolis of Thival and Levadeia 2006, 261–273.

11. "Mark 16:1–8: The Ending of a Biograpy-like Narrative and of a Gospel", in: *Theology & Life* (Hong Kong) 30 (2007) 31–47.

12. "‚Was soll ich tun, damit ich das ewige Leben erbe?' Ein heidenchristlicher Leser vor einigen ethischen Sätzen des Markusevangeliums", in: CHRISTFRIED BÖTTRICH (ed.), *Eschatologie und Ethik im frühen Christentum. Festschrift für Günter Haufe*, Frankfurt am Main: Peter Lang 2006, 75–90.

13. "'Into the Name of Jesus'. A Suggestion Concerning the Earliest Meaning of the Phrase", in: *New Testament Studies* 20 (1973/74), 432–440.

14. "La formule baptismale dans les Actes des Apôtres: quelques observations relatives au style de Luc", in: FRANÇOIS REFOULÉ (ed.), *À cause de l'Évangile. Mélanges offerts à Dom Jacques Dupont* (Lectio Divina 123), Paris: Cerf 1985, 727–738.

15. "Early Baptism – Early Christology", in: ABRAHAM J. MALHERBE/WAYNE A. MEEKS (eds.), *The Future of Christology. Festschrift Leander E. Keck*, Minneapolis, Minn.: Fortress 1993, 191–201.

16. "Usages – Some Notes on the Baptismal Name-Formulae", in: DAVID HELLHOLM/TOR VEGGE/ØYVIND NORDERVALL/CHRISTER HELLHOLM (eds.), *Ablution, Initiation, and Baptism/Waschungen, Initiation und Taufe. Late Antiquity, Early Judaism, and Early Christianity/Spätantike, Frühes Judentum und Frühes Christentum* (BZNW 176/I), Berlin – New York, N.Y.: de Gruyter 2011, 397–413.

17. "*Psychē* – 'Soul'? Reading the Septuagint as a Greek Text". Swedish Original in: *Svensk Exegetisk Årsbok* 70 (2008) 89–99.

18. "'… with the overseers and servants' – The Opening of Paul's Letter to the Philippians. When Considered in the Light of Certain Letter Conventions of the Time", in: OLLE MATSSON/ÅKE FRÄNDBERG/MONICA HEDLUND/STEN LUNELL/GUNNAR SEDIN (eds.), *Libens merito. Festschrift Stig Strömholm* (Acta Academiae Regiae Scientiarum Upsaliensis 21), Uppsala: Kungl. Vetenskapssamhället 2001, 169–178.

19. "He Spoke of the Tempel of His Body (John 2:13–22)", in: *Svensk Exegetisk Årsbok* 54 (1989) 70–79.

20. "Humble and Confident. On the so-called Philosophy in Colossians", in: DAVID HELLHOLM/HALVOR MOXNES/TURID KARLSEN SEIM (eds.), *Mighty Minorities? Minorities in Early Christianity – Positions and Strategies* (= *Studia Theologica* 49), Oslo – Copenhagen – Stockholm – Boston: Scandinavian University Press 1995, 25–39.

21. "The Human Desire in Converse with the Divine. Dio of Prusa and Philo of Alexandria on Images of God", in: PETER SCHALK (ed.), *Being Religious and Living through the Eyes. Festschrift Jan Bergman* (Acta Universitatis

Upsaliensis. Historia Religionum 14), Uppsala: Almqvist & Wiksell 1998, 163–171.

22. "Hellenistic Elements in Apocalyptic Texts", in: GUNNLAGUR A. JÓNSON/ EINAR SIGURBJÖRNSSON/PÉTUR PÉTURSSON (ed.), *The New Testament in Its Hellenistic Context* (Ritröð Guðfræðistofnunar/Studia Theologica Islandica 10), Reykjavik: Guðfræðistofnun Háskóla Íslands 1996, 113–133.

23. "The Book of Revelation: A Document for Its Time as John Sees It", in: The Holy Monastery of Saint John the Theologian in Patmos (ed.), *1900$^{th}$ Anniversary of St. John's Apocalypse. Proceedings of the International and Interdisciplinary Symposium,* Athens 1999, 205–215.

24. "Universal Reconciliation (Col 1,20)", in: ALBERT FUCHS (ed.), *Studien zum Neuen Testament und seiner Umwelt,* Band 10, Linz: Katholisch-Theologische Privatuniversität Linz 1985, 109–121.

25. "Code and Context: A Few Reflections on the Parenesis of Col 3:6–4:1", in: GERALD F. HAWTHORNE/OTTO BETZ (eds.), *Tradition and Interpretation in the New Testament. Essays in Honor of E. Earle Ellis,* Grand Rapids, Mich.: Eerdmans • Tübingen: Mohr 1987, 237–247.

# Index of Modern Authors

Aagaard, Anne Marie 273
Abrams, Meyer H. 18, 20, 22, 24
Ahlström, Gösta W. 41
Aland, Barbara 92
Aland, Kurt 92
Aletti, Jean-Noël 273, 274, 276, 278, 282
Alexander, Philip S. 167
Almquist, Helge 252
Ambrožič, Alojzij M. 129
Andersen, Francis I. 255
Applebaum, Shimon 205, 206
von Arnim, Hans 238, 242
von Arnim, Johannes 280
Arzt-Grabner, Peter 177, 182
Ascough, Richard S. 204
Aulén, Gustaf 165
Aune, David E. 265
Avemarie, Friedrich 177
Baarlink, Heinrich 129
Bäbler, Balbina 238
Baird, William 13, 14
Bakke, Odd Magne 70
Balabanski, Vicky 129
Balch, David L. 285, 286, 287, 293
von Balthasar, Hans Urs 38
Baltzer, Klaus 42, 43, 44, 50
Barnikol, Ernst 145
Barrett, C. Kingsley 220
Barthchy, S. Scott 295
Barth, Gerhard 159, 168, 177, 180
Bauer, Walter 92, 184
Beasley-Murray, George R. 146, 267
Becker, Eve-Marie 117
Becker, Jürgen 215
Bekken, Per Jarle 222
Benoit, Pierre 273, 274, 276
Bentzen, Aage 41
Berger, Klaus 32, 48, 51, 137, 138, 139, 140, 208, 273, 289, 290

Bertram, Georg 202
Best, Ernest 293
Betz, Hans Dieter 49, 184, 247, 248
Beyer, Hermann Wolfgang 210
Bickerman, Elias Joseph 254
Bietenhard, Hans 146, 148, 157, 178, 180
Billerbeck, Paul 82, 146, 147, 166, 178, 218
Binder, Hermann 237, 239
Bjerkelund, Carl J. 215
Blanck, Horst 136
Blaß, Friedrich 93, 94, 95, 183, 276
Blomqvist, Jerker 93, 94, 97
Boers, Hendrikus 58
Bogaert, Pierre-Maurice 265
Borgen, Peder 260
Boring, M. Eugene 270
Bornkamm, Günther 232
Bousset, Wilhelm 250, 266, 267, 268
Bovon, François 268
Brandenburger, Egon 32
Brandt, A. J. H. Wilhlem 146, 178
Bratsiotis, Nikolaus Pan 193, 194, 201
Braun, Herbert 5, 58
Breytenbach, Cilliers 128, 133, 134, 139
Brown, Raymond E. 99, 160, 220, 222
Brox, Norbert 268
Bruce, Frederick Fyvie 160, 225, 295
Bryan, Christopher 117
Bujard, Walter 289
Bultmann, Rudolf 16, 19, 20, 48, 49, 51, 58, 59, 65, 104, 145, 149, 152, 153, 168, 169, 178, 215, 220
Burkert, Walter 216, 219
Burridge, Richard A. 117
Caird, George Bradford 267
von Campenhausen, Hans Fr. 73, 153, 159
Carmignac, Jean 31
Cavallin, Hans C. C. 257

Charles, Robert Henry 85, 87, 267, 268
Charlesworth, James H. 227, 253
Chesterton, Gilbert Keith 27
Clarke, William K. L. 156
Cohen, Shaye J. D. 226
Collins, Adela Yarbro 10, 248, 267, 268, 271
Collins, John J. 32, 247, 260
Collins, Raymond F. 43
Conzelmann, Hans 145, 153, 159, 160, 161, 162, 184, 273
Cook, John G. 104, 107, 108, 109, 110
Crossan, John Dominic 99, 258
Crouch, James E. 286, 292, 293, 295
Cullmann, Oscar 153
Cumont, Franz Valery Marie 227, 230
Cuvillier, Elian 114
Dahl, Nils Alstrup 47, 55, 56, 153, 267
Dalman, Gustaf 146, 178
Daniélou, Jean 83
Danove, Paul L. 116
Davies, William David 42, 43, 51, 55
Le Déaut, Roger 78
Debrunner, Albert 93, 94, 95, 183, 197, 276
Deissmann, Adolf 295
Delcor, Matthias 248
Delling, Gerhard 145, 146, 148, 153, 156, 160, 161, 162, 163
Dénis, Albert-Marie 46
Descamps, Albert-Louis 43
Dewey, Joanna 106, 107
Dibelius, Martin 225, 232, 286
Dietrich, Wolfgang 159
Dihle, Albrecht 128, 129, 130, 133, 138, 139, 195
Dillon, John M. 237
Dinkler, Erich 145, 152, 153
Dittenberger, Wilhelm 217
Dodds, Eric Robertson 140
Donahue, John R. 114, 123, 128
Donfried, Karl Paul 99
Dormeyer, Detlev 117, 135
Dunn, James D. G. 145
Dupont, Jacques 162, 163
Du Rand, Jan A. 267
Eckey, Wilfried 104, 113

Eco, Umberto 26, 37
Egelhaaf-Gaiser, Ulrike 205
Ehler, Bernhard 57
Ehrlich, Ernst Ludwig 218
Eichrodt, Walther 42, 82
Eisenhofer, Ludwig 158
Eisen, Ute E. 101
Elliger, Winfried 237, 238, 239
Ellis, E. Earle 285
Engberg-Pedersen, Troels 208
Engnell, Ivan 41, 193
Eppstein, Victor 215
Ernst, Josef 113, 282
Evans, Craig A. 92
Eynikel, Erik 194, 201
Fensham, Frank Charles 48
Ferguson, Charles A. 184
Festugière, André-Jean 227
Fischer, Karl Martin 169, 170, 267, 268
Fitzmyer, Joseph A. 79, 99, 170, 178, 184
Flemington, William Frederick 145
Focant, Camille 9, 117, 121, 123, 128, 137, 139, 141
Foerster, Werner 47
Fohrer, Georg 19, 48
Forschner, Maximilian 133, 138
Fortna, Robert Tomson 215
Fowler, Robert M. 104
France, Richard Thomas 116, 117, 123
Frey, Jean-Baptiste 205, 206
Freyne, Seán 258
Früchtel, Ursula 243
Furberg, Mats 29
Gadamer, Hans-Georg 15
Gärtner, Bertil 219
Garrow, Alan J. P. 268
Gayer, Roland 295
Gehman, Henry S. 148
Genette, Gérard 23
Georgi, Dieter 48
Gerth, Bernhard 94
Giblin, Charles Homer 267
Giesen, Heinz 271
Glover, Richard 160
Gnilka, Joachim 9, 92, 113, 114, 128, 139, 226, 232, 273, 276, 278, 279, 283, 288, 289, 290

Goldammer, Kurt  216, 217, 218, 219
Goodenough, Erwin R.  255
Goodman, Martin  205
Goppelt, Leonhard  82, 172
Gorman, Frank H. Jr  3
Goulder, Michael Douglas  118, 268, 270
Grant, Frederick C.  217
Grant, Robert M.  13, 285, 289, 290
Greßmann, Hugo  18, 227, 250
Grundmann, Walter  113
Gülich, Elisabeth  4, 14, 107, 265
Guelich, Robert A.  99
Gundry, Robert H.  92, 111, 115
Hägg, Tomas  117
Haenchen, Ernst  145, 158
Hahn, Ferdinand  177
Hall, Basil  3
Hamel, Gildas H.  258
Hanson, John S.  252
Harl, Marguerite  197
Harrill, J. Albert  295
Harrington, Daniel J.  114, 123, 128
Hartman, Lars  6, 9, 11, 32, 35, 77, 82, 85, 86, 117, 119, 140, 159, 166, 167, 170, 173, 175, 177, 180, 184, 247, 262, 266, 280, 286, 288
Hartvigsen, Kirsten Marie  30, 33, 104
Harvey, Julien  42
Hauck, Friedrich  10
Hauspie, Katrin  194, 201
Heil, John Paul  104, 105
Heitmüller, Wilhelm  145, 149, 158, 160, 166, 175, 176, 177, 178, 181, 183, 186, 187
Hellholm, David  24, 32, 45, 51, 86, 88, 107, 136, 173, 181, 248, 251, 261, 266, 267, 269, 270, 286, 293
Hemer, Colin J.  268, 269
Hengel, Martin  149, 247, 249, 252, 253, 255, 256, 257, 258, 259, 261, 262, 281, 282, 292
Henze, Matthias  294
Hercher, Rudolph  208
Hermerén, Göran  15, 30
Hesseling, Dirk Christiaan  95
Himmelfarb, Martha  252
Hirsch, Eric Donald  15, 26

Hoffmann, Paul  59
Holmberg, Bengt  208
Holmstrand, Jonas  208
Holtz, Traugott  172
Hooker, Morna D.  92, 121
Hooke, Samuel Henry  41
Horsley, Greg H. R.  138
Hovhanessian, Vahan  69, 70, 72, 73, 74
Hübner, Hans  60, 224, 275, 282
Hultgård, Anders  261, 262
van Iersel, Bas M. F.  9, 104, 105, 106
Ilan, Tal  99, 100
Jannaris, Antonius Nicholas  93, 94
Jastrup, Poul Ole  93, 94
Jaubert, Annie  42, 43, 48, 83
Jeremias, Joachim  82, 92, 93, 152, 153
Jervell, Jacob  47, 51, 162
Jewett, Robert  10, 52, 204
Johnson, Gary J.  101
Johnson, Sherman E.  145
Joly, S. Robert  138
Jones, Christopher P.  237, 238
Jones, Douglas Rawlinson  3
Jones, Henry Stuart  136
Kabiersch, Jürgen  133, 134, 138
Käsemann, Ernst  32, 51, 52, 53, 57, 61, 274, 275
Kamlah, Ehrhard  294
Kasper, Walter  123
Kayser, Carl Ludwig  208
Keck, Leander E.  171
Kehl, Medard  31, 38
Kelber, Werner H.  129
Kennedy, Henry Agnus Alexander  43, 53, 54
Kennett, Robert Hatch  96
Kieffer, René  3, 11, 26, 57, 215
Kingsbury, Jack Dean  22, 23
Kirby, John T.  265
Klappert, Bertold  57
Klauck, Hans-Josef  75, 238, 265, 268, 269, 271, 294
Klijn, Albertus F. J.  270
Klostermann, Erich  10, 99, 103, 104
Knibb, Michael A.  77
Koch, Dietrich-Alex  226
Koch, Klaus  32, 262

Köhler, Liselotte 205
Koester, Helmut 177, 294
van Kooten, George H. 230, 273
Kraft, Heinrich 153, 267
Kraus, Samuel 206
Kremer, Jacob 75, 159
Kretschmar, Georg 146
Kristensen, William Brede 216
Küchler, Max 290
Kühner, Raphael 94
Kümmel, Werner Georg 13, 27, 31, 57
Kuhn, Heinz-Wolfgang 60
Kuss, Otto 52, 146
Ladd, George Eldon 32
Lagrange, Marie-Joseph 92
Lambrecht, Jan 270
Lampe, Geoffrey William Hugo 82
Lampe, Peter 92, 95
Lane, William L. 93
Larsson, Edvin 290
Lausberg, Heinrich 234
van der Leeuw, Gerardus 216, 217, 277
Lehmann, Manfred R. 79
Leipoldt, Johannes 148
Levine, Baruch A. 216
Lewis, Jack P. 83
Liddell, Henry George 136
Lietzmann, Hans 227, 283
Lindblom, Johannes 145
Lindemann, Andreas 70, 273
Lohfink, Gerhard 3
Lohmeyer, Ernst 92, 213, 267, 268, 274, 277, 286
Lohse, Eduard 48, 52, 53, 232, 267, 270, 290
Lona, Horacio E. 70, 71
Longenecker, Richard N. 152
Lührmann, Dieter 92, 95, 104, 287
Lundberg, Per Ivar 83
Lust, Johan 194, 201, 202
Luz, Ulrich 24, 57
Lyonnet, Stanislas 275, 279, 280
Lys, Daniel 193, 194, 201
Maas, Fritz 86
MacAdam, Henry I. 205
Mack, Burton Lee 218, 278, 281
Macquarrie, John 282

Maier, Johann 216, 218
Malherbe, Abraham J. 134
Marcus, Joel 10, 92
Martin, Luther H. 255
Martin, Wallace 4
Martini, Carlo M. 161
Martyn, J. Louis 222
Massingberde Ford, Josephine 268
McArthur, Harvey K. 99
Meeks, Wayne A. 222
Meier, John P. 160
Merklein, Helmut 127, 130, 134, 137, 139, 292
Metzger, Bruce M. 266
de Meulenaere, Herman 247
Michel, Otto 51, 52, 53, 133
Milik, Józef Tadeusz 77, 80, 81, 82, 86, 87
Millar, Fergus 205
Milligan, George 136, 184, 205
Moloney, Francis J. 9, 115, 116, 121, 123
Moule, Charles F. D. 92, 95, 96, 180, 276
Moulton, James Hope 136, 184, 205
Mowinckel, Sigmund 41, 277
Müller, Karlheinz 287, 288
Müller, Ulrich B. 64, 267, 268, 269, 270
Munck, Johannes 55
Mussner, Franz 49, 56, 57
Naveh, Joseph 179
Neusner, Jacob 78, 221
Nickelsburg, George W. E. 77, 80, 82, 85, 86, 87, 259
Nilsson, Martin P. 140, 227
Nock, Arthur Darby 128, 246
Nygren, Anders 165
O'Brien, Peter T. 226, 230, 232
Oepke, Albrecht 49, 56, 136, 145
Ohm, Thomas 138
Olsson, Birger 215
Olsson, Tord 248
O'Neill, John Cochrane 161, 273
Ortkemper, Franz-Josef 61
Osgood, Charles E. 42
von der Osten-Sacken, Peter 64
Ottosson, Magnus 215
Otzen, Benedikt 255
Pancaro, Severino 222
Patai, Raphael 219, 276, 277

# Index of Modern Authors

Patte, Daniel 78, 83
Peisker, Carl Heinz 92
Pernot, Hubert 95
Perrin, Norman 32, 140
Pesch, Rudolf 8, 9, 92, 95, 104, 113, 114
Plümacher, Eckhard 156, 158, 159
Pokorný, Petr 165, 169, 170, 171
Pollard, Thomas Evan 274
Popkes, Wiard 266
Portefaix, Lilian 136
Porton, Gary 86
Powell, Mark Allan 18, 22
Preisendanz, Karl 184
Preisigke, Friedrich 182
Prigent, Pierre 268, 270, 271
Quasten, Johannes 186
Rabin, Chaim 148
Räisänen, Heikki 60, 265, 267, 268, 269, 271
Rahner, Karl 38
Raible, Wolfgang 4, 14, 107, 265
Rehkopf, Friedrich 93, 94, 95, 183, 276
Rengstorf, Karl Heinrich 52, 287
Reumann, John 99
Rhoads, David 19
Rian, Dagfinn 248
Richardson, Alan 58
Riesenfeld, Harald 273
Rigaux, Béda 46, 47
Rimmon-Kenan, Shlomith 4, 23
Ringgren, Helmer 41, 262
Roloff, Jürgen 160
Rose, Arnold M. 223
Runia, David T. 237
Russell, David Syme 260
Sandelin, Karl-Gustav 13, 16, 26
Sanders, Ed P. 43, 49, 51, 52, 53, 60, 231, 256
Sanders, Jack T. 127
Sandmel, Samuel 239
Sandnes, Karl Olav 178
Sauter, Gerhard 5, 129
Schäfer, Alfred 205
Schäfer, Peter 47, 173, 219, 277
Schenke, Hans-Martin 267, 268
Schenk, Wolfgang 3, 5, 223, 226
Schillebeeckx, Edward 38

Schlier, Heinrich 33, 49, 51, 52, 56, 227
Schmaus, Michael 121
Schmid, Josef 145
Schmid, Wilhelm 242
Schnackenburg, Rudolf 64, 127, 135, 215, 220
Schneider, Gerhard 161, 162
Schnelle, Udo 177, 183
Schnider, Franz 203, 215, 219, 220
Schrage, Wolfgang 57, 61, 127, 135, 137, 141, 261
Schroeder, David 287
Schröter, Jens 177
Schürer, Emil 85, 167, 202, 205, 218, 221, 256, 258
Schürmann, Heinz 172, 218, 282
Schüssler Fiorenza, Elisabeth 267, 268, 269, 270, 271
Schulz, Siegfried 57
Schwartz, Eduard 130, 133, 140
Schweizer, Eduard 20, 113, 153, 225, 230, 273, 275, 277, 279, 281, 290, 295
Schwyzer, Eduard 93, 94, 197
Scott, Robert 136
Searle, John R. 33
Sebeok, Thomas A. 42
Seebass, Horst 194
Seeligmann, Isac Leo 83, 86
Segal, Alan F. 252
Sellin, Gerhard 293
Sevenster, Jan Nicolaas 149
Shaked, Shaul 179
Siegert, Folker 59
Simon, Louis 114
Sjöberg, Erik 47
Slonimsky, Henry 86
Smalley, Beryl 3
Smyth, Herbert Weir 94
Stanton, Graham N. 172
Stauffer, Ethelbert 99, 138, 273
Stegemann, Hartmut 265
Stemberger, Günther 83
Stendahl, Krister 17, 49, 55
Stenger, Werner 203, 215, 219, 220
Strack, Hermann L. 83, 146, 166, 178
Strathmann, Hermann 229
Strecker, Georg 58, 59, 273

Stuhlmacher, Peter  46, 52, 61, 285, 293, 294
Taatz, Irene  294
Thom, Johan Carl  259
Thompson, Leonard L.  267, 268, 269
Thraede, Klaus  287
Thyen, Hartwig  145, 152, 153
Trocmé, Étienne  215
Turcan, Robert  249
Turner, Nigel  94
Ullmann, Stephen  147
van Unnik, Willem Cornelis  43, 45, 46, 48, 159
VanderKam, James C  77, 80
Vanderveken, Daniel  33
van Veldhuizen, Adrianus  95
Vermès, Géza  78, 86, 205
Via, Dan Otto  127
Vielhauer, Philipp  255, 267, 273, 293
Vögtle, Anton  289
Volz, Paul  34, 82, 85
Vorgrimmler, Herbert  123
Vorster, Johannes N.  24
Vouga, François  122
Walaskay, Paul W.  271
Walser, Georg  185
Walter, Nikolaus  265
Watson, Duane F.  267
Watt, Jonathan M.  184
Weidinger, Karl  286

Weiser, Alfons  162
Wendland, Paul  255
Whiteley, Dennis Edward Hugh  43
Wibbing, Siegfried  289
Widengren, Geo  41, 216, 217, 219, 247, 260, 277
Wilckens, Ulrich  128, 161, 162
Wilcox, Max E.  156, 161
Wilder, Amos Niven  24, 26, 32, 36, 127, 140
Williamson, Ronald  239, 243
Wilson, Robert McL.  224, 275
Wilson, Walter T.  290
Wimsatt, William K.  22
Windisch, Hans  95
Wingren, Gustaf  273
Winston, David  194
Wintermute, Orval S.  253, 258
Witherington, Ben  92
Witulski, Thomas  35, 249, 268, 271
Wolff, Hans Walter  194
Wolfson, Harry A.  239, 244, 245
Wrede, William  59
Wright, Addison G.  78, 83
Wülfing von Martitz, Peter  19
Ysebaert, Joseph  146
Zahn, Theodor  267
Zeller, Dieter  53
Ziebarth, Erich  205

# Index of Passages (selected)

## I. Israelite and Jewish Texts

### A. Old Testament

**Genesis**
| | |
|---|---|
| 1:20 | 197 |
| 2:7 | 198 |
| 2:19 | 198 |
| 5:24 | 118 |
| 6 | 262 |
| 6:1–5 | 80 |
| 6:11 | 80 |
| 6:13 | 80 |
| 6:17 | 80 |
| 8:21f. | 79 |
| 9:1 | 84 |
| 9:4 | 197 |
| 9:7 | 84 |
| 9:9ff. | 84 |
| 12:5 | 197 |
| 17:7 | 53 |
| 18:22f. | 243 |
| 19:17 | 197 |
| 23:8 | 199 |
| 27:4 | 199 |
| 42:21 | 198 |
| 46:15 | 200 |
| 46:30 | 245 |
| 49:6 | 199 |

**Exodus**
| | |
|---|---|
| 3:6 | 122 |
| 5:23 | 156 |
| 6:7 | 53 |
| 13:8 | 118 |
| 16:16 | 200 |
| 19:5 | 47 |
| 19:5–6 | 290 |
| 19–34 | 44 |
| 25:8 | 46 |
| 29:45 | 46 |
| 32:32 | 256 |
| 33:13 | 243 |
| 33:17 | 156 |
| 40:34 | 216 |

**Exodus [LXX]**
| | |
|---|---|
| 34:7 | 51 |

**Leviticus**
| | |
|---|---|
| 19 | 290 |
| 19:28 | 200 |
| 26 | 44 |
| 26:11 | 46 |
| 26:17 | 54 |
| 26:25 | 54 |
| 26:33 | 54 |
| 26:36 | 54 |

**Numeri**
| | |
|---|---|
| 17 | 71 |

**Deuteronomium**
| | |
|---|---|
| 4:5 | 46 |
| 4:19 | 167 |
| 4:37 | 290 |
| 4:37–40 | 290 |
| 6:5 | 198 |
| 6:6 | 52 |
| 6:13 | 180 |
| 7:6 | 46, 47 |
| 7:8 | 290 |
| 10:8 | 157, 180 |
| 12:2 | 166, 167, 179 |

| | | | |
|---|---|---|---|
| 14:1 | 48 | 18:24 | 180 |
| 14:24 | 157 | **Regum II (Regnum IV)** | |
| 17:3 | 167 | 2:11f. | 118 |
| 17:12 | 157 | 2:24 | 180 |
| 18:20 | 160, 181 | 13:20f. | 74 |
| 18:22 | 160 | 16–18 | 118 |
| 21:23 | 62 | **Esra (Esdras)** | |
| 26:18 | 47 | 9 | 44 |
| 27:26 | 48 | 9:14f. | 51 |
| 28:1 | 52 | 11:23 | 216 |
| 28:9 | 46 | 25:6 | 198 |
| 28:12 | 83 | **Nehemia** | |
| 28:13 | 52 | 9 | 44 |
| 28:15 | 52 | **Iob** | |
| 28:48 | 54 | 7:15 | |
| 28:53 | 52, 54 | ms A | 200, 201 |
| 28:55 | 54 | 33:17f. | 200, 201 |
| 28:57 | 54 | **Psalmi** | |
| 29:13 | 53 | 2 | 9, 260 |
| 29:19 | 51 | 2:7 | 36 |
| 29:22ff. | 51 | 2:9 | 36 |
| 29–30 | 44 | 4 | 198 |
| 30 | 49 | 6:5 | 197, 198 |
| 30:2 | 46 | 9:24 | 198 |
| 30:6 | 52 | 10:1 | 199 |
| 30:7 | 54 | 10:5 | 200 |
| 30:10 | 49 | 11:4 | 216 |
| 30:15ff. | 47 | 19:8 | 199 |
| 30:19 | 50 | 21:30 | 201 |
| 30:19f. | 243 | 23:4 | 200 |
| 32 | 44 | 24:1 | 199 |
| 32:5f. | 48 | 24:13 | 199 |
| 32:24f. | 54 | 25:9 | 197 |
| **Deuteronomium [LXX]** | | 29:4 | 201 |
| 18 | 160 | 33:22f. | 201 |
| **Josua (=Jesus Nave)** | | 34:9 | 198 |
| 19:49 | 226 | 40:5 | 199 |
| 24:18 | 53 | 43:26 | 198 |
| **Samuel II (Regnum II)** | | 48:16 | 201 |
| 7:13 | 187 | 56:8 | 256 |
| **Regum I (Regnum III)** | | 65:16 | 199 |
| 8:11 | 216 | 68:1 | 199 |
| 8:13 | 216 | 68:11 | 199 |
| 8:27ff. | 217 | 68:21 | 198 |
| 8:29 | 216 | 68:33 | 199, 201 |
| 18:3 | 180 | | |

## Index of Passages (selected)

| | | | |
|---|---|---|---|
| 69:10 | 219 | **Ezechiel** | |
| 85:4 | 199 | 14:14 | 80 |
| 85:11ff. | 84 | 36 | 44 |
| 88:49 | 201 | 36:22–32 | 169 |
| 89:13 | 180 | 36:26 | 51 |
| 89:17 | 180 | 36:27 | 46 |
| 104:18 | 198 | 36:27f. | 50 |
| 110 | 123 | 36:29ff. | 47 |
| 114:8 | 201 | 37:14 | 46 |
| 118 | 112 | 37:27 | 46 |
| 118:22f. | 120 | **Daniel** | |
| 118:26 | 176 | 1:8 | 250 |
| 119:5f. | 200 | 1:17 | 250 |
| 142:8 | 199 | 2 | 249, 260, 261 |
| **Psalmi [LXX]** | | 2:28 | 250 |
| 18:8 | 199 | 2:45 | 261 |
| 53:1 | 156 | 2:47 | 250 |
| **Isaias** | | 3:26 | 250 |
| 1:1 | 128 | 5:11 | 250 |
| 6:9–10 | 91 | 6:10 | 250 |
| 11:2 | 173 | 7 | 260, 261 |
| 14:49 | 128 | 7:10 | 257 |
| 40 | 259 | 7:13 | 123, 173 |
| 54:13 | 46 | 8 | 253 |
| 58:10 | 198 | 9 | 44 |
| 65:20ff. | 84 | 9:16 | 51 |
| **Jeremias** | | 9:17 | 249 |
| 9:24 | 61 | 11:22 | 262 |
| 11:21 | 181 | 11:28 | 262 |
| 14:14 | 181 | 11:30 | 262 |
| 23:25 | 181 | 11:31 | 249 |
| 31 | 44 | 12:1 | 262 |
| 31:20 | 48 | 12:2f. | 257 |
| 31:33 | 47, 53 | **Michaeas** | |
| 31:33f. | 46 | 4:5 | 180 |
| | | **Malachias** | |
| | | 1:11 | 157, 187 |

# B. Apocrypha, Pseudepigrapha and Other Early Jewish Texts

| | | | |
|---|---|---|---|
| **2 (Syriac) Apocalypse** | | 24:1 | 256 |
| **of Baruch** | 260 | 29:8 | 33 |
| 3:1 | 266 | 32:1 | 270 |
| 4 | 266 | 78–86 | 294 |
| 22:1 | 265 | 84:8 | 270 |

| | | | |
|---|---|---|---|
| 85:3–9 | 270 | 46:7 | 259 |
| **Apocalypse of Abraham** | | 50:2 | 181 |
| | 260 | 60:17–23 | 253 |
| 7 | 254 | 67:1 | 80 |
| 15 | 252 | 72–82 | 254 |
| **Apocalypsis Sophoniae** | | 82:4 | 254 |
| | 258 | 82:7–20 | 258 |
| **Ecclesiasticus** | | 89:1ff. | 80 |
| 14:12 | 257 | 90:20 | 256 |
| 14:16f. | 257 | 90:30 | 82 |
| 24:10 | 218 | 90:33 | 82 |
| 39:8 | 53 | 91:9 | 257 |
| 43:26 | 278 | 93:2 | 85 |
| 44:17 | 80 | 94:7f. | 259 |
| 47:18 | 180 | 98:7 | 256 |
| 50:20 | 180 | 99:7 | 259 |
| **1 (Ethiopic) Enoch** | | 100:8 | 51 |
| 1–5 | 260 | 100:10 | 256 |
| 1–36 | 77, 252 | 101:3 | 51 |
| 2–5 | 260 | 102:4–7 | 259 |
| 5:4 | 51 | 102:6 | 262 |
| 5:8f. | 47 | 102:9 | 259 |
| 5:9 | 51 | 103:2ff. | 256 |
| 7f. | 85 | 103:3 | 257 |
| 8:1 | 262, 263 | 104:2 | 257 |
| 8:3 | 254 | 104:7 | 256 |
| 8:3f. | 255 | **2 (Slavonic) Enoch** | |
| 8:4 | 263 | 10:4 | 255 |
| 9:28f. | 84 | **4 Esdras** | |
| 10:2 | 176 | 3:1 | 266 |
| 10:16 | 80, 81 | 4:23 | 266 |
| 10:16–11:2 | 77, 79 | 4:26 | 266 |
| 10:17 | 81 | 4:35f. | 256 |
| 10:18 | 81 | **Pseudo-Eupolemus** | |
| 10:19 | 81 | *Fragmentum* | |
| 10:20 | 80, 82 | 1 | 253 |
| 10:21 | 82 | **Joseph et Aseneth** | |
| 10:22 | 82 | 9:1 | 176 |
| 10f. | 83, 85 | 15:7 | 176 |
| 11:1 | 82, 83 | **Josephus (Flavius)** | |
| 11:2 | 82 | *Antiquitates judaicae* | |
| 16:1 | 261 | 3.7,7 | 277 |
| 17f. | 253 | 4.214 | 206 |
| 18:1–4 | 253 | 8.45–49 | 255 |
| 22 | 257 | 12.152 | 206 |
| 33–36 | 254 | | |

*Index of Passages (selected)* 367

| | |
|---|---|
| 13.10,3 | 218 |
| 20.11 | 207 |

**Contra Apionem**
| | |
|---|---|
| 2.146 | 138 |

**De bello Judaico**
| | |
|---|---|
| 1.632 | 197 |
| 2.292 | 212 |
| 6.299 | 216 |
| 6.312f. | 33 |

**Judith**
| | |
|---|---|
| 10:3-4 | 263 |

**Liber Jubilaeorum**
| | |
|---|---|
| 1 | 44 |
| 1:16ff. | 47 |
| 1:22-25 | 169 |
| 1:23 | 46 |
| 1:24 | 48 |
| 4:17-23 | 79 |
| 5:13-16 | 79 |
| 5:17-19 | 79 |
| 12:16-18 | 253 |
| 21 | 44 |
| 21:3ff. | 259 |
| 22 | 44 |
| 23:30 | 257 |

**1 Macchabaei**
| | |
|---|---|
| 8:27 | 198 |

**2 Macchabaei**
| | |
|---|---|
| 1:10f. | 207 |
| 6:5 | 167 |
| 6:30 | 200, 201 |
| 7:37 | 200 |
| 8:4 | 176 |

**Oracula Sibyllina 3**
| | |
|---|---|
| 228 | 254 |
| 716ff. | 82 |
| 772ff. | 82 |

**Oracula Sibyllina 4** 251, 260
| | |
|---|---|
| 4-22 | 265 |
| 4ff. | 251 |
| 10-14 | 259 |
| 24-39 | 266, 290 |
| 25-30 | 290 |
| 25f. | 245 |
| 41-47 | 266 |
| 43 | 257 |
| 166ff. | 270 |
| 173ff. | 261 |
| 187 | 270 |
| 192 | 270 |

**Philo (Alexandrinus)**

*De Abrahamo*
| | |
|---|---|
| 28 | 291 |

*De agricultura*
| | |
|---|---|
| 9 | 85 |
| 50ff. | 279 |

*De cherubim*
| | |
|---|---|
| 36 | 278 |
| 98-101 | 216 |

*De decalogo*
| | |
|---|---|
| 32 | 240 |
| 52 | 239 |
| 52-81 | 238 |
| 58 | 240 |
| 59 | 240 |
| 61 | 239 |
| 64 | 240, 242 |
| 67 | 242 |
| 69f. | 242 |
| 70 | 242 |
| 72 | 242 |
| 98 | 292 |
| 100 | 292 |
| 101 | 111 |
| 107-120 | 292 |
| 158-161 | 228 |
| 165 | 292 |
| 178 | 240, 280 |

*De ebrietate*
| | |
|---|---|
| 66 | 217 |

*De gigantibus*
| | |
|---|---|
| 47 | 245 |

*De migratione Abrahami*
| | |
|---|---|
| 9 | 233 |
| 130 | 280 |

*De mutatione nominum*
| | |
|---|---|
| 216f. | 245 |

*De opificio mundi*
| | |
|---|---|
| 3 | 260, 280 |
| 8 | 240 |
| 61 | 253 |
| 143 | 280 |

*De plantatione*
| | |
|---|---|
| 8–10 | 279 |
| 126 | 243, 244 |
| 130 | 243, 244 |

*De posteritate Caini*
| | |
|---|---|
| 26 | 233 |
| 27 | 243 |
| 69 | 243 |

*De praemiis et poenis*
| | |
|---|---|
| 22f. | 80 |

*De providentia, fragm. II*
| | |
|---|---|
| 64 | 243 |

*De somniis I*
| | |
|---|---|
| 140 | 256, 258 |
| 140–141 | 227 |
| 149 | 216 |
| 215 | 216, 217 |

*De somniis II*
| | |
|---|---|
| 221 | 282 |

*De virtutibus*
| | |
|---|---|
| 188 | 216 |

*De vita contemplativa*
| | |
|---|---|
| 29 | 292 |
| 75–80 | 292 |

*De vita Mosis II*
| | |
|---|---|
| 48 | 280 |
| 133f. | 278 |
| 174 | 217 |

*Legatio ad Gaium*
| | |
|---|---|
| 222 | 212 |
| 229 | 212 |

*Legum allegoriae III*
| | |
|---|---|
| 4 | 282 |

*Quis rerum divinarum heres sit*
| | |
|---|---|
| 141 | 279 |

| | |
|---|---|
| 205f. | 278 |

*Quod deteriius potiori*
| | |
|---|---|
| 149 | 280 |
| 170 | 81 |

*Quod Deus sit immutabilis*
| | |
|---|---|
| 8 | 217 |
| 55 | 240 |

*Quod omnis probus liber sit*
| | |
|---|---|
| 82 | 292 |

*Specialibus legibus I*
| | |
|---|---|
| 12–50 | 238 |
| 13 | 239 |
| 13ff. | 276 |
| 14 | 239, 240 |
| 18 | 240 |
| 20 | 243 |
| 28f. | 242 |
| 40f. | 243 |
| 55 | 243 |
| 67 | 217, 243 |
| 68 | 244 |
| 68f. | 243 |
| 69–70 | 219 |
| 77 | 217 |
| 97 | 277, 278 |
| 152 | 217 |
| 209 | 240 |
| 271 | 244 |
| 272 | 245 |
| 300 | 245 |

*Specialibus legibus II*
| | |
|---|---|
| 45 | 291 |
| 62 | 292 |
| 188ff. | 279, 280 |
| 190ff. | 275 |
| 225–227 | 292 |
| 226–227 | 292 |

*Specialibus legibus III*
| | |
|---|---|
| 1 | 243 |

**Pseudo-Phocylides**
| | |
|---|---|
| 3–21 | 290 |
| 5 | 291 |
| 7 | 291 |

| | | | | |
|---|---|---|---|---|
| **Prayer of Joseph** | | | 13 | 51 |
| *Fragmenta* | | | 19:29 | 277 |
| 190 | 176 | | **Testamenta XII Patriarcharum** | |
| **Psalmi Salomonis** | | | *Asher* | |
| 17 | 172 | | 2:4 | 176 |
| 17:37 | 173 | | *Judah* | |
| **Sapientia Salomonis** | | | 13:4 | 148 |
| 2:2f. | 201 | | 18–25 | 44 |
| 2:22 | 201 | | *Levi* | |
| 7:12 | 278 | | 13–18 | 44 |
| 7:17f. | 228 | | **Testamentum Salomonis** | |
| 7:25 | 281 | | 67 | 176 |
| 7:27 | 281 | | 115 | 176 |
| 9:9 | 278 | | **Tobias** | |
| 9:15 | 200 | | 13:11ff. | 82 |
| 10–19 | 44 | | | |

## C. Qumran and Related Texts

| | | | | |
|---|---|---|---|---|
| Cairo [Genizah of the] | | | CAVE 4 | |
| Damascus [Document] | | | 4Q292 | |
| I, 21 | 51 | | fragm. 3 | 181 |
| I-li | 44 | | 4Q403 | |
| II, 4f. | 53 | | 1.9 | 181 |
| **CAVE 1** | | | 12 | 181 |
| 1QH VI | | | **CAVE 11** | |
| 15 | 85 | | 11Q14 | |
| 1QM I | 33 | | 1.1 | 181 |
| 1QS IV | | | 3 | 181 |
| 19–23 | 169 | | **Temple Scroll** | |
| 1QS VIII | | | 61.3 | 181 |
| 5 | 85 | | | |

## D. Rabbinic Texts and Jewish Mysticism

| | | | | |
|---|---|---|---|---|
| ʾAbot | | | 32:14ff. | 261 |
| 2:2 | 151 | | **Babylonian Talmud** | |
| 2:12 | 151, 167 | | ʿAbodah Zarah | |
| 4:6 | 167 | | 27a | 150 |
| 4:11 | 148, 151, 166, 179 | | 48a | 149, 180 |
| **Apocalypse of Elijah (Hebrew)** | | | Ḥullin | |
| 28:12 | 261 | | 40 | 151, 167 |
| 31:9ff. | 261 | | | |

|  |  |  |  |
|---|---|---|---|
| 40a | 150, 166, 167 | *Menaḥot* | |
| *Pesaḥim* | | 1:3 | 153 |
| 38b | 150 | *Nedarim* | |
| 60a | 153 | 4:8 | 150 |
| *Šabbat* | | 8:7 | 151 |
| 50a | 150 | *Niddah* | |
| *Sanhedrin* | | 5:6 | 151, 160, 166, 167, 168, 179 |
| 34a | 83 | | |
| 44b | 221 | 5:6 (3 (c)) | 152 |
| 76a | 151 | *Pesaḥim* | |
| 99b | 147, 150, 221 | 5:2 | 147, 150 |
| *Yebamot* | | *Sanhedrin* | |
| 24b | 150, 151 | 7:6 | 160, 167, 180 |
| 39b | 151 | 11:2 | 218 |
| 45b | 150 | *Šeqalim* | |
| *Zebaḥim* | | 3:4 | 150 |
| 30a | 149, 153 | *Sukkah* | |
| **Jerusalem Talmud** | | 1:1 | 151 |
| *Yebamot* | | *Zebaḥim* | |
| 1:1 | 150, 151 | 1:1 | 150 |
| **Mišnah** | | 1:2 | 150 |
| *ʿAbodah Zarah* | | 2:4 | 153 |
| 3:6 | 180 | 4 | 179 |
| 3:7 | 149, 151 | 4:6 | 147, 148, 150, 151, 166, 178 |
| *Bekorot* | | | |
| 1:7 | 151 | **Sipre Numeri** | |
| *Giṭṭin* | | 136 | 151, 159, 167, 179 |
| 3:1 | 151 | **Tosefta** | |
| 3:2 | 151 | *ʿAbodah Zarah* | |
| 4:4 | 149 | 3:12 | 150 |
| *Ḥullin* | | 3:13 | 150, 151, 159, 166, 167, 179 |
| 2:8 | 150, 166, 179 | | |
| 2:10 | 150 | *Giṭṭin* | |
| *Kelim* | | 2:7 | 151 |
| 30:2 | 149 | *Šeqalim* | |
| | | 2:4 | 150 |

# E. Jewish-Christian Texts

**Oracula Sibyllina 1**
148f.                    80

# II. Early Christian Texts

## A. New Testament

**Evangelium Matthaei**
| | |
|---|---|
| 3:13–17 | 17, 18 |
| 3:17 | 36 |
| 4:10 | 20 |
| 5:17 | 20 |
| 5:21–22 | 290 |
| 5:43–48 | 291 |
| 10:35 | 294 |
| 10:41–42 | 176 |
| 10:41f. | 152, 158 |
| 12:28 | 171 |
| 13 | 34 |
| 15:19 | 289 |
| 16:21–23 | 20 |
| 18:5 | 176, 186 |
| 18:20 | 148, 152, 158, 168, 176, 180, 183 |
| 23:39 | 176 |
| 24:5 | 176 |
| 26:24 | 71 |
| 26:39 | 20 |
| 28:19 | 145, 148, 158, 175, 180, 186, 187, 188 |

**Evangelium Marci**
| | |
|---|---|
| 1:1 | 124 |
| 1:2f. | 9 |
| 1:9–11 | 7, 8, 10 |
| 1:10 par. | 171 |
| 1:11 | 9 |
| 1:15 | 129 |
| 1:20 | 129 |
| 3:6 | 111 |
| 3:14 | 129 |
| 4:11–12 | 91 |
| 4:17–19 | 141 |
| 4:19 | 134 |
| 6:25 | 11 |
| 7:21–22 | 289 |
| 8:29 | 171 |
| 8:31–33 | 111 |
| 8:34 | 129 |
| 8:38 | 132, 139 |
| 9:1 | 129, 139 |
| 9:2–8 | 8, 123 |
| 9:35 | 132 |
| 9:37 | 157 |
| 9:38 | 156, 176 |
| 9:39 | 176 |
| 9:47 | 129, 130 |
| 10:1–31 | 135 |
| 10:2–12 | 135 |
| 10:14 | 130 |
| 10:17 | 127 |
| 10:17–31 | 129, 134 |
| 10:21 | 129 |
| 10:42f. | 134 |
| 10:43f. | 132 |
| 10:45 | 111, 132 |
| 11:1–12:44 | 105 |
| 11–12 | 105 |
| 11:12–12:12 | 110 |
| 12:1–12 | 120 |
| 12:13–34 | 109 |
| 12:13–44 | 110 |
| 12:28–33 | 291 |
| 12:28–34 | 137 |
| 12:34 | 130 |
| 12:35–44 | 109 |
| 12:36 | 123 |
| 12:41–44 | 103 |
| 13:6 | 157, 176 |
| 13:9–13 | 112 |
| 13:11–13 | 10 |
| 13:13 | 141 |
| 13:14 | 249 |
| 13:26 | 139 |
| 13:30 | 139 |
| 13:33–37 | 141 |
| 14:3–9 | 119 |
| 14:24 | 111 |
| 14:25 | 129 |
| 14:28 | 121 |
| 14:58 | 109 |
| 14:62 | 123 |

| | |
|---|---|
| 15:19 | 290 |
| 15:39 | 8 |
| 15:43 | 129 |
| 16:1–8 | 115 |
| 16:1–20 | 117 |
| 16:6 | 121 |

**Evangelium Lucae**

| | |
|---|---|
| 1:11–22 | 218 |
| 4:20 | 205 |
| 10:17 | 156 |
| 11:20 | 171 |
| 12:11 | 227 |
| 16:9 | 197 |
| 17:2 | 71 |
| 20:20 | 227 |
| 24:26 | 172 |
| 24:47 | 156 |

**Evangelium Joannis**

| | |
|---|---|
| 1:12 | 176 |
| 1:17 | 222 |
| 1:18 | 221 |
| 2:11 | 220 |
| 2:13–22 | 215 |
| 2:17 | 219 |
| 2:20 | 219 |
| 3:3 | 65 |
| 3:5 | 222 |
| 3:5–8 | 65 |
| 3:14 | 65 |
| 3:14–15 | 65 |
| 3:20f. | 220 |
| 3:36 | 220 |
| 4:21ff. | 220 |
| 4:53 | 221 |
| 5:19 | 221 |
| 5:21 | 221 |
| 5:24 | 221 |
| 6:35f. | 220 |
| 6:45 | 46 |
| 6:53ff. | 222 |
| 6:69 | 220 |
| 7:37f. | 220 |
| 7:39 | 222 |
| 10:11 | 221 |
| 10:16 | 221 |
| 10:25 | 176 |
| 10:36 | 220 |
| 10:38 | 220 |
| 11:40 | 220 |
| 11:52 | 221 |
| 12:13 | 65 |
| 13:3 | 65 |
| 13:31f. | 65 |
| 14:1 | 221 |
| 14:6 | 220 |
| 14:9 | 220 |
| 14:10 | 220 |
| 14:13 | 157 |
| 14:16ff. | 171, 222 |
| 14:24 | 221 |
| 15:1–11 | 222 |
| 15:4f. | 221 |
| 16:7 | 220 |
| 16:7–14 | 222 |
| 16:23 | 220 |
| 16:24 | 220 |
| 17:1 | 65 |
| 17:19 | 221 |
| 17:20 | 222 |
| 17:22 | 221 |
| 18:36 | 65 |
| 19:19 | 65 |
| 19:30 | 65 |
| 20:17 | 65 |
| 20:22f. | 222 |
| 20:23 | 221 |
| 21:9 | 222 |
| 21:15–19 | 222 |

**Acta Apostolorum**

| | |
|---|---|
| 2:33ff. | 171 |
| 2:38 | 145, 155, 157, 158, 161, 162, 175, 184, 187 |
| 3:6 | 156, 161 |
| 4:7 | 156 |
| 4:10 | 156, 161 |
| 4:12 | 156 |
| 4:17 | 156, 176 |
| 5:31 | 169 |
| 8:12 | 147 |
| 8:16 | 145, 155, 158, 161, 166, 175 |
| 9:15 | 147 |

| | | | |
|---|---|---|---|
| 9:22 | 171 | 4:10 | 54 |
| 9:34 | 161 | 4:13–18 | 54 |
| 10:36 | 161 | 4:18 | 200 |
| 10:48 | 155, 157, 158, 161, 162, 167, 171, 175 | 5:7 | 133 |
| | | 5:8f. | 53 |
| 11:17 | 161 | 6:1 | 55 |
| 13:37–39 | 169 | 6:1–14 | 10 |
| 14:11–13 | 219 | 6:3 | 145, 175 |
| 14:23 | 209 | 6:6 | 63 |
| 15:23 | 162 | 8:32 | 169 |
| 15:26 | 161 | 8:38f. | 227, 276, 283 |
| 17:3 | 171 | 9:3ff. | 45 |
| 19:1–6 | 158 | 9:4f. | 45, 50 |
| 19:3 | 170 | 9–11 | 55 |
| 19:5 | 145, 155, 158, 161, 167, 175 | 10:9 | 163 |
| | | 11:1 | 45 |
| 20:28–30 | 213 | 11:17 | 55 |
| 28:19 | 167 | 12:6 | 209 |
| | | 12:7f. | 204, 212 |
| | | 12:8 | 204 |

## Epistula ad Romanos

| | | | |
|---|---|---|---|
| 1:16f. | 53 | 13:8–10 | 291, 293 |
| 1:18 | 51 | 14:15 | 169 |
| 1:18–3:20 | 49, 51, 53 | 15:3 | 282 |
| 1:18–32 | 128 | 16:1 | 204 |
| 1:23 | 51 | | |

## Epistula ad Corinthios I

| | | | |
|---|---|---|---|
| 1:24–31 | 51 | 1 | 75 |
| 1:28 | 51 | 1–3 | 61 |
| 1:32 | 51 | 1:10 | 71 |
| 2:1ff. | 51 | 1:12 | 61 |
| 2:3 | 51 | 1:13 | 61, 72, 145, 158, 166, 175, 177, 180 |
| 2:4 | 51 | | |
| 2:5 | 51 | 1:13–15 | 183 |
| 2:7–10 | 51 | 1:14–16 | 61 |
| 2:17ff. | 53 | 1:15 | 158, 175 |
| 2:25ff. | 52 | 1:17 | 61 |
| 3:2 | 52 | 1:18 | 61 |
| 3:3 | 52 | 1:23 | 172 |
| 3:5 | 52 | 1:29 | 62 |
| 3:7 | 52 | 1:31 | 61 |
| 3:8 | 55 | 2:1–4 | 61 |
| 3:9 | 52 | 2:2 | 63 |
| 3:19 | 52 | 3:23 | 61 |
| 3:21 | 51, 53 | 5:4 | 176 |
| 3:21–27 | 53 | 6:11 | 167, 171, 177, 183 |
| 3:23 | 53 | 7:1 | 72, 231 |
| 3:25 | 53 | 8:4f. | 276 |
| 3:29f. | 53 | 8:5f. | 233 |
| 4 | 54 | | |

| | | | |
|---|---|---|---|
| 9:21 | 55 | 3:26ff. | 48 |
| 10:2 | 145, 175 | 3:27 | 145, 175, 180 |
| 11:24 | 169 | 4:6 | 48 |
| 11:25 | 45, 53 | 4:6f. | 49 |
| 12 | 71, 75 | 4:8 | 49 |
| 12:3 | 163 | 4:9f. | 49 |
| 12:8–9 | 71 | 5:16 | 50 |
| 12–14 | 209 | 5:21 | 50 |
| 12:18 | 209 | 5:24 | 62 |
| 12:28 | 204, 212 | 6:6 | 209, 212 |
| 14:24f. | 212 | 6:7ff. | 50 |
| 15 | 34, 72, 145 | 6:12 | 62 |
| 15:1f. | 73 | 6:13 | 62 |
| 15:3 | 169 | 6:14 | 62 |
| 15:12 | 73 | 6:15f. | 56 |
| 15:24 | 227 | | |
| 15:36–38 | 73 | | |
| 15:59 | 75 | | |
| 16:15 | 204, 206 | | |

Epistula ad Ephesios

| | |
|---|---|
| 2:10 | 200 |
| 2:16 | 64 |
| 5:8 | 128 |
| 5:20 | 157 |
| 5:22–6:9 | 285 |
| 6:2–3 | 292 |
| 6:12 | 227 |

Epistula ad Corinthios II

| | |
|---|---|
| 3 | 45 |
| 3:3 | 45 |
| 3:17 | 171 |
| 4:5 | 163 |
| 5:19 | 275 |
| 5:21 | 169 |
| 8:9 | 282 |
| 12:2 | 226 |

Epistula ad Galatas

| | |
|---|---|
| 1:4 | 169 |
| 2:19 | 62 |
| 2:19f. | 62 |
| 3:1 | 63 |
| 3:1f. | 62 |
| 3:2 | 47, 171 |
| 3:3 | 62 |
| 3:6 | 48 |
| 3:7 | 48 |
| 3:10 | 48 |
| 3:13 | 62 |
| 3:14 | 48, 62 |
| 3:15ff. | 48 |
| 3:18 | 48 |
| 3:19–25 | 49 |
| 3:20–29 | 62 |
| 3:26–4:6 | 48 |

Epistula ad Philippenses

| | |
|---|---|
| 1:1 | 203, 205, 208, 210, 211 |
| 1:12–26 | 211 |
| 1:18 | 211 |
| 1:23 | 141 |
| 1:27 | 212 |
| 1:27–29 | 211 |
| 1:29 | 211 |
| 2:5 | 212 |
| 2:5–11 | 123, 211 |
| 2:7–9 | 112 |
| 2:10 | 157, 176 |
| 2:11 | 163 |
| 2:12 | 212 |
| 2:15f. | 212 |
| 2:17 | 211 |
| 2:18 | 211 |
| 2:30 | 211 |
| 3:1 | 211 |
| 3:5 | 45 |
| 3:6 | 49 |
| 3:10 | 211 |

| | | | |
|---|---|---|---|
| 3:17 | 211 | 2:16 | 224, 225, 227, 230, 234, 288, 291, 295 |
| 4:2f. | 212 | | |
| 4:6 | 211 | 2:16–23 | 288 |
| 4:9 | 211 | 2:16ff. | 277 |
| | | 2:17 | 234 |
| **Epistula ad Colossenses** | | 2:18 | 224, 225, 226, 228, 229, 230, 231, 232, 234, 295 |
| 1:5 | 234 | | |
| 1:6 | 234, 235 | | |
| 1:7 | 233 | 2:20 | 230, 234 |
| 1:9 | 288 | 2:20–23 | 288 |
| 1:9f. | 234 | 2:21 | 224, 225, 231 |
| 1:12 | 234 | 2:22 | 294 |
| 1:13 | 234 | 2:23 | 225, 232, 234, 295 |
| 1:13–20 | 288 | 3:1 | 288 |
| 1:15–20 | 63, 276, 280, 282 | 3:1–4 | 288 |
| 1:16 | 227, 234 | 3:1–4:1 | 293 |
| 1:18–22 | 64 | 3:1–4:6 | 288 |
| 1:19 | 230, 235 | 3:2 | 288 |
| 1:19f. | 234 | 3:3 | 288 |
| 1:20 | 233, 234, 273, 278, 283 | 3:5 | 290, 291 |
| | | 3:5–4:6 | 288 |
| 1:21–23 | 288 | 3:5–9 | 290 |
| 1:22 | 234, 235 | 3:5–17 | 288, 289 |
| 1:23 | 234, 235 | 3:6–4:1 | 285 |
| 1:24 | 282 | 3:10–4:1 | 290 |
| 1:24–2:5 | 288 | 3:12–17 | 291 |
| 1:24–2:23 | 288 | 3:12ff. | 282, 284 |
| 1:26f. | 232 | 3:14 | 291 |
| 1:27 | 234 | 3:16 | 118, 292, 295 |
| 2:1 | 224 | 3:17 | 289 |
| 2:2 | 232, 234 | 3:18–4:1 | 285, 286, 291, 292 |
| 2:4 | 224, 225, 233, 234 | 3:20–4:1 | 292 |
| 2:6 | 163, 295 | 4:2 | 289 |
| 2:6–7 | 288 | 4:12 | 233 |
| 2:6–8 | 288 | 4:15 | 224, 295 |
| 2:7 | 294 | 8 | 290 |
| 2:8 | 223, 224, 225, 226, 230, 231, 234, 288, 294 | 13 | 229 |
| | | **Epistula ad Thessalonicenses I** | |
| 2:8–15 | 63 | 1:10 | 140 |
| 2:9 | 230, 234, 235 | 2:15f. | 55 |
| 2:9–15 | 288 | 2:16 | 47 |
| 2:10 | 227, 230 | 4:3f. | 46 |
| 2:11 | 226, 231 | 4–5 | 34, 46 |
| 2:11–15 | 234 | 4:5 | 200 |
| 2:13 | 226, 231 | 4:7 | 46 |
| 2:14 | 227, 234, 288 | 4:9 | 46 |
| 2:15 | 227, 283 | 4:14 | 172 |

| | | | |
|---|---|---|---|
| 4:17 | 141 | 1:7 | 266 |
| 5:9 | 46 | 1:9–20 | 265 |
| 5:10 | 47 | 2:2 | 267 |
| 5:12 | 204 | 2:3 | 268 |
| 5:20 | 209 | 2:4 | 267 |
| | | 2:5 | 269 |

**Epistula ad Timotheum I**

| | | | |
|---|---|---|---|
| 1:8–10 | 289 | 2:7 | 266 |
| 2:8–15 | 285 | 2:10 | 269 |
| 3 | 209 | 2:13 | 249, 267, 268 |
| 4:3 | 231 | 2:14 | 268, 269 |
| 5:17–20 | 209 | 2:16 | 269 |
| | | 2:20 | 268, 269 |

**Epistula ad Timotheum II**

| | | | |
|---|---|---|---|
| 1:6 | 209 | 2:25 | 269 |
| 2:25 | 95 | 2:27 | 36 |
| | | 3:1 | 267 |

**Epistula ad Titum**

| | | | |
|---|---|---|---|
| 2:1–10 | 285 | 3:2 | 269 |
| | | 3:3 | 266, 269 |
| | | 3:4 | 269 |

**Epistula Jacobi**

| | | | |
|---|---|---|---|
| 2:7 | 153 | 3:8 | 268 |
| 5:14 | 157 | 3:11 | 269 |
| | | 3:15 | 267 |

**Epistula Petri I**

| | | | |
|---|---|---|---|
| 2:18–3:7 | 285 | 3:19 | 269 |
| | | 4:1f. | 226 |

**Epistula Johannis I**

| | | | |
|---|---|---|---|
| 3:15 | 290 | 4–5 | 266 |
| 5:3 | 95 | 4–22 | 269 |
| | | 6 | 267 |
| | | 13 | 249 |

**Epistula Judae**

| | | | |
|---|---|---|---|
| 8f. | 276 | 13:5 | 252 |
| | | 16:5 | 248, 258 |
| | | 19:6 | 271 |

**Apocalypsis Joannis**

| | | | |
|---|---|---|---|
| 1:1 | 265, 271 | 19:7 | 247 |
| 1:1–2 | 267 | 20:12 | 256 |
| 1:3 | 266 | 21:5–8 | 269 |
| 1:5 | 270 | 21:7f. | 269 |

# B. Apostolic Fathers and Other Early Christian Texts

**Athanasius Alexandrinus**
*Adversus Arianos*

| | |
|---|---|
| II.42 | 158 |

**Barnabae Epistula**

| | |
|---|---|
| 16:17f. | 152 |
| 19:5–7 | 285 |

**Basilius Caesariensis Cappadociae**
*Adversus Eunomium*

| | |
|---|---|
| 29.720 | 188 |

*Prologus 8*

| | |
|---|---|
| 31.688 | 187 |

**Clemens Alexandrinus**
*Stromateis*

| | |
|---|---|
| 1:11 | 231 |

## Index of Passages (selected)

| | |
|---|---|
| 6:8 | 231 |

**Clemens Romanus**
*Epistula Clementis ad Corinthios*

| | |
|---|---|
| 1:1 | 70 |
| 5:5–7 | 70 |
| 21:6–9 | 285 |
| 40:1–44:2 | 70 |
| 44:3 | 71 |
| 44:3f. | 70 |
| 46:7 | 71 |
| 47:1–6 | 71 |
| 47:6 | 70 |
| 48:5 | 71 |

**Pseudo-Clementina**
*Homiliae*

| | |
|---|---|
| 8:12 | 81 |

**Cyrillus Hierosolymitanus**
*Mystagogicae Catecheses*

| | |
|---|---|
| 3.1 | 158 |
| 3.4 | 188 |
| 17.21 | 188 |

**Didache XII Apostolorum**

| | |
|---|---|
| 4:9–11 | 285 |
| 7:1 | 158, 175, 185 |
| 7:3 | 158, 185 |
| 9:5 | 158, 175, 185 |

**Didymus Caecus Alexandrinus**
*Commentarii in Psalmos*

| | |
|---|---|
| 67 | 200 |

*De trinitate*

| | |
|---|---|
| 39.697 AB | 81 |
| 39.733 | 188 |

**Epiphanius Constantiensis**
*Ancoratus*

| | |
|---|---|
| 7.1 | 186 |
| 8.8 | 187 |
| 13.8 | 187 |
| 22.6 | 187 |
| 81.2 | 186 |

*Fragmentum alchemicum*

| | |
|---|---|
| 299.3r | 186 |

*Panarion*

| | |
|---|---|
| 1.159 | 187 |
| 1.192 | 186 |
| 1.202 | 188 |
| 1.209 | 187 |
| 1.231 | 187 |
| 1.278 | 187 |
| 1.284 | 187 |
| 1.292 | 187 |
| 1.373 | 187 |
| 2.36 | 187 |
| 2.275 | 187 |
| 3.299 | 188 |
| 76.54,33 | 158 |

**Epistula ad Corinthios III**

| | |
|---|---|
| 1:2 | 73 |
| 1:5 | 73 |
| 1:12 | 73 |
| 2:26 | 73 |
| 2:31 | 74 |
| 4 | 73 |
| 15:44 | 73 |
| 15:59 | 73 |

**Eusebius Caesariensis**
*Contra Marcellum*

| | |
|---|---|
| 1.1,9 | 186 |

*Historia ecclesiastica*

| | |
|---|---|
| 3.16 | 70 |
| 4.22,2 | 72 |
| 4.23,11 | 70 |
| 5.6,3 | 70 |

*Praeparatio evangelica*

| | |
|---|---|
| 8.7 | 292 |
| 8.12–13 | 292 |
| 13.12,13 | 228 |

**Ignatius Antiochenus**
*Epistula ad Romanos*

| | |
|---|---|
| 9.3 | 186 |

**Ioannes Damascenus**
*Expositio fidei*

| | |
|---|---|
| 82 | 187 |

**Irenaeus Lugdunensis**
*Adversus haereses*

| | |
|---|---|
| 1.21,3 | 158 |
| 4.41,4 | 73 |

**Iulius Firmicus Maternus**
De errore profanarum religionum
2.30,1 — 230

Libri Matheseos — 229

**Johannes Chrysostomos**
Adversus Judaeos
PG 48, 863 — 69

Catechesis ad illuminandos
2.22 — 187

Catechesis ultima ad baptizandos
170 — 186

Commentarius in Job
173 — 199

Homiliae in Acta apostolotum
60.63 — 188
60.65 — 188

Homiliae in epistulam ii ad Corinthios
61.458 — 188
61.608 — 188

**Pseudo-Johannes Chrysostomos**
In epistulam ad Ephesos
62.71 — 198

In Psalmos
101–107 — 198

**Justinus Martyr**
Apologia I
61 — 158
61.3 — 185
61.11 — 153

Dialogus cum Tryphone
39.2 — 158

**Origenes**
De Principiis (Peri archōn)
3.16 — 96

**Papias**
Fragmenta
11.2 — 187

**Pastor Hermae**
Similitudines
8.6,4 — 153

Visiones
3.7 — 158
3.7,3 — 175, 185

**Polykarpos Smyrnensis**
Epistula ad Philippenses
4:2–6:3 — 285

**Procopius Gazaeus**
Commentarius in Isaiam
2244 — 188

**Synesius Cyrenensis**
De regno
6 — 134

**Tertullianus**
Adversus Praxean
26 — 158

De baptismo
8 — 81

**Theodoret Cyrrhensis**
Explanatio in Canticum Canticorum
81.204 — 188

**Victorinus Petorionensis**
Commentarius in Apocalypsin
I, 7 — 267

# III. Egyptian Texts

## A. Literary Texts, Papyri and Ostraca

**Bertrand**
Inscriptions métriques
26 — 195

**Potter's Oracle** — 261
Fragmenta
1.1,14–15 — 252

## B. Published Compliations and Inscriptions

Mendes             247

## IV. Classical Texts

### A. Greek Texts

**Achilleus Tatios**
*Leucippe*
8.3,1             196

**Aelianus**
*Epistulae*
8.1                183

**Aelius Aristides**
*Ars rhetorica*
1.12.2.5          137

**Apollonius Tyanensis**
*Apollonii Epistulae*    208

**Appianos**
*Libyca*
403.5            138

**Aristophanes**
*Pax*
832ff.           257

**Artemidorus**
*Oneirokritikos*
V.43             196

**Cephalion**
*Fragmenta*
6                  182

**Cleomedes**
*de motu*
II.1,86–87        229

**Pseudo-Demetrius**
*De elocutione*
227              195

**Dio Cassius**
*Hist.*
30–35.109.1     138
79.13.1         136

*Historia Romana*
45,1,1.          100

**Dio Chrysostomos**
*De aegritudine (Or. 16)*
7f.             242
8              242

*De concordia cum Apamensibus (Or. 40)*
28            242

*De dei cognitione (Or. 12)*
22            239
25f.           238
27            239
29            239
32            239
35            239
37            239
42            239
52            241
54            241
59            240, 241
60            241, 242
61            241
74            239
74f.           241
75            239
84f.           238

*Defensio (Or. 45)*
1              242

*De regno iii (Or. 3)*
52            242

*De virtute (Or. 8)*
28f.           242

*Fragmentum*
459             197

| | |
|---|---|
| *Rhodaica (Or. 31)* | |
| 11 | 239 |
| 15 | 242 |
| *Trojana (Or. 11)* | |
| 59 | 242 |

**Diodorus Siculus**
*Bibliotheca historica*
| | |
|---|---|
| 3.56.2 | 138 |
| 6.5.2 | 182 |

**Diogenes Laertius**
| | |
|---|---|
| VI.63 | 280 |
| VII.87 | 280 |

**Epictetus**
*Diatribes*
| | |
|---|---|
| 3:22.18 | 195 |

*Dissertationes*
| | |
|---|---|
| 1:29.1–4 | 131 |
| 2:17.31 | 286 |
| I.12.5 | 131 |
| I.12,8–16 | 131 |
| I.12.8ff. | 132 |
| I.20.15 | 131 |
| I.24 | 132 |
| I.29.6 | 132 |
| I.30 | 132 |
| II.22.15 | 133 |
| III.13.5 | 133 |
| IV.10.14 | 133 |

*Gnomologium*
| | |
|---|---|
| 21 | 196 |

**Epikuros**
*Fragmentum*
| | |
|---|---|
| 668 | 229 |

**Herodianus**
*Historia*
| | |
|---|---|
| 2.2.10 | 183 |
| 2.13.2 | 183 |

**Isocrates**
*Ad Nicoclem*
| | |
|---|---|
| 12 | 197 |

**Libanios**
*Declamationes*
| | |
|---|---|
| 1.1,128 | 199 |

*Epistulae*
| | |
|---|---|
| 120.1 | 136 |
| 125.2 | 100 |

*Fragmentum*
| | |
|---|---|
| 90 | 195 |

**Lucianus Samosatensis**
*Dialogi mortuorum*
| | |
|---|---|
| 24.1 | 140 |

*Philopseudes*
| | |
|---|---|
| 29 | 201 |

**Menander Rhetor**
Περὶ ἐπιδεικτικῶν (Spengel III)
| | |
|---|---|
| 399 | 136 |
| 404 | 136 |
| 405 | 136 |

**Musonius Rufus**
*Dissertationes*
| | |
|---|---|
| 13A | 136 |
| 13B | 136 |
| 14 | 136 |

**Pausanias**
*Fragmentum*
| | |
|---|---|
| 407, line 107 | 182 |

**Philolaos**
*Fragmentum*
| | |
|---|---|
| 13 | 100 |

**Philostratos**
*Vita Apollonii*
| | |
|---|---|
| 7.12 | 133 |

**Plato**
*Leges*
| | |
|---|---|
| 715 E–716 A | 131 |

*Theaetetus*
| | |
|---|---|
| 162 E | 225 |

**Plutarchos**
*Cato Minor*
| | |
|---|---|
| 14.2 | 199 |

*Conjugalia praecepta*
| | |
|---|---|
| 140A | 136 |

*Consolatio ad uxorem*
| | |
|---|---|
| 120B | 138 |

*De defectu oraculorum*
  425F–426A    130

*De exilio*
  601B    131

*De facie quae in orbe lunae apparet*
  925 F    111

*Fragmenta*
  157, line 89    136

*Lucullus*
  29.6    199

*Marcius Coriolanus*
  37.232    252
  38.3    138

*Numa*
  2    277

*Pericles*
  4    182

*Quaestionum convivalium libri IX*
  614B    138

**Pseudo-Plutarchos**
*De fato*
  572 F–574 C    227

**Proklos**
*In Platonis Timaeum commentaria*
  II.14    136

**Ptolemaios**
*Anthologia Palatina*
  IX.577    228

**Sophocles**
*Oidipus Rex*
  533    197

**Stobaios**
*Anthologium*
  2.7,3a    136
  4.28,17    136

**Strabo**
*Geographica*
  17.1,54    100

**Vettius Valens**
*Anthologiae*
  VI.1,8f.    229
  VI.1,16    229

**Xenophon**
*Cyropaedia*
  3.1,36    196
  8.17,19    196

## B. Latin Texts

**Amminianus Marcellinus**
*Res gestae*
  29.1,25ff.    255

**Apuleius**
*Metamorphoses*
  11.23,8    252

**Chrysippus**
*Fragmenta logica*
  1029    130

**Lucius Iunius Moderatus Columella**
*De re rustica*
  12    136

*Praefatio*
  7–8    136

**Pseudo-Manilius**
*Astronomica*
  I.25–32    228
  II.115–123    228
  IV.407    230

**Marcus Tullius Cicero**
*De legibus*
  1.33f.    138

**Plautus**
*Rudens*
  prol. 9ff.    256

**Seneca major**
*Suasoriae*
  4.1    228

Seneca minor
   Epistulae Lucilium
     6.6               132

Epistulae morales
    11.88,30       138
    94.1            289

# V. Published Compilations, Papyri and Inscriptions

**Aegyptische (Griechische) Urkunden**
   15.2495        182
   1052             136
   1099             136

**Corpus Inscriptionum Iudaicarum**
   1510             194

**Inscriptiones Graecae**
   12.7,409       183
   958              101
   3177             207
   3984             102

   *Attica*
     II. 12595      136
   II.23            207
   II.12142       140
   II.13009a      140

   *Italia*
     XIV. 607      136
   IV.2             207
   IX.1,882       140
   IX.2,913       101

   V.2.268.
     33              195
   XIV.940        140
   II2,3954       101
   II2,3985       102

**Inscriptiones Graecae ad res Romanas pertinentes**
   1204             196

**Inscriptiones Graecae urbis Romae**
   1204             140
   III.1329       140

**Inscription from Afrodisias**    195

**Monumenta Asiae Minoris Antiqua**
   7.366           136
   10.150          101

**Oxyrhynchus Papyri**
   2.237           200
   12.1473        136
   45.3242        184

**Papyri Osloenses**
   107              184

**Papyrus Columbia 123**
   8.209           184

**Papyrus London**
   2.180           182
   3.908           182

**Papyrus Merton**
   1.23             182
   I 8,8–9         182

**Papyrus Meyer**
   8.13             182

**Patrologiae Cursus, series Graeca**
   55. 656, 65     198

**PBabatha**
   18               136

**Supplementum epigraphicum Graecum**
   11.384         140, 196
   17.172         140, 196
   28.323         140
   30.268         140

# Wissenschaftliche Untersuchungen zum Neuen Testament
*Alphabetical Index of the First and Second Series*

*Ådna, Jostein:* Jesu Stellung zum Tempel. 2000. *Vol. II/119.*
*Ådna, Jostein* (Ed.): The Formation of the Early Church. 2005. *Vol. 183.*
– and *Kvalbein, Hans* (Ed.): The Mission of the Early Church to Jews and Gentiles. 2000. *Vol. 127.*
*Ahearne-Kroll, Stephen P., Paul A. Holloway,* and *James A. Kelhoffer* (Ed.): Women and Gender in Ancient Religions. 2010. *Vol. 263.*
*Aland, Barbara:* Was ist Gnosis? 2009. *Vol. 239.*
*Alexeev, Anatoly A., Christos Karakolis* and *Ulrich Luz* (Ed.): Einheit der Kirche im Neuen Testament. Dritte europäische orthodox-westliche Exegetenkonferenz in Sankt Petersburg, 24.–31. August 2005. 2008. *Vol. 218.*
*Alkier, Stefan:* Wunder und Wirklichkeit in den Briefen des Apostels Paulus. 2001. *Vol. 134.*
*Allen, David M.:* Deuteronomy and Exhortation in Hebrews. 2008. *Vol. II/238.*
*Anderson, Charles A.:* Philo of Alexandria's Views of the Physical World. 2011. *Vol. II/309.*
*Anderson, Paul N.:* The Christology of the Fourth Gospel. 1996. *Vol. II/78.*
*Appold, Mark L.:* The Oneness Motif in the Fourth Gospel. 1976. *Vol. II/1.*
*Arnold, Clinton E.:* The Colossian Syncretism. 1995. *Vol. II/77.*
*Ascough, Richard S.:* Paul's Macedonian Associations. 2003. *Vol. II/161.*
*Asiedu-Peprah, Martin:* Johannine Sabbath Conflicts As Juridical Controversy. 2001. *Vol. II/132.*
*Assel, Heinrich, Stefan Beyerle* and *Christfried Böttrich* (Ed.): Beyond Biblical Theologies. 2012. *Vol. 295.*
*Attridge, Harold W.:* Essays on John and Hebrews. 2010. *Vol. 264.*
– see *Zangenberg, Jürgen.*
*Aune, David E.:* Apocalypticism, Prophecy and Magic in Early Christianity. 2006. *Vol. 199.*
– Jesus, Gospel Tradition and Paul in the Context of Jewish and Greco-Roman Antiquity. 2013. *Vol. 303.*
*Avemarie, Friedrich:* Die Tauferzählungen der Apostelgeschichte. 2002. *Vol. 139.*
*Avemarie, Friedrich* and *Hermann Lichtenberger* (Ed.): Auferstehung – Ressurection. 2001. *Vol. 135.*

– Bund und Tora. 1996. *Vol. 92.*
*Baarlink, Heinrich:* Verkündigtes Heil. 2004. *Vol. 168.*
*Bachmann, Michael:* Sünder oder Übertreter. 1992. *Vol. 59.*
*Bachmann, Michael* (Ed.): Lutherische und Neue Paulusperspektive. 2005. *Vol. 182.*
*Back, Frances:* Verwandlung durch Offenbarung bei Paulus. 2002. *Vol. II/153.*
– Gott als Vater der Jünger im Johannesevangelium. 2012. *Vol. II/336.*
*Backhaus, Knut:* Der sprechende Gott. 2009. *Vol. 240.*
*Baker, William R.:* Personal Speech-Ethics in the Epistle of James. 1995. *Vol. II/68.*
*Bakke, Odd Magne:* 'Concord and Peace'. 2001. *Vol. II/143.*
*Balch, David L.:* Roman Domestic Art and Early House Churches. 2008. *Vol. 228.*
– see *Weissenrieder, Annette.*
*Baldwin, Matthew C.:* Whose *Acts of Peter*? 2005. *Vol. II/196.*
*Balla, Peter:* Challenges to New Testament Theology. 1997. *Vol. II/95.*
– The Child-Parent Relationship in the New Testament and its Environment. 2003. *Vol. 155.*
*Baltes, Guido:* Hebräisches Evangelium und synoptische Überlieferung. 2011. *Bd. II/312.*
*Bammel, Ernst:* Judaica. Vol. I 1986. *Vol. 37.*
– Vol. II 1997. *Vol. 91.*
*Barclay, John M.G.:* Pauline Churches and Diaspora Jews. 2011. *Vol. 275.*
*Barnard, Jody A.:* The Mysticism of Hebrews. 2012. *Vol. II/331.*
*Barreto, Eric D.:* Ethnic Negotiations. 2010. *Vol. II/294.*
*Barrier, Jeremy W.:* The Acts of Paul and Thecla. 2009. *Vol. II/270.*
*Barton, Stephen C.:* see *Stuckenbruck, Loren T.*
*Bash, Anthony:* Ambassadors for Christ. 1997. *Vol. II/92.*
*Bauckham, Richard:* The Jewish World around the New Testament. Collected Essays Volume I. 2008. *Vol. 233.*
*Bauer, Thomas Johann:* Paulus und die kaiserzeitliche Epistolographie. 2011. *Vol. 276.*
*Bauernfeind, Otto:* Kommentar und Studien zur Apostelgeschichte. 1980. *Vol. 22.*

*Baum, Armin Daniel:* Pseudepigraphie und literarische Fälschung im frühen Christentum. 2001. *Vol. II/138.*
*Bayer, Hans Friedrich:* Jesus' Predictions of Vindication and Resurrection. 1986. *Vol. II/20.*
*Becker, Eve-Marie:* Das Markus-Evangelium im Rahmen antiker Historiographie. 2006. *Vol. 194.*
*Becker, Eve-Marie* and *Peter Pilhofer* (Ed.): Biographie und Persönlichkeit des Paulus. 2005. *Vol. 187.*
- and *Anders Runesson* (Ed.): Mark and Matthew I. 2011. *Vol. 271.*
- Mark and Matthew II. 2013. *Vol. 304.*
*Becker, Michael:* Wunder und Wundertäter im frührabbinischen Judentum. 2002. *Vol. II/144.*
*Becker, Michael* and *Markus Öhler* (Ed.): Apokalyptik als Herausforderung neutestamentlicher Theologie. 2006. *Vol. II/214.*
*Bell, Richard H.:* Deliver Us from Evil. 2007. *Vol. 216.*
- The Irrevocable Call of God. 2005. *Vol. 184.*
- No One Seeks for God. 1998. *Vol. 106.*
- Provoked to Jealousy. 1994. *Vol. II/63.*
*Bennema, Cornelis:* The Power of Saving Wisdom. 2002. *Vol. II/148.*
*Bergman, Jan:* see *Kieffer, René.*
*Bergmeier, Roland:* Das Gesetz im Römerbrief und andere Studien zum Neuen Testament. 2000. *Vol. 121.*
*Bernett, Monika:* Der Kaiserkult in Judäa unter den Herodiern und Römern. 2007. *Vol. 203.*
*Betho, Benjamin:* see *Clivaz, Claire.*
*Betz, Otto:* Jesus, der Messias Israels. 1987. *Vol. 42.*
- Jesus, der Herr der Kirche. 1990. *Vol. 52.*
*Beyerle, Stefan:* see *Assel, Heinrich.*
*Beyschlag, Karlmann:* Simon Magus und die christliche Gnosis. 1974. *Vol. 16.*
*Bieringer, Reimund:* see *Koester, Craig.*
*Bird, Michael F.* and *Jason Maston* (Ed.): Earliest Christian History. 2012. *Vol. II/320.*
*Bittner, Wolfgang J.:* Jesu Zeichen im Johannesevangelium. 1987. *Vol. II/26.*
*Bjerkelund, Carl J.:* Tauta Egeneto. 1987. *Vol. 40.*
*Blackburn, Barry Lee:* Theios Aner and the Markan Miracle Traditions. 1991. *Vol. II/40.*
*Blackwell, Ben C.:* Christosis. 2011. *Vol. II/314.*
*Blanton IV, Thomas R.:* Constructing a New Covenant. 2007. *Vol. II/233.*
*Bock, Darrell L.:* Blasphemy and Exaltation in Judaism and the Final Examination of Jesus. 1998. *Vol. II/106.*
- and *Robert L. Webb* (Ed.): Key Events in the Life of the Historical Jesus. 2009. *Vol. 247.*
*Bockmuehl, Markus:* The Remembered Peter. 2010. *Vol. 262.*

- Revelation and Mystery in Ancient Judaism and Pauline Christianity. 1990. *Vol. II/36.*
*Bøe, Sverre:* Cross-Bearing in Luke. 2010. *Vol. II/278.*
- Gog and Magog. 2001. *Vol. II/135.*
*Böhlig, Alexander:* Gnosis und Synkretismus. Vol. 1 1989. *Vol. 47* – Vol. 2 1989. *Vol. 48.*
*Böhm, Martina:* Samarien und die Samaritai bei Lukas. 1999. *Vol. II/111.*
*Börstinghaus, Jens:* Sturmfahrt und Schiffbruch. 2010. *Vol. II/274.*
*Böttrich, Christfried:* Weltweisheit – Menschheitsethik – Urkult. 1992. *Vol. II/50.*
- and *Herzer, Jens* (Ed.): Josephus und das Neue Testament. 2007. *Vol. 209.*
- see *Assel, Heinrich.*
*Bolyki, János:* Jesu Tischgemeinschaften. 1997. *Vol. II/96.*
*Bosman, Philip:* Conscience in Philo and Paul. 2003. *Vol. II/166.*
*Bovon, François:* New Testament and Christian Apocrypha. 2009. *Vol. 237.*
- Studies in Early Christianity. 2003. *Vol. 161.*
*Brändl, Martin:* Der Agon bei Paulus. 2006. *Vol. II/222.*
*Braun, Heike:* Geschichte des Gottesvolkes und christliche Identität. 2010. *Vol. II/279.*
*Breytenbach, Cilliers:* see *Frey, Jörg.*
*Broadhead, Edwin K.:* Jewish Ways of Following Jesus Redrawing the Religious Map of Antiquity. 2010. *Vol. 266.*
*Brocke, Christoph vom:* Thessaloniki – Stadt des Kassander und Gemeinde des Paulus. 2001. *Vol. II/125.*
*Brunson, Andrew:* Psalm 118 in the Gospel of John. 2003. *Vol. II/158.*
*Büchli, Jörg:* Der Poimandres – ein paganisiertes Evangelium. 1987. *Vol. II/27.*
*Bühner, Jan A.:* Der Gesandte und sein Weg im 4. Evangelium. 1977. *Vol. II/2.*
*Burchard, Christoph:* Untersuchungen zu Joseph und Aseneth. 1965. *Vol. 8.*
- Studien zur Theologie, Sprache und Umwelt des Neuen Testaments. Ed. by D. Sänger. 1998. *Vol. 107.*
*Burnett, Richard:* Karl Barth's Theological Exegesis. 2001. *Vol. II/145.*
*Byron, John:* Slavery Metaphors in Early Judaism and Pauline Christianity. 2003. *Vol. II/162.*
*Byrskog, Samuel:* Story as History – History as Story. 2000. *Vol. 123.*
*Calhoun, Robert M.:* Paul's Definitions of the Gospel in Romans 1. 2011. *Vol. II/316.*
*Canavan, Rosemary:* Clothing the Body of Christ at Colossae. 2012. *Vol. II/334.*
*Cancik, Hubert* (Ed.): Markus-Philologie. 1984. *Vol. 33.*

*Wissenschaftliche Untersuchungen zum Neuen Testament*

*Capes, David B.:* Old Testament Yaweh Texts in Paul's Christology. 1992. *Vol. II/47.*
*Caragounis, Chrys C.:* The Development of Greek and the New Testament. 2004. *Vol. 167.*
− The Son of Man. 1986. *Vol. 38.*
− see *Fridrichsen, Anton.*
*Carleton Paget, James:* The Epistle of Barnabas. 1994. *Vol. II/64.*
− Jews, Christians and Jewish Christians in Antiquity. 2010. *Vol. 251.*
*Carson, D.A., O'Brien, Peter T.* and *Mark Seifrid* (Ed.): Justification and Variegated Nomism. Vol. 1: The Complexities of Second Temple Judaism. 2001. *Vol. II/140.*
Vol. 2: The Paradoxes of Paul. 2004. *Vol. II/181.*
*Caulley, Thomas Scott* and *Hermann Lichtenberger* (Ed.): Die Septuaginta und das frühe Christentum – The Septuagint and Christian Origins. 2011. *Vol. 277.*
− see *Lichtenberger, Hermann.*
*Chae, Young Sam:* Jesus as the Eschatological Davidic Shepherd. 2006. *Vol. II/216.*
*Chapman, David W.:* Ancient Jewish and Christian Perceptions of Crucifixion. 2008. *Vol. II/244.*
*Chester, Andrew:* Future Hope and Present Reality. Vol. I: Eschatology and Transformation in the Hebrew Bible. 2012. *Vol. 293.*
− Messiah and Exaltation. 2007. *Vol. 207.*
*Chibici-Revneanu, Nicole:* Die Herrlichkeit des Verherrlichten. 2007. *Vol. II/231.*
*Ciampa, Roy E.:* The Presence and Function of Scripture in Galatians 1 and 2. 1998. *Vol. II/102.*
*Classen, Carl Joachim:* Rhetorical Criticsm of the New Testament. 2000. *Vol. 128.*
*Claußen, Carsten* (Ed.): see *Frey, Jörg.*
*Clivaz, Claire, Andreas Dettwiler, Luc Devillers, Enrico Norelli* with *Benjamin Bertho* (Ed.): Infancy Gospels. 2011. *Vol. 281.*
*Colpe, Carsten:* Griechen – Byzantiner – Semiten – Muslime. 2008. *Vol. 221.*
− Iranier – Aramäer – Hebräer – Hellenen. 2003. *Vol. 154.*
*Cook, John G.:* Roman Attitudes Towards the Christians. 2010. *Vol. 261.*
*Coote, Robert B.* (Ed.): see *Weissenrieder, Annette.*
*Coppins, Wayne:* The Interpretation of Freedom in the Letters of Paul. 2009. *Vol. II/261.*
*Crump, David:* Jesus the Intercessor. 1992. *Vol. II/49.*
*Dahl, Nils Alstrup:* Studies in Ephesians. 2000. *Vol. 131.*
*Daise, Michael A.:* Feasts in John. 2007. *Vol. II/229.*

*Deines, Roland:* Die Gerechtigkeit der Tora im Reich des Messias. 2004. *Vol. 177.*
− Jüdische Steingefäße und pharisäische Frömmigkeit. 1993. *Vol. II/52.*
− Die Pharisäer. 1997. *Vol. 101.*
*Deines, Roland, Jens Herzer* and *Karl-Wilhelm Niebuhr* (Ed.): Neues Testament und hellenistisch-jüdische Alltagskultur. III. Internationales Symposium zum Corpus Judaeo-Hellenisticum Novi Testamenti. 21.–24. Mai 2009 in Leipzig. 2011. *Vol. 274.*
− and *Karl-Wilhelm Niebuhr* (Ed.): Philo und das Neue Testament. 2004. *Vol. 172.*
*Dennis, John A.:* Jesus' Death and the Gathering of True Israel. 2006. *Vol. 217.*
*Dettwiler, Andreas* and *Jean Zumstein* (Ed.): Kreuzestheologie im Neuen Testament. 2002. *Vol. 151.*
− see *Clivaz, Claire.*
*Devillers, Luc:* see *Clivaz, Claire.*
*Dickson, John P.:* Mission-Commitment in Ancient Judaism and in the Pauline Communities. 2003. *Vol. II/159.*
*Dietzfelbinger, Christian:* Der Abschied des Kommenden. 1997. *Vol. 95.*
*Dimitrov, Ivan Z., James D.G. Dunn, Ulrich Luz* and *Karl-Wilhelm Niebuhr* (Ed.): Das Alte Testament als christliche Bibel in orthodoxer und westlicher Sicht. 2004. *Vol. 174.*
*Dobbeler, Axel von:* Glaube als Teilhabe. 1987. *Vol. II/22.*
*Docherty, Susan E.:* The Use of the Old Testament in Hebrews. 2009. *Vol. II/260.*
*Dochhorn, Jan:* Schriftgelehrte Prophetie. 2010. *Vol. 268.*
*Doering, Lutz:* Ancient Jewish Letters and the Beginnings of Christian Epistolography. 2012. *Vol. 298.*
*Doole, J. Andrew:* What was Mark for Matthew? 2013. *Vol. II/344.*
*Downs, David J.:* The Offering of the Gentiles. 2008. *Vol. II/248.*
*Dryden, J. de Waal:* Theology and Ethics in 1 Peter. 2006. *Vol. II/209.*
*Dübbers, Michael:* Christologie und Existenz im Kolosserbrief. 2005. *Vol. II/191.*
*Dunn, James D.G.:* The New Perspective on Paul. 2005. *Vol. 185.*
*Dunn , James D.G.* (Ed.): Jews and Christians. 1992. *Vol. 66.*
− Paul and the Mosaic Law. 1996. *Vol. 89.*
− see *Dimitrov, Ivan Z.*
−, *Hans Klein, Ulrich Luz,* and *Vasile Mihoc* (Ed.): Auslegung der Bibel in orthodoxer und westlicher Perspektive. 2000. *Vol. 130.*
*Dunson, Ben C.:* Individual and Community in Paul's Letter to the Romans. 2012. *Vol. II/332.*

## Wissenschaftliche Untersuchungen zum Neuen Testament

*Ebel, Eva:* Die Attraktivität früher christlicher Gemeinden. 2004. *Vol. II/178.*
*Eberhart, Christian A.:* Kultmetaphorik und Christologie. 2013. *Vol. 306.*
*Ebertz, Michael N.:* Das Charisma des Gekreuzigten. 1987. *Vol. 45.*
*Eckstein, Hans-Joachim:* Der Begriff Syneidesis bei Paulus. 1983. *Vol. II/10.*
– Verheißung und Gesetz. 1996. *Vol. 86.*
–, *Christoph Landmesser* and *Hermann Lichtenberger* (Ed.): Eschatologie – Eschatology. The Sixth Durham-Tübingen Research Symposium. 2011. *Vol. 272.*
*Edwards, J. Christopher:* The Ransom Logion in Mark and Matthew. 2012. *Vol. II/327.*
*Ego, Beate:* Im Himmel wie auf Erden. 1989. *Vol. II/34.*
*Ego, Beate, Armin Lange* and *Peter Pilhofer* (Ed.): Gemeinde ohne Tempel – Community without Temple. 1999. *Vol. 118.*
– and *Helmut Merkel* (Ed.): Religiöses Lernen in der biblischen, frühjüdischen und frühchristlichen Überlieferung. 2005. *Vol. 180.*
*Eisele, Wilfried:* Welcher Thomas? 2010. *Vol. 259.*
*Eisen, Ute E., Christine Gerber* and *Angela Standhartinger* (Ed.): Doing Gender – Doing Religion. 2013. *Vol. 302.*
*Eisen, Ute E.:* see *Paulsen, Henning.*
*Elledge, C.D.:* Life after Death in Early Judaism. 2006. *Vol. II/208.*
*Ellis, E. Earle:* Prophecy and Hermeneutic in Early Christianity. 1978. *Vol. 18.*
– The Old Testament in Early Christianity. 1991. *Vol. 54.*
*Elmer, Ian J.:* Paul, Jerusalem and the Judaisers. 2009. *Vol. II/258.*
*Endo, Masanobu:* Creation and Christology. 2002. *Vol. 149.*
*Ennulat, Andreas:* Die 'Minor Agreements'. 1994. *Vol. II/62.*
*Ensor, Peter W.:* Jesus and His 'Works'. 1996. *Vol. II/85.*
*Eskola, Timo:* Messiah and the Throne. 2001. *Vol. II/142.*
– Theodicy and Predestination in Pauline Soteriology. 1998. *Vol. II/100.*
*Farelly, Nicolas:* The Disciples in the Fourth Gospel. 2010. *Vol. II/290.*
*Fatehi, Mehrdad:* The Spirit's Relation to the Risen Lord in Paul. 2000. *Vol. II/128.*
*Feldmeier, Reinhard:* Die Krisis des Gottessohnes. 1987. *Vol. II/21.*
– Die Christen als Fremde. 1992. *Vol. 64.*
*Feldmeier, Reinhard* and *Ulrich Heckel* (Ed.): Die Heiden. 1994. *Vol. 70.*
*Felsch, Dorit:* Die Feste im Johannesevangelium. 2011. *Vol. II/308.*

*Finnern, Sönke:* Narratologie und biblische Exegese. 2010. *Vol. II/285.*
*Fletcher-Louis, Crispin H.T.:* Luke-Acts: Angels, Christology and Soteriology. 1997. *Vol. II/94.*
*Förster, Niclas:* Jesus und die Steuerfrage. 2012. *Vol. 294.*
– Marcus Magus. 1999. *Vol. 114.*
*Forbes, Christopher Brian:* Prophecy and Inspired Speech in Early Christianity and its Hellenistic Environment. 1995. *Vol. II/75.*
*Fornberg, Tord:* see *Fridrichsen, Anton.*
*Fossum, Jarl E.:* The Name of God and the Angel of the Lord. 1985. *Vol. 36.*
*Foster, Paul:* Community, Law and Mission in Matthew's Gospel. *Vol. II/177.*
*Fotopoulos, John:* Food Offered to Idols in Roman Corinth. 2003. *Vol. II/151.*
*Frank, Nicole:* Der Kolosserbrief im Kontext des paulinischen Erbes. 2009. *Vol. II/271.*
*Frenschkowski, Marco:* Offenbarung und Epiphanie. Vol. 1 1995. *Vol. II/79* – Vol. 2 1997. *Vol. II/80.*
*Frey, Jörg:* Eugen Drewermann und die biblische Exegese. 1995. *Vol. II/71.*
– Die Herrlichkeit des Gekreuzigten. Studien zu den Johanneischen Schriften I. 2013. *Vol. 307.*
– Die johanneische Eschatologie. Vol. I. 1997. *Vol. 96.* – Vol. II. 1998. *Vol. 110.* – Vol. III. 2000. *Vol. 117.*
*Frey, Jörg, Carsten Claußen* and *Nadine Kessler* (Ed.): Qumran und die Archäologie. 2011. *Vol. 278.*
– and *Cilliers Breytenbach* (Ed.): Aufgabe und Durchführung einer Theologie des Neuen Testaments. 2007. *Vol. 205.*
– *Jens Herzer, Martina Janßen* and *Clare K. Rothschild* (Ed.): Pseudepigraphie und Verfasserfiktion in frühchristlichen Briefen. 2009. *Vol. 246.*
– *James A. Kelhoffer* and *Franz Tóth* (Ed.): Die Johannesapokalypse. 2012. *Vol. 287.*
– *Stefan Krauter* and *Hermann Lichtenberger* (Ed.): Heil und Geschichte. 2009. *Vol. 248.*
– and *Udo Schnelle (Ed.):* Kontexte des Johannesevangeliums. 2004. *Vol. 175.*
– and *Jens Schröter* (Ed.): Deutungen des Todes Jesu im Neuen Testament. 2005. *Vol. 181.*
– Jesus in apokryphen Evangelienüberlieferungen. 2010. *Vol. 254.*
–, *Jan G. van der Watt,* and *Ruben Zimmermann* (Ed.): Imagery in the Gospel of John. 2006. *Vol. 200.*
*Freyne, Sean:* Galilee and Gospel. 2000. *Vol. 125.*
*Fridrichsen, Anton:* Exegetical Writings. Edited by C.C. Caragounis and T. Fornberg. 1994. *Vol. 76.*

*Gadenz, Pablo T.:* Called from the Jews and from the Gentiles. 2009. *Vol. II/267.*

*Gäbel, Georg:* Die Kulttheologie des Hebräerbriefes. 2006. *Vol. II/212.*

*Gäckle, Volker:* Die Starken und die Schwachen in Korinth und in Rom. 2005. *Vol. 200.*

*Garlington, Don B.:* 'The Obedience of Faith'. 1991. *Vol. II/38.*

- Faith, Obedience, and Perseverance. 1994. *Vol. 79.*

*Garnet, Paul:* Salvation and Atonement in the Qumran Scrolls. 1977. *Vol. II/3.*

*Garský, Zbyněk:* Das Wirken Jesu in Galiläa bei Johannes. 2012. *Vol. II/325.*

*Gemünden, Petra von* (Ed.): see *Weissenrieder, Annette.*

*Gerber, Christine* (Ed.): see *Eisen, Ute E.*

*Gese, Michael:* Das Vermächtnis des Apostels. 1997. *Vol. II/99.*

*Gheorghita, Radu:* The Role of the Septuagint in Hebrews. 2003. *Vol. II/160.*

*Gordley, Matthew E.:* The Colossian Hymn in Context. 2007. *Vol. II/228.*

- Teaching through Song in Antiquity. 2011. *Vol. II/302.*

*Gräbe, Petrus J.:* The Power of God in Paul's Letters. 2000, ²2008. *Vol. II/123.*

*Größer, Erich:* Der Alte Bund im Neuen. 1985. *Vol. 35.*

- Forschungen zur Apostelgeschichte. 2001. *Vol. 137.*

*Grappe, Christian* (Ed.): Le Repas de Dieu / Das Mahl Gottes. 2004. *Vol. 169.*

*Gray, Timothy C.:* The Temple in the Gospel of Mark. 2008. *Vol. II/242.*

*Green, Joel B.:* The Death of Jesus. 1988. *Vol. II/33.*

*Gregg, Brian Han:* The Historical Jesus and the Final Judgment Sayings in Q. 2005. *Vol. II/207.*

*Gregory, Andrew:* The Reception of Luke and Acts in the Period before Irenaeus. 2003. *Vol. II/169.*

*Grindheim, Sigurd:* The Crux of Election. 2005. *Vol. II/202.*

*Gundry, Robert H.:* The Old is Better. 2005. *Vol. 178.*

*Gundry Volf, Judith M.:* Paul and Perseverance. 1990. *Vol. II/37.*

*Häußer, Detlef:* Christusbekenntnis und Jesusüberlieferung bei Paulus. 2006. *Vol. 210.*

*Hafemann, Scott J.:* Suffering and the Spirit. 1986. *Vol. II/19.*

- Paul, Moses, and the History of Israel. 1995. *Vol. 81.*

*Hahn, Ferdinand:* Studien zum Neuen Testament.

Vol. I: Grundsatzfragen, Jesusforschung, Evangelien. 2006. *Vol. 191.*

Vol. II: Bekenntnisbildung und Theologie in urchristlicher Zeit. 2006. *Vol. 192.*

*Hahn, Johannes* (Ed.): Zerstörungen des Jerusalemer Tempels. 2002. *Vol. 147.*

*Hamid-Khani, Saeed:* Relevation and Concealment of Christ. 2000. *Vol. II/120.*

*Hanges, James C.:* Paul, Founder of Churches. 2012. *Vol. 292.*

*Hannah, Darrel D.:* Michael and Christ. 1999. *Vol. II/109.*

*Hardin, Justin K.:* Galatians and the Imperial Cult? 2007. *Vol. II /237.*

*Harrison, James R.:* Paul and the Imperial Authorities at Thessolanica and Rome. 2011. *Vol. 273.*

- Paul's Language of Grace in Its Graeco-Roman Context. 2003. *Vol. II/172.*

*Hartman, Lars:* Approaching New Testament Texts and Contexts. 2013. *Vol. 311.*

- Text-Centered New Testament Studies. Ed. von D. Hellholm. 1997. *Vol. 102.*

*Hartog, Paul:* Polycarp and the New Testament. 2001. *Vol. II/134.*

*Hasselbrook, David S.:* Studies in New Testament Lexicography. 2011. *Vol. II/303.*

*Hays, Christopher M.:* Luke's Wealth Ethics. 2010. *Vol. 275.*

*Heckel, Theo K.:* Der Innere Mensch. 1993. *Vol. II/53.*

- Vom Evangelium des Markus zum viergestaltigen Evangelium. 1999. *Vol. 120.*

*Heckel, Ulrich:* Kraft in Schwachheit. 1993. *Vol. II/56.*

- Der Segen im Neuen Testament. 2002. *Vol. 150.*

- see *Feldmeier, Reinhard.*

- see *Hengel, Martin.*

*Heemstra, Marius:* The Fiscus Judaicus and the Parting of the Ways. 2010. *Vol. II/277.*

*Heiligenthal, Roman:* Werke als Zeichen. 1983. *Vol. II/9.*

*Heininger, Bernhard:* Die Inkulturation des Christentums. 2010. *Vol. 255.*

*Heliso, Desta:* Pistis and the Righteous One. 2007. *Vol. II/235.*

*Hellholm, D.:* see *Hartman, Lars.*

*Hemer, Colin J.:* The Book of Acts in the Setting of Hellenistic History. 1989. *Vol. 49.*

*Henderson, Timothy P.:* The Gospel of Peter and Early Christian Apologetics. 2011. *Vol. II/301.*

*Hengel, Martin:* Jesus und die Evangelien. Kleine Schriften V. 2007. *Vol. 211.*

- Die johanneische Frage. 1993. *Vol. 67.*

- Judaica et Hellenistica. Kleine Schriften I. 1996. *Vol. 90.*

- Judaica, Hellenistica et Christiana. Kleine Schriften II. 1999. *Vol. 109.*
- Judentum und Hellenismus. 1969, ³1988. *Vol. 10.*
- Paulus und Jakobus. Kleine Schriften III. 2002. *Vol. 141.*
- Studien zur Christologie. Kleine Schriften IV. 2006. *Vol. 201.*
- Studien zum Urchristentum. Kleine Schriften VI. 2008. *Vol. 234.*
- Theologische, historische und biographische Skizzen. Kleine Schriften VII. 2010. *Vol. 253.*
- and *Anna Maria Schwemer:* Paulus zwischen Damaskus und Antiochien. 1998. *Vol. 108.*
- Der messianische Anspruch Jesu und die Anfänge der Christologie. 2001. *Vol. 138.*
- Die vier Evangelien und das eine Evangelium von Jesus Christus. 2008. *Vol. 224.*
- Die Zeloten. ³2011. *Vol. 283.*

*Hengel, Martin* and *Ulrich Heckel* (Ed.): Paulus und das antike Judentum. 1991. *Vol. 58.*
- and *Hermut Löhr* (Ed.): Schriftauslegung im antiken Judentum und im Urchristentum. 1994. *Vol. 73.*
- and *Anna Maria Schwemer* (Ed.): Königsherrschaft Gottes und himmlischer Kult. 1991. *Vol. 55.*
- Die Septuaginta. 1994. *Vol. 72.*
-, *Siegfried Mittmann* and *Anna Maria Schwemer* (Ed.): La Cité de Dieu / Die Stadt Gottes. 2000. *Vol. 129.*

*Hentschel, Anni:* Diakonia im Neuen Testament. 2007. *Vol. 226.*

*Hernández Jr., Juan:* Scribal Habits and Theological Influence in the Apocalypse. 2006. *Vol. II/218.*

*Herrenbrück, Fritz:* Jesus und die Zöllner. 1990. *Vol. II/41.*

*Herzer, Jens:* Paulus oder Petrus? 1998. *Vol. 103.*
- see *Böttrich, Christfried.*
- see *Deines, Roland.*
- see *Frey, Jörg.*
- (Ed.): Papyrologie und Exegese. 2012. *Vol. II/341.*

*Hill, Charles E.:* From the Lost Teaching of Polycarp. 2005. *Vol. 186.*

*Hoegen-Rohls, Christina:* Der nachösterliche Johannes. 1996. *Vol. II/84.*

*Hoffmann, Matthias Reinhard:* The Destroyer and the Lamb. 2005. *Vol. II/203.*

*Hofius, Otfried:* Katapausis. 1970. *Vol. 11.*
- Der Vorhang vor dem Thron Gottes. 1972. *Vol. 14.*
- Der Christushymnus Philipper 2,6–11. 1976, ²1991. *Vol. 17.*
- Paulusstudien. 1989, ²1994. *Vol. 51.*
- Neutestamentliche Studien. 2000. *Vol. 132.*
- Paulusstudien II. 2002. *Vol. 143.*
- Exegetische Studien. 2008. *Vol. 223.*
- and *Hans-Christian Kammler:* Johannesstudien. 1996. *Vol. 88.*

*Holloway, Paul A.:* Coping with Prejudice. 2009. *Vol. 244.*
- see *Ahearne-Kroll, Stephen P.*

*Holmberg, Bengt* (Ed.): Exploring Early Christian Identity. 2008. *Vol. 226.*
- and *Mikael Winninge* (Ed.): Identity Formation in the New Testament. 2008. *Vol. 227.*

*Holmén, Tom* (Ed.): Jesus in Continuum. 2012. *Vol. 289.*

*Holtz, Traugott:* Geschichte und Theologie des Urchristentums. 1991. *Vol. 57.*

*Hommel, Hildebrecht:* Sebasmata.
Vol. 1 1983. *Vol. 31.*
Vol. 2 1984. *Vol. 32.*

*Horbury, William:* Herodian Judaism and New Testament Study. 2006. *Vol. 193.*

*Horn, Friedrich Wilhelm* and *Ruben Zimmermann* (Ed.): Jenseits von Indikativ und Imperativ. Vol. 1. 2009. *Vol. 238.*

*Horst, Pieter W. van der:* Jews and Christians in Their Graeco-Roman Context. 2006. *Vol. 196.*

*Hultgård, Anders* and *Stig Norin* (Ed): Le Jour de Dieu / Der Tag Gottes. 2009. *Vol. 245.*

*Hume, Douglas A.:* The Early Christian Community. 2011. *Vol. II/298.*

*Hvalvik, Reidar:* The Struggle for Scripture and Covenant. 1996. *Vol. II/82.*

*Inselmann, Anke:* Die Freude im Lukasevangelium. 2012. *Vol. II/322.*

*Jackson, Ryan:* New Creation in Paul's Letters. 2010. *Vol. II/272.*

*Janßen, Martina:* see *Frey, Jörg.*

*Jauhiainen, Marko:* The Use of Zechariah in Revelation. 2005. *Vol. II/199.*

*Jensen, Morten H.:* Herod Antipas in Galilee. 2006; ²2010. *Vol. II/215.*

*Johns, Loren L.:* The Lamb Christology of the Apocalypse of John. 2003. *Vol. II/167.*

*Joseph, Simon J.:* Jesus, Q, and the Dead Sea Scrolls. 2012. *Vol. II/333.*

*Jossa, Giorgio:* Jews or Christians? 2006. *Vol. 202.*

*Joubert, Stephan:* Paul as Benefactor. 2000. *Vol. II/124.*

*Judge, E. A.:* The First Christians in the Roman World. 2008. *Vol. 229.*
- Jerusalem and Athens. 2010. *Vol. 265.*

*Jungbauer, Harry:* „Ehre Vater und Mutter". 2002. *Vol. II/146.*

*Kähler, Christoph:* Jesu Gleichnisse als Poesie und Therapie. 1995. *Vol. 78.*

*Kamlah, Ehrhard:* Die Form der katalogischen Paränese im Neuen Testament. 1964. *Vol. 7.*

*Kammler, Hans-Christian:* Christologie und Eschatologie. 2000. *Vol. 126.*

- Kreuz und Weisheit. 2003. *Vol. 159.*
- see *Hofius, Otfried.*

*Karakolis, Christos,* Karl-Wilhelm Niebuhr and *Sviatoslav Rogalsky* (Ed.): Gospel Images of Jesus Christ in Church Tradition and in Biblical Scholarship. Fifth International East-West Symposium of New Testament Scholars, Minsk, September 2 to 9, 2010. 2012. *Vol. 288.*
- see *Alexeev, Anatoly A.*

*Karrer, Martin* und *Wolfgang Kraus* (Ed.): Die Septuaginta – Texte, Kontexte, Lebenswelten. 2008. *Vol. 219.*
- see *Kraus, Wolfgang.*

*Kelhoffer, James A.:* The Diet of John the Baptist. 2005. *Vol. 176.*
- Miracle and Mission. 2000. *Vol. II/112.*
- Persecution, Persuasion and Power. 2010. *Vol. 270.*
- see *Ahearne-Kroll, Stephen P.*
- see *Frey, Jörg.*

*Kelley, Nicole:* Knowledge and Religious Authority in the Pseudo-Clementines. 2006. *Vol. II/213.*

*Kennedy, Joel:* The Recapitulation of Israel. 2008. *Vol. II/257.*

*Kensky, Meira Z.:* Trying Man, Trying God. 2010. *Vol. II/289.*

*Kessler, Nadine* (Ed.): see *Frey, Jörg.*

*Kieffer, René* and *Jan Bergman* (Ed.): La Main de Dieu / Die Hand Gottes. 1997. *Vol. 94.*

*Kierspel, Lars:* The Jews and the World in the Fourth Gospel. 2006. *Vol. 220.*

*Kim, Seyoon:* The Origin of Paul's Gospel. 1981, [2]1984. *Vol. II/4.*
- Paul and the New Perspective. 2002. *Vol. 140.*
- "The 'Son of Man'" as the Son of God. 1983. *Vol. 30.*

*Klauck, Hans-Josef:* Religion und Gesellschaft im frühen Christentum. 2003. *Vol. 152.*

*Klein, Hans, Vasile Mihoc* und *Karl-Wilhelm Niebuhr* (Ed.): Das Gebet im Neuen Testament. Vierte, europäische orthodox-westliche Exegetenkonferenz in Sambata de Sus, 4. – 8. August 2007. 2009. Vol. 249.
- see Dunn, James D.G.

*Kleinknecht, Karl Th.:* Der leidende Gerechtfertigte. 1984, [2]1988. *Vol. II/13.*

*Klinghardt, Matthias:* Gesetz und Volk Gottes. 1988. *Vol. II/32.*

*Kloppenborg, John S.:* The Tenants in the Vineyard. 2006, student edition 2010. *Vol. 195.*

*Koch, Michael:* Drachenkampf und Sonnenfrau. 2004. *Vol. II/184.*

*Koch, Stefan:* Rechtliche Regelung von Konflikten im frühen Christentum. 2004. *Vol. II/174.*

*Köhler, Wolf-Dietrich:* Rezeption des Matthäusevangeliums in der Zeit vor Irenäus. 1987. *Vol. II/24.*

*Köhn, Andreas:* Der Neutestamentler Ernst Lohmeyer. 2004. *Vol. II/180.*

*Koester, Craig* and *Reimund Bieringer* (Ed.): The Resurrection of Jesus in the Gospel of John. 2008. *Vol. 222.*

*Konradt, Matthias:* Israel, Kirche und die Völker im Matthäusevangelium. 2007. *Vol. 215.*

*Kooten, George H. van:* Cosmic Christology in Paul and the Pauline School. 2003. *Vol. II/171.*
- Paul's Anthropology in Context. 2008. *Vol. 232.*

*Korn, Manfred:* Die Geschichte Jesu in veränderter Zeit. 1993. *Vol. II/51.*

*Koskenniemi, Erkki:* Apollonios von Tyana in der neutestamentlichen Exegese. 1994. *Vol. II/61.*
- The Old Testament Miracle-Workers in Early Judaism. 2005. *Vol. II/206.*

*Kraus, Thomas J.:* Sprache, Stil und historischer Ort des zweiten Petrusbriefes. 2001. *Vol. II/136.*

*Kraus, Wolfgang:* Das Volk Gottes. 1996. *Vol. 85.*
- see *Karrer, Martin.*
- see *Walter, Nikolaus.*
- and *Martin Karrer* (Hrsg.): Die Septuaginta – Texte, Theologien, Einflüsse. 2010. *Bd. 252.*
- and *Karl-Wilhelm Niebuhr* (Ed.): Frühjudentum und Neues Testament im Horizont Biblischer Theologie. 2003. *Vol. 162.*

*Krauter, Stefan:* Studien zu Röm 13,1-7. 2009. *Vol. 243.*
- see *Frey, Jörg.*

*Kreplin, Matthias:* Das Selbstverständnis Jesu. 2001. *Vol. II/141.*

*Kreuzer, Siegfried, Martin Meiser* and *Marcus Sigismund* (Ed.): Die Septuaginta – Entstehung, Sprache, Geschichte. 2012. *Vol. 286.*

*Kuhn, Karl G.:* Achtzehngebet und Vaterunser und der Reim. 1950. *Vol. 1.*

*Kvalbein, Hans:* see *Ådna, Jostein.*

*Kwon, Yon-Gyong:* Eschatology in Galatians. 2004. *Vol. II/183.*

*Laansma, Jon:* I Will Give You Rest. 1997. *Vol. II/98.*

*Labahn, Michael:* Offenbarung in Zeichen und Wort. 2000. *Vol. II/117.*

*Lambers-Petry, Doris:* see *Tomson, Peter J.*

*Lampe, Peter:* Die stadtrömischen Christen in den ersten beiden Jahrhunderten. 1987, [2]1989. *Vol. II/18.*

*Landmesser, Christof:* Wahrheit als Grundbegriff neutestamentlicher Wissenschaft. 1999. *Vol. 113.*

- Jüngerberufung und Zuwendung zu Gott. 2000. *Vol. 133.*
- see *Eckstein, Hans-Joachim.*
*Lange, Armin:* see *Ego, Beate.*
*Lau, Andrew:* Manifest in Flesh. 1996. *Vol. II/86.*
*Lawrence, Louise:* An Ethnography of the Gospel of Matthew. 2003. *Vol. II/165.*
*Lee, Aquila H.I.:* From Messiah to Preexistent Son. 2005. *Vol. II/192.*
*Lee, DooHee:* Luke-Acts and 'Tragic History'. 2013. *Vol. II/346.*
*Lee, Pilchan:* The New Jerusalem in the Book of Relevation. 2000. *Vol. II/129.*
*Lee, Sang M.:* The Cosmic Drama of Salvation. 2010. *Vol. II/276.*
*Lee, Simon S.:* Jesus' Transfiguration and the Believers' Transformation. 2009. *Vol. II/265.*
*Lichtenberger, Hermann:* Das Ich Adams und das Ich der Menschheit. 2004. *Vol. 164.*
- see *Avemarie, Friedrich.*
- see *Caulley, Thomas Scott.*
- see *Eckstein, Hans-Joachim.*
- see *Frey, Jörg.*
*Lierman, John:* The New Testament Moses. 2004. *Vol. II/173.*
- (Ed.): Challenging Perspectives on the Gospel of John. 2006. *Vol. II/219.*
*Lieu, Samuel N.C.:* Manichaeism in the Later Roman Empire and Medieval China. ²1992. *Vol. 63.*
*Lindemann, Andreas:* Die Evangelien und die Apostelgeschichte. 2009. *Vol. 241.*
- Glauben, Handeln, Verstehen. Studien zur Auslegung des Neuen Testaments. 2011. *Vol. II/282.*
*Lincicum, David:* Paul and the Early Jewish Encounter with Deuteronomy. 2010. *Vol. II/284.*
*Lindgård, Fredrik:* Paul's Line of Thought in 2 Corinthians 4:16–5:10. 2004. *Vol. II/189.*
*Liu, Yulin:* Temple Purity in 1-2 Corinthians. 2013. *Vol. II/343.*
*Livesey, Nina E.:* Circumcision as a Malleable Symbol. 2010. *Vol. II/295.*
*Loader, William R.G.:* Jesus' Attitude Towards the Law. 1997. *Vol. II/97.*
*Löhr, Gebhard:* Verherrlichung Gottes durch Philosophie. 1997. *Vol. 97.*
*Löhr, Hermut:* Studien zum frühchristlichen und frühjüdischen Gebet. 2003. *Vol. 160.*
- see *Hengel, Martin.*
*Löhr, Winrich Alfried:* Basilides und seine Schule. 1995. *Vol. 83.*
*Lorenzen, Stefanie:* Das paulinische Eikon-Konzept. 2008. *Vol. II/250.*
*Luomanen, Petri:* Entering the Kingdom of Heaven. 1998. *Vol. II/101.*
*Luz, Ulrich:* see *Alexeev, Anatoly A.*
- see *Dunn, James D.G.*
*Lykke, Anne* und *Friedrich T. Schipper* (Ed.): Kult und Macht. 2011. *Vol. II/319.*
*Lyu, Eun-Geol:* Sünde und Rechtfertigung bei Paulus. 2012. *Vol. II/318.*
*Mackay, Ian D.:* John's Relationship with Mark. 2004. *Vol. II/182.*
*Mackie, Scott D.:* Eschatology and Exhortation in the Epistle to the Hebrews. 2006. *Vol. II/223.*
*Magda, Ksenija:* Paul's Territoriality and Mission Strategy. 2009. *Vol. II/266.*
*Maier, Gerhard:* Mensch und freier Wille. 1971. *Vol. 12.*
- Die Johannesoffenbarung und die Kirche. 1981. *Vol. 25.*
*Marguerat, Daniel:* Paul in Acts and Paul in His Letters. 2013. *Vol. 310.*
*Markschies, Christoph:* Valentinus Gnosticus? 1992. *Vol. 65.*
*Marshall, Jonathan:* Jesus, Patrons, and Benefactors. 2009. *Vol. II/259.*
*Marshall, Peter:* Enmity in Corinth: Social Conventions in Paul's Relations with the Corinthians. 1987. *Vol. II/23.*
*Martin, Dale B.:* see *Zangenberg, Jürgen.*
*Maston, Jason:* Divine and Human Agency in Second Temple Judaism and Paul. 2010. *Vol. II/297.*
- see *Bird, Michael F.*
*Mayer, Annemarie:* Sprache der Einheit im Epheserbrief und in der Ökumene. 2002. *Vol. II/150.*
*Mayordomo, Moisés:* Argumentiert Paulus logisch? 2005. *Vol. 188.*
*McDonough, Sean M.:* YHWH at Patmos: Rev. 1:4 in its Hellenistic and Early Jewish Setting. 1999. *Vol. II/107.*
*McDowell, Markus:* Prayers of Jewish Women. 2006. *Vol. II/211.*
*McGlynn, Moyna:* Divine Judgement and Divine Benevolence in the Book of Wisdom. 2001. *Vol. II/139.*
*McNamara, Martin:* Targum and New Testament. 2011. *Vol. 279.*
*Meade, David G.:* Pseudonymity and Canon. 1986. *Vol. 39.*
*Meadors, Edward P.:* Jesus the Messianic Herald of Salvation. 1995. *Vol. II/72.*
*Meiser, Martin:* see *Kreuzer, Siegfried.*
*Meißner, Stefan:* Die Heimholung des Ketzers. 1996. *Vol. II/87.*
*Mell, Ulrich:* Die „anderen" Winzer. 1994. *Vol. 77.*
- see *Sänger, Dieter.*
*Mengel, Berthold:* Studien zum Philipperbrief. 1982. *Vol. II/8.*

Merkel, Helmut: Die Widersprüche zwischen den Evangelien. 1971. *Vol. 13.*
- see *Ego, Beate.*

Merklein, Helmut: Studien zu Jesus und Paulus. Vol. 1 1987. *Vol. 43.* – Vol. 2 1998. *Vol. 105.*

Merkt, Andreas: see *Nicklas, Tobias*

Metzdorf, Christina: Die Tempelaktion Jesu. 2003. *Vol. II/168.*

Metzler, Karin: Der griechische Begriff des Verzeihens. 1991. *Vol. II/44.*

Metzner, Rainer: Die Rezeption des Matthäusevangeliums im 1. Petrusbrief. 1995. *Vol. II/74.*
- Das Verständnis der Sünde im Johannesevangelium. 2000. *Vol. 122.*

Michalak, Aleksander: Angels as Warriors in Late Second Temple Jewish Literature. 2012. *Vol. II/330.*

Mihoc, Vasile: see *Dunn, James D.G.*
- see *Klein, Hans.*

Mineshige, Kiyoshi: Besitzverzicht und Almosen bei Lukas. 2003. *Vol. II/163.*

Mittmann, Siegfried: see *Hengel, Martin.*

Mittmann-Richert, Ulrike: Magnifikat und Benediktus. *1996. Vol. II/90.*
- Der Sühnetod des Gottesknechts. 2008. *Vol. 220.*

Miura, Yuzuru: David in Luke-Acts. 2007. *Vol. II/232.*

Moll, Sebastian: The Arch-Heretic Marcion. 2010. *Vol. 250.*

Morales, Rodrigo J.: The Spirit and the Restorat. 2010. *Vol. 282.*

Mournet, Terence C.: Oral Tradition and Literary Dependency. 2005. *Vol. II/195.*

Mußner, Franz: Jesus von Nazareth im Umfeld Israels und der Urkirche. Ed. von M. Theobald. 1998. *Vol. 111.*

Mutschler, Bernhard: Das Corpus Johanneum bei Irenäus von Lyon. 2005. *Vol. 189.*
- Glaube in den Pastoralbriefen. 2010. *Vol. 256.*

Myers, Susan E.: Spirit Epicleses in the Acts of Thomas. 2010. *Vol. 281.*

Myers, Susan E. (Ed.): Portraits of Jesus. 2012. *Vol. II/321.*

Nguyen, V. Henry T.: Christian Identity in Corinth. 2008. *Vol. II/243.*

Nicklas, Tobias, Andreas Merkt und *Joseph Verheyden* (Ed.): Gelitten – Gestorben – Auferstanden. 2010. *Vol. II/273.*
- see *Verheyden, Joseph*

Nicolet-Anderson, Valérie: Constructing the Self. 2012. *Vol. II/324.*

Niebuhr, Karl-Wilhelm: Gesetz und Paränese. 1987. *Vol. II/28.*
- Heidenapostel aus Israel. 1992. *Vol. 62.*
- see *Deines, Roland.*

- see *Dimitrov, Ivan Z.*
- see *Karakolis, Christos.*
- see *Klein, Hans.*
- see *Kraus, Wolfgang.*

Nielsen, Anders E.: "Until it is Fullfilled". 2000. *Vol. II/126.*

Nielsen, Jesper Tang: Die kognitive Dimension des Kreuzes. 2009. *Vol. II/263.*

Nissen, Andreas: Gott und der Nächste im antiken Judentum. 1974. *Vol. 15.*

Noack, Christian: Gottesbewußtsein. 2000. *Vol. II/116.*

Noormann, Rolf: Irenäus als Paulusinterpret. 1994. *Vol. II/66.*

Norelli, Enrico: see *Clivaz, Claire.*

Norin, Stig: see *Hultgård, Anders.*

Novakovic, Lidija: Messiah, the Healer of the Sick. 2003. *Vol. II/170.*

Obermann, Andreas: Die christologische Erfüllung der Schrift im Johannesevangelium. 1996. *Vol. II/83.*

Öhler, Markus: Barnabas. 2003. *Vol. 156.*
- see *Becker, Michael.*
- (Ed.): Aposteldekret und antikes Vereinswesen. 2011. *Vol. 280.*

Oestreich, Bernhard: Performanzkritik der Paulusbriefe. 2012. *Vol. 296.*

Okure, Teresa: The Johannine Approach to Mission. 1988. *Vol. II/31.*

Onuki, Takashi: Heil und Erlösung. 2004. *Vol. 165.*

Oppong-Kumi, Peter Y.: Matthean Sets of Parables. 2013. *Vol. II/340.*

Oropeza, B. J.: Paul and Apostasy. 2000. *Vol. II/115.*

Ostmeyer, Karl-Heinrich: Kommunikation mit Gott und Christus. 2006. *Vol. 197.*
- Taufe und Typos. 2000. *Vol. II/118.*

Ounsworth, Richard: Joshua Typology in the New Testament. 2012. *Vol. II/328.*

Pale Hera, Marianus: Christology and Discipleship in John 17. 2013. *Vol. II/342.*

Pao, David W.: Acts and the Isaianic New Exodus. 2000. *Vol. II/130.*

Pardee, Nancy: The Genre and Development of the Didache. 2012. *Vol. II/339.*

Park, Eung Chun: The Mission Discourse in Matthew's Interpretation. 1995. *Vol. II/81.*

Park, Joseph S.: Conceptions of Afterlife in Jewish Insriptions. 2000. *Vol. II/121.*

Parsenios, George L.: Rhetoric and Drama in the Johannine Lawsuit Motif. 2010. *Vol. 258.*

Pate, C. Marvin: The Reverse of the Curse. 2000. *Vol. II/114.*

Paulsen, Henning: Studien zur Literatur und Geschichte des frühen Christentums. Ed. von Ute E. Eisen. 1997. *Vol. 99.*

*Pearce, Sarah J.K.:* The Land of the Body. 2007.
Vol. 208.
*Peres, Imre:* Griechische Grabinschriften und neutestamentliche Eschatologie. 2003.
Vol. 157.
*Perry, Peter S.:* The Rhetoric of Digressions. 2009. Vol. II/268.
*Pierce, Chad T.:* Spirits and the Proclamation of Christ. 2011. Vol. II/305.
*Philip, Finny:* The Origins of Pauline Pneumatology. 2005. Vol. II/194.
*Philonenko, Marc* (Ed.): Le Trône de Dieu. 1993. Vol. 69.
*Pilhofer, Peter:* Presbyteron Kreitton. 1990. Vol. II/39.
- Philippi. Vol. 1 1995. Vol. 87. - Vol. 2 ²2009. Vol. 119.
- Die frühen Christen und ihre Welt. 2002. Vol. 145.
- see *Becker, Eve-Marie.*
- see *Ego, Beate.*
*Pitre, Brant:* Jesus, the Tribulation, and the End of the Exile. 2005. Vol. II/204.
*Plümacher, Eckhard:* Geschichte und Geschichten. 2004. Vol. 170.
*Pöhlmann, Wolfgang:* Der Verlorene Sohn und das Haus. 1993. Vol. 68.
*Poirier, John C.:* The Tongues of Angels. 2010. Vol. II/287.
*Pokorný, Petr* and *Josef B. Souček:* Bibelauslegung als Theologie. 1997. Vol. 100.
- and *Jan Roskovec* (Ed.): Philosophical Hermeneutics and Biblical Exegesis. 2002. Vol. 153.
*Popkes, Enno Edzard:* Das Menschenbild des Thomasevangeliums. 2007. Vol. 206.
- Die Theologie der Liebe Gottes in den johanneischen Schriften. 2005. Vol. II/197.
- and *Gregor Wurst* (Ed.): Judasevangelium und Codex Tchacos. 2012. Vol. 297.
*Porter, Stanley E.:* The Paul of Acts. 1999. Vol. 115.
*Prieur, Alexander:* Die Verkündigung der Gottesherrschaft. 1996. Vol. II/89.
*Probst, Hermann:* Paulus und der Brief. 1991. Vol. II/45.
*Puig i Tàrrech, Armand:* Jesus: An Uncommon Journey. 2010. Vol. II/288.
*Rabens, Volker:* The Holy Spirit and Ethics in Paul. 2010. Vol. II/283.
*Räisänen, Heikki:* Paul and the Law. 1983, ²1987. Vol. 29.
*Rehfeld, Emmanuel L.:* Relationale Ontologie bei Paulus. 2012. Vol. II/326.
*Rehkopf, Friedrich:* Die lukanische Sonderquelle. 1959. Vol. 5.
*Rein, Matthias:* Die Heilung des Blindgeborenen (Joh 9). 1995. Vol. II/73.

*Reinmuth, Eckart:* Pseudo-Philo und Lukas. 1994. Vol. 74.
*Reiser, Marius:* Bibelkritik und Auslegung der Heiligen Schrift. 2007. Vol. 217.
- Syntax und Stil des Markusevangeliums. 1984. Vol. II/11.
*Reynolds, Benjamin E.:* The Apocalyptic Son of Man in the Gospel of John. 2008. Vol. II/249.
*Rhodes, James N.:* The Epistle of Barnabas and the Deuteronomic Tradition. 2004. Vol. II/188.
*Richards, E. Randolph:* The Secretary in the Letters of Paul. 1991. Vol. II/42.
*Richardson, Christopher A.:* Pioneer and Perfecter of Faith. 2012. Vol. II/338.
*Riesner, Rainer:* Jesus als Lehrer. 1981, ³1988. Vol. II/7.
- Die Frühzeit des Apostels Paulus. 1994. Vol. 71.
*Rissi, Mathias:* Die Theologie des Hebräerbriefs. 1987. Vol. 41.
*Röcker, Fritz W.:* Belial und Katechon. 2009. Vol. II/262.
*Röhser, Günter:* Metaphorik und Personifikation der Sünde. 1987. Vol. II/25.
*Rogalsky, Sviatoslav:* see *Karakolis, Christos.*
*Rose, Christian:* Theologie als Erzählung im Markusevangelium. 2007. Vol. II/236.
- Die Wolke der Zeugen. 1994. Vol. II/60.
*Roskovec, Jan:* see *Pokorný, Petr.*
*Rothschild, Clare K.:* Baptist Traditions and Q. 2005. Vol. 190.
- Hebrews as Pseudepigraphon. 2009. Vol. 235.
- Luke Acts and the Rhetoric of History. 2004. Vol. II/175.
- see *Frey, Jörg.*
- and *Jens Schröter* (Ed.): The Rise and Expansion of Christianity in the First Three Centuries of the Common Era. 2013. Vol. 301.
- and *Trevor W. Thompson* (Ed.): Christian Body, Christian Self. 2011. Vol. 284.
*Rudolph, David J.:* A Jew to the Jews. 2011. Vol. II/304.
*Rüegger, Hans-Ulrich:* Verstehen, was Markus erzählt. 2002. Vol. II/155.
*Rüger, Hans Peter:* Die Weisheitsschrift aus der Kairoer Geniza. 1991. Vol. 53.
*Ruf, Martin G.:* Die heiligen Propheten, eure Apostel und ich. 2011. Vol. II/300.
*Runesson, Anders:* see *Becker, Eve-Marie.*
*Sänger, Dieter:* Antikes Judentum und die Mysterien. 1980. Vol. II/5.
- Die Verkündigung des Gekreuzigten und Israel. 1994. Vol. 75.
- see *Burchard, Christoph*
- and *Ulrich Mell* (Ed.): Paulus und Johannes. 2006. Vol. 198.

*Salier, Willis Hedley:* The Rhetorical Impact of the Semeia in the Gospel of John. 2004. *Vol. II/186.*
*Salzmann, Jörg Christian:* Lehren und Ermahnen. 1994. *Vol. II/59.*
*Samuelsson, Gunnar:* Crucifixion in Antiquity. 2011. *Vol. II/310.*
*Sandelin, Karl-Gustav:* Attraction and Danger of Alien Religion. 2012. *Vol. 290.*
*Sandnes, Karl Olav:* Paul – One of the Prophets? 1991. *Vol. II/43.*
*Sato, Migaku:* Q und Prophetie. 1988. *Vol. II/29.*
*Schäfer, Ruth:* Paulus bis zum Apostelkonzil. 2004. *Vol. II/179.*
*Schaper, Joachim:* Eschatology in the Greek Psalter. 1995. *Vol. II/76.*
*Schimanowski, Gottfried:* Die himmlische Liturgie in der Apokalypse des Johannes. 2002. *Vol. II/154.*
 – Weisheit und Messias. 1985. *Vol. II/17.*
*Schipper, Friedrich T.:* see *Lykke, Anne.*
*Schlichting, Günter:* Ein jüdisches Leben Jesu. 1982. *Vol. 24.*
*Schließer, Benjamin:* Abraham's Faith in Romans 4. 2007. *Vol. II/224.*
*Schnabel, Eckhard J.:* Law and Wisdom from Ben Sira to Paul. 1985. *Vol. II/16.*
*Schnelle, Udo:* see *Frey, Jörg.*
*Schröter, Jens:* Von Jesus zum Neuen Testament. 2007. *Vol. 204.*
 – see *Frey, Jörg.*
 – see *Rothschild, Clare K.*
*Schultheiß, Tanja:* Das Petrusbild im Johannesevangelium. 2012. *Vol. II/329.*
*Schutter, William L.:* Hermeneutic and Composition in I Peter. 1989. *Vol. II/30.*
*Schwartz, Daniel R.:* Reading the First Century. 2013. *Vol. 300.*
 – Studies in the Jewish Background of Christianity. 1992. *Vol. 60.*
*Schwemer, Anna Maria:* see *Hengel, Martin*
*Scott, Ian W.:* Implicit Epistemology in the Letters of Paul. 2005. *Vol. II/205.*
*Scott, James M.:* Adoption as Sons of God. 1992. *Vol. II/48.*
 – Paul and the Nations. 1995. *Vol. 84.*
*Shi, Wenhua:* Paul's Message of the Cross as Body Language. 2008. *Vol. II/254.*
*Shum, Shiu-Lun:* Paul's Use of Isaiah in Romans. 2002. *Vol. II/156.*
*Siegert, Folker:* Drei hellenistisch-jüdische Predigten. Teil I 1980. *Vol. 20* – Teil II 1992. *Vol. 61.*
 – Nag-Hammadi-Register. 1982. *Vol. 26.*
 – Argumentation bei Paulus. 1985. *Vol. 34.*
 – Philon von Alexandrien. 1988. *Vol. 46.*

*Siggelkow-Berner, Birke:* Die jüdischen Feste im Bellum Judaicum des Flavius Josephus. 2011. *Vol. II/306.*
*Sigismund, Marcus:* see *Kreuzer, Siegfried.*
*Simon, Marcel:* Le christianisme antique et son contexte religieux I/II. 1981. *Vol. 23.*
*Smit, Peter-Ben:* Fellowship and Food in the Kingdom. 2008. *Vol. II/234.*
*Smith, Claire S.:* Pauline Communities as 'Scholastic Communities'. 2012. *Vol. II/335.*
*Smith, Julien:* Christ the Ideal King. 2011. *Vol. II/313.*
*Snodgrass, Klyne:* The Parable of the Wicked Tenants. 1983. *Vol. 27.*
*Söding, Thomas:* Das Wort vom Kreuz. 1997. *Vol. 93.*
 – see *Thüsing, Wilhelm.*
*Sommer, Urs:* Die Passionsgeschichte des Markusevangeliums. 1993. *Vol. II/58.*
*Sorensen, Eric:* Possession and Exorcism in the New Testament and Early Christianity. 2002. *Vol. II/157.*
*Souček, Josef B.:* see *Pokorný, Petr.*
*Southall, David J.:* Rediscovering Righteousness in Romans. 2008. *Vol. 240.*
*Spangenberg, Volker:* Herrlichkeit des Neuen Bundes. 1993. *Vol. II/55.*
*Spanje, T.E. van:* Inconsistency in Paul? 1999. *Vol. II/110.*
*Speyer, Wolfgang:* Frühes Christentum im antiken Strahlungsfeld. Vol. I: 1989. *Vol. 50.*
 – Vol. II: 1999. *Vol. 116.*
 – Vol. III: 2007. *Vol. 213.*
*Spittler, Janet E.:* Animals in the Apocryphal Acts of the Apostles. 2008. *Vol. II/247.*
*Sprinkle, Preston:* Law and Life. 2008. *Vol. II/241.*
*Stadelmann, Helge:* Ben Sira als Schriftgelehrter. 1980. *Vol. II/6.*
*Standhartinger, Angela* (Ed.): see *Eisen, Ute E.*
*Stein, Hans Joachim:* Frühchristliche Mahlfeiern. 2008. *Vol. II/255.*
*Stenschke, Christoph W.:* Luke's Portrait of Gentiles Prior to Their Coming to Faith. *Vol. II/108.*
*Stephens, Mark B.:* Annihilation or Renewal? 2011. *Vol. II/307.*
*Sterck-Degueldre, Jean-Pierre:* Eine Frau namens Lydia. 2004. *Vol. II/176.*
*Stettler, Christian:* Der Kolosserhymnus. 2000. *Vol. II/131.*
 – Das letzte Gericht. 2011. *Vol. II/299.*
*Stettler, Hanna:* Die Christologie der Pastoralbriefe. 1998. *Vol. II/105.*
*Stökl Ben Ezra, Daniel:* The Impact of Yom Kippur on Early Christianity. 2003. *Vol. 163.*
*Strobel, August:* Die Stunde der Wahrheit. 1980. *Vol. 21.*

*Stroumsa, Guy G.:* Barbarian Philosophy. 1999. Vol. 112.
*Stuckenbruck, Loren T.:* Angel Veneration and Christology. 1995. Vol. II/70.
–, *Stephen C. Barton* and *Benjamin G. Wold* (Ed.): Memory in the Bible and Antiquity. 2007. Vol. 212.
*Stuhlmacher, Peter* (Ed.): Das Evangelium und die Evangelien. 1983. Vol. 28.
– Biblische Theologie und Evangelium. 2002. Vol. 146.
*Sung, Chong-Hyon:* Vergebung der Sünden. 1993. Vol. II/57.
*Svendsen, Stefan N.:* Allegory Transformed. 2009. Vol. II/269.
*Tajra, Harry W.:* The Trial of St. Paul. 1989. Vol. II/35.
– The Martyrdom of St.Paul. 1994. Vol. II/67.
*Tellbe, Mikael:* Christ-Believers in Ephesus. 2009. Vol. 242.
*Theißen, Gerd:* Studien zur Soziologie des Urchristentums. 1979, ³1989. Vol. 19.
*Theobald, Michael:* Studien zum Corpus Iohanneum. 2010. Vol. 267.
– Studien zum Römerbrief. 2001. Vol. 136.
– see *Mußner, Franz.*
*Thompson, Trevor W.:* see *Rothschild, Clare K.*
*Thornton, Claus-Jürgen:* Der Zeuge des Zeugen. 1991. Vol. 56.
*Thüsing, Wilhelm:* Studien zur neutestamentlichen Theologie. Ed. von Thomas Söding. 1995. Vol. 82.
*Thurén, Lauri:* Derhethorizing Paul. 2000. Vol. 124.
*Thyen, Hartwig:* Studien zum Corpus Iohanneum. 2007. Vol. 214.
*Tibbs, Clint:* Religious Experience of the Pneuma. 2007. Vol. II/230.
*Tilling, Chris:* Paul's Divine Christology. 2012. Vol. II/323.
*Toit, David S. du:* Theios Anthropos. 1997. Vol. II/91.
*Tolmie, D. Francois:* Persuading the Galatians. 2005. Vol. II/190.
*Tomson, Peter J.* and *Doris Lambers-Petry* (Ed.): The Image of the Judaeo-Christians in Ancient Jewish and Christian Literature. 2003. Vol. 158.
*Toney, Carl N.:* Paul's Inclusive Ethic. 2008. Vol. II/252.
– siehe *Frey, Jörg.*
*Tóth, Franz:* see *Frey, Jörg.*
*Trebilco, Paul:* The Early Christians in Ephesus from Paul to Ignatius. 2004. Vol. 166.
*Treloar, Geoffrey R.:* Lightfoot the Historian. 1998. Vol. II/103.

*Trofigruben, Troy M.:* A Conclusion Unhindered. 2010. Vol. II/280.
*Tso, Marcus K.M.:* Ethics in the Qumran Community. 2010. Vol. II/292.
*Tsuji, Manabu:* Glaube zwischen Vollkommenheit und Verweltlichung. 1997. Vol. II/93.
*Twelftree, Graham H.:* Jesus the Exorcist. 1993. Vol. II/54.
*Ulrichs, Karl Friedrich:* Christusglaube. 2007. Vol. II/227.
*Urban, Christina:* Das Menschenbild nach dem Johannesevangelium. 2001. Vol. II/137.
*Vahrenhorst, Martin:* Kultische Sprache in den Paulusbriefen. 2008. Vol. 230.
*Vegge, Ivar:* 2 Corinthians – a Letter about Reconciliation. 2008. Vol. II/239.
*Verheyden, Joseph, Korinna Zamfir* and *Tobias Nicklas* (Ed.): Prophets and Prophecy in Jewish and Early Christian Literature. 2010. Vol. II/286.
– see *Nicklas, Tobias*
*Visotzky, Burton L.:* Fathers of the World. 1995. Vol. 80.
*Vollenweider, Samuel:* Horizonte neutestamentlicher Christologie. 2002. Vol. 144.
*Vos, Johan S.:* Die Kunst der Argumentation bei Paulus. 2002. Vol. 149.
*Waaler, Erik:* The Shema and The First Commandment in First Corinthians. 2008. Vol. II/253.
*Wagener, Ulrike:* Die Ordnung des „Hauses Gottes". 1994. Vol. II/65.
*Wagner, J. Ross:* see *Wilk, Florian.*
*Wahlen, Clinton:* Jesus and the Impurity of Spirits in the Synoptic Gospels. 2004. Vol. II/185.
*Walker, Donald D.:* Paul's Offer of Leniency (2 Cor 10:1). 2002. Vol. II/152.
*Walter, Nikolaus:* Praeparatio Evangelica. Ed. von Wolfgang Kraus und Florian Wilk. 1997. Vol. 98.
*Wander, Bernd:* Gottesfürchtige und Sympathisanten. 1998. Vol. 104.
*Wardle, Timothy:* The Jerusalem Temple and Early Christian Identity. 2010. Vol. II/291.
*Wasserman, Emma:* The Death of the Soul in Romans 7. 2008. Vol. 256.
*Waters, Guy:* The End of Deuteronomy in the Epistles of Paul. 2006. Vol. 221.
*Watt, Jan G. van der* (Ed.): Eschatology of the New Testament and Some Related Documents. 2011. Vol. II/315.
– and *Ruben Zimmermann* (Ed.): Rethinking the Ethics of John. 2012. Vol. 291.
– see *Frey, Jörg*
– see *Zimmermann, Ruben*

*Wissenschaftliche Untersuchungen zum Neuen Testament*

*Watts, Rikki:* Isaiah's New Exodus and Mark. 1997. *Vol. II/88.*
*Webb, Robert L.:* see *Bock, Darrell L.*
*Wedderburn, Alexander J.M.:* Baptism and Resurrection. 1987. *Vol. 44.*
– The Death of Jesus. 2013. *Vol. 299.*
– Jesus and the Historians. 2010. *Vol. 269.*
*Wegner, Uwe:* Der Hauptmann von Kafarnaum. 1985. *Vol. II/14.*
*Weiß, Hans-Friedrich:* Frühes Christentum und Gnosis. 2008. *Vol. 225.*
*Weissenrieder, Annette:* Images of Illness in the Gospel of Luke. 2003. *Vol. II/164.*
–, and *David L. Balch* (Ed.): Contested Spaces. 2012. *Vol. 285.*
–, and *Robert B. Coote* (Ed.): The Interface of Orality and Writing. 2010. *Vol. 260.*
–, *Friederike Wendt* and *Petra von Gemünden* (Ed.): Picturing the New Testament. 2005. *Vol. II/193.*
*Welck, Christian:* Erzählte ,Zeichen'. 1994. *Vol. II/69.*
*Wendt, Friederike* (Ed.): see *Weissenrieder, Annette.*
*Wiarda, Timothy:* Peter in the Gospels. 2000. *Vol. II/127.*
*Wifstrand, Albert:* Epochs and Styles. 2005. *Vol. 179.*
*Wilk, Florian* and *J. Ross Wagner* (Ed.): Between Gospel and Election. 2010. *Vol. 257.*
– see *Walter, Nikolaus.*
*Williams, Catrin H.:* I am He. 2000. *Vol. II/113.*
*Wilson, Todd A.:* The Curse of the Law and the Crisis in Galatia. 2007. *Vol. II/225.*
*Wilson, Walter T.:* Love without Pretense. 1991. *Vol. II/46.*
*Winn, Adam:* The Purpose of Mark's Gospel. 2008. *Vol. II/245.*
*Winninge, Mikael:* see *Holmberg, Bengt.*
*Wischmeyer, Oda:* Von Ben Sira zu Paulus. 2004. *Vol. 173.*
*Wisdom, Jeffrey:* Blessing for the Nations and the Curse of the Law. 2001. *Vol. II/133.*
*Witmer, Stephen E.:* Divine Instruction in Early Christianity. 2008. *Vol. II/246.*
*Witulski, Thomas:* Apk 11 und der Bar Kokhba-Aufstand. 2012. *Vol. II/337.*
*Wold, Benjamin G.:* Women, Men, and Angels. 2005. *Vol. II/2001.*

*Wolter, Michael:* Theologie und Ethos im frühen Christentum. 2009. *Vol. 236.*
– see *Stuckenbruck, Loren T.*
*Worthington, Jonathan:* Creation in Paul and Philo. 2011. *Vol. II/317.*
*Wright, Archie T.:* The Origin of Evil Spirits. 2005. *Vol. II/198.*
*Wucherpfennig, Ansgar:* Heracleon Philologus. 2002. *Vol. 142.*
*Wurst, Gregor:* see *Popkes, Enno Edzard.*
*Wypadlo, Adrian:* Die Verklärung Jesu nach dem Markusevangelium. 2013. *Vol. 308.*
*Yates, John W.:* The Spirit and Creation in Paul. 2008. *Vol. II/251.*
*Yeung, Maureen:* Faith in Jesus and Paul. 2002. *Vol. II/147.*
*Young, Stephen E.:* Jesus Tradition in the Apostolic Fathers. 2011. *Vol. II/311.*
*Zamfir, Corinna:* see *Verheyden, Joseph*
*Zangenberg, Jürgen, Harold W. Attridge* and *Dale B. Martin* (Ed.): Religion, Ethnicity and Identity in Ancient Galilee. 2007. *Vol. 210.*
*Zelyck, Lorne R.:* John among the Other Gospels 2013. *Vol. II/347.*
*Zimmermann, Alfred E.:* Die urchristlichen Lehrer. 1984, ²1988. *Vol. II/12.*
*Zimmermann, Johannes:* Messianische Texte aus Qumran. 1998. *Vol. II/104.*
*Zimmermann, Ruben:* Christologie der Bilder im Johannesevangelium. 2004. *Vol. 171.*
– Geschlechtermetaphorik und Gottesverhältnis. 2001. *Vol. II/122.*
– (Ed.): Hermeneutik der Gleichnisse Jesu. 2008. *Vol. 231.*
– and *Jan G. van der Watt* (Ed.): Moral Language in the New Testament. Vol. II. 2010. *Vol. II/296.*
– see *Frey, Jörg.*
– see *Horn, Friedrich Wilhelm.*
– see *Watt, Jan G. van der.*
*Zugmann, Michael:* „Hellenisten" in der Apostelgeschichte. 2009. *Vol. II/264.*
*Zumstein, Jean:* see *Dettwiler, Andreas*
*Zwiep, Arie W.:* Christ, the Spirit and the Community of God. 2010. *Vol. II/293.*
– Judas and the Choice of Matthias. 2004. *Vol. II/187.*

*For a complete catalogue please write to the publisher*
Mohr Siebeck • P.O. Box 2030 • D–72010 Tübingen/Germany
*Up-to-date information on the internet at www.mohr.de*